21ST ANNUAL EDITION

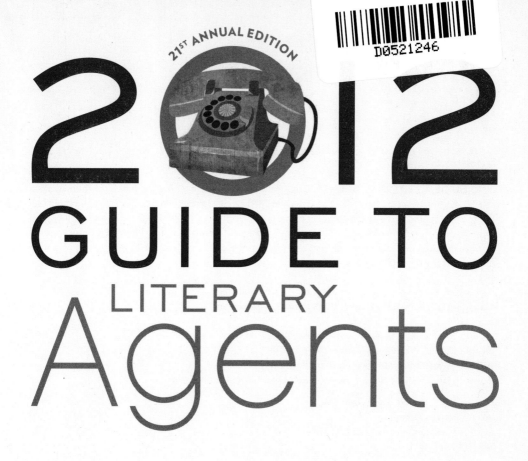

2012
GUIDE TO
LITERARY
Agents

Chuck Sambuchino, Editor

WD

WRITER'S DIGEST
BOOKS

WritersDigest.com
Cincinnati, Ohio

Publisher & Editorial Director, Writing Community: Phil Sexton
Managing Editor, Writer's Digest Market Books: Adria Haley

Writer's Market website: www.writersmarket.com
Writer's Digest website: www.writersdigest.com
Writer's Digest Bookstore: www.writersdigestshop.com
Guide to Literary Agents Blog: www.guidetoliteraryagents.com/blog

Distributed in Canada by Fraser Direct
100 Armstrong Avenue
Georgetown, Ontario, Canada L7G 5S4
Tel: (905) 877-4411

Distributed in the U.K. and Europe by F&W Media International
Brunel House, Newton Abbot, Devon, TQ12 4PU, England
Tel: (+44) 1626-323200, Fax: (+44) 1626-323319
E-mail: postmaster@davidandcharles.co.uk

Distributed in Australia by Capricorn Link
P.O. Box 704, Windsor, NSW 2756 Australia
Tel: (02) 4577-3555

ISSN: 1078-6945
ISBN-13: 978-1-59963-229-2

Attention Booksellers: This is an annual directory of F+W Media, Inc. Return deadline for this edition is December 31, 2012.

Edited by: Chuck Sambuchino
Cover designed by: Jessica Boonstra
Interior designed by: Claudean Wheeler
Page layout by: Terri Woesner
Production coordinated by: Greg Nock
Cover illustration by: Emily Keafer

CONTENTS

FROM THE EDITOR

As the publishing industry continues to evolve, writers need literary agents now more than ever. If you want to get published by a big publishing house that can distribute and promote your book—and ebook—everywhere, you need an agent who can access editors and negotiate the best deal for you. So if you're in the middle of your writing journey and you're looking for a trusted database of literary reps, you've come to the right place.

The *Guide to Literary Agents* is now in its 21st year. It *works*. Just ask 15 published writers who got an agent using *GLA*. (Hear from them in this book's "Success Stories" article. And those 15 are just the tip of the iceberg.) With each agency listing, you get information on how they want to be contacted, what categories they represent, recent sales and how they respond to writers.

Besides its many listings, this book has informative articles to help you get started in the submission process. The upfront article "Query Letter Writing" not only has instruction on how to compose your first contact with an agent, but also includes several successful examples of queries that snagged agents—*with* commentary from the agents themselves. Then check out our "How I Got My Agent" stories: five quick tales from writers relaying their journey to representation and publication. Also, I am pleased to say that *GLA* once again includes agents and managers looking for screenplays, and our upfront instruction as well as our listing content reflects that.

As always, stay in touch with me at guidetoliteraryagents.com/blog. In the meantime, good luck. Hopefully we'll cross paths at a writers conference soon, or maybe I'll feature *your* success story in next year's edition.

Chuck Sambuchino,
literaryagent@fwmedia.com
Author, *How to Survive a Garden Gnome Attack*

HOW TO USE
GUIDE TO
LITERARY AGENTS

Searching for a literary agent can be overwhelming, whether you've just finished your first book or you have several publishing credits on your résumé. More than likely, you're eager to start pursuing agents and anxious to see your name on the spine of a book. But before you go directly to the listings of agencies in this book, take time to familiarize yourself with the way agents work and how you should approach them. By doing so, you will be more prepared for your search, and ultimately save yourself effort and unnecessary grief.

Read the articles

This book begins with feature articles that explain how to prepare for representation, offer strategies for contacting agents and provide perspectives on the author/agent relationship. The articles are organized into three sections appropriate for each stage of the search process: **Getting Started**, **Contacting Agents** and **Sealing the Deal**. You may want to start by reading through each article, and then refer back to relevant articles during each stage of your search.

Because there are many ways to make that initial contact with an agent, we've also provided a section called **Perspectives**. These personal accounts from agents and published authors offer information and inspiration for any writer hoping to find representation.

Decide what you're looking for

A literary agent will present your work directly to editors or producers. It's the agent's job to get her client's work published or sold, and to negotiate a fair contract. In the **Literary Agents** section, we list each agent's contact information and explain what type of work the agency represents as well as how to submit your work for consideration.

1. **WHY DO YOU INCLUDE AGENTS WHO ARE NOT SEEKING NEW CLIENTS?** Some agents ask that their listings indicate they are currently closed to new clients. We include them so writers know the agents exist and know not to contact them at this time.

2. **WHY DO YOU EXCLUDE FEE-CHARGING AGENTS?** We have received a number of complaints in the past regarding fees, and therefore have chosen to list only those agents who do not charge reading fees.

3. **WHY ARE SOME AGENTS NOT LISTED?** Some agents may not have responded to our requests for information. We have taken others out of the book after receiving serious complaints about them.

4. **DO I NEED MORE THAN ONE AGENT IF I WRITE IN DIFFERENT GENRES?** It depends. If you have written in one genre and want to switch to a new style of writing, ask your agent if she is willing to represent you in your new endeavor. Most agents will continue to represent clients no matter what genre they choose to write. Occasionally, an agent may feel she has no knowledge of a certain genre and will recommend an appropriate agent to her client. Regardless, you should always talk to your agent about any potential career move.

5. **WHY DON'T YOU LIST MORE FOREIGN AGENTS?** Most American agents have relationships with foreign co-agents in other countries. It is more common for an American agent to work with a co-agent to sell a client's book abroad than for a writer to work directly with a foreign agent. We do, however, list agents in the United Kingdom, Australia, Canada and other countries who sell to publishers both internationally and in the United States. If you decide to query a foreign agent, make sure they represent American writers (if you're American). Some may request to only receive submissions from Canadians, for example, or UK residents.

6. **DO AGENTS EVER CONTACT A SELF-PUBLISHED WRITER?** If a self-published author attracts the attention of the media or if his book sells extremely well, an agent might approach the author in hopes of representing him.

7. **WHY WON'T THE AGENT I QUERIED RETURN MY MATERIAL?** An agent may not answer your query or return your manuscript for several reasons. Perhaps you did not include a self-addressed, stamped envelope (SASE). Many agents will discard a submission without a SASE. Or, the agent may have moved. To avoid using expired addresses, use the most current edition of *Guide to Literary Agents* or access the information online at WritersMarket.com. Another possibility is that the

> agent is swamped with submissions. An agent can be overwhelmed with queries, especially if the agent recently has spoken at a conference or has been featured in an article or book. Also, some agents specify in their listings that they never return materials of any kind.

For face-to-face contact, many writers prefer to meet agents at **Conferences**. By doing so, writers can assess an agent's personality, attend workshops and have the chance to get more feedback on their work than they get by mailing submissions and waiting for a response. The conferences section lists conferences agents and/or editors attend. In many cases, private consultations are available, and agents attend with the hope of finding new clients to represent.

Utilize the extras

Aside from the articles and listings, this book offers a section of **Resources**. If you come across a term with which you aren't familiar, check out the Resources section for a quick explanation. Also, note the gray tabs along the edge of each page. The tabs block off each section so they are easier to flip to as you conduct your search.

Finally—and perhaps most importantly—are the **Indexes** in the back of the book. These can serve as an incredibly helpful way to start your search because they categorize the listings according to different criteria. For example, you can look for literary agents according to their specialties (fiction/nonfiction genres).

LISTING POLICY AND COMPLAINT PROCEDURE

Listings in *Guide to Literary Agents* are compiled from detailed questionnaires, phone interviews and information provided by agents. The industry is volatile, and agencies change frequently. We rely on our readers for information on their dealings with agents, as well as changes in policies or fees that differ from what has been reported to the editor of this book. Write to us (Guide to Literary Agents, 4700 E. Galbraith Road, Cincinnati, OH 45236) or e-mail us (literaryagent@fwmedia.com) if you have new information, questions or problems dealing with the agencies listed.

Listings are published free of charge and are not advertisements. Although the information is as accurate as possible, the listings are not endorsed or guaranteed by the editor or publisher of *Guide to Literary Agents*. If you feel you have not been treated fairly by an agent or representative listed in *Guide to Literary Agents*, we advise you to take the following steps:

- First try to contact the agency. Sometimes one letter or e-mail can clear up the matter. Politely relate your concern.
- Document all your correspondence with the agency. When you write to us with a complaint, provide the name of your manuscript, the date of your first contact with the agency and the nature of your subsequent correspondence.
- We will keep your letter on file and attempt to contact the agency. The number, frequency and severity of complaints will be considered when deciding whether or not to delete an agency's listing from the next edition.
- *Guide to Literary Agents* reserves the right to exclude any agency for any reason.

Don't forget your webinar!

To access the webinar that is included with your book, go to writersmarket.com/2012gla and learn how to build your author platform.

WHAT AN AGENT DOES

The scoop on day-to-day agent responsibilities.

A writer's job is to write. A literary agent's job is to find publishers for her clients' books. Because publishing houses receive more and more unsolicited manuscripts each year, securing an agent is becoming increasingly necessary. But finding an eager and reputable agent can be a difficult task. Even the most patient writer can become frustrated or disillusioned. As a writer seeking agent representation, you should prepare yourself before starting your search. Learn when to approach agents, as well as what to expect from an author/agent relationship. Beyond selling manuscripts, an agent must keep track of the ever-changing industry, writers' royalty statements, fluctuating market trends—and the list goes on.

So, once again, you face the question: Do I need an agent? The answer, much more often than not, is yes.

WHAT CAN AN AGENT DO FOR YOU?

For starters, today's competitive marketplace can be difficult to break into, especially for unpublished writers. Many larger publishing houses will only look at manuscripts from agents—and rightfully so, as they would be inundated with unsatisfactory writing if they did not. In fact, approximately 80 percent of books published by the six major houses are acquired through agents.

But an agent's job isn't just getting your book through a publisher's door. The following describes the various jobs agents do for their clients, many of which would be difficult for a writer to do without outside help.

AGENTS KNOW EDITORS' TASTES AND NEEDS

An agent possesses information on a complex web of publishing houses and a multitude of editors to ensure her clients' manuscripts are placed in the right hands. This knowledge is gathered through relationships she cultivates with acquisitions editors—the people who decide which books to present to their publisher for possible publication. Through her industry connections, an agent becomes aware of the specializations of publishing houses and their imprints, knowing that one publisher wants only contemporary romances while another is interested solely in nonfiction books about the military. By networking with editors, an agent also learns more specialized information—which editor is looking for a crafty Agatha Christie–style mystery for the fall catalog, for example.

AGENTS TRACK CHANGES IN PUBLISHING

Being attentive to constant market changes and shifting trends is another major requirement of an agent. An agent understands what it may mean for clients when publisher A merges with publisher B and when an editor from house C moves to house D. Or what it means when readers—and therefore editors—are no longer interested in Westerns, but can't get their hands on enough thriller and suspense novels.

AGENTS GET YOUR WORK READ FASTER

Although it may seem like an extra step to send your manuscript to an agent instead of directly to a publishing house, the truth is an agent can prevent you from wasting months sending manuscripts that end up in the wrong place or buried in someone's slush pile. Editors rely on agents to save them time, as well. With little time to sift through the hundreds of unsolicited submissions arriving weekly in the mail, an editor is naturally going to prefer a work that has already been approved by a qualified reader (i.e., the agent) who knows the editor's preferences. For this reason, many of the larger publishers accept agented submissions only.

AGENTS UNDERSTAND CONTRACTS

When publishers write contracts, they are primarily interested in their own bottom line rather than the best interests of the author. Writers unfamiliar with contractual language may find themselves bound to a publisher with whom they no longer want to work. Or, they may find themselves tied to a publisher that prevents them from getting royalties on their first book until subsequent books are written. Agents use their experiences and knowledge to negotiate a contract that benefits the writer while still respecting the publisher's needs. After all, more money for the author will almost always mean more money for the agent— another reason they're on your side.

BEFORE YOU SUBMIT YOUR FICTION BOOK:

1. Finish your novel or short-story collection. An agent can do nothing for fiction without a finished product. Never query with an incomplete novel.
2. Revise your manuscript. Seek critiques from other writers or an independent editor to ensure your work is as polished as possible.
3. Proofread. Don't ruin a potential relationship with an agent by submitting work that contains typos or poor grammar.
4. Publish short stories or novel excerpts in literary journals, which will prove to prospective agents that editors see quality in your writing.
5. Research to find the agents of writers whose works you admire or are similar to yours.
6. Use the Internet and resources like *Guide to Literary Agents* to construct a list of agents who are open to new writers and looking for your category of fiction. (Jump to the listings sections of this book to start now.)
7. Rank your list according to the agents most suitable for you and your work.
8. Write your novel synopsis. (See this book's article for more on how to do just that.)
9. Write your query letter. As an agent's first impression of you, this brief letter should be polished and to the point.
10. Educate yourself about the business of agents so you will be prepared to act on any offer. This guide is a great place to start.

AGENTS NEGOTIATE—AND EXPLOIT—SUBSIDIARY RIGHTS

Beyond publication, a savvy agent keeps in mind other opportunities for your manuscript. If your agent believes your book also will be successful as an audio book, a Book-of-the-Month-Club selection or even a blockbuster movie, she will take these options into consideration when shopping your manuscript. These additional opportunities for writers are called subsidiary rights. Part of an agent's job is to keep track of the strengths and weaknesses of different publishers' subsidiary rights offices to determine the deposition of these rights regarding your work. After contracts are negotiated, agents will seek additional moneymaking opportunities for the rights they kept for their clients.

AGENTS GET ESCALATORS

An escalator is a bonus that an agent can negotiate as part of the book contract. It is commonly given when a book appears on a bestseller list or if a client appears on a popular television show. For example, a publisher might give a writer a $30,000 bonus if he is picked for a book club. Both the agent and the editor know such media attention will sell more books, and the agent negotiates an escalator to ensure the writer benefits from this increase in sales.

AGENTS TRACK PAYMENTS

Because an agent receives payment only when the publisher pays the writer, it's in the agent's best interest to make sure the writer is paid on schedule. Some publishing houses are notorious for late payments. Having an agent distances you from any conflict regarding payment and allows you to spend time writing instead of making phone calls.

AGENTS ARE ADVOCATES

Besides standing up for your right to be paid on time, agents can ensure your book gets a better cover design, more attention from the publisher's marketing department or other benefits you may not know to ask for during the publishing process. An agent also can provide advice during each step of the way, as well as guidance about your long-term writing career.

ARE YOU READY FOR AN AGENT?

Now that you know what an agent is capable of, ask yourself if you and your work are at a stage where you need an agent. Look at the to-do lists for fiction and nonfiction writers in this article, and judge how prepared you are for contacting an agent. Have you spent enough time researching or polishing your manuscript? Does your nonfiction book proposal include everything it should? Is your novel completely finished? Sending an agent an incomplete project not only wastes your time, but also may turn off the agent in the process. Is the work thoroughly revised? If you've finished your project, set it aside for a few weeks, then examine it again with fresh eyes. Give your novel or proposal to critique group partners ("beta readers") for feedback. Join up with writing peers in your community or online.

Moreover, your work may not be appropriate for an agent. Most agents do not represent poetry, magazine articles, short stories or material suitable for academic or small presses; the agent's commission does not justify spending time submitting these types of works. Those agents who do take on such material generally represent authors on larger projects first, and then adopt the smaller items as a favor to the client.

If you believe your work is ready to be placed with an agent, make sure you're personally ready to be represented. In other words, consider the direction in which your writing career is headed. Besides skillful writers, agencies want clients with the ability to produce more than one book. Most agents say they're looking to represent careers, not books.

WHEN DON'T YOU NEED AN AGENT?

Although there are many reasons to work with an agent, some authors can benefit from submitting their own work directly to book publishers. For example, if your project focuses on a very specific area, you may want to work with a small or specialized press. These houses usually are open to receiving material directly from writers. Small presses often can give more attention to writers than large houses can, providing editorial help, marketing expertise and other advice. Academic books or specialized nonfiction books (such as a book about the history of Rhode Island) are good bets for unagented writers.

Beware, though, as you will now be responsible for reviewing and negotiating all parts of your contract and payment. If you choose this path, it's wise to use a lawyer or entertainment attorney to review all contracts. Lawyers who specialize in intellectual property can help writers with contract negotiations. Instead of earning a commission on resulting book sales, lawyers are paid for their time only.

And, of course, some people prefer working independently instead of relying on others. If you're one of these people, it's probably better to submit your own work instead of constantly butting heads with an agent. Let's say you manage to sign with one of the few literary agents who represent short-story collections. If the collection gets shopped around to publishers for several months and no one bites, your agent may suggest retooling the work into a novel or novella(s). Agents suggest changes—some bigger than others—and not all writers think their work is malleable. It's all a matter of what you're writing and how you feel about it.

BEFORE YOU SUBMIT YOUR NONFICTION BOOK:

1. Formulate a concrete idea for your book. Sketch a brief outline, making sure you'll have enough material for a book-length manuscript.
2. Research works on similar topics to understand the competition and determine how your book is unique.
3. Write sample chapters. This will help you estimate how much time you'll need to complete the work, and determine whether or not your writing will need editorial help. You will also need to include 1–4 sample chapters in the proposal itself.
4. Publish completed chapters in journals and/or magazines. This validates your work to agents and provides writing samples for later in the process.
5. Polish your nonfiction book proposal so you can refer to it while drafting a query letter—and you'll be prepared when agents contact you.
6. Brainstorm three to four subject categories that best describe your material.
7. Use the Internet and resources like *Guide to Literary Agents* to construct a list of agents who are open to new writers and looking for your category of nonfiction.
8. Rank your list. Research agent websites and narrow your list further, according to your preferences.
9. Write your query. Give an agent an excellent first impression by professionally and succinctly describing your premise and your experience.
10. Educate yourself about the business of agents so you will be prepared to act on any offer. This guide is a great place to start.

AGENTS TELL ALL

Leading literary reps answer some of writers' most frequently asked questions.

by Chuck Sambuchino, Ricki Schultz and Donna Gambale

ON QUERIES & PITCHING

I simultaneously queried six agents to represent my literary novel and received three favorable responses requesting sample chapters. Is it acceptable for me to reply to them all at once, or should I send material only to one and wait for a decision before sending to others?

As a courtesy, I would let agents know that other agents have also requested the material. Some agencies prefer exclusive submissions, though they realize you may have been querying a variety of agents prior to that request. If an agent asks for an exclusive read, it's reasonable for the author to ask that it be time-limited. I admit to being a bit dismayed when I spend many hours reading something only to find the author has signed with someone else. Requesting sample chapters should allow faster answers than having sent the agent the whole manuscript. I see no problem sending all the agents sample chapters as long as you extend the courtesy to let them know others are interested, especially if and when they ask for the whole manuscript.

—**MICHAEL MANCILLA**, *founder, Greystone Literary Agency*

If I submit a novel to a publisher who agrees to publish it, would it be in bad taste to write to an agent who had rejected me earlier and ask for representation again? I don't know anything about publishing contracts and would like someone to help walk me through it should the time come.

It's fine to approach an agent at any point in the process. We've taken on new clients in cases where we're the first person to see the work and also in cases where there's already an offer on the table. In fact, sometimes, the editor who has made the offer will recommend the author contact us. As your question implies, agents do more than just secure an offer. They also negotiate contracts, act as the author's advocate and champion, and help the author navigate the path after publication. It's an agent's job to deal with issues and (sometimes) the problems that can arise after a publishing contract is secured. That way, the author can have a productive and creative relationship with her editor. A good agent will also think not just about fostering the success of a single book but also the big picture of a client's career.

—LAURA RENNERT, *senior agent,*
Andrea Brown Literary Agency

What are the most common problems you see in a query letter from an unknown author?

First, mistakes in grammar, spelling, word usage or sentence structure. Anything like that is going to put me right off. Second, not saying what the book is about right away. I am only able to spend a minute at most reading your query letter—tell me exactly what I should know immediately, because I may not read all the way to the end. Third, being boring or unoriginal—writers don't seem to realize how many query letters we read in a day or a week. We've seen everything and are looking, more than anything, for our attention to be caught, to be taken by surprise. Be surprising!

—ELLEN PEPUS, *co-founder,*
Signature Literary

Let's say you're looking through the slush pile at query letters. What are common elements you see in a query letter that don't truly need to be there?

If your query letter is more than one page long, there are things in there that are superfluous. The most common unnecessary addition is a description of the writer's family/personal life if the book is not a memoir. Some personal background is good, but I would much prefer to know about the amazing novel you wrote. The personal information can come later. The other most common misstep is listing weak qualifications for writing the book. What I mean by that is when someone says, "I have a daughter, so I am qualified to write this very general book about how to raise daughters." In today's very crowded book market, you must have a strong platform to write nonfiction.

—ABIGAIL KOONS, *literary agent,*
The Park Literary Group

I've heard that you shouldn't (can't?) have two different agents represent your work, but what if your varying genres demand it? I write chick lit and thrillers, but my agent handles only the latter. What should I do?

Most agents handle a smattering of fiction and nonfiction, and so in most cases, there won't be a problem with an agent handling whatever work, categorically, his or her client turns to. However, if one's agent, obviously wanting to serve each and every book optimally, says honestly that he or she truly wouldn't do the job for whatever reason—they don't, let's say, *understand* the genre in question, or they really don't know the editors who publish it to make the proper targeted submissions—then the client should certainly feel free to seek appropriate representation for the book in the "new" genre. What's more, if the situation is succinctly explained to the new agent(s) being approached, they will certainly be understanding (in my view, anyway), and evaluate the submission on merit. And if the writer plans to continue in the new genre, so that the submission in question is not a one-shot, the new agent is even more likely to be open to acting as the writer's "second" agent—even if he or she won't be doing the usual, representing all of that writer's work.

—JOHN WARE, *founder,*
John A. Ware Literary Agency

Do you see many query letters that come in too long?

Length is an issue. Even though I accept online queries, I still want the query to come in somewhere close to one page. I think that writers often think that because it's online, I have no way of knowing that it's more than a page. Believe me, I do. Queries that are concise and compelling are the most intriguing.

—REGINA BROOKS, *founder,*
Serendipity Literary Agency

ON FICTION & GENRES

With literary fiction, what do you look for? What gets you to keep reading?

With literary fiction, I often look for a track record of previous publications. If you've been published in *Tin House* or *McSweeney's* or *GlimmerTrain*, I want to know. It tells me that the writer is, in fact, committed to their craft and building an audience out there in the journals. But if you have a good story and are a brilliant writer, I wouldn't mind if you lived in a cave in the Ozarks. For the record, I have yet to sign anyone who lives in a cave in the Ozarks.

—MICHELLE BROWER, *literary agent,*
Folio Literary

What elements do you believe are integral to a good suspense genre book?

These suggestions come to mind:

1. Learn the formula by reading and studying this genre. (Of course, you won't let your readers know you're following a formula.) Analyze your favorite book to see how the writer adds suspense, to the book in general and to individual scenes.

2. Your central problem or issue must be serious enough to engage readers' attention. What's at stake? Don't go overboard (like saving the earth from giant insects),

but make sure your protagonist faces a life-changing threat. Make it personal for the hero.

3. You'll need a sympathetic protagonist, complete with flaws, quirks and a reason for us to care what happens to her.

4. Have a great ending in mind before you start the book.

5. Your bad guys should be interesting, entertaining and smart. Don't use cardboard villains. The hero should be fully tested by his adversaries.

—SAMMIE JUSTESEN, *founder,*
Northern Lights Literary Services

If you were speaking to someone who was sitting down to write a romance book but had never done so before, what would you tell them about the basics of the genre?

The word count should range from 50,000 to about 100,000. There is a formula to writing good romance. The hero must be a man the reader would like to date, and the heroine should be the type of girl who is bigger than life, who the reader would like to be like. They should meet, overcome obstacles and in the end get together. There are dozens of different kind of romances. The author could join the Romance Writers of America for support and get into critique groups. All my published authors have critique groups.

—MARY SUE SEYMOUR, *founder,*
The Seymour Agency

How does a writer know if her writing falls into the category of women's fiction, as opposed to perhaps literary fiction?

I think I have a fairly good definition of women's fiction. These are not simply stories with female characters but stories that tell us the female journey. Women's fiction is a way for women to learn and grow, and to relate to others what it is to be a woman. When I think of literary fiction, the emphasis is placed more on the telling of a good story instead of making the female journey the centerpiece.

—SCOTT EAGAN, *founder,*
Greyhaus Literary

Can you help define the category "Christian Living" and give a few examples?

The Christian Living category of books represents a huge umbrella that covers a multitude of topics. Christian Living works can include books on issues of importance to women, men and teenagers; Christian Living books can be about parenting, marriage, family life, divorce, breast cancer, healing, health, faith journeys, spiritual challenges, leadership and devotionals. [One] series that I've contracted is for three books with a theme of taking faith to the next level. These were written by a pastor of a large church, and the audience will be members of churches across the country who are interested in working through a study program that deals with parenting and other similar topics.

—JANET BENREY, *founder,*
Benrey Literary

ON NONFICTION & MEMOIR

A lot of people want to write a memoir, but few are good. What do you look for in a memoir?

Memoir is such a tricky genre. Everyone has a story (when I go to writing conferences, memoir writers are usually the overwhelming majority), and, unfortunately, you are right—few are good and many are overly sentimental. I look for two main things: a unique story and great writing. Memoirs should read like novels; they should have suspense, conflict, emotion, character development, dialogue and narrative arc. On top of all that, it's a tough question to ask about one's own story, but authors should ask it: Why will people be interested in me?

—TARYN FAGERNESS, *founder,*
Taryn Fagerness Literary Agency

What's the most important advice you can give for writing nonfiction book proposals?

Three things. 1) Spill the beans. Don't try to tantalize and hold back the juice. 2) No BS! We learn to see right through BS, or we fail rapidly. 3) Get published small. Local papers, literary journals, websites, anything. The more credits you have, the better. And list them all (although not to the point of absurdity) in your query. Why does everyone want to pole-vault from being an unpublished author to having a big book contract? It makes no sense. You have to learn to drive before they'll let you pilot the Space Shuttle.

—GARY HEIDT, *co-founder,*
Signature Literary

Nonfiction writers are always hearing about the importance of building a platform. What does that really mean?

Build your base. I've given workshops at writers' conferences about establishing an author platform, and it all boils down to one basic concept: Develop a significant following before you go out with your nonfiction book. If you build it, they (publishers) will come. Think about that word *platform*. What does it mean? If you are standing on a physical platform, it gives you greater visibility. And that's what it's all about: visibility. How visible are you to the world? That's what determines your level of platform. Someone with real platform is the "go-to" person in their area of expertise. If a reporter from the *New York Times* is doing a story on what you know about most, they will want to go to you for an interview first. But if you don't make yourself known to the world as the expert in your field, then how will the *NYT* know to reach out to you? RuPaul used to say, "If you don't love yourself, how the hell else is anybody else gonna love you?" I'm not saying be egotistical. I'm just saying, know your strengths, and learn to toot your own horn. Get out there. Make as many connections as you possibly can. We live in a celebrity-driven world. Love it or hate it, either way we all have to live with it. So, celebrate what you have to offer, and if it's genuine and enough people respond to it, then you will become a celebrity in your own right. Get out there and prove to the world that you are the be-all and end-all when it comes to what you know about most. Publishers don't expect you to be as big as Oprah, or Martha, or the Donald, but they do expect you to be the next Oprah, or Martha, or the next Donald in your own field.

—JEFFERY MCGRAW, *literary agent,*
The August Agency

Your bio says you seek "travel narrative nonfiction." Can you help define this category for writers?

Travel and adventure narrative nonfiction is the type of book that takes you away to another place. It is often a memoir, but can be a journalistic story of a particular event or even a collection of essays. The key here is that it tells an interesting and engaging story. It is also very important these days that the story is fresh and new—you'd be surprised at how many people have had the exact same experience with the rickshaw in Bangkok that you had. Some successful examples of this genre are Jon Krakauer's *Into Thin Air*, Elizabeth Gilbert's *Eat, Pray, Love*, and most things by Paul Theroux and Bill Bryson.

—ABIGAIL KOONS, *literary agent,*
The Park Literary Group

What stands out for you in a nonfiction book proposal? What immediately draws you into a project?

There are several factors that can help a book's ultimate prospects: great writing, great platform or great information, and ideally all three. For narrative works, the writing should be gorgeous, not just functional. For practical works, the information should be insightful, comprehensive and preferably new. And for any work of nonfiction, of course, the author's platform is enormously important.

—TED WEINSTEIN, *founder,*
Ted Weinstein Literary

What's a common mistake writers make when composing book proposals?

Nonfiction proposals should be fairly easy to write. There's a lot of information available to writers on how to write "the greatest," "the most compelling," "the no-fail" nonfiction proposal, so I'm often surprised when authors fail to mention their reasons and credentials for writing the work. Like publishers, I often jump to the credentials section of the proposal before getting to the meat of the proposal. I need to know why an author is qualified to write what they're writing and how their work differs from what has already been published on the topic they've chosen.

—**JANET BENREY**, *founder,*
Benrey Literary

When you receive a nonfiction book proposal, how detailed should the author's promotional plan be?

As long as it needs to be and still be realistic. I see marketing plans all the time along the lines of "I'll be happy to talk with Oprah," or other things that the author hopes will happen. I just want to hear what the author can really do that will help sell the book, not pie-in-the-sky wishful thinking.

—**JIM DONOVAN**, *founder,*
Jim Donovan Literary

ON CHILDREN'S & YOUNG ADULT

Can you offer some basic tips for writing children's nonfiction?

You can write about almost anything when it comes to children's nonfiction, even if it's been done before. But you need to come at the subject from a different angle. If there is already a book on tomatoes and how they grow, then try writing about tomatoes from a cultural angle. There are a ton of books on slavery, but not many on slaves in Haiti during the Haitian Revolution (Is there even one? There's an idea—someone take it and query me!). Another thing to always consider is your audience. Kids already have textbooks at school, so you shouldn't write your book like one. Come at the subject in a way that kids can relate to and find interesting. Humor is always a useful tool in nonfiction for kids.

—**JOANNA STAMPFEL-VOLPE**, *literary agent,*
Nancy Coffey Literary & Media Representation

Where are writers going wrong in picture book submissions?

Rhyming! So many writers think picture books need to rhyme. There are some editors who won't even look at books in rhyme, and a lot more who are extremely wary of them, so it limits an agent on where it can go and the likelihood of it selling. It's also particularly hard to execute perfectly. Aside from rhyming, I see way too many picture books about a family pet or bedtime.

—**KELLY SONNACK**, *literary agent,*
Andrea Brown Literary Agency

I've heard that nothing is taboo anymore in young adult books, and you can write about topics such as sex and drugs. Is this true?

I would say this: Nothing is taboo if it's done well. Each scene needs to matter in a novel. I've read a number of "edgy" young adult books where writers seem to add in scenes just for shock value, and it doesn't work with the flow of the rest of the novel. "Taboo" subjects need to have a purpose in the progression of the novel. Taboo topics do, however, affect whether the school and library market will pick up the book—and this can have an effect on whether a publisher feels they can sell enough copies.

—JESSICA REGEL, *literary agent,*
Jean V. Naggar Literary Agency

Simply put, concerning middle grade and young adult—how are they different? Subject matter? Length?

As a disclaimer, there are exceptions to these rules, with the fantasy genre being a big one. But, typically, middle grade novels run between 20,000–40,000 words and feature protagonists ages 9–13. Young adult novels run between 40,000–65,000 words and feature protagonists ages 14–17. The type of relationship at the core of a project can also tell you how to characterize it: MG often revolves around a protagonist's relationships with family and friends, while a story heavily driven by a romantic relationship is going to be YA.

—MICHELLE ANDELMAN, *literary agent,*
Regal Literary

In young adult and teen manuscripts, what are some page-one clichés you come across?

The most common problem I see is a story that's been told a million times before, without any new twists to make it unique enough to stand out. Same plot, same situations, same set up = the same ol' story. For example: abusive parents/kid's a rebel; family member(s) killed tragically/kid's a loner; divorced parents/kid acts out. Another problem I often see is when the protagonist/main characters don't have an age-appropriate voice. For example: if your main character is 14, let him talk like a 14-year-old. And lastly, being unable to "connect" with the main character(s). For example: Characters are too whiny or bratty, or character shows no emotion/angst.

—CHRISTINE WITTHOHN, *founder,*
Book Cents Literary

What are some reasons you stop reading a young adult manuscript?

Once I've determined that the writing is strong enough, it's usually a question of plot (we receive many works that are derivative or otherwise unoriginal) or voice. As we know from the young adults in our lives, anything that sounds even vaguely parental will not be well received. And there's nothing worse than narration that reads like a text message from a grandmother. In the past month, I've received 29 YA partials. Looking back on my notes, I see that I rejected eight for writing, seven for voice, six for derivative or unoriginal plots, four because they were inappropriate for the age group and two that simply weren't a good fit for the agency but may find a home elsewhere. Then there were two I liked and passed them on to others in my office. Also, I think a lot of writers, seeing the success of *Twilight*, have tried to force their manuscripts into this genre. I know you've heard it before, but it's so true: Write what you love—don't write what you think will sell.

—JESSICA SINSHEIMER, *literary agent,*
Sarah Jane Freymann Literary Agency

Are there any subjects you feel are untapped and would, therefore, be a refreshing change from the typical YA story?

When I was a (buyer for a bookstore), I was tired of certain subject matters only because those subjects have been explored so well, so often, that you really needed to bring something special to the page to make anyone take notice. Send me some modern immigrant stories, some multi-generational stuff, like the forthcoming (in the U.S.) YA novels of Carlos Ruiz Zafón. There are deeply rich stories about being an outsider, and yet how assimilation means a compromise and loss. I'd also love to see more issues of race discussed in modern terms, where there is the melting pot happening across the U.S., yet the tensions are still there. I think these stories, when done well, are universal stories, as we all feel that way at some point. Look at Junot Diaz's *The Brief Wondrous Life of Oscar Wao* as exhibit A.

—JOE MONTI, *literary agent,*
Barry Goldblatt Literary

What can writers do to enhance their chances of getting a picture book published?

I know it sounds simplistic, but write the very best picture books you can. I think the market contraction has been a good thing, for the most part. I'm only selling the very best picture books my clients write—but I'm definitely selling them. Picture books are generally skewing young, and have been for some time, so focus on strong read-alouds and truly kid-friendly styles. I'm having a lot of luck with projects that have the feel of being created by an author-illustrator even if the author is not an artist, in that they're fairly simple, have all kinds of room for fun and interpretation in the illustrations, and have a lot of personality. I see a lot of picture book manuscripts that depend too heavily on dialogue, which tends to give them the feel of a chapter book or middle grade novel. The style isn't a picture book style.

—ERIN MURPHY, *founder,*
Erin Murphy Literary Agency

Does "tween" exist as a category?

Tween *does* exist, and various publishers even have specific tween imprints in place. As for queries, the same standard holds true for me in terms of tween as it does with YA or MG: If the voice is authentic, then I'm probably interested. However, I do look more at plot with tween novels: right now, it's not enough just to have a great tween voice—the storyline also needs to be unique enough to stand out in the marketplace.

—MEREDITH KAFFEL, *literary agent,*
Charlotte Sheedy Literary Agency

ON OTHER AGENT MATTERS

Do agents usually hold out for a good deal on a book, or do they take the first acceptable offer that comes along?

Well, an offer in your pocket is always better than none. Certainly, if an agent feels she can demand more for a book, she should hold out; however, usually the editor who makes the first offer is the most enthusiastic and thoroughly understands the book, and may turn out to be the best editor and in-house advocate for that book. The most money is not necessarily the best deal for an author. That enthusiasm, commitment and support from all divisions within a publishing house often means more than those dollars in your bank account. An agent's experience regarding what editors are looking to buy, what publishers are currently paying and what the marketplace is like should lead that agent to advise her client regarding whether or not an offer on the table is the *best* (whatever its true meaning) that can be expected. We do *see* editors on a regular basis. Again, working from experience, an agent helps her client make the best possible decision. We all want our authors to accomplish their goals.

—LAURA LANGLIE, *founder,*
Laura Langlie, Literary Agent

Do you need a conservative agent to represent a conservative-minded book about religion or politics? A liberal agent to represent a liberal book? Do agents cross over?

I suspect many agents prefer to work only with political authors whose views are at least in the same quadrant as their own. Some, though, including myself, are open to and enjoy the chance to work with clients whose views challenge us, and are no less effective at selling those books to the right editor and publisher. I have represented a number of liberal, conservative and libertarian authors writing on a range of interesting topics, and sold their books to a mix of publishers. As always, the best way for an author to see if an agent might be right for them, regardless of their political views, is to read the good directories/guides to agents and then visit any prospective agent's website to get a more thorough understanding of their work with other clients.

—TED WEINSTEIN, *founder,*
Ted Weinstein Literary

Can you throw out some examples so writers can get a feel for what constitutes a "pop culture" work?

I think of "pop culture" as anything that's an up-to-the-minute trend. For example, playing off of our current economic situation, I sold a book called *Bitches on a Budget* to New American Library. It's a smart, witty (sometimes snarky) guide for women who want to survive a recession in style. I'm also interested in blog culture, fashion, style, film and entertainment.

—**ALANNA RAMIREZ**, *literary agent,*
Trident Media Group

What advice would you give writers who have had work rejected by agents?

It still surprises me how many writers are angry or defensive when agents reject their work. It's a wasted opportunity. We invest countless hours reading book proposals and giving each proposal careful thought. We have firsthand knowledge of what's selling (or easy to sell) and what's not. Rather than firing off a counter-response (which has probably never convinced an agent in the history of agenting), authors should use the opportunity to find out why they were rejected and improve their future chances of success. It is not rude to ask for more detailed feedback following a rejection, as long as the request is polite. We may be able to give advice or point out character, dialogue, pacing, pitch or structural issues that you might have missed. It could also lead to a referral or a request to resubmit.

—**BRANDI BOWLES**, *literary agent,*
Foundry Literary + Media

A week from now, my self-published novel will come rolling off the presses. Can I use the finished product as bait to hook a reputable agent?

Frankly, my sense is that providing an agent or editor with an already produced book only reduces its attractiveness as a potential property. First, the extra effort and expense smacks of trying too hard. And second, it conveys the sense that the material may already have made the rounds before—else why the desperation to self-publish? Agents, in particular, want the sense that they are discovering something precious and unknown. And to that end, less really is more, in terms of presentation. A simple and straightforward cover letter without any cheesy come-ons, complete with an appropriately modest listing of awards or other writing credentials, is all that should accompany a manuscript. The rest is up to the work itself.

—**ROB MCQUILKIN**, *literary agent,*
Lippincott Massie McQuilkin

I've read some articles that say "Agents agent," meaning that their job is to sell your work, rather than do other tasks such as assisting to edit a manuscript. But other articles say agents are now responsible for lots of editing throughout the process. Which is correct?

I can only speak for what we do at our agency, but it's been a long time since any good agent I know has *just* sold books. Agenting is a full-service business and, in this day and age, when editors sometimes seem to be playing musical chairs and projects are orphaned almost as soon as they're bought, providing editorial feedback for our clients is increasingly important. Here at Dystel & Goderich, we edit an author's work before it goes out on submission in order to optimize its chances in the marketplace. Occasionally, we also offer editorial support once the book is sold and the acquiring editor is unable or unwilling to edit. We like to think that our role is to "cause" books to be published, and for that to happen, we need to be involved at every step of the way.

—Miriam Goderich, *founding agent,*
Dystel & Goderich Literary Management

Is it wise to follow trends? I've heard that politics is a hot topic and YA is a hot genre right now. Should I strike while the iron's hot?

It's always tempting to write something that seems trendy. Much of this business is about the selling aspect, so writers often think that if they write what publishers seem to be publishing, or what seems to be appearing on bestseller lists, then they have a greater chance of getting a contract—but I honestly don't think it's the wisest way to go. Sure, a writer needs to be aware of what's out there, both so you're not reinventing the wheel (i.e., writing a book that's essentially already been published), as well as so you know how to position your book—but you really need to write what you write best. This means if you've never written for the YA market and have little sense of that audience, then starting now probably doesn't make sense, nor for that matter does reinventing yourself as a political writer if you don't already have a column or blog that's well known in that arena. You're not likely to "fool" publishers simply by trying to do what's hot.

Beyond this, though, there's the issue of timing. This is a business where things move slowly, so whatever it is you'd be selling today most likely won't come out for a year to two-and-a-half years. Who knows where the market will be at that point? Being conscious of the market is key—but above all, your book needs to be the best it can be. Who knows—maybe if it's terrific, you'll start the next trend.

—Felicia Eth, *founder,*
Felicia Eth Literary Representation

I'm talking with an agent who politely refused to share a list of who he represents and what he's recently sold. Is this normal?

I understand agencies that don't list clients in directories and public access places. That's a personal choice. Hartline (my agency) lists authors and books sold right on their website. To get down to the point of considering representation, however, not knowing anything about who they have represented and what success they've had would, to me, be like agreeing to surgery without knowing for sure that my doctor has a medical degree. If someone applies for a job, they have to provide a résumé and show their experience and qualifications. An agent is not going to take on a client without knowing the critical details about them, and I believe the client is entitled to the same consideration. Before you sign with an agent, know who they are, who they represent and what titles they've sold.

—TERRY W. BURNS, *literary agent,*
Hartline Literary Agency

What are the most common things you see writers do wrong during an in-person pitch at a writers' conference?

Two things: One, some authors don't seem to understand their true "hook," or most interesting aspect of their work. One writer I met spoke about his young adult fantasy novel, but it wasn't until the end of his pitch that he mentioned how his book was inspired by Japanese folklore and myths. How cool! That is what I would have wanted to hear first. Until then, it sounded like just another young adult fantasy. Two: Some authors over-praise their work. Some people told me how wonderful, great, amazing, funny, etc. their projects are. Coming from the author, such statements make me a bit skeptical. Of course the writer thinks his or her own work is amazing, but what is it about your work that makes it so fabulous? Why is it wonderful? I want more concrete information about an author's work so I can really think about where the book might fit in the market.

—TARYN FAGERNESS, *founder,*
Taryn Fagerness Literary Agency

If I envision a five-book series for my story and even have three manuscripts completed, is it still best to query regarding the first one only? Will the "series talk" come later?

We've been seeing a lot more of these types of "series" presentations lately—the feeling being that the author needs to present a future "franchise" for the agent and publisher to get them more interested in representation and publishing their work. This is not necessarily the case. In fact, it may send up a red flag about the author's expectations. I always try to downplay the series pitch (to publishers) unless there has already been a strong brand presence established in the marketplace. My advice to writers is to sell the first one; when it sells well, the editor and publisher will be very happy to listen to ideas for books two and three. Also, feedback can come from the publisher's sales and marketing teams, who will suggest (based on the success of book one) that the author write another book or make a series out of the original. With that in mind, stick to pitching one book at a time.

—JOHN WILLIG, *founder,*
Literary Services Inc.

Let's say an acquaintance calls you and says, "An agent wants to represent me, but she's new to the scene and has no sales. Is that OK?" How would you answer that?

An agent with little or no sales who has been an assistant at a leading agency will have just as much clout getting to an editor perhaps as an established agent, at least initially. One of the things I always advise writers to do is to ask an interested agent—that is, one who's made an offer of representation—"Why do you want to be my agent?" They will then hear a very clear thumbnail sketch of how that agent will sound agenting.

—Katharine Sands, *literary agent,*
Sarah Jane Freymann Literary Agency

CHUCK SAMBUCHINO is an editor and a writer. He works for Writer's Digest Books and edits *Guide to Literary Agents* (guidetoliteraryagents.com/blog) as well as *Children's Writer's & Illustrator's Market*. His humor book, *How to Survive a Garden Gnome Attack* (gnomeattack.com), was released in Sept. 2010 and has been featured by *Reader's Digest, USA Today*, the *New York Times* and AOL News. His first book was writing-related: the third edition of *Formatting & Submitting Your Manuscript* (2009). Besides that, he is a playwright, magazine freelancer, husband, cover band guitarist, chocolate chip cookie fiend, and owner of a flabby-yet-lovable dog named Graham.

RICKI SCHULTZ (rickischultz.com) is a Virginia-based freelance writer and recovering high school English teacher. In addition to interviewing literary agents for the Guide to Literary Agents Blog, she speaks at writers' conferences. Her work has been featured in several publications, including past editions of *Guide to Literary Agents* and *Children's Writer's & Illustrator's Market* as well as *Northern Virginia Magazine, St. Ignatius Magazine* and *The John Carroll Review*. She also writes young adult fiction. Originally from Ohio, Schultz taught English and journalism for five years, and she holds a BA in English and an M.Ed. in secondary education, both from John Carroll University in Cleveland. As coordinator of the Write-Brained Network (writebrainednetwork.com), she is planning the group's inaugural writing workshop to be held in September 2011 in Virginia—where she lives with her husband and beagle.

DONNA GAMBALE works an office job by day, writes young adult novels by night, and travels when possible. She is a contributing editor for the Guide to Literary Agents Blog, and freelances as a copyeditor and proofreader of both fiction and nonfiction. She is the author of a mini kit, *Magnetic Kama Sutra* (Running Press, 2009). You can find her online at firstnovelsclub.com, where she and her critique group blog about writing, reading, networking and the rest of life.

ASSESSING CREDIBILITY

Check out agents before you query.

//

Many people wouldn't buy a used car without at least checking the odometer, and savvy shoppers would consult the blue books, take a test drive and even ask for a mechanic's opinion. Much like the savvy car shopper, you want to obtain the best possible agent for your writing, so you should do some research on the business of agents before sending out query letters. Understanding how agents operate will help you find an agent appropriate for your work, as well as alert you about the types of agents to avoid.

Many writers take for granted that any agent who expresses interest in their work is trustworthy. They'll sign a contract before asking any questions and simply hope everything will turn out all right. We often receive complaints from writers regarding agents *after* they have lost money or have work bound by contract to an ineffective agent. If writers put the same amount of effort into researching agents as they did writing their manuscripts, they would save themselves unnecessary grief.

The best way to educate yourself is to read all you can about agents and other authors. Organizations such as the Association of Authors' Representatives (AAR; aar-online.org), the National Writers Union (NWU; nwu.org), American Society of Journalists and Authors (ASJA; asja.org) and Poets & Writers, Inc. (pw.org), all have informational material on finding and working with an agent.

Publishers Weekly (publishersweekly.com) covers publishing news affecting agents and others in the publishing industry. The Publishers Lunch newsletter (publishersmarketplace.com) comes free via e-mail every workday and offers news on agents and editors, job postings, recent book sales and more.

Even the Internet has a wide range of sites where you can learn basic information about preparing for your initial contact, as well as specific details on individual agents. You can also find online forums and listservs, which keep authors connected and allow them to share experiences they've had with different editors and agents. Keep in mind, however, that not everything printed on the Web is solid fact; you may come across the site of a writer who is bitter because an agent rejected his manuscript. Your best bet is to use the Internet to supplement your other research.

Once you've established what your resources are, it's time to see which agents meet your criteria. Below are some of the key items to pay attention to when researching agents.

LEVEL OF EXPERIENCE

Through your research, you will discover the need to be wary of some agents. Anybody can go to the neighborhood copy center and order business cards that say "literary agent," but that title doesn't mean she can sell your book. She may lack the proper connections with others in the publishing industry, and an agent's reputation with editors can be a major strength or weakness.

Agents who have been in the business awhile have a large number of contacts and carry the most clout with editors. They know the ins and outs of the industry and are often able to take more calculated risks. However, veteran agents can be too busy to take on new clients or might not have the time to help develop an author. Newer agents, on the other hand, may be hungrier, as well as more open to unpublished writers. They probably have a smaller client list and are able to invest the extra effort to make your book a success.

If it's a new agent without a track record, be aware that you're taking more of a risk signing with her than with a more established agent. However, even a new agent should not be new to publishing. Many agents were editors before they were agents, or they worked at an agency as an assistant. This experience is crucial for making contacts in the publishing industry, and learning about rights and contracts. The majority of listings in this book explain how long the agent has been in business, as well as what she did before becoming an agent. You could also ask the agent to name a few editors off the top of her head who she thinks may be interested in your work and why they sprang to mind. Has she sold to them before? Do they publish books in your genre?

If an agent has no contacts in the business, she has no more clout than you do. Without publishing prowess, she's just an expensive mailing service. Anyone can make photocopies, slide them into an envelope and address them to "Editor." Unfortunately, without a contact name and a familiar return address on the envelope, or a phone call from a trusted colleague letting an editor know a wonderful submission is on its way, your work will land in the slush pile with all the other submissions that don't have representation. You can do your own mailings with higher priority than such an agent could.

PAST SALES

Agents should be willing to discuss their recent sales with you: how many, what type of books and to what publishers. Keep in mind, though, that some agents consider this information confidential. If an agent does give you a list of recent sales, you can call the publishers' contracts department to ensure the sale was actually made by that agent. While it's true that even top agents are not able to sell every book they represent, an inexperienced agent who proposes too many inappropriate submissions will quickly lose her standing with editors.

You can also find out details of recent sales on your own. Nearly all of the listings in this book offer the titles and authors of books with which the agent has worked. Some of them also note to which publishing house the book was sold. Again, you can call the publisher and affirm the sale. If you don't have the publisher's information, simply go to your local library or bookstore to see if they carry the book. Consider checking to see if it's available on websites like Amazon.com, too. You may want to be wary of the agent if her books are nowhere to be found or are only available through the publisher's website. Distribution is a crucial component to getting published, and you want to make sure the agent has worked with competent publishers

TYPES OF FEES

Becoming knowledgeable about the different types of fees agents may charge is vital to conducting effective research. Most agents make their living from the commissions they receive after selling their clients' books, and these are the agents we've listed. Be sure to ask about any expenses you don't understand so you have a clear grasp of what you're paying for. Described below are some types of fees you may encounter in your research.

Office fees

Occasionally, an agent will charge for the cost of photocopies, postage and long-distance phone calls made on your behalf. This is acceptable, so long as she keeps an itemized account of the expenses and you've agreed on a ceiling cost. The agent should only ask for office expenses after agreeing to represent the writer. These expenses should be discussed up front, and the writer should receive a statement accounting for them. This money is sometimes returned to the author upon sale of the manuscript. Be wary if there is an upfront fee amounting to hundreds of dollars, which is excessive.

Reading fees

Agencies that charge reading fees often do so to cover the cost of additional readers or the time spent reading that could have been spent selling. Agents also claim that charging reading fees cuts down on the number of submissions they receive. This practice can save the agent time and may allow her to consider each manuscript more extensively. Whether such promises are kept depends upon the honesty of the agency. You may pay a fee and never receive a response from the agent, or you may pay someone who never submits your manuscript to publishers.

Officially, the Association of Authors' Representatives' (AAR) Canon of Ethics prohibits members from directly or indirectly charging a reading fee, and the Writers Guild of America (WGA) does not allow WGA signatory agencies to charge a reading fee to WGA members, as stated in the WGA's Artists' Manager Basic Agreement. A signatory may charge you a fee if you are not a member, but most signatory agencies do not charge a reading fee as an across-the-board policy.

WARNING SIGNS! BEWARE OF . . .

- Excessive typos or poor grammar in an agent's correspondence.

- A form letter accepting you as a client and praising generic things about your book that could apply to any book. A good agent doesn't take on a new client very often, so when she does, it's a special occasion that warrants a personal note or phone call.

- Unprofessional contracts that ask you for money up front, contain clauses you haven't discussed or are covered with amateur clip-art or silly borders.

- Rudeness when you inquire about any points you're unsure of. Don't employ any business partner who doesn't treat you with respect.

- Pressure, by way of threats, bullying or bribes. A good agent is not desperate to represent more clients. She invites worthy authors but leaves the final decision up to them.

- Promises of publication. No agent can guarantee you a sale. Not even the top agents sell everything they choose to represent. They can only send your work to the most appropriate places, have it read with priority and negotiate you a better contract if a sale does happen.

- A print-on-demand book contract or any contract offering you no advance. You can sell your own book to an e-publisher any time you wish without an agent's help. An agent should pursue traditional publishing routes with respectable advances.

- Reading fees from $25–$500 or more. The fee is usually nonrefundable, but sometimes agents agree to refund the money if they take on a writer as a client, or if they sell the writer's manuscript. Keep in mind, however, that payment of a reading fee does not ensure representation.

- No literary agents who charge reading fees are listed in this book. It's too risky of an option for writers, plus non-fee-charging agents have a stronger incentive to sell your work. After all, they don't make a dime until they make a sale. If you find that a literary agent listed in this book charges a reading fee, please contact the editor at literaryagent@fwmedia.com.

Critique fees

Sometimes a manuscript will interest an agent, but the agent will point out areas requiring further development and offer to critique it for an additional fee. Like reading fees, payment of a critique fee does not ensure representation. When deciding if you will benefit from having someone critique your manuscript, keep in mind that the quality and quantity of comments varies from agent to agent. The critique's usefulness will depend on the agent's knowledge of the market. Also be aware that agents who spend a significant portion of their time commenting on manuscripts will have less time to actively market work they already represent.

In other cases, the agent may suggest an editor who understands your subject matter or genre, and has some experience getting manuscripts into shape. Occasionally, if your story is exceptional, or your ideas and credentials are marketable but your writing needs help, you will work with a ghostwriter or co-author who will share a percentage of your commission, or work with you at an agreed-upon cost per hour.

An agent may refer you to editors she knows, or you may choose an editor in your area. Many editors do freelance work and would be happy to help you with your writing project. Of course, before entering into an agreement, make sure you know what you'll be getting for your money. Ask the editor for writing samples, references or critiques he's done in the past. Make sure you feel comfortable working with him before you give him your business.

An honest agent will not make any money for referring you to an editor. We strongly advise writers not to use critiquing services offered through an agency. Instead, try hiring a freelance editor or joining a writer's group until your work is ready to be submitted to agents who don't charge fees.

AVENUES TO AN AGENT

Get your foot in the door.

Once your work is prepared and you have a solid understanding of how literary agents operate, the time is right to contact an agent. Your initial contact determines the agent's first impression of you, so you want to be professional and brief.

Again, research plays an important role in getting an agent's attention. You want to show agents you've done your homework. Consult resources like *Guide to Literary Agents* to learn agents' areas of interest, check out agent websites to learn more about how they do business, and find out the names of some of their clients. If there's a book you admire that's similar to yours, check the Acknowledgments page to see if the author thanked her agent there. If that fails, try calling the publisher; someone in the contracts department can tell you the name of the agent who sold the title, provided an agent was used. When you contact that agent, impress him with your knowledge of the agency.

There are four main ways to connect with an agent: Submit a query letter to the specifications of an agent's submission guidelines; obtain a referral from someone who knows the agent; meet the agent in person at a writing conference; or attract the agent's attention with your own published writing. Let's look at each of them here.

SUBMISSIONS

The most common way to contact an agent is through a query letter or a proposal package. Most agents accept unsolicited queries. Some also review outlines and sample chapters. Almost none want unsolicited complete manuscripts.

Like publishers, agencies have specialties. Some are interested only in novels or children's books. Others are open to a variety of subjects and may actually have member agents within the company who specialize in just some of the many topics covered by the entire agency.

Agents agree to be listed in directories such as *Guide to Literary Agents*—and post information on their own websites—to indicate what they want to see and how they wish to receive submissions from writers. As you start to query agents, make sure you follow their individual guidelines.

REFERRALS

As in many industries, one of the best ways to get your foot in an agent's door is through a referral from one of her clients, an editor or another agent she has worked with in the past. Because agents trust their clients, they'll usually read referred work before over-the-transom submissions. If you have personal connections to anyone in the publishing business, ask politely for a referral. However, don't be offended if another writer will not share the name of his agent.

CONFERENCES

Going to a writing conference is your best bet for meeting an agent in person. Many conferences invite agents to give presentations or simply be available for meetings with authors, and agents view conferences as a way to find new clients. Often agents set aside time for one-on-one discussions with writers, and occasionally they may even look at material writers bring to the conference. These critiques may cost an extra fee, but if an agent is impressed with you and your work, she'll ask to see writing samples after the conference. When you send your query, be sure to mention the specific conference where you met and that she asked to see your work.

When you're face to face with an agent, it's important to be friendly, prepared and professional. Always wait for the agent to invite you to submit your work. Offering to send pages before they've agreed to consider anything can come off wrong. Don't bring sample chapters or a copy of your manuscript unless you've arranged a professional critique beforehand. Agents will almost never take writers' work home (they don't have the suitcase space), and writers nervously asking agents to take a look at their work and provide feedback could be considered gauche.

Remember, at these conferences, agents' time is very valuable—as is yours. If you discover that an agent who's high on your list recently stopped handling your genre, don't hunt her down and try to convince her to take it on again. Thank the agent for her time and move on to your next target.

If you plan to pitch agents, practice your speech—and make sure you prepare a verbal pitch that clocks in at less than one minute. Keep your in-person pitch simple and exciting; let the agent become interested and ask follow-up questions.

Because this is an effective way to connect with writers, agents often indicate on their websites which writing conferences and retreats they will attend in the near future. To find writing conferences in the area, consult market resources such as *Guide to Literary Agents*, ask local writing groups if they sponsor annual events, and simply try basic Google searches.

PUBLISHING CREDITS

Some agents read magazines or journals to find writers to represent. If you've had an outstanding piece published in a periodical, an agent may take notice and contact you regarding representation. In such cases, make sure the agent has really read your work. There are less-than-reputable individuals who send form letters to writers, and such representatives often make their living entirely from charging reading fees (a practice frowned upon by the Association of Authors' Representatives, the accrediting agency for literary agents) and not from commissions on sales.

For them, you already possess attributes of a good client: You have publishing credits and an editor has validated your work. To receive a letter from a reputable agent who has read your material and wants to represent you is an honor.

Occasionally, writers who have self-published or who have had their work published electronically may attract an agent's attention, especially if the self-published book has sold well.

Recently, writers have been posting their work on the Internet with the hope of attracting an agent's eye. With all the submissions most agents receive, they probably have little time to peruse writers' websites. Nevertheless, there are agents who do consider the Internet a resource for finding fresh voices. If you do post writing samples online, make sure you're not just waiting for agents to find you; be sure to try querying, as well.

COMMUNICATION ETIQUETTE

VIA MAIL

- Address the agent formally and make sure her name is spelled correctly.

- Double-check the agency's address.

- Include a self-addressed, stamped envelope.

- Use a clear font and standard paragraph formatting.

- A short handwritten thank-you note can be appropriate if the agent helped you at a conference or if she provided editorial feedback along with your rejection.

- Don't include any extraneous materials.

- Don't try to set yourself apart by using fancy stationery. Standard paper and envelopes are preferable.

VIA E-MAIL

- Address the agent as you would in a paper letter—be formal.

- If it's not listed on the website, call the company to get the appropriate agent's e-mail address.

- Include a meaningful subject line.

- Keep your emotions in check: Resist the temptation to send an angry response after being rejected, or to send a long, mushy note after being accepted. Keep your e-mails businesslike.

- Don't type in all caps or all lowercase. Use proper punctuation, and pay attention to grammar and spelling always.

- Don't overuse humor—it can be easily misinterpreted.

- Don't e-mail about trivial things.

ON THE PHONE

- Be polite: Ask if she has time to talk, or set up a time to call in advance.

- Get over your "phone phobia." Practice your conversation beforehand if necessary.

- Resist the urge to follow up with an agent too quickly. Give time to review your material.

- Never make your first contact over the phone unless the agent calls you first or requests you do so in her submission guidelines.

- Don't demand information from her immediately. Your phone call is interrupting her busy day and she should be given time to respond to your needs.

- Don't call to get information you could obtain from the Internet or other resources.

- Don't have your spouse, secretary, best friend or parent call for you.

IN PERSON

- Be clear and concise.

- Shake the agent's hand and greet her with your name.

- Be yourself, but be professional.

- Maintain eye contact.

- Don't monopolize her time. Either ask a brief question or ask if you can contact her later (via phone/mail/e-mail) with a more in-depth question.

- Don't be too nervous—agents are human!

RESEARCHING AGENTS

Get personal using the Web.

....

by C. Hope Clark

I clicked from website to website, one blog to another, all telling me my chances of finding an agent were slim in the current publishing environment. Statistics spouted success rates of one half of one percent. One agent read 8,000 queries in a year and only signed five new clients. Some agents even posted the number of queries they received each week versus the number of manuscripts requested. All too often the percentage equaled zero. Hellbent on beating the odds, I devised a plan to find my agent.

Throughout the course of 20 months, I submitted 72 queries, opened 55 rejections and received invitations for seven complete manuscripts. I landed an 88 percent response rate, and finally, a contract with an agent. How did I do it? I got personal.

WHERE TO FIND AGENTS

Many writers cringe at the thought of researching the publishing business. You must be better than that. Embrace the research, especially if it leads to representation. The more you analyze the rules, the players, the successes and failures, the more you increase your chances of signing a contract with a representative. Set aside time (i.e., days, weeks) to educate yourself about these professionals. You have your manuscript, your synopsis, a list of published books like yours and a biography. You've edited and re-edited your query so it's tight as a drum. Now focus. Who do you see as your handler, your mentor, your guide through the publishing maze? And where do you find him or her?

Agency websites

Most literary houses maintain a website. They post guidelines and books they've pushed into the marketplace. They also inform you about the individual agents on staff—including bios, favorite reads, writing styles they prefer, photos and maybe where they attended school. Read all the website has to offer, taking notes. If any agent represents your type of work, record what they prefer in a query and move on to their blog, if they keep one.

Blogs

Agent blogs reveal clues about what agents prefer. While websites are static in design, blogs allow comments. Here agents offer information about publishing changes, new releases—even their vacations and luncheons with movers and shakers in the industry. Some agents solicit feedback with dynamic dilemmas or ethical obstacles. Nathan Bransford of Curtis Brown, Mary Kole of the Andrea Brown Literary Agency and Rachelle Gardner of WordServe Literary Agency have been known to post short contests for their blog readers, if for no other reason than to emphasize what they seek in a client. For a complete list of agent blogs, go to the GLA Blog (guidetoliteraryagents.com/blog) and see them on the left.

Guidebooks and databases

The *Guide to Literary Agents* is a premier example of a guidebook resource. Use it to cull the agents who seek writers just like you. PublishersMarketplace.com and WritersMarket.com offer online, fingertip access to the websites, addresses and desires of most agents—and also point you in other directions to learn more.

Facebook and Twitter

Social networking has enabled writers to see yet another side of agents. These mini-versions of agents' lives can spark ideas for you to use in a query as well as help you digest the publishing world through professional eyes.

Conferences

Margot Starbuck, author of *The Girl in the Orange Dress* and *Unsqueezed: Springing Free from Skinny Jeans*, met her agent at a writers conference. "He had given a seminar that was essentially themed, 'My Perfect Client,' describing the type of writer he'd want to represent. When I got home, I crafted my letter to his own specs!"

It's easier to query an agent you've met, who you've heard, who has articulated what he likes. That subtle Midwestern accent you would not have heard otherwise might trigger you to pitch about your travel book or romance set in Nebraska. A one-hour class might empower you to query a particular agent after hearing her pet peeves and desires.

Online interviews

Google an agent's name and the word "interview." Authors, writers' organizations, magazines and commercial writing sites post such interviews to attract readers. A current Q&A

might prompt you to reword that query opening and tag an agent's interest. The agent might express a wish to read less women's fiction and more young adult novels these days—information not spelled out on her website profile. She might reveal a weakness for Southern writing. Reps also hop from agency to agency, and a timely interview might let you know she's changed location.

THE PLAN

Not wanting to collaborate with a complete stranger, I began dissecting agents' information to get a better feel for them. After noting 1) name, 2) agency, 3) query preferences, and 4) an address for each potential agent on a spreadsheet column, I dug down more for what I deemed the "zing" factor—the human factor. As a previous human resource director, I knew the power of connection. An applicant attending the same university as the manager often warranted a second glance. A first-time interviewee who played golf might reap a return invitation. Why couldn't this concept apply to literary agents? I was a job seeker; they were hiring. How could I make them take a second look at me and the fabulous writing I offered?

I reread bios and Googled deeper; I studied interviews and deciphered blogs. I read between the lines, earnestly seeking what made these people more than agents. Just like I canvassed the doctors and hairdressers in my life, I investigated these people for characteristics that bridged their preferences with mine.

Zing factors

The human connection between you and an agent is what I call the "zing" factor. These agents receive hundreds of queries per week, most skimmed or unread. You never know when an agent has been up all night with a sick child or arrived at work fighting the flu. You have no control over the timing that places your query in an agent's hands. What you can control is a creative opening that doesn't echo like the 30 before it and the 20 after, and rises to the top even if the reader hasn't had his coffee.

Agents hate to be taken for granted or treated like an anonymous personality (i.e., "Dear Agent"). The attention you give to zing factors will demonstrate that you respect the agent as a person. Suddenly you have that magical connection that holds his attention at least long enough to read your dead-on synopsis.

What makes for a great conduit between you and your agent? Anything and everything.

CLIENTELE—Signing good authors and landing great contracts make an agent proud. If you intend to become part of an agency's stable of authors, become familiar with who occupies the neighboring stalls. Recognize agents for what they have accomplished.

Author Tanya Egan Gibson not only emphasized her knowledge of Susan Golomb's clients, but she contacted one of the authors and asked permission to use him as a reference after meeting at a conference. The query won her representation and, later, a contract with Dutton Publishers.

Christine Chitnis introduced herself to other authors at a retreat where they shared critiques and ideas. Once she completed her manuscript, she pitched to the agents of those authors, knowing they could vouch for the quality of her work. She acquired an agent after two attempts.

PREVIOUS MEETINGS—A dinner table discussion with an agent at a conference could provide the lead for your next query. Make a point to meet and greet agents at these functions. They expect it. Give and take in the conversations. Don't smother them with your views. Listen for advice. Be polite. Afterward, before the experience evaporates, record notes about the topics discussed, the locale, maybe even the jokes or awkward speaker. The zing factor becomes instant recall when you remind an agent you met over dinner, during a fast-pitch or over drinks. You evolve into a person instead of another faceless query.

RECOGNITION—In your query, include where you found the agent's name. Congratulate him or her on recent contracts for books that sound similar to yours. You'll find this information through a website called Publishers Marketplace, or on the agency's website, blog, tweets or Facebook page.

FAVORITE READS—Agents are voracious readers, and, like any word geeks, they have favorite genres, authors and styles. Website bios often mention what sits on their nightstand, and blogs might post writers they admire. Note where you uncovered this information and marvel at your similarities, particularly if your work parallels the subjects.

GEOGRAPHY—All agents aren't born and reared in New York. With the ease of communication these days, agents live everywhere and telecommute. They also come from other places, and those roots might marry with yours. A New York agent who grew up in Georgia might have a soft spot for Civil War nonfiction.

PERSONAL INTERESTS—Agents have lives and off-duty pastimes. When author Nina Amir first contacted her agent, she also noted a mutual love of horses—in particular, a desire to save ex-racehorses from slaughter. The agent immediately called her.

In pitching to literary agent Verna Dreisbach, I revealed a common interest in mentoring teenage writers, knowing Verna founded Capitol City Young Writers, a nonprofit for youth interested in writing and publishing. Because my proposal was a mystery and I married a federal agent, I also admired her past work in law enforcement. Later, when asked if those initial items caught her attention, Verna responded in the positive. "Of course it made an impact. Writing with a degree of expertise in any field is crucial, including law enforcement. I looked forward to reading your work. I choose to represent authors that

I have a connection with, and your interests and aspirations certainly fit well with mine. As I expected, we hit it off immediately."

PASSION

Nothing, however, replaces the ability to show passion in your work. Genuine excitement over your book is contagious, and agents spot it in an instant. Carole Bartholomeaux unknowingly personalized her query through her passion. Her agent, an expectant father at the time, was touched by her story about a small town putting their lives on the line to save a group of Jewish children during World War II. You are the biggest advocate for your book, with your agent a close second. Everyone in your path should feel that energy. When agents sense it, they jump on your bandwagon knowing that readers will do the same.

When asked which grabbed her attention more, the personalization or the writing, Dreisbach replied diplomatically yet succinctly: "Both are equally important—authors who are personal and professional. Just as in any business, it is important to stand out from the crowd. I do not mean by being bizarre or unusual, but through the expression of a writer's passion, honesty and talent."

Don't cheapen yourself, though. Nathan Bransford, agent and award-winning blogger, gives his opinion about personalizing a query: "The goal of personalization isn't to suck up to the agent and score cheap points. As much as some people think we agents just want people to suck up to us, it's really not true. There is an art to personalization. Dedication and diligence are important, so if you query me, I hope you'll do your homework, and sure, if you've read books by my clients, mention that. Just don't try and trick me."

So be genuine. Be your passionate self and the person who obviously has done the research. A relationship with an agent is to be entered seriously and practically, with both parties sharing excitement for a common goal.

C. HOPE CLARK is the founder of FundsforWriters.com, chosen by *Writer's Digest* for its 101 Best Websites for Writers for the past 10 years. Her newsletters reach 40,000 readers weekly. She's published in numerous online and print publications, including *Writer's Digest*, *The Writer Magazine* and many Chicken Soups. Currently, she's preparing for the first release in her Carolina Slade suspense series, expected in winter 2011/2012 from Bell Bridge Books. Hope speaks at several writers conferences each year, and you can find her at hopeclark.blogspot.com, twitter.com/hopeclark, and facebook.com/chopeclark. She writes from the banks of Lake Murray, S.C.

CRAFTING A QUERY

How to Write a Great Letter

by Kara Gebhart Uhl

So you've written a book. And now you want an agent. If you're new to publishing, you probably assume that the next step is to send your finished, fabulous book out to agents, right? Wrong. Agents don't want your finished, fabulous book. In fact, they probably don't even want *part* of your finished, fabulous book—at least, not yet. First, they want your query.

A query is a short, professional way of introducing yourself to an agent. If you're frustrated by the idea of this step, imagine yourself at a cocktail party. Upon meeting someone new, you don't greet them with a boisterous hug and kiss and, in three minutes, reveal your entire life story including the fact that you were late to the party because of some gastrointestinal problems. Rather, you extend your hand. You state your name. You comment on the hors d'oeuvres, the weather, the lovely shade of someone's dress. Perhaps, after this introduction, the person you're talking to politely excuses himself. Or, perhaps, you become best of friends. It's basic etiquette, formality, professionalism—it's simply how it's done.

Agents receive hundreds of submissions every month. Often they read these submissions on their own time—evenings, weekends, on their lunch break. Given the number of writers submitting, and the number of agents reading, it would simply be impossible for agents to ask for and read entire book manuscripts off the bat. Instead, a query is a quick way for you to, first and foremost, pitch your book. But it's also a way to pitch yourself. If an agent is intrigued by your query, she may ask for a partial (say, the first three chapters of your book). Or she may ask for your entire manuscript. And only then may you be signed.

As troublesome as it may first seem, try not to be frustrated by this process. Because, honestly, a query is a really great way to help speed up what is already a monumentally slow-paced industry. Have you ever seen pictures of slush piles—those piles of unread queries on many well-known agents' desks? Imagine the size of those slush piles if they held full manuscripts instead of one-page query letters. Thinking of it this way, query letters begin to make more sense.

Here we share with you the basics of a query, including its three parts and a detailed list of dos and don'ts.

PART I: THE INTRODUCTION

Whether you're submitting a 100-word picture book or a 90,000-word novel, you must be able to sum up the most basic aspects of it in one sentence. Agents are busy. And they constantly receive submissions for types of work they don't represent. So upfront they need to know that, after reading your first paragraph, the rest of your query is going to be worth their time.

An opening sentence designed to "hook" an agent is fine—if it's good and if it works. But this is the time to tune your right brain down and your left brain up—agents desire professionalism and queries that are short and to-the-point. Remember the cocktail party. Always err on the side of formality. Tell the agent, in as few words as possible, what you've written, including the title, genre and length.

Within the intro you also must try to connect with the agent. Simply sending 100 identical query letters out to "Dear Agent" won't get you published. Instead, your letter should be addressed not only to a specific agency but a specific agent within that agency. (And double, triple, quadruple check that the agent's name is spelled correctly.) In addition, you need to let the agent know why you chose her specifically. A good author-agent relationship is like a good marriage. It's important that both sides invest the time to find a good fit that meets their needs. So how do you connect with an agent you don't know personally? Research.

1. Make a connection based on an author or book the agent already represents.

Most agencies have websites that list who and what they represent. Research those sites. Find a book similar to yours and explain that, because such-and-such book has a similar theme or tone or whatever, you think your book would be a great fit. In addition, many agents will list specific topics they're looking for, either on their websites or in interviews. If your book is a match, state that.

2. Make a connection based on an interview you read.

Search by agents' names online and read any and all interviews they've participated in. Perhaps they mentioned a love for X and your book is all about X. Or, perhaps they mentioned that they're looking for Y and your book is all about Y. Mention the specific interview. Prove that you've invested as much time researching them as they're about to spend researching you.

3. Make a connection based on a conference you both attended.

Was the agent you're querying the keynote speaker at a writing conference you were recently at? Mention it, specifically commenting on an aspect of his speech you liked. Even better, did you meet the agent in person? Mention it, and if there's something you can say to jog her memory about the meeting, say it. And better yet, did the agent specifically ask you to send your manuscript? Mention it.

Finally, if you're being referred to a particular agent by an author who that agent already represents—that's your opening sentence. That referral is guaranteed to get your query placed on the top of the stack.

PART II: THE PITCH

Here's where you really get to sell your book—but in only three to 10 sentences. Consider the jacket flap and its role in convincing readers to plunk down $24.95 to buy what's in between those flaps. Like a jacket flap, you need to hook an agent in the confines of very limited space. What makes your story interesting and unique? Is your story about a woman going through a mid-life crisis? Fine, but there are hundreds of stories about women going through mid-life crises. Is your story about a woman who, because of a mid-life crisis, leaves her life and family behind to spend three months in India? Again, fine, but this story, too, already exists—in many forms. Is your story about a woman who, because of a mid-life crisis, leaves her life and family behind to spend three months in India, falls in love with someone new while there and starts a new life—and family? And then has to deal with everything she left behind upon her return? *Now* you have a hook.

Practice your pitch. Read it out loud, not only to family and friends, but to people willing to give you honest, intelligent criticism. If you belong to a writing group, workshop your pitch. Share it with members of an online writing forum. Know anyone in the publishing industry? Share it with them. Many writers spend years writing their books. We're not talking about querying magazines here, we're talking about querying an agent who could become a lifelong partner. Spend time on your pitch. Perfect it. Turn it into jacket-flap material so detailed, exciting and clear that it would be near impossible to read your pitch and not want to read more. Use active verbs. Write your pitch, put it aside for a week, then look at it again. Don't send a query simply because you finished a book. Send a query because you finished your pitch and are ready to take the next steps.

PART III: THE BIO

If you write fiction, unless you're a household name or you've recently been a guest on some very big TV or radio shows, an agent is much more interested in your pitch than in who you are. If you write nonfiction, who you are—more specifically, your platform and publicity—is much more important. Regardless, these are key elements that must be present in every bio:

1. Publishing credits

If you're submitting fiction, focus on your fiction credits—previously published works and short stories. That said, if you're submitting fiction and all your previously published work is nonfiction—magazine articles, essays, etc.—that's still fine and good to mention. Don't be overly long about it. Mention your publications in bigger magazines or well-known literary journals. If you've never had anything published, don't say you lack official credits. Simply skip this altogether and thank the agent for his time.

2. Contests and awards

If you've won many, focus on the most impressive ones and the ones that most directly relate to your work. Don't mention contests you entered and weren't named in. Also, feel free to leave titles and years out of it. If you took first place at the Delaware Writers Conference for your fiction manuscript, that's good enough. Mentioning details isn't necessary.

3. MFAs

If you've earned or are working toward a Master of Fine Arts in writing, say so and state the program. Don't mention English degrees or online writing courses.

4. Large, recognized writing organizations

Agents don't want to hear about your book club and the fact that there's always great food, or the small critique group you meet with once a week. And they really don't want to hear about the online writing forum you belong to. But if you're a member of something like the

Romance Writers of America (RWA), the Mystery Writers of America (MWA), the Society of Children's Book Writers and Illustrators (SCBWI), the Society of Professional Journalists (SPJ), the American Medical Writers, etc., say so. This shows you're serious about what you do and you're involved in groups that can aid with publicity and networking.

5. Platform and publicity

If you write nonfiction, who you are and how you're going to help sell the book once it's published becomes very important. Why are you the best person to write it and what do you have now—public speaking engagements, an active website or blog, substantial cred in your industry—that will help you sell this book?

Finally, be cordial. Thank the agent for taking the time to read your query and consider your manuscript. Ask if you may send more, in the format she desires (partial, full, etc.).

Think of the time you spent writing your book. Unfortunately, you can't send your book to an agent for a first impression. Your query *is* that first impression. Give it the time it deserves. Keep it professional. Keep it formal. Let it be a firm handshake—not a sloppy kiss. Let it be a first meeting that evolves into a lifetime relationship—not a rejection slip. But expect those slips. Just like you don't become lifelong friends with everyone you meet at a cocktail party, you can't expect every agent you pitch to sign you. Be patient. Keep pitching. And in the meantime, start writing that next book.

DOS AND DON'TS FOR QUERYING AGENTS

DO:

- Keep the tone professional.
- Query a specific agent at a specific agency.
- Proofread. Double-check the spelling of the agency and the agent's name.
- Keep the query concise, limiting the overall length to one page (single space, 12-point type in a commonly used font).
- Focus on the plot, not your bio, when pitching fiction.
- Pitch agents who represent the type of material you write.
- Check an agency's submission guidelines to see how it would like to be queried—for example, via e-mail or mail—and whether or not to include a SASE.
- Keep pitching, despite rejections.

DON'T:

- Include personal info not directly related to the book. For example, stating that you're a parent to three children doesn't make you more qualified than someone else to write a children's book.

- Say how long it took you to write your manuscript. Some bestselling books took 10 years to write—others, six weeks. An agent doesn't care how long it took—an agent only cares if it's good. Same thing goes with drafts—an agent doesn't care how many drafts it took you to reach the final product.

- Mention that this is your first novel or, worse, the first thing you've ever written aside from grocery lists. If you have no other publishing credits, don't advertise that fact. Don't mention it at all.

- State that your book has been edited by peers or professionals. Agents expect manuscripts to be edited, no matter how the editing was done.

- Bring up screenplays or film adaptations—you're querying an agent about publishing a book, not making a movie.

- Mention any previous rejections.

- State that the story is copyrighted with the U.S. Copyright Office or that you own all rights. Of course you own all rights. You wrote it.

- Rave about how much your family and friends loved it. What matters is that the agent loves it.

- Send flowers, baked goods or anything else except a self-addressed stamped envelope (and only if the SASE is required).

- Follow up with a phone call. After the appropriate time has passed (many agencies say how long it will take to receive a response) follow up in the manner you queried— via e-mail or mail.

KARA GEBHART UHL was formerly a managing editor at *Popular Woodworking Magazine* and later, *Writer's Digest* magazine, Kara Gebhart Uhl now freelance writes and edits for trade and consumer publications from her 100-year-old four-square in Fort Thomas, KY. She also actively writes about the joys and challenges of raising a 3-year-old daughter and twin 1-year-old boys at pleiadesbee.com, which is part of Cincinnati.com's Locals on Living blog network. An essay she wrote, which she originally read for WVXU's "This I Believe" program, is included in *This I Believe: Life Lessons* (Wiley) in fall 2011. You can read more of her work at karagebhartuhl.com.

From: Garth Stein
To: Jeff Kleinman
Subject: Query: "The Art of Racing in the Rain" ①

Dear Mr. Kleinman:

② Saturday night I was participating in a fundraiser for the King County Library System out here in the Pacific Northwest, and I met your client Layne Maheu. He spoke very highly of you and suggested that I contact you.

③ I am a Seattle writer with two published novels. I have recently completed my third novel, *The Art of Racing in the Rain*, and I find myself in a difficult situation: My new book is narrated by a dog, and my current agent ④ told me that he cannot (or will not) sell it for that very reason. Thus, I am seeking new representation.

⑤ *The Art of Racing in the Rain* is the story of Denny Swift, a race car driver who faces profound obstacles in his life, and ultimately overcomes them by applying the same techniques that have made him successful on the track. His story is narrated by his "philosopher dog," Enzo, who, having a nearly human soul (and an obsession with opposable thumbs), believes he will return as a man in his next lifetime.

⑥ My last novel, *How Evan Broke His Head and Other Secrets*, won a 2006 Pacific Northwest Booksellers Association Book Award, and since the award ceremony a year ago, I have given many readings, workshops and lectures promoting the book. When time has permitted, I've read the first chapter from *The Art of Racing in the Rain*. Audience members have been universally enthusiastic and vocal in their response, and the first question asked is always: "When can I buy the book about the dog?" Also very positive.

⑦ I'm inserting, below, a short synopsis of *The Art of Racing in the Rain*, and my biography. Please let me know if the novel interests you; I would be happy to send you the manuscript.

Sincerely,
Garth Stein

① Putting the word "Query" and the title of the book on the subject line of an e-mail often keeps your e-mail from falling into the spam folder. ② One of the best ways of starting out correspondence is figuring out your connection to the agent. ③ The author has some kind of track record. Who's the publisher, though? Were these both self-published novels, or were there reputable publishers involved? (I'll read on, and hope I find out.) ④ This seems promising, but also know this kind of approach can backfire, because we agents tend to be like sheep—what one doesn't like, the rest of us are wary of, too (or, conversely, what one likes, we all like). But in this case getting in the "two published novels" early is definitely helpful. ⑤ The third paragraph is the key pitch paragraph and Garth gives a great description of the book—he sums it up, gives us a feel for what we're going to get. This is the most important part of your letter. ⑥ Obviously it's nice to see the author's winning awards. Also good: The author's not afraid of promoting the book. ⑦ The end is simple and easy—it doesn't speak of desperation, or doubt, or anything other than polite willingness to help.

❷ SAMPLE QUERY 2: YOUNG ADULT
Agent's Comments: Ted Malawer (Upstart Crow Literary)

Dear Mr. Malawer:

I would like you to represent my 65,000-word contemporary teen novel *My Big Nose & Other Natural Disasters*.

❶ Seventeen-year-old Jory Michaels wakes up on the first day of summer vacation with her same old big nose, no passion in her life (in the creative sense of the word), and all signs still pointing to her dying a virgin. Plus, her mother is busy roasting a chicken for Day #6 of the Dinner For Breakfast Diet.

❷ In spite of her driving record (it was an accident!), Jory gets a job delivering flowers and cakes to Reno's casinos and wedding chapels. She also comes up with a new summer goal: saving for a life-altering nose job. She and her new nose will attract a fabulous boyfriend. Nothing like the shameless flirt Tyler Briggs, or Tom who's always nice but never calls. Maybe she'll find someone kind of like Gideon at the Jewel Café, except better looking and not quite so different. Jory survives various summer disasters like doing yoga after sampling Mom's Cabbage Soup Diet, Enforced Mother Bonding With Crazy Nose Obsessed Daughter Night, and discovering Tyler's big secret. But will she learn to accept herself and maybe even find her passion, in the creative (AND romantic!) sense of the word?

❸ I have written for *APPLESEEDS, Confetti, Hopscotch, Story Friends, Wee Ones Magazine*, the *Deseret News, Children's Playmate* and Blooming Tree Press' *Summer Shorts* anthology. I won the Utah Arts Council prize for *Not-A-Dr. Logan's Divorce Book*. My novels *Jungle Crossing* and *Going Native!* each won first prize in the League of Utah Writers contest. I currently serve as an SCBWI Regional Advisor.

❹ I submitted *My Big Nose & Other Natural Disasters* to Krista Marino at Delacorte because she requested it during our critique at the summer SCBWI conference (no response yet).

Thank you for your time and attention. I look forward to hearing from you.

Sincerely,
Sydney Salter Husseman

❶ With hundreds and hundreds of queries each month, it's tough to stand out. Sydney, however, did just that. First, she has a great title that totally made me laugh. Second, she sets up her main character's dilemma in a succinct and interesting way. In one simple paragraph, I have a great idea of who Jory is and what her life is about—the interesting tidbits about her mother help show the novel's sense of humor, too. ❷ Sydney's largest paragraph sets up the plot and the conflict, and introduces some exciting potential love interests and misadventures that I was excited to read about. Again, Sydney really shows off her fantastic sense of humor, and she leaves me hanging with a question that I needed an answer to. ❸ She has writing experience and has completed other manuscripts that were prize-worthy. Her SCBWI involvement—while not a necessity—shows me that she has an understanding of and an interest in the children's publishing world. ❹ The fact that an editor requested the manuscript is always a good sign. That I knew Krista personally and highly valued her opinion was, as Sydney's main character Jory would say, "The icing on the cake."

Dear Ms. Wolfson:

① Have you ever wanted to know the best day of the week to buy groceries or go out to dinner? Have you ever wondered about the best time of day to send an e-mail or ask for a raise? What about the best time of day to schedule a surgery or a haircut? What's the best day of the week to avoid lines at the Louvre? What's the best day of the month to make an offer on a house? What's the best time of day to ask someone out on a date? **②**

My book, *Buy Ketchup in May and Fly at Noon: A Guide to the Best Time to Buy This, Do That, and Go There*, has the answers to these questions and hundreds more.

③ As a long-time print journalist, I've been privy to readership surveys that show people can't get enough of newspaper and magazine stories about the best time to buy or do things. This book puts several hundreds of questions and answers in one place—a succinct, large-print reference book that readers will feel like they need to own. Why? Because it will save them time and money, and it will give them valuable information about issues related to health, education, travel, the workplace and more. In short, it will make them smarter, so they can make better decisions. **④**

Best of all, the information in this book is relevant to anyone, whether they live in Virginia or the Virgin Islands, Portland, Oregon, or Portland, Maine. In fact, much of the book will find an audience in Europe and Australia.

⑤ I've worked as a journalist since 1984. In 1999, the Virginia Press Association created an award for the best news writing portfolio in the state—the closest thing Virginia had to a reporter-of-the-year award. I won it that year and then again in 2000. During the summer of 2007, I left newspapering to pursue book projects and long-form journalism.

⑥ I saw your name on a list of top literary agents for self-help books, and I read on your website that you're interested in books that offer practical advice. *Buy Ketchup in May and Fly at Noon* offers plenty of that. Please let me know if you'd like to read my proposal.

Sincerely,
Mark Di Vincenzo

① I tend to prefer it when authors jump right into the heart of their book, the exception being if we've met at a conference or have some other personal connection. Mark chose clever questions for the opening of the query. All of those questions are, in fact, relevant to my life—with groceries, dinner, e-mail and a raise—and yet I don't have a definitive answer to them. **②** He gets a little more offbeat and unusual with questions regarding surgery, the Louvre, buying a house and dating. This shows a quirkier side to the book and also the range of topics it is going to cover, so I know right away there is going to be a mix of useful and quirky information on a broad range of topics. **③** By starting with "As a long-time print journalist," Mark immediately establishes his credibility for writing on this topic. **④** This helps show that there is a market for this book, and establishes the need for such a book. **⑤** Mark's bio paragraph offers a lot of good information. **⑥** It's nice when I feel like an author has sought me out specifically and thinks we would be a good fit.

❹ SAMPLE QUERY 4: WOMEN'S FICTION
Agent's Comments: Elisabeth Weed (Weed Literary)

Dear Ms. Weed:

❶ Natalie Miller had a plan. She had a goddamn plan. Top of her class at Dartmouth. Even better at Yale Law. Youngest aide ever to the powerful Senator Claire Dupris. Higher, faster, stronger. This? Was all part of the plan. True, she was so busy ascending the political ladder that she rarely had time to sniff around her mediocre relationship with Ned, who fit the three Bs to the max: basic, blond and boring, and she definitely didn't have time to mourn her mangled relationship with Jake, her budding rock star ex-boyfriend.

The lump in her right breast that Ned discovers during brain-numbingly bland morning sex? That? Was most definitely not part of the plan. And Stage IIIA breast cancer? Never once had Natalie jotted this down on her to-do list for conquering the world. When her (tiny-penised) boyfriend has the audacity to dump her on the day after her diagnosis, Natalie's entire world dissolves into a tornado of upheaval, and she's left with nothing but her diary to her ex-boyfriends, her mornings lingering over "The Price is Right," her burnt-out stubs of pot that carry her past the chemo pain, and finally, the weight of her life choices—the ones in which she might drown if she doesn't find a buoy.

❷ *The Department of Lost and Found* is a story of hope, of resolve, of digging deeper than you thought possible until you find the strength not to crumble, and ultimately, of making your own luck, even when you've been dealt an unsteady hand.

❸ I'm a freelance writer and have contributed to, among others, *American Baby, American Way, Arthritis Today, Bride's, Cooking Light, Fitness, Glamour, InStyle Weddings, Men's Edge, Men's Fitness, Men's Health, Parenting, Parents, Prevention, Redbook, Self, Shape, Sly, Stuff, USA Weekend, Weight Watchers, Woman's Day, Women's Health,* and ivillage.com, msn.com and women.com. I also ghostwrote *The Knot Book of Wedding Flowers.*

If you are interested, I'd love to send you the completed manuscript. Thanks so much! Looking forward to speaking with you soon.

Allison Winn Scotch

❶ The opening sentence reads like great jacket copy, and I immediately know who our protagonist is and what the conflict for her will be. (And it's funny, without being silly.) ❷ The third paragraph tells me where this book will land: upmarket women's fiction. (A great place to be these days!) ❸ This paragraph highlights impressive credentials. While being able to write nonfiction does not necessarily translate over to fiction, it shows me that she is someone worth paying more attention to. And her magazine contacts will help when it comes time to promote the book.

Dear Michelle Brower:

❶ "I spent two days in a cage at the SPCA until my parents finally came to pick me up. The stigma of bringing your undead son home to live with you can wreak havoc on your social status, so I can't exactly blame my parents for not rushing out to claim me. But one more day and I would have been donated to a research facility."

Andy Warner is a zombie.

After reanimating from a car accident that killed his wife, Andy is resented by his parents, abandoned by his friends, and vilified by society. Seeking comfort and camaraderie in Undead Anonymous, a support group for zombies, Andy finds kindred souls in Rita, a recent suicide who has a taste for consuming formaldehyde in cosmetic products, and Jerry, a 21-year-old car crash victim with an artistic flair for Renaissance pornography.

❷ With the help of his new friends and a rogue zombie named Ray, Andy embarks on a journey of personal freedom and self-discovery that will take him from his own casket to the SPCA to a media-driven, class-action lawsuit for the civil rights of all zombies. And along the way, he'll even devour a few Breathers.

Breathers is a contemporary dark comedy about life, or undeath, through the eyes of an ordinary zombie. In addition to *Breathers*, I've written three other novels and more than four dozen short stories—a dozen of which have appeared in small press publications. Currently, I'm working on my fifth novel, also a dark comedy, about fate.

Enclosed is a two-page synopsis and the first chapter of *Breathers*, with additional sample chapters or the entire manuscript available upon request. I appreciate your time and interest in considering my query and I look forward to your response.

Sincerely,
Scott G. Browne

❶ What really draws me to this query is the fact that it has exactly what I'm looking for in my commercial fiction—story and style. Scott includes a brief quote from the book that manages to capture his sense of humor as an author and his uniquely relatable main character (hard to do with someone who's recently reanimated). I think this is a great example of how query letters can break the rules and still stand out in the slush pile. I normally don't like quotes as the first line, because I don't have a context for them, but this quote both sets up the main concept of the book *and* gives me a sense of the character's voice. This method won't necessarily work for most fiction, but it absolutely is successful here. ❷ The letter quickly conveys that this is an unusual book about zombies, and being a fan of zombie literature, I'm aware that it seems to be taking things in a new direction. I also appreciate how Scott conveys the main conflict of his plot and his supporting cast of characters—we know there is an issue for Andy beyond coming back to life as a zombie, and that provides momentum for the story.

SYNOPSIS WORKSHOP

Compose an effective novel summary.

by Chuck Sambuchino

Before you submit your novel to an agent or publisher, there are things you need to do. First and foremost, you must finish the work. If you contact an agent and she likes your idea, she will ask to see some or all of the manuscript. You don't want to have to tell her it won't be finished for another six months. If your novel is complete and polished, it's time to write your query and synopsis. After that, you're ready to test the agent and editor waters.

How you submit your novel package will depend on each agent or publisher's specified submission guidelines. You'll find that some want only a query letter; others request a query letter and the complete manuscript; some prefer a query letter plus three sample chapters and a synopsis; and still others request a query letter, a few sample chapters, an outline *and* a synopsis. All want a SASE (self-addressed, stamped envelope) with |adequate postage, unless they request an electronic submission. To determine what you need to submit, visit the agent or publisher's website for guidelines, or consult a current edition of a market resource such as *Novel & Short Story Writer's Market*, *Writer's Market* or *Guide to Literary Agents*. These sources have submission specifications that come straight from the editors and agents telling you just what to send, how to send it and when to anticipate a response.

Be prepared to send at least a query letter, a synopsis and three consecutive sample chapters. These are the most important—and most requested—parts of your novel package. You may not need to send them all in the same submission package, but you probably will need to use each of them at one time or another, so prepare everything before you start submitting. Here we'll focus on what writers often find the most difficult component of their novel submission package: the synopsis.

DEFINING SYNOPSIS

The synopsis supplies key information about your novel (plot, theme, characterization, setting), while also showing how these coalesce to form the big picture. You want to quickly tell what your novel is about without making an editor or agent read the novel in its entirety.

There are no hard and fast rules about the synopsis. In fact, there's conflicting advice about the typical length of a synopsis. Most editors and agents agree, though: The shorter, the better.

When writing your synopsis, focus on the essential parts of your story, and try not to include sections of dialogue unless you think they're absolutely necessary. (It's OK to inject a few strong quotes from your characters, but keep them brief.) Finally, even though the synopsis is only a condensed version of your novel, it must seem complete.

Keep events in the same order as they happen in the novel (but don't break them down into individual chapters). Remember that your synopsis should have a beginning, a middle and an ending (yes, you must tell how the novel ends to round out your story).

That's what's required of a synopsis: You need to be concise, compelling and complete, all at the same time.

CRAFTING TWO SYNOPSES

Because there is no definitive length to a synopsis, it's recommended you have two versions: a long synopsis and a short synopsis.

In past years, there used to be a fairly universal system regarding synopses. For every 35 or so pages of your manuscript, you would have one page of synopsis explanation, up to a maximum of eight pages.

So, if your book was 245 pages, double-spaced, your synopsis would be approximately seven pages. This was fairly standard, and allowed writers a decent amount of space to explain their story. You should write a synopsis following these guidelines first. This will be your long synopsis.

The problem is that during the past few years, agents have gotten busier and busier, and now they want to hear your story now-now-now. Many agents today request synopses of no more than two pages. Some even say one page, but two pages is generally acceptable. To be ready to submit to these agents, you'll also need to draft a new, more concise summary—the short synopsis.

So, once you've written both, which do you submit? If you think your short synopsis is tight and effective, always use that. However, if you think the long synopsis is actually more effective, then you will sometimes submit one and sometimes submit the other. If an agent requests two pages max, send only the short one.

If she says simply, "Send a synopsis," and you feel your longer synopsis is superior, submit the long one. If you're writing plot-heavy fiction, such as thrillers and mysteries, you might really benefit from submitting a longer, more thorough synopsis.

Your best bet on knowing what to submit is to follow the guidelines of the agency or publisher in question.

There are no hard and fast rules about the synopsis. In fact, there's conflicting advice about the typical length of a synopsis. Most editors and agents agree, though: The shorter, the better.

FORMATTING ELECTRONIC SUBMISSIONS

Some editors or agents might ask you to submit your synopsis via e-mail or on a CD. The editor or agent can provide you with specific formatting guidelines indicating how she wants it sent and the type of files she prefers.

If an agent or editor does request an electronic submission, keep the following four points in mind:

1. Follow the same formatting specs as for a paper (hard copy) synopsis submission.
2. When sending your synopsis via e-mail, put the name of your novel in the subject line (but don't use all capital letters—it's just obnoxious).
3. Send the synopsis as an attachment to your e-mail unless the agent requests you cut and paste it in the e-mail body.
4. Include a cover letter in the body of your e-mail, and your cover page and table of contents in the file along with the synopsis.

PUTTING IT ALL TOGETHER

Now you know the basics of synopsis writing. Read on for explanations of mistakes to avoid in your synopsis, as well as an example of what a well-crafted, properly formatted synopsis should look like.

Excerpted from *Formatting & Submitting Your Manuscript, 3rd edition* © 2009 by Chuck Sambuchino and the Editors of Writer's Digest Books, with permission from Writer's Digest Books.

MISTAKES TO AVOID IN YOUR SYNOPSIS

John Q. Writer **(1)**
123 Author Lane
Writerville, USA 95355 **(2)**

Officer on the Run **(3)**

Investigative officer **(4)** David Black doesn't know where to begin when he gets word Police Chief John Murphy is found dead on his bed—with a silver bullet between his eyes and half-inch nail marks running down his back. Black has to answer two questions: Who would kill the Chief, and why?

It turns out quite a few people aren't too pleased with the Chief. He's been on the force for 23 years and no doubt made some enemies. On the home front, the Chief was completely out of control. He'd lost all affection for his wife, Mary, who was once the apple of his eye.

Black interviews all of the women that the Chief had affairs with, whom he called his "Seven Deadly Sins," and finds no leads until Marlene Preston, the Chief's seventh "sin." **(5)** She reveals how the Chief repeatedly would handcuff her arms and legs to four metal poles under the bleachers at the school football stadium. Black drinks himself into a stupor and pours out his problems to a young barmaid, who tells him that the Chief deserved to die.

Black continues investigating the Chief and uncovers all kinds of sordid details. **(6)** The killer is revealed at the end, and it is a total shock and surprise **(7)** to all, especially Black. **(8)**

(1) The genre of the novel is not mentioned, nor is the word length. **(2)** Phone number and e-mail address are missing; make sure the agent or editor will be able to contact you. **(3)** The title of the book should be in all caps, or at the very least bold and italicized. **(4)** The first time a character is introduced, the name should be in all caps. **(5)** Pivotal plot points are glossed over—they should be highlighted. **(6)** Be sure to reveal your novel's ending. **(7)** A short synopsis is preferable, but this is actually too short; it doesn't give enough information about the characters or the plot to make it compelling. **(8)** The characters' motivations and emotions aren't conveyed at all in this synopsis, leaving the editor or agent to think, "Why should I care about these characters?"

THE MAKING OF A SUCCESSFUL SYNOPSIS ❸

John Q. Writer
123 Author Lane
Writerville, CA 95355
(323) 555-0000
johnqwriter@e-mail.com ❶

❷ Mystery
70,000 words

❶ List contact information on the top left corner of first page. ❷ Include novel's genre and word length here. ❸ Avoid numbering the first page. ❹ Center title in all caps. ❺ Use all caps the first time a character is introduced. ❻ Double-space all text. ❼ Establish a good hook, introduce important characters and set up a key conflict.

❹ OFFICER ON THE RUN
Synopsis

Investigative officer ❺ DAVID BLACK doesn't know where to begin when he gets word Police Chief JOHN MURPHY is found dead on his bed—with a silver bullet between his eyes and half-inch nail marks running down his back. Black has to answer two questions: ❻ Who would kill the Chief, and why? ❼

It turns out quite a few people aren't too pleased with the Chief. He'd been on the force for 23 years and no doubt made some enemies. All the townspeople called him Bulldog because he looked like a pit bull, and certainly acted like one.

Countless stories passed through City Hall about how the Chief wouldn't hesitate to roll up his cuffs and beat suspects into submission until they would confess to a crime. That was his method and it worked. He could take control of any person and any situation.

Except his wife and his marriage. On that front, the Chief was completely out of control. He'd lost all affection for his wife, MARY, who was once the apple of his eye but now weighs in at 260 lbs. That was fine with the Chief—the less he had to see Mary, the more time for his own pursuits. But he really had only one pursuit: younger women. That fact he didn't hide. He'd often brag to guys on the force about being the only Chief in the history of law enforcement to "burn through seven dispatchers in just as many years." He even called them his "Seven Deadly Sins." Little did he know that one day they'd all be suspects for his murder.

❷ Black interviews all seven women and finds no leads until MAR-LENE PRESTON, the Chief's "Seventh Deadly Sin," reveals how the Chief repeatedly would handcuff her arms and legs to four metal poles under the bleachers at the school football stadium. Marlene says she's never told anyone about any of it. Black then interrogates ❸ the six other "sins" to see if they had also been physically mistreated. They all say the Chief never tried anything like that with them.

Black drinks himself into a stupor and pours out his problems to a young barmaid, SARAH, who just happens to be the best friend of the Police Lieutenant's daughter, KELLY LIEBERMAN. Sarah tells Black the Chief deserved to die and that he was a jerk, especially to Kelly when she'd baby-sit for the Chief and his wife. According to Sarah, the Chief used to talk dirty to Kelly and then warn her not to tell her father because LIEUTENANT LIEBERMAN was in line for a promotion.

Black interviews Kelly. She denies the Chief did anything but make a few lewd comments on occasion. When Black approaches Kelly's father, Lieutenant Lieberman says Kelly never mentioned a word about the Chief. Black returns to talk with Kelly and asks why she's never mentioned anything to her father. She says she's afraid he'd get upset at her for bringing it up. Black presses further, asking Kelly if the Chief ever did anything other than verbally harass her. Kelly says no.

❹ Black decides to walk back under the bleachers to the spot where Marlene says the Chief repeatedly handcuffed her. There, he notices two sneaker shoestrings on the ground by the four poles Marlene pointed out. The strings had been tied in knots and then cut. Black shows the strings to Marlene and asks if the Chief ever tied her to the poles with them. "Not once," she says. "Handcuffs every time."

❶ Format headers with your name, the title, the word "Synopsis" and the page number. ❷ Begin text three lines below the header. ❸ Write your synopsis in third person, present tense. ❹ In a long synopsis, begin a new scene or twist with the start of a new paragraph (there is not enough room to do this in a short synopsis).

NONFICTION BOOK PROPOSALS

Why you need one, and how to write it.

·····································

by Rachelle Gardner

As a literary agent, I receive queries every day. When one interests me, I ask to see more material. If it's fiction, I'll ask for the manuscript, but if it's nonfiction, I'll ask for a book proposal. Occasionally I receive an e-mail back from the writer: What's a book proposal? Needless to say, that's not the answer I want. A book proposal is the basic sales tool for a nonfiction book—a business plan, if you will. An agent can't sell your book to a publisher without it. You've got to have one, and it's got to be good. Let me put it to you straight: If you don't know what a book proposal is, you're not quite ready to approach an agent. You shouldn't even query an agent with your nonfiction project until your proposal is complete. So if the proposal is your key tool to getting an agent's attention for your book, let's review why you need one and how to compose it.

THE NEED FOR PROPOSALS

If you have a completed manuscript, you may be tempted to think that's enough. It's not. You still need a proposal. Here are a few reasons why:

PUBLISHERS USUALLY DON'T LOOK AT NONFICTION MANUSCRIPTS. The proposal itself provides information publishers need in order to make a purchasing decision. Before they even want to read sample chapters, they will review elements such as the author's platform, how the book fits into the marketplace, and what titles already exist on your topic.

THE BOOK PROPOSAL CAN BE USED THROUGHOUT THE PUBLISHING PROCESS—to help the editorial, marketing and sales teams understand your book. They'll refer to it when they write copy for your book—copy that goes on to your book cover or into marketing, advertising and sales pieces. Therefore you'll want to write the best and most effective "sell language" into your proposal.

A PROPOSAL HELPS YOUR OWN UNDERSTANDING OF THE PROJECT—its structure, theme and execution—and you may be able to identify and correct any problems. If done correctly, your proposal will also help you understand and be able to explain who your audience is and why they would buy your book.

THE PROPOSAL SHOWS THE PUBLISHER THAT YOU'VE DONE YOUR HOMEWORK. It shows you're a professional, and you have a good understanding of the business of publishing. Alternatively, a shoddy proposal makes it easy for an editor to quickly say "No" and toss it in the reject pile.

READING ENTIRE MANUSCRIPTS IS EXTREMELY TIME-CONSUMING. Proposals give editors the information they need to make decisions as quickly and effectively as possible.

ELEMENTS OF A PROPOSAL

Here's a basic rundown of what you should include. The four questions agents and editors will be asking when they sit down to review your project are: What is the project? What is its place in the market? Why is this writer the best individual to write it? And, finally: Can the writer write?

Addressing "What is the project?"

TITLE PAGE: Title, authors' names, phone numbers and e-mail addresses. Contact information for your agent if you have one. If you've had books traditionally published, you can list them under your name.

ONE-SENTENCE SUMMARY: It's the first sentence of your overview and it captures your book in 25 words or fewer. It should be more hook than description. This could also be a tagline that you might see across the top of the back cover.

BRIEF OVERVIEW: This should read similar to back-cover copy. It should be exciting, informative, and make someone want to read your book. It tells the publisher in a succinct form what the book is about, why this project is necessary and unique, and who the market is. Aim for one page single-spaced, or two at the most.

FELT NEED: What needs will your book fulfill that your audience is already aware of? What questions are they asking that your book will answer? What do they want that you can give them?

DETAILS: How many words will your book be? (Words, not pages.) Is the book complete? If not, how long after the signing of a contract will it take you to complete the book? (Two to six months is typical.) Are you envisioning photos or illustrations as part of the project? Will you be responsible for collecting art or illustrations for the book?

Addressing "What is its place in the market?"

THE MARKET: Whom do you see as the audience for the book? Make sure you identify whether it's a larger, general audience or a niche market. More is not always better. What's important is whether you've accurately identified your audience(s). Don't say your book is for "all adults ages 18 to 68." Find a way to identify and categorize specific groups of people who will want your book. Is it for skateboard enthusiasts? New moms? Pop culture junkies? Fans of college football?

You'll also want to answer such questions as: Why would somebody buy this book? How is this audience reached? Do you have any special relationships to the market? What books and magazines does this audience already read? What radio and TV programs do they tune into? Demonstrate an understanding of exactly who will buy your book and why. For example, instead of naming a potential audience group as "new moms," can you further delve into the audience and describe as "new moms who are on the cutting edge of parenting techniques and read upscale parenting magazines."

COMPETITIVE ANALYSIS: What other books are in print on the same subject? How is your book different and better? (Never say there are no books like yours. There is always competition.) List four to eight books that could be considered most comparable to yours. List the title, author, ISBN and year of publication. (Books in the last two to three years are best.) Then write a couple of sentences explaining what that book is about, and how yours is different, better, and/or a good complement to it. If possible, add book sale numbers. If you see online that a comparative book passed a half million sales in June 2011, say so.

This section is more important than you might think. It forces you to become familiar with what's already been written along the same lines as your book. It shows you whether there is a hole in the market that your book can fill, or whether the topic has already been done to death (in which case, you go back to the drawing board and tweak your idea so that it takes a different approach or says something other than what everyone else is saying). It shows the publisher that you know your genre or category well. It alerts your publisher to any possible sales issues regarding competition. It helps everyone (editors, marketing, sales, design) to capture a vision for your book, to understand it a little better, to know which section of the bookstore it goes in. To find all comparative titles, use Amazon and Google to search for books using a variety of means; don't limit yourself to one particular search term or one method. Go deeper than the titles to make sure you're not missing anything; search using different keywords. I recommend an actual trip to the bookstore (strange concept, I know) rather than solely online research. Lastly, don't criticize the other books or say they're terrible (even if you think they are). Simply highlight the differences.

Addressing "Why is this writer the best individual to write it?"

ABOUT THE AUTHORS: Half page to a full page on each author. Why are you qualified to write this book? Make a good case for you as the best possible author for a book on this topic. Be sure to include any academic or professional credentials, as well as work or life experiences that qualify you. Have you won awards? Possess relevant degrees? This is also where you list any previously published books along with sales figures. Be sure to include the title, publisher, year published, and number of copies sold. You can also include your published magazine or journal articles here. If you have a large number of these, don't list them all individually, but find a way to convey the breadth of your work. For example, one bullet point could be something like, "From 2005 to 2011, (Author) had sixteen articles appear in *Money* magazine."

AUTHOR MARKETING: This is where you'll talk about your platform. How are you able to reach your target audience to market your book? This is not the place for expressing your willingness to participate in marketing. This is the place for concrete facts: what you've already done, what contacts you already have, and what plans you've already made to help market your book.

Feel free to mention things such as speaking engagements already booked, radio or television programs on which you're scheduled to appear (or have in the past), a newsletter you're already sending out regularly, or a blog or website that gets an impressive number of daily page views. This section should be specific, and include numbers wherever possible. For example, on your biggest speaking engagements, list the size of each audience; also, give specific stats on your blog or website traffic. This is not the place to say that your book would be terrific on the "Today" show, unless you can document that the "Today" show has already contacted you.

If you're writing a novel, don't worry about creating a proposal when you're looking for an agent. Concentrate on writing your book and then a terrific query. If your agent prefers to submit fiction business proposals to publishers, he or she will let you know. However, before querying, you should at least have these three things ready: The hook: one sentence. The pitch: This is the one- or two-paragraph pitch for the book that you probably used in your query. The synopsis: These are difficult to write without it being awful to read, but necessary nonetheless. Aim for one to three pages, single-spaced—giving the gist of the entire story, including the main plot twists and the ending.

Addressing "Can the writer write?"

ANNOTATED CHAPTER OUTLINE: This is where it becomes crucial that your book is well organized and completely thought out. You will need chapter titles and a couple of sentences capturing each chapter's theme. From this outline, the editor will gain an understanding of your book as a whole. You'll need to make sure the outline communicates that you will deliver on what your proposal promises.

SAMPLE CHAPTERS: Include the Introduction (if you have one) and Chapter 1, along with one other chapter (either Chapter 2, or one from later in the book). Make sure they're polished and perfect! The two sample chapters should not only be well written, but each one should have a high degree of interest and be designed to grab an editor's attention. Ideally the two chapters should highlight different aspects of your writing. For example, if one is general, the other one can be more specific, covering one aspect of your topic. If one of the chapters is more personal, the other can be instructive or professional. Your goal is to give the editor an idea of your range

WHAT ABOUT FICTION?

If you're writing a novel, don't worry about creating a proposal when you're looking for an agent. Concentrate on writing your book and then a terrific query. If your agent prefers to submit fiction business proposals to publishers, he or she will let you know. However, before querying, you should at least have these three things ready: The hook: one sentence. The pitch: This is the one-or two-paragraph pitch for the book that you probably used in your query. The synopsis: These are difficult to write without it being awful to read, but necessary nonetheless. Aim for one to three pages, double-spaced—giving the gist of the entire story, including the main plot twists and the ending.

as an author. The execution—the quality of writing in the sample chapters—is extremely important. The editor might love your book idea, but they also need to know you can deliver a well-written book.

SOME LAST TIPS

There are many acceptable formats for book proposals, so don't be overly stressed about it. Just make sure it looks nice, and is easy to read and well organized. Always err on the side of more white space—i.e., don't crunch everything together on the page. Aim for a pleasing reading experience. Double-space the overview and sample chapters.

Make sure to demonstrate that you have enough material to fill an entire book. One pitfall of many nonfiction authors is presenting a topic that doesn't seem to warrant a book but rather a long magazine article. Prove you have the content to fill a book.

Remember that the book proposal is a sales tool. Like any good salesperson, you'll need to anticipate all possible objections to your book, and overcome them in your proposal. Imagine the questions the editor will be asking, and answer them.

Lastly, be yourself in the proposal! Just because a book proposal is a professional document and a sales tool does not mean it should be dry and boring. Bring your personality to the page. Whatever voice you've used in your book, be sure to use it in your proposal, too. If you're seeking more information about proposals, seek out either *Write the Perfect Book Proposal* by Jeff Herman and Deborah Levine Herman, or *How to Write a Book Proposal, 4th Ed.*, by Michael Larsen. Both address and dissect real proposals that sold.

RACHELLE GARDNER is a literary agent with WordServe Literary Group, representing both fiction and nonfiction. She has been in the publishing business for 15 years, with experience in marketing, sales, international rights, acquisitions and editorial. Rachelle accepts all genres of adult fiction except fantasy and sci-fi, and prefers stories with strong characters and page-turning plots. In nonfiction, she's looking for health, practical self-help, memoir, books for Christians, and a variety of other topics. She wants nonfiction authors with significant marketing platforms who understand the importance of self-promotion. Her blog is cba-ramblings.blogspot.com.

PHOTO: Heather Sams Fine Portraits

MAKE THE MOST OF A WRITERS CONFERENCE

Meet agents, editors and writing peers.

....

by Ricki Schultz

If you've picked up this book, chances are, you're serious about writing and want to know how to advance to the next level. That said, no matter what the stage of your writing career, as a serious professional, you should attend writers conferences.

Writers conferences are events where writers gather together to see presentations and seminars from accomplished people in the industry. Some events last a day; others last a weekend. Other events may even last a week—but those are most likely *retreats*, which focus on sitting down to relax and write, rather than conferences, which are about mingling and learning. This article will address conferences—and all the reasons you should think about heading out to one this year.

REASONS TO ATTEND

Networking

First off, writing is a business. If you're looking to land an agent or sign a book deal with such-and-such a publisher, the chances of that happening without networking are slim to nonexistent; you have to get out there and make things happen. Conferences are golden opportunities to connect not only with industry professionals but other writers as well.

As well, writing can be a *lonely* business. Although you might get on a roll, you can also lose your flow in an instant. It's during those times that writers most need the advice, ideas and companionship of other writers. Conferences are chockfull of people—just like you—who know what it's like to consider setting their manuscripts ablaze after yet another revision. If you've ever been rereading your manuscript and wished you had a friend who could give a critique, conferences are where you meet such friends.

Seminars

Other than providing you with a place to rub elbows with industry professionals and other write-minded folks, writers conferences offer myriad opportunities for you to learn more about the craft and business of writing. Published authors, as well as editors and agents, teach seminars and sit on panels. Presentation schedules vary, but they usually include sessions on everything from drafting query letters to developing characters.

Some presenters assign in-class exercises or homework; some divulge secrets on how they structure plot; but every conference is packed with tips on how to shape your writing. In addition, most offer group or one-on-one critique sessions with authors, agents and editors, so you can get specific feedback on how to attack your current project.

HOW TO CHOOSE AN EVENT

If you've made up your mind that you want to attend a conference but have no idea which one to attend, it's all a matter of asking yourself some simple questions.

Do you want a general event, a specialized conference or a retreat?

General conferences are just what you think they are—events that are general in nature and geared toward all categories and levels of writers. There are hundreds of these nationwide every year, and most of the biggest fall under this category. Just as there are plenty of general events, there are also conferences that focus on a particular category of writing. If you are writing kids books, romance, Christian themes or mystery/thriller, there are specialized conferences out there for you. Lastly, retreats are longer events designed to let writers write, rather than sit in on panels or pitch agents.

What do you want to get out of the experience?

This question, obviously, is key. Perhaps if you want to just sit down and write—maybe finally finish that novel—then an intensive retreat is just what you need. Do you want to sit down and learn? Are you ready to pitch agents? If so, then you want to look for conferences that not only have agents in attendance, but have agents in attendance who represent the category you're writing. This is where a specialized conference comes in handy. If you're writing Christian fiction, then all agents in attendance at a Christian conference should listen to your pitch. Bigger conferences often have a slew of editors and agents in attendance—but they also cost more. Start by looking local. You may find an event nearby that has a solid list of seminars and professionals as part of the conference.

MAXIMIZE THE EXPERIENCE

Here are some tips on how to maximize your conference experience and make a lasting impression on the industry's finest.

Be prepared

This involves doing some homework before the conference; however, it's worth the time and effort.

1. BUSINESS CARDS. Cards are a quick, inexpensive way to assert professionalism. *Don't* hand them out to literary agents, editors or authors (unless someone specifically asks), but *do* distribute them whenever you make a connection with another writer. Agents and editors will generally hand *you* a card if they're interested, and they will quickly give instructions on what to send them and how.

2. HAVE WORK HANDY. Even though it's extremely rare for agents and editors to request material from you (outside a pitch session), you want to be prepared for anything and everything—which means having your work handy at a moment's notice. Because agents vary in terms of preferences, print out a few hard copies of your first chapter and synopsis and stick them on your person at all times. For a more "green" option, carry a thumb drive with your first chapter and synopsis on it. That way, you can raid your hotel's business center and print or e-mail your work, should the need arise.

3. STUDY THE FACULTY. Another way to stand out from the crowd is to read up on the presenters. Not only will this prior knowledge aid you in choosing which sessions to attend, but it will also help you zero in on with whom to schmooze. Likewise, having studied up on the industry pros will ease the daunting task of talking to them. When you run into the editor from Your Dream Publisher, you will have something more to say than just an awkward hello.

IN PRACTICE: The second day of one of the conferences I attended, I sat with some faculty members—one being an editor who didn't represent my genre. This relieved me, as I was just looking for a friendly dinner that night. No pitching. Someone else asked what I was working on, so I gave a short synopsis of my manuscript. Later, the editor at our table approached me and requested some pages. She said that she had recently worked on a young adult book and was interested in building her list in that area. Even though I wasn't planning to pitch, I had one ready—and I had brought my work on a flash drive—so I was able to e-mail her with a partial right there. Score!

Dress the part

It's the oldest business advice in the world, but this simple tip can help you stand out at writing conferences: Dress for success. As much as we might resist it because we're writers (and, therefore, averse to anything as cold and unfeeling as the business world), writing is a business. You have to be able to sell your writing—and the first way to do that at a conference is to sell people on *you*. You want to stand out in a positive way—and if you achieve that from something as simple as not wearing jeans, good for you. Your attire won't get you a book deal, but dressing in professional garb will make you pop against all the schlubs who didn't.

IN PRACTICE: At another conference, an agent who'd read some of my pages struck up a conversation, saying she liked my look in addition to the premise of my manuscript, and she thought I'd be marketable. This led to several other conversations throughout the conference—some about my manuscript and some about where I wanted my writing career to take me. And she wanted to see the rest of my manuscript.

This was not *all* because I dressed up—but she'd been to my website, my blog and my online community. I not only "dressed the part" in terms of actual clothing, but in building a platform as well.

Be visible

Sign up for any and all extras the conference offers, such as critiques, pitch sessions, slush fests and contests. Some of these things cost extra money, but they make the experience that much more worth it. Think of them as your takeaways, because you can gain much in terms of feedback, networking and experience from each of them. As well, go to as many sessions as possible while you're there. You can't go to everything, but the more activities you attend, the more people you'll meet, the more you'll learn and the more visible you'll become. After all, how can those agents fall in love with you if they never see you? You can sleep when you get home. In addition, don't hide in the corner during sessions. Ask questions. You've got a unique opportunity to pick this pro's brain, so take advantage of it.

IN PRACTICE: I signed up for a query workshop at the last conference I attended. Although I wasn't querying with my manuscript then, I had a query written. Always one for free feedback (sans a rejection), I read my pitch—and the agent gave me a referral to one of her colleagues. All because I took advantage of a conference "extra" and had the guts to be "visible" within the class as well.

Be open

No one said going to these things isn't scary at first, but the more assertive you are, the more you'll get out of a conference.

ATTENDEES

Walking up to complete strangers may threaten your comfort levels—particularly because you might fear everyone there is more accomplished than you—but you need to do it anyway. If you can't think of a conversation starter, simply ask, "What do you write?" Every attendee fears the same things you do, and they're all dying to talk about what they're writing, what they're reading, whom they've queried, etc. If you overcome your initial nervousness, you'll stand out from the wallflowers and make connections.

Furthermore, talk to anyone and everyone. No matter where you are in your writing journey, be just as open to meeting folks with less experience than you as you are to meeting those with more. Who knows? The guy who just asked you what a literary agent is might be the next Stephen King. If you blow him off to schmooze some big-name agent, that will make just as much of an impression on him as if you'd been friendly; it just won't make the kind of impression you want.

IN PRACTICE: With conferences hosting agents, editors and best-selling authors, I always do my homework before arriving. At a recent conference, I approached some fellow writers at a cocktail hour. Because I'd done my research, I was able to give my new pals the scoop on the who's who around the patio.

INDUSTRY PROFESSIONALS

Even more frightening than chatting up conference attendees is approaching the agents, editors and authors of the faculty. Some of these people are famous; some of these people are from—*gasp*—New York City, and they all hold your publishing career in the palms of their hands.

One common misconception is that these people do not want to be bothered; on the contrary, agents and editors *expect* to field questions and hear pitches at conferences. If there is an opportunity to sit with one of them, take it. Don't stalk the person; just use your best judgment about appropriate times. Often at meals, the faculty will distribute themselves among the conference-goers, so these are perfect opportunities to get to know them.

IN PRACTICE: When researching presenters for a previous conference I attended, I saw that Chuck Sambuchino (editor of *this* book) and I actually shared a mutual friend. I used this fact to start up a conversation. That led to an invitation to dinner with other presenters and attendees. That dinner led to talk of freelance work (and this article you're now reading!). As well, at dinner, I ended up sitting next to an agent with whom I had scheduled a pitch session for the next day (eek!). Sharing that meal with her actually helped take the edge off when it came time for my pitch.

FOLLOW THROUGH

A last way you can stand out and make the most of a writers conference happens after you return home—and it lies in the follow-through. If you got to know someone well enough to exchange information, take a few minutes to shoot your conference buddy an e-mail, saying how much you enjoyed chatting with her. Not only is this important in terms of fostering those sanity-saving writer groups, but you never know: The lady from Wichita, with whom you split the last sugar cookie, might snag an agent before you do—and if you stay in touch with her, you might have a potential referral to her agency within your grasp.

Ultimately, however, to start making splashes at a writers conference, you first need to scrape together the dough and get to one. You already consider yourself to be a serious writer—now prove it.

IN PRACTICE: In the days since both conferences, I have followed up with many of the people I met. Some have become beta readers, critique partners—and friends. What's more, I blogged about the events, and agents commented on my posts!

MY OWN CONFERENCE ADVENTURES

I attended two great conferences in 2010: the Society of Southwestern Authors' Wrangling with Writing Conference in Tuscon, Ariz., and the James River Writers Conference in Richmond, Va.

Both were fantastic midsize conferences—SSA welcomed 120 attendees and 50 faculty members; JRW hosted 200 attendees and 40 faculty members.

The SSA was set up a bit more like a traditional conference; it included all meals—with faculty and keynote speeches. The JRW conference mostly offered sessions that were panels of professionals; although, they added a separate afternoon of workshops, new this year. Both hosted a slew of heavy hitters in the publishing industry—from *New York Times* bestselling authors to agents from all over the country to editors from a number of publishing houses. Pitch sessions and critiques were available at both conferences as well.

First-time and regular conference-goers alike would be comfortable at either location. Both were well organized and packed a lot of punch.

ssa-az.org/

jamesriverwriters.org/

"HOW I GOT MY AGENT"

Five stories by agented writers.

....

by Chuck Sambuchino

 EUGENIA KIM
Author of *The Calligrapher's Daughter, a novel.*

Merit Badges

Once I knew I was writing a novel, I also knew it would help to have published work when I was ready to find an agent. With the dreamy optimism of the inexperienced, I submitted stories and essays to the mountaintops: *The Atlantic*, *The Paris Review* and *Granta*. And thus began a decade-long process of manuscript revision paralleled with humbling self-revision. A few pieces did manage to fill some pages in anthologies and regional literary journals, and I gathered these little recognitions like scout merit badges, pinning them to the sash I'd show to prospective agents.

During the years of schooling, reading, writing and revising, I'd collected a fistful of agents' names from book acknowledgments, industry articles and seminars, and—the golden fleece in the agent search—referral promises from author friends. I had learned about the mechanics of the process: the query letter with its pithy opening sentence, the snappy synopsis, the bio (adorned with my merit badges), the strict compliance to submission guidelines, the helmet for the barrage of rejections. Patient and perhaps too-kind friends had read my novel and delivered thumbs-ups. I began querying literary agents partly because I couldn't face revising the manuscript yet again. Instead, I wrote and repeatedly revised the query letter, synopsis and bio. I should have paid more attention to the lessons that rose from boiling down a manuscript into a one-page description. I was seeing my novel in a different light, its themes shifting in emphasis as I tried to write the kind of copy that would sell the book. Like any loving mother, I believed that no one but I could see the flaws in my 500-page child.

Queries And Setbacks

After so many years working on the novel, the relative speed of creating the query package prodded the impetus to send it out. I mailed it to my best hope, careful to give her an exclusive submission. As a fail-safe measure I bought the latest *Guide to Literary Agents*, checked who might be a good fit for my novel and verified their submission guidelines online. The stars shone brightly the day the agent's assistant called asking for the first 50 pages, and I barely slept—until the rejection came. It included a generous paragraph pointing to the weaknesses that I continued to rationalize away. As a salve, I sharpened the query and sent it out again, and yet again, until I'd burnt through the precious commodity of the half-dozen agents with whom I had a meaningful connection. With each rejection came a revision of my writerly worth, a meek reshaping of the image of big-name agents fighting over my pages flying in scattered delight.

Rather than work on my manuscript, I created a detailed list of agent prospects coded by cold-query acceptance levels, for affinity of their represented books to mine, and charted to date-track the process. About 30 queries in, I received an offer, but the agent's request to radically refocus the novel didn't feel right, nor did the tone of the conversation we had. I agonized over this decision, finally choosing to trust my gut over my eagerness to sign. That experience, along with 40 rejections in nine months, made it impossible to deny that my child wasn't communicating properly. I devoted time to rehabilitate her. Plus, there were only 10 more names on my prospective agent list.

An Unexpected Call

A month later, I knew I had a better product. Even the query felt simple to revise and sounded fresh and clear. And as the winter holidays approached, I had better results.

Three agents requested the complete manuscript. I nurtured hope that my novel would have a little fireside attention in a comfortable home setting.

Then came a call from Nat Sobel. The strange thing was: I'd heard of Nat but he was not one of the many agents I queried. He actually called to say that he had admired my short story in a small literary journal and asked if I had anything book-length. I described the novel and, my brain going clickity-clack, told him that three other agents had the full manuscript.

I sent it overnight to his holiday vacation home—the fireside!—and the next day he said Sobel Weber Associates was interested if I was open to revising the material. This time, knowing that revision had improved my "finished" novel and could only make it better, and with all my expectations thoroughly revised after the year-long querying process, it felt completely right.

② DELILAH MARVELLE
Author of historical romance novels.

PHOTO: Cynthia O'Donnell

A Setback

A few months before the release of my second book, *Lord of Pleasure*, I discovered that my publisher, Kensington, was not going to be renewing contracts. It's a writer's worst nightmare to be rejected by your own publisher once you thought you've made it. What could possibly be worse than being rejected by your own publisher? Letting go of your agent beforehand, which, yes, I'd unfortunately just done. Right after my agent and I parted ways, I got the bad news from Kensington.

So without a contract and without an agent, I basically started over. I queried 15 agents and every single one of them came back with the same answer: "Love the writing but it's a tough market. We can't take on this project right now." Considering that it had originally taken me 11 years to get published and that during those 11 years, I had garnered more than 200 rejections, I knew I needed to keep trudging onward. So I did the one thing I could do. I submitted to publishers on my own. Or at least those that would let me query without an agent (which isn't very many). I queried Avon, HQN and Sourcebooks, and waited.

A Life-changing Event

Two weeks later, I went to the National Romance Writers of America Conference, which I attend every year. It's an amazing writing haven where connections and education abound for all romance writers, published or not. I went with no expectations, just the high hopes that I could push my upcoming book and make some friends.

At one of the luncheons, I sat at a table with a group of lovely women I didn't know and we all started to talk. About the same time, a gentleman nabbed the last empty seat at the table and quietly sat there listening to our conversation. I happened to touch upon the topic of my blog, which I post to every first of the month on topics of sex in the context of history. That is exactly when the gentleman spoke up and said, "That sounds very fascinating. Might I have a card?" Seeing I was discussing my blog, I thought "Perve" (because I seem to attract them), so I drawled, "And you *are*?" He paused, then graciously replied, "Donald Maass." Needless to say, after recognizing the name of this top agent, I choked, gave him my card (feeling much like a dolt) and thought, "Well there goes *that* chance." Then, the night before the conference was over, my life completely changed.

Although there are usually tons of desserts available after the event's Golden Heart and Rita Ceremony, for some reason, this year, there were none to be had as the staff wasn't refilling the platters. Being a chef, I immediately flagged down a waiter, handed him an empty plate and kindly asked him to go into the kitchen and bring me whatever dessert he could find. While I waited by the kitchen door, the editor from Sourcebooks approached me and on the spot offered me a four-book contract based on the proposal for the new series I had submitted. As I stood there in complete shock, the waiter came back and delivered a huge piece of chocolate cake. All for me. So yes, I had my cake and ate it, too. I hardly got home and immediately called up the two other publishers who had my series to let them know I had an offer. Avon passed with glowing compliments, but HQN counteroffered. And that's when I realized, "Holy Cow, I need an agent."

A Clean Slate

My good writing buddies, Lisa Hendrix and Kristina McMorris, quickly offered up their fabulous agents, whom I called immediately. My husband, however, kept pestering me and saying, "Why don't you call Donald Maass?" I cringed. After I had insulted the man? I think not. My husband, however, kept pressing, and needless to say, I caved and called. Lo and behold, Donald not only offered representation, but assistance in honing my writing. To get an agent and writing coach all in one? A complete dream! I signed with him and he helped me through the daunting process of choosing which publisher was best for me.

To receive two offers from two amazing publishers may be what every writer dreams about, but it's not quite as fun filled as you might think when you're actually living it. After some back and forth between the two publishers, I eventually decided on HQN, who offered me a three-book deal.

So what did I learn from my roller-coaster experience? Trust your gut and don't ever, ever let an agent decide your career for you.

③ COLIN BRODERICK
Author of *Oragutan*, a memoir.

Rock Bottom

On the sixth day of the sixth month 2006, I left my apartment in Hells Kitchen with the last of my belongings in a small U-Haul truck to drive to farmhouse up north and try to save my life. It might sound like I'm fabricating the facts here for dramatic effect, but as I started the truck and headed north, I glanced at the dash clock and it read 6:06. It occurred to me then, and I still believe it now, that there was some Dante-esque connection at play here; my life had spiraled to its lowest point. I was a 38-year-old, twice-divorced alcoholic weighing in at an astonishing 115 pounds. I was broke and now I had lost my apartment. It was time to start the long crawl out of the hole I had dug for myself. I had witnessed the depths of the inferno and it held little of the allure it once did for me. I wanted nothing more to do with it.

Within three days, I had started writing what was to become my memoir, *Orangutan*. I had been writing for 20 years since moving to New York from Northern Ireland at the age of 20 to work construction. I'd completed a couple of novels, plays, short stories and notebooks full of poetry—but I had managed to get only one short story published, and that had been 10 years before. I'd spent my 20s convinced that I would be "discovered." An agent or editor would read one page of my manuscript and run to the nearest phone to dial my number with an offer that would catapult me into the waiting arms of the Nobel Prize Committee. It didn't happen. I did send my early manuscripts out to a few agents and agencies, but I can't remember even receiving a rejection letter. It seemed finding an agent was more difficult than finding a publisher. I used to say that you needed an agent to get one in this town.

The Referral

After spending a year on *Orangutan*—a year that saw me back on the bottle for a brief but productive period that added a stint in an upstate jail to my résumé—I started dating a girl who had been a bartender of mine once upon a time. She was a writer, also. She read what I had written and was convinced that this was the manuscript that would finally get me published. She took me back to the city and gave me a place to stay and a desk for my work. I married her for her efforts and quit drinking to devote my time and energy to creating a career for myself in the only profession that has ever made any sense to me: writing.

I was at a meeting one night way downtown—one of those meetings you hear about where the alcoholics gather to drink coffee and smoke their cigarettes—when I heard a guy about my age tell his story. He'd escaped from a locked ward at Bellevue Mental Hospital, and had been the first to escape from the institution since the early 1970s. He'd sobered up and written a book about it, and with the help of his wonderful agent had just nailed down a book deal. I lurked around outside the meeting afterward waiting for my moment. He was quite popular and had a lot of goodbyes to say, but I was patient. This was my guy—I was sure of it. When he finally turned to leave, I followed him around the corner and stopped him with a tap on the shoulder.

"Excuse me, my name's Colin. I just heard your story in there, and it was great. Here's the deal: I heard you say you have an agent. Well, I'm a writer myself and I have this manuscript almost finished that could really use an agent." Here he started mumbling some line about how he had introduced someone to his agent already and it hadn't really worked out for him, but I didn't let him finish. "I can assure you," I told him, "that if you introduce me to your agent, you will always remember this as the night you discovered Colin Broderick." He smiled. I had appealed to his cooky sense of happenstance. He laughed and eyed me skeptically.

"I promise," I said. "I will not embarrass you."

The Pitch

Three days later (thanks to a phone call from this nice man), I was seated in the office of Dystel and Goderich down on Union Square. I was on one couch, and two agents, Jane and Miriam, were on another facing me. "OK, shoot," Jane said, clasping her hands in her lap. The two women glared at me with raised eyebrows.

"What?" I had no idea what to do next.

"Well, why are we sitting here with you? Shoot."

This was the moment I had been waiting for my entire adult life. Here was an honest-to-goodness shot at the hoop. I jumped right in with my story, and within a few minutes I could tell they were warming up. We had made a connection. They asked me if I'd brought anything with me for them to read. I had. I gave them a disc with what I had of the manuscript so far, and within three days I was back in their office signing a contract. I had my agent!—the same agency who represented Barack Obama, a Hemingway, Judge Judy and a Bellevue escapee. I had found my home.

It took six months for them to sell *Orangutan* to Three Rivers Press (Random House, no less). Over the past two years, both Jane and Miriam have been working closely with me helping me refine my next book proposal. They have just submitted it to the publishers. It's been a long hard road, but it's been well worth the wait. And that Bellevue escapee (author Chris Campion) and I became fast friends into the bargain.

④ KRISTYN CROW
Author of several children's picture books.

Sneaking In

Carving out time to attend a week-long writing conference wasn't easy for a mother of seven. I had to arrange baby-sitting, swap carpool shifts, stock the refrigerator and leave a trail of reminder notes for my husband. But the dream of getting a children's picture book published had nagged at me since I was a kid, and I couldn't ignore it any longer. I had been writing stories for 20 years.

When I arrived at the conference registration desk, the secretary told me that Rick Walton's workshop—the one I really wanted—had "no spaces available." She insisted I select another. But Rick Walton was the local guru of picture books, having authored more than 50. I wanted to learn from him. So I snuck into his class, finding an open chair in the corner. Gratefully, nobody shooed me out the door.

I'm One Of "Those People"?

Soon manuscript critiques were underway, and after a dozen or so it was my turn. "Who will volunteer to read this one?" Rick asked. A hand went up, and as my story was read aloud, I tried to pretend my guts weren't twisting into knots. I had written a rhyming, jazzy tale of a rat in the city, told in scat. Admittedly, the thing was odd. Would anybody get it? When the reader finished, there was an awkward silence, then a wave of positive comments. Rick seemed enthusiastic. "There's a literary agent here at the conference you should show this to," he said. I was ecstatic.

A meeting was arranged. I remember entering a small classroom and sitting across from the classy-looking agent in high heels. It was the Dollar Store meets Saks Fifth Avenue. I smiled, introduced myself and gave her my manuscript. She looked it over, then got a confused expression and began to chuckle. "Who sent you to me?" she asked. Before I could answer, she looked up at the ceiling, speaking aloud to some invisible force in the universe: "Why do they always send *these people* to me?" I blinked, dumbstruck. I didn't know who "these people" were, but they sounded pitiful. She handed back my story with a verbal pat on the head, and pointed to the door. Needless to say, I was crushed.

Back in workshops, I privately shared the agent's reaction. Rick shook his head. "She's wrong," he said. "Here. Try this agent." He wrote down the name and address of Kendra Marcus of Bookstop Literary Agency. "Send her your manuscript and a few more of your best things. See what happens." I tucked the piece of paper into my purse, thanking him, but wasn't sure I was ready to set myself up for more rejection.

The conference ended, and I returned to my life of refereeing kid-squabbles, finding missing socks in potted plants, and experimenting with macaroni and cheese. It took several months of prodding from my husband before I had the courage to send off "a few of my best things" to the mysterious agent scrawled on the paper in my purse. Yet finally, I did. And I waited. Then tragedy struck. The United States was attacked on September 11th. Everyone was in an awful state of shock, rage and mourning. Church and synagogue attendance was on the rise as our troops prepared for war. Suddenly my whimsical rat story about—of all places—New York City, which mentioned—of all things—the Twin Towers, seemed ridiculous. It was all bad karma. I put my dream away for good.

The Call

Several weeks after the dust had cleared (both literally and figuratively), I was looking through my pantry when the telephone rang. The voice on the line said, "Kristyn, this is Kendra Marcus from Bookstop Literary Agency. And if you're interested, I'd like to represent you." I dropped the can of chili I was holding. She continued: "I've been reading over your manuscripts and they're very good. If you're willing to make some revisions, I think I can sell these stories."

A year later, Kendra sold *Cool Daddy Rat* to G.P. Putnam's sons. It received starred reviews, and Mike Lester won the Rueben award for his illustrations. Since then, she's sold other picture books for me, including *Bedtime at the Swamp* (HarperCollins), *The Middle-Child Blues* (G.P. Putnam's Sons) and *Skeleton Cat* (Scholastic). Kendra and her perceptive associate, Minju Chang, have been more than agents; they've been mentors, advocates and friends. I am thrilled to be represented by Bookstop.

Sure, one agent didn't connect with my work, but the next enthusiastically signed me on as a client. I'm often haunted by the question, "What if I hadn't tried again?"

---

5 **A.C. ARTHUR**
Author of almost two dozen books, mostly romance.

PHOTO: RW Phtography

Not On The Same Page

Since my first book was published in 2003, my search for an agent has been a long and tedious one. One of the first obstacles I faced was that I didn't really know what the job of an agent was, and therefore, didn't have a clue what I was looking for. Of course that led to my first choice not necessarily being the right one (meaning I signed with the first agent who showed any interest in my work). And three years and three additional contracts later, I released that agent. Why? Because we wanted different things from my writing career—and that is a recipe for disaster in an agent/writer relationship.

I continued to get publishing contracts and to write books, all the while knowing there was something or someone missing from taking my career to the next level.

Referral And Rejection

One day in 2006, during a routine rant about not having an agent, an editor friend of mine suggested Christine Witthohn of Book Cents Literary Agency. My friend's exact words were, "She's a new agent, but she's smart. She knows what she's doing and how to work for you." This sounded fantastic, so I sent Christine an e-mail and she, in turn, asked for a proposal.

The phone call I received from her about two weeks later was not what I'd been expecting. You see, I thought that because I had a referral and because Christine had immediately responded by requesting material, I was a sure thing. Not so!

Christine's exact words were, "You don't need me." I was devastated, but had to respect her honesty. Besides, she was so nice to talk to, the fact that she was actually rejecting me stung just a little less. I couldn't really figure out why she said I didn't need her, because I was convinced I did. But I accepted her decision and tried to move on. This meant the search was still on, and I sent out numerous queries to more agents—some who I'd queried in the past and other new ones. This is a very subjective industry; it all depends on the right editor seeing the right manuscript at the right time. I'm persistent, if nothing else.

A Fated Connection

In early 2008 when a very reputable agent expressed interest in my work, I was overjoyed. Again, I was convinced I'd found the right agent. Again, I was wrong. What was it about me that I just couldn't find the right person to represent my work? The funny thing was, after only a couple of months with this agent, I had a feeling I'd once again missed the mark. There was no real connection. And while I thought I'd done a good job of explaining what I wanted, where I wanted my career to go, we still came out on opposite sides. That's not to say that this agent wasn't good; he just wasn't the one for me.

At this point I still had the same problem; I was sans agent. The publishing houses that I wanted to write for accepted only agented submissions. Besides that, the contracts were changing—the language becoming increasingly more technical—and I knew I wasn't getting the best deals for myself. So on this agent search, I researched and researched and sent only material that I thought specific agents would be interested in. Meanwhile, in April 2009, I finally got to meet Christine at the Romantic Times Booklovers Convention. I didn't pitch her; I just wanted to meet her.

A little while later, I had another proposal and needed some honest feedback—so I called on Christine again for advice. Again, she responded immediately, which I'd always been impressed by because I know how busy agents are. And her response was more like a friend would reply to another friend's message, rather than an agent to an author, so that was very cool! Two months later, I was signing a Book Cents Literary Agency contract. We finally decided we were right for each other. It had taken three years, but I firmly believe in timing, especially in this industry. I also believe in fated connections.

HOW NOT TO START YOUR BOOK

Agents dish about all those things they hate to see in Chapter 1.

by Chuck Sambuchino

Ask literary agents what they're looking for in a first chapter and they'll all say the same thing: "Good writing that hooks me in." Agents appreciate the same elements of good writing that readers do. They want action; they want compelling characters and a reason to read on; they want to see your voice come through in the work and feel an immediate connection with your writing style.

Sure, the fact that agents look for great writing and a unique voice is nothing new. But, for as much as you know about what agents *want* to see in chapter one, what about all those things they *don't* want to see? Obvious mistakes such as grammatical errors and awkward writing aside, writers need to be conscious of first-chapter clichés and agent pet peeves—any of which can sink a manuscript and send a form rejection letter your way.

Have you ever begun a story with a character waking up from a dream? Or opened chapter one with a line of salacious dialogue? Both clichés! Chances are, you've started a story with a cliché or touched on a pet peeve (or many!) in your writing and you don't even know it—and nothing turns off an agent like what agent Cricket Freeman of the August Agency calls "nerve-gangling, major turn-off, ugly-as-sin, nails-on-the-blackboard pet peeves."

To help compile a grand list of these poisonous chapter one no-no's, plenty of established literary agents were more than happy to chime in and vent about everything that they can't stand to see in that all-important first chapter. Here's what they had to say.

DESCRIPTION

"I dislike endless 'laundry list' character descriptions. For example: 'She had eyes the color of a summer sky and long blonde hair that fell in ringlets past her shoulders. Her petite nose was the perfect size for her heart-shaped face. Her azure dress—with the empire waist and long, tight sleeves—sported tiny pearl buttons down the bodice and ivory lace peeked out of the hem in front, blah, blah, blah.' Who cares! Work it into the story."

—LAURIE MCLEAN, *Larsen/Pomada, Literary Agents*

"Slow writing with a lot of description will put me off very quickly. I personally like a first chapter that moves quickly and draws me in so I'm immediately hooked and want to read more."

—ANDREA HURST, *Andrea Hurst & Associates Literary Management*

VOICE AND POINT-OF-VIEW

"A pet peeve of mine is ragged, fuzzy point-of-view. How can a reader follow what's happening? I also dislike beginning with a killer's POV. What reader would want to be in such an ugly place? I feel like a nasty voyeur."

—CRICKET FREEMAN, *The August Agency*

"An opening that's predictable will not hook me in. If the average person could have come up with the characters and situations, I'll pass. I'm looking for a unique outlook, voice, or character and situation."

—DEBBIE CARTER, *Muse Literary Management*

"Avoid the opening line 'My name is …,' introducing the narrator to the reader so blatantly. There are far better ways in chapter one to establish an instant connection between narrator and reader."

—MICHELLE ANDELMAN, *Regal Literary*

"I hate reading purple prose, taking the time to set up—to describe something so beautifully and that has nothing to do with the actual story. I also hate when an author starts something and then says '(the main character) would find out later.' I hate gratuitous sex and violence anywhere in the manuscript. If it is not crucial to the story then I don't want to see it in there, in any chapters."

—CHERRY WEINER, *Cherry Weiner Literary*

"I recently read a manuscript when the second line was something like, 'Let me tell you this, Dear Reader …' What do *you* think of that?"

—SHEREE BYKOFSKY, *Sheree Bykofsky Literary*

ACTION (OR LACK THEREOF)

"I don't really like first-day-of-school beginnings, or the 'From the beginning of time,' or 'Once upon a time' starts. Specifically, I dislike a chapter one where nothing happens."

—JESSICA REGEL, *Jean V. Naggar Literary Agency*

" 'The Weather' is always a problem—the author feels he has to take time to set up the scene completely and tell us who the characters are. I like starting a story *in media res*."

—ELIZABETH POMADA, *Larsen/Pomada, Literary Agents*

"I want to feel as if I'm in the hands of a master storyteller, and starting a story with long, flowery, overly descriptive sentences (kind of like this one) makes the writer seem amateurish and the story contrived. Of course, an equally jarring beginning can be nearly as off-putting, and I hesitate to read on if I'm feeling disoriented by the fifth page. I enjoy when writers can find a good balance between exposition and mystery. Too much accounting always ruins the mystery of a novel, and the unknown is what propels us to read further. It is what keeps me up at night saying, 'Just one more chapter, then I'll go to sleep.' If everything is explained away in the first chapter, I'm probably putting the book down and going to sleep."

—**PETER MILLER**, *Peter Miller Literary*

"Characters that are moving around doing little things, but essentially nothing. Washing dishes and thinking, staring out the window and thinking, tying shoes, thinking. Authors often do this to transmit information, but the result is action in a literal sense but no real energy in a narrative sense. The best rule of thumb is always to start the story where the story starts."

—**DAN LAZAR**, *Writers House*

CLICHÉS AND FALSE BEGINNINGS

"I *hate* it when a book begins with an adventure that turns out to be a dream at the end of the chapter."

—**MOLLIE GLICK**, *Foundry Literary + Media*

"Anything cliché such as 'It was a dark and stormy night' will turn me off. I hate when a narrator or author addresses the reader (e.g., 'Gentle reader')."

—**JENNIE DUNHAM**, *Dunham Literary*

"Sometimes a reasonably good writer will create an interesting character and describe him in a compelling way, but then he'll turn out to be some unimportant bit player. I also don't want to read about anyone sleeping, dreaming, waking up or staring at anything. Other annoying, unoriginal things I see too often: some young person going home to a small town for a funeral, someone getting a phone call about a death, a description of a psycho lurking in the shadows or a terrorist planting a bomb."

—**ELLEN PEPUS**, *Signature Literary Agency*

"I don't like it when the main character dies at the end of chapter one. Why did I just spend all this time with this character? I feel cheated."

—**CRICKET FREEMAN**, *The August Agency*

"1. Squinting into the sunlight with a hangover in a crime novel. Good grief—been done a million times. 2. A sci-fi novel that spends the first two pages describing the strange landscape. 3. A trite statement ('Get with the program' or 'Houston, we have a problem' or 'You go girl' or 'Earth to Michael' or 'Are we all on the same page?'), said by a weenie sales guy, usually in the opening paragraph. 4. A rape scene in a Christian novel, especially in the first chapter. 5. 'Years later, Monica would look back and laugh ...' 6. 'The [adjective] [adjective] sun rose in the [adjective] [adjective] sky, shedding its [adjective] light across the [adjective] [adjective] [adjective] land.' "

—CHIP MACGREGOR, *MacGregor Literary*

"A cheesy 'hook' drives me nuts. I know that they say 'Open with a hook!'—something to grab the reader. While that's true, there's a fine line between a hook that's intriguing and a hook that's just silly. An example of a silly hook would be opening with a line of overtly sexual dialogue. Or opening with a hook that's just too convoluted to be truly interesting."

—DAN LAZAR, *Writers House*

"Here are things I can't stand: Cliché openings in fantasy novels can include an opening scene set in a battle (and my peeve is that I don't know any of the characters yet so why should I care about this battle) or with a pastoral scene where the protagonist is gathering herbs (I didn't realize how common this is). Opening chapters where a main protagonist is in the middle of a bodily function (jerking off, vomiting, peeing or what have you) is usually a firm *no* right from the get-go. Gross. Long prologues that often don't have anything to do with the story. (So common in fantasy, again.) Opening scenes that are all dialogue without any context. I could probably go on ..."

—KRISTIN NELSON, *Nelson Literary*

CHARACTERS AND BACKSTORY

"I don't like descriptions of the characters where writers make the characters seem too perfect. Heroines (and heroes) who are described physically as being unflawed come across as unrelatable and boring. No 'flowing, windswept golden locks'; no 'eyes as blue as the sky'; no 'willowy, perfect figures.' "

—LAURA BRADFORD, *Bradford Literary Agency*

"Many writers express the character's backstory before they get to the plot. Good writers will go back and cut that stuff out and get right to the plot. The character's backstory stays with them—it's in their DNA—even after the cut. To paraphrase Bruno Bettelheim: The more the character in a fairy tale is described, the less the audience will identify with him ... The less the character is characterized and described, the more likely the reader is to identify with him."

—ADAM CHROMY, *Artists and Artisans*

"I'm really turned off when a writer feels the need to fill in all the backstory before starting the story; a story that opens on the protagonist's mental reflection of their situation is (usually) a red flag."

—STEPHANY EVANS, *FinePrint Literary Management*

"One of the biggest problems I encounter is the 'information dump' in the first few pages, where the author is trying to tell us everything we supposedly need to know to understand the story. Getting to know characters in a story is like getting to know people in real life. You find out their personality and details of their life over time."

—RACHELLE GARDNER, *Wordserve Literary*

OTHER PET PEEVES

"The most common opening is a grisly murder scene told from the killer's point of view. While this usually holds the reader's attention, the narrative drive often doesn't last once we get into the meat of the story. A catchy opening scene is great, but all too often it falls apart after the initial pages. I often refer people to the opening of *Rosemary's Baby* by Ira Levin, which is about nothing more than a young couple getting an apartment. It is masterfully written and yet it doesn't appear to be about anything sinister at all. And it keeps you reading."

—IRENE GOODMAN, *Irene Goodman Literary*

"Things I dislike include: 1) Telling me what the weather's like in order to set atmosphere. OK, it was raining. It's *always* raining. 2) Not starting with action. I want to have a sense of dread quite quickly—and not from rain! 3) Sending me anything but the beginning of the book; if you tell me that it 'starts getting good' on page 35, then I will tell you to start the book on page 35, because if even you don't like the first 34, neither will I or any other reader."

—JOSH GETZLER, *Hannigan Salky Getzler Agency.*

"One of my biggest pet peeves is when writers try to stuff too much exposition into dialogue rather than trusting their abilities as storytellers to get information across. I'm talking stuff like the mom saying, 'Listen, Jimmy, I know you've missed your father ever since he died in that mysterious boating accident last year on the lake, but I'm telling you, you'll love this summer camp!' "

—CHRIS RICHMAN, *Upstart Crow Literary*

"I hate to see a whiny character who's in the middle of a fight with one of their parents, slamming doors, rolling eyes, and displaying all sorts of other stereotypical behavior. I also tend to have a hard time bonding with characters who address the reader directly."

—KELLY SONNACK, *Andrea Brown Literary*

RETREATS

Writers' retreats are opportunities for relaxation and writing. Is one right for you?

....

by Tom Bentley

A "writer's retreat" has an old-fashioned kind of sound, bringing to mind a monk, quill in hand, withdrawing to a solitary enclave, or maybe a desert ascetic scribbling in a ragged journal, while the sun beats down on a tin-roofed shack. The fact that I chose Big Sur, California, one of the most stunning spots in all of this fair country, for my own writer's retreat doesn't mean that hunkered-down writing wasn't the focus of the trip. It was. It's just when I took my respites from the page, I had a hundred opportunities to say "wow!"

Choosing the location of your personal writer's retreat is a central question—but understanding your motivation for the retreat in the first place trumps locale. My object was to wake from its slumbers a novel I began three years ago, worked on sporadically, and then left to its own decaying devices for more than a year. Not a word-count goal, but renewed focus. Focus is such a significant issue for writers: writers who can zero in, even for relatively short stretches, can be remarkably productive. A novel is a long march, and ground can be gained in sprints as well, but the key is forward movement. I'd stopped.

Thus, my retreat impetus: remove the distractions of the everyday by removing myself from my everyday—get out of town, get into writing. As for where to, that can be tricky. Big Sur was right on some of the same counts where it was wrong: it's a spectacularly beautiful place, where the hiking is stunning, and where there are many intriguing traveler's pursuits. Is it better to be in a drab place, that tin-roofed shack described above, to really focus? Rationalization or not, my thought was that the inviting diversions, which included lots of exercise, were the perfect counterpart to long stretches at the keyboard. Besides, I could easily drive to Big Sur, so no plane flights, or arriving exhausted from hours at the wheel.

WHERE TO STAY AND HOW TO BEGIN?

I chose to stay in a small cottage, a separate studio of a small, rustic hotel. The cottage was down a little woodsy road, a distance away from a couple of other cottages. The setting was semi-private, quiet and serene, and not pricy. It had a fridge and stove so I could make some of my own meals. I did want a site with Internet access, because I wanted to get some business e-mail while I was there. But I'd recommend *not* having the Net access; it was a partial distraction for me that didn't have a real upside. My packed essentials were a laptop, a notebook for jotting when I was out and about, and a camera to record both diverting pictures and anything that might upon later reflection provoke writing. Oh, and good chocolate.

So, to business: have a plan. Mine was to settle in, and then immediately take care of some "secretarial" aspects of the novel. I'd brought with me a number of chapters handed out in the writer's workshop I'd been in a while back, marked up with questions and suggestions that I'd never addressed.

My thought was that beginning this way would refresh me with the novel's flow, as well as provoke me, by virtue of my fellow workshopper's questions, to make a number of scene, character and structural changes. Those changes, though small, once again put me in the novel's world in both an artistic and mechanical "fix this" way. It worked! In inputting workshop criticism, you have to take what you can—some criticism can sting, but it can be helpful to recognize critical validity in some suggestions.

I labored in a transfixed state for a few hours, so much so I forgot where I was. I got up to stretch, and walked a short distance down a path to a riverbed not far from the cabin. A discovery! There was a small waterfall with a flowing pool, making me wish I could come up with a spontaneous haiku. But I was pleased enough with the wild lilies scattered about.

I celebrated my keyboard satisfactions at a nearby restaurant. The novel's fresh stimulation was real: I almost felt smug to be taking a bunch of energetic notes on upcoming scenes while at dinner. The retreat frame was being established, with everything in its time: write, stretch, break, eat, walk—the basics. But basics that seem elusive at home.

NEGATIVE IONS ARE POSITIVE

The next day, I took a short beach walk on one of Big Sur's picturesque, craggy beaches, one with a big blowhole that shot waves through in bright, fluffy bursts of whitewater. I wanted the retreat to be truly about writing, so I tried to return my thoughts to the writing process. It's easy to do, staring at the sea, seeing both the regular and irregular rhythms of waves and thinking of them in terms of the rhythms of words, sometimes swelling, sometimes retreating, sometimes cascading forth. And you can get an energy boost just from drinking in the negative ions of the sea.

I was feeling the rejuvenation of the retreat in small bursts. It reminded me of that F. Scott Fitzgerald quote, "My own happiness in the past often approached such an ecstasy that I could not share it even with the person dearest to me, but had to walk it away in quiet streets and lanes with only fragments of it to distill into little lines in books." I felt pushed to produce on the page, but merrily pushed. But I also felt that welcome pressure to not merely produce, but to pay attention to *everything*—don't slack on a single word. This was retreat energy, new to me.

Focus became easier: there's a happiness in crafting a single sentence, an ephemeral feeling, but akin to that Zen sense of a perfect cup of tea. Crafting sentences made me crave a cigar on my cottage deck, more my cup of tea. I was paranoid the organic police of Big Sur would come out of the mountains to shackle me, but I escaped unscathed. Late that night, the moon was up. I kept turning its reflection to my writing reflection: sometimes the words fell like moonbeams, sometimes the moon was dry and distant like the words, which must be seduced. But the retreat channeling—me and the work—made me trust the process.

My third day, I got a lot of new writing done, as well as a lot of loose outlining of scenes for subsequent chapters. I didn't want to leave my cabin without a line of coaches that were going to pull me further into the writing. I feared a post-retreat retreat, away from the writing. No. Even the drive back was an incubation period for the work. Motivation continued to move me forward into the novel, and I give the retreat full credit for that.

Leaving the standard writing confines of my office provided a sense of renewal and freshness, fed by rhythms of writing, thinking, exercising, writing, thinking, exercising .... Big Sur was perfect: place is important in so many pieces of writing, and so this place was when it was my writing backdrop as well.

But lately, all I've done is *think* about the novel, rather than write it. Lucky for me, Big Sur's only 90 minutes away.

TOM BENTLEY has run a writing and editing business out of his house for more than 10 years. He has published many freelance pieces—ranging from first-person essays to travel pieces to more journalistic subjects—in newspapers, magazines and online. He is a published fiction writer, and was the 1999 winner of the National Steinbeck Center's short story contest; he has also won some nonfiction writing awards. His short-story collection, *Flowering*, will be published by AuthorMike Ink in 2011. He maintains a writing-related blog at tombentley.com.

PHOTO: Alice Bourget

AGENTS AND SELF-PUBLISHING

Why some projects sell and some don't.

by Chuck Sambuchino

Between subsidy publishers, vanity presses, print-on-demand companies and other options, plenty of avenues exist for writers to see their work brought to life outside of the traditional publishing route. While writers young and old will argue all day about the benefits and downsides of self-publishing, one thing is fairly certain: It's very difficult for a self-published book to be available in bookstores all across the country and break out. That's why acquiring a literary agent to rep the book is seen as a logical step in the process.

As inspiring as it is to stare at books like *Eragon* or *The Shack*, know that getting an agent to take on a self-published book is no easy task. In fact, the odds are slim. Some agents won't even consider your book, no matter what. And the many that *will* consider it are already deluged in slush—so your submission better stand out. Before you send out any more queries (or worse, precious copies of the book), keep reading to find out what agents look for—and what they absolutely must see—when considering to take on a self-published book.

TARGETING POTENTIAL REPS

Let's go straight to the good news: Many agents are open to representing self-published books and trying to see those books get traditional contracts. "Most agents will at least hear out an author with a self-published book to the same extent that they would hear out any query letter," says agent Stephany Evans, president of FinePrint Literary Management.

Make sure that, as always, you follow agency submission guidelines to a T. If the agency says "Query only," then don't send the book. Also be certain that the rep you're contacting does indeed handle works in your particular genre or category. Resist the temptation to send out your entire book as a submission; use a query (and a synopsis, if applicable) as your bait.

As you might expect, there are some agents who won't consider self-published works of any kind, no matter what. Those closed to such submissions include high-brow reps in the literary world with full client list who don't need to take a risk on an unproven writer. And then there are just a small number of agents who pass on self-published books because they take pleasure of finding "fresh" projects. "A self-published book is already viewed as a 'used product.' There are so many great new manuscripts out there for editors to choose from, so why take on a book that already has some community?" says Andrea Brown, founder of Andrea Brown Literary Agency in Palo Alto.

Michelle Andelman, with Regal Literary, echoes that stance: "I won't consider self-published books because they deflate that great sense of 'discovery for me. I always feel I can most enthusiastically champion something brand new to editors, who I think are eager to feel that sense of discovery as well."

MAKING YOUR PROJECT STAND OUT

When an author sends in a query for a novel, the *hook* is the most crucial element. An agent wants to know what makes this particular book unique and appealing. Queries for self-published books have the disadvantage of immediately being scanned for not only a clever hook, but also a promising track record of sales.

In fact, your sales may be *the* most important factor in the query, because agents are looking for proof that the book has markets into which to tap. Concerning how many sales constitute a number impressive enough to attract attention, the answer varies greatly; however, a general rule of thumb would be to start querying after you've sold no fewer than 2,000 books. Another guideline to consider is that nonfiction typically sells easier than fiction. A lower number of sales for a novel would be somewhat equal to a higher number of nonfiction sales. Agent Adam Chromy of Artists and Artisans says he also weighs the number of books sold against how long the book has been on the market for purchase. "It's all about momentum," he says. "If it's out two months and has sold 5,000 copies and it's getting press, that's great and will certainly make me consider it. If it's out for years, the number would have to be higher."

When Sharlene Martin, principal of Martin Literary Management, considers a self-published book, she's looking not only for sales information, but also for a mention that the author self-published by choice, not default by rejection of agents and editors on previous submission rounds. Agents are looking for authors who self-published *before* drowning in rejections and who sold enough books to warrant a new life for the project with traditional publishing.

Whether your work is fiction or nonfiction, agents will be looking for a solid platform—meaning all the avenues you possess to sell/market your book to the identified markets of readers who will buy it. "A couple of aspects of a query letter for a self-published book will get me interested," says Jennie Dunham of Dunham Literary. "How much of an expert is the author? Really strong credentials help. Also, what type of platform does the author have? An author who can promote and sell a book is valuable."

If the writer's platform is rock solid, and the book is on its way up (rather than on the downside of the slope sales-wise), then your odds are improved. Agent Andrea Hurst, who founded an agency in Sacramento, came across a proposal from a self-published nonfiction author who had recently appeared on the Dr. Laura Show. Hurst signed the client and made a deal. Other writers have successfully signed with Hurst the same way, she says, though self-published books she reps may sometimes need an overhaul before a publisher's review. "We have taken on a few where we had the author add chapters, possibly change the title, and update it before it sold," she says.

> In fact, your sales may be the most important factor in the query, because agents are looking for proof that the book has markets into which to tap.

In addition to outlining your platform and how you intend to sell the book, include independent praise of your work. Awards, accolades, reviews, press and endorsements—anything of significant value—can all help stir the buzzstorm. Evans says she took on a self-published project when the book picked up several high-profile endorsements that helped trigger a few thousand sales. Diane Freed, another agent at FinePrint, noticed an article in a Maine newspaper about an award-winning self-published book written by a local librarian. The article was enough to get Freed's attention, and that librarian signed a two-book deal with Freed's help.

RECOGNIZING POSSIBLE DEAD ENDS

Knowing that agents immediately look for sales, you may be tempted to head outside right this moment, pack the car full of your books and peddle your wares at the nearest independent bookstore. But the flipside problem to not selling enough copies of your book is selling *too* many copies. Believe it or not, that's actually a bad thing. "There's a bit of a Catch-22 here," says Jessica Regel, agent at the Jean V. Naggar Literary Agency in New York City. "If they haven't sold many copies and the book was just self-published, then you try to convince a mainstream publisher that the book hasn't hit its market yet, because it had no marketing/

publicity. If the book has sold a good number of copies—let's say more than 10,000—then a publisher will worry that it has already hit its market, so you need to convince them that there is still an untapped audience out there."

For example, let's say you printed a book about the history of Mobile, Ala. After five months, you've sold several thousand copies—to local historians, community members, as well as your friends and relatives. Impressive, sure—but there isn't much of a point finding an agent or publisher, as you're probably close to maxing out your sales. Dunham agrees that very strong sales can be a deterrent: "I want to know that the author is off to a solid start. I also have to be convinced, however, that there's a wider audience beyond that," she says. "I've seen a couple of books where I felt there were strong sales, but then I felt like there wouldn't be many more."

Memoir is one of the most common categories where writers self-publish their work. With memoirs in particular, getting an agent to take on the book is a steep hill to climb, as there are just *too many* self-published memoirs out there to compete against. If penning the memoir gave you a new vigor for writing, then set the self-published book aside and start on a new project that you plan to take to agents first. Get the first book out of your system and keep writing. "I have only taken on a couple of self-published books and have sold almost all of them, but I will often look at a self-published author and see if we can't just let the self-pub book go and work on the next book in their career," says Chromy.

BATTLING THE STIGMA

Perhaps the biggest reason why the odds are against self-published books catching the eye of an agent is this: "Often they have not sold well, are not professionally edited, and have been out for quite a while," Hurst says.

Self-published books are constantly fighting against assumptions. Agents and editors will assume the work has been turned down by dozens (or hundreds) of people already—even if this is not the case. If your work is print-on-demand, they'll assume it sold the average amount of copies: 75. They'll assume the writing is below average and the author has no ability to market the work—even if these factors, too, are not the case. That's why your query letter introducing your self-published book must squelch all misconceptions immediately—and that includes the assumption that you, the writer, will be difficult to work with. Books are changed and edited and sometimes drastically reworked throughout the publishing process. Just because your literary fiction book has already sold 2,000 copies won't make it immune to major suggestions from agents and editors on how to rework it.

"I've found that a lot of self-published writers don't want to revise their books," says Debbie Carter of Muse Literary. "These projects can be a waste of time for agents and editors who are looking to develop new talent."

ACKNOWLEDGING PREVIOUS BOOKS

If you've decided to go the route of letting your self-published book stay self-published and move on to Work No. 2, then how do you address your prior books when crafting that next query?

Previous self-published works can easily be found and analyzed if they have ISBNs (and they likely do). Nielsen's BookScan allows the publishing industry to search sales records of books and authors. You must mention all your self-published books upfront in the interest of full disclosure. If you're worried because sales were weak, then include mentions of them at the bottom of the query letter in your "bio" paragraph. Don't even include the titles just yet. This way, you're honest about your publishing past, but not drawing a lot of attention to it. If you mention your self-published books in the first line or two, the agent may stop reading simply because of the stigma. Let agents see your pitch and get hooked in by your idea, platform and enthusiasm. If they are interested enough in the project, your bio details—including a list of any self-published books in your arsenal—should have little effect on their request to see more.

QUERYING YOUR SELF-PUBLISHED BOOK

Composing a good query is vital in getting an agent hooked on your self-published book—so it can help to see a real example of how to do just that. The following letter was written by Suzanne Hansen to query her self-published book, *You'll Never Nanny in This Town Again! The True Adventures of a Hollywood Nanny.* Her letter reached the hands of agent Sharlene Martin, who quickly saw the work's potential. Read on for Hansen's successful pitch, and Martin's insight.

Dear Ms. Martin:

When I was 18 years old, I moved from my hometown in Oregon (population: 7,500) to live with the most powerful man in Hollywood and be a nanny to his three children.

In my memoir: *You'll Never Nanny in this Town Again!—The Adventures and Misadventures of a Hollywood Nanny*, I describe my unusual experiences with the rich and famous and provide a peek into their private lives. I also share humorous stories about my girlfriends who were working for celebrity families. The book describes my short education at the Northwest Nannies Institute in Portland, Oregon. It also describes my journey to being a 24-hour-a-day modern servant, while juggling medical emergencies, as well as toddler *and* adult tantrums.

This book is a cross between *People* magazine and "Seinfeld." One example of the bizarre priorities of the wealthy that I encountered was a family who had a small painting in their family room that cost five times as much as my parents' home, but I was told not to take anything from the hotel honor bar when we were on vacation, because it was too expensive.

I self-published the book last year and was selected for a distribution contract through IPG small publishers program. I have consistently been ranked in the top 5 percent of Amazon sales. I have already sold over 4,000 copies in 12 months and garnered great reviews. I have a popular website: www.HollywoodNanny.com.

Some of the media attention I have received includes an E! Channel "Will Work for Stars" red carpet interview for the Screen Actors Guild awards. I am featured on an upcoming A&E special "Fathers and Sons in Hollywood," have been interviewed on many radio programs, and speak nationally.

So now I'm ready to go mainstream with a major publisher. Apart from writing this book, I am a mother of two, an RN and have worked as a high-risk labor and delivery nurse, lactation specialist and childbirth educator.

I can send you a copy of the book by e-mail or regular mail, and hope to hear from you to discuss this further.

Suzanne Hansen

ANALYSIS BY AGENT SHARLENE MARTIN

The instant appeal of a nanny who worked for a major Hollywood player is obvious. And paragraphs two and three make a clear description of the work, so that when the "spoiler" comes in paragraph four—telling of the book's self-publishing past (a usual deal killer)— she builds upon momentum she has already established, pointing out that her self-published book enjoyed real success in online sales and word-of-mouth.

After Suzanne sent me this letter, the supposedly "impossible" happened: Her previously self-published book sold to Crown Books/Random House for a six-figure advance in auction, and quickly went into multiple printings. It became a *New York Times* and *Los Angeles Times* bestseller.

THE GATEKEEPERS

Think beyond getting an agent; here's who else has a say in what gets published.

....

by Mike Nappa

Here's the deal: *You really only need to impress three key people to get your book published.* No, your agent isn't one of them. Neither is your editor. Those people are only scouts who may or may not get you to the real decision-makers. So who decides if your book gets published, and how do you impress them?

That's what I'm here to tell you. I've spent the last two+ decades working in book acquisitions, both as an editor and as a literary agent. In the pages that follow, I'll put on both my "acquisitions editor" and "literary agent" caps, and we can chat. (If I say something like "when you send me your proposal …" you can assume that "me" in that sentence refers to both "me-the-generic-acquisitions-editor" and "me-the-generic-literary-agent.") When we're done here, you'll know what it really takes to get your next book published. The rest, of course, will be up to you.

Ready? Then let's go.

THE PUBLISH/REJECT DECISION

First, you need to be aware of how the "Publish/Reject" decision is made in a publishing board meeting. Yes, many people weigh in on that decision, including the acquisitions editor (your first gatekeeper), an editorial director, a marketing manager or two, a salesperson or two, a print buyer, sometimes a reader or team of readers, and maybe even an employee's nephew or girlfriend or husband or whatever. But in the end, when it's time for the publishing board to decide whether or not to invest in your book, only three voices count:
- the publisher,
- the vice president of marketing
- the vice-president of sales.

LEARN MORE

This article excerpted and adapted with permission, from the book *77 Reasons Why Your Book Was Rejected* (Sourcebooks, July 2011) by Mike Nappa. The book details the various reasons why editors and agents reject book ideas, and pinpoints the mistakes that writers most often make in their proposals. It provides information on why editors and agents decline some books but say yes to others.

Oh I know. You're already arguing with me. "What about the acquisitions editor?" you say. "What about the VP of editorial? Certainly those people have a say in the publishing decision, right?" The honest answer? Not so much.

You see, the acquisitions editor makes the initial rejection based on what that person thinks his or her publisher, sales VP and marketing VP will approve later in publishing board. If the acquisitions editor doesn't see your book getting a nod from those three executives, the book gets rejected up front.

If an editor does end up taking your book proposal into a publishing committee meeting, he or she gets no real vote on whether or not it gets approved. Fact is, your acquisitions editor is only there as a guest, given a three- or four-minute window to talk about your book. The primary purpose of any editorial presence (acquisitions or executive) at a publishing board is simply as an *advocate* for whatever book is being presented. Yep, your editor and/or the VP of editorial have to literally *sell* their colleagues on your work.

Sometimes this almost feels like used-car hucksterism, with trinkets or gimmicks to capture everyone's attention. (I once knew of an editorial team that dressed up as pirates to pitch a book for their publishing board.) But most often it's a straightforward sales pitch directed toward the publisher, marketing VP and sales VP. You editor presents the product, deflects objections and asks for the sale. Then they vote.

And yes, the VP of editorial is usually given a vote, but that vote is also—almost always—simply a lockstep opinion with whatever the publisher (the VP of editorial's boss) has already decided.

I've worked in acquisitions for three different publishing houses and I've sat in many, many publishing board meetings. In all that time, I've never seen a publisher and VP of editorial split their votes. If a publisher and VP of editorial happen to disagree on a book, they typically work it out between them until they can present a united front. (Sometimes, in fact, the publisher is also the VP of editorial—combining both roles into one person.) If they can't work it out, the publisher *always* overrules the VP of editorial. That's just the way it works. So, if you want to publish a book, you need to convince the publisher, the VP of marketing and the VP of sales that your manuscript is worth it.

If you can win over those three people, then not much is going to stand in the way of publishing your book. Impress those folks and they'll all jump to acquire your soon-to-be masterpiece of literature. Of course, that's easier said than done. But here are a few strategies you can try:

HOW TO IMPRESS THE PUBLISHER...

1. DO THE EDITOR'S JOB. Generally speaking, your only access to the publisher is through an acquisitions editor. Subsequently, my job as editor is to deliver everything my publisher needs to feel confident of your book's success. How do I do that? With a detailed proposal pitch and writing samples.

Hmm. That sounds familiar, doesn't it? In fact, it sounds pretty much like what you sent me in the first place.

Of course, you already know I'm harried, overworked-and-underpaid, time-crunched and a bit short-tempered. So why are you depending on me to fill in the gaps and elevate a publisher's interest in your proposal pitch and writing samples? Heck, you can do a better job of that in your sleep—and you should. (Well, except for the sleeping part.)

So after you've created superb writing samples, carefully put together your proposal with my job as acquisitions editor in your mind. You know I'm going to have to sell your book to my publisher, VP of marketing and VP of sales, so give me everything I need up front to sell those "customers" on your manuscript, including the following elements:

- A compelling title (and subtitle, if applicable)
- Short (one paragraph) at-a-glance summary of the book's content/story
- Short summary of your author bio/credentials
- Short description of series potential (mostly for fiction only)
- Manuscript details (such as word count and shelving category)
- Clear identification of your book's primary target audience, along with potential secondary audiences that could add on sales
- Clear, compelling statements of reader benefits (that could be used in marketing copy)
- Competitive analysis of books like yours that are already in the market
- Annotated table of contents, with chapter-by-chapter summaries (for nonfiction)
- Plot summary (for fiction books; best to keep this at around 500-1,000 words)
- Compelling writing samples (introduction and at least one full chapter for nonfiction; the full manuscript for fiction)

Look, if you do my job for me up front, I'm going to notice—and be grateful. This goes for editors and agents alike. When you make our lives easier, we often become your most ardent advocates to the publisher—and that gets you one vote closer to publication.

2. DON'T DO A SHODDY JOB ON ANYTHING MY PUBLISHER WILL SEE. Some authors live by the rule that "anything is better than nothing" or "good enough is good enough." Unfortunately, neither of those philosophies is true.

The only thing worse than sending me an incomplete proposal is sending me complete crap in your pitch pages. Your proposal should reflect clear, competent thinking that's reinforced by the superb samples of your writing. If you've rushed through your competitive analysis, or don't actually understand how to articulate reader benefits in a compelling way, you've wasted what little time you spent on those things.

Remember, good enough is never good enough. A publisher doesn't care if you got impatient with all the detail work of writing or didn't have time to do a pre-edit on your manuscript or never actually learned how to differentiate your book from the competition. All he sees is what you put on the page—and the publisher will judge it ruthlessly. So make sure you submit only your best, from beginning to end.

HOW TO IMPRESS THE MARKETING VP...

1. BE GOOD TO MAMA. In the hit movie musical *Chicago*, Queen Latifah plays Matron Mama Morton, a media-savvy, happily dishonest warden at a women's penitentiary. When welcoming new inmate Roxie Hart (Renee Zellweger) into prison, Mama sings a little melody explaining the golden rule for success in her jail:

"When you're good to Mama, Mama's good to you."

Why is that important for you to know? Because, in the world of publishing, the role of Matron Mama Morton is played by my marketing VP. That person holds the keys that can set your book free from its unpublished prison and send it on to its rightful renown.

The truth is, professional success as an author depends equally on your ability to write and your ability to market your work. It takes a proactive, productive partnership between editorial and marketing to be the driving force behind any significant sales success.

And so the bottom line is this: If you can make yourself a valuable contributor to my marketing VP's success, you will be successful yourself. Remember that the next time you want to publish a book.

Be good to Mama, and she'll be good to you.

2. GET ON THE MARKETING VP'S TEAM. Honestly, my marketing VP is already biased against you. In a publishing board meeting, she's going to shine a spotlight on all your weaknesses and argue against taking any real risks with an unproven author.

You can either whine about that (and get rejected) or you can picture yourself as a member of the marketing department and make yourself an ally of my VP by creating something that contributes to her team's success.

So before you send anything to an acquisitions editor, ask yourself, "What's this editor's marketing VP going to ask about this proposal?" Seriously, go ahead and make a list of anticipated questions that will concern the marketing team about your book.

Next, figure out how to answer all those questions in ways that are "good to Mama"—that is, in ways that show my VP you're doing the best you can to make the marketing team successful in their work.

This may take some thought on your part, and some questions may strike you as impossible to answer. But if you can think of the questions, you can bet my marketing VP is going to ask them. So tackle them head on, and be that rare author who actually makes Mama happy with a new book proposal.

HOW TO IMPRESS THE SALES VP ...

1. AFTER YOU'VE WRITTEN WORDS, THINK IN NUMBERS. People who write books are *word folks*—that's what empowers us to capture ideas and express them well on the printed page. People who publish books are *numbers folks*—that's what empowers us to actually make money from writing.

Understand this: Regardless of an author's artistry with words or the life-changing ideals on display in a manuscript, *every book* in a publisher's approval process *must pass* a final feasibility report (also called "P&L—profit and loss," "Pro Forma" and "Projected Book Budget") before it sees the light of day. Every possible expense we can think of has been tossed into that P&L statement, along with any possible way we can see to bring income from your writing. Down at the bottom of that report, typically in bold letters that are either red or black, there's a single number that predicts what our ROI (return on investment) will be on your book. If that number shows 50 percent or higher net return in the first year, chances are very good your book will be published. Anything under 50 percent and your prospects dwindle.

If you really want to publish, find out how you can manipulate those bottom line numbers until they make my sales VP smile. That's the only near-guarantee you have for avoiding rejection of your book.

This takes a forced change in perspective because, if you are any good as a writer, up to this point you've been 100 percent focused on creating a work of art with words. That's good, if only because true art is inherently rare and thus infinitely valuable.

But after you've created the art, after you've bled your heart and soul into a manuscript and transformed the intangible idea into actual, physical words, it's time to stop thinking like an artist. It's now time to start thinking like an accountant—to view your spiritual masterpiece as merely another commodity to be bought and sold like pork futures or a shovel on sale at the local Ace Hardware store.

What makes your manuscript something that people will *buy*? And how many will buy it? And how much can your publisher realistically charge for it? And how much will it cost to make it? And how will that paper-and-ink commodity add up on the accounting ledger?

Answer those questions well and you'll make a kindred spirit out of my sales VP—and earn her support when it's time to vote on your book.

2. FIND A WAY TO GUARANTEE A CERTAIN AMOUNT OF SALES FOR YOUR BOOK. Hey, if money really is what matters in publishing, then being able to guarantee sales that make money gets everybody interested. Of course, that's much easier said than done—but you've got to try.

People who are best positioned to do this are those with a built-in demand for what they create. For instance, leaders of an association that'll commit to buy 1,000 copies out of the first print run on their book. University professors who'll require their books as textbooks. Professional public speakers who can buy and sell a significant number of their own books each year. A writer's own online store that demonstrates significant sales already. A business leader of a national retail chain that can promise all her stores will carry her book. You get the idea.

Regardless of your situation, regardless of your writing skill, to get the vote of a sales VP, you've got to be able to realistically convince that person that your book will sell. Figure out how to do that, and very little will keep you from getting published.

NOW WHAT?

Of course, we've barely touched the surface here, but at least now you know what it really takes to publish your next book:

You must impress the publisher, the marketing VP and the sales VP.

Easy? No.

Impossible? Also no.

Worth the effort? Well, if you see yourself as a legitimate threat for success as a published author, then that answer must be yes.

I look forward to seeing your work on bookstore shelves everywhere!

MIKE NAPPA is founder and chief agent at Nappaland Literary Agency. He's also publisher of FamilyFans.com "The Free E-Magazine for Families," and creator of the award-winning serialized kids' comic, *Johnny Grav & The Visioneer*. Over the course of his career, Mike has served as an acquisitions editor for three publishing houses. In addition, he's an award-winning author in his own right, with more than a million copies of his books in print worldwide. Mike's recent books include 77 *Reasons Why Your Book Was Rejected*, *The Jesus Survey* and the children's picture book, *Pogo's Prank-a-Palooza Day*. Oh, and Mike collects Captain America comic books, too. So, you know, he's got that going for him. Learn more at MikeNappa.com and at Nappaland.com.

COPYRIGHT BASICS

A copyright lawyer explains how to protect yourself and your book.

....

by Paul S. Levine

So you've signed with an agent, and he's landed you an offer from a publishing house. He can take it from here, right?

Wrong. You've heard that publishing agreements should not be entered into lightly—but what exactly are those elusive points your agent negotiates on your behalf, anyway? And do you really need to know?

As both an agent and an attorney, I can tell you that most publishing contracts you'll be offered will contain language that can come back to haunt you. It's important to address these issues *before* signing—and just because your agent is the one dealing with the publishing house doesn't mean you can sit back and let him handle it. Being informed about the business you're now in will go a long way in enhancing your writing career. At the very least, you need to have a basic understanding of what questions you should be asking.

Here are some of the most important things to examine, in the order in which they typically appear in most publishing agreements.

DESCRIPTION OF THE "WORK"

This might seem obvious, but it can be surprisingly easy to overlook. Be sure the "work" described in the publishing agreement accurately and completely describes the book you wrote (or are being contracted to write). In the event of an unfortunate agent/editor miscommunication or some other oversight, getting this wrong could result in a bad "surprise" when you deliver your manuscript to your editor.

RIGHTS

Rights are described in terms of media, length of time ("term") and territory. Fairly standard rights for authors to grant publishers include the right to publish the book in printed form in hardcover and/or softcover—that is, trade paperback (the types of books you see in bookstores) and/or mass-market paperback (those sold at grocery stores, pharmacies, etc.)—along with associated rights, such as audiobook and e-book rights. A royalty should be specified for each different media. Beware of catchphrases like "including but not limited to" and "media now known or hereafter devised." They can signal loopholes your publisher could use to its benefit.

You should *not* grant a publisher rights it's not in the business of exploiting. For example, if the house publishes English-language books in the United States only, it doesn't make sense to grant it international publication rights—but the publisher might try to get them anyway (you know, just in case they come in handy in the unforeseeable future).

Give publishers only specific rights they'll actually use, and reserve all rights not specifically granted. If you need to compromise, grant specific rights for a fairly short period of time (say, two years) in a territory not normally "used" by the publisher. Then, if the publisher "sells" your book in that territory within that time frame, great—but if not, your agent can attempt to do so. Otherwise, the term for the grant of rights is typically for the life of the copyright (usually the life of the author plus 70 years) in the version of the work being produced (for example, hardcover books).

SUBSIDIARY RIGHTS

The same principle applies to subsidiary rights, where the income the publisher receives from a third party that exploits them is split with the author (usually 50/50, but in the case of first serialization rights, 90/10, in the author's favor): *Don't* grant the publisher a right it won't "lay off" on a third party. *Do* grant a publisher rights related to the sale of the book itself, such as book-club or large-print rights. *Don't* grant a publisher tangential rights, such as motion picture and TV rights.

It is your agent who can most effectively advocate for you in selling dramatic rights for your book to a studio or network. There's no reason for the publisher to receive any money from the sale of these rights. (It will still benefit, after all, when the movie drives sales of the book!)

Rights can be granted *exclusively*, so no one but the grantee can exploit them, or *nonexclusively*, so you can grant the same right to more than one grantee. If the publisher insists on having dramatic rights (often arguing that if it wasn't for the book, there would be no movie), you can compromise by granting them *nonexclusively*. Then, if the publisher finds the buyer for the movie rights to your book, it can share in the income resulting from its efforts. If, however, (as is much more typically the case) your agent finds the buyer and negotiates the deal, the publisher does *not* share in the profits.

ROYALTIES

Most publishing agreements contain language—usually buried at the end of a long section describing the royalties the publisher will pay for each type of book it publishes—similar to the following: "If the book is sold at other than our usual and customary discount, the above referenced royalties will be reduced by one half."

This means if the publisher sells the book to a wholesaler (Costco, for example) at a fee other than its "usual and customary discount"—say, 51 percent off the cover price, rather than the "usual and customary" 50 percent—the publisher will pay the author *one half* of the royalties it would otherwise pay. You and your agent should advocate for more specific language, like, "If the book is sold at more than 55 percent off the list price, then…"

Speaking of price, all royalties should be specified as a percentage of the "cover" or Suggested Retail List Price (SRLP) of the book. If the contract has royalties based on "publisher's net receipts" or a similar amorphous phrase, push to change it. And when evaluating two different offers, be sure you're comparing apples to apples; royalties should be a percentage of the same thing. If the publisher insists on basing royalties on "publisher's net receipts," a good rule of thumb is to cut the royalty offered in half, because publishers sell books to retailers at roughly 50 percent off the list price. Thus, 20 percent of a publisher's net receipts is roughly equivalent to 10 percent of the cover price.

ADVANCES

Beware of language stating the publisher pays the first part of the advance "upon execution." If given license to do so, the publisher may wait an interminable length of time after you sign the agreement to countersign so it doesn't have to send your agent that first check. Negotiate that the advance be payable as soon as the publisher receives the contract signed by you, or require the publisher to countersign and issue the check within so many days after receiving the contract.

COPYRIGHT

Typically, most contracts provide that "upon publication" the publisher will register the book for copyright in the name of the author. All this means is that the publisher will fill in the copyright registration form and pay the fee (currently $35–50, depending on how the information is submitted) to register the book for copyright. To get the full benefit of all the provisions of copyright law (including statutory damages and attorney's fees, should you have to sue someone for copyright infringement), make sure your contract requires your publisher to register your book for copyright within 90 days of publication.

PAUL S. LEVINE "wears two hats." He is a lawyer (paulslevine.com) and a literary agent (paulslevinelit.com). Mr. Levine has practiced entertainment law for over 29 years, specializing in the representation of writers, producers, actors, directors, composers, musicians, artists, authors, photographers, galleries, publishers, developers, production companies and theatre companies. In 1998, he opened the Paul S. Levine Literary Agency, specializing in the representation of book authors and the sale of motion picture and television rights in and to books. Since starting his literary agency, Mr. Levine has sold more than 100 fiction and nonfiction books to at least 40 different publishers, and has had many books developed as movies-for-television and feature films.

GLA SUCCESS STORIES

Those who came before and succeeded.

I realize there are other places you can turn to for information on agents, but the *Guide to Literary Agents* has always prided itself as being the biggest (we list almost every agent) and the most thorough (guidelines, sales, agent by agent breakdowns, etc.). That's why it's sold more than 250,000 copies. It *works*—and if you keep reading, I'll prove it to you. Here are testimonials from a handful of writers who have used this book to find an agent and publishing success.

❶ Marisha Chamberlain, *The Rose Variations (Soho)*
"*Guide to Literary Agents* oriented me, the lowly first-time novelist, embarking on an agent search. The articles and the listings gave insight into the world of literary agents that allowed me to comport myself professionally and to persist. And I did find a terrific agent."

② **EUGENIA KIM,** *The Calligrapher's Daughter* (Holt)

"After so many years working on the novel, the relative speed of creating the query package
 prodded the impetus to send it out. As a fail-safe measure, I bought the *Guide to Literary
 Agents* and checked who might be a good fit for my novel..."

③ **EVE BROWN-WAITE,** *First Comes Love, Then Comes Malaria* (Broadway)

"I bought the *Guide To Literary Agents* ... and came across Laney Katz Becker. So I sent off a
 very funny query. On March 15, 2007, Laney called. 'I love your book,' she said. 'I'd like to
 represent you.' Three months later, Laney sold my book—at auction—in a six-figure deal."

④ **MARA PURNHAGEN,** *Tagged* (Harlequin Teen)

"I trusted the *Guide to Literary Agents* to provide solid, up-to-date information to help me
 with the process. I now have a wonderful agent and a four-book deal."

⑤ **RICHARD HARVELL,** *The Bells* (Crown)

"*Guide to Literary Agents* contains a wealth of information and advice, and was crucial in my
 successful search for an agent. My book has now sold in 11 (countries) and counting."

⑥ **PATRICK LEE,** *The Breach* (Harper)

"The *GLA* has all the info you need for narrowing down a list of agencies to query."

⑦ **KAREN DIONNE,** *Freezing Point* and *Boiling Point* (Jove)

"I'm smiling as I type this, because I actually got my agent via the *Guide to Literary Agents*.
 I certainly never dreamed that I'd tell my [success] story in the same publication!"

⑧ **HEATHER NEWTON,** *Under the Mercy Trees* (Harper)

"I found my literary agent through the *Guide to Literary Agents*!"

⑨ MICHAEL WILEY, *The Last Striptease* and *The Bad Kitty Lounge* (Minotaur)
"*GLA* was very useful to me when I started. I always recommend it to writers."

⑩ LES EDGERTON, *Hooked* and 11 more books
"Just signed with literary agent Chip MacGregor and I came upon him through the *Guide to Literary Agents*. If not for *GLA*, I'd probably still be looking."

⑪ JENNIFER CERVANTES, *Tortilla Sun* (Chronicle)
"Within 10 days of submitting, I found an amazing agent—and it's all thanks to *GLA*."

⑫ CARSON MORTON, *Stealing Mona Lisa* (St. Martin's / Minotaur)
"I wanted to thank you for the *Guide to Literary Agents*. After contacting 16 literary agencies, number 17 requested my historical novel. Within a few weeks, they offered to represent me. Hard work and good, solid, accurate information makes all the difference. Thanks again."

⑬ DARIEN GEE, *Friendship Bread: A Novel* (Ballatine)
"The *Guide to Literary Agents* was an indispensable tool for me when I was querying agents. I highly recommend it for any aspiring author."

⑭ LEXI GEORGE, *Demon Hunting in Dixie* (Brava)
"The *Guide to Literary Agents* is an invaluable resource for writers."

⑮ STEPHANIE BARDEN, *Cinderella Smith* (HarperCollins)
"When I felt my book was finally ready for eyes other than mine to see it, I got some terrific advice: Go buy the *Guide to Literary Agents*. By the time I was through with it, it looked like it had gone to battle—it was battered and dog-eared and highlighted and Post-It-Noted. But it was victorious; I had an agent. Huge thanks, *GLA*—I couldn't have done it without you!"

THINK LIKE A SCRIPT AGENT OR PRODUCER

Get your script read.

by Trai Cartwright

The foremost priority of writers is to write what's in their heart, right? Obeying the muse is paramount, and no one would have writers shun or shirk their inspiration. No one, that is, except a Hollywood producer.

In Hollywood, different muses call for a different sort of obedience. Generally coming in the guise of a power-suited agent, a jeans-and-cashmere-sweater-clad producer, or even a backwards-baseball-cap-wearing director, they are beholden to the muse of the bottom line. That's because it's the bottom line that ensures a green light to make their movie—your movie.

What does this have to do with you? Isn't the budget their problem? Yes and no. A little production-sensitive script polishing by the writer could be the difference between a yes and a fast pass. Think of screenwriting as 90 percent inspiration and 10 percent consideration.

A producer I know calls it, "Taking Away the No's." He has an uncanny knack for predicting what details in a script will give his targeted investor, director or agent a reason to pass. He also knows that if he can circumvent those "no's" via some savvy tweaking, then he'll have a better chance of getting ahead. Those no's can be obvious to spot—a cameo by President Obama, for example—but others are seated in the subconscious. Understanding the filter through which a producer, director or agent reads a script will help you identify all the potential No's in your script. Below are 10 standard problem "pass points" in a screenplay—and suggestions for how to Take Away the No's!

NO #1: THE TITLE

A great title can get you read; a weak, awkward or "B Movie" title can guarantee an instant "no" by producers and future theater-goers.

Name your film *Rogue Nazi Killers* and you're stalled at the gate. Sure, it tells us exactly what the movie's about, that it's going to be bloody and edgy, but it's not tasteful or clever—and therefore, we assume your screenplay won't be, either. But a title like *Inglourious Basterds*, while still lacking taste, does invites fun—the misspelling is a great touch. It gets the brain churning right away about just what that sort of adventure we're in for. *Man Versus Woman* might be appropriate for a gender war romantic comedy, but again, it's not particularly clever and it's definitely not cute. In fact, it's off-putting and vague. But *The Ugly Truth* is indeed clever; it insinuates that it's an equal-opportunity gender war, and invites the audience in on the joke.

Have a look at your title: Is it catchy but not campy? Intriguing but not too vague? Indicative of the subject matter without being on-the-nose (although *Star Trek* might have an argument for on-the-nose titling)? Is it appropriate for the genre? A good title is the best possible introduction to your film; make sure yours is working as hard as it can for you.

NO #2: LOCATION

This is another rather simple tweak that many writers may not have even considered while writing their script, but it's guaranteed the producer will. *30 Days of Night*, a movie about a vampire attack on an Alaskan village during the month when the sun doesn't rise has a very good reason to shoot in the snow, at night, in Alaska. Otherwise, that set-up would be the kiss of death.

Location and setting should be a part of the writer's thinking process. Finding the right place and time can best complicates the hero's journey, but most of the time, it can and will be fudged due to budgetary concerns. A writer can circumvent these issues. For example, John Hughes specifically wrote *The Breakfast Club* as a small film ideal for his directorial debut. It had one location (a school library—any school library) and was set at the ideal time to get a film crew in to shoot unobstructed (on the weekend when no one's around).

Granted, few movies can plant themselves in a single location for the duration and tell their story effectively, but that doesn't mean there can't be consideration for the resources it takes to build sets or travel from place to place. Would it alter your story too much to shoot zombies after the mall closes instead of during the height of the Memorial Day Sale-a-thon? Would it compromise anything to have your characters confront in a town car with tinted windows as opposed to a convertible Porsche? Does the 18th-century film about courtly manners absolutely have to place each new scene in a new part of a filigreed palace?

Have a good hard look at the locations in your script. You don't want a producer to say "no" just because your settings break the bank.

NO #3: TALENT

Most movies ultimately get made for one of two reasons: star vehicle or commercial appeal. Or, to put it bluntly, Oscar bait or tent-pole pic. If your film falls somewhere in the middle, this is where great roles for actors can help take away the no's. If you've got a vibrant, dynamic protagonist (and a keen antagonist doesn't hurt), you're halfway to having talent attachments—actors with track records at the box office who might convince the moneymen that their investment is sure to be returned.

Does your film have a strong lead role? Is the main character something new for your genre? Just because it's an action film doesn't mean he has to be a two-dimensional tough guy. Just because it's a drama doesn't mean she has to be weepy and sorrowful. Just because it's a horror doesn't mean she can't bring real pathos to the role. Ditto the villain, the romantic interest, even sidekicks and secondary characters. The more life you bring to their lives, the better chance you'll light up a producer or agent with talent possibilities.

NO #4: KIDS AND DOGS

You know the old adage: "Never work with kids or dogs." What you may not know is that it was a producer who said that. The easiest way to go over budget is to cast a monkey. The second easiest way? Cast a child. After all, kids can only work a set number of hours each day, and animals don't always perform on cue.

If your story is about a kid who is kidnapped and saved by a little dog named Benji, then by all means, go forth. But if your film has a single scene in which a team of heavily armed bad guys flee a bank robbery and run right through a mob of grade-school tourists, guns blazing—you just added days to the production and money to the budget. Would it be as effective if they ran through a gaggle of jogging mothers with unseen babies in strollers?

This category is a more minor "no," and may not a deal breaker, but it's one that could compound the lean toward a pass.

NO #5: KNOW YOUR SCOPE

If you've got a story about two best friends on a road trip across the sunny southwest in which they make few stops and speak to a few people, chances are you've got yourself a low-budget film. This is a doable film, even if you write a climax that involves Thelma and Louise being chased down by an FBI task force and their helicopters, and driving their vintage convertible off a cliff.

Now, if you've got a film that takes place in outer space in mostly zero-G conditions, featuring an attack by an army of fully articulated aliens in an armada of ships that are translucent like jellyfish and move like them, too, you've just joined the $150 million club.

In between these two extremes are lots of variations with variables that can be finessed for a reasonable, viable scope for your film. If you've got a one-room drama, you can make that room as elaborate as you want. If you've got an intercontinental thriller, you'd be wise to set much of it indoors so a sound stage can be employed rather than asking the whole production to actually travel to Rome, Siberia, Topeka and Cozumel.

Scope also includes concepts like scene count, interiors vs. exteriors, weather, cast size and set pieces. A lower-budgeted film tends to have fewer scenes: this generally equates to fewer locations and fewer company moves. Low budget films tend to have smaller casts of more developed characters; big-budget films splurge with lots of extras (sometimes computer-generated!). Low-budget films tend to take place mostly indoors, or outside during daylight hours (no lights to rent); big-budget movies don't even think about this. Big-budget movies have towns covered in snow or hurricanes, or even just romantic rain showers during which the lovers share their first kiss; lower-budgeted movies don't try to dictate weather.

Knowing the scope of your film is not just knowing what budget range your film falls in to, but also adjusting production elements to be most appropriate for your film's context. A conscientiously created world doesn't give the producer, director or agent a budgetary reason to say no.

NO #6: ACTION SEQUENCES

Not every movie has action in it, so if your script doesn't feature this particular piece of filmmaking, skip to No. 7. The rest of you, be advised that action sequences are another tricky area where a producer can say no.

A great action sequence features some or all of the following: an original backdrop, like the catacombs under Paris, or a candy factory; maybe a fun, innovative vehicle; a very personal, mano-a-mano fight; and finally, a surprising weapon—what's laying around and how can it be most interestingly applied?

The key to writing great action choreography is pacing, surprise, stakes and climax. Study the pros to see how they do it, because it's important. In fact, a couple of great action sequences can actually buy you "yes's"—reprieves from "no's" elsewhere in the script.

NO #7: GENRE

Yes, horror sells. It is the perennial seller in Hollywood. Comedy sells in phases, but hysterically funny is always marketable. Would you believe that really smart also sells well? But what if you aren't a rocket scientist with a terrifying tale about a ravenous space monster, or a clone of Judd Apatow (or Adam Sandler. Or Christopher Guest. Or whoever's in vogue at the moment)? What does genre have to do with you?

Demonstrating that you've mastered your genre's rules shows the producer that you've got a strong grasp of screenwriting craft, a key component to getting a "yes." Genre is, after all, structure, tone and theme all in one.

So have you mastered your genre's rules? Do the beats fall where they are supposed to? Is your tone consistent and appropriate to your genre? If you've written an action film but it's got multiple multi-page talking head scenes and only two major action sequences, you've missed your target. If you've written a drama about a raging flu epidemic, but it's packed with pratfalls and one-liners, you're way off base. A producer can forgive weak dialogue or a poorly drawn villain, but he can't forgive a story whose very underpinnings aren't solidly built. Do your homework and read a screenwriting how-to book; take a class or join a group of savvy writers.

NO #8: DERIVATIVE/TRENDY

It's only natural that this category follows genre. If your script reads like something the producer or agent just saw in the theater, it's a "no." If it's trying to capitalize on the flash-fire of a new box office success (for example, 2008 was *Cloverfield*; 2009 is *District 9*), just remember that it takes between 18 months and two years to go from script to theater; if your script is too trendy, it's already dated by the time it hits the producer's desk.

As for trends making bigger waves, that's fair game. It's okay to jump on the vampire bandwagon, but you've got to find a unique twist. It's also fine to write the 10,000th romantic comedy, but you've got to ground it in a fun new set-up. The point is that every idea to be had has already been had; you can write anything you want, but if you don't find what's original and fresh about the subject matter, you'll get a "no."

If your script isn't following a trend at all, but rather is your contribution to, for example, the coming-of-age genre, the same rules still apply: Hollywood does not want to see one more crazy night in Vegas/after prom/while-the-hubbies-are-away comedy when everything goes awry, true love is discovered and friendships are forged in fire. Bring us your talent, your voice, your heart—but please don't bring us another unsung WWII hero or *Saw*-like psychopath. At least not until it's in vogue again.

NO #9: RIGHTS TO MATERIAL

This is a very simple one. Don't adapt and try to sell something you don't have the rights to. Don't try to sell something when you're battling with your co-writer over credit. Don't try to sell something that is just your slightly altered spin on someone else's idea. Don't try to sell something that isn't legally yours. Not only will this get you a big fat "no," but it will get you a big fat lawsuit, too.

NO #10: MARKETING

If the bottom line is a fickle muse, then the marketing muse is haranguing harridan. If she can't see your film's poster or tagline, she's going to force a no.

You don't have to be a marketing pro to be sensitive to how important marketing is to Hollywood. It's the interface through which they make back their money; if they can't figure out how to market a film, they won't make it. This is the biggest, most resolute "no" of all.

This brings us full circle to the title: Is there a hook in your concept, a location or world to showcase, a relationship to exploit, a villain to supersize? Even the lowest-budget film starring the least-known actors has something unique about it that will entice an audience. Make sure that something unique gets the attention on the page it deserves. One memorable visual, one pithy catchphrase, one original conceit that makes the brain fizz with expectation—that's all your producer is asking for. If you build it, they will come (the tagline of *Field of Dreams*). The Navy pilots in *Top Gun*. Jack and Rose on the bow of the *Titanic*. Darth Vadar.

Help your producer, your director, your agent help you: Deliver a screenplay that has eliminated the traps and tripwires that make his job tough. You don't have to change your writing, your concept, your genre or anything of major thematic import. Thinking like a producer when you write can help you deliver a more professional, producible product. Take away a few "no's," and he'll be more inclined to give you that golden, glorious "yes."

TRAI CARTWRIGHT is a 20-year entertainment industry veteran recently transplanted to Colorado. While living in Los Angeles, Trai produced three independent films and consulted on hundreds of scripts. She was a studio development executive, spent eight years consulting for HBO, was assistant director of Leonardo DiCaprio's online ventures, worked at a multi-player online role-playing game company, and made ringtones for 20th Century Fox. The most fun she had was as a screenwriter. Trai's work has been optioned four times and has placed in some of Hollywood's most prestigious contests. Currently, Trai is a writing consultant and editor who teaches all kinds of writing for community colleges, writers' groups and one-on-one. She oversees teen writers critique groups and runs the Explorati Teen Writers Boot Camp and Explorati Teens Film & Theater Camp summer programs. To learn more, visit craftwrite.com.

KEN SHERMAN

A script agent talks about searching for that killer writing sample.

by Chuck Sambuchino

It was in Paris, observing French director Claude Sautet shoot a film, that script agent Ken Sherman officially fell in love with writing and movies.

"I observed the making of a Sautet film, standing behind the director the entire shooting," says Sherman, whose company, Ken Sherman & Associates, works out of Beverly Hills. "I also went to movies every day and came back (to Los Angeles) after two years living in Paris—half of that time was spent extensively traveling."

Sherman, a Los Angeles native and University of California-Berkeley psychology graduate, returned from his adventures in Europe and started his career in film and television as a reader for Columbia Pictures. After less than a year reading screenplays, he interviewed at the William Morris Agency and was accepted into a training program the next day. Thus began his foray into the world of agenting.

It wasn't until a few years later, in the early 1980s, however, that Sherman would open his own agency. "I found space and opened my first literary agency where I am today. After two years, The (Robby) Lantz Office in New York bought my company. I worked in their L.A. office for four years. I kept my space here—the first office space—and reopened my agency in 1989. I decided it was time to be on my own again and that's what I've been doing ever since. I really like it. I find the independence and the ability to choose clients and projects much more satisfying than servicing a list of existing clients for other people."

Nowadays, Sherman's agency handles approximately 35 clients; he makes contact with most of his new writers through referrals, and he handles just about every topic you can think of in nonfiction, fiction and scripts. But no matter where a new writer comes from, what Sherman's looking for hasn't changed throughout his years as an agent: "It's about passion. If writers don't feel obsessed about what they're writing, it won't come through on the paper. It's the basic adage to write what you know—better yet, write *about* what you know."

When a writer is composing his first screenplay, should he aim to write something perceived as trendy, marketable or salable? Or should he just write the best he can, even if the script will likely be unproducable?

What I'm looking for, and what every producer, studio, network and agent I know is looking for, is a killer writing sample—meaning something that we can send out in one day to 30 producers and have them say, "This may not be exactly the story I'm looking for, but I need to know this writer." And hopefully, each one of them will call me back and say, "We want the story. We want to option the material or purchase it outright." But most important is that they want to know the writer and meet with the writer and talk about other projects because the writer has a unique voice.

You just finished reading a book that'll make a great television series or movie. How does a work like that get optioned?

One of my internationally known book authors recently had his book on the *New York Times* bestseller list for a couple of months. There was a real flurry of interest in it. Finally, someone who really, really felt passionate about the story and was a proven producer called an executive at one of the movie studios and said, "I want to do this." The head of the studio called me to check if the rights were available because he wanted to make an offer—and he did. The offer of an option is for two things. First, the option guarantees the exclusive rights to the producer for a certain amount of time—in this case, 18 months. Nobody else can have the rights to that story during those 18 months. In that time, the producer can have a screenplay or teleplay developed. Second, the producer can then decide if they want to pay the purchase price and fully own the rights to the book.

Does some work get optioned more than once?

Yes. I have a client whose first book became an Oprah's Book Club book after it was published. We then had it under contract to Dreamworks, attached to a specific writer-director. The one-year option expired and we've just set it up with one of last year's Oscar-nominated producers. Sometimes a project will have many, many homes before it's actually produced. And there's no guarantee that anything will be produced even if the rights have been purchased.

In addition to working with television writers, screenwriters and book writers, you also deal with buying and selling life rights. How does that work?

Here's an example: I was sitting in my office one day and a TV/movie producer I know called me. He said, "I've spoken to a lady and the fireman who saved her life during the Oklahoma City bombing. Would you mind handling the life rights—the option and purchase price and contract for them?" I then negotiated for both (individuals). Their life rights were optioned and then the purchase price for the exclusive use of their stories for the TV movie, "Oklahoma City: A Survivor's Story" was exercised.

. . . .

What I'm looking for, and what every producer, studio, network and agent I know is looking for, is a killer writing sample— meaning something that we can send out in one day to 30 producers and have them say, "This may not be exactly the story I'm looking for, but I need to know this writer."

. . . .

If a writer wishes to see his idea on the big screen, is it more practical to write a good book and get it optioned into a film, rather than try to sell an original screenplay?

It depends in which form the author writes best. If the writer is a great screenwriter, I would hope they'd attack the story and characters as a screenplay, because, traditionally, screenplays take less time to write. I want to preface this by saying that there are no rules or answers to any of these questions. What I'm suggesting today are just a few ideas of a few ways things can happen for individuals—but everybody needs to find their own way in their own time. One prominent client wrote eight screenplays before things finally clicked.

Does an author get the first crack at writing an adapted screenplay of his own novel?

If the author is seriously interested in adapting his or her own book into a screenplay, I highly suggest they write a spec screenplay (or one based on their book) while they're waiting for the book to be published. That way, they can show the studio or the network or whomever is optioning the material that they can deliver the goods.

Do you pay any attention to what studios are buying?

I don't worry too much about that. I prefer to try and find really first-rate material that stands on it own. And even though it may be a genre that's a bit out of favor at the moment—maybe something that was hot three or five years ago for some reason—we can reignite interest with a solid screenplay or book. One thing I've noticed is that many executives in this business are very happy not to take a risk on anything. They're very happy to go along with what other people say, which is why sometimes you can get an auction going with multiple bids on the same project. You say, "Well so-and-so just made an offer on it," or "Such-and-such studio wants it." And they think that if another studio wants it, it must be something good. Of course it is ...

Kind of like the business phrase "Don't sell the steak. Sell the sizzle"?

Sometimes you can sell the sizzle, but more importantly, the material really has to stand on its own. Because don't forget that even with a TV movie, a producer or writer is with the project for a good six months to a year, if not more. A producer needs the passion to stay with the project and to be able to sell it, because they're constantly selling and reselling the material to new people who join the project.

Let's say someone writes a great script. You read it and love it. Before you sign a contract, is it important that the writer has other screenplays waiting in the wings?

That's ideal. Again, as I've said before, I'm looking for that killer writing sample: a screenplay I can send to anybody anywhere anytime and have them sit up and say, "Wow, this is a serious and professional writer." And more often than not, I won't take on clients without knowing that there are three or four or five good pitches behind them if they're to go into a meeting, and ideally another one or two screenplays that are polished and ready to be sent out.

What else should writers know about dealing with Hollywood agents?

I think (writers) should keep in mind that it's a collaborative effort between the writer and the agent. We work as a team. I've found that my reputation is only as good as the quality of writing I send from my office. Therefore the author should do everything they can to help themselves and help me get the material into perfect form so that people will sit up and say, "Yes, we want to be in business with this writer."

SCREENPLAY MANAGERS

3 script reps, 3 perspectives.

....

by Ricki Schultz

It's no secret—there's big money in film and television writing. That, coupled with the fact that screenplays are so much shorter than literary manuscripts (the average film-length screenplay is about 110 pages), it's no wonder script managers are inundated with queries. Likewise, it's no surprise that the screenwriting realm is even more competitive than the cutthroat world of book publishing.

So, how does one break in? What are script managers looking for?

Lucky for us, three such industry professionals, script managers Charlene Kay, Michael L. Shortt and Peter Miller, were kind enough to take time out of their query-battling schedules to give us some insight into the business of screenwriting—including writing tips, their personal preferences and their opinions on the current trends.

CHARLENE KAY has been in the business for more than 30 years. Before founding Charlene Kay Agency in Québec, Canada, she had been writing scripts, mostly for television, under a pseudonym to maintain her anonymity.

MICHAEL SHORTT is one of the leading authorities in the talent and film industry in Savannah, Ga. Not only did he found Talent Source in 1989, but he also started the Georgia Association of Talent and Theatrical Agents (GATTA) and co-authored a bill that sought regulation, state guidelines, bonding and licensing for talent agencies. For his entire career, he has worked to promote legitimate talent agencies as well as protect talent from fraudulent operations, and he had a large hand in establishing the Savannah Film Commission—an organization he still works alongside today.

PETER MILLER has been an active force in the film industry for more than three decades. As president of PMA Literary and Film Management, Inc., and Millennium Lion, Inc., in New York City, he has been involved in the management of several Emmy Award-nominated projects as well as several *New York Times* bestsellers. He currently has more than two dozen film and television projects in active development.

YOUR QUESTIONS ANSWERED

What are you looking for and not getting? Besides a great logline or a referral, how can a new writer get your attention?

CHARLENE KAY: A writer's credentials definitely don't impress us, whether professional or amateur. A referral rarely convinces us to sign a writer to a contract. We often skip the name and the bio, and go straight for the story idea.

If it moves us, we generally pitch the synopsis to a few of our contacts to see what comes out. A positive response will bring us to contact the writer and work at getting the completed script out to the interested party.

MICHAEL SHORTT: Small budget, non-period comedies and dramas. Everybody wants to write a blockbuster!

People need to use their heads. *If* a person has the power to green light a $300 million movie, are they going to do it using a script written by an unproven writer?

Be honest and modest and simply give a clean, concise "Cliff's Notes" rundown of the story.

PETER MILLER: Write a *New York Times* best-selling book that has global marketing potential and film potential.

What does an unsolicited query have to have in order for you to request the script or screenplay? What grabs you?

CHARLENE KAY: The story idea is what grabs us, not the writer's credentials or the pitching technique. The less we know about the writer's background, the better. It tells us that this person is focusing on his/her story, not who he/she is.

MICHAEL SHORTT: They need to follow the guidelines on our website.

My number one pet peeve is a teaser. Tell me the whole story—exposition, conflict and resolution. If you don't, it goes into the "circular file." I do not have the time to be teased, ask you to do it correctly or play games.

A straightforward approach without a bunch of hyperbole and BS [grabs me]. Let the work speak for itself.

PETER MILLER: Making a movie today involves several components, including financing, domestic and foreign distribution, gap financing, tax incentives, movie stars, bankable directors and an extraordinary story. In order for me to be attracted to any new project, it needs to have a few or more of these elements attached to it—unless, of course, the script is extraordinary and/or based on a bestselling or world-renowned book.

What's hot right now?

CHARLENE KAY: Remakes, reality shows, technically-enhanced features and animated pictures.

MICHAEL SHORTT: Unfortunately, what's seems to be "hot" are badly made remakes and sequels. The studios have been castrated and are afraid to spend money on new ideas and concepts because they invest far too much money in feature films.

The oft-quoted "average production price" for a feature is now at an alleged $75 million before promotion costs. That's simply insane.

With the advent of digital technology and the improvements in optics, the costs should be dropping, but they aren't because they are all above-the-line costs. It's a grossly inequitable system that isn't sustainable, and we are seeing the end of it, I'm afraid.

PETER MILLER: Spiritual, life-changing transformation. Gandhi said, "Be the change you wish to see in the world," so I am looking to develop motion picture properties that can manifest change in a positive light.

On the other side of that, what trends do you see becoming worn-out?

MICHAEL SHORTT: Farce comedies, teen horror, family dramas.

PETER MILLER: Certainly movies about the Middle East seem to be overdone. The only romantic comedies that are going to work are those special ones, like *When Harry Met Sally*. The horror genre won't stop, but I'm avoiding getting involved with any horror projects unless they're special.

What's your take on trends vs. originality? Should writers focus on one when starting out?

CHARLENE KAY: We don't follow trends. We prefer originality. Writers should listen to what their inspiration dictates. If they follow the trend and write for money, that's their prerogative; but it definitely doesn't score points with us.

MICHAEL SHORTT: Always be original. Write what you know. If you are a tour guide, write a character who is a tour guide.

You only get to have one "first" work; make it something that you know about. There is nothing worse than a non-lawyer writing a legal thriller, a non-cop writing a crime drama or a non-vet writing a military story right out of the box.

If you can write, show it. Then, take that success and spend the time researching things that you don't know about, and you'll have the proven track record to at least have your non-authority subjects looked at.

PETER MILLER: I always tend to lean towards originality, but certain genres, like vampires and love stories and unique horror movies, never stop.

How perfect do you need a script to be before you offer a writer representation? Do you work with writers to cultivate the script before offering representation, or is the sheer volume of submissions such that you're more likely to pass if the idea and execution are not 100 percent?

CHARLENE KAY: Some of our present clients were once unacquainted with the proper screenplay and teleplay format when they first submitted a script to us, but their story ideas were gripping. When given the right tools and software, they learned how to set their creation in the accepted layout.

In a nutshell, the basic story is what's important. When you build a house, you need to pour in a solid foundation before erecting the walls.

MICHAEL SHORTT: 80 percent of what it should be. Yes, I often point out problems in the story, yet few understand that filmmaking is a collaborative art form and won't make changes. Then, we part company. (None of those who stayed their own course have ever had a film produced.)

The joy is finding a diamond in the rough.

PETER MILLER: We're more likely to pass if the idea and execution are not 100 percent.

When you take on new clients, are you generally in it for the long haul with that person? In your experience, how fluid is the agent/writer relationship in Hollywood?

CHARLENE KAY: Yes, absolutely. The agent-writer relationship is like a marriage. Conflicts of interest may arise when discussing the best avenue for a particular script. Constructive criticism goes both ways. Communication is a huge part of any success, and you eventually find a compromise for the good of the script involved.

An agent *cannot* dictate how a script should be written but, instead, offer suggestions to enhance the salability of such.

MICHAEL SHORTT: Yes. Actors, writers, whores and drug dealers—I think they are all looking for the best deal, and most lack the loyalty gene.

PETER MILLER: I am definitely in it for the long haul with clients, and there is no fluidity in Hollywood because you are only as good as your last project.

How much does a writer's platform matter to you? Do things like writers' websites/blogs/publications of the literary variety carry any weight (especially in a query), or is it primarily the story and the writing first, all else last?

CHARLENE KAY: We're unimpressed by the size of a writer's biography/filmography. We don't waste our time with ego-inflated writers who believe their screenplays are beyond improvement.

Some will say that prior experience will help sell the scripts—and, granted, it does. We will sign those writers only if we find that they are flexible and open to constructive criticism.

MICHAEL SHORTT: None. Absolutely, what is on the page. Nothing more matters.

For at least the last five years, Hollywood has been producing remakes and sequels. In your opinion, is this a good or bad thing? As well, do you take on these kinds of projects, or do you prefer brand-new concepts?

CHARLENE KAY: Remakes and sequels are fine, providing they are done in good taste and capture the main essence of the original.

Reunions of classic TV series are tough to sell to the original producers, but I must say that many story ideas that have come across our desks are highly better than what we have seen produced so far. Those unknown writers recapture the main essence of what made the series successful in the past, and actors will agree.

Many will argue that times have changed and that we must adapt the remakes to today's trend. We totally disagree. New generations are discovering those classic series on the Internet and on DVDs. They enjoy the way they were made back then with the wholesome values that abounded.

MICHAEL SHORTT: Bad, bad, bad. Considering the studios own the rights to the movies, characters and story lines, it is a waste of time for an unknown writer to spend time on these properties unless they were contacted and contracted to work on a sequel. The odds are better to win the lottery.

PETER MILLER: It's very difficult for me to get involved with representing an already-existing brand or franchising because it's already controlled by studios/distributors/financiers—unless, of course, I managed or produced the original property.

What is your take on the quality of film writing? Is it getting better or worse—and why do you think that is?

CHARLENE KAY: We have noticed a sharp decline in quality series and movies. They are often written in haste to capitalize on a current event.

Let's face it: We're all in it for the money—and more so today than in the past 20 to 30 years. Studios want to ride the wave, and who can blame them? But, by doing so, they have [been] destroying the quality of the scripts.

Quantity is what reigns supreme in today's market.

MICHAEL SHORTT: Worse. Society is being dumbed down, generation by generation.

[I'm] not optimistic, based on what I read. Ninety-five percent of submitted scripts are written by hacks, TV babies or outright thieves with no appreciation for those who came before them.

The fact is, there are a limited number of story lines—the old adage, I believe, is that there are only seven stories in Hollywood. I think that's mostly true, but how you structure these seven stories is where the magic happens.

Be a student of film; understand what works. I would take Quentin Tarantino's education as a video clerk over any MFA graduate in a heartbeat, because he watched films that worked and understood *why* they worked.

The human condition has not changed and will not change. A good story is a good story. It doesn't have to be complicated or different; it just has to keep the viewer engaged, and to do that, you have to care about the characters—plain and simple.

PETER MILLER: It depends on the genre of movie, but in my opinion, it varies from brilliant quality writing to garbage—as in certain very successful abnormal horror movies.

Let's say someone tells you Steven Spielberg is looking for a romantic comedy about zombies. When you get wind of opportunities like these, how do you approach them? Keep your eyes peeled for queries fitting the bill, or get on the horn with your top undead-loving client? Something else?

CHARLENE KAY: We will prioritize our present clients and ask if any has an idea for such a script, but we will not push them into hatching a storyline in haste. Next step will be to thumb through the submissions.

MICHAEL SHORTT: I would consider the merits of the opportunity. *If* it were something I believed in, I would let some clients know and see if they wanted to adapt or create something that fits the bill.

PETER MILLER: I pride myself on always trying to connect the dots. When an opportunity arises, if I think it's in the best interest of one of my clients, I absolutely would pursue it and encourage a client to write a script for such a project.

Think about the most recent submissions you've read and passed on. What are a few of the top reasons you turned them down?

CHARLENE KAY: The few we've read we had to turn down because our contacts didn't pan out, and we didn't feel passionate enough about the script to invest our time and money into representing it.

MICHAEL SHORTT: My list is long. Here are instant circular file candidates:

Call yourself a business of any kind. If you do not have a business license, a tax ID number or a bank account in that name, then you are not one.

Call yourself a studio. If you don't own a soundstage, *you are not a studio.*

Call yourself a production company. If you have never produced anything, don't have production insurance, and have never produced anything, *you are not a production company.*

Tell me that you also want to executive produce, produce or direct. Learn what these people do, and develop respect for those who actually do these jobs. I would no more walk into a hospital ER and demand to do a lung transplant than I would submit a script to an agent and say I *must* direct this as well.

Suggest an all-star dream cast. Let your work do all the talking. I do not care whom you want to play "Billy Bob" unless you are writing the check to pay the actor chosen.

I do not care who you know. If it was either true or mattered, then why are you talking to me? I do not care what awards you won in high school or college. I do not care what life-transforming experience/alien abduction led you to this epiphany. I do not care if all your friends think you're a great guy or a crazy hermit asshole. I do not care if you kicked smoking, drugs, alcohol, whores, gambling or were a former Jerry Springer reject.

Just write the script, and make it interesting and properly formatted. If you do not know how, buy a book. Better yet, buy several published screenplays of popular movies and watch them and go through the scripts page by page. *Understand* the process.

PETER MILLER: I have a lot of difficulty dealing with crazy, over-demanding authors.

Getting movies financed these days is extremely difficult, so I always look for additional packaging components, like financing, distribution, etc. That, and wrong subject matter is why I've turned down submissions.

If you were teaching a course called "Qualities Writers Must Have in Order to Break into the Business," what would be item No. 1 on your syllabus?

CHARLENE KAY: Don't write for money. Keep your day job, and write as a hobby. It cannot feel like work, even if you eventually get to write full time. It must remain a fun pastime. Be proud of your work but do not let your ego run wild. You must remain flexible and open to criticisms, even if you disagree with them.

MICHAEL SHORTT: STFU and listen. I want to help you—but if you do all the talking, you aren't going to learn anything, are you?

PETER MILLER: The first quality I am looking for is "magnificence."

Best piece(s) of advice we haven't yet covered for new writers?

CHARLENE KAY: Be yourself. Write something that is dear to your heart, whether it's with the current trend or not. You must live and breathe the story. It has to move you to the core, to lift you away from the world around you.

MICHAEL SHORTT: Be modest, and put yourself in the shoes of a movie patron. Why would I pay $11 to see this movie? Does it teach, educate or entertain? Does it do more than one? Does it do it, or all of them, well?

Be concise. Understand your audience and audience members' motivation as well as their depositions.

Understand the historical trends and be ahead of them—don't follow them. The production cycle is long. If you are writing for what's hot today, by the time your film gets made (if at all), that trend will be old history on basic cable.

Most of all, write as a new writer should write—small and successful, not big and bold. The examples of one are plentiful; the others are almost nonexistent.

PETER MILLER: Write something out of the box, that's never been done before. Write something that's wonderful.

GLOSSARY OF INDUSTRY TERMS

Your guide to every need-to-know term.

#10 ENVELOPE. A standard, business-size envelope.

ACKNOWLEDGMENTS PAGE. The page of a book on which the author credits sources of assistance—both individuals and organizations.

ACQUISITIONS EDITOR. The person responsible for originating and/or acquiring new publishing projects.

ADAPTATION. The process of rewriting a composition (novel, story, film, article, play) into a form suitable for some other medium, such as TV or the stage.

ADVANCE. Money a publisher pays a writer prior to book publication, usually paid in installments, such as one-half upon signing the contract and one-half upon delivery of the complete, satisfactory manuscript. An advance is paid against the royalty money to be earned by the book. Agents take their percentage off the top of the advance as well as from the royalties earned.

ADVENTURE. A genre of fiction in which action is the key element, overshadowing characters, theme and setting.

AUCTION. Publishers sometimes bid for the acquisition of a book manuscript with excellent sales prospects. The bids are for the amount of the author's advance, guaranteed dollar amounts, advertising and promotional expenses, royalty percentage, etc. Auctions are conducted by agents.

AUTHOR'S COPIES. An author usually receives about 10 free copies of his hardcover book from the publisher; more from a paperback firm. He can obtain additional copies at a price that has been reduced by an author's discount (usually 50 percent of the retail price).

AUTOBIOGRAPHY. A book-length account of a person's entire life written by the subject himself.

BACKLIST. A publisher's list of books that were not published during the current season, but that are still in print.

BACKSTORY. The history of what has happened before the action in your story takes place, affecting a character's current behavior.

BIO. A sentence or brief paragraph about the writer; includes work and educational experience.

BIOGRAPHY. An account of a person's life (or the lives of a family or close-knit group) written by someone other than the subject(s). The work is set within the historical framework (i.e., the unique economic, social and political conditions) existing during the subject's life.

BLURB. The copy on paperback book covers or hardcover book dust jackets, either promoting the book and the author or featuring testimonials from book reviewers or well-known people in the book's field. Also called flap copy or jacket copy.

BOILERPLATE. A standardized publishing contract. Most authors and agents make many changes on the boilerplate before accepting the contract.

BOOK DOCTOR. A freelance editor hired by a writer, agent or book editor who analyzes problems that exist in a book manuscript or proposal, and offers solutions to those problems.

BOOK PACKAGER. Someone who draws elements of a book together—from initial concept to writing and marketing strategies—and then sells the book package to a book publisher and/or movie producer. Also known as book producer or book developer.

BOUND GALLEYS. A prepublication, often paperbound, edition of a book, usually prepared from photocopies of the final galley proofs. Designed for promotional purposes, bound galleys serve as the first set of review copies to be mailed out. Also called bound proofs.

CATEGORY FICTION. A term used to include all types of fiction. See *genre*.

CLIMAX. The most intense point in the story line of a fictional work.

CLIPS. Samples, usually from newspapers or magazines, of your published work. Also called tearsheets.

COMMERCIAL FICTION. Novels designed to appeal to a broad audience. These are often broken down into categories such as western, mystery and romance. See *genre*.

CONFESSION. A first-person story in which the narrator is involved in an emotional situation that encourages sympathetic reader identification, concluding with the affirmation of a morally acceptable theme.

CONFLICT. A prime ingredient of fiction that usually represents some obstacle to the main character's (i.e., the protagonist's) goals.

CONTRIBUTOR'S COPIES. Copies of the book sent to the author. The number of contributor's copies is often negotiated in the publishing contract.

CO-PUBLISHING. Arrangement where author and publisher share publication costs and profits of a book. Also called co-operative publishing.

COPYEDITING. Editing of a manuscript for writing style, grammar, punctuation and factual accuracy.

COPYRIGHT. A means to protect an author's work. A copyright is a proprietary right designed to give the creator of a work the power to control that work's reproduction, distribution and public display or performance, as well as its adaptation to other forms.

COVER LETTER. A brief letter that accompanies the manuscript being sent to an agent or publisher.

CREATIVE NONFICTION. Type of writing where true stories are told by employing the techniques usually reserved for novelists and poets, such as scenes, character arc, a three-act structure and detailed descriptions. This category is also called narrative nonfiction or literary journalism.

CRITIQUING SERVICE. An editing service offered by some agents in which writers pay a fee for comments on the salability or other qualities of their manuscript. Sometimes the critique includes suggestions on how to improve the work. Fees vary, as does the quality of the critique.

CURRICULUM VITAE (CV). Short account of one's career or qualifications.

DEADLINE. A specified date and/or time that a project or draft must be turned into the editor. A deadline factors into a preproduction schedule, which involves copyediting, typesetting and production.

DEAL MEMO. The memorandum of agreement between a publisher and author that precedes the actual contract and includes important issues such as royalty, advance, rights, distribution and option clauses.

DEUS EX MACHINA. A term meaning "God from the machine" that refers to any unlikely, contrived or trick resolution of a plot in any type of fiction.

DIALOGUE. An essential element of fiction. Dialogue consists of conversations between two or more people, and can be used heavily or sparsely.

DIVISION. An unincorporated branch of a publishing house/company.

ELECTRONIC RIGHTS. Secondary or subsidiary rights dealing with electronic/multimedia formats (the Internet, CD-ROMs, electronic magazines).

EL-HI. Elementary to high school. A term used to indicate reading or interest level.

EROTICA. A form of literature or film dealing with the sexual aspects of love. Erotic content ranges from subtle sexual innuendo to explicit descriptions of sexual acts.

ETHNIC. Stories and novels whose central characters are African American, Native American, Italian American, Jewish, Appalachian or members of some other specific cultural group. Ethnic fiction usually deals with a protagonist caught between two conflicting ways of life: mainstream American culture and his ethnic heritage.

EVALUATION FEES. Fees an agent may charge to simply evaluate or consider material without further guarantees of representation. Paying upfront evaluation fees to agents is never recommended and strictly forbidden by the Association of Authors' Representations. An agent makes money through a standard commission—taking 15 percent of what you earn through advances and, if applicable, royalties.

EXCLUSIVE. Offering a manuscript, usually for a set period of time such as one month, to just one agent and guaranteeing that agent is the only one looking at the manuscript.

EXPERIMENTAL. Type of fiction that focuses on style, structure, narrative technique, setting and strong characterization rather than plot. This form depends largely on the revelation of a character's inner being, which elicits an emotional response from the reader.

FAMILY SAGA. A story that chronicles the lives of a family or a number of related or interconnected families over a period of time.

FANTASY. Stories set in fanciful, invented worlds or in a legendary, mythic past that rely on outright invention or magic for conflict and setting.

FILM RIGHTS. May be sold or optioned by the agent/author to a person in the film industry, enabling the book to be made into a movie.

FLOOR BID. If a publisher is very interested in a manuscript, he may offer to enter a floor bid when the book goes to auction. The publisher sits out of the auction, but agrees to take the book by topping the highest bid by an agreed-upon percentage (usually 10 percent).

FOREIGN RIGHTS. Translation or reprint rights to be sold abroad.

FOREIGN RIGHTS AGENT. An agent who handles selling the rights to a country other than that of the first book agent. Usually an additional percentage (about 5 percent) will be added on to the first book agent's commission to cover the foreign rights agent.

GENRE. Refers to either a general classification of writing, such as a novel, poem or short story, or to the categories within those classifications, such as problem novels or sonnets.

GENRE FICTION. A term that covers various types of commercial novels, such as mystery, romance, Western, science fiction, fantasy, thriller and horror.

GHOSTWRITING. A writer puts into literary form the words, ideas or knowledge of another person under that person's name. Some agents offer this service; others pair ghostwriters with celebrities or experts.

GOTHIC. Novels characterized by historical settings and featuring young, beautiful women who win the favor of handsome, brooding heroes while simultaneously dealing with some life-threatening menace—either natural or supernatural.

GRAPHIC NOVEL. Contains comic-like drawings and captions, but deals more with everyday events and issues than with superheroes.

HIGH CONCEPT. A story idea easily expressed in a quick, one-line description.

HI-LO. A type of fiction that offers a high level of interest for readers at a low reading level.

HISTORICAL. A story set in a recognizable period of history. In addition to telling the stories of ordinary people's lives, historical fiction may involve political or social events of the time.

HOOK. Aspect of the work that sets it apart from others and draws in the reader/viewer.

HORROR. A story that aims to evoke some combination of fear, fascination and revulsion in its readers—either through supernatural or psychological circumstances.

HOW-TO. A book that offers the reader a description of how something can be accomplished. It includes both information and advice.

IMPRINT. The name applied to a publisher's specific line of books.

IN MEDIAS RES. A Latin term, meaning "into the midst of things," that refers to the literary device of beginning a narrative at a dramatic point in a story well along in the sequence of events to immediately convey action and capture reader interest.

IRC. International Reply Coupon. Buy at a post office to enclose with material sent outside the country to cover the cost of return postage. The recipient turns them in for stamps in their own country.

ISBN. This acronym stands for International Standard Book Number. ISBN is a tool used for both ordering and cataloging purposes.

JOINT CONTRACT. A legal agreement between a publisher and two or more authors that establishes provisions for the division of royalties their co-written book generates.

JUVENILE. Category of children's writing that can be broken down into easy-to-read books (ages 7–9), which run 2,000–10,000 words, and middle-grade books (ages 9–12), which run 20,000–40,000 words.

LIBEL. A form of defamation, or injury to a person's name or reputation. Written or published defamation is called *libel*, whereas spoken defamation is known as *slander*.

LITERARY. A book where style and technique are often as important as subject matter. In literary fiction, character is typically more important than plot, and the writer's voice and skill with words are both very essential. Also called serious fiction.

LOGLINE. A one-sentence description of a plot.

MAINSTREAM FICTION. Fiction on subjects or trends that transcend popular novel categories like mystery or romance. Using conventional methods, this kind of fiction tells stories about people and their conflicts.

MARKETING FEE. Fee charged by some agents to cover marketing expenses. It may be used to cover postage, telephone calls, faxes, photocopying or any other legitimate expense incurred in marketing a manuscript. Recouping expenses associated with submissions and marketing is the one and only time agents should ask for out-of-pocket money from writers.

MASS MARKET PAPERBACKS. Softcover books, usually 4×7 inches, on a popular subject directed at a general audience and sold in groceries, drugstores and bookstores.

MEMOIR. An author's commentary on the personalities and events that have significantly influenced one phase of his life.

MIDLIST. Those titles on a publisher's list expected to have limited sales. Midlist books are mainstream, not literary, scholarly or genre, and are usually written by new or relatively unknown writers.

MULTIPLE CONTRACT. Book contract that includes an agreement for a future book(s).

MYSTERY. A form of narration in which one or more elements remain unknown or unexplained until the end of the story. Subgenres include: amateur sleuth, caper, cozy, heist, malice domestic, police procedural, etc.

NET RECEIPTS. One method of royalty payment based on the amount of money a book publisher receives on the sale of the book after the booksellers' discounts, special sales discounts and returned copies.

NOVELIZATION. A novel created from the script of a popular movie and published in paperback. Also called a movie tie-in.

NOVELLA. A short novel or long short story, usually 20,000–50,000 words. Also called a novelette.

OCCULT. Supernatural phenomena, including ghosts, ESP, astrology, demonic possession, paranormal elements and witchcraft.

ONE-TIME RIGHTS. This right allows a short story or portions of a fiction or nonfiction book to be published again without violating the contract.

OPTION. The act of a producer buying film rights to a book for a limited period of time (usually six months or one year) rather than purchasing said rights in full. A book can be optioned multiple times by different production companies.

OPTION CLAUSE. A contract clause giving a publisher the right to publish an author's next book.

OUTLINE. A summary of a book's content (up to 15 double-spaced pages); often in the form of chapter headings with a descriptive sentence or two under each one to show the scope of the book.

PICTURE BOOK. A type of book aimed at ages 2–9 that tells the story partially or entirely with artwork, with up to 1,000 words. Agents interested in selling to publishers of these books often handle both artists and writers.

PLATFORM. A writer's speaking experience, interview skills, website and other abilities that help form a following of potential buyers for his book.

PROOFREADING. Close reading and correction of a manuscript's typographical errors.

PROPOSAL. An offer to an editor or publisher to write a specific work, usually a package consisting of an outline and sample chapters.

PROSPECTUS. A preliminary written description of a book, usually one page in length.

PSYCHIC/SUPERNATURAL. Fiction exploiting—or requiring as plot devices or themes—some contradictions of the commonplace natural world and materialist assumptions about it (including the traditional ghost story).

QUERY. A letter written to an agent or a potential market to elicit interest in a writer's work.

READER. A person employed by an agent or buyer to go through the slush pile of manuscripts and scripts, and select those worth considering.

REGIONAL. A book faithful to a particular geographic region and its people, including behavior, customs, speech and history.

RELEASE. A statement that your idea is original, has never been sold to anyone else, and that you are selling negotiated rights to the idea upon payment. Some agents may ask that you sign a release before they request pages and review your work.

REMAINDERS. Leftover copies of an out-of-print or slow-selling book purchased from the publisher at a reduced rate. Depending on the contract, a reduced royalty or no royalty is paid to the author on remaindered books.

REPRINT RIGHTS. The right to republish a book after its initial printing.

ROMANCE. A type of category fiction in which the love relationship between a man and a woman pervades the plot. The story is told from the viewpoint of the heroine, who meets a man (the hero), falls in love with him, encounters a conflict that hinders their relationship, and then resolves the conflict with a happy ending.

ROYALTIES. A percentage of the retail price paid to the author for each copy of the book that is sold. Agents take their percentage from the royalties earned and from the advance.

SASE. Self-addressed, stamped envelope. It should be included with all mailed correspondence.

SCHOLARLY BOOKS. Books written for an academic or research audience. These are usually heavily researched, technical and often contain terms used only within a specific field.

SCIENCE FICTION. Literature involving elements of science and technology as a basis for conflict, or as the setting for a story.

SERIAL RIGHTS. The right for a newspaper or magazine to publish sections of a manuscript.

SIMULTANEOUS SUBMISSION. Sending the same query or manuscript to several agents or publishers at the same time.

SLICE OF LIFE. A type of short story, novel, play or film that takes a strong thematic approach, depending less on plot than on vivid detail in describing the setting and/or environment, and the environment's effect on characters involved in it.

SLUSH PILE. A stack of unsolicited submissions in the office of an editor, agent or publisher.

STANDARD COMMISSION. The commission an agent earns on the sales of a manuscript. The commission percentage (usually 15 percent) is taken from the advance and royalties paid to the writer.

SUBAGENT. An agent handling certain subsidiary rights, usually working in conjunction with the agent who handled the book rights. The percentage paid the book agent is increased to pay the subagent.

SUBSIDIARY. An incorporated branch of a company or conglomerate (for example, Crown Publishing Group is a subsidiary of Random House, Inc.).

SUBSIDIARY RIGHTS. All rights other than book publishing rights included in a book publishing contract, such as paperback rights, book club rights and movie rights. Part of an agent's job is to negotiate those rights and advise you on which to sell and which to keep.

SUSPENSE. The element of both fiction and some nonfiction that makes the reader uncertain about the outcome. Suspense can be created through almost any element of a story, including the title, characters, plot, time restrictions and word choice.

SYNOPSIS. A brief summary of a story, novel or play. As a part of a book proposal, it is a comprehensive summary condensed in a page or page-and-a-half, single-spaced. Unlike a query letter or logline, a synopsis is a front-to-back explanation of the work—and will give away the story's ending.

TERMS. Financial provisions agreed upon in a contract, whether between writer and agent, or writer and editor.

TEXTBOOK. Book used in school classrooms at the elementary, high school or college level.

THEME. The point a writer wishes to make. It poses a question—a human problem.

THRILLER. A story intended to arouse feelings of excitement or suspense. Works in this genre are highly sensational, usually focusing on illegal activities, international espionage, sex and violence.

TOC. Table of Contents. A listing at the beginning of a book indicating chapter titles and their corresponding page numbers. It can also include chapter descriptions.

TRADE BOOK. Either a hardcover or softcover book sold mainly in bookstores. The subject matter frequently concerns a special interest for a more general audience.

TRADE PAPERBACK. A soft-bound volume, usually 5×8 inches, published and designed for the general public; available mainly in bookstores.

TRANSLATION RIGHTS. Sold to a foreign agent or foreign publisher.

UNSOLICITED MANUSCRIPT. An unrequested full manuscript sent to an editor, agent or publisher.

VET. A term used by editors when referring to the procedure of submitting a book manuscript to an outside expert (such as a lawyer) for review before publication. Memoirs are frequently vetted to confirm factually accuracy before the book is published.

WESTERNS/FRONTIER. Stories set in the American West, almost always in the 19th century, generally between the antebellum period and the turn of the century.

YOUNG ADULT (YA). The general classification of books written for ages 12–15. They run 40,000–80,000 words and include category novels—adventure, sports, paranormal, science fiction, fantasy, multicultural, mysteries, romance, etc.

LITERARY AGENTS

Agents listed in this section generate 98–100 percent of their income from commission on sales. They do not charge for reading, critiquing or editing your manuscript or book proposal. It's the goal of an agent to find salable manuscripts: Her income depends on finding the best publisher for your manuscript.

Since an agent's time is better spent meeting with editors, she will have little or no time to critique your writing. Agents who don't charge fees must be selective and often prefer to work with established authors, celebrities or those with professional credentials in a particular field.

Some agents in this section may charge clients for office expenses such as photocopying, foreign postage, long-distance phone calls or express mail services. Make sure you have a clear understanding of what these expenses are before signing any agency agreement.

SUBHEADS

Each agency listing is broken down into subheads to make locating specific information easier. In the first section, you'll find contact information for each agency. You'll also learn if the agents within the agency belong to any professional organizations; membership in these organizations can tell you a lot about an agency. For example, members of the Association of Authors' Representatives (AAR) are prohibited from charging reading or evaluating fees. Additional information in this section includes the size of each agency, its willingness to work with new or unpublished writers, and its general areas of interest.

MEMBER AGENTS: Agencies comprised of more than one agent list member agents and their individual specialties. This information will help you determine the appropriate person to whom you should send your query letter.

REPRESENTS: This section allows agencies to specify what nonfiction and fiction subjects they represent. Make sure you query only those agents who represent the type of material you write.

Look for the key icon to quickly learn an agent's areas of specialization. In this portion of the listing, agents mention the specific subject areas they're currently seeking, as well as those subject areas they do not consider.

HOW TO CONTACT: Most agents open to submissions prefer an initial query letter that briefly describes your work. While some agents may ask for an synopsis, book proposal (nonfiction) and/or a specific number of sample chapters, most don't. You should send these items only if the agent requests them. In this section, agents also mention if they accept queries by fax or e-mail, if they consider simultaneous submissions, and how they prefer to obtain new clients.

RECENT SALES: To give you a sense of the types of material they represent, the agents list specific titles they've sold, as well as a sampling of clients' names. Note that some agents consider their client list confidential and may only share client names once they agree to represent you.

TERMS: Provided here are details of an agent's commission, whether a contract is offered and for how long, and what additional office expenses you might have to pay if the agent agrees to represent you. Standard commissions range from 10–15 percent for domestic sales and 15–20 percent for foreign or dramatic sales (with the difference going to the co-agent who places the work).

At the beginning of some listings, you will find one or more of the following symbols:

⊘ agency not currently seeking new clients

☯ Canadian agency

⮌ agency located outside of the U.S. and Canada

◗ comment from the editor of *Guide to Literary Agents*

◯ newer agency actively seeking clients

◐ agency seeking both new and established writers

● agency seeking mostly established writers through referrals

◉ agency has a specialized focus

⤙ tips on agency's specializations

Find a pull-out bookmark with a key to symbols on the inside cover of this book.

WRITERS CONFERENCES: A great way to meet an agent is at a writers conference. Here agents list the conferences they usually attend. For more information about a specific conference, check the Conferences section in this book.

TIPS: In this section, agents offer advice and additional instructions for writers.

SPECIAL INDEXES

LITERARY AGENTS SPECIALTIES INDEX: This index organizes agencies according to the subjects they are interested in receiving. This index should help you compose a list of agents specializing in your areas. Cross-referencing categories and concentrating on agents interested in two or more aspects of your manuscript might increase your chances of success.

GENERAL INDEX: This index lists all agencies and conferences appearing in the book.

2M COMMUNICATIONS, LTD.

33 W. 17 St., PH, New York NY 10011. (212)741-1509. Fax: (212)691-4460. E-mail: morel@2mcommunications.com. Website: www.2mcommunications.com. **Contact:** Madeleine Morel. Member of AAR. Represents 100 clients. 20% of clients are new/unpublished writers. Currently handles: nonfiction books 100%.

- Prior to becoming an agent, Ms. Morel worked at a publishing company.

REPRESENTS nonfiction books. **Considers these nonfiction areas:** autobiography, biography, child guidance, cooking, cultural interests, diet/nutrition, ethnic, foods, health, history, medicine, music, parenting, self-help, women's issues, women's studies, cookbooks.

- This agency specializes in exclusively and non-exclusively representing professional ghostwriters and collaborators. This agency's writers have penned multiple bestsellers. They work closely with other leading literary agents and editors whose high-profile authors require confidential associations.

HOW TO CONTACT Query with SASE. Submit outline, 3 sample chapters. Accepts simultaneous submissions. Responds in 1 week to queries. Responds in 1 month to mss. Obtains most new clients through recommendations from others, solicitations.

TERMS Agent receives 15% commission on domestic sales. Agent receives 20% commission on foreign sales. Offers written contract, binding for 2 years. Charges clients for postage, photocopying, long-distance calls, faxes.

A+B WORKS

E-mail: query@aplusbworks.com. Website: www.aplusbworks.com/literary/submissions. **Contact:** Amy Jameson.

- Prior to her current position, Ms. Jameson worked at Janklow & Nesbit Associates.

REPRESENTS nonfiction books, novels. **Considers these fiction areas:** young adult and middle grade fiction, women's fiction, and select narrative nonfiction.

- This agency specializes in middle grade and young adult fiction, women's fiction and some adult nonfiction. We are only interested in established writers at this time. We do not represent thrillers, literary fiction, erotica, cook books, picture books, poetry, short fic-

tion, or screenplays. Due to the high volume of queries we receive, we cannot guarantee a response to unsolicited queries. We accept very few new clients in order to ensure the best possible representation for each of our authors.

HOW TO CONTACT Query via e-mail only. Please review our submissions policies first. Send queries to query@aplusbworks.com.

DOMINICK ABEL LITERARY AGENCY, INC.

146 W. 82nd St., #1A, New York NY 10024. (212)877-0710. Fax: (212)595-3133. E-mail: dominick@dalainc.com. Member AAR. Represents 100 clients. Currently handles: adult fiction and nonfiction.

HOW TO CONTACT Query via e-mail.

TERMS Agent receives 15% commission on domestic sales. Agent receives 20% commission on foreign sales.

ABOUT WORDS AGENCY

Website: agency.aboutwords.org. **Contact:** Susan Graham. Currently handles: nonfiction books 40%, novels 60%.

- About Words Agency is looking for commercial fiction and nonfiction. Does not want true crime, religious/Christian market, poetry.

HOW TO CONTACT Only accepts e-mail queries now. Send via e-mail with the subject: Query—[title of your book].

TERMS Agent receives 15% commission on domestic sales. Agent receives 20% commission on foreign sales. Offers written contract.

ADAMS LITERARY

7845 Colony Rd., C4 #215, Charlotte NC 28226. E-mail: info@adamsliterary.com. E-mail: submissions@adamsliterary.com. Website: www.adamsliterary.com. **Contact:** Tracey Adams, Josh Adams, Quinlan Lee. Member of AAR. Other memberships include SCBWI and WNBA. Currently handles: juvenile books.

MEMBER AGENTS Tracey Adams, Josh Adams, Quinlan Lee.

HOW TO CONTACT "All submissions and queries must be made through the online form on our website. We will not review—and will promptly recycle—any unsolicited submissions or queries we receive by post. Before submitting your work for consideration, please carefully review our complete guidelines." Responds in 6 weeks "While we have an established client list, we do seek new talent—and we accept submissions from both published and aspiring authors and artists."

TIPS "Guidelines are posted (and frequently updated) on our website."

BRET ADAMS LTD. AGENCY

448 W. 44th St., New York NY 10036. (212)765-5630. E-mail: literary@bretadamsltd.net. Website: bret adamsltd.net. **Contact:** Colin Hunt, Mark Orsini. Member of AAR. Currently handles: movie scripts, TV scripts, stage plays.

MEMBER AGENTS Bruce Ostler, Mark Orsini.

REPRESENTS movie scripts, TV scripts, TV movie of the week, theatrical stage play.

  ⌲ Handles theatre/film and TV projects. No books. Cannot accept unsolicited material.

HOW TO CONTACT Professional recommendation.

AITKEN ALEXANDER ASSOCIATES

18-21 Cavaye Place, London England SW10 9PT UK. (44)(207)373-8672. Fax: (44)(207)373-6002. E-mail: reception@aitkenalexander.co.uk. Website: www.aitkenalexander.co.uk. **Contact:** Submissions Department. Estab. 1976. Represents 300+ clients. 10% of clients are new/unpublished writers.

MEMBER AGENTS Gillon Aitken, agent; Clare Alexander, agent; Andrew Kidd, agent.

REPRESENTS nonfiction books, novels. **Considers these nonfiction areas:** current affairs, government, history, law, memoirs, popular culture, politics. **Considers these fiction areas:** historical, literary.

  ⌲ "We specialize in literary fiction and nonfiction." Does not represent illustrated children's books, poetry or screenplays.

HOW TO CONTACT Query with SASE. Submit synopsis, first 30 pages, and SASE. You can either address your submission to an individual agent, or simply to the Submissions Department. Responds in 6–8 weeks to queries. Obtains most new clients through recommendations from others, solicitations.

TERMS Agent receives 15% commission on domestic sales. Agent receives 20% commission on foreign sales. Offers written contract; 28-day notice must be given to terminate contract. Charges for photocopying and postage.

RECENT SALES Sold 50 titles in the last year. *My Life With George*, by Judith Summers (Voice); *The Separate Heart*, by Simon Robinson (Bloomsbury); *The Fall* *of the House of Wittgenstein*, by Alexander Waugh (Bloomsbury); *Shakespeare's Life*, by Germane Greer (Picador); *Occupational Hazards*, by Rory Stewart.

TIPS "Before submitting to us, we advise you to look at our existing client list to establish whether your work will be of interest. Equally, you should consider whether the material you have written is ready to submit to a literary agency. If you feel your work qualifies, then send us a letter introducing yourself. Keep it relevant to your writing (e.g., tell us about any previously published work, be it a short story or journalism; you may be studying or have completed a post-graduate qualification in creative writing; when it comes to nonfiction, we would want to know what qualifies you to write about the subject)."

ALIVE COMMUNICATIONS, INC.

7680 Goddard St., Suite 200, Colorado Springs CO 80920. (719)260-7080. Fax: (719)260-8223. E-mail: submissions@alivecom.com. Website: www.alivecom.com. **Contact:** Rick Christian. Member of AAR. Other memberships include Authors Guild. Represents 100+ clients. 5% of clients are new/unpublished writers. Currently handles: nonfiction books 50%, novels 40%, juvenile books 10%.

MEMBER AGENTS Rick Christian, president (blockbusters, bestsellers); Lee Hough (popular/commercial nonfiction and fiction, thoughtful spirituality, children's); Andrea Heinecke (thoughtful/inspirational nonfiction, women's fiction/nonfiction, popular/commercial nonfiction & fiction); Joel Kneedler (popular/commercial nonfiction and fiction, thoughtful spirituality, children's).

REPRESENTS nonfiction books, novels, short story collections, novellas. **Considers these nonfiction areas:** autobiography, biography, business, child guidance, economics, how-to, inspirational, parenting, personal improvement, religious, self-help, women's issues, women's studies. **Considers these fiction areas:** adventure, contemporary issues, crime, family saga, historical, humor, inspirational, literary, mainstream, mystery, police, religious, satire, suspense, thriller.

  ⌲ This agency specializes in fiction, Christian living, how-to and commercial nonfiction. Actively seeking inspirational, literary and mainstream fiction, and work from authors with established track records and platforms. Does not want to receive poetry, scripts or dark themes.

HOW TO CONTACT Query via e-mail. "Be advised that this agency works primarily with well-established, bestselling, and career authors. Always looking for a breakout, blockbuster author with genuine talent." New clients come through recommendations from others.

TERMS Agent receives 15% commission on domestic sales. Offers written contract; 2-month notice must be given to terminate contract.

RECENT SALES Sold 300+ titles in the last year. A spiritual memoir by Eugene Peterson (Viking); A biography of Rwandan president Paul Kagame, by Stephen Kinzer (St. Martin's Press); *Ever After*, by Karen Kingsbury (Zondervan); *A Hole in our Gospel*, by Rich Stears (Nelson); *My Life Outside the Ring*, by Hulk Hogan (St. Martin's Press), Tim Pawlenty (Tyndale).

TIPS "Rewrite and polish until the words on the page shine. Endorsements and great connections may help, provided you can write with power and passion. Network with publishing professionals by making contacts, joining critique groups, and attending writers' conferences in order to make personal connections and to get feedback. Alive Communications, Inc., has established itself as a premiere literary agency. We serve an elite group of authors who are critically acclaimed and commercially successful in both Christian and general markets."

❶ ALLEN O'SHEA LITERARY AGENCY

615 Westover Rd., Stamford CT 06902. (203)359-9965. Fax: (203)357-9909. E-mail: marilyn@allenoshea.com; coleen@allenoshea.com. Website: www.allenoshea.com. **Contact:** Marilyn Allen. Represents 100 clients. 20% of clients are new/unpublished writers. Currently handles: nonfiction books 99%.

- Prior to becoming agents, both Ms. Allen and Ms. O'Shea held senior positions in publishing.

MEMBER AGENTS Marilyn Allen; Coleen O'Shea.
REPRESENTS nonfiction books. **Considers these nonfiction areas:** biography, business, cooking, current affairs, health, history, how-to, humor, military, money, popular culture, psychology, sports, interior design/decorating.

- ☞ "This agency specializes in practical nonfiction including cooking, sports, business, pop culture, etc. We look for clients with strong marketing platforms and new ideas coupled with strong writing." Actively seeking narrative nonfiction, health and history writers;

very interested in writers who have a large blog following and interesting topics. Does not want to receive fiction, memoirs, poetry, textbooks or children's.

HOW TO CONTACT Query with via e-mail or mail with SASE. Submit outline, author bio, marketing page. No phone or fax queries. Accepts simultaneous submissions. Responds in 1 week to queries. Responds in 1-2 months to mss. Obtains most new clients through recommendations from others, conferences.

TERMS Agent receives 15% commission on domestic sales. Offers written contract, binding for 2 years; 1-month notice must be given to terminate contract. Charges for photocopying large mss, and overseas postage—"typically minimal costs."

RECENT SALES Sold 45 titles in the last year. "This agency prefers not to share information about specific sales, but see our website."

WRITERS CONFERENCES ASJA, Publicity Submit for Writers, Connecticut Authors and Publishers, Mark Victor Hansen Mega Book Conference.

TIPS "Prepare a strong overview, with competition, marketing and bio. We will consider when your proposal is ready."

❶ MIRIAM ALTSHULER LITERARY AGENCY

53 Old Post Road N., Red Hook NY 12571. (845)758-9408. Website: www.miriamaltshulerliteraryagency.com. **Contact:** Miriam Altshuler. Estab. 1994. Member of AAR. Represents 40 clients. Currently handles: nonfiction books 45%, novels 45%, story collections 5%, juvenile books 5%.

- Ms. Altshuler has been an agent since 1982.

REPRESENTS nonfiction books, novels, short story collections, juvenile. **Considers these nonfiction areas:** biography, ethnic, history, language, memoirs, multicultural, music, nature, popular culture, psychology, sociology, film, women's. **Considers these fiction areas:** literary, mainstream, multicultural, some selective children's books.

- ☞ Literary commercial fiction and nonfiction. Does not want self-help, mystery, how-to, romance, horror, spiritual, fantasy, poetry, screenplays, science fiction or techno-thriller, Western.

HOW TO CONTACT Send query; do not send e-mail. If we want to see your ms we will respond via e-mail (if you do not have an e-mail address, please send a SASE). We will only respond if interested in materials. Submit contact info with e-mail address. Prefers to read materials exclusively. Accepts simultaneous submissions. Responds in 3 weeks to mss. Obtains most new clients through recommendations from others.

TERMS Agent receives 15% commission on domestic sales. Agent receives 20% commission on foreign sales. Charges clients for overseas mailing, photocopies, overnight mail when requested by author.

WRITERS CONFERENCES Bread Loaf Writers' Conference; Washington Independent Writers Conference; North Carolina Writers' Network Conference.

TIPS See the website for specific submission details.

AMBASSADOR LITERARY AGENCY

P.O. Box 50358, Nashville TN 37205. (615)370-4700. E-mail: wes@ambassadoragency.com; info@ambassadoragency.com. Website: www.AmbassadorAgency.com. **Contact:** Wes Yoder. Represents 25-30 clients. 10% of clients are new/unpublished writers. Currently handles: nonfiction books 95%, novels 5%.

- Prior to becoming an agent, Mr. Yoder founded a music artist agency in 1973; he established a speakers bureau division of the company in 1984.

REPRESENTS nonfiction books, novels. **Considers these nonfiction areas:** biography, current affairs, ethnic, government, history, how to, memoirs, popular culture, religion, self-help, women's.

- "This agency specializes in religious market publishing dealing primarily with A-level publishers." Actively seeking popular nonfiction themes, including the following: practical living; Christian spirituality; literary fiction. Does not want to receive short stories, children's books, screenplays or poetry.

HOW TO CONTACT Ambassador's Literary department represents a growing list of best-selling authors. We represent select authors and writers who are published by the leading religious and general market publishers in the United States and Europe, and represent television and major motion picture rights for our clients. Authors should e-mail a short description of their manuscript with a request to submit their work for review. Guidelines for submission will be sent if we agree to review a manuscript. Accepts simultaneous submissions. Responds in 2–4

weeks to queries. Obtains most new clients through recommendations from others.

TERMS Agent receives 15% commission on domestic sales. Agent receives 20% commission on foreign sales. Offers written contract.

RECENT SALES Sold 20 titles in the last year. *The Death and Life of Gabriel Phillips*, by Stephen Baldwin (Hachette); *Amazing Grace: William Wilberforce and the Heroic Campaign to End Slavery*, by Eric Mataxas (Harper San Francisco); *Life@ The Next Level*, by Courtney McBath (Simon and Schuster); *Women, Take Charge of Your Money*, by Carolyn Castleberry (Random House/Multnomah).

MARCIA AMSTERDAM AGENCY

41 W. 82nd St., Suite 9A, New York NY 10024-5613. (212)873-4945. **Contact:** Marcia Amsterdam. Signatory of WGA. Currently handles: nonfiction books 15%, novels 70%, movie scripts 5%, TV scripts 10%.

- Prior to opening her agency, Ms. Amsterdam was an editor.

REPRESENTS novels, movie scripts, feature film, sitcom. **Considers these fiction areas:** adventure, detective, horror, mainstream, mystery, romance (contemporary, historical), science, thriller, young adult. **Considers these script areas:** comedy, romantic comedy.

HOW TO CONTACT Query with SASE. Responds in 1 month to queries.

TERMS Agent receives 15% commission on domestic sales. Agent receives 20% commission on foreign sales. Agent receives 10% commission on film sales. Offers written contract, binding for 1 year. Charges clients for extra office expenses, foreign postage, copying, legal fees (when agreed upon).

RECENT SALES *Hidden Child,* by Isaac Millman (FSG); *Lucky Leonardo*, by Jonathan Canter (Sourcebooks).

TIPS "We are always looking for interesting literary voices."

BETSY AMSTER LITERARY ENTERPRISES

6312 Sw Capitol Hwy #503, Portland OR 97239. Website: www.amsterlit.com. **Contact:** Betsy Amster. Estab. 1992. Member of AAR. Represents more than 65 clients. 35% of clients are new/unpublished writers. Currently handles: nonfiction books 65%, novels 35%.

- Prior to opening her agency, Ms. Amster was an editor at Pantheon and Vintage for 10 years, and served as editorial director for the Globe Pequot Press for 2 years.

REPRESENTS nonfiction books, novels. **Considers these nonfiction areas:** art & design, biography, business, child guidance, cooking/nutrition, current affairs, ethnic, gardening, health/medicine, history, memoirs, money, parenting, popular culture, psychology, science/technology, self-help, sociology, travelogues, social issues, women's issues. **Considers these fiction areas:** ethnic, literary, women's, high quality.

→ "Actively seeking strong narrative nonfiction, particularly by journalists; outstanding literary fiction (the next Richard Ford or Jhumpa Lahiri); witty, intelligent commerical women's fiction (the next Elinor Lipman or Jennifer Weiner); mysteries that open new worlds to us; and high-profile self-help and psychology, preferably research-based." Does not want to receive poetry, children's books, romances, Western, science fiction, action/adventure, screenplays, fantasy, techno-thrillers, spy capers, apocalyptic scenarios, or political or religious arguments.

HOW TO CONTACT For adult titles: b.amster.assistant@gmail.com. See submission requirements online at website. The requirements have changed and only e-mail submissions are accepted. Accepts simultaneous submissions. Responds in 1 month to queries. Responds in 2 months to mss. Obtains most new clients through recommendations from others, solicitations, conferences.

TERMS Agent receives 15% commission on domestic sales. Agent receives 20% commission on foreign sales. Offers written contract, binding for 1 year; 3-month notice must be given to terminate contract. Charges for photocopying, postage, long distance phone calls, messengers, galleys/books used in submissions to foreign and film agents and to magazines for first serial rights.

WRITERS CONFERENCES USC Masters in Professional Writing; San Diego State University Writers' Conference; UCLA Extension Writers' Program; Los Angeles Times Festival of Books; The Loft Literary Center; Willamette Writers Conference.

◑ ANDERSON LITERARY MANAGEMENT, LLC

12 W. 19th St., New York NY 10011. (212)645-6045. Fax: (212)741-1936. E-mail: info@andersonliterary.com; kathleen@andersonliterary.com; christine@andersonliterary.com; tess@andersonliterary.com. Website: www.andersonliterary.com/. **Contact:** Kathleen Anderson. Estab. 2006. Member of AAR. Represents 100+ clients. 20% of clients are new/unpublished writers. Currently handles: nonfiction books 50%, novels 50%.

MEMBER AGENTS Kathleen Anderson, Christine Mervart, Tess Taylor.

REPRESENTS nonfiction books, novels, short story collections, juvenile. **Considers these nonfiction areas:** anthropology, archeology, architecture, art, autobiography, biography, cultural interests, current affairs, dance, design, education, environment, ethnic, gay, government, history, law, lesbian, memoirs, music, nature, politics, psychology, women's issues, women's studies. **Considers these fiction areas:** action, adventure, ethnic, family saga, feminist, frontier, gay, historical, lesbian, literary, mystery, suspense, thriller, Westerns, women's, young adult.

→ "Specializes in adult and young adult literary and commercial fiction, narrative nonfiction, American and European history, literary journalism, nature and travel writing, memoir, and biography. We do not represent science fiction, cookbooks, gardening, craft books or children's picture books. While we love literature in translation, we cannot accept samples of work written in languages other than English."

HOW TO CONTACT Query with SASE. Submit synopsis, first 3 sample chapters, proposal (for nonfiction). Snail mail queries only. Accepts simultaneous submissions. Responds in 6 weeks to queries. Obtains most new clients through recommendations from others, solicitations, conferences.

TERMS Agent receives 15% commission on domestic sales. Offers written contract.

WRITERS CONFERENCES Squaw Valley Conference.

TIPS "We do not represent plays or screenplays."

◑ ARCADIA

31 Lake Place N., Danbury CT 06810. E-mail: arcadialit@sbcglobal.net. **Contact:** Victoria Gould Pryor. Member of AAR.

REPRESENTS nonfiction books, literary and commercial fiction. **Considers these nonfiction areas:** biography, business, current affairs, health, history, psychology, science, true crime, women's, investigative journalism; culture; classical music; life transforming self-help.

8—¬ "I'm a very hands-on agent, which is necessary in this competitive marketplace. I work with authors on revisions until whatever we present to publishers is as strong as possible. I represent talented, dedicated, intelligent and ambitious writers who are looking for a long-term relationship based on professional success and mutual respect." Does not want to receive science fiction/fantasy, horror, humor or children's/young adult. "We are only able to read fiction submissions from previously published authors."

HOW TO CONTACT No unsolicited submissions. Query with SASE. This agency accepts e-queries (no attachments).

⊘ EDWARD ARMSTRONG LITERARY AGENCY

4 Richard Ave., Shrewbury MA 01545. (401)569-7099. **Contact:** Edward Armstrong. Currently handles: 100% fiction.

- Prior to becoming an agent, Mr. Armstrong was a business professional specializing in quality and regulatory compliance. **This agency is not taking submissions at this time 02/07/10.** Please continue to check back.

REPRESENTS novels, short story collections, novellas. **Considers these fiction areas:** mainstream, romance, science, thriller, suspense.

HOW TO CONTACT Obtains most new clients through solicitations.

TERMS Agent receives 5% commission on domestic sales. Agent receives 5% commission on foreign sales. This agency charges for photocopying and postage.

❶ ARTISTS AND ARTISANS INC.

244 Madison Ave., Suite 334, New York NY 10016. Website: www.artistsandartisans.com. **Contact:** Adam Chromy and Jamie Brenner. Represents 70 clients. 80% of clients are new/unpublished writers. Currently handles: nonfiction books 50%, fiction 50%.

MEMBER AGENTS Adam Chromy (fiction and narrative nonfiction); Jamie Brenner (thrillers, commercial and literary fiction, memoir, narrative nonfiction, young adult).

REPRESENTS nonfiction books, novels. **Considers these nonfiction areas:** biography, business, child, current affairs, ethnic, health, how-to, humor, language, memoirs, money, music, popular culture, religion, science, self-help, sports, film, true crime, women's, fashion/style. **Considers these fiction areas:** confession, family, humor, literary, mainstream.

8—¬ "My education and experience in the business world ensure that my clients' enterprise as authors gets as much attention and care as their writing." Working journalists for nonfiction books. No scripts, photo or children's books.

HOW TO CONTACT Query by e-mail only. Start subject line with "query." No unsolicited submissions. All fiction queries must include a brief author's bio, and the setup or premise for the book. Accepts simultaneous submissions. Responds to queries only if interested. Obtains most new clients through recommendations from others, solicitations, conferences.

TERMS Agent receives 15% commission on domestic sales. Agent receives 25% commission on foreign sales. Offers written contract; 1-month notice must be given to terminate contract. "We only charge for extraordinary expenses (e.g., client requests check via FedEx instead of regular mail)."

RECENT SALES *New World Monkeys*, (Shaye Areheart); *World Made by Hand* (Grove Atlantic); *House of Cards*, by David Ellis Dickerson (Penguin).

WRITERS CONFERENCES ASJA Writers Conference, Pacific Northwest Writers Conference, Newbury Port Writers Conference.

TIPS "Please make sure you are ready before approaching us or any other agent. If you write fiction, make sure it is the best work you can do and get objective criticism from a writing group. If you write nonfiction, make sure the proposal exhibits your best work and a comprehensive understanding of the market."

❶ ROBERT ASTLE AND ASSOCIATES LITERARY MANAGEMENT, INC.

419 Lafayette St., 3rd Floor, New York NY 10003. (212)277-8014. Fax: (212)228-6149. E-mail: robert@astleliterary.com. Website: www.astleliterary.com. **Contact:** Robert Astle.

- Prior to becoming an agent, Mr. Astle spent 25 years in theater.

REPRESENTS nonfiction books, novels.

8—¬ "We are especially interested in receiving nonfiction projects with a wide range of topics, including narrative nonfiction, popular culture, arts and culture, theater and performance, sports, travel, celebrity, biography, politics, memoir, history, new media and multi-ethnic. We are actively seeking writers of literary fiction and commercial fiction—mysteries and suspense, thrillers, mainstream literary fiction, historical fiction, women's fiction, humor/satire and graphic novels. We will also seek writers in the genre of young audiences: middle grade and teen."

HOW TO CONTACT Use the online form to query. Specifications for nonfiction and fiction submissions are online. Obtains most new clients through recommendations from others, solicitations.

TIPS "Please read the submission guidelines carefully, and make sure your query letter is the best it can be."

O AVENUE A LITERARY

419 Lafayette St., Second Floor, New York NY 10003. Fax: (212)228-6149. E-mail: submissions@avenuealiterary.com. Website: www.avenuealiterary.com. **Contact:** Jennifer Cayea. Represents 20 clients. 75% of clients are new/unpublished writers. Currently handles: nonfiction books 40%, novels 45%, story collections 5%, juvenile books 10%.

- Prior to opening her agency, Ms. Cayea was an agent and director of foreign rights for Nicholas Ellison, Inc., a division of Sanford J. Greenburger Associates. She was also an editor in the audio and large-print divisions of Random House.

REPRESENTS nonfiction books, novels, short story collections, juvenile. **Considers these nonfiction areas:** cooking, cultural interests, current affairs, dance, ethnic, film, foods, health, history, medicine, memoirs, music, nutrition, personal improvement, popular culture, self-help, sports, theater. **Considers these fiction areas:** contemporary issues, family saga, feminist, historical, literary, mainstream, thriller, young adult, women's/chick lit.

- ⌐ "Our authors are dynamic and diverse. We seek strong new voices in fiction and nonfiction, and are fiercely dedicated to our authors. We are actively seeking new authors of fiction and nonfiction."

HOW TO CONTACT Query via e-mail only. Submit synopsis, publishing history, author bio, full contact info. Paste info in e-mail body. No attachments. Include all information *in the body of your e-mail*: submissions sent as attachments will *not* be read. Accepts simultaneous submissions. Responds in 6–8 weeks to queries. Obtains most new clients through recommendations from others, solicitations, conferences.

TERMS Agent receives 15% commission on domestic sales. Agent receives 15% commission on foreign sales. Offers written contract; 30-day notice must be given to terminate contract.

RECENT SALES *Gunmetal Black*, by Daniel Serrano.

TIPS "Build a résumé by publishing short stories if you are a fiction writer."

O THE BALKIN AGENCY, INC.

P.O. Box 222, Amherst MA 01004. (413)322-8697; (978)656-8389. Fax: (413)322-8697. E-mail: rick62838@crocker.com; christinawardlit@mac.com. Website: http://wardbalkin.com. **Contact:** Rick Balkin, president. Christina Ward: P.O. Box 7144, Lowell, MA 01852. Member of AAR. Represents 50 clients. 10% of clients are new/unpublished writers. Currently handles: nonfiction books 85%, 5% reference books .

- Prior to opening his agency, Mr. Balkin served as executive editor with Bobbs-Merrill Company.

MEMBER AGENTS Christina Ward (literary fiction: contemporary, historical, mysteries, thrillers. literary memoirs; creative nonfiction; narrative history; art and culture; biography; psychology; natural history and animal-related narratives; "green" subject areas [alternative lifestyle, shelter, sustainability, local living, permaculture, food systems]; nutrition [but probably not cookbooks or diet books]; health and medicine; gardening; social thought and commentary).

REPRESENTS nonfiction books. **Considers these nonfiction areas:** animals, anthropology, current affairs, health, history, how to, nature, popular culture, science, sociology, translation, biography, et al.

- ⌐ This agency specializes in adult nonfiction. Does not want to receive fiction, poetry, screenplays, children's books or computer books.

HOW TO CONTACT Query with SASE. Submit proposal package, outline. Responds in 1 week to queries. Responds in 2 weeks to mss. Obtains most new clients through recommendations from others.

TERMS Agent receives 15% commission on domestic sales. Agent receives 20% commission on foreign sales. Offers written contract, binding for 1 year. This agency charges clients for photocopying and express or foreign mail.

RECENT SALES Sold 15 titles in the last year. *No Tongue Shall Speak*, by Utpal Sandesara/Tom Wooten (Prometheus Books); *Wrong*, by David H. Freedman

(Little, Brown); *The Musical Vision of Gustavo Dudamel*, by Tricia Tunstall, (W.W. Norton & Co.).

TIPS "I do not take on books described as bestsellers or potential bestsellers. Any nonfiction work that is either unique, paradigmatic, a contribution, truly witty or a labor of love is grist for my mill."

◑ BARER LITERARY, LLC

270 Lafayette St., Suite 1504, New York NY 10012. (212)691-3513. E-mail: submissions@barerliterary. com. Website: www.barerliterary.com. **Contact:** Julie Barer. Estab. 2004. Member of AAR.

- Before becoming an agent, Julie worked at Shakespeare & Co. Booksellers in New York City. She is a graduate of Vassar College.

MEMBER AGENTS Julie Barer.

REPRESENTS nonfiction books, novels, short story collections., Julie Barer is especially interested in working with emerging writers and developing long-term relationships with new clients. **Considers these nonfiction areas:** biography, ethnic, history, memoirs, popular culture, women's. **Considers these fiction areas:** contemporary issues, ethnic, historical, literary, mainstream.

⌇╍ This agency no longer accepts young adult submissions. No health/fitness, business/investing/finance, sports, mind/body/spirit, reference, thrillers/suspense, military, romance, children's books/picture books, screenplays.

HOW TO CONTACT Query with SASE; no attachments if query by e-mail. We do not respond to queries via phone or fax.

TERMS Agent receives 15% commission on domestic sales. Agent receives 20% commission on foreign sales. Offers written contract. Charges for photocopying and books ordered.

RECENT SALES *The Unnamed*, by Joshua Ferris (Reagan Arthur Books); *Tunneling to the Center of the Earth*, by Kevin Wilson (Ecco Press); *A Disobedient Girl*, by Ru Freeman (Atria Books); *A Friend of the Family*, by Lauren Grodstein (Algonquin); *City of Veils*, by Zoe Ferraris (Little, Brown).

BAROR INTERNATIONAL, INC.

P.O. Box 868, Armonk NY 10504. E-mail: heather@barorint.com. Website: www.barorint.com. **Contact:** Danny Baror; Heather Baror. Represents 300 clients.

⌇╍ "This agency represents authors and publishers in the international market. Currently representing all genres ranging from thrillers to science fiction/fantasy, self-help, spiritual, young adult, commercial fiction, and more."

HOW TO CONTACT Submit by e-mail or mail (with SASE); please include a cover letter.

TIPS No further information on this agency is available.

◑ LORETTA BARRETT BOOKS, INC.

220 E. 23rd St., 11th Floor, New York NY 10010. (212)242-3420. E-mail: query@lorettabarrettbooks. com. Website: www.lorettabarrettbooks.com. **Contact:** Loretta A. Barrett, Nick Mullendore, Gabriel Davis. Estab. 1990. Member of AAR. Currently handles: nonfiction books 50%, novels 50%.

- Prior to opening her agency, Ms. Barrett was vice president and executive editor at Doubleday and editor-in-chief of Anchor Books.

MEMBER AGENTS Loretta A. Barrett; Nick Mullendore.

REPRESENTS nonfiction books, novels. **Considers these nonfiction areas:** biography, child guidance, current affairs, ethnic, government, health/nutrition, history, memoirs, money, multicultural, nature, popular culture, psychology, religion, science, self help, sociology, spirituality, sports, women's, young adult, creative nonfiction. **Considers these fiction areas:** contemporary, psychic, adventure, detective, ethnic, family, historical, literary, mainstream, mystery, thriller, young adult.

⌇╍ "The clients we represent include both fiction and nonfiction authors for the general adult trade market. The works they produce encompass a wide range of contemporary topics and themes including commercial thrillers, mysteries, romantic suspense, popular science, memoirs, narrative fiction and current affairs." No children's, juvenile, cookbooks, gardening, science fiction, fantasy novels, historical romance.

HOW TO CONTACT See guidelines online. Use e-mail (no attachments) or if by post, query with SASE. For hardcopy queries, please send a 1-2 page query letter and a synopsis or chapter outline for your project. In your letter, please include your contact information, any relevant background information on yourself or your project, and a paragraph of description of your project. If you are submitting electronically, then all of this material may be included in the body of your e-mail. Accepts simultaneous submissions. Responds in 3-6 weeks to queries.

TERMS Agent receives 15% commission on domestic sales. Agent receives 20% commission on foreign sales. Offers written contract. Charges clients for shipping and photocopying.

○○ LORELLA BELLI LITERARY AGENCY (LBLA)

54 Hartford House, 35 Tavistock Crescent, Notting Hill, London England W11 1AY United Kingdom. (44)(207)727-8547. Fax: (44)(870)787-4194. E-mail: info@lorellabelliagency.com. Website: www.lorella belliagency.com. **Contact:** Lorella Belli. Other memberships include AAA.

REPRESENTS nonfiction books, novels. **Considers these nonfiction areas:** business, current affairs, economics, history, personal improvement, politics, science, self-help, technology, travel, women's issues, women's studies, food/wine; popular music; lifestyle. **Considers these fiction areas:** historical, literary, genre fiction; women's; crime.

○─π "We are interested in first-time novelists, journalists, multicultural and international writing, and books about Italy." Does not want children's books, fantasy, science fiction, screenplays, short stories, or poetry.

HOW TO CONTACT For fiction, send query letter, first 3 chapters, synopsis, brief CV, SASE. For nonfiction, send query letter, full proposal, chapter outline, 2 sample chapters, SASE.

TERMS Agent receives 15% commission on domestic sales. Agent receives 20% commission on foreign sales.

TIPS "Please send an initial inquiry letter or e-mail before submitting your work to us."

○ FAYE BENDER LITERARY AGENCY

19 Cheever Place, Brooklyn NY 11231. E-mail: info@ fbliterary.com. Website: www.fbliterary.com. **Contact:** Faye Bender. Estab. 2004. Member of AAR.

MEMBER AGENTS Faye Bender.

REPRESENTS nonfiction books, novels, juvenile. **Considers these nonfiction areas:** biography, memoirs, popular culture, women's issues, women's studies, young adult, narrative; health; popular science. **Considers these fiction areas:** commercial, literary, women's, young adult and middle grade.

○─π "I choose books based on the narrative voice and strength of writing. I work with previ-

ously published and first-time authors." Faye does not represent picture books, genre fiction for adults (Western, romance, horror, science fiction, fantasy), business books, spirituality or screenplays.

HOW TO CONTACT Query with SASE and 10 sample pages via mail or e-mail (no attachments). Guidelines online. "Please do not send queries or submissions via registered or certified mail, or by FedEx or UPS requiring signature. We will not return unsolicited submissions weighing more than 16 ounces, even if an SASE is attached. We do not respond to queries via phone or fax."

TIPS "Please keep your letters to the point, include all relevant information, and have a bit of patience."

○ THE BENT AGENCY

204 Park Place, Number 2, Brooklyn NY 11238. E-mail: info@thebentagency.com. Website: www.thebentagency. com. **Contact:** Jenny Bent, Susan Hawk. Estab. 2009.

- Prior to forming her own agency, Ms. Bent was an agent and vice president at Trident Media.

MEMBER AGENTS Jenny Bent (all adult fiction except for science fiction); Susan Hawk (young adult and middle grade books; within the realm of kids stories, she likes fantasy, science fiction, historical fiction and mystery).

REPRESENTS **Considers these fiction areas:** commercial, crime, historical, horror, mystery, picture books, romance, suspense, thriller, women's, young adult literary.

HOW TO CONTACT E-mail queries@thebentagency. com, or if you're writing for children or teens, kidsque ries@thebentagency.com. "Tell us briefly who you are, what your book is, and why you're the one to write it. Then include the first ten pages of your material in the body of your e-mail. We respond to all queries, please resend your query if you haven't had a response within 4 weeks." Accepts simultaneous submissions.

RECENT SALES *Worst Laid Plans*, by Laura Kindred and Alexandra Lydon; *The Dark Ink Chronicles*, by Elle Jasper; *What We Don't Tell*, by Desiree Washington; *Bent Road*, by Lori Roy; *The Art of Saying Goodbye*, by Ellyn Bache; *Through Her Eyes*, by Jenny Archer; *You Don't Sweat Much for a Fat Girl*, by Celia Rivenbark; *When Harry Met Molly*, by Kieran Kramer.

BIDNICK & COMPANY

E-mail: bidnick@comcast.net. Currently handles: 100% nonfiction books.

- Founding member of Collins Publishers. Vice President of HarperCollins, San Francisco.

MEMBER AGENTS Carole Bidnick.

☙ This agency specializes in cookbooks and narrative nonfiction.

HOW TO CONTACT Send queries via e-mail only.

● VICKY BIJUR LITERARY AGENCY

333 West End Ave., Apt. 5B, New York NY 10023. E-mail: assistant@vickybijuragency.com. Estab. 1988. Member of AAR.

- Vicky Bijur worked at Oxford University Press and with the Charlotte Sheedy Literary Agency. Books she represents have appeared on *The New York Times* Bestseller List, in *The New York Times* Notable Books of the Year, *Los Angeles Times* Best Fiction of the Year, *Washington Post* Book World Rave Reviews of the Year.

REPRESENTS nonfiction books, novels. **Considers these nonfiction areas:** cooking, government, health, history, psychology, psychiatry, science, self-help, sociology, biography; child care/development; environmental studies; journalism; social sciences.

☙ Does not want science fiction, fantasy, horror, romance, poetry, children's

HOW TO CONTACT Accepts e-mail queries. Fiction: query and first chapter (if e-mailed, please paste chapter into body of e-mail as I don't open attachments from unfamiliar senders). Nonfiction: query and proposal. No phone or fax queries.

RECENT SALES *Left Neglected* and *Love, Anthony,* by Lisa Genova (Pocket Books, 2011 and 2012); *I'd Know You Anywhere* and two untitled books, by Laura Lippman (William Morrow, 2010, 2011, 2012); *The Serious Eats Guide,* by Ed Levine (Clarkson Potter, 2012); *The Cartoon Guide to Calculus,* by Larry Gonick (HarperCollins, 2012); *Relaxation Revolution,* by Herbert Benson, M.D., and William Proctor (Scribner, 2010).

● DAVID BLACK LITERARY AGENCY

335 Adams St., # 2710, Brooklyn NY 11201-3724. (718)852-5500. **Contact:** David Black, owner. Member of AAR. Represents 150 clients. Currently handles: nonfiction books 90%, novels 10%.

MEMBER AGENTS David Black; Susan Raihofer (general nonfiction, literary fiction); Gary Morris (commercial fiction, psychology); Joy E. Tutela (general nonfiction, literary fiction); Leigh Ann Eliseo; Linda Loewenthal (general nonfiction, health, science, psychology, narrative).

REPRESENTS nonfiction books, novels. **Considers these nonfiction areas:** autobiography, biography, business, economics, finance, government, health, history, inspirational, law, medicine, military, money, multicultural, psychology, religious, sports, war, women's issues, women's studies. **Considers these fiction areas:** literary, mainstream, commercial.

☙ This agency specializes in business, sports, politics, and novels.

HOW TO CONTACT Query with SASE. For nonfiction works, send a formal proposal that includes an overview, author bio, chapter outline, a marketing/publicity section, a competition section, and at least one sample chapter. Please also include writing samples, such as newspaper or magazine clips if relevant. (See questions in Guidelines online.) When submitting fiction, please include a synopsis, author bio, and the first 3 chapters of the book (25-50 pages). Accepts simultaneous submissions. Responds in 2 months to queries.

TERMS Agent receives 15% commission on domestic sales. Charges clients for photocopying and books purchased for sale of foreign rights.

RECENT SALES Some of the agency's best-selling authors include: Mitch Albom, Erik Larson, Ken Davis, Bruce Feiler, Dan Coyle, Jane Leavy, Randy Pausch, Steve Lopez, Jenny Sanford, David Kidder and Noah Oppenheim.

BLEECKER STREET ASSOCIATES, INC.

217 Thompson St., #519, New York NY 10012. (212)677-4492. Fax: (212)388-0001. E-mail: bleeckerst@hotmail.com. **Contact:** Agnes Birnbaum. Member of AAR. Other memberships include RWA, MWA. Represents 60 clients. 20% of clients are new/unpublished writers. Currently handles: nonfiction books 75%, novels 25%.

- Prior to becoming an agent, Ms. Birnbaum was a senior editor at Simon & Schuster, Dutton/Signet, and other publishing houses.

REPRESENTS nonfiction books, novels. **Considers these nonfiction areas:** New Age, animals, biography, business, child, computers, cooking, current affairs, ethnic, government, health, history, how-to, memoirs, military, money, nature, popular culture, psychology, religion, science, self-help, sociology, sports, true crime, women's. **Considers these fiction areas:** ethnic, historical, literary, mystery, romance, thriller, women's.

8—⚓ "We're very hands-on and accessible. We try to be truly creative in our submission approaches. We've had especially good luck with first-time authors." Does not want to receive science fiction, Westerns, poetry, children's books, academic/scholarly/professional books, plays, scripts, or short stories.

HOW TO CONTACT Query with SASE. No e-mail, phone, or fax queries. Accepts simultaneous submissions. Responds in 2 weeks to queries. Responds in 1 month to mss. "Obtains most new clients through recommendations from others, solicitations, conferences, plus, I will approach someone with a letter if his/her work impresses me."

TERMS Agent receives 15% commission on domestic sales. Agent receives 25% commission on foreign sales. Offers written contract; 1-month notice must be given to terminate contract. Charges for postage, long distance, fax, messengers, photocopies (not to exceed $200).

RECENT SALES Sold 14 titles in the last year. *Following Sarah*, by Daniel Brown (Morrow); *Biology of the Brain*, by Paul Swingle (Rutgers University Press); *Santa Miracles*, by Brad and Sherry Steiger (Adams); *Surviving the College Search*, by Jennifer Delahunt (St. Martin's).

TIPS "Keep query letters short and to the point; include only information pertaining to the book or background as a writer. Try to avoid superlatives in description. Work needs to stand on its own, so how much editing it may have received has no place in a query letter."

REID BOATES LITERARY AGENCY

69 Cooks Crossroad, Pittstown NJ 08867. (908)797-8087. Fax: (908)788-3667. E-mail: reid.boates@gmail.com. **Contact:** Reid Boates. Represents 45 clients. 5% of clients are new/unpublished writers. Currently handles: nonfiction books 85%, novels 15%, story collections very rarely.

HOW TO CONTACT No unsolicited queries of any kind. Obtains new clients by personal referral only.

TERMS Agent receives 15% commission on domestic sales. Agent receives 20% commission on foreign sales.

RECENT SALES Sold 15 titles in the last year. New sales include placements at HarperCollins, Wiley, Random House, and other major general-interest publishers.

⊘ BOND LITERARY AGENCY

4340 E. Kentucky Ave, Suite 471, Denver CO 80246. E-mail: sbbond@aol.com. Website: www.bondliteraryagency.com. **Contact:** Sandra Bond.

• Prior to her current position, Ms. Bond worked with agent Jody Rein.

REPRESENTS nonfiction books, novels. **Considers these nonfiction areas:** business, health, history, memoirs, science, narrative nonfiction. **Considers these fiction areas:** literary, general fiction, mystery, juvenile fiction.

8—⚓ Does not represent romance, poetry, sci-fi, or children's picture books.

HOW TO CONTACT Submit query by mail or e-mail (no attachments). "She will let you know if she is interested in seeing more material. *No unsolicited manuscripts.* No phone calls please." Accepts simultaneous submissions.

⊙ BOOK CENTS LITERARY AGENCY, LLC

2011 Quarrier St., Charleston WV 25311. (304)347-2330, ext. 1105. E-mail: cw@bookcentsliteraryagency.com. Website: www.bookcentsliteraryagency.com. **Contact:** Christine Witthohn. Member of AAR. RWA, MWA, SinC, KOD.

MEMBER AGENTS Christine Witthohn (Christine represents both published and unpublished authors. She is currently accepting queries for specific areas of fiction and nonfiction.).

8—⚓ Actively seeking "single-title romance (contemporary, romantic comedy, paranormal, mystery/suspense), women's lit (must have a strong hook), mainstream mystery/suspense, medical or legal fiction, literary fiction. For nonfiction, seeking women's issues/experiences, fun/quirky topics (particularly those of interest to women), cookbooks (fun, ethnic, etc.), gardening (herbs, plants, flowers, etc.), books with a "save-the-planet" theme, how-to books, travel and outdoor adventure." Does not want to receive category romance, erotica, inspirational, historical, sci-fi/fantasy, horror/dark thrillers, short stories/novella, children's picture books, poetry, screenplays.

HOW TO CONTACT "We prefer and respond faster to e-mail queries and submissions."

TIPS "We sponsor the International Women's Fiction Festival in Matera, Italy. See: womensfictionfestival. com for more information."

◑ BOOKENDS, LLC

136 Long Hill Rd., Gillette NJ 07933. Website: www. bookends-inc.com; bookendslitagency.blogspot.com. **Contact:** Jessica Faust, Kim Lionetti, Jessica Alvarez. Member of AAR. RWA, MWA. Represents 50+ clients. 10% of clients are new/unpublished writers. Currently handles: nonfiction books 50%, novels 50%.

MEMBER AGENTS Jessica Faust (fiction: romance, erotica, women's fiction, mysteries and suspense; nonfiction: business, finance, career, parenting, psychology, women's issues, self-help, health, sex); Kim Lionetti (Kim is only currently considering romance, women's fiction, and young adult queries. If your book is in any of these 3 categories, please be sure to specify "romance," "women's fiction," or "young adult" in your e-mail subject line. Any queries that do not follow these guidelines will not be considered); Jessica Alvarez (women's fiction, erotica, urban fantasy/paranormal, romantic suspense, and single title and category romance submissions); Lauren Ruth.

REPRESENTS nonfiction books, novels. **Considers these nonfiction areas:** business, child, ethnic, gay, health, how-to, money, psychology, religion, self-help, sex, true crime, women's. **Considers these fiction areas:** detective, cozies, mainstream, mystery, romance, thriller, women's.

8——¬ "BookEnds is currently accepting queries from published and unpublished writers in the areas of romance (and all its subgenres), erotica, mystery, suspense, women's fiction, and literary fiction. We also do a great deal of nonfiction in the areas of self-help, business, finance, health, pop science, psychology, relationships, parenting, pop culture, true crime, and general nonfiction." BookEnds does not want to receive children's books, screenplays, science fiction, poetry, or technical/military thrillers.

HOW TO CONTACT Review website for guidelines, as they change. BookEnds is no longer accepting unsolicited proposal packages or snail mail queries. Send query in the body of e-mail to only one agent.

● BOOKS & SUCH LITERARY AGENCY

52 Mission Circle, Suite 122, PMB 170, Santa Rosa CA 95409. E-mail: representation@booksandsuch.biz. Website: www.booksandsuch.biz. **Contact:** Janet Kobobel Grant, Etta Wilson, Rachel Kent, Mary Keeley. Member of AAR. Member of CBA (associate), American Christian Fiction Writers. Represents 150 clients. 5% of clients are new/unpublished writers. Currently handles: nonfiction books 50%, novels 50%.

• Prior to becoming an agent, Ms. Grant was an editor for Zondervan and managing editor for *Focus on the Family*; Ms. Lawton was an author, sculptor and designer of porcelein dolls. Ms. Zurakowski concentrates on material for 20-something or 30-something readers. Ms. Keeley accepts both nonfiction and adult fiction. She previously was an acquisition editor for Tyndale publishers.

REPRESENTS nonfiction books, novels. **Considers these nonfiction areas:** humor, religion, self-help, women's. **Considers these fiction areas:** contemporary, family, historical, mainstream, religious, romance.

8——¬ This agency specializes in general and inspirational fiction, romance, and in the Christian booksellers market. Actively seeking well-crafted material that presents Judeo-Christian values, if only subtly.

HOW TO CONTACT Query via e-mail only, no attachments. Accepts simultaneous submissions. Responds in 1 month to queries. "If you don't hear from us asking to see more of your writing within 30 days after you have sent your e-mail, please know that we have read and considered your submission but determined that it would not be a good fit for us." Obtains most new clients through recommendations from others, conferences.

TERMS Agent receives 15% commission on domestic sales. Agent receives 20% commission on foreign sales. Offers written contract; 2-month notice must be given to terminate contract. No additional charges.

RECENT SALES Sold 125 titles in the last year. *One Perfect Gift*, by Debbie Macomber (Howard Books); *Greetings from the Flipside*, by Rene Gutteridge and Cheryl McKay (B&H Publishing); *Key on the Quilt*, by Stephanie Grace Whitson (Barbour Publishing); *Annotated Screwtape Letters, Annotations*, by Paul McCusker, (Harper One). Other clients include: Lauraine Snelling, Lori Copeland, Rene Gutteridge,

Dale Cramer, BJ Hoff, Diann Mills.

WRITERS CONFERENCES Mount Hermon Christian Writers' Conference; Writing for the Soul; American Christian Fiction Writers' Conference; San Francisco Writers' Conference.

TIPS "The heart of our agency's motivation is to develop relationships with the authors we serve, to do what we can to shine the light of success on them, and to help be a caretaker of their gifts and time."

● GEORGES BORCHARDT, INC.

136 E. 57th St., New York NY 10022. Website: www. gbagency.com. Member of AAR.

MEMBER AGENTS Anne Borchardt; Georges Borchardt; Valerie Borchardt.

8—π This agency specializes in literary fiction and outstanding nonfiction.

HOW TO CONTACT *No unsolicited mss.* Obtains most new clients through recommendations from others.

TERMS Agent receives 15% commission on domestic sales. Agent receives 20% commission on foreign sales. Offers written contract.

◐ BRADFORD LITERARY AGENCY

5694 Mission Center Rd., #347, San Diego CA 92108. (619)521-1201. E-mail: query@bradfordlit.com; laura@ bradfordlit.com. Website: www.bradfordlit.com. **Contact:** Laura Bradford, founder; Natalie M. Fischer, agent. Member of AAR. RWA. Represents 35 clients. 20% of clients are new/unpublished writers. Currently handles: nonfiction books 10%, novels 90%.

- Ms. Bradford started with her first literary agency straight out of college and has 14 years of experience as a bookseller in parallel.

REPRESENTS nonfiction books, novels, novellas, stories within a single author's collection, anthology. **Considers these nonfiction areas:** business, child care, current affairs, health, history, how-to, memoirs, money, popular culture, psychology, self-help, women's interest. **Considers these fiction areas:** adventure, detective, erotica, ethnic, historical, humor, mainstream, mystery, romance, thriller, psychic/supernatural.

8—π Actively seeking romance (including category), romantica, women's fiction, mystery, thrillers and young adult. Does not want to receive poetry, short stories, children's books (juvenile) or screenplays.

HOW TO CONTACT Query with SASE. Submit cover letter, first 30 pages of completed ms, synopsis and SASE. Send no attachments via e-mail; only send a query letter with 'query' in the subject line. Accepts simultaneous submissions. Responds in 2-4 weeks to queries. Responds in 10 weeks to mss. Obtains most new clients through solicitations.

TERMS Agent receives 15% commission on domestic sales. Agent receives 20% commission on foreign sales. Offers written contract, non-binding for 2 years; 45-day notice must be given to terminate contract. Charges for photocopies, postage, extra copies of books for submissions.

RECENT SALES Sold 53 titles in the last year. *Tempting Eden*, by Margaret Rowe (Berkley Heat); *Princess Poltergeist*, by Stacey Kade (Hyperion Children's); *Ruthless Heart*, by Emma Lang (Kensington Brava); *Deadly Fear*, by Cynthia Eden (Grand Central); *Precious and Fragile Things*, by Megan Hart (Mira Books); *Cruel Enchantment*, by Anya Bast (Berkley Sensation); *Razorland*, by Elisabeth Naughton (Dorchester); *His Darkest Craving*, by Juliana Stone (Avon).

WRITERS CONFERENCES RWA National Conference; Romantic Times Booklovers Convention.

◐ BRANDT & HOCHMAN LITERARY AGENTS, INC.

1501 Broadway, Suite 2310, New York NY 10036. (212)840-5760. Fax: (212)840-5776. **Contact:** Gail Hochman. Member of AAR. Represents 200 clients.

MEMBER AGENTS Carl Brandt; Gail Hochman; Marianne Merola; Charles Schlessiger; Bill Contardi; Joanne Brownstein.

REPRESENTS nonfiction books, novels, short story collections, juvenile, journalism. **Considers these nonfiction areas:** autobiography, biography, cultural interests, current affairs, ethnic, government, history, law, politics, women's issues, women's studies. **Considers these fiction areas:** contemporary issues, ethnic, historical, literary, mystery, romance, suspense, thriller, young adult.

HOW TO CONTACT Submit through e-mail or if by post, send one-page query letter with SASE. Accepts simultaneous submissions. Responds in 1 month to queries. Obtains most new clients through recommendations from others.

TERMS Agent receives 15% commission on domestic sales. Agent receives 20% commission on foreign sales. Charges clients for ms duplication or other special expenses agreed to in advance.

TIPS "Write a letter which will give the agent a sense of you as a professional writer—your long-term interests as well as a short description of the work at hand."

● BARBARA BRAUN ASSOCIATES, INC.

151 West 19th St., 4th floor, New York NY 10011. Fax: (212)604-9041. E-mail: bbasubmissions@gmail.com. Website: www.barbarabraunagency.com. **Contact:** Barbara Braun. Member of AAR.
MEMBER AGENTS Barbara Braun; John F. Baker.
REPRESENTS nonfiction books, novels. **Considers these nonfiction areas:** "We represent both literary and commercial and serious nonfiction, including psychology, biography, history, women's issues, social and political issues, cultural criticism, as well as art, architecture, film, photography, fashion and design." **Considers these fiction areas:** literary and commercial.

&—☞ "Our fiction is strong on women's stories, historical and multicultural stories, as well as mysteries and thrillers. We're interested in narrative nonfiction and books by journalists. We do not represent poetry, science fiction, fantasy, horror, or screenplays. Look online for more details."

HOW TO CONTACT "E-mail submissions only, marked 'query' in subject line. We no longer accept submissions by regular mail. Your query should include: a brief summary of your book, word count, genre, any relevant publishing experience, and the first 5 pages of your manuscript pasted into the body of the e-mail. (NO attachments—we will not open these.)"
TERMS Agent receives 15% commission on domestic sales. Agent receives 20% commission on foreign sales.
RECENT SALES *Clara and Mr. Tiffany*, by Susan Vreeland.
TIPS "Our clients' books are represented throughout Europe, Asia and Latin America by various subagents. We are also active in selling motion picture rights to the books we represent, and work with various Hollywood agencies."

● PAUL BRESNICK LITERARY AGENCY, LLC

115 W. 29th St., Third Floor, New York NY 10001. (212)239-3166. Fax: (212)239-3165. E-mail: paul@bresnickagency.com. **Contact:** Paul Bresnick, Polly Bresnick.

• Prior to becoming an agent, Mr. Bresnick spent 25 years as a trade book editor.

REPRESENTS nonfiction books, novels. **Considers these nonfiction areas:** autobiography/memoir, biography, health, history, humor, memoirs, multicultural, popular culture, sports, travel, true crime, celebrity-branded books, narrative nonfiction, pop psychology, relationship issues. **Considers these fiction areas:** general fiction.
HOW TO CONTACT For fiction, submit query/SASE and 2 chapters. For nonfiction, submit query/SASE with proposal.

❶ BRICK HOUSE LITERARY AGENTS

80 Fifth Ave., Suite 1101, New York NY 10011. Website: www.brickhouselit.com. **Contact:** Sally Wofford-Girand. Member of AAR.

• Jenni holds an MFA in fiction from the University of Michigan and a BA from Oberlin College. She taught creative writing at the University of Michigan and the Gotham Writers Workshop. She has worked as a reader for *The Paris Review*, and a bookseller at Housing Works. Her short fiction and food writing have been published in numerous magazines. She is the editor of *Alone in the Kitchen With an Eggplant* and a member of the International Association of Culinary Professionals.

MEMBER AGENTS Sally Wofford-Girand; Jenni Ferrari-Adler; Melissa Sarver, assistant.
REPRESENTS nonfiction books, narrative nonfiction. **Considers these nonfiction areas:** cultural interests, ethnic, history, memoirs, nature, science, women's issues, women's studies, biography; food writing; lifestyle; science; natural history. **Considers these fiction areas:** literary, general & juvenile fiction.

&—☞ Sally's particular areas of interest are: history, memoir, women's issues, cultural studies, and fiction that is both literary and hard to put down (novels like *The Road* or *Blindness*). Jenni Ferrari-Adler specializes in representing novels, food narrative and cookbooks, and narrative nonfiction. Actively seeking history, memoir, women's issues, cultural studies, literary fiction and quality commercial fiction.

HOW TO CONTACT "E-mail query letter (in body of e-mail—not as attachment) and first page to either Sally or Jenni. We will ask to see more if interested and are sorry that we cannot respond to all queries."

M. COURTNEY BRIGGS

Derrick & Briggs, LLP, 100 N. Broadway Ave., 28th Floor, Oklahoma City OK 73102-8806. (405)235-1900. Fax: (405)235-1995. Website: www.derrickandbriggs.com.

- Prior to becoming an agent, Ms. Briggs was in subsidiary rights at Random House for 3 years; an associate agent and film rights associate with Curtis Brown, Ltd.; and an attorney for 16 years.

REPRESENTS nonfiction books, novels, juvenile. **Considers these nonfiction areas:** young adult.

8→ "I work primarily, but not exclusively, with children's book authors and illustrators. I will also consult or review a contract on an hourly basis." Actively seeking children's fiction, children's picture books (illustrations and text), young adult novels, fiction, nonfiction.

HOW TO CONTACT Query with SASE. Only published authors should submit queries. Obtains most new clients through recommendations from others.

TERMS Agent receives 15% commission on domestic sales. Agent receives 25% commission on foreign sales. Offers written contract; 60-day notice must be given to terminate contract.

WRITERS CONFERENCES SCBWI Annual Winter Conference.

RICK BROADHEAD & ASSOCIATES LITERARY AGENCY

501-47 St. Clair Ave. W., Toronto ON M4V 3A5, Canada. (416)929-0516. Fax: (416)927-8732. E-mail: info@rbaliterary.com; submissions@rbaliterary.com. Website: www.rbaliterary.com. **Contact:** Rick Broadhead, president. Other memberships include Authors Guild. Represents 125 clients. 50% of clients are new/unpublished writers. Currently handles: nonfiction books 100%.

- With an MBA from the Schulich School of Business, one of the world's leading business schools, Rick Broadhead is one of the few literary agents in the publishing industry with a business and entrepreneurial background, one that benefits his clients at every step of the book development and contract negotiation process. He is also a bestselling author, having authored and co-authored 35 books. He sold 25 titles in the last year.

REPRESENTS nonfiction books. **Considers these nonfiction areas:** crafts, animals, anthropology, bi-

ography, child guidance, cooking, current affairs, government, health, history, how-to, humor, memoirs, military, money, music, nature, popular culture, psychology, sports, true crime, women's. Of special interest are current affairs/politics, business, history, natural history/environment, food/drink, narrative nonfiction, science, pop culture, humor, and health/self-help.

8→ Rick Broadhead & Associates is a leading literary agency that represents nonfiction authors to all of the top publishing houses in North America. The agency has negotiated millions of dollars in royalties for its clients with venerable American and Canadian publishing houses. Bestselling author Rick Broadhead has a proven track record for finding literary talent, developing projects with strong commercial and media potential, and matching authors with publishers. Books represented by the agency have appeared on bestseller lists, been shortlisted for literary awards, translated into multiple languages, and through its partnerships in Hollywood, optioned for film and television development. The agency's clients include accomplished journalists, historians, physicians, television personalities, bloggers and creators of popular websites, successful business executives, and experts in their respective fields. They include Yale University physician Dr. David Katz; survival skills expert and Discovery Channel host Les Stroud ("Survivorman"). The agency is actively seeking compelling proposals from experts in their fields, journalists, and authors with relevant credentials and an established media platform (TV, web, radio, print experience/exposure). Does not want to receive fiction, screenplays, children's or poetry at this time.

HOW TO CONTACT "Please send a short query letter by e-mail or via regular mail with a description of the project, your credentials, and contact info. E-mail queries are welcome. Please do not send entire manuscripts or sample chapters unless requested. If I am interested, I will request a proposal. I am always interested in seeing nonfiction proposals from prospective clients, especially in the following subject categories: history, politics, business, natural history/environment, national security/intelligence, current affairs, biography, science, pop culture, pop science, relationships, self-help, health, medicine, military history, and humor." Accepts simultaneous submissions. Obtains most new clients through recommendations from others, solicitations.

TERMS Agent receives 15% commission on domestic sales. Agent receives 20% commission on foreign sales. Offers written contract. Charges for postage and photocopying expenses.

RECENT SALES Sold 25 titles within the last year. *The Secret Sentry: The Top-Secret History of the National Security Agency,* by intelligence historian Matthew Aid (Bloomsbury Press/Bloomsbury USA); *The Longest Shot: Jack Fleck, Ben Hogan, and Pro Golf's Greatest Upset* (Thomas Dunne Books/ St. Martin's Press); *101 Foods That Could Save Your Life,* by Registered Dietician David Grotto (Bantam Dell/Random House USA); *Do Gentlemen Really Prefer Blondes?* by former Random House editor Jena Pincott (Bantam Dell/Random House USA); *Insultingly Stupid Movie Physics,* by engineer and science teacher Tom Rogers (Sourcebooks); *The Quantum Ten: A Story of Passion, Tragedy, Ambition and Science,* by science journalist Sheilla Jones (Oxford University Press); *The Disappearing Spoon: And Other True Tales of Madness, Love, and the History of the Periodic Table of the Elements,* by science journalist Sam Kean (Little, Brown).

TIPS "Books rarely sell themselves these days, so I look for authors who have a 'platform' (media exposure/experience, university affiliation, recognized expertise, etc.). Remember that a literary agent has to sell your project to an editor, and then the editor has to sell your project internally to his/her colleagues (including the marketing and sales staff), and then the publisher has to sell your book to the book buyers at the chains and bookstores. You're most likely to get my attention if you write a succinct and persuasive query letter that demonstrates your platform/credentials, the market potential of your book, and why your book is different. I love finding great authors, pitching great book ideas, negotiating deals for my clients, and being a part of this exciting and dynamic industry."

❶ ANDREA BROWN LITERARY AGENCY, INC.

1076 Eagle Dr., Salinas CA 93905. E-mail: andrea@ andreabrownlit.com; caryn@andreabrownlit.com. Website: www.andreabrownlit.com. **Contact:** And-

rea Brown, president. Member of AAR. 10% of clients are new/unpublished writers.

• Prior to opening her agency, Ms. Brown served as an editorial assistant at Random House and Dell Publishing and as an editor with Knopf.

MEMBER AGENTS Andrea Brown; Laura Rennert (laura@andreabrownlit.com); Kelly Sonnack; Caryn Wiseman; Jennifer Rofé; Jennifer Laughran, associate agent; Jamie Weiss Chilton, associate agent; Jennifer Mattson, associate agent; Mary Kole.

REPRESENTS Juvenile nonfiction books, novels. **Considers these nonfiction areas:** juvenile nonfiction, memoirs, young adult, narrative. **Considers these fiction areas:** juvenile, literary, picture books, women's, young adult, middle-grade, all juvenile genres.

☞ This agency specializes in children's books, though each agent has differing tastes.

HOW TO CONTACT For picture books, submit complete ms, SASE. For fiction, submit short synopsis, SASE, first 3 chapters. For nonfiction, submit proposal, 1-2 sample chapters. For illustrations, submit 4-5 color samples (no originals). "We only accept queries via e-mail. No attachments, with the exception of jpeg illustrations from illustrators. Visit the agents' bios on our website and choose only one agent to whom you will submit your e-query. Send a short e-mail query letter to that agent with QUERY in the subject field. Accepts simultaneous submissions. If we are interested in your work, we will certainly follow up by e-mail or by phone. However, if you haven't heard from us within 6 to 8 weeks, please assume that we are passing on your project." Obtains most new clients through referrals from editors, clients and agents. Check website for guidelines and information.

TERMS Agent receives 15% commission on domestic sales. Agent receives 20% commission on foreign sales. Offers written contract.

RECENT SALES *Chloe*, by Catherine Ryan Hyde (Knopf); Sasha Cohen Autobiography (HarperCollins); *The Five Ancestors*, by Jeff Stone (Random House); *Thirteen Reasons Why*, by Jay Asher (Penguin); *Identical*, by Ellen Hopkins (S&S).

WRITERS CONFERENCES SCBWI; Asilomar; Maui Writers' Conference; Southwest Writers' Conference; San Diego State University Writers' Conference; Big Sur Children's Writing Workshop; William Saroyan Writers' Conference; Columbus Writers' Conference; Willamette Writers' Conference;

La Jolla Writers' Conference; San Francisco Writers' Conference; Hilton Head Writers' Conference; Pacific Northwest Conference; Pikes Peak Conference.

CURTIS BROWN, LTD.

10 Astor Place, New York NY 10003-6935. (212)473-5400. E-mail: gknowlton@cbltd.com. Website: www.curtisbrown.com. **Contact:** Ginger Knowlton. Alternate address: Peter Ginsberg, president at CBSF, 1750 Montgomery St., San Francisco CA 94111. (415)954-8566. Member of AAR. Signatory of WGA.

MEMBER AGENTS Ginger Clark; Katherine Fausset; Holly Frederick, VP; Emilie Jacobson; Elizabeth Hardin; Ginger Knowlton, Exec. VP; Timothy Knowlton, CEO; Laura Blake Peterson; Mitchell Waters. San Francisco Office: Peter Ginsberg (President).

REPRESENTS nonfiction books, novels, short story collections, juvenile. **Considers these nonfiction areas:** agriculture horticulture, americana, crafts, interior, juvenile, New Age, young, animals, anthropology, art, biography, business, child, computers, cooking, current affairs, education, ethnic, gardening, gay, government, health, history, how-to, humor, language, memoirs, military, money, multicultural, music, nature, philosophy, photography, popular culture, psychology, recreation, regional, religion, science, self-help, sex, sociology, software, spirituality, sports, film, translation, travel, true crime, women's, creative nonfiction. **Considers these fiction areas:** contemporary, glitz, New Age, psychic, adventure, comic, confession, detective, erotica, ethnic, experimental, family, fantasy, feminist, gay, gothic, hi-lo, historical, horror, humor, juvenile, literary, mainstream, military, multicultural, multimedia, mystery, occult, picture books, plays, poetry, regional, religious, romance, science, short, spiritual, sports, thriller, translation, Western, young, women's.

HOW TO CONTACT Prefers to read materials exclusively. *No unsolicited mss.* Responds in 3 weeks to queries. Responds in 5 weeks to mss. Obtains most new clients through recommendations from others, solicitations, conferences.

TERMS Offers written contract. Charges for some postage (overseas, etc.).

RECENT SALES This agency prefers not to share information on specific sales.

MARIE BROWN ASSOCIATES, INC.

412 W. 154th St., New York NY 10032. (212)939-9725. Fax: (212)939-9728. E-mail: mbrownlit@aol.com. **Contact:** Marie Brown. Estab. 1984. Represents 60 clients. Currently handles: nonfiction books 75%, juvenile books 25%, other.

MEMBER AGENTS Janell Walden Agyeman (Miami).

REPRESENTS nonfiction books, juvenile. **Considers these nonfiction areas:** juvenile, biography, business, ethnic, history, music, religion, women's. **Considers these fiction areas:** ethnic, juvenile, literary, mainstream.

8—⚏ This agency specializes in multicultural and African-American writers.

HOW TO CONTACT Query with SASE. Prefers to read materials exclusively. Reports in 6-10 weeks on queries. Obtains most new clients through recommendations from others.

TERMS Agent receives 15% commission on domestic sales. Agent receives 20% commission on foreign sales. Offers written contract.

● BROWNE & MILLER LITERARY ASSOCIATES

410 S. Michigan Ave., Suite 460, Chicago IL 60605-1465. (312)922-3063. E-mail: mail@browneandmiller.com. Website: www.browneandmiller.com. **Contact:** Danielle Egan-Miller. Estab. 1971. Member of AAR. Other memberships include RWA, MWA, Author's Guild. Represents 150 clients. 2% of clients are new/unpublished writers. Currently handles: nonfiction books 25%, novels 75%.

REPRESENTS nonfiction books, most genres of commercial adult fiction and nonfiction, as well as select young adult projects. **Considers these nonfiction areas:** agriculture, animals, anthropology, archeology, autobiography, biography, business, child guidance, cooking, crafts, cultural interests, current affairs, economics, environment, ethnic, finance, foods, health, hobbies, horticulture, how-to, humor, inspirational, investigative, medicine, memoirs, money, nature, nutrition, parenting, personal improvement, popular culture, psychology, religious, satire, science, self-help, sociology, sports, technology, true crime, women's issues, women's studies. **Considers these fiction areas:** contemporary issues, crime, detective, erotica, ethnic, family saga, glitz, historical, inspirational, literary, mainstream, mystery, police, religious, romance, sports, suspense, thriller, paranormal.

8—⚏ "We are partial to talented newcomers and experienced authors who are seeking hands-on career management, highly personal representation, and who are interested in being full partners in their books' successes. We are editorially focused and work closely with our authors through the whole publishing process, from proposal to after publication. We are most interested in commercial women's fiction, especially elegantly crafted, sweeping historicals; edgy, fresh teen/chick/mom/lady lit; and CBA women's fiction by established authors. We are also very keen on literary historical mysteries and literary young adult novels. Topical, timely nonfiction projects in a variety of subject areas are also of interest, especially prescriptive how-to, self-help, sports, humor, and pop culture." Does not represent poetry, short stories, plays, original screenplays, articles, children's picture books, software, horror or sci-fi novels.

HOW TO CONTACT Only accepts e-mail queries. Inquiring authors may initially submit one chapter and a synopsis. *No unsolicited mss.* Prefers to read material exclusively. Put [title] in the subject line. Send no attachments. Also has online submission form. Responds in 2-4 months to queries. Obtains most new clients through referrals, queries by professional/marketable authors.

TERMS Agent receives 15% commission on domestic sales. Agent receives 20% commission on foreign sales. Offers written contract, binding for 2 years. Charges clients for photocopying, overseas postage.

WRITERS CONFERENCES BookExpo America; Frankfurt Book Fair; RWA National Conference; ICRS; London Book Fair; Bouchercon, regional writers conferences.

TIPS "If interested in agency representation, be well informed."

⊘ PEMA BROWNE, LTD.

11 Tena Place, Valley Cottage NY 10989. E-mail: ppbltd@optonline.net. Website: www.pemabrowneltd. com. **Contact:** Pema Browne. Signatory of WGA. Other memberships include SCBWI, RWA. Represents 30 clients. Currently handles: nonfiction books 25%, novels 50%, juvenile books 25%.

- Prior to opening her agency, Ms. Browne was an artist and art buyer.

REPRESENTS nonfiction books, novels, juvenile, reference books. **Considers these nonfiction areas:** business, child guidance, cooking, cultural interests, economics, ethnic, finance, foods, gay, health, how-to, inspirational, juvenile nonfiction, lesbian,

medicine, metaphysics, money, New Age, nutrition, parenting, personal improvement, popular culture, psychology, religious, self-help, spirituality, women's issues, women's studies, reference. **Considers these fiction areas:** contemporary, glitz, adventure, feminist, gay, historical, juvenile, literary, mainstream, commercial, mystery, picture books, religious, romance, contemporary, gothic, historical, regency, young.

☞ "We are not accepting any new projects or authors until further notice."

HOW TO CONTACT Query with SASE. No attachments for e-mail.

TERMS Agent receives 20% commission on domestic sales. Agent receives 20% commission on foreign sales.

RECENT SALES *The Champion*, by Heather Grothaus (Kensington/Zebra); *The Highlander's Bride*, by Michele Peach (Kensington/Zebra); *The Daring Harriet Quimby*, by Suzanne Whitaker (Holiday House); *One Night to Be Sinful*, by Samantha Garver (Kensington); *Taming the Beast*, by Heather Grothaus (Kensington/Zebra); *Kisses Don't Lie* by Alexis Darin (Kensington/Zebra).

TIPS "We do not review manuscripts that have been sent out to publishers. If writing romance, be sure to receive guidelines from various romance publishers. In nonfiction, one must have credentials to lend credence to a proposal. Make sure of margins, double-space, and use clean, dark type."

⊘ BROWN LITERARY AGENCY

410 Seventh St. NW, Naples FL 34120. E-mail: broagent@aol.com. Website: www.brownliteraryagency.com. **Contact:** Roberta Brown. Member of AAR. Other memberships include RWA, Author's Guild. Represents 45 clients. 5% of clients are new/unpublished writers.

REPRESENTS novels. **Considers these fiction areas:** erotica, romance, women's, single title and category.

☞ "This agency is selectively reading material at this time."

HOW TO CONTACT The agency specializes in women's fiction, erotica, single title and category romance. We have eclectic tastes and enjoy romantic comedies to sizzling erotica. Historicals to category romances. We look for unique voices and page-turning plots. We also represent young adult novels and mystery cozies. **At this time, the agency is closed to submissions, except by NY published authors seeking new representation.**

Query via e-mail only. Send synopsis and two chapters in Word attachment. Response time varies.

TERMS Agent receives 15% commission on domestic sales. Agent receives 20% commission on foreign sales. Offers written contract; 30-day notice must be given to terminate contract.

WRITERS CONFERENCES RWA National Conference.

TIPS "Polish your manuscript. Be professional."

❶ TRACY BROWN LITERARY AGENCY

P.O. Box 772, Nyack, New York NY 10960. (914)400-4147. Fax: (914)931-1746. E-mail: tracy@brownlit.com. **Contact:** Tracy Brown. Represents 35 clients. Currently handles: nonfiction books 90%, novels 10%.

- Prior to becoming an agent, Mr. Brown was a book editor for 25 years.

REPRESENTS nonfiction books, novels, anthologies. **Considers these nonfiction areas:** current events, popular history, health, psychology, sports, humor, biography, travel, nature, women's issues, and literary fiction. **Considers these fiction areas:** contemporary issues, feminist, literary, mainstream, women's.

- Specializes in thorough involvement with clients' books at every stage of the process from writing to proposals to publication. Actively seeking serious nonfiction and fiction. Does not want to receive YA, sci-fi or romance.

HOW TO CONTACT Submit outline/proposal, synopsis, author bio. Accepts simultaneous submissions. Responds in 2 weeks to queries. Obtains most new clients through referrals.

TERMS Agent receives 15% commission on domestic sales. Agent receives 20% commission on foreign sales. Offers written contract.

RECENT SALES *Why Have Kids?*, by Jessica Valenti (HarperCollins); *Hotel Notell: A Novel*, by Daphne Uviller (Bantam); *Healing Sexual Pain*, by Deborah Coady, M.D. and Nancy Fish, MSW, MPH (Seal Press).

● SHEREE BYKOFSKY ASSOCIATES, INC.

PO Box 706, Brigantine NJ 08203. E-mail: shereebee@aol.com; submitbee@aol.com. Website: www.shereebee.com. **Contact:** Sheree Bykofsky. Member of AAR. Other memberships include ASJA, WNBA. Currently handles: nonfiction books 80%, novels 20%.

- Prior to opening her agency, Ms. Bykofsky served as executive editor of The Stonesong Press and managing editor of Chiron Press. She is also the author or co-author of more

than 20 books, including *The Complete Idiot's Guide to Getting Published*. Ms. Bykofsky teaches publishing at NYU and SEAK, Inc.

MEMBER AGENTS Janet Rosen, associate.

REPRESENTS nonfiction books, novels. **Considers these nonfiction areas:** Americana, animals, architecture, art, autobiography, biography, business, child guidance, cooking, crafts, creative nonfiction, cultural interests, current affairs, dance, design, economics, education, environment, ethnic, film, finance, foods, gardening, gay, government, health, history, hobbies, humor, language, law, lesbian, memoirs, metaphysics, military, money, multicultural, music, nature, New Age, nutrition, parenting, philosophy, photography, popular culture, politics, psychology, recreation, regional, religious, science, sex, sociology, spirituality, sports, translation, travel, true crime, war, anthropology. **Considers these fiction areas:** contemporary issues, literary, mainstream, mystery, suspense.

- This agency specializes in popular reference nonfiction, commercial fiction with a literary quality and mysteries. "I have wide-ranging interests, but it really depends on quality of writing, originality and how a particular project appeals to me (or not). I take on fiction when I completely love it—it doesn't matter what area or genre." Does not want to receive poetry, material for children, screenplays, Westerns, horror, science fiction or fantasy.

HOW TO CONTACT We only accept e-queries now and will only respond to those in which we are interested. E-mail short queries to submitbee@aol.com. Please, no attachments, snail mail, or phone calls. One-page query, one-page synopsis, and first page of manuscript in the body of the e-mail. Nonfiction: One-page query in the body of the e-mail. We cannot open attached Word files or any other types of attached files. These will be deleted. Accepts simultaneous submissions. Responds in 1 month to requested mss. Obtains most new clients through recommendations from others.

TERMS Agent receives 15% commission on domestic sales. Agent receives 20% commission on foreign sales. Offers written contract, binding for 1 year. Charges for postage, photocopying, fax.

RECENT SALES *Red Sheep: The Search for My Inner Latina*, by Michele Carlo (Citadel/Kensington); *Bang the Keys: Four Steps to a Lifelong Writing*

Practice, by Jill Dearman (Alpha, Penguin); *Signed, Your Student: Celebrities on the Teachers Who Made Them Who They Are Today*, by Holly Holbert (Kaplan); *The Five Ways We Grieve*, by Susan Berger (Trumpeter/Shambhala).

WRITERS CONFERENCES ASJA Writers Conference; Asilomar; Florida Suncoast Writers' Conference; Whidbey Island Writers' Conference; Florida First Coast Writers' Festival; Agents and Editors Conference; Columbus Writers' Conference; Southwest Writers' Conference; Willamette Writers' Conferece; Dorothy Canfield Fisher Conference; Maui Writers' Conference; Pacific Northwest Writers' Conference; IWWG.

TIPS "Read the agent listing carefully and comply with guidelines."

● KIMBERLEY CAMERON & ASSOCIATES

1550 Tiburon Blvd., #704, Tiburon CA 94920. Fax: (415)789-9177. E-mail: info@kimberleycameron.com. Website: www.kimberleycameron.com. **Contact:** Kimberley Cameron. Member of AAR. 30% of clients are new/unpublished writers. Currently handles: nonfiction books 50%; fiction 50%.

- Kimberley Cameron & Associates (formerly The Reece Halsey Agency) has had an illustrious client list of established writers, including the estate of Aldous Huxley, and has represented Upton Sinclair, William Faulkner, and Henry Miller.

MEMBER AGENTS Kimberley Cameron, Amy Burkhardt.

REPRESENTS nonfiction, fiction. **Considers these nonfiction areas:** biography, current affairs, foods, humor, language, memoirs, popular culture, science, true crime, women's issues, women's studies, lifestyle. **Considers these fiction areas:** adventure, contemporary issues, ethnic, family saga, historical, horror, mainstream, mystery, interlinked short story collections, thriller, women's, and sophisticated/crossover young adult.

⚷ "We are looking for a unique and heartfelt voice that conveys a universal truth."

HOW TO CONTACT Query via e-mail. See our website for submission guidelines. Obtains new clients through recommendations from others, solicitations.

TERMS Agent receives 15% on domestic sales; 10% on film sales. Offers written contract, binding for 1 year.

WRITERS CONFERENCES Pacific Northwest Writers Association Conference, Aspen Summer Words, Willamette Writers Conference, San Diego State

University Writers Conference, San Francisco Writers Conference, Killer Nashville, Left Coast Crime, Bouchercon, Book Passage Mystery and Travel Writers Conferences, Antioch Writers Workshop, Florida Writers Association Conference, and others.

TIPS "Please consult our submission guidelines and send a polite, well-written query to our e-mail address."

● MARIA CARVAINIS AGENCY, INC.

1270 Avenue of the Americas, Suite 2320, New York NY 10019. (212)245-6365. Fax: (212)245-7196. E-mail: mca@mariacarvainisagency.com. **Contact:** Maria Carvainis, Chelsea Gilmore. Member of AAR. Signatory of WGA. Other memberships include Authors Guild, Women's Media Group, ABA, MWA, RWA. Represents 75 clients. 10% of clients are new/unpublished writers. Currently handles: nonfiction books 35%, novels 65%.

- Prior to opening her agency, Ms. Carvainis spent more than 10 years in the publishing industry as a senior editor with Macmillan Publishing, Basic Books, Avon Books, and Crown Publishers. Ms. Carvainis has served as a member of the AAR Board of Directors and AAR Treasurer, as well as serving as chair of the AAR Contracts Committee. She presently serves on the AAR Royalty Committee. Ms. Gilmore started her publishing career at Oxford University Press, in the Higher Education Group. She then worked at Avalon Books as associate editor. She is most interested in women's fiction, literary fiction, young adult, pop culture, and mystery/suspense.

MEMBER AGENTS Maria Carvainis, president/literary agent; Chelsea Gilmore, literary agent.

REPRESENTS nonfiction books, novels. **Considers these nonfiction areas:** autobiography, biography, business, economics, history, memoirs, science, technology, women's issues, women's studies. **Considers these fiction areas:** contemporary issues, historical, literary, mainstream, mystery, suspense, thriller, women's, young adult, middle grade.

⚷ Does not want to receive science fiction or children's picture books.

HOW TO CONTACT Query with SASE. No e-mail accepted. Responds in up to 3 months to mss and to queries 1 mo. Obtains most new clients through recommendations from others, conferences, query letters.

TERMS Agent receives 15% commission on domestic sales. Agent receives 20% commission on foreign sales. Offers written contract. Charges clients for foreign postage and bulk copying.

RECENT SALES *A Secret Affair*, by Mary Balogh (Delacorte); *Tough Customer*, by Sandra Brown (Simon & Schuster); *A Lady Never Tells*, by Candace Camp (Pocket Books); *The King James Conspiracy*, by Phillip Depoy (St. Martin's Press).

WRITERS CONFERENCES BookExpo America; Frankfurt Book Fair; London Book Fair; Mystery Writers of America; Thrillerfest; Romance Writers of America.

● ① CASTIGLIA LITERARY AGENCY

1155 Camino Del Mar, Suite 510, Del Mar CA 92014. (858)755-8761. Fax: (858)755-7063. E-mail: deborah@castigliaagency.com; win@castigliaagency.com. Website: home.earthlink.net/~mwgconference/id22.html. Member of AAR. Other memberships include PEN. Represents 65 clients. Currently handles: nonfiction books 55%, novels 45%.

MEMBER AGENTS Julie Castiglia; Winifred Golden (science fiction, ethnic, commercial and thriller novels, plus narrative nonfiction and some health books—prefers referrals); Sally Van Haitsma (actively looking for good proposals by way of query letters, and her wish list covers literary and women's fiction, current affairs, architecture, pop culture, and science fiction); Deborah Ritchken (narrative nonfiction, food/cookbooks, design, France, literary fiction, no genre fiction).

REPRESENTS nonfiction books, novels. **Considers these nonfiction areas:** animals, anthropology, archeology, autobiography, biography, business, child guidance, cooking, cultural interests, current affairs, economics, environment, ethnic, finance, foods, health, history, inspirational, language, literature, medicine, money, nature, nutrition, psychology, religious, science, technology, women's issues, women's studies. **Considers these fiction areas:** contemporary issues, ethnic, literary, mainstream, mystery, suspense, women's.

⊶➞ Does not want to receive horror, screenplays, poetry or academic nonfiction.

HOW TO CONTACT No unsolicited submissions. Query with SASE. No e-mail submissions accepted. Obtains most new clients through recommendations from others, solicitations, conferences.

TERMS Agent receives 15% commission on domestic sales. Agent receives 25% commission on foreign sales. Offers written contract; 6-week notice must be given to terminate contract.

RECENT SALES *Germs Gone Wild*, by Kenneth King (Pegasus); *The Insider* by Reece Hirsch (Berkley/Penguin); *The Leisure Seeker*, by Michael Zadoorian (Morrow/HarperCollins); *Beautiful: The Life of Hedy Lamarr*, by Stephen Shearer (St. Martin's Press); *American Libre*, by Raul Ramos y Sanchez (Grand Central); *The Two Krishnas*, by Ghalib Shiraz Dhalla (Alyson Books).

WRITERS CONFERENCES Santa Barbara Writers' Conference; Southern California Writers' Conference; Surrey International Writers' Conference; San Diego State University Writers' Conference; Willamette Writers' Conference.

TIPS "Be professional with submissions. Attend workshops and conferences before you approach an agent."

CHAMEIN CANTON AGENCY

Canton Smith Agency, E-mail: cantonsmithagency@cantonsmithagency.com. Website: www.cantonsmithagency.com. **Contact:** Eric Smith, senior partner (ericsmith@cantonsmithagency.com); Chamein Canton, partner (chamein@cantonsmithagency.com); James Weil (jamesw@cantonsmithagency.com). Estab. 2001. Represents 28 clients. 100% of clients are new/unpublished writers.

- Prior to becoming agents, Mr. Smith was in advertising and bookstore retail; Ms. Canton was a writer and a paralegal.

MEMBER AGENTS Chamein Canton, managing partner, chamein@cantonsmithagency (women's fiction, chick-lit, business, how-to, fashion, romance, erotica, African American, Latina, women's issues, health, relationships, decorating, cookbooks, lifestyle, literary novels, astrology, numerology, New Age); Eric Smith, senior partner, ericsmith@cantonsmithagency.com (science fiction, sports, literature); James Weil, reviewer, jamesw@cantonsmithagency.com.

REPRESENTS nonfiction books, novels, juvenile, scholarly, textbooks, movie. **Considers these nonfiction areas:** architecture, art, business, child guidance, cooking, cultural interests, dance, design, economics, education, ethnic, foods, health, history, how-to, humor, language, literature, medicine, memoirs, military, music, nutrition, parenting, photography, psychology, satire, sports, translation, war, women's issues, women's studies. **Considers these fiction areas:** fantasy, humor, juvenile, multicultural, romance, young adult, Latina fiction, chick lit, African-American fiction, entertainment. **Considers these script areas:** action/adventure, comedy, romantic comedy, romantic drama, science fiction.

8—¶ "We specialize in helping new and established writers expand their marketing potential for prospective publishers. We are currently focusing on women's fiction (chick lit), Latina fiction, African American fiction, multicultural, romance, memoirs, humor and entertainment, in addition to more nonfiction titles (cooking, how-to, fashion, home improvement, etc.)."

HOW TO CONTACT Only accepts e-queries. E-mail query with synopsis (**only**); include the title and genre in the subject line. Send e-mail to Chamein Canton at chamein@cantonsmithagency.com Accepts simultaneous submissions. Responds in 8-12 weeks to queries. Responds in 3-5 months to mss. Obtains most new clients through recommendations from others.

TERMS Agent receives 15% commission on domestic sales. Agent receives 20% commission on foreign sales. Offers written contract; 2-month notice must be given to terminate contract.

TIPS "Know your market. Agents, as well as publishers, are keenly interested in writers with their finger on the pulse of their market."

○ JANE CHELIUS LITERARY AGENCY

548 Second St., Brooklyn NY 11215. (718)499-0236. Fax: (718)832-7335. E-mail: queries@janechelius.com. Website: www.janechelius.com. Member of AAR.
REPRESENTS nonfiction books, novels. **Considers these nonfiction areas:** biography, humor, medicine, parenting, popular culture, satire, women's issues, women's studies, natural history; narrative. **Considers these fiction areas:** literary, mystery, suspense.

8—¶ Does not want to receive fantasy, science fiction, children's books, stage plays, screenplays, or poetry.

HOW TO CONTACT Please see website for submission procedures. Does not consider e-mail queries with attachments. No unsolicited sample chapters or mss. Responds in 3-4-weeks usually.

○○ ELYSE CHENEY LITERARY ASSOCIATES, LLC

78 Fifth Avenue, 3rd Floor, New York NY 10011. Website: www.cheneyliterary.com. **Contact:** Elyse Cheney, Nicole Steen.

- Prior to her current position, Ms. Cheney was an agent with the literary agency Sanford J. Greenburger Associates.

REPRESENTS nonfiction, novels. **Considers these nonfiction areas:** autobiography, biography, business, cultural interests, current affairs, finance, history, memoirs, multicultural, politics, science, sports, women's issues, women's studies, narrative nonfiction and journalism. **Considers these fiction areas:** upmarket commercial fiction, historical fiction, literary, suspense, upmarket women's fiction, and young adult novels.

HOW TO CONTACT Query this agency with a referral. Include SASE or IRC. No fax queries. Snail mail or e-mail (submissions@cheneyliterary.com) only.

RECENT SALES *Moonwalking with Einstein: The Art and Science of Remembering Everything*, by Joshua Foer; *The Possessed: Adventures with Russian Books and the People Who Read Them*, by Elif Batuman (Farrar, Strauss & Giroux); *The Coldest Winter Ever*, by Sister Souljah (Atria); *A Heartbreaking Work of Staggering Genius*, by Dave Eggers (Simon and Schuster).

CINE/LIT REPRESENTATION

P.O. Box 802918, Santa Clarita CA 91380-2918. (661)513-0268. Fax: (661)513-0915. **Contact:** Mary Alice Kier. Member of AAR.
MEMBER AGENTS Mary Alice Kier; Anna Cottle.
REPRESENTS nonfiction books, novels.

8—¶ "Looking for nonfiction books: mainstream, thrillers, mysteries, supernatural, horror, narrative nonfiction, environmental, adventure, biography, travel and pop culture." Does not want to receive Westerns, sci-fi or romance.

HOW TO CONTACT Send query letter with SASE.

● EDWARD B. CLAFLIN LITERARY AGENCY, LLC

128 High Ave., Suite #2, Nyack NY 10960. (845)358-1084. E-mail: edclaflin@aol.com. **Contact:** Edward Claflin. Represents 30 clients. 10% of clients are new/unpublished writers.

- Prior to opening his agency, Mr. Claflin worked at Banbury Books, Rodale and Prentice Hall Press. He is the co-author of 13 books.

REPRESENTS nonfiction books. **Considers these nonfiction areas:** business, cooking, current affairs, economics, finance, foods, health, history, how-to, medicine, military, money, nutrition, psychology, sports, war.

🔑 This agency specializes in consumer health, narrative history, psychology/self-help and business. Actively seeking compelling and authoritative nonfiction for specific readers. Does not want to receive fiction.

HOW TO CONTACT Query with synopsis, bio, SASE or e-mail attachment in Word. Responds in 1 month to queries. Obtains most new clients through recommendations from others.

TERMS Agent receives 15% commission on domestic sales.

● WM CLARK ASSOCIATES

186 Fifth Ave., Second Floor, New York NY 10010. (212)675-2784. Fax: (347)-649-9262. E-mail: general@wmclark.com. Website: www.wmclark.com. Estab. 1997. Member of AAR. 50% of clients are new/unpublished writers. Currently handles: nonfiction books 50%, novels 50%.

- Prior to opening WCA, Mr. Clark was an agent at the William Morris Agency.

REPRESENTS nonfiction books, novels. **Considers these nonfiction areas:** architecture, art, autobiography, biography, cultural interests, current affairs, dance, design, ethnic, film, history, inspirational, memoirs, music, politics, popular culture, religious, science, sociology, technology, theater, translation, travel memoir, Eastern philosophy. **Considers these fiction areas:** contemporary issues, ethnic, historical, literary, mainstream, Southern fiction.

🔑 William Clark represents a wide range of titles across all formats to the publishing, motion picture, television, and new media fields on behalf of authors of first fiction and award-winning, bestselling narrative nonfiction, international authors in translation, chefs, musicians, and artists. Offering individual focus and a global presence, the agency undertakes to discover, develop and market today's most interesting content and the talent that create it, and forge sophisticated and innova-tive plans for self-promotion, reliable revenue streams, and an enduring creative career. Referral partners are available to provide services including editorial consultation, media training, lecture booking, marketing support and public relations. Agency does not respond to screenplays or screenplay pitches. It is advised that before querying you become familiar with the kinds of books we handle by browsing our Book List, which is available on our website.

HOW TO CONTACT Accepts queries via online form only at www.wmclark.com/queryguidelines.html. We respond to all queries submitted via this form. Responds in 1-2 months to queries.

TERMS Agent receives 15% commission on domestic sales. Agent receives 20% commission on foreign sales. Offers written contract.

TIPS "WCA works on a reciprocal basis with Ed Victor Ltd. (U.K.) in representing select properties to the U.S. market and vice versa. Translation rights are sold directly in the German, Italian, Spanish, Portuguese, Latin American, French, Dutch and Scandinavian territories in association with Andrew Nurnberg Associates Ltd. (UK); through offices in China, Bulgaria, Czech Republic, LaTVia, Poland, Hungary and Russia; and through corresponding agents in Japan, Greece, Israel, Turkey, Korea, Taiwan and Thailand."

● NANCY COFFEY LITERARY & MEDIA REPRESENTATION

240 W. 35th St., Suite 500, New York NY 10001. Fax: (212)279-0927. E-mail: assist@nancycoffeyliterary.com. Website: www.nancycoffeyliterary.com. **Contact:** Nancy Coffey. Member of AAR. Currently handles: nonfiction books 5%, novels 90%, juvenile books 5%.

MEMBER AGENTS Nancy Coffey (hard-copy queries only); Joanna Stampfel-Volpe (joanna@nancycoffeyliterary.com).

REPRESENTS nonfiction books, novels, juvenile, young adult, from cutting-edge material to fantasy. **Considers these fiction areas:** family, fantasy, military, espionage, mystery, romance, science, thriller, young adult, women's.

HOW TO CONTACT Query via e-mail (to query@nancycoffeyliterary.com with the word "QUERY" in the subject line, plus appropriate agent's name) or regular mail with SASE to above address. See website for complete submission guidelines.

⊘ COLCHIE AGENCY, GP

324 85th St., Brooklyn NY 11209-4604. (718)921-7468. E-mail: ColchieLit@earthlink.net. **Contact:** Thomas or Elaine Colchie. Currently handles: 100% fiction.

REPRESENTS novels.

✂—ᵀ Does not want to receive nonfiction.

HOW TO CONTACT This listing does not take or respond to unsolicited queries or submissions.

RECENT SALES *The Prince of Mist*, by Carlos Ruizz Zafon (Little Brown Books); *White Masks*, by Elias Khoury (Archipelago); *The Philosopher's Kiss*, by Peter Prange (Atria); *The Woman Who Dove Into the Heart of the World*, by Sabina Berman (Holt).

● FRANCES COLLIN, LITERARY AGENT

P.O. Box 33, Wayne PA 19087-0033. E-mail: queries@francescollin.com. Website: www.francescollin.com. **Contact:** Sarah Yake, associate agent. Member of AAR. Represents 90 clients. 1% of clients are new/unpublished writers. Currently handles: nonfiction books 50%, fiction 50%.

REPRESENTS nonfiction books, fiction, young adult.

✂—ᵀ Does not want to receive cookbooks, craft books, poetry, screenplays, or books for young children.

HOW TO CONTACT Query via e-mail describing project (text in the body of the e-mail only, no attachments) to queries@francescollin.com. "Please note that all queries are reviewed by both agents." No phone or fax queries. You may mail queries with a SASE. Accepts simultaneous submissions.

TERMS Agent receives 15% commission on domestic sales. Agent receives 20% commission on foreign sales. Offers written contract.

● DON CONGDON ASSOCIATES INC.

156 Fifth Ave., Suite 625, New York NY 10010-7002. (212)645-1229. Fax: (212)727-2688. E-mail: dca@doncongdon.com. **Contact:** Don Congdon, Michael Congdon, Susan Ramer, Cristina Concepcion, Maura Kye-Casella, Katie Kotchman, Katie Grimm. Member of AAR. Represents 100 clients. Currently handles: nonfiction books 60%, other 40% fiction.

REPRESENTS nonfiction books, fiction. **Considers these nonfiction areas:** anthropology, archeology, autobiography, biography, child guidance, cooking, current affairs, dance, environment, film, foods, government, health, history, humor, language, law, literature, medicine, memoirs, military, music, na-

ture, nutrition, parenting, popular culture, politics, psychology, satire, science, technology, theater, travel, true crime, war, women's issues, women's studies, creative nonfiction. **Considers these fiction areas:** action, adventure, contemporary issues, crime, detective, literary, mainstream, mystery, police, short story collections, suspense, thriller, women's.

✂—ᵀ Especially interested in narrative nonfiction and literary fiction.

HOW TO CONTACT Query with SASE or via e-mail (no attachments). Responds in 3 weeks to queries. Responds in 1 month to mss. Obtains most new clients through recommendations from other authors.

TERMS Agent receives 15% commission on domestic sales. Agent receives 19% commission on foreign sales. Charges client for extra shipping costs, photocopying, copyright fees, book purchases.

TIPS "Writing a query letter with a SASE is a must. We cannot guarantee replies to foreign queries via standard mail. No phone calls. We never download attachments to e-mail queries for security reasons, so please copy and paste material into your e-mail."

CONNOR LITERARY AGENCY

2911 W. 71st St., Minneapolis MN 55423. (612)866-1486. E-mail: connoragency@aol.com; coolmkc@aol.com. **Contact:** Marlene Connor Lynch. Represents 50 clients. 30% of clients are new/unpublished writers. Currently handles: nonfiction books 50%, novels 50%.

• Prior to opening her agency, Ms. Connor served at the Literary Guild of America, Simon & Schuster and Random House. She is the author of *Welcome to the Family: Memories of the Past for a Bright Future* (Broadway Books) and *What is Cool: Understanding Black Manhood in America* (Crown).

MEMBER AGENTS Marlene Connor Lynch (all categories with an emphasis on these nonfiction areas: Child guidance/parenting; cooking/foods/nutrition; crafts/hobbies; current affairs; ethnic/cultural interests; government/politics/law; health/medicine; how-to; humor/satire; interior design/decorating; language/literature/criticism; money/finance; photography; popular culture; self-help/personal improvement; women's issues/studies; relationships. Considers these fiction areas: historical; horror; literary; mainstream/contemporary; multicultural; thriller; women's; suspense); Deborah Coker (mainstream and literary fiction, multicultural fiction, children's books, humor, politics, memoirs, narrative nonfiction, true crime/investigative).

REPRESENTS nonfiction books, novels.

👌— Actively seeking illustrated books. We are currently accepting manuscripts; and we are expanding our interest to include more mainstream and multicultural fiction.

HOW TO CONTACT Query with one page and synopsis, SASE. All unsolicited mss returned unopened. Obtains most new clients through recommendations from others, conferences, grapevine.

TERMS Agent receives 15% commission on domestic sales. Agent receives 25% commission on foreign sales. Offers written contract, binding for 1 year.

RECENT SALES *Beautiful Hair at Any Age*, by Lisa Akbari; *12 Months of Knitting*, by Joanne Yordanou; *The Warrior Path: Confessions of a Young Lord* by Felipe Luciano.

WRITERS CONFERENCES National Writers Union, Midwest Chapter; Agents, Agents, Agents; Texas Writers' Conference; Detroit Writers' Conference; Annual Gwendolyn Brooks Writers' Conference for Literature and Creative Writing; Wisconsin Writers' Festival.

TIPS "Previously published writers are preferred; new writers with national exposure or potential to have national exposure from their own efforts preferred."

⊘ CORNERSTONE LITERARY, INC.

4525 Wilshire Blvd., Ste. 208, Los Angeles CA 90010. (323)930-6039. Fax: (323)930-0407. E-mail: info@cornerstoneliterary.com. Website: www.cornerstoneliterary.com. **Contact:** Helen Breitwieser. Member of AAR. Other memberships include Author's Guild, MWA, RWA, PEN, Poets & Writers. Represents 40 clients. 30% of clients are new/unpublished writers.

• Prior to founding her own boutique agency, Ms. Breitwieser was a literary agent at The William Morris Agency.

REPRESENTS novels. **Considers these fiction areas:** crime, detective, erotica, ethnic, family saga, glitz, graphic novels, historical, literary, mainstream, memoirs, multicultural, mystery, police, romance, suspense, thriller, women's fiction, Christian fiction.

👌— "We are not taking new clients at this time. We do not respond to unsolicited e-mail inquiries. All unsolicited manuscripts will be returned unopened." Does not want to receive science fiction, Western, poetry, screenplays, fantasy, gay/

lesbian, horror, self-help, psychology, business or diet.

HOW TO CONTACT Does not respond to unsolicited e-mail. Obtains most new clients through recommendations from others.

TERMS Agent receives 15% commission on domestic sales. Agent receives 20% commission on foreign sales. Offers written contract, binding for 1 year; 2-month notice must be given to terminate contract.

CRAWFORD LITERARY AGENCY

92 Evans Rd., Barnstead NH 03218. (603)269-5851. Fax: (603)269-2533. E-mail: crawfordlit@att.net. **Contact:** Susan Crawford. Winter Office: 3920 Bayside Rd., Fort Myers Beach FL 33931. (239)463-4651. Fax: (239)463-0125.

REPRESENTS nonfiction books, novels.

👌— This agency specializes in celebrity and/or media-based books and authors. Actively seeking action/adventure stories, medical thrillers, self-help, inspirational, how-to, and women's issues. No short stories, or poetry.

HOW TO CONTACT Query with cover letter, SASE. Accepts simultaneous submissions. Responds in 3 weeks. Obtains most new clients through recommendations from others, solicitations, conferences.

TERMS Agent receives 15% commission on domestic sales. Agent receives 20% commission on foreign sales. Offers written contract.

RECENT SALES *Thriving After Divorce*, by Tonja Weimer; *Something About You*, by Julie James; *The Golden Temple*, by Mingmei Yip; *Untitled Memoir*, by John Travolta; *Final Finesse* by Karna Bodman; *Tunnel Vision*, by Gary Braver; *White House Doctor*, by Dr. Connie Mariano.

WRITERS CONFERENCES International Film & Television Workshops; Maui Writers Conference; Emerson College Conference; Suncoast Writers Conference; San Diego Writers Conference; Simmons College Writers Conference; Cape Cod Writers Conference; Writers Retreats on Maui; Writers Alaskan Cruise; Western Caribbean Cruise and Fiji Island.

TIPS "Keep learning to improve your craft. Attend conferences and network."

CREATIVE TRUST, INC.

5141 Virginia Way, Suite 320, Brentwood TN 37027. 615-297-5010. Fax: 615-297-5020. E-mail: info@creativetrust. com. Website: www.creativetrust.com/. Currently handles: novella, graphic novels, movie scripts, multimedia, other video scripts.

MEMBER AGENTS Dan Raines, President. See website for list.

HOW TO CONTACT "Creative Trust Literary Group does not accept unsolicited manuscripts or book proposals from unpublished authors. We do accept unsolicited inquiries from previously published authors under the following requisites: e-mail inquiries only, which must not be accompanied by attachments of any kind. If we're interested, we'll e-mail you an invitation to submit additional materials and instructions on how to do so."

● CRICHTON & ASSOCIATES

6940 Carroll Ave., Takoma Park MD 20912. (301)495-9663. Fax: (202)318-0050. E-mail: query@crichton-associates.com. Website: www.crichton-associates.com. **Contact:** Sha-Shana Crichton. 90% of clients are new/unpublished writers. Currently handles: nonfiction books 50%, fiction 50%.

- Prior to becoming an agent, Ms. Crichton did commercial litigation for a major law firm.

REPRESENTS nonfiction books, novels. **Considers these nonfiction areas:** child guidance, cultural interests, ethnic, gay, government, investigative, law, lesbian, parenting, politics, true crime, women's issues, women's studies, African-American studies. **Considers these fiction areas:** ethnic, feminist, inspirational, literary, mainstream, mystery, religious, romance, suspense, chick lit.

- Actively seeking women's fiction, romance, and chick lit. Looking also for multicultural fiction and nonfiction. Does not want to receive poetry, children's, young adult, science fiction, or screenplays.

HOW TO CONTACT In the subject line of e-mail, please indicate whether your project is fiction or nonfiction. Please do not send attachments. Your query letter should include a description of the project and your biography. If you wish to send your query via snail mail, please include your telephone number and e-mail address. We will respond to you via e-mail. For fiction, include short synopsis and first 3 chapters with query. For nonfiction, send a book proposal. Responds in 3-5 weeks to queries.

TERMS Agent receives 15% commission on domestic sales. Agent receives 20% commission on foreign

sales. Offers written contract, binding for 45 days. Only charges fees for postage and photocopying.

RECENT SALES *The African American Entrepreneur*, by W. Sherman Rogers (Praeger); *The Diversity Code*, by Michelle Johnson (Amacom); *Secret & Lies*, by Rhonda McKnight (Urban Books); *Love on the Rocks*, by Pamela Yaye (Harlequin). Other clients include Kimberley White, Beverley Long, Jessica Trap, Altonya Washington, Cheris Hodges.

WRITERS CONFERENCES Silicon Valley RWA; BookExpo America.

THE CROCE AGENCY

PO Box 449, Leonia NJ 07605. (201)248-3175. E-mail: submissions@thecroceagency.com. Website: www.thecroceagency.com. **Contact:** Nicholas Croce, president. 25% of clients are new/unpublished writers. Currently handles: 75% fiction; 25% nonfiction.

- Prior to becoming an agent, Mr. Croce was an editor. He is also a writer.

REPRESENTS novels. **Considers these nonfiction areas:** biography, business, current affairs, ethnic, history, popular culture, psychology, science, true crime. **Considers these fiction areas:** commercial genre fiction including historical, women's, romance, mystery, thriller/suspense, sci-fi, Western, horror, fantasy, paranormal, select literary fiction.

- Actively seeking commercial fiction and narrative nonfiction. Does not want to receive poetry or screenplays.

HOW TO CONTACT Query with SASE. Submit for fiction, a one-paragraph synopsis, author bio, 3 sample chapters. For nonfiction, send a one-paragraph synopsis, book outline and author credentials and platform. Accepts simultaneous submissions. Responds in 1 week to queries, 2-4 weeks to mss.

TERMS Agent receives 15% commission on domestic sales. Agent receives 20% commission on foreign sales. This agency charges for postage if a sale is made.

RECENT SALES *The Stolen Crown*, by Susan Higginbotham; *The Boleyn Wife*, by Brandy Purdy (Kensington); *Mr. Darcy's Little Sister*, by Allyn Pierson.

WRITERS CONFERENCES Thrillerfest, San Diego State Univ. Writers' Conference, BookExpo, Crime Bake, International Women's Writing Guild Conference, Houston Writer's Guild Conference.

● RICHARD CURTIS ASSOCIATES, INC.

171 E. 74th St., New York NY 10021. (212)772-7363. Fax: (212)772-7393. Website: www.curtisagency. com. Other memberships include RWA, MWA, ITW, SFWA. Represents 100 clients. 1% of clients are new/unpublished writers. Currently handles: nonfiction books 50%, other 50% genre fiction.

- Mr. Curtis authored more than 50 published books.

REPRESENTS Mostly nonfiction. **Considers these nonfiction areas:** autobiography, biography, business, economics, health, history, medicine, science, technology.

HOW TO CONTACT Considers only authors published by national houses.

TERMS Agent receives 15% commission on domestic sales. Agent receives 25% commission on foreign sales. Offers written contract. Charges for photocopying, express mail, international freight, book orders.

RECENT SALES Sold 100 titles in the last year. *Morpheus*, by DJ MacHale; *Hull 03*, by Greg Bear; *Black Magic Sanction*, by Kim Harrison.

WRITERS CONFERENCES RWA National Conference.

●○ CURTIS BROWN (AUST) PTY LTD

P.O. Box 19, Paddington NSW 2021 Australia. (61)(2)9361-6161; +61 2 9331-5301. Fax: (61)(2)9360-3935. E-mail: info@curtisbrown.com.au. Website: www.curtisbrown.com.au. **Contact:** Submissions Department. 10% of clients are new/unpublished writers. Currently handles: nonfiction books 30%, novels 30%, juvenile books 25%, other 15% other.

- Prior to joining Curtis Brown, most of our agents worked in publishing or the film/theatre industries in Australia and the United Kingdom.

MEMBER AGENTS Fiona Inglis, managing director; Fran Moore, agent/deputy managing director; Tara Wynne, agent; Pippa Masson, agent; Clare Forster, agent.

REPRESENTS nonfiction books, novels, novellas, juvenile.

- "We are the oldest and largest literary agency in Australia and we look after a wide variety of clients." No poetry, short stories, stage/screenplays, picture books or translations.

HOW TO CONTACT Submit 3 sample chapters, cover letter with biographical information, synopsis (2-3 pages), SASE. We do not accept e-mailed or faxed submissions. No responsibility is taken for the receipt or loss of manuscripts. We are currently taking between 8-10 weeks to assess submissions. We do not offer specific comments on the manuscripts we reject and we do not charge a reading fee.

D4EO LITERARY AGENCY

7 Indian Valley Rd., Weston CT 06883. (203)544-7180. Fax: (203)544-7160. E-mail: d4eo@optonline. net. Website: www.d4eo.com. **Contact:** Bob Diforio. Represents more than 100 clients. 50% of clients are new/unpublished writers. Currently handles: nonfiction books 70%, novels 25%, juvenile books 5%.

- Prior to opening his agency, Mr. Diforio was a publisher.

MEMBER AGENTS Kristin Miller (kristin@d4eo. com; middle grade, young adult and picture books), Mandy Hubbard (mandy@d4eo.com; middle grade and young adult), Joyce Holland (joyce@d4eo.com; mysteries, romance, science fiction, thrillers and nonfiction; no picture books or young adult.).

REPRESENTS nonfiction books, novels. **Considers these nonfiction areas:** juvenile, art, biography, business, child, current affairs, gay, health, history, how-to, humor, memoirs, military, money, psychology, religion, science, self-help, sports, true crime, women's. **Considers these fiction areas:** adventure, detective, erotica, historical, horror, humor, juvenile, literary, mainstream, mystery, picture books, romance, science, sports, thriller, Western, young adult.

HOW TO CONTACT Query with SASE. Accepts and prefers e-mail queries. Prefers to read material exclusively. Responds in 1 week to queries. Obtains most new clients through recommendations from others.

TERMS Agent receives 15% commission on domestic sales. Agent receives 25% commission on foreign sales. Offers written contract, binding for 2 years; 60-day notice must be given to terminate contract. Charges for photocopying and submission postage.

● LAURA DAIL LITERARY AGENCY, INC.

350 Seventh Ave., Suite 2003, New York NY 10010. (212)239-7477. Fax: (212)947-0460. E-mail: queries@ ldlainc.com. Website: www.ldlainc.com. Member of AAR.

MEMBER AGENTS Laura Dail; Tamar Rydzinski.

REPRESENTS nonfiction books, novels.

⚷━⚓ "Due to the volume of queries and manuscripts received, we apologize for not answering every e-mail and letter. Specializes in historical, literary and some young adult fiction, as well as both practical and idea-driven nonfiction." None of us handles children's picture books or chapter books. No New Age. We do not handle screenplays or poetry.

HOW TO CONTACT Query with SASE or e-mail. This agency prefers e-queries. Include the word "query" in the subject line. If you are mailing your query, please include a SASE.

◑ DANIEL LITERARY GROUP

1701 Kingsbury Dr., Suite 100, Nashville TN 37215. (615)730-8207. E-mail: submissions@danielliterarygroup.com. Website: www.danielliterarygroup.com. **Contact:** Greg Daniel. Represents 45 clients. 30% of clients are new/unpublished writers. Currently handles: nonfiction books 85%, novels 15%.

- Prior to becoming an agent, Mr. Daniel spent 10 years in publishing—six at the executive level at Thomas Nelson Publishers.

REPRESENTS nonfiction books, novels. **Considers these nonfiction areas:** autobiography, biography, business, child guidance, current affairs, economics, environment, film, health, history, how-to, humor, inspirational, medicine, memoirs, nature, parenting, personal improvement, popular culture, religious, satire, self-help, sports, theater, women's issues, women's studies. **Considers these fiction areas:** action, adventure, contemporary issues, crime, detective, family saga, historical, humor, inspirational, literary, mainstream, mystery, police, religious, satire, suspense, thriller.

⚷━⚓ The agency currently accepts all fiction topics, except for children's, romance and sci-fi. "We take pride in our ability to come alongside our authors and help strategize about where they want their writing to take them in both the near and long term. Forging close relationships with our authors, we help them with such critical factors as editorial refinement, branding, audience, and marketing." The agency is open to submissions in almost every popular category of nonfiction, especially if authors are recognized experts in their fields.

No screenplays, poetry, science fiction/fantasy, romance, children's, or short stories.

HOW TO CONTACT Query via e-mail only. Submit publishing history, author bio, brief synopsis of work, key selling points. E-queries only. Send no attachments. For fiction, send first 5 pages pasted in e-mail. Check Submissions Guidelines before querying or submitting. Please do not query via telephone. Responds in 2-3 weeks to queries.

⬤ DARHANSOFF & VERRILL LITERARY AGENTS

236 W. 26th St., Suite 802, New York NY 10001. (917)305-1300. Fax: (917)305-1400. E-mail: chuck@dvagency.com. Website: www.dvagency.com. Member of AAR. Represents 120 clients. 10% of clients are new/unpublished writers. Currently handles: nonfiction books 25%, novels 60%, story collections 15%.

MEMBER AGENTS Liz Darhansoff; Chuck Verrill, Michele Mortimer.

REPRESENTS novels, juvenile books, narrative nonfiction, literary fiction, mystery & suspense, young adult.

HOW TO CONTACT Queries welcome via website or with SASE. Obtains most new clients through recommendations from others.

↩⬤ CAROLINE DAVIDSON LITERARY AGENCY

5 Queen Anne's Gardens, London England W4 ITU United Kingdom. (44)(208)995-5768. Fax: (44)(208)994-2770. E-mail: cdliterary@btinternet.com. Website: www.cdla.co.uk. **Contact:** Caroline Davidson.

REPRESENTS nonfiction books, serious material only, novels.

⚷━⚓ Does not consider autobiographies, chick lit, children's, crime, erotica, fantasy, horror, local history, murder mysteries, occult, self-help, short stories, sci-fi, thrillers, individual short stories, or memoir.

HOW TO CONTACT Send e-mail or query with SASE. See website for additional details and what to include for fiction and nonfiction. Responds in 2 weeks to queries. Obtains most new clients through recommendations from others, solicitations.

TIPS "Visit our website before submitting any work to us."

DAVIS WAGER LITERARY AGENCY

419 N. Larchmont Blvd., #317, Los Angeles CA 90004. E-mail: submissions@daviswager.com. Website: www. daviswager.com. **Contact:** Timothy Wager. Estab. 2004. Represents 12 clients.

- Prior to his current position, Mr. Wager was with the Sandra Dijkstra Literary Agency, where he worked as a reader and associate agent.

REPRESENTS nonfiction books, novels. **Considers these fiction areas:** literary.

⚷ Actively seeking: literary fiction and general-interest nonfiction. "I do not handle screenplays, children's books, romance, or science fiction. Memoirs and most genre fiction (other than crime or noir) are a serious long shot, too."

HOW TO CONTACT Query with SASE. Submit author bio, synopsis for fiction, book proposal or outline for nonfiction. Query via e-mail. No author queries by phone.

LIZA DAWSON ASSOCIATES

350 7th Ave., Ste. 2003, New York NY 10001. (212)465-9071. Fax: (212)947-0460. E-mail: queryliza@lizadawsonassociates.com. Website: www. lizadawsonassociates.com. Member of AAR. Other memberships include MWA, Women's Media Group. Represents 50+ clients. 15% of clients are new/unpublished writers. Currently handles: nonfiction books 60%, novels 40%.

- Prior to becoming an agent, Ms. Dawson was an editor for 20 years, spending 11 years at William Morrow as vice president and 2 years at Putnam as executive editor. Ms. Blasdell was a senior editor at HarperCollins and Avon. Ms. Miller is an *Essence*-best-selling author and niche publisher. Ms. Olswanger is an author.

MEMBER AGENTS Liza Dawson (plot-driven literary fiction, historicals, thrillers, suspense, parenting books, history, psychology [both popular and clinical], politics, narrative nonfiction and memoirs); Caitlin Blasdell (science fiction, fantasy (both adult and young adult), parenting, business, thrillers and women's fiction); Anna Olswanger (gift books for adults, young adult fiction and nonfiction, children's illustrated books, and Judaica); Havis Dawson (business books, how-to and practical books, spirituality, fantasy, Southern-culture fiction and military memoirs); David Austern (fiction and nonfiction, with an interest in young adult, pop culture, sports, and male-interest works); and Judith Engracia (literary fiction, urban fantasy, paranormal romance, thrillers, mysteries, young adult, and middle grade).

REPRESENTS nonfiction books, novels and gift books (Olswanger only). **Considers these nonfiction areas:** autobiography, biography, business, health, history, medicine, memoirs, parenting, politics, psychology, sociology, women's issues, women's studies. **Considers these fiction areas:** literary, mystery, regional, suspense, thriller, African-American (Miller only), fantasy and science fiction (Blasdell only).

⚷ "This agency specializes in readable literary fiction, thrillers, mainstream historicals, women's fiction, academics, historians, business, journalists and psychology."

HOW TO CONTACT Query only with SASE. Individual query e-mails are query[agentfirstname]@ lizadawsonassociates.com. We prefer to see only a query letter first. If we are intrigued, we'll ask to see a portion of the manuscript. Responds in 3 weeks to queries. Responds in 6 weeks to mss. Obtains most new clients through recommendations from others, conferences.

TERMS Agent receives 15% commission on domestic sales. Agent receives 20% commission on foreign sales. Offers written contract. Charges clients for photocopying and overseas postage.

JACQUES DE SPOELBERCH ASSOCIATES

9 Shagbark Rd., Wilson Point, South Norwalk CT 06854. (203)838-7571. Fax: (203)866-2713. E-mail: Jjdespoel@aol.com. **Contact:** Jacques de Spoelberch. Represents 50 clients.

MEMBER AGENTS Jacques de Spoelberch.

REPRESENTS Represents nonfiction books, novels.

HOW TO CONTACT Query with SASE. Responds in 2 months to queries. Obtains most new clients through recommendations from others.

TERMS Agent receives 15% commission on domestic sales; 20% commission on foreign sales.

DEFIORE & CO.

47 E. 19th St., 3rd Floor, New York NY 10003. (212)925-7744. Fax: (212)925-9803. E-mail: info@defioreandco. com; submissions@defioreandco.com. Website: www. defioreandco.com. **Contact:** Lauren Gilchrist. Member of AAR. Represents 75 clients. 50% of clients are

new/unpublished writers. Currently handles: nonfiction books 70%, novels 30%.

- Prior to becoming an agent, Mr. DeFiore was publisher of Villard Books (1997-1998), editor-in-chief of Hyperion (1992-1997), and editorial director of Delacorte Press (1988-1992).

MEMBER AGENTS Brian DeFiore (popular nonfiction, business, pop culture, parenting, commercial fiction); Laurie Abkemeier (memoir, parenting, business, how-to/self-help, popular science); Kate Garrick (literary fiction, memoir, popular nonfiction); Debra Goldstein (health and diet, wellness); Laura Nolan (cookbooks, memoir, nonfiction); Matthew Elblonk (young adult, popular culture, narrative nonfiction); Karen Gerwin (popular culture, memoir); Caryn Karmatz-Rudy (popular fiction, self-help, narrative nonfiction).

REPRESENTS nonfiction books, novels. **Considers these nonfiction areas:** autobiography, biography, business, child guidance, cooking, economics, foods, how-to, inspirational, money, multicultural, parenting, popular culture, psychology, religious, self-help, sports, young adult, middle grade. **Considers these fiction areas:** ethnic, literary, mainstream, mystery, suspense, thriller.

⚷ "Please be advised that we are not considering children's picture books, poetry, adult science fiction and fantasy, romance, or dramatic projects at this time."

HOW TO CONTACT Query with SASE or e-mail to submissions@defioreandco.com. Please include the word "Query" in the subject line. All attachments will be deleted; please insert all text in the body of the e-mail. "For more information about our agents, their individual interests, and their query guidelines, please visit our 'About Us' page." Accepts simultaneous submissions. Responds in 3 weeks to queries. Responds in 2 months to mss. Obtains most new clients through recommendations from others.

TERMS Agent receives 15% commission on domestic sales. Agent receives 20% commission on foreign sales. Offers written contract; 10-day notice must be given to terminate contract. Charges clients for photocopying and overnight delivery (deducted only after a sale is made).

WRITERS CONFERENCES Maui Writers Conference; Pacific Northwest Writers Conference; North Carolina Writers' Network Fall Conference.

● JOELLE DELBOURGO ASSOCIATES, INC.

101 Park St., 3rd Floor, Montclair NJ 07042. (973)783-6800. Fax: (973)783-6802. E-mail: info@delbourgo.com. Website: www.delbourgo.com. **Contact:** Joelle Delbourgo, Molly Lyons, Jacquie Flynn. Represents more than 100 clients. Currently handles: nonfiction books 75%, novels 25%.

- Prior to becoming an agent, Ms. Delbourgo was an editor and senior publishing executive at HarperCollins and Random House.

MEMBER AGENTS Joelle Delbourgo (narrative nonfiction, serious "expert-driven" nonfiction, self-help, psychology, business, history, science, medicine, quality fiction); Molly Lyons (memoir, narrative nonfiction, biography, current events, cultural issues, pop culture, health, psychology, smart, fresh practical nonfiction, fiction, young adult and middle grade); Jacquie Flynn (thought-provoking and practical business, parenting, education, personal development, current events, science and other select nonfiction and fiction titles).

REPRESENTS nonfiction books, novels. **Considers these nonfiction areas:** autobiography, biography, business, child guidance, cooking, cultural interests, current affairs, decorating, diet/nutrition, economics, education, environment, ethnic, foods, gay/lesbian, government, health, history, how-to, inspirational, investigative, law, medicine, metaphysics, money, popular culture, politics, psychology, religious, science, sociology, technology, true crime, women's issues, women's studies, New Age/metaphysics, interior design/decorating. **Considers these fiction areas:** historical, literary, mainstream, mystery, suspense.

⚷ "We are former publishers and editors, with deep knowledge and an insider perspective. We have a reputation for individualized attention to clients, strategic management of authors' careers, and creating strong partnerships with publishers for our clients." Actively seeking history, narrative nonfiction, science/medicine, memoir, literary fiction, psychology, parenting, biographies, current affairs, politics, young adult fiction and nonfiction. Does not want to receive genre fiction, science fiction, fantasy, or screenplays.

HOW TO CONTACT Query by mail with SASE. Accepts simultaneous submissions. Responds in 3 weeks to queries. Responds in 2 months to mss.

TERMS Agent receives 15% commission on domestic sales. Agent receives 20% commission on foreign sales. Offers written contract. Charges clients for postage and photocopying.

RECENT SALES *Alexander the Great*, by Philip Freeman; *The Big Book of Parenting Solutions*, by Dr. Michele Borba; *The Secret Life of Ms. Finkelman*, by Ben H. Wintners; *Not Quite Adults*, by Richard Settersten Jr. and Barbara Ray; *Tabloid Medicine*, by Robert Goldberg, Ph.D.; *Table of Contents*, by Judy Gerlman and Vicky Levi Krupp.

TIPS "Do your homework. Do not cold call. Read and follow submission guidelines before contacting us. Do not call to find out if we received your material. No e-mail queries. Treat agents with respect, as you would any other professional, such as a doctor, lawyer or financial advisor."

DH LITERARY, INC.

P.O. Box 805, Nyack NY 10960-0990. **Contact:** David Hendin. Member of AAR. Represents 10 clients. Currently handles: nonfiction books 80%, novels 10%, scholarly books 10%.

- Prior to opening his agency, Mr. Hendin served as president and publisher for Pharos Books/World Almanac, as well as senior VP and COO at sister company United Feature Syndicate.

☞ *Not accepting new clients. Please do not send queries or submissions.*

TERMS Agent receives 15% commission on domestic sales. Agent receives 20% commission on foreign sales. Offers written contract, binding for 1 year. Charges for out-of-pocket expenses for overseas postage specifically related to the sale.

RECENT SALES *Big Nate, Strikes Again* and *Zacula* (3 titles), by Lincoln Peirce to Harper Collins; *Miss Manners Guide to a Surprisingly Dignified Wedding*, by Judith and Jacobina Martin (Norton); *Pumped for Murder*, by Elaine Viets (NAL/Signet); *The New Time Travelers*, by David Toomey (Norton).

ⓞ SANDRA DIJKSTRA LITERARY AGENCY

1155 Camino del Mar, PMB 515, Del Mar CA 92014. (858)755-3115. Fax: (858)794-2822. E-mail: elise@dijkstraagency.com. Website: www.dijkstraagency.com. Member of AAR. Other memberships include Authors Guild, PEN West, Poets and Editors, MWA. Represents 100+ clients. 30% of clients are new/unpublished writers. Currently handles: nonfiction books 50%, novels 45%, juvenile books 5%.

MEMBER AGENTS Sandra Dijkstra; Elise Capron; Jill Marr; Taylor Martindale.

REPRESENTS nonfiction books, novels. **Considers these nonfiction areas:** Americana, animals, anthropology, archeology, art, business, child guidance, cooking, cultural interests, diet/nutrition, economics, environment, ethnic, foods, gay/lesbian, government, health, history, inspirational, language, law, literature, medicine, memoirs, military, money, parenting, politics, psychology, regional, science, self-help, sociology, technology, travel, war, women's issues, women's studies, Asian studies, juvenile nonfiction, accounting, transportation. **Considers these fiction areas:** erotica, ethnic, fantasy, juvenile, literary, mainstream, mystery, picture books, science fiction, suspense, thriller, graphic novels.

☞ Does not want to receive Westerns, screenplays, short-story collections or poetry.

HOW TO CONTACT "Please see guidelines on our website and please note that we now only accept e-mail submissions. Due to the large number of unsolicited submissions we receive, we are now *only* able to respond those submissions in which we are interested. Unsolicited submissions in which we are not interested will receive no response." Accepts simultaneous submissions. Responds in about 6 weeks to queries. Obtains most new clients through recommendations from others, solicitations, conferences.

TERMS Agent receives 15% commission on domestic sales. Agent receives 20% commission on foreign sales. Offers written contract. Charges clients for expenses for foreign postage and copying costs if a client requests a hard copy submission to publishers.

TIPS "Be professional and learn the standard procedures for submitting your work. Be a regular patron of bookstores, and study what kind of books are being published and will appear on the shelves next to yours. Read! Check out your local library and bookstores—you'll find lots of books on writing and the publishing industry that will help you. At conferences, ask published writers about their agents. Don't believe the myth that an agent has to be in New York to be successful. We've already disproved it!"

⊙ DONADIO & OLSON, INC.

121 W. 27th St., Suite 704, New York NY 10001. (212)691-8077. Fax: (212)633-2837. E-mail: mail@donadio.com. **Contact:** Neil Olson. Member of AAR.

MEMBER AGENTS Neil Olson (no queries); Edward Hibbert (no queries); Carrie Howland (represents literary fiction and nonfiction as well as young adult fiction. She can be reached at carrie@donadio.com).

REPRESENTS nonfiction books, novels.

☞ This agency represents mostly fiction, and is very selective.

HOW TO CONTACT Query by snail mail is preferred; for e-mail use mail@donadio.com; only send submissions to open agents. Obtains most new clients through recommendations from others.

● JANIS A. DONNAUD & ASSOCIATES, INC.

525 Broadway, Second Floor, New York NY 10012. (212)431-2664. Fax: (212)431-2667. E-mail: jdonnaud@aol.com; donnaudassociate@aol.com. **Contact:** Janis A. Donnaud. Member of AAR. Signatory of WGA. Represents 40 clients. 5% of clients are new/unpublished writers. Currently handles: nonfiction books 100%.

• Prior to opening her agency, Ms. Donnaud was vice president and associate publisher of Random House Adult Trade Group.

REPRESENTS nonfiction books. **Considers these nonfiction areas:** autobiography, African-American, biography, business, celebrity, child guidance, cooking, current affairs, diet/nutrition, foods, health, humor, medicine, parenting, psychology, satire, women's issues, women's studies, lifestyle.

☞ This agency specializes in health, medical, cooking, humor, pop psychology, narrative nonfiction, biography, parenting, and current affairs. We give a lot of service and attention to clients. Does not want to receive "fiction, poetry, mysteries, juvenile books, romances, science fiction, young adult, religious or fantasy."

HOW TO CONTACT Query with SASE. Submit description of book, 2-3 pages of sample material. Prefers to read materials exclusively. No phone calls. Responds in 1 month to queries. Responds in 1 month to mss. Obtains most new clients through recommendations from others.

TERMS Agent receives 15% commission on domestic sales. Agent receives 20% commission on foreign sales. Agent receives 20% commission on film sales.

Offers written contract; 1-month notice must be given to terminate contract. Charges clients for messengers, photocopying and purchase of books.

RECENT SALES *The Coupon Mom's Guide to Cutting Your Grocery Bill in Half* by Stephanie Nelson; *Jim Lahey's Pizza Book*, by Jim Lahey and Rick Flaste; *Cook Like a Rock Star*, by Anne Burrell; *Paula Deen's Bible of Southern Cooking*, by Paula Deen and Melissa Clark.

◐◉ JIM DONOVAN LITERARY

4515 Prentice St., Suite 109, Dallas TX 75206-5028. E-mail: jdlqueries@sbcglobal.net. **Contact:** Melissa Shultz, agent. Represents 30 clients. 10% of clients are new/unpublished writers. Currently handles: nonfiction books 75%, novels 25%.

MEMBER AGENTS Jim Donovan (history—particularly American, military and Western; biography; sports; popular reference; popular culture; fiction—literary, thrillers and mystery); Melissa Shultz (parenting, women's issues, memoir).

REPRESENTS nonfiction books, novels. **Considers these nonfiction areas:** autobiography, biography, business, child guidance, current affairs, economics, environment, health, history, how-to, investigative, law, medicine, memoirs, military, money, music, parenting, popular culture, politics, sports, true crime, war, women's issues, women's studies. **Considers these fiction areas:** action, adventure, crime, detective, literary, mainstream, mystery, police, suspense, thriller.

☞ This agency specializes in commercial fiction and nonfiction. "Does not want to receive poetry, children's, short stories, inspirational or anything else not listed above."

HOW TO CONTACT "For nonfiction, I need a well-thought query letter telling me about the book: What it does, how it does it, why it's needed now, why it's better or different than what's out there on the subject, and why the author is the perfect writer for it. For fiction, the novel has to be finished, of course; a short (2 to 5 page) synopsis—not a teaser, but a summary of all the action, from first page to last—and the first 30-50 pages is enough. This material should be polished to as close to perfection as possible." Accepts simultaneous submissions. Responds in 3 weeks to queries. Responds in 1 month to mss. Obtains most new clients through recommendations from others.

TERMS Agent receives 15% commission on domestic sales. Agent receives 20% commission on foreign sales. Offers written contract, binding for 1 year; 30-day notice must be given to terminate contract. This agency charges for things such as overnight delivery and manuscript copying. Charges are discussed beforehand.

RECENT SALES Sold 27 titles in the last year. *The Last Gunfight*, by Jeff Guinn (Simon and Schuster); *Resurrection* by Jim Dent (St. Martin's Press); *The Battling Bastards of Bataan* by Bill Sloan (Simon and Schuster); *Perfect*, by Lew Paper (NAL); *Honor in the Dust*, by Gregg Jones (NAL); *First in War* by David Clary (Simon and Schuster); *Desperadoes* by Mark Gardner (HarperCollins); *Apocalypse of the Dead* by Joe McKinney (Kensington).

TIPS "Get published in short form—magazine reviews, journals, etc.—first. This will increase your credibility considerably, and make it much easier to sell a full-length book."

● DOYEN LITERARY SERVICES, INC.

1931 660th St., Newell IA 50568-7613. (712)272-3300. Website: www.barbaradoyen.com. **Contact:** Ms. B.J. Doyen, president. Represents over 100 clients. 20% of clients are new/unpublished writers. Currently handles: nonfiction books 100%.

- Prior to opening her agency, Ms. Doyen worked as a published author, teacher, guest speaker, and wrote and appeared in her own weekly TV show airing in 7 states. She is also the co-author of *The Everything Guide to Writing a Book Proposal* (Adams 2005) and *The Everything Guide to Getting Published* (Adams 2006).

REPRESENTS nonfiction for adults, no children's. **Considers these nonfiction areas:** agriculture, Americana, animals, anthropology, archeology, architecture, art, autobiography, biography, business, child guidance, computers, cooking, crafts, cultural interests, current affairs, diet/nutrition, design, economics, education, environment, ethnic, film, foods, gardening, government, health, history, hobbies, horticulture, language, law, medicine, memoirs, metaphysics, military, money, multicultural, music, parenting, photography, popular culture, politics, psychology, recreation, regional, science, self-help, sex, sociology, software, technology, theater, true crime, women's issues, women's studies, creative nonfiction, electronics.

8— This agency specializes in nonfiction. Actively seeking business, health, science, how-to, self-help—all kinds of adult nonfiction suitable for the major trade publishers. Does not want to receive pornography, screenplays, children's books, fiction, or poetry.

HOW TO CONTACT Send a query letter initially. Do not send us any attachments.Your text must be in the body of the e-mail. Prefers e-mail query through the website, using the contact button. Please read the website before submitting a query. Include your background information in a bio. Send no unsolicited attachments. Accepts simultaneous submissions. Responds immediately to queries. Responds in 3 weeks to mss.

TERMS Agent receives 15% commission on domestic sales. Agent receives 20% commission on foreign sales. Offers written contract, binding for 2 years.

RECENT SALES *Stem Cells For Dummies*, by Lawrence S.B. Goldstein and Meg Schneider; *The Complete Idiot's Guide to Country Living*, by Kimberly Willis; *The Complete Illustrated Pregnancy Companion* by Robin Elise Weiss; *The Complete Idiot's Guide to Playing the Fiddle*, by Ellery Klein; *Healthy Aging for Dummies*, by Brent Agin, M.D. and Sharon Perkins, R.N.

TIPS "Our authors receive personalized attention. We market aggressively, undeterred by rejection. We get the best possible publishing contracts. We are very interested in nonfiction book ideas at this time and will consider most topics. Many writers come to us from referrals, but we also get quite a few who initially approach us with query letters. Do not call us regarding queries. It is best if you do not collect editorial rejections prior to seeking an agent, but if you do, be upfront and honest about it. Do not submit your manuscript to more than 1 agent at a time—querying first can save you (and us) much time. We're open to established or beginning writers—just send us a terrific letter!"

● DREISBACH LITERARY MANAGEMENT

PO Box 5379, El Dorado Hills CA 95762. (916)804-5016. E-mail: verna@dreisbachliterary.com. Website: www.dreisbachliterary.com. **Contact:** Verna Dreisbach. Estab. 2007.

REPRESENTS fiction and nonfiction. **Considers these nonfiction areas:** animals, biography, business, health, multicultural, parenting, religious, spirituality, travel, true crime, women's issues. **Considers these fiction areas:** literary, mystery, thriller.

8—π "The agency has a particular interest in books with a political, economic or social context. Open to most types of nonfiction. Fiction interests include literary, commercial and young adult. Verna's first career as a law enforcement officer gives her a genuine interest and expertise in the genres of mystery, thriller and true crime. " Does not want to receive sci-fi, fantasy, horror, poetry, screenplay, Christian or children's books.

HOW TO CONTACT E-mail queries only please. No attachments in the query. They will not be opened. No unsolicited manuscripts.

RECENT SALES *Walnut Wine and Truffle Groves* (Running Press); *Coming to the Fire* (BenBella Books); *Off the Street* (Behler); *Hog-Tied* (Bell Bridge); Divine Injustice (New Horizon).

ⓞ DUNHAM LITERARY, INC.

156 Fifth Ave., Suite 625, New York NY 10010-7002. (212)929-0994. Website: www.dunhamlit.com. **Contact:** Jennie Dunham. Member of AAR, SCBWI. Represents 50 clients. 15% of clients are new/unpublished writers. Currently handles: nonfiction books 25%, novels 25%, juvenile books 50%.

- Prior to opening her agency, Ms. Dunham worked as a literary agent for Russell & Volkening. The Rhoda Weyr Agency is now a division of Dunham Literary, Inc.

MEMBER AGENTS Blair Hewes. Represents authors of literary and commercial fiction, narrative nonfiction, and books for children of all ages. She is interested in representing authors of nonfiction books in the categories of pop-culture, historical biography, lifestyle, and women's issues. She is not interested in Western, hard-boiled crime fiction, or political or medical thrillers.

REPRESENTS nonfiction books, novels, short story collections, juvenile. **Considers these nonfiction areas:** anthropology, archeology, autobiography, biography, cultural interests, environment, ethnic, government, health, history, language, law, literature, medicine, popular culture, politics, psychology, science, technology, women's issues, women's studies. **Considers these fiction areas:** ethnic, juvenile, literary, mainstream, picture books, young adult.

HOW TO CONTACT Query with SASE. Responds in 1 week to queries. Responds in 2 months to mss. Obtains most new clients through recommendations from others, solicitations.

TERMS Agent receives 15% commission on domestic sales. Agent receives 20% commission on foreign sales.

RECENT SALES Sold 30 books for young readers in the last year. *Peter Pan*, by Robert Sabuda (Little Simon); *Flamingos On the Roof*, by Calef Brown (Houghton); *Adele and Simon In America*, by Barbara McClintock (Farrar, Straus & Giroux); *Caught Between the Pages*, by Marlene Carvell (Dutton); *Waiting For Normal*, by Leslie Connor (HarperCollins); *The Gollywhopper Games*, by Jody Feldman (Greenwillow); *America the Beautiful* by Robert Sabuda; *Dahlia*, by Barbara McClintock; *Living Dead Girl* by Tod Goldberg; *In My Mother's House* by Margaret McMulla; *Black Hawk Down* by Mark Bowden; *Look Back All the Green Valley* by Fred Chappell; *Under a Wing* by Reeve Lindbergh; *I Am Madame X* by Gioia Diliberto.

ⓞ DUNOW, CARLSON, & LERNER AGENCY

27 W. 20th St., #1107, New York NY 10011. E-mail: mail@dclagency.com. Website: www.dclagency.com. **Contact:** Jennifer Carlson, Henry Dunow, Betsy Lerner. Member of AAR.

MEMBER AGENTS Jennifer Carlson (young adult and middle grade, some fiction and nonfiction); Henry Dunow (quality fiction—literary, historical, strongly written commercial—and with voice-driven nonfiction across a range of areas—narrative history, biography, memoir, current affairs, cultural trends and criticism, science, sports); Erin Hosier (nonfiction: popular culture, music, sociology and memoir); Betsy Lerner (nonfiction writers in the areas of psychology, history, cultural studies, biography, current events, business; fiction: literary, dark, funny, voice-driven); Yishai Seidman (broad range of fiction: literary, postmodern, and thrillers; nonfiction: sports, music, and pop culture).

REPRESENTS nonfiction books, novels, juvenile.

HOW TO CONTACT Query with SASE or by e-mail to mail@dclagency.com. No attachments. Unable to respond to queries except when interested.

ⓞ DUPREE/MILLER AND ASSOCIATES, INC. LITERARY

100 Highland Park Village, Suite 350, Dallas TX 75205. (214)559-BOOK. Fax: (214)559-PAGE. Website: www.

dupreemiller.com. **Contact:** Submissions Department. Other memberships include ABA. Represents 200 clients. 20% of clients are new/unpublished writers. Currently handles: nonfiction books 90%, novels 10%.

MEMBER AGENTS Jan Miller, president/CEO; Shannon Miser-Marven, senior executive VP; Annabelle Baxter; Nena Madonia; Cheri Gillis.

REPRESENTS nonfiction books, novels, scholarly, syndicated, religious/inspirational/spirituality. **Considers these nonfiction areas:** animals, anthropology, archeology, architecture, art, autobiography, biography, business, child guidance, cooking, crafts, current affairs, dance, diet/nutrition, design, economics, education, environment, ethnic, film, foods, gardening, government, health, history, how-to, humor, language, literature, medicine, memoirs, money, multicultural, music, parenting, philosophy, photography, popular culture, psychology, recreation, regional, satire, science, self-help, sex, sociology, sports, technology, theater, translation, true crime, women's issues, women's studies. **Considers these fiction areas:** action, adventure, crime, detective, ethnic, experimental, family saga, feminist, glitz, historical, humor, inspirational, literary, mainstream, mystery, picture books, police, psychic, religious, satire, sports, supernatural, suspense, thriller. ⊶ This agency specializes in commercial fiction and nonfiction.

HOW TO CONTACT Submit 1-page query, summary, bio, how to market, SASE through U.S. postal service. Obtains most new clients through recommendations from others, conferences, lectures.

TERMS Agent receives 15% commission on domestic sales. Offers written contract.

WRITERS CONFERENCES Aspen Summer Words Literary Festival.

TIPS "If interested in agency representation, it is vital to have the material in the proper working format. As agents' policies differ, it is important to follow their guidelines. Work on establishing a strong proposal that provides sample chapters, an overall synopsis (fairly detailed), and some biographical information on yourself. Do not send your proposal in pieces; it should be complete upon submission. Your work should be in its best condition."

Ø DWYER & O'GRADY, INC.

Agents for Writers & Illustrators of Children's Books, P.O. Box 790, Cedar Key FL 32625-0790. (352)543-9307. Fax: (603)375-5373. Website: www.dwyerogrady.com. **Contact:** Elizabeth O'Grady. Estab. 1990. Other memberships include SCBWI. Represents 30 clients. Currently handles: juvenile books 100%.

• Prior to opening their agency, Mr. Dwyer and Ms. O'Grady were booksellers and publishers.

MEMBER AGENTS Elizabeth O'Grady; Jeff Dwyer.

REPRESENTS juvenile. **Considers these nonfiction areas:** juvenile. **Considers these fiction areas:** juvenile, picture books, young.

⊶ "We are not accepting new clients at this time. This agency represents only writers and illustrators of children's books."

HOW TO CONTACT Do not send unsolicited material. "We are not adding new clients. Check website to see if policy changes. Obtains most new clients through recommendations from others, direct approach by agent to writer whose work they've read."

TERMS Agent receives 15% commission on domestic sales. Agent receives 20% commission on foreign sales. Offers written contract; 1-month notice must be given to terminate contract. This agency charges clients for photocopying of longer mss or mutually agreed, upon marketing expenses.

WRITERS CONFERENCES BookExpo America; American Library Association Annual Conference; SCBWI.

TIPS "This agency previously had an address in New Hampshire. Mail all materials to the new Florida address."

◐ DYSTEL & GODERICH LITERARY MANAGEMENT

1 Union Square W., Suite 904, New York NY 10003. (212)627-9100. Fax: (212)627-9313. Website: www.dystel.com. **Contact:** Michael Bourret and Jim McCarthy. Member of AAR, SCBWI. Represents 617 clients. 50% of clients are new/unpublished writers. Currently handles: nonfiction books 65%, novels 35%.

• Dystel & Goderich Literary Management recently acquired the client list of Bedford Book Works.

MEMBER AGENTS Jane Dystel; Stacey Glick; Michael Bourret; Jim McCarthy; Jessica Papin; Lauren Abramo; Chasya Milgrom; Rachel Oakley; Rachel Stout.

REPRESENTS nonfiction books, novels, cookbooks. **Considers these nonfiction areas:** animals, anthropology, archeology, autobiography, biography, business, child guidance, cultural interests, current affairs, economics, ethnic, gay/lesbian, health, history, humor, inspirational, investigative, medicine, metaphysics, military, New Age, parenting, popular culture, psychology, religious, science, technology, true crime, women's issues, women's studies. **Considers these fiction areas:** action, adventure, crime, detective, ethnic, family saga, gay, lesbian, literary, mainstream, mystery, police, suspense, thriller.

○━┳ "This agency specializes in cookbooks and commercial and literary fiction and nonfiction." No plays, screenplays, or poetry.

HOW TO CONTACT Query with SASE. Please include the first 3 chapters in the body of the e-mail. E-mail queries preferred (Michael Bourret only accepts e-mail queries); will accept mail. See website for full guidelines. You can find our e-mail addresses there. Accepts simultaneous submissions. Responds in 6 to 8 weeks to queries. Responds within 8 weeks to mss. Obtains most new clients through recommendations from others, solicitations, conferences.

TERMS Agent receives 15% commission on domestic sales. Agent receives 19% commission on foreign sales. Offers written contract.

WRITERS CONFERENCES Backspace Writers' Conference; Pacific Northwest Writers' Association; Pike's Peak Writers' Conference; Writers League of Texas; Love Is Murder; Surrey International Writers Conference; Society of Children's Book Writers and Illustrators; International Thriller Writers; Willamette Writers Conference; The South Carolina Writers Workshop Conference; Las Vegas Writers Conference; Writer's Digest; Seton Hill Popular Fiction; Romance Writers of America; Geneva Writers Conference.

TIPS "DGLM prides itself on being a full-service agency. We're involved in every stage of the publishing process, from offering substantial editing on mss and proposals, to coming up with book ideas for authors looking for their next project, negotiating contracts and collecting monies for our clients. We follow a book from its inception through its sale to a publisher, its publication, and beyond. Our commitment to our writers does not, by any means, end when we have collected our commission. This is one of the many things that makes us unique in a very competitive business."

◖◗ TOBY EADY ASSOCIATES

Third Floor, 9 Orme Court, London England W2 4RL, United Kingdom. (44)(207)792-0092. Fax: (44)(207)792-0879. E-mail: zaria@tobyeady associates.co.uk. E-mail: submissions@tobyeadyassociates.co.uk. Website: www.tobyeadyassociates. co.uk. **Contact:** Jamie Coleman. Estab. 1968. Represents 53 clients. 13% of clients are new/unpublished writers. Currently handles: nonfiction books 50%, novels 50%.

MEMBER AGENTS Toby Eady (China, the Middle East, Africa, politics of a Swiftian nature); Laetitia Rutherford (fiction and nonfiction from around the world).

REPRESENTS nonfiction books, novels, short-story collections, novellas, anthologies. **Considers these nonfiction areas:** architecture, art, cooking, cultural interests, current affairs, diet/nutrition, design, ethnic, foods, government, health, history, law, medicine, memoirs, popular culture, politics. **Considers these fiction areas:** action, adventure, confession, historical, literary, mainstream.

○━┳ "We handle fiction and nonfiction for adults, and we specialize in China, the Middle East and Africa." Actively seeking "stories that demand to be heard." Does not want to receive poetry, screenplays or children's books.

HOW TO CONTACT Send the first 50 pages of your work, double-spaced and unbound, with a synopsis and a brief bio; attn: Jamie Coleman. Accepts simultaneous submissions. Responds in 2 weeks to queries. Responds in 2 weeks to mss. Obtains most new clients through recommendations from others, solicitations, conferences.

TERMS Agent receives 15% commission on domestic sales. Agent receives 20% commission on foreign sales. Offers written contract; 3-month notice must be given to terminate contract.

WRITERS CONFERENCES City Lit; Winchester Writers' Festival.

TIPS "Send submissions to this address: Jamie Coleman, Third Floor, 9 Orme Court, London W2 4RL."

⬤ EAST/WEST LITERARY AGENCY, LLC

1158 26th St., Suite 462, Santa Monica CA 90403. (310)573-9303. Fax: (310)453-9008. E-mail: dwarren@ eastwestliteraryagency.com; mgjames@eastwestliteraryagency.com; rpfeffer@eastwestliteraryagency.com. Estab. 2000. Represents 100 clients. 70% of clients are new/unpublished writers. Currently handles: juvenile books 80%, adult books 20%.

MEMBER AGENTS Deborah Warren, founder; Mary Grey James, partner literary agent (special interest: southern writers and their stories, literary fiction); Rubin Pfeffer, partner content agent and digital media strategist.

HOW TO CONTACT By referral only. Submit proposal and first 3 sample chapters, table of contents (2 pages or fewer), synopsis (1 page). For picture books, submit entire ms. Requested submissions should be sent by mail as a Word document in Courier, 12-pt., double-spaced with 1.20 inch margin on left, ragged right text, 25 lines per page, continuously paginated, with all your contact info on the first page. Only responds if interested, no need for SASE. Responds in 60 days. Obtains new clients through recommendations from others.

TERMS Agent receives 15% commission on domestic sales. Agent receives 25% commission on foreign sales. Offers written contract; 30-day notice must be given to terminate contract. Charges for out-of-pocket expenses, such as postage and copying.

● ANNE EDELSTEIN LITERARY AGENCY

20 W. 22nd St., Suite 1603, New York NY 10010. (212)414-4923. Fax: (212)414-2930. E-mail: info@aeliterary.com. Website: www.aeliterary.com. Member of AAR.

MEMBER AGENTS Anne Edelstein; Krista Ingebretson.

REPRESENTS nonfiction books, fiction. **Considers these nonfiction areas:** history, inspirational, memoirs, psychology, religious, Buddhist thought. **Considers these fiction areas:** literary.

8—▼ This agency specializes in fiction and narrative nonfiction.

HOW TO CONTACT Query with SASE; submit 25 sample pages.

RECENT SALES *Confessions of a Buddhist Atheist*, by Stephen Batchelor (Spiegel & Grau); *April & Oliver*, by Tess Callahan (Doubleday).

◉ EDUCATIONAL DESIGN SERVICES, LLC

5750 Bou Ave., Suite 1508, Bethesda MD 20852. (301)881-8611. E-mail: blinder@educationaldesignservices.com. Website: www.educationaldesignservices.com. **Contact:** Bertram L. Linder, president. Represents 14 clients. 95% of clients are new/unpublished writers. Currently handles: 100% textbooks and professional materials for education.

• Prior to becoming an agent, Mr. Linder was an author and a teacher.

MEMBER AGENTS Bertram Linder (textbooks and professional materials for education).

REPRESENTS scholarly, textbooks.

8—▼ "We are one of the few agencies that specialize exclusively in materials for the education market. We handle text materials for grades pre K-12, text materials for college/university use, and materials for professionals in the field of education, staff development and education policy." Does not want to receive children's fiction and nonfiction, or picture books.

HOW TO CONTACT Query with SASE. Submit proposal package, outline, outline/proposal, 2–3 sample chapters, SASE. Prefers e-mail submission. Accepts simultaneous submissions. Responds in 4–6 weeks to queries and mss. Obtains most new clients through recommendations from others, solicitations, conferences.

TERMS Agent receives 15% commission on domestic sales. Agent receives 25% commission on foreign sales. Offers written contract; 30 days notice must be given to terminate contract. Charges clients for extraordinary expenses in postage and shipping, as well as long distance telephone calls.

RECENT SALES Sold 5 titles in the last year. *No Parent Left Behind*, by P. Petrosino and L. Spiegel (Rowman & Littlefield Education); *Preparing for the 8th Grade Test in Social Studies* by E. Farran and A. Paci (Amsco Book Company); *Teaching Test-Taking Skills*, by G. Durham (Rowman & Littlefield Education); *Teacher's Quick Guide to Communicating*, by G. Sundem (Corwin Press); *Being Grown Up In a Teenage World*, by Susan Porter (R&L Education).

❶ JUDITH EHRLICH LITERARY MANAGEMENT, LLC

880 Third Ave., Eighth Floor, New York NY 10022. (646)505-1570. Fax: (646)505-1570. E-mail: jehrlich@judithehrlichliterary.com. Website: www.judithehrlichliterary.com. Other memberships include Author's Guild, the American Society of Journalists and Authors.

• Prior to her current position, Ms. Ehrlich was an award-winning journalist; she is the co-author of *The New Crowd: The Changing of the Jewish Guard on Wall Street* (Little, Brown). Emmanuelle Alspaugh was an agent at Wendy Sherman Associates and an editor at Fodor's, the travel division of Random House.

MEMBER AGENTS Judith Ehrlich; Emmanuelle Morgen: emorgen@judithehrlichliterary.com (upmarket fiction, historical fiction, women's fiction and romance, urban fantasy, thrillers, young adult fiction, and select memoir, narrative nonfiction, and how-to projects); Sophia Seidner: sseidner@judithehrlichliterary.com (strong literary fiction and nonfiction including self-help, narrative nonfiction, memoir, and biography. Areas of special interest include medical and health-related topics, science [popular, political and social], animal welfare, current events, politics, law, history, ethics, parody and humor, sports, art and business self-help).

REPRESENTS nonfiction books, novels.

8—— "Special areas of interest include compelling narrative nonfiction, outstanding biographies and memoirs, lifestyle books, works that reflect our changing culture, women's issues, psychology, science, social issues, current events, parenting, health, history, business, and prescriptive books offering fresh information and advice." Does not want to receive children's or young adult books, novellas, poetry, textbooks, plays or screenplays.

HOW TO CONTACT Query with SASE. Queries should include a synopsis and some sample pages. Send e-queries to jehrlich@judithehrlichliterary.com. The agency will respond only if interested.

RECENT SALES Fiction: *Breaking the Bank*, by Yona Zeldis McDonough (Pocket); *Sinful Surrender*, by Beverley Kendall (Kensington). Nonfiction: *Strategic Learning: How to be Smarter Than Your Competition and Turn Key Insights Into Competitive Advantage*, by William Pieterson (Wiley); *Paris Under Water: How the City of Light Survived the Great Flood of 1910*, by Jeffrey Jackson (Palgrave Macmillan); *When Growth Stalls: How It Happens, Why You're Stuck & What to Do About It*, by Steve McKee (Jossey-Bass); *I'm Smarter Than My Boss. Now What?* by Diane Garnick (Bloomberg Press).

⊙ THE LISA EKUS GROUP, LLC

57 North St., Hatfield MA 01038. (413)247-9325. Fax: (413)247-9873. E-mail: LisaEkus@lisaekus.com. Website: www.lisaekus.com. **Contact:** Lisa Ekus-Saffer. Member of AAR.

REPRESENTS nonfiction books. **Considers these nonfiction areas:** cooking, diet/nutrition, foods, occasionally health/well-being and women's issues.

HOW TO CONTACT Submit a one-page query via e-mail or submit your complete hardcopy proposal with title page, proposal contents, concept, bio, marketing, TOC, etc. Include SASE for the return of materials.

RECENT SALES Please see the regularly updated client listing on website.

TIPS "Please do not call. No phone queries."

⊙ ETHAN ELLENBERG LITERARY AGENCY

548 Broadway, #5-E, New York NY 10012. (212)431-4554. Fax: (212)941-4652. E-mail: agent@ethanellenberg.com. Website: ethanellenberg.com. **Contact:** Ethan Ellenberg. Estab. 1984. Represents 80 clients. 10% of clients are new/unpublished writers. Currently handles: nonfiction books 25%, novels 75%.

• Prior to opening his agency, Mr. Ellenberg was contracts manager of Berkley/Jove and associate contracts manager for Bantam.

MEMBER AGENTS Denise Little: deniselitt@aol.com. (accepts romance, paranormal, young adult, science fiction, fantasy, Christian fiction, and commercial nonfiction. Send a short query letter telling about your writing history, and including the first 15 pages of the work you want her to represent. If she is interested in your work, she'll reply to you within four weeks); Evan Gregory (accepting clients).

REPRESENTS nonfiction books, novels, children's books. **Considers these nonfiction areas:** biography, current affairs, health, history, medicine, military, science, technology, war, narrative. **Considers these fiction areas:** commercial, fantasy, mystery, romance, science fiction, suspense, thriller, young adult, children's (all types).

8—— "This agency specializes in commercial fiction—especially thrillers, romance/women's, and specialized nonfiction. We also do a lot of children's books. Actively seeking commercial fiction as noted above—romance/fiction for women, science fiction and fantasy, thrillers, suspense and mysteries. Our other two main areas of interest are children's books and narrative nonfiction. We are actively seeking clients, follow the directions on our website." Does not want to receive poetry, short stories, or screenplays.

HOW TO CONTACT For fiction, send introductory letter, outline, first 3 chapters, SASE. For nonfiction, send query letter, proposal, 1 sample chapter, SASE.

For children's books, send introductory letter, up to 3 picture book mss, outline, first 3 chapters, SASE. Accepts simultaneous submissions. Responds in 2 weeks to queries (no attachments); 4–6 weeks to mss.

TERMS Agent receives 15% commission on domestic sales. Agent receives 10% commission on foreign sales. Offers written contract. Charges clients (with their consent) for direct expenses limited to photocopying and postage.

WRITERS CONFERENCES RWA National Conference; Novelists, Inc.; and other regional conferences.

TIPS "We do consider new material from unsolicited authors. Write a good, clear letter with a succinct description of your book. We prefer the first 3 chapters when we consider fiction. For all submissions, you must include a SASE or the material will be discarded. It's always hard to break in, but talent will find a home. Check our website for complete submission guidelines. We continue to see natural storytellers and nonfiction writers with important books."

THE NICHOLAS ELLISON AGENCY

Affiliated with Sanford J. Greenburger Associates, 55 Fifth Ave., 15th Floor, New York NY 10003. (212)206-5600. Fax: (212)463-8718. E-mail: nellison@sjga.com. Website: www.greenburger.com. **Contact:** Nicholas Ellison. Represents 70 clients. Currently handles: nonfiction books 50%, novels 50%.

- Prior to becoming an agent, Mr. Ellison was an editor at Minerva Editions and Harper & Row, and editor-in-chief at Delacorte.

MEMBER AGENTS Nicholas Ellison; Sarah Dickman; Chelsea Lindman;

REPRESENTS nonfiction books, novels (literary, mainstream, children's books). **Considers these fiction areas:** literary, mainstream.

HOW TO CONTACT Query with SASE. Responds in 6 weeks to queries.

TERMS Agent receives 15% commission on domestic sales. Agent receives 20% commission on foreign sales.

ANN ELMO AGENCY, INC.

305 Seventh Avenue, # 1101, New York NY 10001. (212)661-2880. Fax: (212)661-2883. E-mail: aalitagent@sbcglobal.net; elmolit@aol.com. **Contact:** Lettie Lee. Member of AAR. Other memberships include Authors Guild.

MEMBER AGENTS Lettie Lee; Mari Cronin (plays); A.L. Abecassis (nonfiction).

REPRESENTS nonfiction books, novels. **Considers these nonfiction areas:** biography, current affairs, health, history, how-to, popular culture, science. **Considers these fiction areas:** ethnic, family, mainstream, romance, contemporary, gothic, historical, regency, thriller, women's.

HOW TO CONTACT Only accepts referrals; mail queries with SASE. Do not send full ms unless requested. Responds in 3 months to queries. Obtains most new clients through recommendations from others.

TERMS Agent receives 15% commission on domestic sales. Agent receives 20% commission on foreign sales. Offers written contract.

TIPS "Query first, and **only** when asked send a double-spaced, readable manuscript. Include a SASE, of course."

◑ THE ELAINE P. ENGLISH LITERARY AGENCY

4710 41st St. NW, Suite D, Washington DC 20016. (202)362-5190. Fax: (202)362-5192. E-mail: queries@elaineenglish.com. E-mail: elaine@elaineenglish.com; naomi@elaineenglish.com. Website: www.elaineenglish.com/literary.php. **Contact:** Elaine English; Naomi Hackenberg. Member of AAR. Represents 20 clients. 25% of clients are new/unpublished writers. Currently handles: novels 100%.

- Ms. English has been working in publishing for more than 20 years. She is also an attorney specializing in media and publishing law.

MEMBER AGENTS Elaine English (novels); Naomi Hackenberg (Young Adult fiction).

REPRESENTS novels. **Considers these fiction areas:** historical, multicultural, mystery, suspense, thriller, women's, romance (single-title, historical, contemporary, romantic, suspense, chick lit, erotic), general women's fiction. The agency is slowly but steadily acquiring in all mentioned areas.

- Actively seeking women's fiction, including single-title romances, and young adult fiction. Does not want to receive any science fiction, time travel, or picture books.

HOW TO CONTACT Generally prefers e-queries sent to queries@elaineenglish.com or young adult sent to naomi@elaineenglish.com. If requested, submit synopsis, first 3 chapters, SASE. Please check website for further details. Responds in 4-8 weeks to queries; 3 months to requested submissions. Obtains most new clients through recommendations from others, conferences, submissions.

TERMS Agent receives 15% commission on domestic sales. Agent receives 20% commission on foreign sales. Offers written contract; 30-day notice must be given to terminate contract. Charges only for shipping expenses; generally taken from proceeds.

RECENT SALES Have been to Sourcebooks, Tor, Harlequin.

WRITERS CONFERENCES RWA National Conference; Novelists, Inc.; Malice Domestic; Washington Romance Writers Retreat, among others.

◯ THE EPSTEIN LITERARY AGENCY

P.O. Box 392, Randolph MA 02368. (781)718-4025. E-mail: kate@epsteinliterary.com. Website: www.epsteinliterary.com. **Contact:** Kate Epstein. See website for most current location. Member of AAR. Currently handles: nonfiction books 70%; 30% fiction.

- Prior to opening her literary agency, Ms. Epstein was an acquisitions editor at Adams Media. Ms. Epstein has been a literary agent since 2005.

MEMBER AGENTS Kate Epstein represents: practical nonfiction, memoir, narrative nonfiction, young adult fiction, middle grade fiction, popular science, sociology, and psychology.

REPRESENTS nonfiction books for adults and novels for young adults and middle grade. No children's picture books. **Considers these nonfiction areas:** animals, autobiography, biography, business, child guidance, cooking, crafts, current affairs, diet/nutrition, economics, foods, health, hobbies, how-to, humor, medicine, memoirs, metaphysics, New Age, parenting, popular culture, psychology, satire, self-help, sociology, travel, women's issues, women's studies.

⊶ "My background as an editor means that I'm extremely good at selling to them. It also means I'm a careful and thorough line editor. I'm particularly skilled at hardening concepts to make them sellable and proposing the logical follow-up for any book. Most of my list is practical nonfiction, and I have a particular affinity for pets. It's exciting to be doing something new with fiction for young people, and I believe that most of the best work being done in fiction today is for children. At the same time nonfiction is the core of my business and I'm very proud of what I've built in those areas. Crafts books are outrageously

fun, and, while I take on maybe .05% of the memoirs sent me the genre is in fact my favorite." Actively seeking commercial nonfiction for adults. Does not want scholarly works.

HOW TO CONTACT Query via e-mail (no attachments). Accepts simultaneous submissions. Responds in 3 months to queries. Obtains most new clients through solicitations.

TERMS Agent receives 25% commission on domestic sales. Agent receives 20% commission on foreign sales. Offers written contract; 30-day notice must be given to terminate contract.

RECENT SALES *Silver Like Dust*, by Kimi Cunningham Grant (Pegasus); *Knits For Nerds*, by Toni Carr (Andrews McMeel); *Chasing the Jaguar*, by Peter Allison (Globe Pequot Press/Allen & Unwin).

◑ FELICIA ETH LITERARY REPRESENTATION

555 Bryant St., Suite 350, Palo Alto CA 94301-1700. (650)375-1276. Fax: (650)401-8892. E-mail: felicia eth@aol.com. **Contact:** Felicia Eth. Member of AAR. Represents 25-35 clients. Currently handles: nonfiction books 75%, novels 25%.

REPRESENTS nonfiction books, novels. **Considers these nonfiction areas:** animals, anthropology, autobiography, biography, business, child guidance, cultural interests, current affairs, economics, ethnic, gay/lesbian, government, health, history, investigative, law, medicine, parenting, popular culture, politics, psychology, science, sociology, technology, true crime, women's issues, women's studies. **Considers these fiction areas:** literary, mainstream.

⊶ This agency specializes in high-quality fiction (preferably mainstream/contemporary) and provocative, intelligent, and thoughtful nonfiction on a wide array of commercial subjects.

HOW TO CONTACT Query with SASE. Accepts simultaneous submissions. Responds in 3 weeks to queries. Responds in 4-6 weeks to mss.

TERMS Agent receives 15% commission on domestic sales. Agent receives 20% commission on foreign sales. Agent receives 20% commission on film sales. Charges clients for photocopying and express mail service.

RECENT SALES *Bumper Sticker Philosophy*, by Jack Bowen (Random House); *Boys Adrift* by Leonard Sax (Basic Books); *A War Reporter*, by Barbara Quick (HarperCollins); *Pantry*, by Anna Badkhen (Free

Press/S&S).

WRITERS CONFERENCES "Wide Array—from Squaw Valley to Mills College."

TIPS "For nonfiction, established expertise is certainly a plus—as is magazine publication—though not a prerequisite. I am highly dedicated to those projects I represent, but highly selective in what I choose."

● MARY EVANS, INC.

242 E. Fifth St., New York NY 10003. (212)979-0880. Fax: (212)979-5344. Website: www.maryevansinc.com. Member of AAR.

MEMBER AGENTS Mary Evans (no unsolicited queries); Devin McIntyre, devin@maryevansinc.com (commercial and literary fiction, narrative nonfiction, pop culture, graphic novels, multicultural, pop science, sports, food).

REPRESENTS nonfiction books, novels.

HOW TO CONTACT Query with SASE. Query by snail mail. Non-query correspondence can be sent to info(at)maryevansinc.com. Obtains most new clients through recommendations from others, solicitations.

◑ FAIRBANK LITERARY REPRESENTATION

P.O. Box 6, Hudson NY 12534-0006. (617)576-0030. Fax: (617)576-0030. E-mail: queries@fairbankliterary.com. Website: www.fairbankliterary.com. **Contact:** Sorche Fairbank. Member of AAR. Represents 45 clients. 20% of clients are new/unpublished writers. Currently handles: nonfiction books 60%, novels 22%, story collections 3%, other 15% illustrated.

MEMBER AGENTS Sorche Fairbank (narrative nonfiction, commercial and literary fiction, memoir, food and wine); Matthew Frederick (scout for sports nonfiction, architecture, design).

REPRESENTS nonfiction books, novels, short story collections. **Considers these nonfiction areas:** agriculture, architecture, art, autobiography, biography, cooking, crafts, cultural interests, current affairs, decorating, diet/nutrition, design, environment, ethnic, foods, gay/lesbian, government, hobbies, horticulture, how-to, interior design, investigative, law, memoirs, photography, popular culture, politics, science, sociology, sports, technology, true crime, women's issues, women's studies. **Considers these fiction areas:** action, adventure, feminist, gay, lesbian, literary, mainstream, mystery, sports, suspense, thriller, women's, Southern voices.

☞ "I have a small agency in Harvard Square, where I tend to gravitate toward literary fiction and narrative nonfiction, with a strong interest in women's issues and women's voices, international voices, class and race issues, and projects that simply teach me something new about the greater world and society around us. We have a good reputation for working closely and developmentally with our authors and love what we do." Actively seeking literary fiction, international and culturally diverse voices, narrative nonfiction, topical subjects (politics, current affairs), history, sports, architecture/design and pop culture. Does not want to receive romance, poetry, science fiction, pirates, vampire, young adult or children's works.

HOW TO CONTACT Query with SASE. Submit author bio. Accepts simultaneous submissions. Responds in 6 weeks to queries. Responds in 10 weeks to mss. Obtains most new clients through recommendations from others, solicitations, conferences, ideas generated in-house.

TERMS Agent receives 15% commission on domestic sales. Agent receives 20% commission on foreign sales. Offers written contract, binding for 12 months; 45-day notice must be given to terminate contract.

WRITERS CONFERENCES San Francisco Writers' Conference, Muse and the Marketplace/Grub Street Conference, Washington Independent Writers' Conference, Murder in the Grove, Surrey International Writers' Conference.

TIPS "Be professional from the very first contact. There shouldn't be a single typo or grammatical flub in your query. Have a reason for contacting me about your project other than I was the next name listed on some website. Please do not use form query software! Believe me, we can get a dozen or so a day that look identical—we know when you are using a form. Show me that you know your audience—and your competition. Have the writing and/or proposal at the very, very best it can be before starting the querying process. Don't assume that if someone likes it enough they'll 'fix' it. The biggest mistake new writers make is starting the querying process before they—and the work—are ready. Take your time and do it right."

ⓘ DIANA FINCH LITERARY AGENCY

116 W. 23rd St., Suite 500, New York NY 10011. E-mail: diana.finch@verizon.net. Website: dianafinchlit eraryagency.blogspot.com/. **Contact:** Diana Finch. Member of AAR. Represents 40 clients. 20% of clients are new/unpublished writers. Currently handles: nonfiction books 75%, novels 15%, juvenile books 5%, multimedia 5%.

- Seeking to represent books that change lives. Prior to opening her agency in 2003, Ms. Finch worked at Ellen Levine Literary Agency for 18 years.

REPRESENTS nonfiction books, novels, scholarly. **Considers these nonfiction areas:** autobiography, biography, business, child guidance, computers, cultural interests, current affairs, dance, economics, environment, ethnic, film, government, health, history, how-to, humor, investigative, juvenile nonfiction, law, medicine, memoirs, military, money, music, parenting, photography, popular culture, politics, psychology, satire, science, self-help, sports, technology, theater, translation, true crime, war, women's issues, women's studies, electronic. **Considers these fiction areas:** action, adventure, crime, detective, ethnic, historical, literary, mainstream, police, thriller, young adult.

○➤ Actively seeking narrative nonfiction, popular science, memoir and health topics. "Does not want romance, mysteries, or children's picture books."

HOW TO CONTACT Query with SASE or via e-mail (no attachments). Accepts simultaneous submissions. Obtains most new clients through recommendations from others.

TERMS Agent receives 15% commission on domestic sales. Agent receives 20% commission on foreign sales. Offers written contract. "I charge for photocopying, overseas postage, galleys, and books purchased, and try to recoup these costs from earnings received for a client, rather than charging outright."

RECENT SALES *Heidegger's Glasses,* by Thaisa Frank; *Genetic Rounds,* by Robert Marion, M.D. (Kaplan); *Honeymoon In Tehran,* by Azadeh Moaveni (Random House); *Darwin Slept Here* by Eric Simons (Overlook); *Black Tide,* by Antonia Juhasz (HarperCollins); *Stalin's Children,* by Owen Matthews (Bloomsbury); *Radiant Days,* by Michael Fitzgerald (Shoemaker & Hoard); *The Queen's Soprano,* by Carol Dines (Harcourt Young Adult); *What To Say to a Porcupine,* by Richard Gallagher (Amacom); *The Language of Trust,* by Michael Maslansky.

TIPS "Do as much research as you can on agents before you query. Have someone critique your query letter before you send it. It should be only 1 page and describe your book clearly—and why you are writing it—but also demonstrate creativity and a sense of your writing style."

FINEPRINT LITERARY MANAGEMENT

240 West 35th St., Suite 500, New York NY 10001. (212)279-1282. E-mail: (agent's first name)@fine printlit.com. Website: www.fineprintlit.com. Member of AAR.

MEMBER AGENTS Peter Rubie, CEO (nonfiction interests include narrative nonfiction, popular science, spirituality, history, biography, pop culture, business, technology, parenting, health, self help, music, and food; fiction interests include literate thrillers, crime fiction, science fiction and fantasy, military fiction and literary fiction); Stephany Evans, president (nonfiction interests include health and wellness—especially women's health, spirituality, lifestyle, home renovating/decorating, entertaining, food and wine, popular reference, and narrative nonfiction; fiction interests include stories with a strong and interesting female protagonist, both literary and upmarket commercial—including chick lit, romance, mystery, and light suspense); June Clark (nonfiction: entertainment, self-help, parenting, reference/how-to books, teen books, food and wine, style/beauty, and prescriptive business titles); Diane Freed (nonfiction: health/fitness, women's issues, memoir, baby boomer trends, parenting, popular culture, self-help, humor, young adult, and topics of New England regional interest); Meredith Hays (both fiction and nonfiction: commercial and literary; she is interested in sophisticated women's fiction such as urban chick lit, pop culture, lifestyle, animals, and absorbing nonfiction accounts); Janet Reid (mysteries and offbeat literary fiction); Colleen Lindsay; Marissa Walsh; Ward Calhoun; Laura Wood; Suzie Townsend; Rachel Vater Coyne.

REPRESENTS nonfiction books, novels. **Considers these nonfiction areas:** business, child guidance, cooking, dance, diet/nutrition, economics, foods, government, health, history, humor, law, medicine, memoirs, music, parenting, politics, psychology, science, spirituality, true crime, women's issues, women's studies, narrative nonfiction, young adult, popular science. **Considers these fiction areas:** crime, detective, fantasy, literary, military, mystery, police, romance, science fiction, suspense, war, women's, young adult.

HOW TO CONTACT Query with SASE. Submit synopsis and first two chapters for fiction; proposal for nonfiction. Do not send attachments or manuscripts without a request. See contact page online at website for e-mails. Obtains most new clients through recommendations from others, solicitations.

TERMS Agent receives 15% commission on domestic sales. Agent receives 20% commission on foreign sales.

JAMES FITZGERALD AGENCY

118 Waverly Pl., #1B, New York NY 10011. (212)308-1122. E-mail: submissions@jfitzagency.com. Website: www.jfitzagency.com. **Contact:** James Fitzgerald.

- Prior to his current position, Mr. Fitzgerald was an editor at St. Martin's Press, Doubleday, and the *New York Times.*

MEMBER AGENTS James Fitzgerald.

REPRESENTS books that reflect the popular culture of today being in the forms of fiction, nonfiction, graphic and packaged books.

8→ Does not want to receive poetry or screenplays.

HOW TO CONTACT Query with SASE. Submit proposal package, outline/proposal, publishing history, author bio, overview.

RECENT SALES *Gimme Something Better: The Profound, Progressive, and Occasionally Pointless History of Punk in the Bay Area*, by Jack Boulware and Silke Tudor (Viking/Penguin); *Black Dogs: The Possibly True Story of Classic Rock's Greatest Robbery*, by Jason Buhrmester (Three Rivers/Crown); *Theo Gray's Med Science: Experiments You Can Do at Home—But Probably Shouldn't* (Black Dog and Loenthal).

TIPS "Please submit all information in English, even if your manuscript is in Spanish."

FLAMING STAR LITERARY ENTERPRISES

11 Raup Rd., Chatham NY 12037. E-mail: flamingstarlit@aol.com; janvall@aol.com. Website: www.flamingstarlit.com for Joseph Vallely; www.janisvallely.com for Janis Vallely. **Contact:** Joseph B. Vallely, Janis C. Vallely. Represents 100 clients. 25% of clients are new/unpublished writers. Currently handles: nonfiction books 100%.

- Prior to opening the agency, Mr. Vallely served as national sales manager for Dell; Ms. Vallely was V.P. and Associate Publisher of Doubleday.

REPRESENTS nonfiction books. **Considers these nonfiction areas:** current affairs, diet/nutrition, government, health, law, memoirs, politics, psychology, self-help. Note: Health, science, memoir and psychology are represented through our separate offices at www.janisvallely.com.

8→ This agency specializes in upscale commercial nonfiction. No poetry, screenplays, fiction, young adult, children's lit.

HOW TO CONTACT E-mail only (no attachments). Responds in one week to queries. Obtains most new clients through recommendations from others, solicitations.

TERMS Agent receives 15% commission on domestic sales. Agent receives 20% commission on foreign sales. Offers written contract. Charges clients for photocopying and postage only.

RECENT SALES *Diabetes Without Drugs*, by Suzy Cohen (Rodale).

TIPS "See website."

FLANNERY LITERARY

1140 Wickfield Ct., Naperville IL 60563. (630)428-2682. Fax: (630)428-2683. E-mail: FlanLit@aol.com. **Contact:** Jennifer Flannery. Represents 40 clients. 50% of clients are new/unpublished writers. Currently handles: juvenile books 100%.

8→ This agency specializes in children's and young adult fiction and nonfiction. It also accepts picture books.

HOW TO CONTACT Query with SASE. No e-mail submissions or queries. Responds in 2 weeks to queries. Responds in 1 month to mss. Obtains most new clients through recommendations from others, submissions.

TERMS Agent receives 15% commission on domestic sales. Agent receives 20% commission on foreign sales. Offers written contract, binding for life of book in print; 1-month notice must be given to terminate contract.

TIPS "Write an engrossing, succinct query describing your work. We are always looking for a fresh new voice."

PETER FLEMING AGENCY

P.O. Box 458, Pacific Palisades CA 90272. (310)454-1373. E-mail: peterfleming@earthlink.net. **Contact:** Peter Fleming. Currently handles: nonfiction books 100%.

⚷ This agency specializes in nonfiction books that unearth innovative and uncomfortable truths with bestseller potential. "Greatly interested in journalists in the free press (the Internet)."

HOW TO CONTACT Query with SASE. Obtains most new clients through a different, one-of-a-kind idea for a book often backed by the writer's experience in that area of expertise.

TERMS Agent receives 15% commission on domestic sales. Agent receives 25% commission on foreign sales. Offers written contract, binding for 1 year. Charges clients only those fees agreed to in writing.

RECENT SALES *Stop Foreclosure*, by Lloyd Segol; *Rulers of Evil*, by F. Tupper Saussy (HarperCollins); *Why Is It Always About You—Saving Yourself from the Narcissists in Your Life*, by Sandy Hotchkiss (Free Press).

TIPS "You can begin by starting your own blog."

FLETCHER & COMPANY

78 Fifth Ave., 3rd Floor, New York NY 10011. (212)614-0778. Fax: (212)614-0728. E-mail: mail@fletcherpar ry.com. Website: www.fletcherandco.com. **Contact:** Christy Fletcher. Member of AAR.

MEMBER AGENTS Melissa Chinchilla (current affairs/politics, multicultural literature, smart women's fiction, horror, thrillers, crime and the paranormal—as well as select, high concept children's books, academic/trade books); Swanna MacNair (Southern literature and music, literary fiction, nonfiction, narrative journalism, investigative journalism, international fictions, thrillers, crime, paranormal, cultural studies, medical investigation, Young Adult, self-help, minority literature and smart romance); Grainne Fox (looking for Irish literary fiction and more smart, upmarket fiction); Rebecca Gradinger (literary fiction, upmarket commercial fiction, narrative nonfiction, self-help, memoir, humor, parenting, young adult, and pop culture, health and medicine, women's issues, cultural studies, and fiction); Donald Lamm (history, biography, investigative journalism, politics, current affairs, and business books for the trade); Anne Loder (nonfiction, literary fiction, popular culture, poetry, and narrative journalism) Lucinda Blumenfeld (reps journalists, specialists, and emerging, young voices; specific categories include: narrative and prescriptive nonfiction, business, memoir, young adult, cultural studies, commercial and literary fiction).

REPRESENTS nonfiction books, novels. **Considers these nonfiction areas:** biography, business, current affairs, health, history, memoirs, science, sports, travel, African-American, narrative, lifestyle. **Considers these fiction areas:** literary, young adult, commercial.

⚷ Does not want genre fiction.

HOW TO CONTACT Query with SASE or e-mail according to our guidelines. NO ATTACHMENTS. Responds in 6 weeks to queries.

FOLIO LITERARY MANAGEMENT, LLC

505 Eighth Ave., Suite 603, New York NY 10018. Website: www.foliolit.com. Member of AAR. Represents 100+ clients.

- Prior to creating Folio Literary Management, Mr. Hoffman worked for several years at another agency; Mr. Kleinman was an agent at Graybill & English; Ms. Wheeler was an agent at Creative Media Agency; Ms. Fine was an agent at Vigliano Associates and Trident Media Group; Ms. Brower was an agent at Wendy Sherman Associates; Ms. Niumata was an editor at Simon & Schuster, HarperCollins, and Avalon Books.

MEMBER AGENTS Scott Hoffman; Jeff Kleinman; Paige Wheeler; Celeste Fine; Erin Niumata; Michelle Brower, Marcy Posner, Steve Troha, Molly Jaffa; Michael Harriot; Shawna Morey; Sarah S. McLellan; Emily van Beek.

REPRESENTS nonfiction books, novels, short story collections. **Considers these nonfiction areas:** animals, art, biography, business, child guidance, economics, environment, health, history, how-to, humor, inspirational, memoirs, military, parenting, popular culture, politics, psychology, religious, satire, science, self-help, technology, war, women's issues, women's studies, animals (equestrian), narrative nonfiction, espionage; fitness, lifestyle, relationship, culture, cookbooks. **Considers these fiction areas:** erotica, fantasy, literary, mystery, religious, romance, science, thriller, psychological, young, womens, Southern; legal; edgy crime, young adult, middle grade.

⚷ No poetry, stage plays, or screenplays.

HOW TO CONTACT Query via e-mail only (no attachments). Read agent bios online for specific submission guidelines and e-mail addresses. Responds in 1 month to queries.

TIPS "Please do not submit simultaneously to more than one agent at Folio. If you're not sure which of us is exactly right for your book, don't worry. We work closely as a team, and if one of our agents gets a query that might be more appropriate for someone else, we'll always pass it along. It's important that you check each agent's bio page for clear directions as to how to submit, as well as when to expect feedback."

FOUNDRY LITERARY + MEDIA

33 West 17th St., PH, New York NY 10011. (212)929-5064. Fax: (212)929-5471. Website: www.foundrymedia.com.

MEMBER AGENTS Peter H. McGuigan (smart, offbeat nonfiction, particularly works of narrative nonfiction on pop culture, niche history, biography, music and science; fiction interests include commercial and literary, across all genres, especially first-time writers); Yfat Reiss Gendell (favors nonfiction books focusing on all manners of prescriptive: how-to, science, health and well-being, memoirs, adventure, travel stories and lighter titles appropriate for the gift trade genre; Yfat also looks for commercial fiction highlighting the full range of women's experiences—young and old-and also seeks science fiction, thrillers and historical fiction); Stéphanie Abou (in fiction and nonfiction alike, Stéphanie is always on the lookout for authors who are accomplished storytellers with their own distinctive voice, who develop memorable characters, and who are able to create psychological conflict with their narrative; she is an across-the-board fiction lover, attracted to both literary and smart upmarket commercial fiction; in nonfiction she leans towards projects that tackle big topics with an unusual approach in th realm of pop culture, health, science, parenting, women's and multicultural issues are of special interest); Chris Park (memoirs, narrative nonfiction, Christian nonfiction and character-driven fiction); David Patterson (outstanding narratives and/or idea-driven works of nonfiction); Hannah Brown Gordon (fiction, young adult, memoir, narrative nonfiction, history, current events, science, psychology and pop-culture); Lisa Grubka; Mollie Glick (literary fiction, narrative nonfiction, young adult, and a bit of practical nonfiction); Stephen Barbara (all categories of books for young readers in addition to servicing writers for the adult market); Brandi Bowles (idea and platform-driven nonfiction in all categories, including music and pop culture, humor, business, sociology, philosophy, health, and relationships; quirky, funny, or contrarian proposals are always welcome in her inbox, as are big-idea books that change the way we think about the world; Brandi also represents fiction in the categories of literary fiction, women's fiction, urban fantasy, and young adult).

REPRESENTS Considers these nonfiction areas: biography, child, health, memoirs, multicultural, music, popular culture, science. Considers these fiction areas: literary, religious.

HOW TO CONTACT Query with SASE. Should be addressed to one agent only. Submit synopsis, 3 sample chapters, author bio. For nonfiction, submit query, proposal, sample chapter, TOC, bio. Put "Submisssions" on your snail mail submission.

●⊙ FOX CHASE AGENCY, INC.

701 Lee Road, Suite 102, Chesterbrook Corporate Center, Chesterbrook PA 19087. Member of AAR.
MEMBER AGENTS A.L. Hart; Jo C. Hart.
REPRESENTS nonfiction books, novels.
HOW TO CONTACT No unsolicited mss. Query with SASE.

FOX LITERARY

168 Second Ave., PMB 180, New York NY 10003. E-mail: submissions@foxliterary.com. Website: www.foxliterary.com.

REPRESENTS Considers these nonfiction areas: memoirs, biography, pop culture, narrative nonfiction, history, science, spirituality, self-help, celebrity, dating/relationships, women's issues, psychology, film & entertainment, cultural/social issues, journalism. Considers these fiction areas: erotica, fantasy, romance, science, young adult, science fiction, thrillers, historical fiction, literary fiction, graphic novels, commercial fiction, women's fiction, gay & lesbian, erotica, historical romance.

Does not want to receive screenplays, poetry, category Western, horror, Christian/inspirational, or children's picture books.

HOW TO CONTACT E-mail query and first 5 pages in body of e-mail. E-mail queries preferred. For snail mail queries, must include an e-mail address for response. Do not send SASE.

LYNN C. FRANKLIN ASSOCIATES, LTD.

1350 Broadway, Suite 2015, New York NY 10018. (212)868-6311. Fax: (212)868-6312. **Contact:** Lynn Franklin, President; Claudia Nys, Foreign Rights; Weronika Janczuk, agent. Other memberships include PEN America. Represents 30-35 clients. 50% of clients are new/unpublished writers. Currently handles: nonfiction books 90%, novels 10%.

REPRESENTS nonfiction books, novels. **Considers these nonfiction areas:** New Age, biography, current affairs, health, history, memoirs, psychology, religion, self-help, spirituality. **Considers these fiction areas:** literary, mainstream, commercial; juvenile, middle-grade, and young adult.

⌐► "This agency specializes in general nonfiction with a special interest in self-help, biography/memoir, alternative health, and spirituality."

HOW TO CONTACT Query via e-mail to agency@franklinandsiegal.com. No unsolicited mss. No attachments. For nonfiction, query letter with short outline and synopsis. For fiction, query letter with short synopsis and a maximum of 10 sample pages (in the body of the e-mail). Please indicate "query adult" or "query children's) in the subject line. Accepts simultaneous submissions. Responds in 2 weeks to queries. Responds in 6 weeks to mss. Obtains most new clients through recommendations from others, solicitations.

TERMS Agent receives 15% commission on domestic sales. Agent receives 20% commission on foreign sales. Offers written contract.

RECENT SALES Adult: *Made for Goodness*, by Archbishop Desmond Tutu and Reverend Mpho Tutu (HarperOne); *Children of God Storybook Bible*, by Archbishop Desmond Tutu (Zondervan for originating publisher Lux Verbi); *Playing Our Game: Why China's Economic Rise Doesn't Threaten the West*, by Edward Steinfeld (Oxford University Press); *The 100 Year Diet*, by Susan Yager (Rodale); Children's/ young adult: *I Like Mandarin*, by Kirsten Hubbard (Delacorte/Random House); *A Scary Scene in a Scary Movie*, by Matt Blackstone (Farrar, Straus & Giroux).

◐ JEANNE FREDERICKS LITERARY AGENCY, INC.

221 Benedict Hill Rd., New Canaan CT 06840. (203)972-3011. Fax: (203)972-3011. E-mail: jeanne.fredericks@gmail.com. Website: jeannefredericks.com. **Contact:** Jeanne Fredericks. Member of AAR. Other memberships include Authors Guild. Represents 90 clients. 10% of clients are new/unpublished writers. Currently handles: nonfiction books 100%.

• Prior to opening her agency, Ms. Fredericks was an agent and acting director with the Susan P. Urstadt, Inc. Agency.

REPRESENTS nonfiction books. **Considers these nonfiction areas:** animals, autobiography, biography, child guidance, cooking, decorating, finance, foods, gardening, health, history, how-to, interior design, medicine, money, nature, nutrition, parenting, personal improvement, photography, psychology, self-help, sports (not spectator sports), women's issues.

⌐► This agency specializes in quality adult nonfiction by authorities in their fields. Does not want to receive children's books or fiction.

HOW TO CONTACT Query first with SASE, then send outline/proposal, 1-2 sample chapters, SASE. See submission guidelines online first. Accepts simultaneous submissions. Responds in 3-5 weeks to queries. Responds in 2-4 months to mss. Obtains most new clients through recommendations from others, solicitations, conferences.

TERMS Agent receives 15% commission on domestic sales. Agent receives 25% commission on foreign sales with co-agent. Offers written contract, binding for 9 months; 2-month notice must be given to terminate contract. Charges client for photocopying of whole proposals and mss, overseas postage, priority mail, express mail services.

RECENT SALES *The Green Market Baking Book* by Laura Martin (Sterling); *Tales of the Seven Seas*, by Dennis Powers (Taylor); *The Monopoly® Guide to Real Estate* by Carolyn Janik (Sterling); *The Generosity Plan* by Kathy LeMay (Beyond Words/Atria); *Canadian Vegetable Gardening* by Doug Green (Cool Springs).

WRITERS CONFERENCES Connecticut Authors and Publishers Association-University Conference; ASJA Writers' Conference; BookExpo America; Garden Writers' Association Annual Symposium; Harvard Medical School CME Course in Publishing.

TIPS "Be sure to research competition for your work and be able to justify why there's a need for your book. I enjoy building an author's career, particularly if he/she is professional, hardworking, and courteous. Aside from 17 years of agenting experience, I've had 10 years of editorial experience in adult trade book publishing that enables me to help an author polish a proposal so that it's more appealing to prospective editors. My MBA in marketing also distinguishes me from other agents."

● GRACE FREEDSON'S PUBLISHING NETWORK

375 North Broadway, Suite 102, Jericho NY 11753. (516)931-7757. Fax: (516)931-7759. E-mail: gfreedson@worldnet.att.net. **Contact:** Grace Freedson, 17 Center Dr., Syosset, NY 11791-6113. Represents 100 clients. 10% of clients are new/unpublished writers. Currently handles: nonfiction books 90%, juvenile books 10%.

- Prior to becoming an agent, Ms. Freedson was a managing editor and director of acquisition for Barron's Educational Series.

REPRESENTS nonfiction books, juvenile. **Considers these nonfiction areas:** animals, business, cooking, crafts, current affairs, diet/nutrition, economics, education, environment, foods, health, history, hobbies, how-to, humor, medicine, money, popular culture, psychology, satire, science, self-help, sports, technology.

8—ℼ "In addition to representing many qualified authors, I work with publishers as a packager of unique projects—mostly series." Does not want to receive fiction.

HOW TO CONTACT Query with SASE. Submit synopsis, SASE. Responds in 2-6 weeks to queries. Obtains most new clients through recommendations from others.

TERMS Agent receives 15% commission on domestic sales. Offers written contract; 30-day notice must be given to terminate contract.

RECENT SALES Sold 50 titles in the last year. *The Dangers Lurking Beyond the Glass Ceiling*, by D. Sherr Bourierg Carter (Prometheus); *Threats, Lies and Intimidation: Inside Debt Collection*, by Fred Williams (FT Press); *Plastic Planet*, by Kathryn Jones (FT Press).

WRITERS CONFERENCES BookExpo of America.

TIPS "At this point, I am only reviewing proposals on nonfiction topics by credentialed authors with platforms."

◑ FREDRICA S. FRIEDMAN AND CO., INC.

136 E. 57th St., 14th Floor, New York NY 10022. (212)829-9600. Fax: (212)829-9669. E-mail: info@fredricafriedman.com; submissions@fredricafriedman.com. Website: www.fredricafriedman.com/agency.htm. **Contact:** Ms. Chandler Smith. Represents 75+ clients. 50% of clients are new/unpublished writers. Currently handles: nonfiction books 95%, novels 5%.

REPRESENTS nonfiction books, novels, anthologies. **Considers these nonfiction areas:** art, biography, business, child, cooking, current affairs, education, ethnic, gay, government, health, history, how-to, humor, language, memoirs, money, music, photography, popular culture, psychology, self-help, sociology, film, true crime, women's, interior design/decorating. **Considers these fiction areas:** literary.

8—ℼ "We represent a select group of outstanding nonfiction and fiction writers. We are particularly interested in helping writers expand their readership and develop their careers." Does not want poetry, plays, screenplays, children's books, sci-fi/fantasy, or horror.

HOW TO CONTACT Submit e-query, synopsis; be concise, and include any pertinent author information, including relevant writing history. If you are a fiction writer, we also request a one-page sample from your manuscript to provide its voice. We ask that you keep all material in the body of the e-mail. Accepts simultaneous submissions. Responds in 4-6 weeks to queries. Responds in 4-6 weeks to mss. Obtains most new clients through recommendations from others.

TERMS Agent receives 15% commission on domestic sales. Agent receives 25% commission on foreign sales. Offers written contract. Charges for photocopying and messenger/shipping fees for proposals.

RECENT SALES *A World of Lies: The Crime and Consequences of Bernie Madoff*, by Diana B. Henriques (Times Books/Holt); *Polemic and Memoir: The Nixon Years* by Patrick J. Buchanan (St. Martin's Press); *Angry Fat Girls: Five Women, Five Hundred Pounds, and a Year of Losing It ... Again*, by Frances Kuffel (Berkley/Penguin); *Life With My Sister Madonna*, by Christopher Ciccone with Wendy Leigh (Simon & Schuster Spotlight); *The World Is Curved: Hidden Dangers to the Global Economy*, by David Smick (Portfolio/Penguin); *Going to See the Elephant*, by Rodes Fishburne (Delacorte/Random House); *Seducing the Boys Club: Uncensored Tactics from a Woman at the Top*, by Nina DiSesa (Ballantine/Random House); *The Girl from Foreign: A Search for Shipwrecked Ancestors, Forgotten Histories, and a Sense of Home*, by Sadia Shepard (The Penguin Press).

TIPS "Spell the agent's name correctly in your query letter."

◐ FREDERICK HILL BONNIE NADELL, INC.

8899 Beverly Blvd., Suite 805, Los Angeles CA 90048. (310)860-9605. Fax: (310)860-9672. Website: www. hillnadell.com. Represents 100 clients.

MEMBER AGENTS Bonnie Nadell; Elise Proulx, associate.

REPRESENTS nonfiction books, novels. **Considers these nonfiction areas:** current affairs, environment, health, history, language, literature, medicine, popular culture, politics, science, technology, biography; government/politics, narrative. **Considers these fiction areas:** literary, mainstream.

HOW TO CONTACT Query with SASE. Keep your query to one page. Send via snail mail or e-mail. Do not send the same query to multiple locations. Accepts simultaneous submissions.

TERMS Agent receives 15% commission on domestic sales. Agent receives 20% commission on foreign sales. Agent receives 15% commission on film sales. Charges clients for photocopying and foreign mailings.

RECENT SALES *Living the Sweet Life in Paris* by David Lebovitz (memoir); *Next Stop, Reloville: Inside America's New Rootless Professional Class* by Peter Kilborn.

◐◉ FRESH BOOKS LITERARY AGENCY

231 Diana St., Placerville CA 95667. E-mail: matt@ fresh-books.com. Website: www.fresh-books.com. **Contact:** Matt Wagner. Represents 30+ clients. 5% of clients are new/unpublished writers. Currently handles: nonfiction books 95%, multimedia 5%.

• Prior to becoming an agent, Mr. Wagner was with Waterside Productions for 15 years.

REPRESENTS nonfiction books. **Considers these nonfiction areas:** animals, anthropology, archeology, architecture, art, business, child guidance, comput-

ers, cooking, crafts, cultural interests, current affairs, dance, design, economics, education, environment, ethnic, gay/lesbian, government, health, history, hobbies, humor, law, medicine, military, money, music, parenting, photography, popular culture, politics, psychology, satire, science, sports, technology.

🗝 "I specialize in tech and how-to. I love working with books and authors, and I've repped many of my clients for upwards of 15 years now." Actively seeking popular science, natural history, adventure, how-to, business, education and reference. Does not want to receive fiction, children's books, screenplays, or poetry.

HOW TO CONTACT Query with SASE. No phone calls. Accepts simultaneous submissions. Responds in 1-4 weeks to queries. Responds in 1-4 weeks to mss. Obtains most new clients through recommendations from others.

TERMS Agent receives 15% commission on domestic sales. Agent receives 20% commission on foreign sales.

RECENT SALES *The Myth of Multitasking: How Doing It All Gets Nothing Done* (Jossey-Bass); *Wilderness Survival for Dummies* (Wiley); and *The Zombie Combat Manual* (Berkley).

TIPS "Do your research. Find out what sorts of books and authors an agent represents. Go to conferences. Make friends with other writers—most of my clients come from referrals."

● SARAH JANE FREYMANN LITERARY AGENCY

59 W. 71st St., Suite 9B, New York NY 10023. (212)362-9277. E-mail: sarah@sarahjanefreymann.com; Submissions@SarahJaneFreymann.com. Website: www. sarahjanefreymann.com. **Contact:** Sarah Jane Freymann, Steve Schwartz. Represents 100 clients. 20% of clients are new/unpublished writers. Currently handles: nonfiction books 75%, novels 23%, juvenile books 2%.

MEMBER AGENTS Sarah Jane Freymann; (nonfiction books, novels, illustrated books); Jessica Sinsheimer, Jessica@sarahjanefreymann.com (young adult fiction); Steven Schwartz, steve@sarahjanefreymann. com; Katharine Sands.

REPRESENTS **Considers these nonfiction areas:** animals, anthropology, architecture, art, autobiography, biography, business, child guidance, cooking, current affairs, decorating, diet/nutrition, design, economics, ethnic, foods, health, history, interior design, medicine, memoirs, parenting, psychology, self-help, women's issues, women's studies, lifestyle. **Considers these fiction areas:** ethnic, literary, mainstream.

HOW TO CONTACT Query with SASE. Responds in 2 weeks to queries. Responds in 6 weeks to mss. Obtains most new clients through recommendations from others.

TERMS Agent receives 15% commission on domestic sales. Agent receives 20% commission on foreign sales. Offers written contract. Charges clients for long distance, overseas postage, photocopying. 100% of business is derived from commissions on ms sales.

RECENT SALES *How to Make Love to a Plastic Cup: And Other Things I Learned While Trying to Knock Up My Wife*, by Greg Wolfe (Harper Collins); *I Want to Be Left Behind: Rapture Here on Earth*, by Brenda Peterson (a Merloyd Lawrence Book); *That Bird Has My Name: The Autobiography of an Innocent Man on Death Row*, by Jarvis Jay Masters with an Introduction by Pema Chodrun (HarperOne); *Perfect One-Dish Meals*, by Pam Anderson (Houghton Mifflin); *Birdology*, by Sy Montgomery (Simon & Schuster); *Emptying the Nest: Launching Your Reluctant Young Adult*, by Dr. Brad Sachs (Macmillan); *Tossed & Found*, by Linda and John Meyers (Steward, Tabori & Chang); *32 Candles*, by Ernessa Carter; *God and Dog*, by Wendy Francisco.

TIPS "I love fresh, new, passionate works by authors who love what they are doing and have both natural talent and carefully honed skill."

◑ FULL CIRCLE LITERARY, LLC

7676 Hazard Center Dr., Suite 500, San Diego CA 92108. E-mail: submissions@fullcircleliterary.com. Website: www.fullcircleliterary.com. **Contact:** Lilly Ghahremani, Stefanie Von Borstel. Represents 55 clients. 60% of clients are new/unpublished writers. Currently handles: nonfiction books 70%, novels 10%, juvenile books 20%.

- Before forming Full Circle, Ms. Von Borstel worked in both marketing and editorial capacities at Penguin and Harcourt; Ms. Ghahremani received her law degree from UCLA, and has experience in representing authors on legal affairs.

MEMBER AGENTS Lilly Ghahremani (Lilly is mostly retired and only taking referrals: young adult, pop culture, crafts, "green" living, narrative nonfiction, business, relationships, Middle Eastern interest, multicultural); Stefanie Von Borstel (Latino interest, crafts, parenting, wedding/relationships, how-to, self-help, middle grade/teen fiction/young adult, green living, multicultural/bilingual picture books); Adriana Dominguez (fiction areas of interest: children's books—picture books, middle grade novels, and (literary) young adult novels; on the adult side, she is looking for literary, women's, and historical fiction. Nonfiction areas of interest: multicultural, pop culture, how-to, and titles geared toward women of all ages).

REPRESENTS nonfiction books, juvenile. **Considers these nonfiction areas:** animals, autobiography, biography, business, child guidance, crafts, cultural interests, current affairs, dance, diet/nutrition, ethnic, foods, health, hobbies, how-to, humor, juvenile nonfiction, medicine, parenting, popular culture, satire, self-help, women's issues, women's studies. **Considers these fiction areas:** ethnic, literary, young adult.

⌥ "Our full-service boutique agency, representing a range of nonfiction and children's books (limited fiction), provides a one-stop resource for authors. Our extensive experience in the realms of law and marketing provide Full Circle clients with a unique edge. Actively seeking nonfiction by authors with a unique and strong platform, projects that offer new and diverse viewpoints, and literature with a global or multicultural perspective. We are particularly interested in books with a Latino or Middle Eastern angle and books related to pop culture." Does not want to receive "screenplays, poetry, commercial fiction or genre fiction (horror, thriller, mystery, Western, sci-fi, fantasy, romance, historical fiction)."

HOW TO CONTACT Agency accepts e-queries. See website for fiction guidelines, as they are in flux. For nonfiction, send full proposal. Accepts simultaneous submissions. Responds in 1-2 weeks to queries. Responds in 4-6 weeks to mss. Obtains most new clients through recommendations from others, solicitations, conferences.

TERMS Agent receives 15% commission on domestic sales. Agent receives 20% commission on foreign

sales. Offers written contract; up to 30-day notice must be given to terminate contract. Charges for copying and postage.

TIPS "Put your best foot forward. Contact us when you simply can't make your project any better on your own, and please be sure your work fits with what the agent you're approaching represents. Little things count, so copyedit your work. Join a writing group and attend conferences to get objective and constructive feedback before submitting. Be active about building your platform as an author before, during, and after publication. Remember this is a business and your agent is a business partner."

⊙ NANCY GALLT LITERARY AGENCY

273 Charlton Ave., South Orange NJ 07079. (973)761-6358. Fax: (973)761-6318. E-mail: submissions@nancygallt.com. Website: www.nancygallt.com. **Contact:** Nancy Gallt. Represents 40 clients. 30% of clients are new/unpublished writers. Currently handles: juvenile books 100%.

- Prior to opening her agency, Ms. Gallt was subsidiary rights director of the children's book division at Morrow, Harper and Viking.

MEMBER AGENTS Nancy Gallt; Marietta Zacker.

REPRESENTS juvenile.

⚯ "I only handle children's books." Actively seeking picture books, middle grade and young adult novels. Does not want to receive rhyming picture book texts.

HOW TO CONTACT Submit a novel or chapter book by copying and pasting the first 5 pages onto the body of the e-mail and attach the first three chapters to submissions@nancygallt.com. Do not send to individual e-mail address, but do address submission to specific agent. If submitting a picture book: please copy and paste the entire manuscript into the body of the e-mail and attach it, as well. A response from one agent is a response from the entire company. Please see website for more submission details. Accepts simultaneous submissions. Responds in 3 months to queries. Responds in 3 months to mss. Obtains most new clients through recommendations from others, solicitations.

TERMS Agent receives 15% commission on domestic sales. Agent receives 20% commission on foreign sales. Offers written contract; 30-day notice must be given to terminate contract.

RECENT SALES Sold 50 titles in the last year. *Kane*

Chronicles series, by Rick Riordan (Hyperion); *Nightshade City*, by Hilary Wagner (Holiday House); *Cinderella Smith*, by Stephanie Barden (HarperCollins); *The Square Cat*, by Elizabeth Schoonmaker (Simon & Schuster); *Granddaughter's Necklace*, illustrated by Bagram Ibatoulline (Scholastic).

TIPS "Writing and illustrations stand on their own, so submissions should tell the most compelling stories possible—whether visually, in words, or both."

MAX GARTENBERG LITERARY AGENCY

912 N. Pennsylvania Ave., Yardley PA 19067. (215)295-9230. Website: www.maxgartenberg.com. **Contact:** Anne Devlin. Estab. 1954. Represents 50 clients. 5% of clients are new/unpublished writers. Currently handles: nonfiction books 90%, novels 10%.

MEMBER AGENTS Max Gartenberg, president, (biography, environment, and narrative nonfiction); Anne G. Devlin (current events, women's issues, health, lifestyle, literary fiction, romance, and celebrity); Will Devlin (sports, popular culture, humor and politics).

REPRESENTS nonfiction books, novels. **Considers these nonfiction areas:** agriculture horticulture, animals, art, biography, child, current affairs, health, history, money, music, nature, psychology, science, self-help, sports, film, true crime, women's.

HOW TO CONTACT Writers desirous of having their work handled by this agency should first send a one- or two-page query letter directed to an agent on staff. Send queries via snail mail with SASE. Accepts simultaneous submissions. Responds in 2 weeks to queries. Responds in 6 weeks to mss. Obtains most new clients through recommendations from others, following up on good query letters.

TERMS Agent receives 15% commission on domestic sales. Agent receives 20% commission on foreign sales.

RECENT SALES *What Patients Taught Me*, by Audrey Young, MD (Sasquatch Books); *Unorthodox Warfare: The Chinese Experience*, by Ralph D. Sawyer (WesTView Press); *Encyclopedia of Earthquakes and Volcanoes*, by Alexander E. Gates (Facts on File); *Homebirth in the Hospital*, by Stacey Kerr, MD (Sentient Publications).

TIPS "We have recently expanded to allow more access for new writers."

GELFMAN SCHNEIDER LITERARY AGENTS, INC.

250 W. 57th St., Suite 2122, New York NY 10107. (212)245-1993. Fax: (212)245-8678. E-mail: mail@gelfmanschneider.com. Website: www.gelfmanschneider.com. **Contact:** Jane Gelfman, Deborah Schneider. Member of AAR. Represents 300+ clients. 10% of clients are new/unpublished writers.

REPRESENTS fiction and nonfiction books. **Considers these fiction areas:** literary, mainstream, mystery, women's.

☞ Does not want to receive romance, science fiction, Westerns, or children's books.

HOW TO CONTACT Query with SASE. Send queries via snail mail only. No unsolicited mss. Please send a query letter, a synopsis, and a SAMPLE CHAPTER ONLY. Responds in 1 month to queries. Responds in 2 months to mss.

TERMS Agent receives 15% commission on domestic sales. Agent receives 20% commission on foreign sales. Agent receives 15% commission on film sales. Offers written contract. Charges clients for photocopying and messengers/couriers.

BARRY GOLDBLATT LITERARY, LLC

320 Seventh Ave., #266, Brooklyn NY 11215. Fax: (718)360-5453. Website: www.bgliterary.com. **Contact:** Barry Goldblatt. Member of AAR, SCBWI.

MEMBER AGENTS Barry Goldblatt, Joe Monti, Beth Fleisher (kids work and graphic novels; she is particularly interested in finding new voices in middle grade and young adult fantasy, science fiction, mystery, historicals and action adventure).

REPRESENTS juvenile books. **Considers these fiction areas:** picture books, young adult, middle grade, all genres.

☞ This agency specializes in children's books of all kinds from picture books to young adult novels, across all genres.

HOW TO CONTACT E-mail queries to query@bgliterary.com, and include the first five pages and a synopsis of the novel pasted into the text of the e-mail. No attachments or links.

RECENT SALES *Prophecy: The Dragon King Chronicles*, by Ellen Oh; *Kiss Number Eight*, by Colleen af Venable; *The Mysterious Four Series*, by Dan Poblocki.

TIPS "We're a group of hands-on agents, with wide-ranging interests. Get us hooked with a great query letter, then convince us with an unforgettable manuscript."

FRANCES GOLDIN LITERARY AGENCY, INC.

57 E. 11th St., Suite 5B, New York NY 10003. (212)777-0047. Fax: (212)228-1660. E-mail: agency@goldinlit.com. Website: www.goldinlit.com. Estab. 1977. Member of AAR. Represents over 100 clients.

MEMBER AGENTS Frances Goldin, principal/agent; Ellen Geiger, agent (commercial and literary fiction and nonfiction, cutting-edge topics of all kinds); Matt McGowan, agent/rights director (innovative works of fiction and nonfiction); Sam Stoloff, agent (literary fiction, memoir, history, accessible sociology and philosophy, cultural studies, serious journalism, narrative and topical nonfiction with a progressive orientation); Sarah Bridgins, agent/office manager (literary fiction and nonfiction).

REPRESENTS nonfiction books, novels.

☞ "We are hands-on and we work intensively with clients on proposal and manuscript development." Does not want anything that is racist, sexist, agist, homophobic, or pornographic. No screenplays, children's books, art books, cookbooks, business books, diet books, romance, self-help, or genre fiction.

HOW TO CONTACT Query with SASE. No unsolicited mss or work previously submitted to publishers. Prefers hard-copy queries. If querying by e-mail, put word "query" in subject line. For queries to Sam Stoloff or Ellen Geiger, please use online submission form. Responds in 4–6 weeks to queries.

THE SUSAN GOLOMB LITERARY AGENCY

875 Avenue of the Americas, Suite 2302, New York NY 10001. Fax: (212)239-9503. E-mail: susan@sgolombagency.com; eliza@sgolombagency.com. **Contact:** Susan Golomb. Represents 100 clients. 20% of clients are new/unpublished writers. Currently handles: nonfiction books 50%, novels 40%, story collections 10%.

MEMBER AGENTS Susan Golomb (accepts queries); Sabine Hrechdakian (accepts queries); Kim Goldstein (no unsolicited queries).

REPRESENTS nonfiction books, novels, short story collections, novellas. **Considers these nonfiction areas:** animals, anthropology, archeology, autobiography, biography, business, current affairs, economics, environment, government, health, history, law, memoirs, military, money, popular culture, politics, psychology, science, sociology, technology, war, women's issues, women's studies. **Considers these fiction areas:** ethnic, historical, humor, literary, mainstream, satire, thriller, women's, young adult, chick lit.

8→ "We specialize in literary and upmarket fiction and nonfiction that is original, vibrant and of excellent quality and craft. Nonfiction should be edifying, paradigm-shifting, fresh and entertaining." Actively seeking writers with strong voices. Does not want to receive genre fiction.

HOW TO CONTACT Query with SASE. Submit outline/proposal, synopsis, 1 sample chapter, author bio, SASE. Query via mail or e-mail. Responds in 2 week to queries. Responds in 8 weeks to mss. Obtains most new clients through recommendations from others, solicitations.

TERMS Agent receives 15% commission on domestic sales. Agent receives 20% commission on foreign sales. Offers written contract.

RECENT SALES Sold 20 titles in the last year. *Sunnyside*, by Glen David Gold (Knopf); *How to Buy a Love of Reading*, by Tanya Egan Gibson (Dutton); *Telex From Cuba*, by Rachel Kushner (Scribner); *The Imperfectionists* by Tom Rachman (Dial).

⊙ GOODMAN ASSOCIATES

500 West End Ave., New York NY 10024-4317. (212)873-4806. Member of AAR.

8→ Accepting new clients by recommendation only.

① IRENE GOODMAN LITERARY AGENCY

27 W. 24th Street, Suite 700B, New York NY 10010. E-mail: queries@irenegoodman.com. Website: www.irenegoodman.com. **Contact:** Irene Goodman, Miriam Kriss. Member of AAR.

MEMBER AGENTS Irene Goodman; Miriam Kriss; Barbara Poelle; Jon Sternfeld.

REPRESENTS nonfiction books, novels. **Considers these nonfiction areas:** narrative nonfiction dealing with social, cultural and historical issues; an occasional memoir and current affairs book, parenting, social issues, francophilia, anglophilia, Judaica, lifestyles, cooking, memoir. **Considers these fiction areas:** historical, intelligent literary, modern urban fantasies, mystery, romance, thriller, women's.

8→ "Specializes in the finest in commercial fiction and nonfiction. We have a strong background in women's voices, including mysteries, romance, women's fiction, thrillers, suspense. Historical fiction is one of Irene's particular passions and Miriam is fanatical about modern urban fantasies. In nonfiction, Irene is looking for topics on narrative history, social issues and trends, education, Judaica, francophilia, anglophilia, other cultures, animals, food, crafts, and memoir." Barbara is looking for commercial thrillers with strong female protagonists; Miriam is looking for urban fantasy and edgy sci-fi/young adult. No children's picture books, screenplays, poetry, or inspirational fiction.

HOW TO CONTACT Query. Submit synopsis, first 10 pages. E-mail queries only! See the website submission page. No e-mail attachments. Responds in 2 months to queries.

RECENT SALES *The Ark*, by Boyd Morrison; *Isolation*, by C.J. Lyons; *The Sleepwalkers*, by Paul Grossman; *Dead Man's Moon*, by Devon Monk; *Becoming Marie Antoinette*, by Juliet Grey; *What's Up Down There*, by Lissa Rankin; *Beg for Mercy*, by Toni Andrews; *The Devil Inside*, by Jenna Black.

TIPS "We are receiving an unprecedented amount of e-mail queries. If you find that the mailbox is full, please try again in two weeks. E-mail queries to our personal addresses will not be answered. E-mails to our personal inboxes will be deleted."

◐ GOUMEN & SMIRNOVA LITERARY AGENCY

Nauki pr., 19/2 fl. 293, St. Petersburg 195220 Russia. E-mail: info@gs-agency.com. Website: www.gs-agency.com. **Contact:** Julia Goumen, Natalia Smirnova. Represents 20 clients. 10% of clients are new/unpublished writers. Currently handles: nonfiction books 10%, novels 80%, story collections 5%, juvenile books 5%.

• Prior to becoming agents, both Ms. Goumen and Ms. Smirnova worked as foreign rights managers with an established Russian publisher selling translation rights for literary fiction.

MEMBER AGENTS Julia Goumen (translation rights, Russian language rights, film rights); Natalia Smirnova (translation rights, Russian language rights, film rights).

REPRESENTS nonfiction books, novels, short story collections, novellas, movie, TV, TV movie, sitcom. **Considers these nonfiction areas:** biography, current affairs, ethnic, humor, memoirs, music. **Considers these fiction areas:** adventure, experimental, family, historical, horror, literary, mainstream, mystery, romance, thriller, young adult, women's. **Considers these script areas:** action, comedy, detective, family, mainstream, romantic comedy, romantic drama, teen, thriller.

⊶🖝 "We are the first full-service agency in Russia, representing our authors in book publishing, film, television, and other areas. We are also the first agency, representing Russian authors worldwide, based in Russia. The agency also represents international authors, agents and publishers in Russia. Our philosophy is to provide an individual approach to each author, finding the right publisher both at home and across international cultural and linguistic borders, developing original marketing and promotional strategies for each title." Actively seeking manuscripts written in Russian, both literary and commercial; and foreign publishers and agents with the high-profile fiction and general nonfiction list—to represent in Russia. Does not want to receive unpublished manuscripts in languages other then Russian, or any information irrelevant to our activity.

HOW TO CONTACT Query with SASE. Submit synopsis, author bio. Accepts simultaneous submissions. Responds in 14 days to mss. Obtains most new clients through recommendations from others, solicitations.

TERMS Agent receives 20% commission on domestic sales. Agent receives 20% commission on foreign sales. Offers written contract, binding for 1 year; 2-month notice must be given to terminate contract.

➊🌑 DOUG GRAD LITERARY AGENCY, INC.

156 Prospect Park West, Brooklyn NY 11215. (718)788-6067. E-mail: doug.grad@dgliterary.com. E-mail: query@dgliterary.com. Website: www.dgliterary.com. **Contact:** Doug Grad. Estab. 2008.

- Prior to being an agent, Doug Grad spent the last 22 years as an editor at 4 major publishing houses.

HOW TO CONTACT Query by e-mail first at query@dgliterary.com. No sample material unless requested.
RECENT SALES *Drink the Tea*, by Thomas Kaufman (St. Martin's); *15 Minutes: The Impossible Math of Nuclear War*, by L. Douglas Keeney (St. Martin's).

➋🌑 GRAHAM MAW CHRISTIE LITERARY AGENCY

19 Thornhill Crescent, London England N1 1BJ United Kingdom. (44)(207)812-9937; 0(207) 609 1326. E-mail: enquiries@grahammawchristie.com; info@grahammawchristie.com. Website: www.grahammawchristie.com. Represents 40 clients. 30% of clients are new/unpublished writers. Currently handles: nonfiction books 100%.

- Prior to opening her agency, Ms. Graham Maw was a publishing director at HarperCollins and worked in rights, publicity and editorial. She has ghostwritten several nonfiction books, which gives her an insider's knowledge of both the publishing industry and the pleasures and pitfalls of authorship. Ms. Christie has a background in advertising and journalism.

MEMBER AGENTS Jane Graham Maw; Jennifer Christie.

REPRESENTS nonfiction books. **Considers these nonfiction areas:** autobiography, biography, child guidance, cooking, diet/nutrition, foods, health, how-to, medicine, memoirs, parenting, popular culture, psychology, self-help.

⊶🖝 "We aim to make the publishing process easier and smoother for authors. We work hard to ensure that publishing proposals are watertight before submission. We aim for collaborative relationships with publishers so that we provide the right books to the right editor at the right time. We represent ghostwriters as well as authors." Actively seeking work from UK writers only. Does not want to receive fiction, poetry, children's books, plays or e-mail submissions.

HOW TO CONTACT "Our books are currently full. We will open them again: please check the website for updates." Query with synopsis, chapter outline, bio, SASE. Responds in 2 weeks to queries. Obtains most new clients through recommendations from others.

TERMS Agent receives 15% commission on domestic sales. Agent receives 20% commission on foreign

sales. Offers written contract; 30-day notice must be given to terminate contract.

WRITERS CONFERENCES London Book Fair, Frankfurt Book Fair.

TIPS "UK clients only!"

GRAND STREET LITERARY AGENCY

66 Grand St., Suite 1, New York NY 10013. (212)226-1398. E-mail: mecoy@aol.com. Website: www.grand streetliterary.com. **Contact:** Bob Mecoy.

MEMBER AGENTS Bob Mecoy.

○━┳ Fiction (literary, crime, romance); nonfiction (true crime, finance, memoir, literary, prescriptive self-help & graphic novelists). No Westerns.

HOW TO CONTACT Query with sample chapters and synopsis.

● ASHLEY GRAYSON LITERARY AGENCY

1342 W. 18th St., San Pedro CA 90732. Fax: (310)514-1148. E-mail: graysonagent@earthlink.net. Website: www.graysonagency.com/blog. Estab. 1976. Member of AAR. Represents 100 clients. 5% of clients are new/unpublished writers. Currently handles: nonfiction books 20%, novels 50%, juvenile books 30%.

MEMBER AGENTS Ashley Grayson (fantasy, mystery, thrillers, young adult); Carolyn Grayson (chick lit, mystery, children's, nonfiction, women's fiction, romance, thrillers); Denise Dumars (mind/body/spirit, women's fiction, dark fantasy/horror); Lois Winston (women's fiction, chick lit, mystery).

REPRESENTS nonfiction books, novels. **Considers these nonfiction areas:** business, computers, economics, history, investigative, popular culture, science, self-help, sports, technology, true crime, mind/body/spirit, lifestyle. **Considers these fiction areas:** fantasy, juvenile, multicultural, mystery, romance, science fiction, suspense, women's, young adult, chick lit.

○━┳ "We prefer to work with published (traditional print), established authors. We will give first consideration to authors who come recommended to us by our clients or other publishing professionals. We accept a very small number of new, previously unpublished authors. The agency is temporarily closed to queries from writers who are not published at book length (self published or print-on-demand do not count). There are only three exceptions to this policy: (1) Unpublished authors who have re- ceived an offer from a reputable publisher, who need an agent before beginning contract negotiations; (2) Authors who are recommended by a published author, editor or agent who has read the work in question; (3) Authors whom we have met at conferences and from whom we have requested submissions." **Unpublished authors - Nonfiction:** "Authors who are recognized within their field or area may still query with proposals. We are seeking more mysteries and thrillers."

HOW TO CONTACT As of early 2011, the agency was only open to fiction authors with publishing credits (no self-published). For nonfiction, only writers with great platforms will be considered.

TERMS Agent receives 15% commission on domestic sales. Agent receives 20% commission on foreign sales.

● SANFORD J. GREENBURGER ASSOCIATES, INC.

55 Fifth Ave., New York NY 10003. (212)206-5600. Fax: (212)463-8718. E-mail: queryHL@sjga.com. Website: www.greenburger.com. Member of AAR. Represents 500 clients.

MEMBER AGENTS Heide Lange; Faith Hamlin; Dan Mandel; Matthew Bialer; Courtney Miller-Callihan, Michael Harriot, Brenda Bowen (authors and illustrators of children's books for all ages as well as graphic novelists); Lisa Gallagher.

REPRESENTS nonfiction books and novels. **Considers these nonfiction areas:** Americana, animals, anthropology, archeology, architecture, art, biography, business, computers, cooking, crafts, current affairs, decorating, diet/nutrition, design, education, environment, ethnic, film, foods, gardening, gay/lesbian, government, health, history, horticulture, how-to, humor, interior design, investigative, juvenile nonfiction, language, law, literature, medicine, memoirs, metaphysics, military, money, multicultural, music, New Age, philosophy, photography, popular culture, psychology, recreation, regional, romance, science, sex, sociology, software, sports, theater, translation, travel, true crime, women's issues, women's studies, young adult. **Considers these fiction areas:** action, adventure, crime, detective, ethnic, family saga, feminist, gay, glitz, historical, humor, lesbian, literary, mainstream, mystery, police, psychic, regional, satire, sports, supernatural, suspense, thriller.

○━┳ No Westerns. No screenplays.

HOW TO CONTACT Submit query, first 3 chapters, synopsis, brief bio, SASE. Accepts simultaneous submissions. Responds in 2 months to queries and mss. Responds to mss. Obtains most new clients through recommendations from others.

TERMS Agent receives 15% commission on domestic sales. Agent receives 20% commission on foreign sales. Charges for photocopying and books for foreign and subsidiary rights submissions.

◑ KATHRYN GREEN LITERARY AGENCY, LLC

250 West 57th St., Suite 2302, New York NY 10107. (212)245-2445. Fax: (212)245-2040. E-mail: query@ kgreenagency.com. **Contact:** Kathy Green. Other memberships include Women's Media Group. Represents approximately 20 clients. 50% of clients are new/unpublished writers. Currently handles: nonfiction books 50%, novels 25%, juvenile books 25%.

- Prior to becoming an agent, Ms. Green was a book and magazine editor.

REPRESENTS nonfiction books, novels, short story collections, juvenile, middle grade and young adult only). **Considers these nonfiction areas:** autobiography, biography, business, child guidance, cooking, current affairs, diet/nutrition, economics, education, foods, history, how-to, humor, interior design, investigative, juvenile nonfiction, memoirs, parenting, popular culture, psychology, satire, self-help, sports, true crime, women's issues, women's studies. **Considers these fiction areas:** crime, detective, family saga, historical, humor, juvenile, literary, mainstream, mystery, police, romance, satire, suspense, thriller, women's, young adult.

⊶ Keeping the client list small means that writers receive my full attention throughout the process of getting their project published. Does not want to receive science fiction or fantasy.

HOW TO CONTACT Query to query@kgreenagency.com. Send no samples unless requested. Accepts simultaneous submissions. Responds in 1-2 months to mss. Obtains most new clients through recommendations from others, solicitations, conferences.

TERMS Agent receives 15% commission on domestic sales. Agent receives 20% commission on foreign sales. No written contract.

RECENT SALES *The Touch Series* by Laurie Stolarz; *How Do You Light a Fart,* by Bobby Mercer; *Creepiosity,* by David Bickel; *Hidden Facets: Diamonds For the Dead* by Alan Orloff; *Don't Stalk the Admissions Officer,* by Risa Lewak; *Designed Fat Girl,* by Jennifer Joyner.

TIPS "This agency offers a written agreement."

◔◑ GREGORY & CO. AUTHORS' AGENTS

3 Barb Mews, Hammersmith, London W6 7PA England. (44)(207)610-4676. Fax: (44)(207)610-4686. E-mail: info@gregoryandcompany.co.uk. E-mail: mary jones@gregoryandcompany.co.uk. Website: www.greg oryandcompany.co.uk. **Contact:** Jane Gregory. Other memberships include AAA. Represents 60 clients. Currently handles: nonfiction books 10%, novels 90%.

MEMBER AGENTS Stephanie Glencross.

REPRESENTS nonfiction books, novels. **Considers these nonfiction areas:** autobiography, biography, history. **Considers these fiction areas:** crime, detective, historical, literary, mainstream, police, thriller, contemporary women's fiction.

⊶ As a British agency, we do not generally take on American authors. Actively seeking well-written, accessible modern novels. Does not want to receive horror, science fiction, fantasy, mind/body/spirit, children's books, screenplays, plays, short stories or poetry.

HOW TO CONTACT Query with SASE. Submit outline, first 10 pages by e-mail or post, publishing history, author bio. Send submissions to Mary Jones, submissions editor: maryjones@gregoryandcompany. co.uk. Accepts simultaneous submissions. Returns materials only with SASE. Obtains most new clients through recommendations from others, conferences.

TERMS Agent receives 15% commission on domestic sales. Agent receives 20% commission on foreign sales. Offers written contract; 1-month notice must be given to terminate contract. Charges clients for photocopying of whole typescripts and copies of book for submissions.

RECENT SALES *Ritual,* by Mo Hader (Bantam UK/ Grove Atlantic); *A Darker Domain,* by Val McDermid (HarperCollins UK); *The Chameleon's Shadow,* by Minette Walters (Macmillan UK/Knopf, Inc); *Stratton's War,* by Laura Wilson (Orion UK/St. Martin's).

WRITERS CONFERENCES CWA Conference; Bouchercon.

● BLANCHE C. GREGORY, INC.

2 Tudor City Place, New York NY 10017. (212)697-0828. E-mail: info@bcgliteraryagency.com. Website: www.bcgliteraryagency.com. Member of AAR.

REPRESENTS nonfiction books, novels, juvenile.

8—**π** This agency specializes in adult fiction and nonfiction; children's literature is also considered. Does not want to receive screenplays, stage plays or teleplays.

HOW TO CONTACT Submit query, brief synopsis, bio, SASE. No e-mail queries. Online submission form available at website. Obtains most new clients through recommendations from others.

● GREYHAUS LITERARY

3021 20th St., PL SW, Puyallup WA 98373. E-mail: scott@greyhausagency.com. Website: www.greyhausagency.com. **Contact:** Scott Eagan, member RWA. Estab. 2003.

REPRESENTS fiction, novels. **Considers these fiction areas:** romance, women's.

8—**π** "We specialize in romance, women's fiction and young adult romance." Actively seeking contemporary romance, and stories that are 75,000-100,000 words in length. Does not want sci-fi, fantasy, inspirational, literary, futuristic, erotica, writers targeting e-pubs, young adult.

HOW TO CONTACT Send a query, the first 3 pages and a synopsis of no more than 3 pages. There is also a submission form on this agency's website.

● JILL GRINBERG LITERARY AGENCY

16 Court St., Suite 3306, Brooklyn NY 11241. (212)620-5883. Fax: (212)627-4725. E-mail: info@grinbergliterary.com. Website: www.grinbergliterary.com.

• Prior to her current position, Ms. Grinberg was at Anderson Grinberg Literary Management.

MEMBER AGENTS Jill Grinberg; Kirsten Wolf (foreign rights).

REPRESENTS nonfiction books, novels. **Considers these nonfiction areas:** autobiography, biography, business, current affairs, economics, government, health, history, law, medicine, multicultural, politics, psychology, science, spirituality, technology, travel, women's issues, women's studies. **Considers these fiction areas:** commercial, fantasy, historical, juvenile, literary, romance, science fiction, women's, young adult, middle grade.

HOW TO CONTACT Query with SASE. Send a proposal and author bio for nonfiction; send a query, synopsis and the first 50 pages for fiction.

TIPS "We prefer submissions by mail."

● JILL GROSJEAN LITERARY AGENCY

1390 Millstone Road, Sag Harbor NY 11963-2214. (631)725-7419. Fax: (631)725-8632. E-mail: jill6981@aol.com. **Contact:** Jill Grosjean. Represents 40 clients. 100% of clients are new/unpublished writers. Currently handles: novels 100%.

• Prior to becoming an agent, Ms. Grosjean was manager of an independent bookstore. She has also worked in publishing and advertising.

REPRESENTS novels. **Considers these fiction areas:** historical, literary, mainstream, mystery, regional, romance, suspense.

8—**π** This agency offers some editorial assistance (i.e., line-by-line edits). Actively seeking literary novels and mysteries.

HOW TO CONTACT E-mail queries only, no attachments. No cold calls, please. Accepts simultaneous submissions. Responds in 1 week to queries. Responds in 1 month to mss. Obtains most new clients through recommendations from others, solicitations.

TERMS Agent receives 15% commission on domestic sales. Agent receives 20% commission on foreign sales. No written contract. Charges clients for photocopying and mailing expenses.

RECENT SALES *Threading the Needle,* by Marie Bostwick (Kensington Publishers); *A Spark Of Death,* by Bernadette Pajer, (Poison Pen Press); *A Single Thread* and *Thread of Truth, A Thread So Thin, Snow Angels,* by Marie Bostwick (Kensington); *Greasing the Pinata* and *Jump,* by Tim Maleeny (Poison Pen Press); *Shame and No Idea,* by Greg Garrett, David C. Cook; *The Reluctant Journey of David Conners.*

WRITERS CONFERENCES Book Passage's Mystery Writers' Conference; Agents and Editors Conference; Texas Writers' and Agents' Conference.

● LAURA GROSS LITERARY AGENCY

39 Chester Street, Suite 301, Newton Highlands MA 02461. (617)964-2977. Fax: (617)964-3023. E-mail: query@lg-la.com. **Contact:** Laura Gross. Represents 30 clients. Currently handles: nonfiction books 40%, novels 50%, scholarly books 10%.

• Prior to becoming an agent, Ms. Gross was an editor.

REPRESENTS nonfiction books, novels. **Considers these nonfiction areas:** autobiography, biography, child guidance, cultural interests, current affairs, ethnic, government, health, history, law, medicine, memoirs, parenting, popular culture, politics, psychology, sports, women's issues, women's studies. **Considers these fiction areas:** historical, literary, mainstream, mystery, suspense, thriller.

HOW TO CONTACT Submit online at: http://lauragrossliteraryagency.com/submission. Query with SASE or by e-mail. Submit author bio. Responds in several days to queries. Obtains most new clients through recommendations from others.

TERMS Agent receives 15% commission on domestic sales. Agent receives 20% commission on foreign sales. Offers written contract.

HALSTON FREEMAN LITERARY AGENCY, INC.

140 Broadway, 46th Floor, New York NY 10005. E-mail: queryhalstonfreemanliterary@hotmail.com. **Contact:** Molly Freeman, Betty Halston. Currently handles: nonfiction books 65%, novels 35%.

• Prior to becoming an agent, Ms. Halston was a marketing and promotion director for a local cable affiliate; Ms. Freeman was a television film editor and ad agency copywriter.

MEMBER AGENTS Molly Freeman, Betty Halston.
REPRESENTS nonfiction books, novels. **Considers these nonfiction areas:** autobiography, biography, business, child guidance, cultural interests, current affairs, economics, ethnic, gay/lesbian, government, health, history, horticulture, how-to, humor, investigative, law, medicine, memoirs, metaphysics, New Age, parenting, politics, psychology, satire, self-help, true crime, women's issues, women's studies. **Considers these fiction areas:** action, adventure, crime, detective, ethnic, feminist, frontier, historical, horror, humor, literary, mainstream, mystery, police, romance, satire, science fiction, suspense, thriller, Westerns, women's.

➛ "We are a hands-on agency specializing in quality nonfiction and fiction. As a new agency, it is imperative that we develop relationships with good writers who are smart, hardworking and understand what's required of them to promote their books." Does not want

to receive children's books, textbooks or poetry. Send no e-mail attachments.

HOW TO CONTACT Query with SASE. For nonfiction, include sample chapters, synopsis, platform, bio and competitive titles. For fiction, include synopsis, bio and three sample chapters. No e-mail attachments. Accepts simultaneous submissions. Responds in 2-6 weeks to queries. Responds in 1-2 months to mss. Obtains most new clients through recommendations from others, solicitations, conferences.

TERMS Agent receives 15% commission on domestic sales. Agent receives 20% commission on foreign sales. This agency charges clients for copying and postage directly related to the project.

HARTLINE LITERARY AGENCY

123 Queenston Dr., Pittsburgh PA 15235-5429. (412)829-2483. Fax: (412)829-2432. E-mail: joyce@hartlineliterary.com. Website: www.hartlineliterary.com. **Contact:** Joyce A. Hart. Represents 40 clients. 20% of clients are new/unpublished writers. Currently handles: nonfiction books 40%, novels 60%.

MEMBER AGENTS Joyce A. Hart, principal agent; Terry Burns: terry@hartlineliterary.com; Tamela Hancock Murray: tamela@hartlineliterary.com; Diana Flegal: diana@hartlineliterary.com.

REPRESENTS nonfiction books, novels. **Considers these nonfiction areas:** business, child guidance, cooking, diet/nutrition, economics, foods, inspirational, money, parenting, religious, self-help, women's issues, women's studies. **Considers these fiction areas:** action, adventure, contemporary issues, family saga, historical, inspirational, literary, mystery, regional, religious, suspense, thriller, amateur sleuth, cozy, contemporary, gothic, historical, and regency romances.

➛ "This agency specializes in the Christian bookseller market." Actively seeking adult fiction, self-help, nutritional books, devotional, and business. Does not want to receive erotica, gay/lesbian, fantasy, horror, etc.

HOW TO CONTACT Submit summary/outline, author bio, 3 sample chapters. Accepts simultaneous submissions. Responds in 2 months to queries. Responds in 3 months to mss. Obtains most new clients through recommendations from others.

TERMS Agent receives 15% commission on domestic sales. Offers written contract.

RECENT SALES *Aurora, An American Experience*

in *Quilt, Community and Craft*, and *A Flickering Light*, by Jane Kirkpatrick (Waterbrook Multnomah); *Oprah Doesn't Know My Name* by Jane Kirkpatrick (Zondervan); *Paper Roses, Scattered Petals, and Summer Rains*, by Amanda Cabot (Revell Books); *Blood Ransom*, by Lisa Harris (Zondervan); *I Don't Want a Divorce*, by David Clark (Revell Books); *Love Finds You in Hope, Kansas*, by Pamela Griffin (Summerside Press); Journey to the Well, by Diana Wallis Taylor (Revell Books); *Paper Bag Christmas, The Nine Lessons* by Kevin Milne (Center Street); *When Your Aging Parent Needs Care* by Arrington & Atchley (Harvest House); *Katie at Sixteen* by Kim Vogel Sawyer (Zondervan); *A Promise of Spring*, by Kim Vogel Sawyer (Bethany House); *The Big 5-OH!*, by Sandra Bricker (Abingdon Press); A *Silent Terror & A Silent Stalker*, by Lynette Eason (Steeple Hill); Extreme Devotion series, by Kathi Macias (New Hope Publishers); *On the Wings of the Storm*, by Tamira Barley (Whitaker House); Tribute, by Graham Garrison (Kregel Publications); *The Birth to Five Book*, by Brenda Nixon (Revell Books); *Fat to Skinny Fast and Easy*, by Doug Varrieur (Sterling Publishers).

ANTONY HARWOOD LIMITED

103 Walton St., Oxford OX2 6EB England. +44 01865 559 615. Fax: +44 01865 310 660. E-mail: mail@antonyharwood.com. Website: www.antonyharwood.com. **Contact:** Antony Harwood, James Macdonald Lockhart. Estab. 2000. Represents 52 clients.

- Prior to starting this agency, Mr. Harwood and Mr. Lockhart worked at publishing houses and other literary agencies.

MEMBER AGENTS Antony Harwood, James Macdonald Lockhart, Jo Williamson (children's).
REPRESENTS nonfiction books, novels. **Considers these nonfiction areas:** Americana, animals, anthropology, archeology, architecture, art, autobiography, biography, business, child guidance, computers, cooking, current affairs, design, economics, education, environment, ethnic, film, gardening, gay/lesbian, government, health, history, horticulture, how-to, humor, language, memoirs, military, money, multicultural, music, parenting, philosophy, photography, popular culture, psychology, recreation, regional, science, self-help, sex, sociology, software, spirituality, sports, technology, translation, travel, true crime, war, women's issues, women's studies. **Considers these fiction areas:** action, adventure,

cartoon, comic books, confession, crime, detective, erotica, ethnic, experimental, family saga, fantasy, feminist, frontier, gay, hi-lo, historical, horror, humor, lesbian, literary, mainstream, military, multicultural, multimedia, mystery, occult, picture books, plays, police, regional, religious, romance, satire, science fiction, spiritual, sports, suspense, thriller, translation, war, Westerns, young adult, gothic.

☞ "We accept every genre of fiction and nonfiction except for children's fiction for readers ages 10 and younger." No poetry or screenplays.

HOW TO CONTACT Submit outline, 2-3 sample chapters via e-mail in a Word or RTF format or postal mail (include SASE or IRC). Responds in 2 months to queries.

TERMS Agent receives 15% commission on domestic sales. Agent receives 20% commission on foreign sales.

JOHN HAWKINS & ASSOCIATES, INC.

71 W. 23rd St., Suite 1600, New York NY 10010. (212)807-7040. Fax: (212)807-9555. E-mail: jha@jhalit.com. Website: www.jhalit.com. **Contact:** Moses Cardona (moses@jhalit.com). Member of AAR. Represents over 100 clients. 5-10% of clients are new/unpublished writers. Currently handles: nonfiction books 40%, novels 40%, juvenile books 20%.

MEMBER AGENTS Moses Cardona; Anne Hawkins (ahawkins@jhalit.com); Warren Frazier (frazier@jhalit.com); William Reiss (reiss@jhalit.com).
REPRESENTS nonfiction books, novels, young adult. **Considers these nonfiction areas:** agriculture, Americana, anthropology, archeology, architecture, art, autobiography, biography, business, cultural interests, current affairs, design, economics, education, ethnic, film, gardening, gay/lesbian, government, health, history, horticulture, how-to, investigative, language, law, medicine, memoirs, money, multicultural, music, philosophy, popular culture, politics, psychology, recreation, science, self-help, sex, sociology, software, theater, travel, true crime, young adult, music, creative nonfiction. **Considers these fiction areas:** action, adventure, crime, detective, ethnic, experimental, family saga, feminist, frontier, gay, glitz, hi-lo, historical, inspirational, lesbian, literary, mainstream, military, multicultural, multimedia, mystery, police, psychic, religious, short story collections, sports, supernatu-

ral, suspense, thriller, translation, war, Westerns, women's, young adult.

HOW TO CONTACT Submit query, proposal package, outline, SASE. Accepts simultaneous submissions. Responds in 1 month to queries. Obtains most new clients through recommendations from others.

TERMS Agent receives 15% commission on domestic sales. Agent receives 20% commission on foreign sales. Charges clients for photocopying.

RECENT SALES *Celebration of Shoes*, by Eileen Spinelli; *Chaos*, by Martin Gross; *The Informationist*, by Taylor Stevens; *The Line*, by Olga Grushin.

● HEACOCK HILL LITERARY AGENCY, INC.

West Coast Office, 1020 Hollywood Way, #439, Burbank CA 91505. (505)585-0111. E-mail: agent@heacockhill.com. Website: www.heacockhill.com. **Contact:** Catt LeBaigue or Tom Dark. Member of AAR. Other memberships include SCBWI.

- Prior to becoming an agent, Ms. LeBaigue spent 18 years with Sony Pictures and Warner Bros.

MEMBER AGENTS Tom Dark (adult fiction, nonfiction); Catt LeBaigue (juvenile fiction, adult nonfiction including arts, crafts, anthropolgy, astronomy, nature studies, ecology, body/mind/spirit, humanities, self-help).

REPRESENTS nonfiction, fiction. **Considers these nonfiction areas:** hiking.

HOW TO CONTACT E-mail queries only. No unsolicited manuscripts. No e-mail attachments. Responds in 1 week to queries. Obtains most new clients through recommendations from others, solicitations.

TERMS Offers written contract.

TIPS "Write an informative original e-query expressing your book idea, your qualifications, and short excerpts of the work. No unfinished work, please."

☉ HELEN HELLER AGENCY INC.

4-216 Heath Street West, Toronto Ontario M5P 1N7 Canada. (416)489-0396. E-mail: info@helenhelleragency.com. Website: www.helenhelleragency.com. **Contact:** Helen Heller. Represents 30+ clients.

- Prior to her current position, Ms. Heller worked for Cassell & Co. (England), was an editor for Harlequin Books, a senior editor for Avon Books, and editor-in-chief for Fitzhenry & Whiteside.

MEMBER AGENTS Helen Heller, helen@helenhelleragency.com; Daphne Hart, daphne.hart@sympatico.ca; Sarah Heller, sarah@helenhelleragency.com.

REPRESENTS nonfiction books, novels.

⊶ Actively seeking adult fiction and nonfiction (excluding children's literature, screenplays or genre fiction). Does not want to receive screenplays, poetry, or young children's picture books.

HOW TO CONTACT Submit synopsis, publishing history, author bio. Online submission form available at website. Responds in 6 weeks. Obtains most new clients through recommendations from others, solicitations.

RECENT SALES *Break on Through*, by Jill Murray (Doubleday Canada); *Womankind: Faces of Change Around the World*, by Donna Nebenzahl (Raincoast Books); *One Dead Indian: The Premier, The Police, and the Ipperwash Crisis*, by Peter Edwards (McClelland & Stewart); a full list of deals is available online.

TIPS "Whether you are an author searching for an agent, or whether an agent has approached you, it is in your best interest to first find out who the agent represents, what publishing houses has that agent sold to recently and what foreign sales have been made. You should be able to go to the bookstore, or search online and find the books the agent refers to. Many authors acknowledge their agents in the front or back or their books."

◑ RICHARD HENSHAW GROUP

22 W. 23rd St., 5th Floor, New York NY 10010. E-mail: submissions@henshaw.com. Website: www.richh.addr.com. **Contact:** Rich Henshaw. Member of AAR. Other memberships include SinC, MWA, HWA, SFWA, RWA. 20% of clients are new/unpublished writers. Currently handles: nonfiction books 35%, novels 65%.

- Prior to opening his agency, Mr. Henshaw served as an agent with Richard Curtis Associates, Inc.

REPRESENTS nonfiction books, novels. **Considers these nonfiction areas:** animals, autobiography, biography, business, child guidance, cooking, current affairs, dance, economics, environment, foods, gay/lesbian, health, humor, investigative, money, music, New Age, parenting, popular culture, politics, psychology, science, self-help, sociology, sports, technology, true crime, women's issues, women's studies, electronic. **Considers these fiction areas:** action, adventure, crime, detective, ethnic, family saga, historical, humor, literary, mainstream, mystery, police, psychic, romance, satire, science fiction, sports, supernatural, suspense, thriller.

☞ This agency specializes in thrillers, mysteries, science fiction, fantasy and horror.

HOW TO CONTACT Query with SASE. Accepts multiple submissions. Responds in 3 weeks to queries. Responds in 6 weeks to mss. Obtains most new clients through recommendations from others, solicitations, conferences.

TERMS Agent receives 15% commission on domestic sales. Agent receives 20% commission on foreign sales. No written contract. Charges clients for photocopying and book orders.

RECENT SALES *Though Not Dead*, by Dana Stabenow; *The Perfect Suspect*, by Margaret Coel; *City of Ruins*, by Kristine Kathryn Rusch; *A Dead Man's Tale*, by James D. Doss; *Wickedly Charming*, by Kristine Grayson, History of the World series by Susan Wise Bauer; *Notorious Pleasures*, by Elizabeth Hoyt.

TIPS "While we do not have any reason to believe that our submission guidelines will change in the near future, writers can find up-to-date submission policy information on our website. Always include a SASE with correct return postage."

◑ HIDDEN VALUE GROUP

1240 E. Ontario Ave., Ste. 102-148, Corona CA 92881. (951)549-8891. Fax: (951)549-8891. Website: www.hiddenvaluegroup.com. **Contact:** Nancy Jernigan. Represents 55 clients. 10% of clients are new/unpublished writers.

MEMBER AGENTS Jeff Jernigan, jjernigan@hiddenvaluegroup.com (men's nonfiction, fiction, Bible studies/curriculum, marriage and family); Nancy Jernigan, njernigan@hiddenvaluegroup.com (nonfiction, women's issues, inspiration, marriage and family, fiction).

REPRESENTS nonfiction books and adult fiction; no poetry. **Considers these nonfiction areas:** autobiography, biography, business, child guidance, economics, history, how-to, inspirational, juvenile nonfiction, language, literature, memoirs, money, parenting, psychology, religious, self-help, women's issues, women's studies. **Considers these fiction areas:** action, adventure, crime, detective, fantasy, frontier, inspirational, literary, police, religious, thriller, Westerns, women's.

☞ "The Hidden Value Group specializes in helping authors throughout their publishing career. We believe that every author has a special message to be heard and we specialize in getting that message out." Actively seeking established fiction authors, and authors who are focusing on women's issues. Does not want to receive poetry or short stories.

HOW TO CONTACT Query with SASE. Submit synopsis, 2 sample chapters, author bio, and marketing and speaking summary. Accepts queries to bookquery@hiddenvaluegroup.com. No fax queries. Responds in 1 month to queries. Responds in 1 month to mss. Obtains most new clients through recommendations from others, solicitations.

TERMS Agent receives 15% commission on domestic sales. Agent receives 15% commission on foreign sales. Offers written contract.

WRITERS CONFERENCES Glorieta Christian Writers' Conference; CLASS Publishing Conference.

● JULIE A. HILL AND ASSOC, LLC

1155 Camino Del Mar, #530, Del Mar CA 92014. (858)259-2595. Fax: (858)259-2777. **Contact:** Julie Hill. Represents 50 clients. 20% of clients are new/unpublished writers. Currently handles: nonfiction books 90%, story collections 5%, other 5% books that accompany films.

MEMBER AGENTS Julie Hill, agent and publicist.

REPRESENTS nonfiction books. **Considers these nonfiction areas:** biography, cooking, ethnic, health, history, how-to, language, memoirs, music, New Age, popular culture, psychology, religious, self-help, women's issues.

☞ Currently interested in finding memoirs from wives and adult children of drug lords, known criminals, and those in polygamist marriages. Actively seeking travel, health, and media tie-ins. Does not want to receive horror, juvenile, sci-fi, thrillers or autobiographies of any kind.

HOW TO CONTACT Snail mail: Query with SASE. Submit outline/proposal, SASE. Accepts simultaneous submissions: Yes. Responds in 4-6 weeks to queries. E-submissions, please send to: Hillagent@aol.com. Accepts simultaneous submissions. Responds in 4-6 weeks to queries. Obtains most new clients through recommendations from other authors, editors, and agents.

RECENT SALES best-selling *Publish This Book,* by Stephen Markley, reviewed by PW, Huff Post and many many others. *Cracking Up*, from the book *The Happy Neurotic*, by David Granirer, to GRBTV. Travel: multiple titles to Frommers (Wiley) for kids travel and theme parks guides, by Laura Lea Miller, Barnes and Noble travel bestsellers. Falcon (Globe Pequot) hiking guides: *Best Easy Day Hikes to Long Island*, and others by Susan Finch. *Insiders Guides, Off the Beaten Path*, Best Day Trips to multiple US cities by multiple authors, including New York City, Chicago, Seattle, Houston, Palm Beach (Fla.) and many more.

● BARBARA HOGENSON AGENCY

165 West End Ave., Suite 19-C, New York NY 10023. (212)874-8084. Fax: (212)362-3011. E-mail: bhogenson@aol.com. **Contact:** Barbara Hogenson, Lori Styler, Contract Manager. Member of AAR.

HOW TO CONTACT Query with SASE. Obtains most new clients through recommendations from other clients only.

TIPS "We do not specialize in mystery."

HOPKINS LITERARY ASSOCIATES

2117 Buffalo Rd., Suite 327, Rochester NY 14624-1507. (585)352-6268. **Contact:** Pam Hopkins. Member of AAR. Other memberships include RWA. Represents 30 clients. 5% of clients are new/unpublished writers. Currently handles: novels 100%.

REPRESENTS novels. **Considers these fiction areas:** mostly women's genre romance, historical, contemporary, category, women's.

8→ This agency specializes in women's fiction, particularly historical, contemporary, and category romance, as well as mainstream work.

HOW TO CONTACT Regular mail with synopsis, 3 sample chapters, SASE. Accepts simultaneous submissions. Responds in 2 weeks to queries. Responds in 1 month to mss. Obtains most new clients through recommendations from others, solicitations, conferences.

TERMS Agent receives 15% commission on domestic sales. Agent receives 20% commission on foreign sales. No written contract.

RECENT SALES Sold 50 titles in the last year. *The Wilting Bloom Series* by Madeline Hunter (Berkley);

The Dead Travel Fast, by Deanna Raybourn; *Baggage Claim*, by Tanya Michna (NAL).

WRITERS CONFERENCES RWA National Conference.

● HORNFISCHER LITERARY MANAGEMENT

P.O. Box 50544, Austin TX 78763. E-mail: queries@hornfischerlit.com. Website: www.hornfischerlit.com. **Contact:** James D. Hornfischer, president. Represents 45 clients. 10% of clients are new/unpublished writers. Currently handles: nonfiction books 100%.

• Prior to opening his agency, Mr. Hornfischer held editorial positions at HarperCollins and McGraw-Hill. "My New York editorial background working with a variety of bestselling authors, such as Erma Bombeck, Jared Diamond, and Erica Jong, is useful in this regard. In 17 years as an agent, I've handled twelve *New York Times* nonfiction bestsellers, including three No. 1's."

REPRESENTS nonfiction books. **Considers these nonfiction areas:** anthropology, archeology, autobiography, biography, business, child guidance, current affairs, economics, environment, government, health, history, how-to, humor, inspirational, investigative, law, medicine, memoirs, military, money, multicultural, parenting, popular culture, politics, psychology, religious, satire, science, self-help, sociology, sports, technology, true crime, war.

8→ Actively seeking the best work of terrific writers. Does not want poetry or genre fiction.

HOW TO CONTACT E-mail queries only. Submit proposal package, outline, 2 sample chapters. Accepts simultaneous submissions. Responds in 5-6 weeks to submissions. Obtains most new clients through referrals from clients, reading books and magazines, pursuing ideas with New York editors.

TERMS Agent receives 15% commission on domestic sales. Agent receives 25% commission on foreign sales. Offers written contract. Reasonable expenses deducted from proceeds after book is sold.

RECENT SALES *The Next 100 Years*, by George Friedman (Doubleday); *Traitor to His Class* by H. W. Brands (Doubleday); *Scent of the Missing,* by Susannah Charleson (Houghton Mifflin Harcourt); *Red November* by W. Craig Reed (Morrow); and *Abigail Adams,* by Woody Holton (Free Press). See agency website for more sales information.

TIPS "When you query agents and send out proposals, present yourself as someone who's in command of his material and comfortable in his own skin. Too many writers have a palpable sense of anxiety and insecurity. Take a deep breath and realize that—if you're good—someone in the publishing world will want you."

● ANDREA HURST LITERARY MANAGEMENT

For Andrea Hurst and Vickie Motter P.O. Box 1467, Coupeville WA 98239. For Gordon Warnock: P.O. Box 19010, Sacramento CA 95819. E-mail: andrea@andreahurst.com. Website: www.andreahurst.com. **Contact:** Andrea Hurst, Judy Mikalonis, Gordon Warnock, Vickie Motter. Represents 100+ clients. 50% of clients are new/unpublished writers. Currently handles: nonfiction books 50%, novels 50%.

- Prior to becoming an agent, Ms. Hurst was an acquisitions editor as well as a freelance editor and published writer; Ms. Mikalonis was in marketing and branding consulting; Gordon Warnock was a freelance editor and marketing consultant.

MEMBER AGENTS Andrea Hurst, andrea@andreahurst.com (adult fiction, women's fiction, nonfiction—including personal growth, health and wellness, science, business, parenting, relationships, women's issues, animals, spirituality, metaphysical, psychological, cookbooks and self help); Judy Mikalonis, judy@andreahurst.com (young adult fiction, Christian fiction, Christian nonfiction). Gordon Warnock, gordon@andreahurst.com. Gordon represents nonfiction: Memoir, political and current affairs, health, humor and cookbooks. Fiction: Commercial narrative with a literary edge. Vickie Motter, vickie@andreahurst.com. Vickie represents young adult fiction and nonfiction and adult nonfiction.

REPRESENTS nonfiction books, novels, juvenile. **Considers these fiction areas:** inspirational, juvenile, literary, mainstream, psychic, religious, romance, supernatural, thriller, women's, young adult. ☛ "We work directly with our signed authors to help them polish their work and their platform for optimum marketability. Our staff is always available to answer phone calls and e-mails from our authors and we stay with a project until we have exhausted all publishing avenues." Actively seeking "well written nonfiction by authors with a strong platform; su-perbly crafted fiction with depth that touches the mind and heart and all of our listed subjects." Does not want to receive sci-fi, horror, Western, poetry or screenplays.

HOW TO CONTACT E-mail query with SASE. Submit outline/proposal, synopsis, 2 sample chapters, author bio. Query a specific agent after reviewing website. Use (agentfirstname)@andreahurst.com. Accepts simultaneous submissions. Obtains most new clients through recommendations from others, solicitations, conferences.

TERMS Agent receives 15% commission on domestic sales. Agent receives 20% commission on foreign sales. Offers written contract, binding for 6 to 12 months; 30-day notice must be given to terminate contract. This agency charges for postage. No reading fees. Visit our new blog: www.andreahurst.com.

RECENT SALES *No Buddy Left Behind,* by Terri Crisp and Cindy Hurn (Lyons Press); *A Year of Miracles*, by Dr. Bernie Siegel (NWL); *Selling Your Crafts on Etsy* (St. Martin's); *The Underground Detective Agency*, (Kensington); *Alaskan Seafood Cookbook*, (Globe Pequot); *Faith, Hope and Healing*, by Dr. Bernie Siegel (Rodale); *Code Name: Polar Ice*, by Jean-Michel Cousteau and James Fraioli (Gibbs Smith); *How to Host a Killer Party*, by Penny Warner (Berkley/Penguin).

WRITERS CONFERENCES San Francisco Writers' Conference; Willamette Writers' Conference; PNWA; Whidbey Island Writers Conference.

TIPS "Do your homework and submit a professional package. Get to know the agent you are submitting to by researching their website or meeting them at a conference. Perfect your craft: Write well and edit ruthlessly over and over again before submitting to an agent. Be realistic: Understand that publishing is a business and be prepared to prove why your book is marketable and how you will market it on your own. Be persistent! Andrea Hurst is no longer accepting unsolicited query letters. Unless you have been referred by one of our authors, an agent or publisher, please check our website for another appropriate agent."

● INKWELL MANAGEMENT, LLC

521 Fifth Ave., 26th Floor, New York NY 10175. (212)922-3500. Fax: (212)922-0535. E-mail: info@inkwellmanagement.com. Website: www.inkwellmanagement.com. Represents 500 clients. Currently handles: nonfiction books 60%, novels 40%.

MEMBER AGENTS Michael Carlisle; Richard Pine; Kimberly Witherspoon; George Lucas; Catherine Drayton; David Forrer; Susan Arellano; Alexis Hurley; Patricia Burke, Susan Hobson; Nat Jacks; Ethan Bassoff, Julie Schilder, Libby O'Neill; Elisa Petrini, Mairead Duffy; David Hale Smith.

REPRESENTS nonfiction books, novels.

HOW TO CONTACT Query with SASE or via e-mail to submissions@inkwellmanagement.com. Obtains most new clients through recommendations from others.

TERMS Agent receives 15% commission on domestic sales. Agent receives 20% commission on foreign sales. Offers written contract.

TIPS "We will not read manuscripts before receiving a letter of inquiry."

⬤ INTERNATIONAL CREATIVE MANAGEMENT

825 Eighth Ave., New York NY 10019. (212)556-5600. Website: www.icmtalent.com. **Contact:** Literary Department. Member of AAR. Signatory of WGA.

MEMBER AGENTS Lisa Bankoff, lbankoff@icmtalent.com (fiction interests include: literary fiction, family saga, historical fiction, offbeat/quirky; nonfiction interests include: history, biography, memoirs, narrative); Patrick Herold, pherold@icmtalent.com; Jennifer Joel, jjoel@icmtalent.com (fiction interests include: literary fiction, commercial fiction, historical fiction, thrillers/suspense; nonfiction interests include: history, sports, art, adventure/true story, pop culture); Esther Newberg; Sloan Harris; Amanda Binky Urban; Heather Schroder; Kristine Dahl; Andrea Barzvi, abarzvi@icmtalent.com (fiction interests include: chick lit, commercial fiction, women's fiction, thrillers/suspense; nonfiction interests include: sports, celebrity, self-help, dating/relationships, women's issues, pop culture, health and fitness); Tina Dubois Wexler, twexler@icmtalent.com (literary fiction, chick lit, young adult, middle grade, memoir, narrative nonfiction); Kate Lee, klee@icmtalent.com (mystery, commercial fiction, short stories, memoir, dating/relationships, pop culture, humor, journalism); Michelle Humphrey.

REPRESENTS nonfiction books, novels.

⁂➤ *We do not accept unsolicited submissions.*

HOW TO CONTACT Query with SASE. Send queries via snail mail and include an SASE. Target a specific agent. Obtains most new clients through recommendations from others.

TERMS Agent receives 15% commission on domestic sales. Agent receives 20% commission on foreign sales.

⬤ INTERNATIONAL LITERARY ARTS

RR 5, Box 5391 A, Moscow PA 18444. E-mail: query@InternationalLiteraryArts.com. Website: www.InternationalLiteraryArts.com. **Contact:** Pamela K. Brodowsky.

- Prior to her current position, Ms. Fazio worked at Prentice Hall, Random House, M.E. Sharpe and Baker & Taylor; Ms. Brodowsky is a public speaker, as well as the author of *Secrets of Successful Query Letters* and *Bulletproof Book Proposals*.

MEMBER AGENTS Pamela K. Brodowsky; Evelyn Fazio.

REPRESENTS nonfiction books, movie. **Considers these nonfiction areas:** autobiography, biography, business, cooking, current affairs, diet/nutrition, economics, foods, health, history, humor, medicine, money, parenting, satire, science, self-help, sports, technology, travel, reference, lifestyle.

⁂➤ "ILA is a full-service literary property agency representing authors in all areas of nonfiction across the creative spectrum. The agency is committed to the clients it represents and to the publishers with whom we match our talent. Our goal is to provide for our publishers talented authors with long-term career goals. Our mission is to create the continuance of the discovery of new talent and thriving careers for our represented clients." No longer accepting fiction.

HOW TO CONTACT Query with SASE. For nonfiction, send an e-mail cover letter, contact info, proposal and sample chapter. Send no e-attachments. When sending your query please be sure to address it to the correct department to ensure your material is submitted to the correct division. Responds in 4-6 weeks to queries.

WRITERS CONFERENCES BookExpo America.

TIPS "If you are inquiring about a nonfiction book project, please address your material to the attention of the Book Department. For screenplays, please address your material to the attention of the Motion Picture Department. Due to the enormous amount of submissions we receive, we will only respond to queries that we feel are a good fit for our agency."

● INTERNATIONAL TRANSACTIONS, INC.

P.O. Box 97, Gila NM 88038-0097. (845)373-9696. Fax: (845)373-7868. E-mail: submissions@intltrans.com; submission-fiction@intltrans.com; submission-non fiction@intltrans.com. Website: www.intltrans.com. **Contact:** Peter Riva. Represents 40+ clients. 10% of clients are new/unpublished writers. Currently handles: nonfiction books 60%, novels 25%, story collections 5%, juvenile books 5%, scholarly books 5%.

MEMBER AGENTS Peter Riva (nonfiction, fiction, illustrated; television and movie rights placement); Sandra Riva (fiction, juvenile, biographies); JoAnn Collins (fiction, women's fiction, medical fiction).

REPRESENTS nonfiction books, novels, short story collections, juvenile, scholarly, illustrated books, anthologies. **Considers these nonfiction areas:** anthropology, archeology, architecture, art, autobiography, biography, computers, cooking, cultural interests, current affairs, diet/nutrition, design, ethnic, foods, gay/lesbian, government, health, history, humor, investigative, language, law, literature, medicine, memoirs, military, music, photography, politics, satire, science, sports, translation, true crime, war, women's issues, women's studies. **Considers these fiction areas:** action, adventure, crime, detective, erotica, experimental, family saga, feminist, gay, historical, humor, lesbian, literary, mainstream, mystery, police, satire, spiritual, sports, suspense, thriller, women's, young adult, chick lit.

⌖ "We specialize in large and small projects, helping qualified authors perfect material for publication." Actively seeking intelligent, well-written innovative material that breaks new ground. Does not want to receive material influenced by TV (too much dialogue); a rehash of previous successful novels' themes or poorly prepared material.

HOW TO CONTACT First, e-query with an outline or synopsis. E-queries only. Responds in 3 weeks to queries. Responds in 5 weeks to mss. Obtains most new clients through recommendations from others, solicitations.

TERMS Agent receives 15% (25% on illustrated books) commission on domestic sales. Agent receives 20% commission on foreign sales. Offers written contract; 120-day notice must be given to terminate contract.

TIPS " 'Book'—a published work of literature. That last word is the key. Not a string of words, not a book of (TV or film) 'scenes,' and never a stream of consciousness unfathomable by anyone outside of the writer's coterie. A writer should only begin to get 'interested in getting an agent' if the work is polished, literate and ready to be presented to a publishing house. Anything less is either asking for a quick rejection or is a thinly disguised plea for creative assistance—which is often given but never fiscally sound for the agents involved. Writers, even published authors, have difficulty in being objective about their own work. Friends and family are of no assistance in that process either. Writers should attempt to get their work read by the most unlikely and stern critic as part of the editing process, months before any agent is approached. In another matter: the economics of our job have changed as well. As the publishing world goes through the transition to e-books (much as the music industry went through the change to downloadable music)—a transition we expect to see at 95% within 10 years—everyone is nervous and wants "assured bestsellers" from which to eke out a living until they know what the new e-world will bring. This makes the sales rate and, especially, the advance royalty rates, plummet. Hence, our ability to take risks and take on new clients' work is increasingly perilous financially for us and all agents."

● JABBERWOCKY LITERARY AGENCY

P.O. Box 4558, Sunnyside NY 11104-0558. (718)392-5985. Website: www.awfulagent.com. **Contact:** Joshua Bilmes. Other memberships include SFWA. Represents 40 clients. 15% of clients are new/unpublished writers. Currently handles: nonfiction books 15%, novels 75%, scholarly books 5%, other 5%.

MEMBER AGENTS Joshua Bilmes; Eddie Schneider; Jessie Cammack.

REPRESENTS novels. **Considers these nonfiction areas:** autobiography, biography, business, cooking, current affairs, diet/nutrition, economics, film, foods, gay/lesbian, government, health, history, humor, language, law, literature, medicine, money, popular culture, politics, satire, science, sociology, sports, theater, war, women's issues, women's studies, young adult. **Considers these fiction areas:** action, adventure, contemporary issues, crime, detective, ethnic, family saga, fantasy, gay, glitz, historical, horror, humor, lesbian, literary, mainstream, police, psychic, regional, satire, science fiction, sports, supernatural, thriller.

☛ This agency represents quite a lot of genre fiction and is actively seeking to increase the amount of nonfiction projects. It does not handle children's or picture books. Book-length material only—no poetry, articles, or short fiction.

HOW TO CONTACT We are currently closed to un-solicited queries. No e-mail queries, please. Query with SASE. Please check our website as there may be times during the year when we are not accepting queries. Query letter only; no manuscript material unless requested. Accepts simultaneous submissions. Responds in 3 weeks to queries. Obtains most new clients through solicitations, recommendation by current clients.

TERMS Agent receives 15% commission on domestic sales. Agent receives 20% commission on foreign sales. Offers written contract, binding for 1 year. Charges clients for book purchases, photocopying, international book/ms mailing.

RECENT SALES Sold 30 US and 100 foreign titles in the last year. *Dead in the Family*, by Charlaine Harris; *The Way of Kings*, by Brandon Sanderson; *The Desert Spear*, by Peter V. Brett; *Oath of Fealty*, by Elizabeth Moon. Other clients include Tanya Huff, Simon Green, Jack Campbell, Kat Richardson and Jon Sprunk.

WRITERS CONFERENCES World SF Convention; World Fantasy; Boucheron; full schedule of appearances can be found on our website.

TIPS "In approaching with a query, the most important things to us are your credits and your biographical background to the extent it's relevant to your work. I (and most agents) will ignore the adjectives you may choose to describe your own work."

🌐⊘ JANKLOW & NESBIT ASSOCIATES

445 Park Ave., New York NY 10022. (212)421-1700. Fax: (212)980-3671. E-mail: info@janklow.com. Web-site: janklowandnesbit.com. **Contact:** Julie Just, Literary Agent. Estab. 1989.

REPRESENTS nonfiction, fiction, trade books, mass market books. **Considers these nonfiction areas:** juvenile nonfiction, Accepts all genres; picture books (age preschool-8), young readers (age 5-8), middle readers (age 9-11), young adult/teens (age 12 and up). Query or submit outline/synopsis and 6 sample chapters. **Considers these fiction areas:** juvenile, Accepts all genres. Query or submit outline/synopsis and 6 sample chapters.

☛ Does not want to receive unsolicited submissions or queries. Do not contact this agency without a referral.

HOW TO CONTACT Considers electronic submissions. Accepts simultaneous submissions. Responds in 8 weeks to queries and mss. Obtains most new clients through recommendations from others.

TIPS "Please send a short query with sample chapters or artwork."

🌐 JET LITERARY ASSOCIATES

2570 Camino San Patricio, Santa Fe NM 87505. (505)474-9139. E-mail: etp@jetliterary.com. Web-site: www.jetliterary.com. **Contact:** Liz Trupin-Pulli. Represents 75 clients. 35% of clients are new/unpublished writers.

MEMBER AGENTS Liz Trupin-Pulli (adult and young adult fiction/nonfiction; romance, mysteries, parenting); Jim Trupin (adult fiction/nonfiction, military history, pop culture); Jessica Trupin, associate agent based in Seattle (adult fiction and nonfiction, children's and young adult, memoir, pop culture).

REPRESENTS nonfiction books, novels, short story collections. **Considers these nonfiction areas:** autobiography, biography, business, child guidance, cultural interests, current affairs, economics, ethnic, gay/lesbian, government, humor, investigative, law, memoirs, military, parenting, popular culture, politics, satire, sports, true crime, war, women's issues, women's studies. **Considers these fiction areas:** action, adventure, crime, detective, erotica, ethnic, gay, glitz, historical, humor, lesbian, literary, mainstream, mystery, police, romance, suspense, thriller, women's, young adult.

☛ "JET was founded in New York in 1975, so we bring a wealth of knowledge and contacts, as well as quite a bit of expertise to our representation of writers." Actively seeking women's fiction, mysteries and narrative nonfiction. JET represents the full range of adult and young adult fiction and nonfiction, including humor and cookbooks. Does not want to receive sci-fi, fantasy, horror, poetry, children's or religious.

HOW TO CONTACT Only e-queries accepted. Responds in 1 week to queries. Responds in 8 weeks to mss. Obtains most new clients through recommendations from others, solicitations, conferences.

TERMS Agent receives 15% commission on domestic sales. Agent receives 10% commission on foreign sales. Offers written contract, binding for 3 years. This agency charges for reimbursement of mailing and any photocopying.

RECENT SALES Sold 22 books in 2009 including several ghostwriting contracts. *Mom-In-chief,* by Jamie Woolf (Wiley); *Dangerous Games* by Charlotte Mede (Kensington); *So You Think You Can Spell!,* by David Grambs and Ellen Levine (Perigee, 2009); *Cut, Drop & Die,* by Joanna Campbell Slan (Midnight Ink).

WRITERS CONFERENCES Women Writing the West; Southwest Writers Conference; Florida Writers Association Conference.

TIPS "Do not write 'cute' queries—stick to a straightforward message that includes the title and what your book is about, why you are suited to write this particular book, and what you have written in the past (if anything), along with a bit of a bio."

● CAREN JOHNSON LITERARY AGENCY

132 East 43rd St., No. 216, New York NY 10017. E-mail: caren@johnsonlitagency.com. Website: www.johnsonliterary.com. **Contact:** Caren Estesen, Elana Roth. Represents 20 clients. 50% of clients are new/unpublished writers. Currently handles: nonfiction books 35%, juvenile books 35%, romance/women's fiction 30%.

- Prior to her current position, Ms. Estesen was with Firebrand Literary and the Peter Rubie Agency.

MEMBER AGENTS Caren Estesen, Elana Roth, Katie Shea.

REPRESENTS nonfiction books, novels. **Considers these nonfiction areas:** history, popular culture, science, technology. **Considers these fiction areas:** detective, erotica, ethnic, romance, young adult, middle grade, women's fiction.

- Does not want to receive poetry, plays or screenplays/scripts. Elana Roth will consider picture books but is very selective of what she takes on.

HOW TO CONTACT Query via e-mail only, directing your query to the appropriate person; responds in 12 weeks to all materials sent. Include 4-5 sample pages withing the body of your e-mail when pitching us. Accepts simultaneous submissions. Responds in 4-6 weeks to queries. Responds in 6-8 weeks to mss. Obtains most new clients through recommendations from others.

TERMS Agent receives 15% commission on domestic sales. Agent receives 20% commission on foreign sales. Offers written contract; 30-day notice must be given to terminate contract. This agency charges for postage and photocopying, though the author is consulted before any charges are incurred.

RECENT SALES "Please check out our website for a complete client list."

WRITERS CONFERENCES RWA National; Book-Expo America; SCBWI.

●⊙ KELLER MEDIA INC.

23852 West Pacific Coast Hwy., Suite 701, Malibu CA 90265. (800)278-8706. E-mail: query@KellerMedia.com. Website: www.KellerMedia.com. **Contact:** Megan Collins, associate agent. Other memberships include National Speakers Association. 25% of clients are new/unpublished writers. Currently handles: nonfiction books 100%.

- Prior to becoming an agent, Ms. Keller was an award-winning journalist and worked for PR Newswire and several newspapers.

REPRESENTS nonfiction. **Considers these nonfiction areas:** business, current affairs, finance, health, history, nature, politics, psychology, science, self-help, sociology, spirituality, women's issues.

- "We focus a great deal of attention on authors who want to also become paid professional speakers, and current speakers who want to become authors. All of our authors are highly credible experts, who have or want a significant platform in media, academia, politics, paid professional speaking, syndicated columns or regular appearances on radio/TV." Does not want (and absolutely will not respond to) fiction, scripts, teleplays, poetry, juvenile, anything Christian, picture books, illustrated books, first-person stories of mental or physical illness, wrongful incarceration, or abduction by aliens, books channeled by aliens, demons, or dead celebrities.

HOW TO CONTACT Accepts e-mail queries only. Make sure to include your credentials and a good, short overview of the proposed book. Do not send attachments; just a simple, succinct e-mail. Please do not send hard copy mss without permission! Send your one-page query briefly stating your subject and credentials, plus your contact info and website URL (if applicable) to Query@KellerMedia.com. If we're interested, you'll hear back within a few business days. Accepts simultaneous submissions. Responds in 7 days. Obtains most new clients through referral.

TERMS Agent receives 15% commission on domestic sales. Agent receives 20% commission on foreign sales.

TIPS "Don't send a query to any agent unless you're certain they handle the type of book you're writing. 90% of all rejections happen because what you offered us doesn't fit our established, advertised, printed, touted and shouted guidelines. Be organized! Have your proposal in order before you query. Never make apologies for 'bad writing' or sloppy content—get it right before you waste your one shot with us. Have something new, different or interesting to say and be ready to dedicate your whole heart to marketing it."

ⓘ NATASHA KERN LITERARY AGENCY

P.O. Box 1069, White Salmon WA 98672. (509)493-3803. E-mail: agent@natashakern.com. Website: www.natashakern.com. **Contact:** Natasha Kern. Other memberships include RWA, MWA, SinC, The Authors Guild, and American Society of Journalists and Authors

- Prior to opening her agency, Ms. Kern worked as an editor and publicist for Simon & Schuster, Bantam and Ballantine. This agency has sold more than 700 books.

MEMBER AGENTS Natasha Kern.

REPRESENTS **Considers these nonfiction areas:** animals, child guidance, cultural interests, current affairs, environment, ethnic, gardening, health, inspirational, medicine, metaphysics, New Age, parenting, popular culture, psychology, religious, self-help, spirituality, women's issues, women's studies, investigative journalism. **Considers these fiction areas:** commercial, historical, inspirational, mainstream, multicultural, mystery, religious, romance, suspense, thriller, women's.

⚷ "This agency specializes in commercial fiction and nonfiction for adults. We are a full-service agency." Historical novels from any country or time period; contemporary fiction including novels with romance or suspense elements; and multi-cultural fiction. We are also seeking inspirational fiction in a broad range of genres, including: suspense and mysteries, historicals, romance, and contemporary novels. Does not represent horror, true crime, erotica, children's books, short stories or novellas, poetry, screenplays, technical, photography or art/craft books, cookbooks, travel, or sports books.

HOW TO CONTACT See submission instructions online. Send query to queries@natashakern. com. Please include the word "query" in the subject line. "We do not accept queries by snail mail or phone." Accepts simultaneous submissions. Responds in 3 weeks to queries.

TERMS Agent receives 15% commission on domestic sales. Agent receives 20% commission on foreign sales. Agent receives 15% commission on film sales.

RECENT SALES Sold 43 titles in the last year. *China Dolls*, by Michelle Yu and Blossom Kan (St. Martin's); *Bastard Tongues*, by Derek Bickerton (Farrar Strauss); *Bone Rattler*, by Eliot Pattison; *Wicked Pleasure*, by Nina Bangs (Berkley); *Inviting God In*, by David Aaron (Shambhala); *Unlawful Contact*, by Pamela Clare (Berkley); *Dead End Dating*, by Kimberly Raye (Ballantine); *A Scent of Roses*, by Nikki Arana (Baker Book House); *The Sexiest Man Alive*, by Diana Holquist (Warner Books).

WRITERS CONFERENCES RWA National Conference; MWA National Conference; ACFW Conference; and many regional conferences.

TIPS "Your chances of being accepted for representation will be greatly enhanced by going to our website first. Our idea of a dream client is someone who participates in a mutually respectful business relationship, is clear about needs and goals, and communicates about career planning. If we know what you need and want, we can help you achieve it. A dream client has a storytelling gift, a commitment to a writing career, a desire to learn and grow, and a passion for excellence. We want clients who are expressing their own unique voice and truly have something of their own to communicate. This client understands that many people have to work together for a book to succeed and that everything in publishing takes far longer than one imagines. Trust and communication are truly essential."

ⓘ LOUISE B. KETZ AGENCY

414 E. 78th St., Suite 1B, New York NY 10075. (212)249-0668. E-mail: ketzagency@aol.com. **Contact:** Louise B. Ketz. Represents 25 clients. 15% of clients are new/unpublished writers. Currently handles: nonfiction books 100%.

REPRESENTS nonfiction books. **Considers these nonfiction areas:** business, current affairs, history, military, science, sports, economics.

☛ This agency specializes in science, history and reference.

HOW TO CONTACT Query with SASE. Submit outline, 1 sample chapter, author bio (with qualifications for authorship of work). Responds in 6 weeks to mss. Obtains most new clients through recommendations from others, idea development.

TERMS Agent receives 15% commission on domestic sales.

⬤ VIRGINIA KIDD AGENCY, INC.

538 E. Harford St., P.O. Box 278, Milford PA 18337. (570)296-6205. Fax: (570)296-7266. Website: www.vk-agency.com. Other memberships include SFWA, SFRA. Represents 80 clients.

MEMBER AGENTS Christine Cohen.

REPRESENTS novels. **Considers these fiction areas:** fantasy, historical, mainstream, mystery, science fiction, suspense, women's, speculative.

☛ This agency specializes in science fiction and fantasy.

HOW TO CONTACT This agency is not accepting queries from unpublished authors at this time. Submit synopsis (1-3 pages), cover letter, first chapter, SASE. Snail mail queries only. Responds in 6 weeks to queries.

TERMS Agent receives 15% commission on domestic sales. Agent receives 20-25% commission on foreign sales. Agent receives 20% commission on film sales. Offers written contract; 2-month notice must be given to terminate contract. Charges clients occasionally for extraordinary expenses.

RECENT SALES *Sagramanda*, by Alan Dean Foster (Pyr); *Incredible Good Fortune*, by Ursula K. Le Guin (Shambhala); *The Wizard and Soldier of Sidon*, by Gene Wolfe (Tor); *Voices and Powers*, by Ursula K. Le Guin (Harcourt); *Galileo's Children*, by Gardner Dozois (Pyr); *The Light Years Beneath My Feet* and *Running From the Deity*, by Alan Dean Foster (Del Ray); *Chasing Fire*, by Michelle Welch. Other

clients include Eleanor Arnason, Ted Chiang, Jack Skillingstead, Daryl Gregory, Patricia Briggs, and the estates for James Tiptree, Jr., Murray Leinster, E.E. "Doc" Smith, R.A. Lafferty.

TIPS "If you have a completed novel that is of extraordinary quality, please send us a query."

⊙ KIRCHOFF/WOHLBERG, INC.

897 Boston Post Rd., Madison CT 06443. (203)245-7308. Fax: (203)245-3218. E-mail: trade@kirchoffwohlberg.com. Website: www.kirchoffwohlberg.com/literaryagent. **Contact:** Ronald Zollshan. Member of AAR. Other memberships include SCBWI, AAP, Society of Illustrators, SPAR, Bookbuilders of Boston, New York Bookbinders' Guild, AIGA. 10% of clients are new/unpublished writers. Currently handles: nonfiction books 5%, novels 25%, other 5% young adult.

• Kirchoff/Wohlberg has been in business for over 60 years.

☛ This agency specializes in juvenile fiction and nonfiction through Young Adult.

HOW TO CONTACT Submit by mail to address above. We welcome the submission of manuscripts from first-time or established children's book authors. Please enclose a SASE but note that while we endeavor to read all submissions we cannot guarantee a reply or their return. Accepts simultaneous submissions.

TERMS Offers written contract, binding for at least 1 year. Agent receives standard commission, depending upon whether it is an author-only, illustrator-only, or an author/illustrator book.

ⓘ HARVEY KLINGER, INC.

300 W. 55th St., Suite 11V, New York NY 10019. (212)581-7068. E-mail: queries@harveyklinger.com. Website: www.harveyklinger.com. **Contact:** Harvey Klinger. Member of AAR. Represents 100 clients. 25% of clients are new/unpublished writers. Currently handles: nonfiction books 50%, novels 50%.

MEMBER AGENTS David Dunton (popular culture, music-related books, literary fiction, young adult fiction, and memoirs); Sara Crowe (children's and young adult authors, adult fiction and nonfiction, foreign rights sales); Andrea Somberg (literary fiction, commercial fiction, romance, sci-fi/fantasy, mysteries/thrillers, young adult, middle grade, quality narrative nonfiction, popular culture, how-to, self-help, humor, interior design, cookbooks, health/fitness).

REPRESENTS nonfiction books, novels. **Considers these nonfiction areas:** autobiography, biography, cooking, diet/nutrition, foods, health, investigative, medicine, psychology, science, self-help, spirituality, sports, technology, true crime, women's issues, women's studies. **Considers these fiction areas:** action, adventure, crime, detective, family saga, glitz, literary, mainstream, mystery, police, suspense, thriller.

○━┮ This agency specializes in big, mainstream, contemporary fiction and nonfiction.

HOW TO CONTACT Use online e-mail submission form, or query with SASE. No phone or fax queries. Don't send unsolicited manuscripts or e-mail attachments. Responds in 2 months to queries and mss. Obtains most new clients through recommendations from others.

TERMS Agent receives 15% commission on domestic sales. Agent receives 25% commission on foreign sales. Offers written contract. Charges for photocopying mss and overseas postage for mss.

RECENT SALES *Woman of a Thousand Secrets*, by Barbara Wood; *I am Not a Serial Killer*, by Dan Wells; untitled memoir, by Bob Mould; *Children of the Mist*; by Paula Quinn; *Tutored*, by Allison Whittenberg; *Will You Take Me As I Am*, by Michelle Mercer. Other clients include: George Taber, Terry Kay, Scott Mebus, Jacqueline Kolosov, Jonathan Maberry, Tara Altebrando, Eva Nagorski, Greg Kot, Justine Musk, Alex McAuley, Nick Tasler, Ashley Kahn, Barbara De Angelis.

● KNEERIM & WILLIAMS

90 Canal St., Boston MA 02114. (617)303-1650. Fax: (617)542-1660. E-mail: jill@kwlit.com; jtwilliams@ kwlit.com. Website: www.kwlit.com. Also located in New York and Washington D.C. Estab. 1990.

• Prior to becoming an agent, Mr. Williams was a lawyer; Ms. Kneerim was a publisher and editor; Mr. Wasserman was an editor and journalist; Ms. Bloom worked in magazines; Ms. Flynn in academia; and Ms. Zimmerman in newspapers.

MEMBER AGENTS John Taylor "Ike" Williams (accepts queries); Jill Kneerim (accepts queries); Steve Wasserman (not currently accepting submissions); Brettne Bloom (not currently accepting submissions).

REPRESENTS nonfiction books, novels. **Considers these nonfiction areas:** anthropology, archeology, autobiography, biography, business, child guidance, current affairs, economics, environment, government, health, history, inspirational, language, law, literature, medicine, memoirs, parenting, popular culture, politics, psychology, religious, science, sociology, sports, technology, women's issues, women's studies. **Considers these fiction areas:** historical, literary, mainstream.

○━┮ "This agency specializes in narrative nonfiction, history, science, business, women's issues, commercial and literary fiction, film, and television. We have 5 agents and 4 scouts in Boston, New York, Washington DC and Santa Fe." Actively seeking distinguished authors, experts, professionals, intellectuals, and serious writers. Does not want to receive blanket multiple submissions, genre fiction or original screenplays.

HOW TO CONTACT Submit query via e-mail only at: submissions@kwlit.com. No hard copies will be accepted. Submissions should contain a cover letter explaining your book and why you are qualified to write it, a two-page synopsis of the book, one sample chapter, and your c.v. or a history of your publications. Accepts simultaneous submissions. Responds in 4-6 weeks to queries. Responds in 2 months to mss. Obtains most new clients through recommendations from others.

RECENT SALES *The Inner Circle*, by Brad Meltzer; *First Family*, by Joe Ellis; *Commencement*, by J. Courtney Sullivan; *Hitch-22*, by Christopher Hitchens.

● LINDA KONNER LITERARY AGENCY

10 W. 15th St., Suite 1918, New York NY 10011-6829. (212)691-3419. E-mail: ldkonner@cs.com. Website: www.lindakonnerliteraryagency.com. **Contact:** Linda Konner. Member of AAR. Signatory of WGA. Other memberships include ASJA. Represents 85 clients. 30-35% of clients are new/unpublished writers. Currently handles: nonfiction books 100%.

REPRESENTS nonfiction books. **Considers these nonfiction areas:** diet/nutrition, gay/lesbian, health, medicine, money, parenting, popular culture, psychology, self-help, women's issues, biography (celebrity), African American and Latino issues, relation-ships.

☞ This agency specializes in health, self-help, and how-to books. Authors/co-authors must be top experts in their field with a substantial media platform.

HOW TO CONTACT Query by e-mail or by mail with SASE, synopsis, author bio, sufficient return postage. Prefers to read materials exclusively for 2 weeks. Accepts simultaneous submissions. Obtains most new clients through recommendations from others, occasional solicitation among established authors/journalists.

TERMS Agent receives 15% commission on domes-tic sales. Agent receives 25% commission on foreign sales. Offers written contract. Charges one-time fee for domestic expenses; additional expenses may be incurred for foreign sales.

RECENT SALES *Organize Your Mind, Organize Your Life*, by Paul Hammerness, PhD, Margaret Moore and John Hanc, with the editors of Harvard Health Publications; *Southern Plate: Cherished Recipes and Stories From My Grandparents*, by Christy Jordan (Harper Studio); *Second Acts: Finding a Passionate New Career*, by Kerry Hannon (Chronicle Books); *Who Do You Think You Are?: Tracing Your Family History*, a tie-in to the NBC TV series, by Megan Smolenyak (Viking).

WRITERS CONFERENCES ASJA Writers Confer-ence, Harvard Medical School's "Publishing Books, Memoirs, and Other Creative Nonfiction" Annual Conference.

BARBARA S. KOUTS, LITERARY AGENT

P.O. Box 560, Bellport NY 11713. (631)286-1278. Fax: (631) 286-1538. **Contact:** Barbara S. Kouts. Member of AAR. Represents 50 clients. 10% of clients are new/unpublished writers.

REPRESENTS juvenile.

☞ This agency specializes in children's books.

HOW TO CONTACT Query with SASE. Accepts simultaneous submissions. Responds in 1 week to queries. Responds in 2 months to mss. Obtains most new clients through recommendations from others, solicitations, conferences.

TERMS Agent receives 10% commission on domes-tic sales. Agent receives 20% commission on foreign sales. This agency charges clients for photocopying.

RECENT SALES *Code Talker*, by Joseph Bruchac

(Dial); *The Penderwicks*, by Jeanne Birdsall (Knopf); *Froggy's Baby Sister*, by Jonathan London (Viking).

TIPS "Write, do not call. Be professional in your writing."

⊙ KRAAS LITERARY AGENCY

E-mail: irenekraas@sbcglobal.net. Website: www.kraasliteraryagency.com. **Contact:** Irene Kraas. Rep-resents 35 clients. 75% of clients are new/unpublished writers. Currently handles: novels 100%.

MEMBER AGENTS Irene Kraas, principal.

REPRESENTS novels. **Considers these fiction ar-eas:** literary, thriller, young adult.

☞ This agency is interested in working with pub-lished writers, but that does not mean self-published writers. "The agency is ONLY ac-cepting new manuscripts in the genre of adult thrillers and mysteries. Submissions should be the first ten pages of a completed manu-script embedded in an e-mail. I do not open attachments or go to websites." Does not want to receive short stories, plays or poetry. This agency no longer represents adult fantasy or science fiction.

HOW TO CONTACT Query and e-mail the first 10 pages of a completed ms. Requires exclusive read on mss. Accepts simultaneous submissions.

TERMS Offers written contract.

TIPS "I am interested in material—in any genre—that is truly, truly unique."

⊙ BERT P. KRAGES

6665 SW Hampton St., Suite 200, Portland OR 97223. (503)597-2525. E-mail: krages@onemain.com. Web-site: www.krages.com. **Contact:** Bert Krages. Repre-sents 10 clients. 80% of clients are new/unpublished writers. Currently handles: nonfiction books 95%, scholarly books 5%.

• Mr. Krages is also an attorney.

REPRESENTS nonfiction books. **Considers these nonfiction areas:** agriculture, animals, anthropology, archeology, architecture, art, autobiography, biogra-phy, business, child guidance, computers, cultural in-terests, current affairs, design, economics, education, environment, ethnic, health, history, horticulture, medicine, memoirs, military, parenting, psychology, science, self-help, sociology, technology, war.

☞ "I handle a small number of literary clients and concentrate on trade nonfiction (science, health, psychology, and history)." No fiction submissions until further notified—check the website.

HOW TO CONTACT Keep queries to one page—nonfiction only. E-mail submissions preferred. Queries should concisely describe the subject of the book, the intended audience, and your qualifications to write the book. Accepts simultaneous submissions. Responds in 1-6 weeks to queries. Obtains most new clients through solicitations.

TERMS Agent receives 15% commission on domestic sales. Agent receives 20% commission on foreign sales. Offers written contract, binding for 1 year; 60-day notice must be given to terminate contract. Charges for photocopying and postage only if the book is placed.

TIPS "Read at least 2 books on how to prepare book proposals before sending material. An extremely well-prepared proposal will make your material stand out."

STUART KRICHEVSKY LITERARY AGENCY, INC.

381 Park Ave. S., Suite 428, New York NY 10016. (212)725-5288. Fax: (212)725-5275. E-mail: query@skagency.com. Website: www.skagency.com. Member of AAR.

MEMBER AGENTS Stuart Krichevsky; Shana Cohen (science fiction, fantasy); Jennifer Puglisi (assistant).

REPRESENTS nonfiction books, novels.

HOW TO CONTACT Submit query, synopsis, 1 sample page via e-mail (no attachments). Snail mail queries also acceptable. Obtains most new clients through recommendations from others, solicitations.

EDITE KROLL LITERARY AGENCY, INC.

20 Cross St., Saco ME 04072. (207)283-8797. Fax: (207)283-8799. E-mail: ekroll@maine.rr.com. **Contact:** Edite Kroll. Represents 45 clients. 20% of clients are new/unpublished writers. Currently handles: nonfiction books 40%, novels 5%, juvenile books 40%, scholarly books 5%, other.

• Prior to opening her agency, Ms. Kroll served as a book editor and translator.

REPRESENTS nonfiction books, novels (very selective), juvenile, scholarly. **Considers these nonfiction areas:** juvenile (selectively), biography, current affairs, ethnic, gay, government, health, no diet books, humor, memoirs (selectively), popular culture, psychology, religion (selectively), self help (selectively),

women's, issue-oriented nonfiction. **Considers these fiction areas:** juvenile, literary, picture books, young adult, middle grade, adult.

"We represent writers and writer-artists of both adult and children's books. We have a special focus on international feminist writers, women writers and artists who write their own books (including children's and humor books)." Actively seeking artists who write their own books and international feminists who write in English. Does not want to receive genre (mysteries, thrillers, diet, cookery, etc.), photography books, coffee table books, romance or commercial fiction.

HOW TO CONTACT Query with SASE. Submit outline/proposal, synopsis, 1–2 sample chapters, author bio, entire ms if sending picture book. No phone queries. Responds in 2–4 weeks to queries. Responds in 4-8 weeks to mss. Obtains most new clients through recommendations from others.

TERMS Agent receives 15% commission on domestic sales. Agent receives 20% commission on foreign sales. Offers written contract; 30-day notice must be given to terminate contract. Charges clients for photocopying and legal fees with prior approval from writer.

RECENT SALES Sold 12 domestic/30 foreign titles in the last year. This agency prefers not to share information on specific sales. Clients include Shel Silverstein estate, Suzy Becker, Geoffrey Hayes, Henrik Drescher, Charlotte Kasl, Gloria Skurzynski, Fatema Mernissa.

TIPS "Please do your research so you won't send me books/proposals I specifically excluded."

KT LITERARY, LLC

9249 S. Broadway, #200-543, Highlands Ranch CO 80129. (720)344-4728. Fax: (720)344-4728. E-mail: contact@ktliterary.com. Website: http://ktliterary.com. **Contact:** Kate Schafer Testerman. Member of AAR. Other memberships include SCBWI. Represents 20 clients. 60% of clients are new/unpublished writers. Currently handles: nonfiction books 5%, novels 5%, juvenile books 90%.

• Prior to her current position, Ms. Schafer was an agent with Janklow & Nesbit.

REPRESENTS nonfiction books, novels, juvenile books. **Considers these nonfiction areas:** popular culture. **Considers these fiction areas:** action, adventure, fantasy, historical, juvenile, romance, science fiction, women's, young adult.

⊶ "I'm bringing my years of experience in the New York publishing scene, as well as my lifelong of reading, to a vibrant area for writers, proving that great work can be found, and sold, from anywhere. Actively seeking brilliant, funny, original middle grade and young adult fiction, both literary and commercial; witty women's fiction (chick lit); and pop culture, narrative nonfiction. Quirky is good." Does not want picture books, serious nonfiction, and adult literary fiction.

HOW TO CONTACT E-mail queries only. Ms. Testerman is closed to submissions until June of 2011. Keep an eye on the KT Literary blog for updates. Responds in 2 weeks to queries. Responds in 2 months to mss. Obtains most new clients through recommendations from others, solicitations, conferences.

TERMS Agent receives 15% commission on domestic sales. Agent receives 20% commission on foreign sales. Offers written contract; 30-day notice must be given to terminate contract.

WRITERS CONFERENCES Various SCBWI conferences, BookExpo.

TIPS "If we like your query, we'll ask for (more). Continuing advice is offered regularly on my blog 'Ask Daphne,' which can be accessed from my website."

◯ KT PUBLIC RELATIONS & LITERARY SERVICES

1905 Cricklewood Cove, Fogelsville PA 18051. (610)395-6298. Fax: (610)395-6299. Website: www.ktpublicrelations.com; Blog: http://newliteraryagents.blogspot.com. **Contact:** Jon Tienstra. Represents 12 clients. 75% of clients are new/unpublished writers. Currently handles: nonfiction books 50%, novels 50%.

• Prior to becoming an agent, Kae Tienstra was publicity director for Rodale, Inc. for 13 years and then founded her own publicity agency; Mr. Tienstra joined the firm in 1995 with varied corporate experience and a master's degree in library science.

MEMBER AGENTS Kae Tienstra (health, parenting, psychology, how-to, women's fiction, general fiction); Jon Tienstra (nature/environment, history, cooking/foods/nutrition, war/military, automotive, health/medicine, gardening, general fiction, science fiction/contemporary fantasy, popular fiction).

REPRESENTS nonfiction books, novels. **Considers these nonfiction areas:** animals, child guidance, cooking, decorating, diet/nutrition, environment, foods, health, history, hobbies, horticulture, how-to, interior design, medicine, military, parenting, popular culture, psychology, science, self-help, technology, interior design/decorating. **Considers these fiction areas:** action, adventure, crime, detective, family saga, historical, literary, mainstream, mystery, police, romance, science fiction, suspense, thriller, contemporary fantasy (no swords or dragons).

⊶ "We have worked with a variety of authors and publishers over the years and have learned what individual publishers are looking for in terms of new acquisitions. We are both mad about books and authors and we look forward to finding publishing success for all our clients. Specializes in parenting, history, cooking/foods/nutrition, war, health/medicine, psychology, how-to, gardening, science fiction, contemporary fantasy, women's fiction, and popular fiction." Does not want to see unprofessional material.

HOW TO CONTACT Query with SASE. Prefers snail mail queries. Will accept e-mail queries. Responds in 3 months to chapters; 6-9 months for mss. Accepts simultaneous submissions. Responds in 4 weeks to queries.

TERMS Agent receives 15% commission on domestic sales. Agent receives 20% commission on foreign sales. Offers written contract. Charges clients for long-distance phone calls, fax, postage, photocopying (only when incurred). No advance payment for these out-of-pocket expenses.

● PETER LAMPACK AGENCY, INC.

551 Fifth Ave., Suite 1613, New York NY 10176-0187. (212)687-9106. Fax: (212)687-9109. E-mail: alampack@verizon.net. **Contact:** Andrew Lampack. Represents 50 clients. 10% of clients are new/unpublished writers. Currently handles: nonfiction books 20%, novels 80%.

MEMBER AGENTS Peter Lampack (president); Rema Delanyan (foreign rights); Andrew Lampack (new writers).

REPRESENTS nonfiction books, novels. **Considers these fiction areas:** adventure, crime, detective, family saga, literary, mainstream, mystery, police, suspense, thriller, contemporary relationships.

⚷— "This agency specializes in commercial fiction and nonfiction by recognized experts." Actively seeking literary and commercial fiction, thrillers, mysteries, suspense, and psychological thrillers. Does not want to receive horror, romance, science fiction, Westerns, historical literary fiction or academic material.

HOW TO CONTACT Query via e-mail. *No unsolicited mss.* Responds within 2 months to queries. Obtains most new clients through referrals made by clients.

TERMS Agent receives 15% commission on domestic sales. Agent receives 20% commission on foreign sales.

RECENT SALES *Spartan Gold*, by Clive Cussler with Grant Blackwood; *The Wrecker*, by Clive Cussler with Justin Scott; *Medusa*, by Clive Cussler and Paul Kemprecos; *Silent Sea* by Clive Cussler with Jack Dubrul; *Summertime*, by J.M. Coetzee; *Dreaming in French*, by Megan McAndrew; *Time Pirate*, by Ted Bell.

WRITERS CONFERENCES BookExpo America; Mystery Writers of America.

TIPS "Submit only your best work for consideration. Have a very specific agenda of goals you wish your prospective agent to accomplish for you. Provide the agent with a comprehensive statement of your credentials—educational and professional accomplishments."

❶ LAURA LANGLIE, LITERARY AGENT

63 Wyckoff St., Brooklyn NY 11201. (718)855-8102. Fax: (718)855-4450. E-mail: laura@lauralanglie.com. **Contact:** Laura Langlie. Represents 25 clients. 50% of clients are new/unpublished writers. Currently handles: nonfiction books 15%, novels 58%, story collections 2%, juvenile books 25%.

- Prior to opening her agency, Ms. Langlie worked in publishing for 7 years and as an agent at Kidde, Hoyt & Picard for 6 years.

REPRESENTS nonfiction books, novels, short story collections, novellas, juvenile. **Considers these nonfiction areas:** autobiography, biography, cultural interests, current affairs, environment, film, history, language, law, literature, memoirs, popular culture, politics, psychology, satire, theater, women's issues, women's studies, history of medicine and science, animals (not how-to). **Considers these fiction areas:** crime, detective, ethnic, feminist, historical, humor, juvenile, literary, mainstream, mystery, police, suspense, thriller, young adult.

⚷— "I'm very involved with and committed to my clients. I also employ a publicist to work with all my clients to make the most of each book's publication. Most of my clients come to me via recommendations from other agents, clients and editors. I've met very few at conferences. I've often sought out writers for projects, and I still find new clients via the traditional query letter." Does not want to receive how-to, children's picture books, science fiction, poetry, men's adventure or erotica.

HOW TO CONTACT Query with SASE. Accepts queries via fax. Accepts simultaneous submissions. Responds in 1 week to queries. Responds in 1 month to mss. Obtains most new clients through recommendations, submissions.

TERMS Agent receives 15% commission on domestic sales. Agent receives 20% commission on foreign and dramatic sales. No written contract.

RECENT SALES Sold 15 titles in the last year. *Autobiography of Mrs. Tom Thumb*, by Melanie Benjamin (Delacorte Press); *A Body of Water*, by Sarah Dooley (Feiwel & Friends/Macmillan); *Miss Dimple Rallies to the Cause*, by Mignon F. Ballard (St. Martin's Press); *Abandon* by Meg Cabot (Scholastic, Inc.); *Overbite*, by by Meg Cabot (William Morrow); *Huntress*, by Malinda Lo (Little, Brown & Co Books for Young Readers); *Everybody Bugs Out*, by Leslie Margolis (Bloomsbury); *The Elite Gymnasts*, by Dominique Moceanu and Alicia Thompson (Disney/Hyperion); *Safe From the Sea*, by Peter Geye (Unbridled Books).

TIPS "Be complete, forthright and clear in your communications. Do your research as to what a particular agent represents."

LANGTONS INTERNATIONAL AGENCY

124 West 60th St., #42M, New York NY 10023. (646)344-1801. E-mail: langton@langtonsinternational@com; llangton@langtonsinternational.com. Website: www.langtonsinternational.com. **Contact:** Linda Langton, President.

- Prior to becoming an agent, Ms. Langton was a co-founding director and publisher of the international publishing company, The Ink Group.

REPRESENTS nonfiction books and literary fiction. **Considers these nonfiction areas:** biography, health, history, how-to, politics, self-help, true crime. **Considers these fiction areas:** literary, political thrillers, young adult and middle grade books.

8—🛪 "Langtons International Agency is a multimedia literary and licensing agency specializing in nonfiction, inspirational, thrillers and children's middle grade and young adult books as well as the the visual world of photography."

HOW TO CONTACT Please submit all queries via hard copy to the address above or e-mail outline/ proposal, synopsis, publishing history, author bio. Only published authors should query this agency. Accepts simultaneous submissions.

RECENT SALES *Talking With Jean-Paul Sartre: Conversations and Debates*, by Professor John Gerassi (Yale University Press); *The Obama Presidency and the Politics of Change*, by Professor Stanley Renshon (Routledge Press); *I Would See a Girl Walking*, by Diana Montane and Kathy Kelly (Berkley Books); *Begin 1913-1992*, by Avi Shilon (Yale University Press); *This Borrowed Earth*, by Robert Emmet Hernan (Palgrave McMillan); *The Perfect Square*, by Nancy Heinzen (Temple Uni Press); *The Honey Trail* by Grace Pundyk (St. Martin's Press); *Dogs of Central Park* by Fran Reisner (Rizzoli/Universe Publishing).

◑ MICHAEL LARSEN/ELIZABETH POMADA, LITERARY AGENTS

1029 Jones St., San Francisco CA 94109-5023. (415)673-0939. E-mail: larsenpoma@aol.com. Website: www.larsen-pomada.com. **Contact:** Mike Larsen, Elizabeth Pomada. Member of AAR. Other memberships include Authors Guild, ASJA, PEN, WNBA, California Writers Club, National Speakers Association. Represents 100 clients. 40-45% of clients are new/unpublished writers. Currently handles: nonfiction books 70%, novels 30%.

• Prior to opening their agency, Mr. Larsen and Ms. Pomada were promotion executives for major publishing houses. Mr. Larsen worked for Morrow, Bantam and Pyramid (now part of Berkley); Ms. Pomada worked at Holt, David McKay and The Dial Press. Mr. Larsen is the author of the 4th edition of *How to Write a Book Proposal* and *How to Get a Literary Agent*

as well as the coauthor of *Guerilla Marketing for Writers: 100 Weapons for Selling Your Work*, which was republished in September 2009.

MEMBER AGENTS Michael Larsen (nonfiction); Elizabeth Pomada (fiction & narrative nonfiction); Laurie McLean (kids, genre, more); Lindsey Clemons (literary, thriller mystery).

REPRESENTS Considers these nonfiction areas: anthropology, archeology, architecture, art, autobiography, biography, business, current affairs, diet/ nutrition, design, economics, environment, ethnic, film, foods, gay/lesbian, health, history, how-to, humor, inspirational, investigative, law, medicine, memoirs, metaphysics, money, music, New Age, popular culture, politics, psychology, religious, satire, science, self-help, sociology, sports, travel, women's issues, women's studies, futurism. **Considers these fiction areas:** action, adventure, contemporary issues, crime, detective, ethnic, experimental, family saga, feminist, gay, glitz, historical, humor, inspirational, lesbian, literary, mainstream, mystery, police, religious, romance, satire, suspense, chick lit.

8—🛪 "We have diverse tastes. We look for fresh voices and new ideas. We handle literary, commercial and genre fiction, and the full range of nonfiction books." Actively seeking commercial, genre and literary fiction. Does not want to receive children's books, plays, short stories, screenplays, pornography, poetry or stories of abuse.

HOW TO CONTACT Query with SASE. **Elizabeth Pomada** handles literary and commercial fiction, romance, thrillers, mysteries, narrative nonfiction and mainstream women's fiction. If you have completed a novel, **please e-mail the first 10 pages and 2 page synopsis to larsenpoma@aol.com**. Use 14-point typeface, double-spaced, as an e-mail letter with no attachments. For nonfiction, please read Michael's **How to Write a Book Proposal** book—available through your library or bookstore, and through our website—so you will know exactly what editors need. Then, before you start writing, send him the title, subtitle and your promotion plan via conventional mail (with SASE) or e-mail. If sent as e-mail, please include the information in the body of your e-mail with NO attachments. Please allow up to two weeks for a response. Responds in 8 weeks to pages or submissions.

TERMS Agent receives 15% commission on domestic sales. Agent receives 20% (30% for Asia) commission on foreign sales. May charge for printing, postage for multiple submissions, foreign mail, foreign phone calls, galleys, books, legal fees.

RECENT SALES Sold at least 15 titles in the last year. *Secrets of the Tudor Court*, by D. Bogden (Kensington); *Zen & the Art of Horse Training*, by Allan Hamilton, M.D. (Storey Pub.); *The Solemn Lantern Maker* by Merlinda Bobis (Delta); *Bite Marks*, the fifth book in an urban fantasy series by J.D. Rardin (Orbit/Grand Central); *The Iron King*, by Julie Karawa (Harlequin Teen).

WRITERS CONFERENCES This agency organizes the annual San Francisco Writers' Conference (www.sfwriters.org).

TIPS "We love helping writers get the rewards and recognition they deserve. If you can write books that meet the needs of the marketplace and you can promote your books, now is the best time ever to be a writer. We must find new writers to make a living, so we are very eager to hear from new writers whose work will interest large houses, and nonfiction writers who can promote their books. For a list of recent sales, helpful info, and three ways to make yourself irresistible to any publisher, please visit our website."

◉ THE STEVE LAUBE AGENCY

5025 N. Central Ave., #635, Phoenix AZ 85012. (602)336-8910. E-mail: krichards@stevelaube.com. Website: www.stevelaube.com. **Contact:** Steve Laube. Other memberships include CBA. Represents 60+ clients. 5% of clients are new/unpublished writers. Currently handles: nonfiction books 48%, novels 48%, novella 2%, scholarly books 2%.

• Prior to becoming an agent, Mr. Laube worked 11 years as a Christian bookseller and 11 years as editorial director of nonfiction with Bethany House Publishers.

REPRESENTS nonfiction books, novels. **Considers these nonfiction areas:** religious. **Considers these fiction areas:** religious.

⛓ Primarily serves the Christian market (CBA). Actively seeking Christian fiction and religious nonfiction. Does not want to receive children's picture books, poetry or cookbooks.

HOW TO CONTACT Submit proposal package, outline, 3 sample chapters, SASE. No e-mail submissions. Consult website for guidelines. Accepts simultaneous submissions. Responds in 6-8 weeks to

queries. Obtains most new clients through recommendations from others, solicitations, conferences.

TERMS Agent receives 15% commission on domestic sales. Agent receives 20% commission on foreign sales. Offers written contract; 30-day notice must be given to terminate contract.

RECENT SALES Sold 80 titles in the last year. Other clients include Deborah Raney, Allison Bottke, H. Norman Wright, Ellie Kay, Jack Cavanaugh, Karen Ball, Tracey Bateman, Susan May Warren, Lisa Bergren, John Rosemond, Cindy Woodsmall, Karol Ladd, Judith Pella, Michael Phillips, Margaret Daley, William Lane Craig, Tosca Lee, Ginny Aiken.

WRITERS CONFERENCES Mount Hermon Christian Writers' Conference; American Christian Fiction Writers' Conference.

◎ LAUNCHBOOKS LITERARY AGENCY

566 Sweet Pea Place, Encinitas CA 92024. (760)944-9909. E-mail: david@launchbooks.com. Website: www.launchbooks.com. **Contact:** David Fugate. Represents 45 clients. 35% of clients are new/unpublished writers. Currently handles: nonfiction books 100%.

• David Fugate has been an agent for more than 18 years and has successfully represented more than 1,000 book titles. He left another agency to found Launchbooks in 2005.

REPRESENTS nonfiction books, novels, textbooks. **Considers these nonfiction areas:** anthropology, archeology, autobiography, biography, business, child guidance, computers, cooking, cultural interests, current affairs, dance, diet/nutrition, economics, education, environment, ethnic, foods, government, health, history, how-to, humor, investigative, law, medicine, memoirs, military, money, music, parenting, popular culture, politics, satire, science, sociology, sports, technology, true crime, war.

⛓ Actively seeking a wide variety of nonfiction, including business, technology, adventure, popular culture, science, creative nonfiction, current events, history, politics, reference, memoirs, health, how-to, lifestyle, parenting and more.

HOW TO CONTACT E-mail query is preferred, or query with SASE. Submit outline/proposal, synopsis, 1 sample chapter, author bio. Accepts simultaneous submissions. Responds in 1 week to queries. Responds in 4 weeks to mss. Obtains most new clients through recommendations from others, solicitations.

TERMS Agent receives 15% commission on domestic sales. Agent receives 25% commission on foreign sales. Offers written contract; 30-day notice must be given to terminate contract. Charges occur very seldom. This agency's agreement limits any charges to $50 unless the author gives a written consent.

RECENT SALES *The Wall Street Virus*, by Christopher Steiner (Portfolio); *Kingpin*, by Kevin Poulsen (Crown); *Inventing Green*, by Alexis Madrigal (Da Capo); *Always On*, by Brian Chen (Basic Books); *When Gadgets Betray Us*, by Robert Vamosi (Basic Books); *The Art of Non-Conformity* (Perigee) and *The $100 Startup* (Crown), both books by Chris Guillebeau; *When A Billion Chinese Jump*, by Jonathan Watts (Scribner); *Ghost in The Wires*, by Kevin Mitnick (Little, Brown); *The Things You Would Have Said*, (Hudson Street Press) by Jackie Hooper.

⬤ SUSANNA LEA ASSOCIATES

28, rue Bonaparte, 75006 Paris France. E-mail: us-submissions@susannalea.com; uk-submissions@susannalea.com; fr-submissions@susannalea.com (France). Website: www.susannaleaassociates.com. **Contact:** Submissions Department. 331 W. 20th Street, New York, NY 10011.

REPRESENTS nonfiction books, novels.

⛏ "Keeps list small; prefers to focus energies on a limited number of projects rather than spreading themselves too thinly. The company is currently developing new international projects—selective, yet broad in their reach, their slogan is: 'Published in Europe, Read by the World.'" Does not want to receive poetry, plays, screenplays, science fiction, educational textbooks, short stories or illustrated works.

HOW TO CONTACT To submit your work, please send the following by e-mail: a concise query letter, including your e-mail address, telephone number, any relevant information about yourself (previous publications, etc.), a brief synopsis, the first three chapters and/or proposal.

TIPS "Your query letter should be concise and include any pertinent information about yourself, relevant writing history, etc."

❶ ROBERT LECKER AGENCY

4055 Melrose Ave., Montreal QC H4A 2S5, Canada. (514)830-4818. Fax: (514)483-1644. E-mail: leckerlink@aol.com. Website: www.leckeragency.com. **Contact:** Robert Lecker. Represents 20 clients. 20% of clients are new/unpublished writers. Currently handles: nonfiction books 80%, novels 10%, scholarly books 10%.

- Prior to becoming an agent, Mr. Lecker was the co-founder and publisher of ECW Press and professor of English literature at McGill University. He has 30 years of experience in book and magazine publishing.

MEMBER AGENTS Robert Lecker (popular culture, music), Mary Williams (travel, food, popular science).

REPRESENTS nonfiction books, novels, scholarly, syndicated material. **Considers these nonfiction areas:** autobiography, biography, cooking, cultural interests, dance, diet/nutrition, ethnic, film, foods, how-to, language, literature, music, popular culture, science, technology, theater. **Considers these fiction areas:** action, adventure, crime, detective, erotica, literary, mainstream, mystery, police, suspense, thriller.

⛏ RLA specializes in books about popular culture, popular science, music, entertainment, food and travel. The agency responds to articulate, innovative proposals within 2 weeks. Actively seeking original book mss only after receipt of outlines and proposals.

HOW TO CONTACT Query first. Only responds to queries of interest. Discards the rest. Accepts simultaneous submissions. Responds in 2 weeks to queries. Responds in 1 month to mss. Obtains most new clients through recommendations from others, conferences, interest in website.

TERMS Agent receives 15% commission on domestic sales. Agent receives 15-20% commission on foreign sales. Offers written contract, binding for 1 year; 6-month notice must be given to terminate contract.

⬤ LESCHER & LESCHER, LTD.

346 E. 84th St., New York NY 10028. (212)396-1999. Fax: (212)396-1991. E-mail: cl@lescherltd.com. **Contact:** Carolyn Larson, agent. Member of AAR. Represents 150 clients. Currently handles: nonfiction books 80%, novels 20%.

REPRESENTS nonfiction books, novels. **Considers these nonfiction areas:** biography, cooking, current affairs, history, law, memoirs, popular culture, cookbooks/wines, narrative nonfiction. **Considers these fiction areas:** commercial, literary, mystery, suspense.

- Does not want to receive screenplays, science fiction or romance.

HOW TO CONTACT Query with SASE. Obtains most new clients through recommendations from others.

TERMS Agent receives 15% commission on domestic sales. Agent receives 10% commission on foreign sales.

LEVINE GREENBERG LITERARY AGENCY, INC.

307 Seventh Ave., Suite 2407, New York NY 10001. (212)337-0934. Fax: (212)337-0948. E-mail: submit@levinegreenberg.com. Website: www.levinegreenberg.com. Member of AAR. Represents 250 clients. 33% of clients are new/unpublished writers. Currently handles: nonfiction books 70%, novels 30%.

- Prior to opening his agency, Mr. Levine served as vice president of the Bank Street College of Education.

MEMBER AGENTS James Levine, Daniel Greenberg, Stephanie Kip Rostan, Lindsay Edgecombe, Danielle Svetcov, Elizabeth Fisher, Victoria Skurnick.

REPRESENTS nonfiction books, novels. **Considers these nonfiction areas:** New Age, animals, art, biography, business, child, computers, cooking, gardening, gay, health, money, nature, religion, science, self-help, sociology, spirituality, sports, women's. **Considers these fiction areas:** literary, mainstream, mystery, thriller, psychological, women's.

- This agency specializes in business, psychology, parenting, health/medicine, narrative nonfiction, spirituality, religion, women's issues, and commercial fiction.

HOW TO CONTACT See website for full submission procedure at "How to Submit." Or use our e-mail address if you prefer or online submission form. Do not submit directly to agents. Prefers electronic submissions. Cannot respond to submissions by mail. Obtains most new clients through recommendations from others.

TERMS Agent receives 15% commission on domestic sales. Agent receives 20% commission on foreign sales. Offers written contract. Charges clients for out-of-pocket expenses—telephone, fax, postage, photocopying—directly connected to the project.

WRITERS CONFERENCES ASJA Writers' Conference.

TIPS "We focus on editorial development, business representation, and publicity and marketing strategy."

PAUL S. LEVINE LITERARY AGENCY

1054 Superba Ave., Venice CA 90291-3940. (310)450-6711. Fax: (310)450-0181. E-mail: paul@paulslevinelit.com. Website: www.paulslevinelit.com. **Contact:** Paul S. Levine. Other memberships include the State Bar of California. Represents over 100 clients. 75% of clients are new/unpublished writers. Currently handles: nonfiction books 60%, novels 20%, movie scripts 10%, TV scripts 5%, juvenile books 5%.

MEMBER AGENTS Paul S. Levine (children's and young adult fiction and nonfiction, adult fiction and nonfiction except sci-fi, fantasy, and horror); Loren R. Grossman (archaeology, art/photography/architecture, gardening, education, health, medicine, science).

REPRESENTS nonfiction books, novels, episodic drama, movie, TV, movie scripts, feature film, TV movie of the week, sitcom, animation, documentary, miniseries, syndicated material, reality show. **Considers these nonfiction areas:** architecture, art, autobiography, biography, business, child guidance, computers, cooking, crafts, cultural interests, current affairs, diet/nutrition, design, economics, education, ethnic, film, foods, gay/lesbian, government, health, history, hobbies, how-to, humor, investigative, language, law, medicine, memoirs, military, money, music, New Age, parenting, photography, popular culture, politics, psychology, science, self-help, sociology, sports, theater, true crime, women's issues, women's studies, creative nonfiction, animation. **Considers these fiction areas:** action, adventure, comic books, confession, crime, detective, erotica, ethnic, experimental, family saga, feminist, frontier, gay, glitz, historical, humor, inspirational, lesbian, literary, mainstream, mystery, police, regional, religious, romance, satire, sports, suspense, thriller, Westerns. **Considers these script areas:** action, biography, cartoon, comedy, contemporary, detective, erotica, ethnic, experimental, family, feminist, gay, glitz, historical, horror, juvenile, mainstream, multimedia, mystery, religious, romantic comedy, romantic drama, sports, teen, thriller, Western.

- Does not want to receive science fiction, fantasy, or horror.

HOW TO CONTACT Query with SASE. Accepts simultaneous submissions. Responds in 1 day to queries. Responds in 6-8 weeks to mss. Obtains most new clients through conferences, referrals, listings on various websites and in directories.
TERMS Agent receives 15% commission on domestic sales. Offers written contract. Charges for postage and actual, out-of-pocket costs only.
RECENT SALES Sold 8 books in the last year.
WRITERS CONFERENCES Willamette Writers Conference; San Francisco Writers Conference; Santa Barbara Writers Conference and many others.
TIPS "Write good, sellable books."

⊙ ROBERT LIEBERMAN ASSOCIATES

400 Nelson Rd., Ithaca NY 14850-9440. (607)273-8801. E-mail: rhl10@cornell.edu. Website: www.people.cornell.edu/pages/rhl10. **Contact:** Robert Lieberman. Represents 30 clients. 50% of clients are new/unpublished writers. Currently handles: nonfiction books 100%.
REPRESENTS nonfiction books, trade, scholarly, college-level textbooks. **Considers these nonfiction areas:** agriculture, anthropology, archeology, architecture, art, business, computers, design, economics, education, environment, film, health, horticulture, medicine, money, music, psychology, science, sociology, technology, theater, memoirs by authors with high public recognition.

    • This agency only accepts nonfiction ideas and specializes in university/college-level textbooks, CD-ROM/software for the university/college-level textbook market, and popular trade books in math, engineering, economics, and other subjects. Does not want to receive any fiction, self-help, or screenplays.

HOW TO CONTACT Prefers to read materials exclusively. Responds in 2 weeks to queries. Responds in 1 month to mss. Obtains most new clients through referrals.
TERMS Agent receives 15% commission on domestic sales. Agent receives 20% commission on foreign sales. Offers written contract; 1-month notice must be given to terminate contract. Fees are sometimes charged to clients for shipping and when special reviewers are required.
TIPS "The trade books we handle are by authors who are highly recognized in their fields of expertise. Our client list includes Nobel Prize winners and others

with high name recognition, either by the public or within a given area of expertise."

⥀⊙ LIMELIGHT CELEBRITY MANAGEMENT, LTD.

33 Newman St., London W1T 1PY England. (44)(207)637-2529. E-mail: mary@limelightmanagement.com. Website: www.limelightmanagement.com. **Contact:** Fiona Lindsay. Estab. 1989. Other memberships include AAA. Represents 70 clients. Currently handles: nonfiction books 100%, multimedia.

    • Prior to becoming an agent, Ms. Lindsay was a public relations manager at the Dorchester and was working on her law degree.

MEMBER AGENTS Fiona Lindsay.
REPRESENTS nonfiction books. **Considers these nonfiction areas:** agriculture, architecture, art, cooking, crafts, decorating, diet/nutrition, design, environment, foods, gardening, health, hobbies, horticulture, interior design, medicine, metaphysics, New Age, photography, self-help, sports, travel.

    • "We are celebrity agents for TV celebrities, broadcasters, writers, journalists, celebrity speakers and media personalities, after dinner speakers, motivational speakers, celebrity chefs, TV presenters and TV chefs." Specializes in nonfiction books in the lifestyle areas, particularly cookery, gardening, health & beauty, nutrition, relationships, business motivation and interior design. Do not send large attachments via e-mail. This agency will consider women's fiction, as well.

HOW TO CONTACT Prefers to read materials exclusively. Query with SASE/IRC via e-mail. Agents will be in contact if they want to see more. No attachments to e-mails. Responds in 1 week to queries. Obtains most new clients through recommendations from others.
TERMS Agent receives 15% commission on domestic sales. Agent receives 20% commission on foreign sales. Offers written contract; 2-month notice must be given to terminate contract.

⓿ LINDSTROM LITERARY MANAGEMENT, LLC

871 N. Greenbrier St., Arlington VA 22205. Fax: (703)527-7624. E-mail: submissions@lindstromliterary.com; kristin@lindstromliterary.com. Website: www.lindstromliterary.com. **Contact:** Kristin Lind-

strom. Other memberships include Author's Guild. Represents 9 clients. 30% of clients are new/unpublished writers. Currently handles: nonfiction books 30%, novels 70%.

- Prior to her current position, Ms. Lindstrom started her career as an editor of a monthly magazine in the energy industry, and was employed as a public relations manager for a national software company before becoming an independent marketing and publicity consultant.

REPRESENTS nonfiction books, novels. **Considers these nonfiction areas:** animals, autobiography, biography, business, current affairs, economics, history, investigative, memoirs, popular culture, science, technology, true crime. **Considers these fiction areas:** action, adventure, crime, detective, erotica, inspirational, mainstream, mystery, police, religious, suspense, thriller, women's.

8—π "In 2006, I decided to add my more specific promotion/publicity skills to the mix in order to support the marketing efforts of my published clients." Actively seeking commercial fiction and narrative nonfiction. Does not want to receive young adult or children's books, or books of poetry.

HOW TO CONTACT Query via e-mail only. Submit author bio, synopsis and first four chapters if submitting fiction. For nonfiction, send the first 4 chapters, synopsis, proposal, outline and mission statement. "You will only hear from us again if we decide to ask for a complete manuscript or further information." Accepts simultaneous submissions. Responds in 6 weeks to queries. Responds in 8 weeks to requested mss. Obtains most new clients through referrals and solicitations.

TERMS Agent receives 15% commission on domestic sales. Agent receives 20% commission on performance rights and foreign sales. Offers written contract. This agency charges for postage, UPS, copies and other basic office expenses.

RECENT SALES A memoir by Agathe von Trapp (It Books/Harper); two-book deal for Alice Wisler (Bethany House); a thriller by J.C. Hutchins (St. Martin's Press).

TIPS "Do your homework on accepted practices; make sure you know what kind of book the agent handles."

◑ LIPPINCOTT MASSIE MCQUILKIN

27 West 20th Street, Suite 305, New York NY 10011. Fax: (212)352-2059. E-mail: info@lmqlit.com. Website: www.lmqlit.com.

MEMBER AGENTS Maria Massie (fiction, memoir, cultural criticism); Will Lippincott (politics, current affairs, history); Rob McQuilkin (fiction, history, psychology, sociology, graphic material); Jason Anthony (young adult, pop culture, memoir, true crime, and general psychology).

REPRESENTS nonfiction books, novels, short story collections, scholarly, graphic novels. **Considers these nonfiction areas:** animals, anthropology, archeology, architecture, art, autobiography, biography, business, child guidance, cultural interests, current affairs, design, economics, ethnic, film, gay/lesbian, government, health, history, inspirational, language, law, literature, medicine, memoirs, military, money, music, parenting, popular culture, politics, psychology, religious, science, self-help, sociology, technology, true crime, women's issues, women's studies, young adult. **Considers these fiction areas:** action, adventure, cartoon, comic books, confession, family saga, feminist, gay, historical, humor, lesbian, literary, mainstream, regional, satire.

8—π "LMQ focuses on bringing new voices in literary and commercial fiction to the market, as well as popularizing the ideas and arguments of scholars in the fields of history, psychology, sociology, political science, and current affairs. Actively seeking fiction writers who already have credits in magazines and quarterlies, as well as nonfiction writers who already have a media platform or some kind of a university affiliation." Does not want to receive romance, genre fiction or children's material.

HOW TO CONTACT "We accepts electronic queries only. Only send additional materials if requested." Accepts simultaneous submissions. Responds in 1 week to queries. Responds in 1 month to mss. Obtains most new clients through recommendations from others, solicitations, conferences.

TERMS Agent receives 15% commission on domestic sales. Agent receives 20% commission on foreign sales. Offers written contract; 30-day notice must be given to terminate contract. Only charges for reasonable business expenses upon successful sale.

RECENT SALES Clients include: Peter Ho Davies,

Kim Addonizio, Natasha Trethewey, Anne Carson, David Sirota, Katie Crouch, Uwen Akpan, Lydia Millet, Tom Perrotta, Jonathan Lopez, Chris Hayes, Caroline Weber.

● LITERARY AND CREATIVE ARTISTS, INC.

3543 Albemarle St., N.W., Washington D.C. 20008-4213. E-mail: lca9643@lcadc.com. Website: www.lcadc.com. **Contact:** Muriel Nellis. Member of AAR. Other memberships include Authors Guild, American Bar Association, American Booksellers Association. Currently handles: nonfiction books 50%, novels 50%.

MEMBER AGENTS Prior to becoming an agent, Mr. Powell was in sales and contract negotiation.

REPRESENTS nonfiction books, novels, art, biography, business, photography, popular culture, religion, self-help, literary, regional, religious, satire. **Considers these nonfiction areas:** autobiography, biography, business, cooking, diet/nutrition, economics, foods, government, health, how-to, law, medicine, memoirs, philosophy, politics, human drama; lifestyle.

⛐ "Specializles in adult trade fiction and nonfiction. Current, we are only accepting projects by established authors. Actively seeking quality projects by authors with a vision of where they want to be in 10 years and a plan of how to get there. We do not handle poetry, or purely academic/technical work."

HOW TO CONTACT Query via e-mail first and include a synopsis. **We do not accept unsolicited manuscripts, faxed manuscripts, manuscripts sent by e-mail or manuscripts on computer disk.** Accepts simultaneous submissions. Responds in 3 weeks to queries. Responds in 1 week to mss. Obtains new clients through recommendations from others.

TERMS Agent receives 15% commission on domestic sales. Agent receives 25% commission on foreign sales. Offers written contract. Charges clients for long-distance phone/fax, photocopying, shipping.

TIPS "If you are an unpublished author, join a writers group, even if it is on the Internet. You need good honest feedback. Don't send a manuscript that has not been read by at least five people. Don't send a manuscript cold to any agent without first asking if they want it. Try to meet the agent face to face before signing. Make sure the fit is right."

● LITERARY MANAGEMENT GROUP, INC.

(615)812-4445. E-mail: brucebarbour@literarymanagementgroup.com; brb@brucebarbour.com. Website: http://literarymanagementgroup.com; www.brucebarbour.com. **Contact:** Bruce Barbour.

• Prior to becoming an agent, Mr. Barbour held executive positions at several publishing houses, including Revell, Barbour Books, Thomas Nelson, and Random House.

REPRESENTS nonfiction books, novels. **Considers these nonfiction areas:** biography, Christian living; spiritual growth; women's and men's issues; prayer; devotional; meditational; Bible study; marriage; business; family/parenting.

⛐ "Although we specialize in the area of Christian publishing from an Evangelical perspective, we have editorial contacts and experience in general interest books as well." Does not want to receive gift books, poetry, children's books, short stories, or juvenile/young adult fiction. No unsolicited mss or proposals from unpublished authors.

HOW TO CONTACT Query with SASE. E-mail proposal as an attachment.

TERMS Agent receives 15% commission on domestic sales.

ⓘ LITERARY SERVICES, INC.

P.O. Box 888, Barnegat NJ 08005. (609)698-7162. Fax: (609)698-7163. E-mail: john@literaryservicesinc.com; shane@literaryservicesinc.com. Website: www.LiteraryServicesInc.com. **Contact:** John Willig. Other memberships include Author's Guild. Represents 90 clients. 25% of clients are new/unpublished writers. Currently handles: nonfiction books 100%. Beginning to accept and consider crime fiction projects.

MEMBER AGENTS John Willig (business, personal growth, narratives, history, health); Cynthia Zigmund (personal finance, investments, entrepreneurship).

REPRESENTS nonfiction books. **Considers these nonfiction areas:** architecture, art, biography, business, child guidance, cooking, crafts, design, economics, health, history, politics, how-to, humor, language, literature, metaphysics, money, New Age, popular culture, psychology, satire, science, self-help, sports, technology, true crime.

⛐ We work primarily with nonfiction and mystery/crime fiction authors. "Our publishing experience and 'inside' knowledge of how companies and editors really work sets us apart from many agencies; our specialties are noted above, but we are open to unique presentations in all nonfiction topic areas." Actively seeking business, work/life topics, story-driven narratives. Does not want to receive fiction (except crime fiction), children's books, science fiction, religion or memoirs.

HOW TO CONTACT Query with SASE. For starters, a one-page outline sent via e-mail is acceptable. See our website and our Submissions section to learn more about our questions. Do not send mss unless requested. Accepts simultaneous submissions. Responds in 3-4 weeks to queries. Responds in 4 weeks to mss. Obtains most new clients through recommendations from others, solicitations, conferences.

TERMS Agent receives 15% commission on domestic sales. Agent receives 20% commission on foreign sales. Offers written contract. This agency charges administrative fees for copying, postage, etc.

RECENT SALES Sold 32 titles in the last year. *In Pursuit of Elegance* (Doubleday/Currency). A full list of new books are noted on the website.

WRITERS CONFERENCES Author 101; Publicity Summit; Writer's Digest.

TIPS "Be focused. In all likelihood, your work is not going to be of interest to 'a very broad audience' or 'every parent,' so I appreciate when writers put aside their passion and do some homework, i.e., positioning, special features and benefits of your work. Be a marketer. How have you tested your ideas and writing (beyond your inner circle of family and friends)? Have you received any key awards for your work or endorsements from influential persons in your field? What steps, especially social media, have you taken to increase your presence in the market?"

✚ ❶ LIVING WORD LITERARY AGENCY

PO Box 40974, Eugene OR 97414. E-mail: livingwordliterary@gmail.com. Website: livingwordliterary.wordpress.com. **Contact:** Kimberly Shumate/Agent. Estab. 2008. Member Evangelical Christian Publishers Association.

- Kimberly began her employment with Harvest House Publishers as the assistant to the National Sales Manager as well as the International Sales Director.

REPRESENTS Considers these nonfiction areas: health, parenting, self-help, relationships. **Considers these fiction areas:** inspirational, adult fiction, Christian living.

⊶ Does not want to receive cookbooks, children's books, science fiction or fantasy, memoirs, screenplays or poetry.

HOW TO CONTACT Submit a query with short synopsis and first chapter via Word document. Agency only responds if interested.

LJK LITERARY MANAGEMENT

708 Third Ave., 16th Floor, New York NY 10018. (212)221-8797. Fax: (212)221-8722. E-mail: submissions@ljkliterary.com. Website: www.ljkliterary.com. Represents 20+ clients.

- Larry Kirshbaum is the former head of Time Warner Book group; Jud Laghi worked for ICM; Susanna Einstein worked for Maria B. Campbell Associates; Meg Thompson worked for Bill Clinton and Charlie Rose before joining Larry in starting LJK; Lisa Leshne co-founded *The Prague Post*.

MEMBER AGENTS Larry Kirshbaum; Susanna Einstein (contemporary fiction, literary fiction, romance, suspense, historical fiction, middle grade, young adult, crime fiction, narrative nonfiction, memoir and biography); Meg Thompson (new media, narrative nonfiction, politics, pop culture, humor); Lisa Leshne (nonfiction, memoirs, literary and popular fiction, business, politics, pop culture).

REPRESENTS nonfiction books, novels.

⊶ "We are not considering picture books or poetry collections."

HOW TO CONTACT As of Friday, April 15, 2011 we will not be accepting any unsolicited submissions. Any submissions received after this date will be deleted and will not be considered. This is a temporary policy; check our website for updates. Send query letter in the body of an e-mail to submissions@ljkliterary.com with 25-page sample (fiction) or proposal (nonfiction) as an attachment; if sending a paper query, include SASE. E-mail is preferred. No fax queries. Responds in 8 weeks to queries. Responds in 8 weeks to mss.

RECENT SALES *Think Big and Kick Ass*, by Donald Trump and Bill Zanker; *The Book of Love*, by Kathleen McGowan; *The Christmas Pearl*, by Dorothea Benton Frank; *The Hidden Man*, by David

Ellis; *Maphead*, by Ken Jennings; *Grandma's Dead*, by Ben Schwartz and Amanda McCall; *Found II*, by Davy Rothbart; *Amberville*, by Tim Davys; *Moses Never Closes*, by Jenny Wingfield; *Daily Routines*, by Mason Currey.

TIPS "All submissions will receive a response from us if they adhere to our submission guidelines. Please do not contact us to inquire about your submission unless 8 weeks have passed."

🌑 LOUD LITERARY AGENCY

Box 4244, Hyregatan 14, SE-203 13 Malmö, Sweden. (46)(0)40 30 52 40. E-mail: info@loudagency.com. **Contact:** Joakim Hansson.

MEMBER AGENTS Joakim Hansson (managing director and literary agent); Hanserik Tönnheim (senior advisor and literary agent); Karin Stangertz (literary agent).

REPRESENTS nonfiction books, novels.

⌐━ The agency is a co-operation between veteran agent Hanserik Tönnheim and newcomer Joakim Hansson. The agency represents a number of bestselling Scandinavian authors in many categories of writing—mainly fiction, contemporary journalism, self-help and humor. For direct representation, the agency mainly works with established European authors. It also represents various English and American writers.

HOW TO CONTACT Submit a one-page synopsis of the work and the author.

⬤ LOWENSTEIN ASSOCIATES, INC.

121 W. 27th St., Suite 601, New York NY 10001. (212)206-1630. Fax: (212)727-0280. E-mail: assistant@bookhaven.com. Website: www.lowensteinassociates.com. **Contact:** Barbara Lowenstein. Member of AAR. Represents 150 clients. 20% of clients are new/unpublished writers. Currently handles: nonfiction books 60%, novels 40%.

MEMBER AGENTS Barbara Lowenstein, president (nonfiction interests include narrative nonfiction, health, money, finance, travel, multicultural, popular culture and memoir; fiction interests include literary fiction and women's fiction); Meredith Barnes, associate agent. She is seeking children's books (chapter, middle grade, and young adult) and young adult nonfiction.

REPRESENTS nonfiction books, novels. **Considers these nonfiction areas:** animals, anthropology, archeology, autobiography, biography, business, child guidance, current affairs, education, ethnic, film, government, health, history, how-to, language, literature, medicine, memoirs, money, multicultural, parenting, popular culture, psychology, science, sociology, travel, music; narrative nonfiction; science; film. **Considers these fiction areas:** crime, detective, erotica, ethnic, fantasy, feminist, historical, literary, mainstream, mystery, police, romance, suspense, thriller, young adult.

⌐━ "This agency specializes in health, business, creative nonfiction, literary fiction and commercial fiction—especially suspense, crime and women's issues. We are a full-service agency, handling domestic and foreign rights, film rights and audio rights to all of our books." Barbara Lowenstein is currently looking for writers who have a platform and are leading experts in their field, including business, women's issues, psychology, health, science and social issues, and is particularly interested in strong new voices in fiction and narrative nonfiction.

HOW TO CONTACT Please send us a one-page query letter, along with the first 10 pages pasted in the body of the message (if fiction; for nonfiction, please send only a query letter), by e-mail. Please put the word "Query" and the title of your project in the subject field of your e-mail and address it to the agent of your choice. Please do not send an attachment. We reply to all queries and generally send a response within 2-4 weeks. By mail: For Fiction: Mail a query letter, short synopsis, first chapter and a SASE. For nonfiction: Mail a query letter, proposal, if available, or else a project overview and a SASE. Responds in 4 weeks to queries. Obtains most new clients through recommendations from others, solicitations, conferences.

TERMS Agent receives 15% commission on domestic sales. Agent receives 20% commission on foreign sales. Offers written contract. Charges for large photocopy batches, messenger service, international postage.

WRITERS CONFERENCES Malice Domestic.

TIPS "Know the genre you are working in and read! Also, please see our website for details on which agent to query for your project."

●① ANDREW LOWNIE LITERARY AGENCY, LTD.

36 Great Smith St., London SW1P 3BU England. (44)(207)222-7574. Fax: (44)(207)222-7576. E-mail: lownie@globalnet.co.uk. Website: www.andrewlownie.co.uk. **Contact:** Andrew Lownie. Other memberships include AAA. Represents 130 clients. 20% of clients are new/unpublished writers. Currently handles: nonfiction books 90%, novels 10%.

- Prior to becoming an agent, Mr. Lownie was a journalist, bookseller, publisher, author of 12 books and director of the Curtis Brown Agency.

REPRESENTS nonfiction books. **Considers these nonfiction areas:** autobiography, biography, current affairs, government, history, investigative, law, memoirs, military, popular culture, politics, true crime, war.

- ⚷⚞ "This agent has wide publishing experience, extensive journalistic contacts, and a specialty in showbiz/celebrity memoir." Showbiz memoirs, narrative histories, and biographies. No poetry, short stories, children's fiction, academic or scripts.

HOW TO CONTACT Query with SASE and/or IRC. Submit outline, 1 sample chapter. Accepts simultaneous submissions. Responds in 1 week to queries. Responds in 1 month to mss. Obtains most new clients through recommendations from others.

TERMS Agent receives 15% commission on domestic sales. Agent receives 15% commission on foreign sales. Offers written contract; 30-day notice must be given to terminate contract.

RECENT SALES Sold 50 titles in the last year, with over a dozen top ten bestsellers including two number 1's, as well as the memoirs of actor Warwick Davis, Multiple Personality Disorder sufferer Alice Jamieson, round-the-world yachtsman Mike Perham, poker player Dave 'Devilfish' Ulliott. Other clients: Juliet Barker, Guy Bellamy, Joyce Cary estate, Roger Crowley, Duncan Falconer, Laurence Gardner, Cathy Glass, Timothy Good, Lawrence James, Christopher Lloyd, Sian Rees, Desmond Seward, Daniel Tammet and Christian Wolmar.

➕ MARSAL LYON LITERARY AGENCY, LLC

PMB 121, 665 San Rodolfo Dr. 124, Solana Beach CA 92075. (858)492-8009. E-mail: Kevan@MarsalLyonLiteraryAgency.com; Jill@MarsalLyonLiteraryAgency.com. Website: www.marsallyonliteraryagency.com. **Contact:** Kevan Lyon, Jill Marsal; Kathleen Rushall. **REPRESENTS** nonfiction books, novels. **Considers these nonfiction areas:** animals, biography, business, cooking, current affairs, diet/nutrition, foods, health, history, investigative, memoirs, music, parenting, popular culture, politics, psychology, science, self-help, sports, women's issues, relationships, advice. **Considers these fiction areas:** commercial, mainstream, multicultural, mystery, romance, suspense, thriller, women's, young adult.

HOW TO CONTACT Query by e-mail to either Jill Marsal at jill@marsallyonliteraryagency.com or Kevan Lyon at kevan@marsallyonliteraryagency.com. "Please visit our website to determine who is best suited for your work. Write 'query' in the subject line of your e-mail. Please allow up to several weeks to hear back on your query."

TIPS "Our Agency's mission is to help writers achieve their publishing dreams. We want to work with authors not just for a book but for a career; we are dedicated to building long-term relationships with our authors and publishing partners. Our goal is to help find homes for books that engage, entertain, and make a difference."

① LYONS LITERARY, LLC

27 West 20th St., Suite 10003, New York NY 10011. (212)255-5472. Fax: (212)851-8405. E-mail: info@lyonsliterary.com. Website: www.lyonsliterary.com. **Contact:** Jonathan Lyons. Member of AAR. Other memberships include The Author's Guild, American Bar Association, New York State Bar Association, New York State Intellectual Property Law Section. Represents 37 clients. 15% of clients are new/unpublished writers. Currently handles: nonfiction books 60%, novels 40%.

REPRESENTS nonfiction books, novels. **Considers these nonfiction areas:** animals, autobiography, biography, cooking, crafts, cultural interests, current affairs, diet/nutrition, ethnic, foods, gay/lesbian, government, health, history, hobbies, how-to, humor, law, medicine, memoirs, military, money, multicultural, popular culture, politics, psychology, science, sociology, sports, technology, translation, travel, true crime, women's issues, women's studies. **Considers these fiction areas:** contemporary issues, crime, detective, fantasy, feminist, gay, historical, humor, lesbian, literary, mainstream, mystery, police, psychic, regional, satire, science fiction, sports, supernatural, suspense, thriller, women's, chick lit.

⚷▬ "With my legal expertise and experience selling domestic and foreign language book rights, paperback reprint rights, audio rights, film/TV rights and permissions, I am able to provide substantive and personal guidance to my clients in all areas relating to their projects. In addition, with the advent of new publishing technology, Lyons Literary, LLC is situated to address the changing nature of the industry while concurrently handling authors' more traditional needs."

HOW TO CONTACT Only accepts queries through online submission form. Accepts simultaneous submissions. Responds in 8 weeks to queries. Responds in 12 weeks to mss. Obtains most new clients through recommendations from others.

TERMS Agent receives 15% commission on domestic sales. Agent receives 20% commission on foreign sales. Offers written contract.

WRITERS CONFERENCES Agents and Editors Conference.

TIPS "Please submit electronic queries through our website submission form."

⬤ DONALD MAASS LITERARY AGENCY

121 W. 27th St., Suite 801, New York NY 10001. (212)727-8383. E-mail: info@maassagency.com. Website: www.maassagency.com. Member of AAR. Other memberships include SFWA, MWA, RWA. Represents more than 100 clients. 5% of clients are new/unpublished writers. Currently handles: novels 100%.

- Prior to opening his agency, Mr. Maass served as an editor at Dell Publishing (New York) and as a reader at Gollancz (London). He also served as the president of AAR.

MEMBER AGENTS Donald Maass (mainstream, literary, mystery/suspense, science fiction, romance); Jennifer Jackson (commercial fiction, romance, science fiction, fantasy, mystery/suspense); Cameron McClure (literary, mystery/suspense, urban, fantasy, narrative nonfiction and projects with multicultural, international, and environmental themes, gay/lesbian); Stacia Decker (fiction, memoir, narrative nonfiction, pop-culture [cooking, fashion, style, music, art], smart humor, upscale erotica/erotic memoir and multicultural fiction/nonfiction); Amy Boggs (fantasy and science fiction, especially urban fantasy,

paranormal romance, steampunk, young adult/children's, and alternate history. historical fiction, multicultural fiction, Westerns).

REPRESENTS novels. **Considers these nonfiction areas:** narrative nonfiction (and see J.L's bio for subject interest). **Considers these fiction areas:** crime, detective, fantasy, historical, horror, literary, mainstream, mystery, police, psychic, science fiction, supernatural, suspense, thriller, women's, romance (historical, paranormal, and time travel).

⚷▬ This agency specializes in commercial fiction, especially science fiction, fantasy, mystery and suspense. Actively seeking to expand in literary fiction and women's fiction. We are fiction specialists. All genres are welcome. Does not want to receive nonfiction, picture books, prescriptive nonfiction, or poetry.

HOW TO CONTACT Query with SASE. Returns material only with SASE. Accepts simultaneous submissions. Responds in 2 weeks to queries. Responds in 3 months to mss.

TERMS Agent receives 15% commission on domestic sales. Agent receives 20% commission on foreign sales.

RECENT SALES *Codex Alera 5: Princep's Fury*, by Jim Butcher (Ace); *Fonseca 6: Bright Futures*, by Stuart Kaimsky (Forge): *Fathom*, by Cherie Priest (Tor); *Gospel Grrls 3: Be Strong and Curvaceous*, by Shelly Adina (Faith Words); *Ariane 1: Peacekeeper*, by Laura Reeve (Roc); *Execution Dock*, by Anne Perry (Random House).

WRITERS CONFERENCES Donald Maass: World Science Fiction Convention; Frankfurt Book Fair; Pacific Northwest Writers Conference; Bouchercon. Jennifer Jackson: World Science Fiction Convention; RWA National Conference.

TIPS "We are fiction specialists, also noted for our innovative approach to career planning. Few new clients are accepted, but interested authors should query with a SASE. Works with subagents in all principle foreign countries and Hollywood. No prescriptive nonfiction, picture books or poetry will be considered."

⬤ GINA MACCOBY LITERARY AGENCY

P.O. Box 60, Chappaqua NY 10514. (914)238-5630. **Contact:** Gina Maccoby. Member of AAR. Ethics and Contracts subcommittee; Authors Guild Represents 25 clients. Currently handles: nonfiction books 33%, novels 33%, juvenile books 33%, other illustrators of children's books.

MEMBER AGENTS Gina Maccoby.

REPRESENTS nonfiction books, novels, juvenile. **Considers these nonfiction areas:** autobiography, biography, cultural interests, current affairs, ethnic, history, juvenile nonfiction, popular culture, women's issues, women's studies. **Considers these fiction areas:** juvenile, literary, mainstream, mystery, thriller, young adult.

HOW TO CONTACT Query with SASE. If querying by e-mail, put "query" in subject line. Accepts simultaneous submissions. Responds in 3 months to queries. Obtains most new clients through recommendations from clients and publishers.

TERMS Agent receives 15% commission on domestic sales. Agent receives 25% commission on foreign sales. Charges clients for photocopying. May recover certain costs, such as legal fees or the cost of shipping books by air to Europe or Japan.

RECENT SALES This agency sold 21 titles last year.

● MACGREGOR LITERARY INC.

2373 N.W. 185th Ave., Suite 165, Hillsboro OR 97124. (503)277-8308. E-mail: submissions@macgregorlit erary.com. Website: www.macgregorliterary.com. **Contact:** Chip MacGregor. Signatory of WGA. Represents 40 clients. 10% of clients are new/unpublished writers. Currently handles: nonfiction books 40%, novels 60%.

> • Prior to his current position, Mr. MacGregor was the senior agent with Alive Communications. Most recently, he was associate publisher for Time-Warner Book Group's Faith Division, and helped put together their Center Street imprint.

MEMBER AGENTS Chip MacGregor, Sandra Bishop, Amanda Luedeke.

REPRESENTS nonfiction books, novels. **Considers these nonfiction areas:** business, current affairs, economics, history, how-to, humor, inspirational, parenting, popular culture, satire, self-help, sports, marriage. **Considers these fiction areas:** crime, detective, historical, inspirational, mainstream, mystery, police, religious, romance, suspense, thriller, women's, chick lit.

> ✂━ "My specialty has been in career planning with authors—finding commercial ideas, then helping authors bring them to market, and in the midst of that assisting the authors as they get firmly established in their writing careers.

I'm probably best known for my work with Christian books over the years, but I've done a fair amount of general market projects as well." Actively seeking authors with a Christian worldview and a growing platform. Does not want to receive fantasy, sci-fi, children's books, poetry or screenplays.

HOW TO CONTACT Query with SASE. Accepts simultaneous submissions. Responds in 3 weeks to queries. Obtains most new clients through recommendations from others. Not looking to add unpublished authors except through referrals from current clients.

TERMS Agent receives 15% commission on domestic sales. Agent receives 15% commission on foreign sales. Offers written contract; 30-day notice must be given to terminate contract. Charges for exceptional fees after receiving authors' permission.

WRITERS CONFERENCES Blue Ridge Christian Writers' Conference; Write to Publish.

TIPS "Seriously consider attending a good writers' conference. It will give you the chance to be face-to-face with people in the industry. Also, if you're a novelist, consider joining one of the national writers' organizations. The American Christian Fiction Writers (ACFW) is a wonderful group for new as well as established writers. And if you're a Christian writer of any kind, check into The Writers View, an online writing group. All of these have proven helpful to writers."

◑ RICIA MAINHARDT AGENCY (RMA)

612 Argyle Rd., #L5, Brooklyn NY 11230. (718)434-1893. Fax: (718)434-2157. E-mail: ricia@ricia.com. Website: www.ricia.com. **Contact:** Ricia Mainhardt. Represents 10 clients. 50% of clients are new/unpublished writers. Currently handles: nonfiction books 40%, novella 50%, juvenile books 10%.

REPRESENTS nonfiction books, novels, juvenile. **Considers these fiction areas:** action, adventure, confession, crime, detective, erotica, ethnic, family saga, fantasy, feminist, frontier, gay, glitz, historical, horror, humor, juvenile, lesbian, literary, mainstream, mystery, police, psychic, regional, romance, satire, science fiction, sports, supernatural, suspense, thriller, Westerns, women's, young adult.

> ✂━ "We are a small boutique agency that provides hands-on service and attention to clients." Actively seeking adult and young adult fiction, nonfiction, picture books for early

readers. Does not want to receive poetry, children's books or screenplays.

HOW TO CONTACT Query with SASE or by e-mail. See guidelines on website depending on type of ms. No attachments or diskettes. Accepts simultaneous submissions. Responds in 1 month to queries. Responds in 4 months to mss. Obtains most new clients through recommendations from others, solicitations.

TERMS Agent receives 15% commission on domestic sales. Offers written contract; 90-day notice must be given to terminate contract.

WRITERS CONFERENCES Science Fiction Worldcon, Lunacon, World Fantasy, RWA.

TIPS "Be professional; be patient. It takes a long time for me to evaluate all the submissions that come through the door. Pestering phone calls and e-mails are not appreciated. Write the best book you can in your own style and keep an active narrative voice."

◑ KIRSTEN MANGES LITERARY AGENCY

115 West 29th St., Third Floor, New York NY 10001. E-mail: kirsten@mangeslit.com. Website: www.mangeslit.com. **Contact:** Kirsten Manges.

- Prior to her current position, Ms. Manges was an agent at Curtis Brown.

REPRESENTS nonfiction books, novels. **Considers these nonfiction areas:** cooking, diet/nutrition, foods, history, memoirs, multicultural, psychology, science, spirituality, sports, technology, travel, women's issues, women's studies, journalism, narrative. **Considers these fiction areas:** commercial, women's, chick lit.

☞ This agency has a focus on women's issues. "Actively seeking high-quality fiction and nonfiction. I'm looking for strong credentials, an original point of view and excellent writing skills. With fiction, I'm looking for well written commercial novels, as well as compelling and provocative literary works."

HOW TO CONTACT Query with SASE. Obtains most new clients through recommendations from others, solicitations.

◑ CAROL MANN AGENCY

55 Fifth Ave., New York NY 10003. (212)206-5635. Fax: (212)675-4809. Website: www.carolmannagency.com/. **Contact:** Eliza Dreier. Member of AAR. Represents roughly 200 clients. 15% of clients are new/unpublished writers. Currently handles: nonfiction books 90%, novels 10%.

MEMBER AGENTS Carol Mann (health/medical, religion, spirituality, self-help, parenting, narrative nonfiction, current affairs); Laura Yorke; Gareth Esersky; Myrsini Stephanides (Nonfiction areas of interest: pop culture and music, humor, narrative nonfiction and memoir, cookbooks; fiction areas of interest: offbeat literary fiction, graphic works, and edgy young adult fiction). Joanne Wyckoff (Nonfiction areas of interest: memoir, narrative nonfiction, personal narrative, psychology, women's issues, education, health and wellness, parenting, serious self-help, natural history); fiction.

REPRESENTS nonfiction books, novels. **Considers these nonfiction areas:** anthropology, archeology, architecture, art, autobiography, biography, business, child guidance, cultural interests, current affairs, design, ethnic, government, health, history, law, medicine, money, music, parenting, popular culture, politics, psychology, self-help, sociology, sports, women's issues, women's studies. **Considers these fiction areas:** commercial, literary.

☞ This agency specializes in current affairs, self-help, popular culture, psychology, parenting, and history. Does not want to receive genre fiction (romance, mystery, etc.).

HOW TO CONTACT Please see website for submission guidelines. Responds in 4 weeks to queries.

TERMS Agent receives 15% commission on domestic sales. Agent receives 20% commission on foreign sales. Offers written contract.

◑ MANUS & ASSOCIATES LITERARY AGENCY, INC.

425 Sherman Ave., Suite 200, Palo Alto CA 94306. (650)470-5151. Fax: (650)470-5159. E-mail: manuslit@manuslit.com. Website: www.manuslit.com. **Contact:** Jillian Manus, Jandy Nelson, Penny Nelson. Member of AAR. Represents 75 clients. 30% of clients are new/unpublished writers. Currently handles: nonfiction books 70%, novels 30%.

- Prior to becoming an agent, Ms. Manus was associate publisher of two national magazines and director of development at Warner Bros. and Universal Studios; she has been a literary agent for 20 years.

MEMBER AGENTS Jandy Nelson, jandy@manuslit.com (self-help, health, memoirs, narrative nonfiction, women's fiction, literary fiction, multicultural fiction, thrillers). Nelson is currently on sabbatical and not taking on new clients. Jillian Manus, jillian@manuslit.com (political, memoirs, self-help, history, sports, women's issues, Latin fiction and nonfiction, thrillers); Penny Nelson, penny@manuslit.com (memoirs, self-help, sports, nonfiction); Dena Fischer (literary fiction, mainstream/commercial fiction, chick lit, women's fiction, historical fiction, ethnic/cultural fiction, narrative nonfiction, parenting, relationships, pop culture, health, sociology, psychology); Janet Wilkens Manus (narrative fact-based crime books, religion, pop psychology, inspiration, memoirs, cookbooks); Stephanie Lee (not currently taking on new clients).

REPRESENTS nonfiction books, novels. **Considers these nonfiction areas:** autobiography, biography, business, child guidance, cultural interests, current affairs, economics, environment, ethnic, health, how-to, medicine, memoirs, money, parenting, popular culture, psychology, science, self-help, technology, women's issues, women's studies, Gen X and Gen Y issues; creative nonfiction. **Considers these fiction areas:** literary, mainstream, multicultural, mystery, suspense, thriller, women's, quirky/edgy fiction.

☞ "Our agency is unique in the way that we not only sell the material, but we edit, develop concepts, and participate in the marketing effort. We specialize in large, conceptual fiction and nonfiction, and always value a project that can be sold in the TV/feature film market." Actively seeking high-concept thrillers, commercial literary fiction, women's fiction, celebrity biographies, memoirs, multicultural fiction, popular health, women's empowerment and mysteries. No horror, romance, science fiction, fantasy, Western, young adult, children's, poetry, cookbooks or magazine articles.

HOW TO CONTACT Query with SASE. If requested, submit outline, 2-3 sample chapters. All queries should be sent to the California office. Accepts simultaneous submissions. Responds in 3 months to queries. Responds in 3 months to mss. Obtains most new clients through recommendations from others, solicitations, conferences.

TERMS Agent receives 15% commission on domestic sales. Agent receives 20-25% commission on foreign sales. Offers written contract, binding for 2 years; 60-day notice must be given to terminate contract. Charges for photocopying and postage/UPS.

RECENT SALES *Nothing Down for the 2000s* and *Multiple Streams of Income for the 2000s*, by Robert Allen; *Missed Fortune 101*, by Doug Andrew; *Cracking the Millionaire Code*, by Mark Victor Hansen and Robert Allen; *Stress Free for Good*, by Dr. Fred Luskin and Dr. Ken Pelletier; *The Mercy of Thin Air*, by Ronlyn Domangue; *The Fine Art of Small Talk*, by Debra Fine; *Bone Men of Bonares*, by Terry Tamoff.

WRITERS CONFERENCES Maui Writers' Conference; San Diego State University Writers' Conference; Willamette Writers' Conference; BookExpo America; MEGA Book Marketing University.

TIPS "Research agents using a variety of sources."

● MARCH TENTH, INC.

24 Hillside Terrace, MonTVale NJ 07645. (201)387-6551. Fax: (201)387-6552. E-mail: hchoron@aol.com; schoron@aol.com. Website: www.marchtenthinc.com. **Contact:** Harry Choron, vice president. Represents 40 clients. 30% of clients are new/unpublished writers. Currently handles: nonfiction books 100%.

REPRESENTS nonfiction books. **Considers these nonfiction areas:** autobiography, biography, current affairs, film, health, history, humor, language, literature, medicine, music, popular culture, satire, theater.

☞ "We prefer to work with published/established writers." Does not want to receive children's or young adult novels, plays, screenplays or poetry.

HOW TO CONTACT Query with SASE. Include your proposal, a short bio, and contact information. Accepts simultaneous submissions. Responds in 1 month to queries.

TERMS Agent receives 15% commission on domestic sales. Agent receives 20% commission on foreign sales. Agent receives 20% commission on film sales. Does not require expense money upfront.

● THE EVAN MARSHALL AGENCY

6 Tristam Place, Pine Brook NJ 07058-9445. (973)882-1122. Fax: (973)882-3099. E-mail: evanmarshall@optonline.net. **Contact:** Evan Marshall. Member of AAR. Other memberships include MWA, Sisters in Crime. Currently handles: novels 100%.

REPRESENTS novels. **Considers these fiction areas:** action, adventure, erotica, ethnic, frontier, historical, horror, humor, inspirational, literary, mainstream, mystery, religious, satire, science fiction, suspense, Westerns, romance (contemporary, gothic, historical, regency).

HOW TO CONTACT Do not query. Currently accepting clients only by referal from editors and our own clients. Responds in 1 week to queries. Responds in 3 months to mss. Obtains most new clients through recommendations from others.

TERMS Agent receives 15% commission on domestic sales. Agent receives 20% commission on foreign sales. Offers written contract.

RECENT SALES *Watch Me Die*, by Erica Spindler (St. Martin's Press); *The First Day of the Rest of My Life*, by Cathy Lamb (Kensington); *Highland Protector*, by Hannah Howell (Zebra); *Devoured by Darkness*, by Alexandra Ivy (Kensington).

● THE MARTELL AGENCY

1350 Avenue of the Americas, Suite 1205, New York NY 10019. Fax: (212)317-2676. E-mail: afmartell@aol. com. **Contact:** Alice Martell.

REPRESENTS nonfiction. **Considers these nonfiction areas:** business, economics, health, history, medicine, memoirs, multicultural, psychology, self-help, women's issues, women's studies. **Considers these fiction areas:** commercial, novels (NO mystery).

HOW TO CONTACT Query with SASE. Submit sample chapters. Submit via snail mail. No e-mail or fax queries.

RECENT SALES *Peddling Peril: The Secret Nuclear Arms Trade* by David Albright and Joel Wit (Five Press); *America's Women: Four Hundred Years of Dolls, Drudges, Helpmates, and Heroines*, by Gail Collins (William Morrow). Other clients include Serena Bass, Janice Erlbaum, David Cay Johnston, Mark Derr, Barbara Rolls, Ph.D.

◑ MARTIN LITERARY MANAGEMENT

7683 SE 27th St., #307, Mercer Island WA 98040. (206)486-1773. Fax: 206)466-1774. E-mail: sharlene@martinliterarymanagement.com; bree@martinliterarymanagement.com; kate@martinliterarymanagement.com. Website: www.MartinLiteraryManagement.com. **Contact:** Sharlene Martin. 75% of clients are new/unpublished writers.

- Prior to becoming an agent, Ms. Martin worked in film/TV production and acquisitions.

MEMBER AGENTS Sharlene Martin (nonfiction). Bree Ogden (children's books and graphic novels only; Bree@MartinLiteraryManagement.com). Kate Folkers (adult fiction).

REPRESENTS **Considers these nonfiction areas:** autobiography, biography, business, child guidance, current affairs, economics, health, history, how-to, humor, inspirational, investigative, medicine, memoirs, parenting, popular culture, psychology, satire, self-help, true crime, women's issues, women's studies.

�'➔ This agency has strong ties to film/TV. Actively seeking nonfiction that is highly commercial and that can be adapted to film. "We are being inundated with queries and submissions that are wrongfully being submitted to us, which only results in more frustration for the writers."

HOW TO CONTACT Query via e-mail with MS Word only. No attachments on queries; place letter in body of e-mail. Accepts simultaneous submissions. Responds in 2 weeks to queries. Responds in 3-4 weeks to mss. Obtains most new clients through recommendations from others.

TERMS Agent receives 15% commission on domestic sales. Agent receives 25% commission on foreign sales. Offers written contract, binding for 1 year; 1-month notice must be given to terminate contract. Charges author for postage and copying if material is not sent electronically. 99% of materials are sent electronically to minimize charges to author for postage and copying.

RECENT SALES *Notes Left Behind*, by Keith and Brooke Desserich and *Publish Your Nonfiction*, by Sharlene Martin and Anthony Flacco.

TIPS "Have a strong platform for nonfiction. Please don't call. I welcome e-mail. I'm very responsive when I'm interested in a query and work hard to get my clients' materials in the best possible shape before submissions. Do your homework prior to submission and only submit your best efforts. Please review our website carefully to make sure we're a good match for your work. If you read my book, *Publish Your Nonfiction Book: Strategies For Learning the Industry, Selling Your Book and Building a Successful Career* (Writer's Digest Books), you'll know exactly how to charm me."

JED MATTES, INC.

PO Box 116, Stuyvesant NY 12173. (212)595-5228. Fax: (212)595-5232. E-mail: fmorris@jedmattes.com; gener al@jedmattes.com. Website: www.jedmattes.com. **Contact:** Fred Morris. Member of AAR. **MEMBER AGENTS** Fred Morris. **REPRESENTS** Nonfiction, fiction. **HOW TO CONTACT** Query with SASE.

ⓘ MAX AND CO., A LITERARY AGENCY AND SOCIAL CLUB

3929 Coliseum St., New Orleans LA 70115. (504)377-7745; (201)704-2483. E-mail: mmurphy@maxlit.com. Website: www.maxliterary.org. **Contact:** Michael Murphy.

- Max & Co. was established in the Fall of 2007 by Michael Murphy. Prior to the literary agency, Michael began in book publishing in 1981 at Random House. He left in 1995 as a Vice President and later ran William Morrow as their Publisher. Co-agent Jack Perry joined publishing in 1994 and has been a Vice President in Sales & Marketing for Random House, Source Books, and Scholastic.

MEMBER AGENTS Michael Murphy, Nettie Hartsock (literary fiction, business books and popular nonfiction, and the occasional Southern fiction book), Jack Perry (nonfiction books with a foundation in history, sports, business, politics, narrative nonfiction, math, and science).

REPRESENTS Considers these nonfiction areas: business, history, humor, memoirs, politics, science, sports, narrative nonfiction. **Considers these fiction areas:** literary.

- ☛ Seeking work in literary or eclectic fiction. In nonfiction, seeks narrative or creative nonfiction. Does not represent romance, science fiction, fantasy, tea-cozy or whodunnit mysteries. Does not represent self-help or prescriptive (how-to) nonfiction. Represents no children's or young adult work.

HOW TO CONTACT Agency desires e-mailed submissions and will not accept nor respond to mailed submissions. There are four agents—two in New York, one in Austin, Texas, and Michael Murphy in New Orleans.

ⓘ MARGRET MCBRIDE LITERARY AGENCY

P.O. Box 9128, La Jolla CA 92038. (858)454-1550. Fax: (858)454-2156. E-mail: staff@mcbridelit.com. Website: www.mcbrideliterary.com. **Contact:** Michael Daley, submissions manager. Other address: 7744 Fay Ave., Suite 201, La Jolla, CA 92037. Member of AAR.

Other memberships include Authors Guild. Represents 55 clients.

- Prior to opening her agency, Ms. McBride worked at Random House, Ballantine Books, and Warner Books.

REPRESENTS nonfiction books, novels. **Considers these nonfiction areas:** autobiography, biography, business, cooking, cultural interests, current affairs, dance, diet/nutrition, economics, ethnic, foods, government, health, history, how-to, law, medicine, money, music, popular culture, politics, psychology, science, self-help, sociology, technology, women's issues, women's studies, style. **Considers these fiction areas:** action, adventure, crime, detective, ethnic, frontier, historical, humor, literary, mainstream, mystery, police, satire, suspense, thriller, Westerns.

- ☛ This agency specializes in mainstream fiction and nonfiction. Does not want to receive screenplays, romance, poetry, or children's/young adult.

HOW TO CONTACT The agency is only accepting new clients by referral at this time. Query with synopsis, bio, SASE. No e-mail or fax queries. Accepts simultaneous submissions. Responds in 4-6 weeks to queries. Responds in 6-8 weeks to mss.

TERMS Agent receives 15% commission on domestic sales. Agent receives 25% commission on foreign sales. Charges for overnight delivery and photocopying.

THE MCCARTHY AGENCY, LLC

7 Allen St., Rumson NJ 07660. Phone/Fax: (732)741-3065. E-mail: McCarthylit@aol.com; ntfrost@hotmail.com. **Contact:** Shawna McCarthy. Member of AAR. Currently handles: nonfiction books 25%, novels 75%.

MEMBER AGENTS Shawna McCarthy, Nahvae Frost.

REPRESENTS nonfiction books, novels. **Considers these nonfiction areas:** biography, history, philosophy, science. **Considers these fiction areas:** fantasy, juvenile, mystery, romance, science, women's.

HOW TO CONTACT Query via e-mail or regular mail to The McCarthy Agency, c/o Nahvae Frost, 101 Clinton Avenue, Apartment #2, Brooklyn, NY 11205. Accepts simultaneous submissions.

MCCARTHY CREATIVE SERVICES

625 Main St., Suite 834, New York NY 10044-0035. (212)832-3428. Fax: (212)829-9610. E-mail: paulmc carthy@mccarthycreative.com. Website: www.mccar thycreative.com. **Contact:** Paul D. McCarthy. Other memberships include The Authors Guild, American Society of Journalists & Authors, National Book Critics Circle, Authors League of America. Represents 5 clients. 0% of clients are new/unpublished writers. Currently handles: nonfiction books 95%, novels 5%.

- Prior to his current position, Mr. McCarthy was a professional writer, literary agent at the Scott Meredith Literary Agency, senior editor at publishing companies (Simon & Schuster, HarperCollins and Doubleday) and a public speaker. Learn much more about Mr. McCarthy by visiting his website.

MEMBER AGENTS Paul D. McCarthy.

REPRESENTS nonfiction books, novels. **Considers these nonfiction areas:** animals, anthropology, art, biography, business, child, current affairs, education, ethnic, gay, government, health, history, how-to, humor, language, memoirs, military, money, music, nature, popular culture, psychology, religion, science, self-help, sociology, sports, translation, true crime, women's. **Considers these fiction areas:** glitz, adventure, confession, detective, erotica, ethnic, family, fantasy, feminist, gay, historical, horror, humor, literary, mainstream, mystery, regional, romance, science, sports, thriller, Western, young adult, women's.

- ⊶ "I deliberately founded my company to be unlimited in its range. That's what I offer, and the world has responded. My agency was founded so that I could maximize and build on the value of my combined experience for my authors and other clients, in all of my capacities and more. I think it's *very* important for authors to know that because I'm so exclusive as an agent, I may not be able to offer representation on the basis of the manuscript they submit. However, if they decide to invest in their book and lifetime career as authors, by engaging my professional, near-unique editorial services, there is the possibility that at the end of the process, when they've achieved the very best, most salable and competitive book they can write, I may see sufficient potential in the book and their

next books, that I do offer to be their agent. Representation is never guaranteed." Established authors of serious and popular nonfiction, who want the value of being one of MCS's very exclusive authors who receive special attention, and of being represented by a literary agent who brings such a rich diversity and depth of publishing/creative/professorial experience, and distinguished reputation. No first novels. "Novels by established novelists will be considered very selectively."

HOW TO CONTACT Submit outline, one chapter (either first or best). Queries and submissions by e-mail only. Send as e-mail attachment. Responds in 3-4 weeks to queries. Obtains most new clients through recommendations from others.

TERMS Agent receives 15% commission on domestic sales. Agent receives 20% commission on foreign sales. Offers written contract; 30-day notice must be given to terminate contract. "All reading done in deciding whether or not to offer representation is free. Editorial services are available. Mailing and postage expenses that incurred on the author's behalf are always approved by them in advance."

TIPS "Always keep in mind that your query letter/proposal is only one of hundreds and thousands that are competing for the agent's attention. Therefore, your presentation of your book and yourself as author has to be immediate, intense, compelling, and concise. Make the query letter one-page, and after short, introductory paragraph, write a 150-word KEYNOTE description of your manuscript."

☺⊘ ANNE MCDERMID & ASSOCIATES, LTD

83 Willcocks St., Toronto ON M5S 1C9 Canada. (416)324-8845. Fax: (416)324-8870. E-mail: info@mc dermidagency.com. Website: www.mcdermidagency. com. **Contact:** Anne McDermid. Other address: 64 Bloem Ave., Toronto, ON M6E 1S1. Estab. 1996. Represents 60+ clients.

MEMBER AGENTS Anne McDermid, Martha Magor, Monica Pacheco, and Chris Bucci.

REPRESENTS nonfiction books, novels. **Considers these nonfiction areas:** The agency represents literary novelists and commercial novelists of high quality, and also writers of nonfiction in the areas of memoir, biography, history, literary travel, narrative science, and investigative journalism. We also represent a certain number of children's and young adult writers and writers in the fields of science fiction and fantasy.

HOW TO CONTACT Query via e-mail or mail with a brief bio, description, and first 5 pages of project only. *No unsolicited manuscripts.* Obtains most new clients through recommendations from others.

◑ MCINTOSH & OTIS

353 Lexington Ave., New York NY 10016. (212)687-7400. Fax: (212)687-6894. E-mail: info@mcintoshan dotis.com. Website: www.mcintoshandotis.net/. **Contact:** Attn: *reference your department*. Estab. 1928. Member of AAR.

MEMBER AGENTS Eugene H. Winick; Elizabeth Winick (literary fiction, women's fiction, historical fiction, and mystery/suspense, along with narrative nonfiction, spiritual/self-help, history and current affairs); Edward Necarsulmer IV; Rebecca Strauss (nonfiction, literary and commercial fiction, women's fiction, memoirs, and pop culture); Cate Martin; Ina Winick (psychology, self-help, and mystery/suspense); Ian Polonsky (film/TV/stage/radio).

REPRESENTS nonfiction books, novels, movie, movie scripts, feature film. M&O represents a broad range of adult and children's fiction and nonfiction, including many bestsellers, literary icons, Pulitzer Prize and National Book Award winners.

HOW TO CONTACT Adult fiction: Please send a query letter, synopsis, author bio, the first two chapters, and a SASE. Adult nonfiction: Send an outline and all that is required for fiction guidelines above. Children: middle grade and young adult: Query letter, the first 3 pages of manuscript, and a SASE. Picture Books: Please send a query letter. One picture book manuscript only, and a SASE. Film and dramatic rights: Please send query, synopsis, and a SASE. Does not accept e-mail queries. Responds in 8 weeks to queries.

TIPS No phone calls please.

● MENDEL MEDIA GROUP, LLC

115 W. 30th St., Suite 800, New York NY 10001. (646)239-9896. Fax: (212)685-4717. E-mail: scott@mendelmedia.com. Website: www.mendelmedia.com. Member of AAR. Represents 40-60 clients.

• Prior to becoming an agent, Mr. Mendel was an academic. "I taught American literature, Yiddish, Jewish studies, and literary theory at the University of Chicago and the University of Illinois at Chicago while working on my PhD in English. I also worked as a freelance technical writer and as the managing editor of a health-care magazine. In 1998, I began working for the late Jane Jordan Browne, a long-time agent in the book publishing world."

REPRESENTS nonfiction books, novels, scholarly, with potential for broad/popular appeal. **Considers these nonfiction areas:** Americana, animals, anthropology, architecture, art, biography, business, child guidance, cooking, current affairs, dance, diet/nutrition, education, environment, ethnic, foods, gardening, gay/lesbian, government, health, history, how-to, humor, investigative, language, medicine, memoirs, military, money, multicultural, music, parenting, philosophy, popular culture, psychology, recreation, regional, religious, science, self-help, sex, sociology, software, spirituality, sports, true crime, war, women's issues, women's studies, Jewish topics; creative nonfiction. **Considers these fiction areas:** action, adventure, contemporary issues, crime, detective, erotica, ethnic, feminist, gay, glitz, historical, humor, inspirational, juvenile, lesbian, literary, mainstream, mystery, picture books, police, religious, romance, satire, sports, thriller, young adult, Jewish fiction.

➤ "I am interested in major works of history, current affairs, biography, business, politics, economics, science, major memoirs, narrative nonfiction, and other sorts of general nonfiction." Actively seeking new, major or definitive work on a subject of broad interest, or a controversial, but authoritative, new book on a subject that affects many people's lives. I also represent more light-hearted nonfiction projects, such as gift or novelty books, when they suit the market particularly well." Does not want "queries about projects written years ago that were unsuccessfully shopped to a long list of trade publishers by either the author or another agent. I am specifically not interested in reading short, category romances (regency, time travel, paranormal, etc.), horror novels, supernatural stories, poetry, original plays, or film scripts."

HOW TO CONTACT Query with SASE. Do not e-mail or fax queries. For nonfiction, include a complete, fully edited book proposal with sample chapters. For fiction, include a complete synopsis and no more than 20 pages of sample text. Responds in 2 weeks to queries. Responds in 4-6 weeks to mss. Obtains most new clients through recommendations from others.

TERMS Agent receives 15% commission on domestic sales. Agent receives 20% commission on foreign sales.

WRITERS CONFERENCES BookExpo America; Frankfurt Book Fair; London Book Fair; RWA National Conference; Modern Language Association Convention; Jerusalem Book Fair.

TIPS "While I am not interested in being flattered by a prospective client, it does matter to me that she knows why she is writing to me in the first place. Is one of my clients a colleague of hers? Has she read a book by one of my clients that led her to believe I might be interested in her work? Authors of descriptive nonfiction should have real credentials and expertise in their subject areas, either as academics, journalists, or policy experts, and authors of prescriptive nonfiction should have legitimate expertise and considerable experience communicating their ideas in seminars and workshops, in a successful business, through the media, etc."

SCOTT MEREDITH LITERARY AGENCY

200 W. 57th St., Suite 904, New York NY 10019. (646)274-1970. Fax: (212)977-5997. E-mail: info@scottmeredith.com. Website: www.scottmeredith.com. **Contact:** Arthur Klebanoff, CEO. Adheres to the AAR canon of ethics. Represents 20 clients. 5% of clients are new/unpublished writers. Currently handles: nonfiction books 85%, novels 10%, textbooks 5%.

 • Prior to becoming an agent, Mr. Klebanoff was a lawyer.

REPRESENTS nonfiction books, textbooks.

This agency's specialty lies in category nonfiction publishing programs. Actively seeking category leading nonfiction. Does not want to receive first fiction projects.

HOW TO CONTACT Query with SASE. Submit proposal package, author bio. Accepts simultaneous submissions. Responds in 1 week to queries. Responds in 2 weeks to mss. Obtains most new clients through recommendations from others.

TERMS Agent receives 15% commission on domestic sales. Offers written contract.

RECENT SALES *The Conscience of a Liberal*, by Paul

Krugman; *The King of Oil: The Secret Lives of Marc Rich*, by Daniel Ammann; *Ten*, by Sheila Lukins; *Peterson Field Guide to Birds of North America*.

DORIS S. MICHAELS LITERARY AGENCY, INC.

1841 Broadway, Suite 903, New York NY 10023. (212)265-9474. Fax: (212)265-9480. E-mail: query@dsmagency.com. Website: www.dsmagency.com. **Contact:** Doris S. Michaels, President. Member of AAR. Other memberships include WNBA.

REPRESENTS novels. **Considers these nonfiction areas:** specialties are business and self-help books from top professionals in their fields of expertise. We are also looking for books in categories such as current affairs, narrative, biography and memoir, lifestyle, social sciences, gender, history, health, classical music, sports, and women's issues. In the fiction camp, we are currently interested in representing literary fiction that has commercial appeal and strong screen potential. Go to our biography section to find out more. **Considers these fiction areas:** literary, with commercial appeal and strong screen potential., "Go to our biography section online to find out more.".

"Our specialties are business and self-help books from top professionals in their fields of expertise." "We are also looking for books in categories such as current affairs, narrative, biography and memoir, lifestyle, social sciences, gender, history, health, classical music, sports, and women's issues." No romance, coffee table books, art books, trivia, pop culture, humor, Westerns, occult and supernatural, horror, poetry, textbooks, children's books, picture books, film scripts, articles, cartoons, and professional manuals.

HOW TO CONTACT Query by e-mail; synopsis of your project in one page or less, and include a short paragraph that details your credentials. Do not send attachments or URL links. See submission guidelines on website. Obtains most new clients through recommendations from others, conferences.

TERMS Agent receives 15% commission on domestic sales. Agent receives 20% commission on foreign sales. Offers written contract, binding for 1 year; 1-month notice must be given to terminate contract. Charges clients for office expenses, not to exceed $150 without written permission.

WRITERS CONFERENCES BookExpo America; Frankfurt Book Fair; London Book Fair; Maui Writers Conference.

● MARTHA MILLARD LITERARY AGENCY

420 Central Park West, #5H, New York NY 10025. (212)662-1030; (212)787-1030. **Contact:** Martha Millard. Estab. 1980. Member of AAR. Other memberships include SFWA. Represents 50 clients. Currently handles: nonfiction books 25%, novels 65%, story collections 10%.

- Prior to becoming an agent, Ms. Millard worked in editorial departments of several publishers and was vice president at another agency for more than four years.

REPRESENTS nonfiction books, novels. **Considers these nonfiction areas:** architecture, art, autobiography, biography, business, child guidance, cooking, cultural interests, current affairs, design, economics, education, ethnic, film, health, history, how-to, memoirs, metaphysics, money, music, New Age, parenting, photography, popular culture, psychology, self-help, theater, true crime, women's issues, women's studies. **Considers these fiction areas:** fantasy, mystery, romance, science fiction, suspense.

HOW TO CONTACT No unsolicited queries. **Referrals only.** Obtains most new clients through recommendations from others.

TERMS Agent receives 15% commission on domestic sales. Agent receives 20% commission on foreign sales. Offers written contract.

● THE MILLER AGENCY

Film Center, 630 Ninth Ave., Suite 1102, New York NY 10036. (212)206-0913. Fax: (212)206-1473. E-mail: angela@milleragency.net. **Contact:** Angela Miller, Sharon Bowers, Jennifer Griffin. Represents 100 clients. 5% of clients are new/unpublished writers.

REPRESENTS nonfiction books. **Considers these nonfiction areas:** child guidance, cooking, design, foods, health, parenting.

☞ This agency specializes in nonfiction, multicultural arts, psychology, self-help, cookbooks, biography, travel, memoir, and sports. Fiction is considered selectively. This agency specializes in cookbooks.

HOW TO CONTACT Accepts simultaneous submissions. Obtains most new clients through referrals.

TERMS Agent receives 15% commission on domestic sales. Agent receives 20-25% commission on foreign sales. Offers written contract, binding for 2 years; 2-month notice must be given to terminate contract. Charges clients for postage (express mail or messenger services) and photocopying.

⊘ MARK B. MILLER MANAGEMENT

PO Box 2442, Warminster PA 18974. (267)988-4226. **Contact:** Mark B. Miller.

TIPS "Inquiries welcome; no unsolicited manuscripts accepted."

MOORE LITERARY AGENCY

10 State St., Newburyport MA 01950. (978)465-9015. Fax: (978)465-8817. E-mail: cmoore@moorelit.com. **Contact:** Claudette Moore. Estab. 1989. 10% of clients are new/unpublished writers. Currently handles: nonfiction books 100%.

REPRESENTS nonfiction books. **Considers these nonfiction areas:** computers, technology.

☞ This agency specializes in trade computer books (90% of titles).

HOW TO CONTACT Query with SASE. Submit proposal package. Query by e-mail. Send proposals by snail mail. Obtains most new clients through recommendations from others, conferences.

TERMS Agent receives 15% commission on domestic sales. Agent receives 15% commission on foreign sales. Agent receives 15% commission on film sales. Offers written contract.

● HOWARD MORHAIM LITERARY AGENCY

30 Pierrepont St., Brooklyn NY 11201. (718)222-8400. Fax: (718)222-5056. Website: www.morhaimliterary.com/. Member of AAR.

MEMBER AGENTS Howard Morhaim, Kate McKean, Katie Menick (assistant; no submissions).

☞ Actively seeking fiction, nonfiction and young-adult novels.

HOW TO CONTACT Query via e-mail with cover letter and three sample chapters. See each agent's listing for specifics.

● WILLIAM MORRIS AGENCY, INC.

1325 Avenue of the Americas, New York NY 10019. (212)586-5100. Fax: (212)246-3583. Website: www.wma.com. **Contact:** Literary Department Coordinator. Alternate address: One William Morris Place,

Beverly Hills CA 90212. (310)285-9000. Fax: (310)859-4462. Member of AAR.

MEMBER AGENTS Owen Laster; Jennifer Rudolph Walsh; Suzanne Gluck; Joni Evans; Tracy Fisher; Mel Berger; Jay Mandel; Peter Franklin; Lisa Grubka; Jonathan Pecursky.

REPRESENTS nonfiction books, novels, TV, movie scripts, feature film.

⊶ Does not want to receive screenplays.

HOW TO CONTACT Query with synopsis, publication history, SASE. Send book queries to the NYC address. Accepts simultaneous submissions.

TERMS Agent receives 15% commission on domestic sales. Agent receives 20% commission on foreign sales.

TIPS "If you are a prospective writer interested in submitting to the William Morris Agency in **London**, please follow these guidelines: For all queries, please send a cover letter, synopsis, and the first three chapters (up to 50 pages) by e-mail only to: dkar@wmeentertainment.com."

⊘ MORTIMER LITERARY AGENCY

41769 Enterprise Circle N., Suite 107, Temecula CA 92590. (951)208-5674. E-mail: kmortimer@mortimerliterary.com. E-mail: queries@mortimerliterary.com. Website: www.mortimerliterary.com. **Contact:** Kelly Gottuso Mortimer. Romance Writers of America. Represents 16 clients. 80% of clients are new/unpublished writers. Currently handles: nonfiction books 40%, novels 40%, young adult books 20%.

- Prior to becoming an agent, Ms. Mortimer was a freelance writer and the CFO of Microvector, Inc. She has a degree in contract law, finance and is a winner of The American Christian Fiction Writers Literary Agent of the Year Award in 2008 and the OCC-RAW Volunteer of the Year award. Was Top 5: Publishers marketplace Top 100 Dealmakers (romance category, 2008).

REPRESENTS nonfiction books, novels, young adult. **Considers these nonfiction areas:** Please refer to submissions page on website, as the list changes. **Considers these fiction areas:** Please refer to submissions page on website, as the list changes.

⊶ "I keep a short client list to give my writers personal attention. I edit my clients' manuscripts as necessary. I send manuscripts out to pre-selected editors in a timely fashion, and send my clients monthly reports. I only sign writers not yet published, or not published in the last 3 years. Those are the writers who need my help the most."

HOW TO CONTACT See website for submission guidelines. Accepts simultaneous submissions. Responds in 3 months to mss. Obtains most new clients through query letters.

TERMS Agent receives 15% commission on domestic sales. Agent receives 20% commission on foreign sales. Offers written contract. "I charge for postage—only the amount I pay and it comes out of the author's advance. The writer provides me with copies of their manuscripts if needed."

WRITERS CONFERENCES RWA, several conference. See schedule on website.

TIPS "Follow submission guidelines on the website, submit your best work and don't query unless your manuscript is finished. Don't send material or mss that I haven't requested."

① DEE MURA LITERARY

269 West Shore Dr., Massapequa NY 11758-8225. (516)795-1616. Fax: (516)795-8797. E-mail: query@deemuraliterary.com. Website: http://deemuraliterary.com/. **Contact:** Dee Mura. Signatory of WGA. 50% of clients are new/unpublished writers.

- Prior to opening her agency, Ms. Mura was a public relations executive with a roster of film and entertainment clients and worked in editorial for major weekly news magazines.

MEMBER AGENTS Dee Mura, Karen Roberts, Bobbie Sokol, David Brozain.

REPRESENTS Considers these nonfiction areas: animals, anthropology, biography, business, child guidance, computers, current affairs, education, ethnic, finance, gay, government, health, history, how-to, humor, juvenile nonfiction, law, lesbian, medicine, memoirs, military, money, nature, personal improvement, politics, science, self-help, sociology, sports, technology, travel, true crime, women's issues, women's studies. **Considers these fiction areas:** action, adventure, contemporary issues, crime, detective, ethnic, experimental, family saga, fantasy, feminist, gay, glitz, historical, humor, juvenile, lesbian, literary, mainstream, military, mystery, psychic, regional, romance, science fiction, sports, thriller, Westerns, young adult, political. **Considers these script areas:** action, cartoon, comedy, contemporary, detective, (and espionage), family, fantasy, feminist, gay/lesbian, glitz, historical, horror, juvenile, mainstream, mystery, psychic, romantic comedy, romantic drama, science, sports, teen, thriller, Western.

☞ "Some of us have special interests, and some of us encourage you to share your passion and work with us." Does not want to receive "ideas for sitcoms, novels, films, etc., or queries without SASEs."

HOW TO CONTACT Query with SASE. Accepts e-mail queries (no attachments). If via e-mail, please include the type of query and your genre in the subject line. If via regular mail, you may include the first few chapters, outline, or proposal. Mark envelope "Attn: Query Dept." No fax queries. Accepts simultaneous submissions. Only responds if interested; responds as soon as possible. Obtains most new clients through recommendations from others, queries.

TERMS Agent receives 15% commission on domestic sales. Agent receives 20% commission on foreign sales. Offers written contract. Charges clients for photocopying, mailing expenses, overseas/long distance phone calls/faxes.

RECENT SALES Sold more than 40 titles and 35 scripts in the last year.

TIPS "Please include a paragraph on your background, even if you have no literary background, and a brief synopsis of the project."

⊘ ERIN MURPHY LITERARY AGENCY

2700 Woodlands Village, #300-458, Flagstaff AZ 86001-7172. (928)525-2056. Fax: (928)525-2480. Website: emliterary.com. **Contact:** Erin Murphy, president; Ammi-Joan Paquette, associate agent.

☞ "This agency only represents children's books. We do not accept unsolicited manuscripts or queries. We consider new clients by referral or personal contact only."

① MUSE LITERARY MANAGEMENT

189 Waverly Place, #4, New York NY 10014-3135. (212)925-3721. E-mail: museliterarymgmt@aol.com. Website: www.museliterary.com. **Contact:** Deborah Carter. Associations: NAWE, International Thriller Writers, Historical Novel Society, Associations of Booksellers for Children, The Authors Guild, Children's Literature Network, and American Folklore Society. Represents 5 clients. 80% of clients are new/unpublished writers.

• Prior to starting her agency, Ms. Carter trained with an AAR literary agent and worked in the music business and as a talent scout for record companies in artist management. She has a BA in English and music from Washington Square University College at NYU.

REPRESENTS novels, short story collections, poetry books. **Considers these nonfiction areas:** , narrative nonfiction (no prescriptive nonfiction), children's. **Considers these fiction areas:** adventure, detective, juvenile, mystery, picture books, suspense, thriller, young adult, espionage; middle grade novels; literary short story collections, literary fiction with popular appeal.

☞ Specializes in manuscript development, the sale and administration of print, performance, and foreign rights to literary works, and post-publication publicity and appearances. Actively seeking "writers with formal training who bring compelling voices and a unique outlook to their manuscripts. Those who submit should be receptive to editorial feedback and willing to revise during the submission provess in order to remain competitive." Does not want "manuscripts that have been worked over by book doctors (collaborative projects OK, but writers must have chops); category romance, chick lit, sci-fi, fantasy, horror, stories about cats and dogs, vampires or serial killers, fiction or nonfiction with religious or spiritual subject matter."

HOW TO CONTACT Query with SASE. Query via e-mail (no attachments). Discards unwanted queries. Responds in 2 weeks to queries. Responds in 2-3 weeks to mss. Obtains most new clients through recommendations from others, conferences.

TERMS Agent receives 15% commission on domestic sales. Agent receives 20% commission on foreign sales. One-year contract offered when writer and agent agree that the manuscript is ready for submission; manuscripts in development are not bound by contract. Sometimes charges for postage and photocopying. All expenses are preapproved by the client.

TIPS "I give editorial feedback and work on revisions on spec. Agency agreement is offered when the writer and I feel the manuscript is ready for submission to publishers. Writers should also be open to doing revisions with editors who express serious interest in their work, prior to any offer of a publishing contract. All aspects of career strategy are discussed with writers, and all decisions are ultimately theirs. I make multiple and simultaneous submissions when looking for rights opportunities, and share all correspondence. All agreements are signed by the writers. Reimbursement for expenses is subject to client's approval, limited to photocopying (usually press clips) and postage. I always submit fresh manuscripts to publishers printed in my office with no charge to the writer."

● JEAN V. NAGGAR LITERARY AGENCY, INC.

216 E. 75th St., Suite 1E, New York NY 10021. (212)794-1082. E-mail: jweltz@jvnla.com; jvnla@jvnla.com. E-mail: jweltz@jvnla.com; jregel@jvnla.com; atasman@jvnla.com. Website: www.jvnla.com. **Contact:** Jean Naggar. Member of AAR. Other memberships include PEN, Women's Media Group, Women's Forum. Represents 80 clients. 20% of clients are new/unpublished writers. Currently handles: nonfiction books 35%, novels 45%, juvenile books 15%, scholarly books 5%.

• Ms. Naggar has served as president of AAR.

MEMBER AGENTS Jennifer Weltz (subrights, children's, adults); Jessica Regel (young adult, adult, subrights); Jean Naggar taking no new clients. See website for client list; Alice Tasman (adult, children's); Elizabeth Evans (adult nonfiction, some fiction and young adult).

REPRESENTS nonfiction books, novels. **Considers these nonfiction areas:** biography, child guidance, current affairs, government, health, history, juvenile nonfiction, law, medicine, memoirs, New Age, parenting, politics, psychology, self-help, sociology, travel, women's issues, women's studies. **Considers these fiction areas:** action, adventure, crime, detective, ethnic, family saga, feminist, historical, literary, mainstream, mystery, police, psychic, supernatural, suspense, thriller.

⚷ This agency specializes in mainstream fiction and nonfiction and literary fiction with commercial potential.

HOW TO CONTACT Query via e-mail. Prefers to read materials exclusively. No fax queries. Responds in 1 day to queries. Responds in 2 months to mss. Obtains most new clients through recommendations from others.

TERMS Agent receives 15% commission on domestic sales. Agent receives 20% commission on foreign

sales. Offers written contract. Charges for overseas mailing, messenger services, book purchases, long-distance telephone, photocopying—all deductible from royalties received.

RECENT SALES *Night Navigation* by Ginnah Howard; *After Hours At the Almost Home*, by Tara Yelen; *An Entirely Synthetic Fish: A Biography of Rainbow Trout* by Anders Halverson; *The Patron Saint of Butterflies* by Cecilia Galante; *Wondrous Strange* by Lesley Livingston; *6 Sick Hipsters* by Rayo Casablanca; *The Last Bridge* by Teri Coyne; *Gypsy Goodbye* by Nancy Springer; *Commuters* by Emily Tedrowe; *The Language of Secrets* by Dianne Dixon; *Smiling to Freedom* by Martin Benoit Stiles; *The Tale of Halcyon Crane* by Wendy Webb; *Fugitive* by Phillip Margolin; *BlackBerry Girl* by Aidan Donnelley Rowley; *Wild Girls* by Pat Murphy.

WRITERS CONFERENCES Willamette Writers Conference; Pacific Northwest Writers Conference; Bread Loaf Writers Conference; Marymount Manhattan Writers Conference; SEAK Medical & Legal Fiction Writing Conference.

TIPS "Use a professional presentation. Because of the avalanche of unsolicited queries that flood the agency every week, we have had to modify our policy. We will now only guarantee to read and respond to queries from writers who come recommended by someone we know. Our areas are general fiction and nonfiction—no children's books by unpublished writers, no multimedia, no screenplays, no formula fiction, and no mysteries by unpublished writers. We recommend patience and fortitude: the courage to be true to your own vision, the fortitude to finish a novel and polish it again and again before sending it out, and the patience to accept rejection gracefully and wait for the stars to align themselves appropriately for success."

❶ NELSON LITERARY AGENCY

1732 Wazee St., Suite 207, Denver CO 80202. (303)292-2805. E-mail: query@nelsonagency.com. Website: www. nelsonagency.com. **Contact:** Kristin Nelson, president and senior literary agent; Sara Megibow, associate literary agent. Member of AAR, RWA, SCBWI, SFWA.

• Prior to opening her own agency, Ms. Nelson worked as a literary scout and subrights agent for agent Jody Rein.

REPRESENTS novels, select nonfiction. **Considers these nonfiction areas:** memoirs. **Considers these fiction areas:** commercial, literary, mainstream, women's, chick lit (includes mysteries), romance (includes fantasy with romantic elements, science fiction, fantasy, young adult).

⚯ NLA specializes in representing commercial fiction and high caliber literary fiction. Actively seeking Latina writers who tackle contemporary issues in a modern voice (think *Dirty Girls Social Club*). Does not want short story collections, mysteries (except chick lit), thrillers, Christian, horror, or children's picture books.

HOW TO CONTACT Query by e-mail only.

RECENT SALES *New York Times* best-selling author of *I'd Tell You I Love You, But Then I'd Have to Kill You*, Ally Carter's fourth novel in the Gallagher Girls series; *Hester* (historical fiction), by Paula Reed; *Proof by Seduction* (debut romance), by Courtney Milan; *Soulless* (fantasy debut), by Gail Carriger; *The Shifter* (debut children's fantasy), by Janice Hardy; *Real Life & Liars* (debut women's fiction), by Kristina Riggle; *Hotel on the Corner of Bitter and Sweet* (debut literary fiction), by Jamie Ford.

◑ KIRSTEN NEUHAUS LITERARY AGENCY

267 West 17th St., Suite 22, New York NY 10011. E-mail: submissions@kirstenneuhausliterary.com. Website: www.kirstenneuhausliterary.com. **Contact:** Kirsten Neuhaus.

• Prior to becoming an agent, Kirsten Neuhaus has worked at Elaine Markson Agency, Sanford J. Greenburger Associates and Vigliano Associates, developing her own client list as well as handling foreign rights. She began her publishing career as an intern at Where Books Begin, a freelance editing company.

REPRESENTS Considers these nonfiction areas: Kirsten Neuhaus Literary is a full-service boutique agency specializing in nonfiction, particularly current events, business, science, biographies, international affairs, pop cultural studies, and narratives with strong female voices, as well as up-market, commercial fiction.

HOW TO CONTACT "Our preferred method for receiving queries is via e-mail. Please send a query letter, including a bio, and approximately ten sample pages." Paste copy into the e-mail body. No attachments.

NINE MUSES AND APOLLO, INC.

525 Broadway, Suite 201, New York NY 10012. (212)431-2665. **Contact:** Ling Lucas. Represents 50 clients. 10% of clients are new/unpublished writers. Currently handles: nonfiction books 100%.

• Prior to her current position, Ms. Lucas served as vice president, sales/marketing director and associate publisher of Warner Books.

REPRESENTS nonfiction books.

⚯ This agency specializes in nonfiction. Does not want to receive children's or young adult material.

HOW TO CONTACT Submit outline, 2 sample chapters, SASE. Prefers to read materials exclusively.

TERMS Agent receives 15% commission on domestic sales. Agent receives 20-25% commission on foreign sales. Offers written contract. Charges clients for photocopying, postage.

TIPS "Your outline should already be well developed, cogent, and reveal clarity of thought about the general structure and direction of your project."

◑ NORTHERN LIGHTS LITERARY SERVICES, LLC

2323 State Road, 252, Martinsville IN 46151. (888)558-4354. Fax: (208)265-1948. E-mail: queries@northern lightsls.com. Website: www.northernlightsls.com. **Contact:** Sammie Justesen. Represents 25 clients. 35% of clients are new/unpublished writers. Currently handles: nonfiction books 90%, novels 10%.

MEMBER AGENTS Sammie Justesen (fiction and nonfiction); Vorris Dee Justesen (business and current affairs).

REPRESENTS nonfiction books, novels. **Considers these nonfiction areas:** animals, autobiography, biography, business, child guidance, cooking, crafts, current affairs, diet/nutrition, economics, environment, ethnic, foods, health, inspirational, investigative, memoirs, metaphysics, New Age, parenting, popular culture, psychology, religious, self-help, sports, true crime, women's issues, women's studies. **Considers these fiction areas:** action, adventure, crime, detective, ethnic, family saga, feminist, glitz, historical, inspirational, mainstream, mystery, police, psychic, regional, religious, romance, supernatural, suspense, thriller, women's.

⚯ "Our goal is to provide personalized service to clients and create a bond that will endure throughout the writer's career. We seriously consider each query we receive and will accept hardworking new authors who are willing to develop their talents and skills. We enjoy working with healthcare professionals and writers who clearly understand their market and have a platform." Actively seeking general nonfiction—especially if the writer has a platform. Does not want to receive fantasy, horror, erotica, children's books, screenplays, poetry or short stories.

HOW TO CONTACT Query with SASE. Submit outline/proposal, synopsis, 3 sample chapters, author bio. E-queries preferred. No phone queries. All queries considered, but the agency only replies if interested. If you've completed and polished a novel, send a query letter, a one-or-two page synopsis of the plot, and the first chapter. Also include your biography as it relates to your writing experience. Do not send an entire ms unless requested. If you'd like to submit a nonfiction book, send a query letter, along with the book proposal. Include a bio showing the background that will enable you to write the book. Accepts simultaneous submissions. Responds in 2 months to queries. Responds in 2 months to mss. Obtains most new clients through solicitations, conferences.

TERMS Agent receives 15% commission on domestic sales. Agent receives 20% commission on foreign sales. Offers written contract; 30-day notice must be given to terminate contract.

RECENT SALES *Intuitive Parenting*, by Debra Snyder, Ph.D. (Beyond Words); *The Confidence Trap* by Russ Harris (Penguin); *The Never Cold Call Again Toolkit*, by Frank Rumbauskas, Jr. (Wiley); *Thank You for Firing Me*, by Candace Reed and Kitty Martini (Sterling); *The Wal-Mart Cure: Ten Lifesaving Supplements for Under $10* (Sourcebooks).

TIPS "If you're fortunate enough to find an agent who answers your query and asks for a printed manuscript, always include a letter and cover page containing your name, physical address, e-mail address and phone number. Be professional!"

● HAROLD OBER ASSOCIATES

425 Madison Ave., New York NY 10017. (212)759-8600. Fax: (212)759-9428. Website: www.haroldober. com. **Contact:** Craig Tenney. Member of AAR. Represents 250 clients. 10% of clients are new/unpublished writers. Currently handles: nonfiction books 35%, novels 50%, juvenile books 15%.

• Mr. Elwell was previously with Elwell & Weiser.

MEMBER AGENTS Phyllis Westberg; Pamela Malpas; Craig Tenney (few new clients, mostly Ober backlist); Jake Elwell (previously with Elwell & Weiser).

HOW TO CONTACT Submit concise query letter addressed to a specific agent with the first 5 pages of the manuscript or proposal and SASE. No fax or e-mail. Does not handle scripts. Responds as promptly as possible. Obtains most new clients through recommendations from others.

TERMS Agent receives 15% commission on domestic sales. Agent receives 20% commission on foreign sales. Charges clients for photocopying and express mail/package services.

ONK AGENCY LTD.

(formerly) ONK Copyright Agency, Cumhuriyet Cad. 30, Pak Apt. Kt: 4 Daire: 9 Elmadağ Şişli, İstanbul 34367 Turkey. +90 212 241 77 00. Fax: +90 212 241 77 31. E-mail: info@onkagency.com. Website: www. onkagency.com/english/. Estab. 1959.

● FIFI OSCARD AGENCY, INC.

110 W. 40th St., 16th Floor, New York NY 10018. (212)764-1100. Fax: (212)840-5019. E-mail: agency@ fifioscard.com. Website: www.fifioscard.com. **Contact:** Literary Department. Signatory of WGA.

MEMBER AGENTS Peter Sawyer; Carmen La Via; Kevin McShane; Carolyn French.

REPRESENTS nonfiction books, novels, stage plays. **Considers these nonfiction areas:** biography, business, cooking, economics, health, history, inspirational, religious, science, sports, technology, women's issues, women's studies, African American, body/mind/spirit, lifestyle, cookbooks.

HOW TO CONTACT Query through online submission form preferred, though snail mail queries are acceptable. *No unsolicited mss.* Responds in 2 weeks to queries.

TERMS Agent receives 15% commission on domestic sales. Agent receives 20% commission on foreign sales. Agent receives 10% commission on film sales. Charges clients for photocopying expenses.

PARAVIEW, INC.

A Division of Cosimo, Inc., P.O. Box 416, Old Chelsea Station, New York NY 10011-0416. (212)989-3616. Fax: (212)989-3662. E-mail: lhagan@paraview.com. Website: www.paraview.com. **Contact:** Lisa Hagan. Represents 75 clients. 15% of clients are new/unpublished writers. Currently handles: nonfiction books 100%.

REPRESENTS nonfiction books. **Considers these nonfiction areas:** agriculture horticulture, New Age, animals, anthropology, art, biography, business, cooking, current affairs, education, ethnic, gay, government, health, history, how to, humor, language, memoirs, military, money, multicultural, nature, philosophy, popular culture, psychology, recreation, regional, religion, science, self help, sex, sociology, spirituality, travel, true crime, women's, Americana; creative nonfiction.

☛ This agency specializes in business, science, gay/lesbian, spiritual, New Age, and self-help nonfiction.

HOW TO CONTACT Submit query, synopsis, author bio via e-mail. Responds in 1 month to queries. Responds in 3 months to mss. Obtains most new clients through recommendations from editors and current clients.

TERMS Agent receives 15% commission on domestic sales. Agent receives 20% commission on foreign sales.

WRITERS CONFERENCES BookExpo America; London Book Fair; E3—Electronic Entertainment Exposition.

TIPS "New writers should have their work edited, critiqued, and carefully reworked prior to submission. First contact should be via e-mail."

◑ PARK LITERARY GROUP, LLC

270 Lafayette St., Suite 1504, New York NY 10012. (212)691-3500. Fax: (212)691-3540. E-mail: info@parkliterary.com. Website: www.parkliterary.com.

• Prior to their current positions, Ms. Park and Ms. O'Keefe were literary agents at Sanford J. Greenburger Associates. Prior to 1994, Ms. Park was a practicing attorney.

MEMBER AGENTS Theresa Park (plot-driven fiction and serious nonfiction); Abigail Koons (quirky, edgy and commercial fiction, as well as superb thrillers and mysteries; adventure and travel narrative nonfiction, exceptional memoirs, popular science, history, politics and art); Emily Sweet (not an agent—liaison to film and media industries).

REPRESENTS nonfiction books, novels.

☛ The Park Literary Group represents fiction and nonfiction with a boutique approach: an emphasis on servicing a relatively small number of clients, with the highest professional stan-

dards and focused personal attention. Does not want to receive poetry or screenplays.

HOW TO CONTACT Query with SASE or by e-mail at queries@parkliterary.com. Submit synopsis, 1-3 sample chapters, SASE. Responds in 4-6 weeks to queries.

● THE RICHARD PARKS AGENCY

P.O. Box 693, Salem NY 12865. (518)854-9466. Fax: (518)854-9466. E-mail: rp@richardparksagency.com. Website: www.richardparksagency.com. **Contact:** Richard Parks. Member of AAR. Currently handles: nonfiction books 55%, novels 40%, story collections 5%.

REPRESENTS nonfiction books, novels. **Considers these nonfiction areas:** animals, anthropology, archeology, art, autobiography, biography, business, child guidance, cooking, crafts, cultural interests, current affairs, dance, diet/nutrition, economics, environment, ethnic, film, foods, gardening, gay/lesbian, government, health, history, hobbies, how-to, humor, language, law, memoirs, military, money, music, parenting, popular culture, politics, psychology, science, self-help, sociology, technology, theater, travel, women's issues, women's studies.

☛ Actively seeking nonfiction. Considers fiction by referral only. Does not want to receive unsolicited material.

HOW TO CONTACT Query with SASE. Does not accept queries by e-mail or fax. Responds in 2 weeks to queries. Obtains most new clients through recommendations/referrals.

TERMS Agent receives 15% commission on domestic sales. Agent receives 20% commission on foreign sales. Charges clients for photocopying or any unusual expense incurred at the writer's request.

● KATHI J. PATON LITERARY AGENCY

P.O. Box 2236, Radio City Station, New York NY 10101. (212)265-6586. E-mail: KJPLitBiz@optonline.net. Website: www.PatonLiterary.com. **Contact:** Kathi Paton. Currently handles: nonfiction books 85%, novels 15%.

REPRESENTS nonfiction books, novels, short story collections, book-based film rights. **Considers these nonfiction areas:** business, child guidance, economics, environment, humor, investigative, money, parenting, psychology, religious, satire, personal investing. **Considers these fiction areas:** literary, mainstream, multicultural, short stories.

8—π This agency specializes in adult nonfiction.

HOW TO CONTACT Accepts e-mail queries only. Accepts simultaneous submissions. Accepts new clients through recommendations from current clients.

TERMS Agent receives 15% commission on domestic sales. Agent receives 20% commission on foreign sales. Offers written contract. Charges clients for photocopying.

WRITERS CONFERENCES Attends major regional panels, seminars and conferences.

⊙ PAVILION LITERARY MANAGEMENT

660 Massachusetts Ave., Suite 4, Boston MA 02118. (617)792-5218. E-mail: jeff@pavilionliterary.com. Website: www.pavilionliterary.com. **Contact:** Jeff Kellogg.

- Prior to his current position, Mr. Kellogg was a literary agent with The Stuart Agency, and an acquiring editor with HarperCollins.

REPRESENTS nonfiction books, novels, memoir. **Considers these nonfiction areas:** narrative nonfiction (topical and historical) and cutting-edge popular science from experts in their respective fields. **Considers these fiction areas:** adventure, fantasy, juvenile, mystery, thriller, general fiction, genre-blending fiction.

8—π "We are presently accepting fiction submissions only from previously published authors and/or by client referral. Nonfiction projects, specifically narrative nonfiction and cutting-edge popular science from experts in their respective fields, are most welcome."

HOW TO CONTACT Query first by e-mail (no attachments). The subject line should specify fiction or nonfiction and include the title of the work. If submitting nonfiction, include a book proposal (no longer than 75 pages), with sample chapters.

◐ PEARSON, MORRIS & BELT

3000 Connecticut Ave., NW, Suite 317, Washington DC 20008. (202)723-6088. E-mail: dpm@morrisbelt.com; llb@morrisbelt.com. Website: www.morrisbelt.com.

- Prior to their current positions, Ms. Belt and Ms. Morris were agents with Adler & Robin Books, Inc.

MEMBER AGENTS Laura Belt (nonfiction and computer books); Djana Pearson Morris (fiction, nonfiction, and computer books. Her favorite subjects are self-help, narrative nonfiction, African-American fiction and nonfiction, health and fitness, women's fiction, technology, and parenting).

REPRESENTS nonfiction books, novels, computer books.

8—π This agency specializes in nonfiction, computer books and exceptional fiction. Does not want to receive poetry, children's literature or screenplays. Regarding fiction, this agency does not accept science fiction, thrillers or mysteries.

HOW TO CONTACT Query with SASE. Submit proposal (nonfiction); detailed synopsis and 2-3 sample chapters (fiction). Only query with a finished ms. Accepts e-mail queries but no attachments. Responds in 6-8 weeks to queries. Obtains most new clients through recommendations from others, solicitations.

TIPS "Many of our books come from ideas and proposals we generate in-house. We retain a proprietary interest in and control of all ideas we create and proposals we write."

◐ PELHAM LITERARY AGENCY

PMB 315, 2650 Jamacha Rd., Suite 147, El Cajon CA 92019. (619)447-4468. E-mail: jmeals@pelhamliterary.com. Website: pelhamliterary.com. **Contact:** Jim Meals. Currently handles: nonfiction books 10%, novels 90%.

- Before becoming agents, both Mr. Pelham and Mr. Meals were writers.

MEMBER AGENTS Howard Pelham; Jim Meals.

REPRESENTS nonfiction books, novels.

8—π "Every manuscript that comes to our agency receives a careful reading and assessment. When a writer submits a promising manuscript, we work extensively with the author until the work is ready for marketing."

HOW TO CONTACT Query by mail or e-mail first; do not send unsolicited mss.

TERMS Agent receives 15% commission on domestic sales. Offers written contract. Charges for photocopying and postage.

TIPS "Only phone if it's necessary."

◑ L. PERKINS AGENCY

5800 Arlington Ave., Riverdale NY 10471. (718)543-5344. Fax: (718)543-5354. E-mail: submissions@lperkinsagency.com. Website: http://lperkinsagency.com. **Contact:** Sandy Lu, sandy@lperkinsagency.com; Louise Fury, lfury@lperkinsagency.com; Marisa Corvisiero, marisa@lperkinsagency.com; Saritza Hernandez, sh@lperkinsagency.com. Member of AAR.

Represents 90 clients. 10% of clients are new/unpublished writers.

- Ms. Perkins has been an agent for 20 years. She is also the author of *The Insider's Guide to Getting an Agent* (Writer's Digest Books), as well as three other nonfiction books. She has also edited 12 erotic anthologies, and is also the editorial director of Ravenousromance.com, an e-publisher.

MEMBER AGENTS Lori Perkins (no longer takes submissions, but maintains her client list and blog); Sandy Lu (fiction areas of interest: literary and commercial fiction, upscale women's fiction, mystery, thriller, psychological horror, and historical fiction. She is especially interested in edgy, contemporary urban fiction. Nonfiction areas of interest: narrative nonfiction, history, biography, memoir, science, psychology, pop culture, and food writing. She also has a particular interest in Asian or Asian-American writing, both original and in translation, fiction and nonfiction); Marisa Iozzi Corvisiero (fiction interests include cross genre romance, science fiction, fantasy and urban fantasy, horror, literary, quality chick lit, young adult and children's books. Nonfiction interest include memoirs, how-to, guides and tales about the legal practice, parenting, self-help, and mainstream science); Saritza Hernandez (e-pub agent; looking for strong erotic romance in these sub-genres: paranormal, sci-fi, steampunk, cyberpunk, fantasy, BDSM, historical [emphasis on Ancient Egypt, Caribbean/MesoAmerican], intercultural and all GLBT-themed erotica for the digital marketplace).

REPRESENTS nonfiction books, novels. **Considers these nonfiction areas:** how-to, law, memoirs, parenting, popular culture, science, self-help. **Considers these fiction areas:** erotica, fantasy, horror, literary, science fiction, women's, young adult.

⸻ "Most of my clients write both fiction and nonfiction. This combination keeps my clients publishing for years. I am also a published author, so I know what it takes to write a good book." Actively seeking a Latino *Gone With the Wind* and *Waiting to Exhale*, and urban ethnic horror. Does not want to receive anything outside of the above categories (Westerns, romance, etc.).

HOW TO CONTACT E-queries only. Accepts simultaneous submissions. Responds in 12 weeks to queries. Responds in 3-6 months to mss. Obtains most new clients through recommendations from others, solicitations, conferences.

TERMS Agent receives 15% commission on domestic sales. Agent receives 20% commission on foreign sales. No written contract. Charges clients for photocopying.

WRITERS CONFERENCES NECON; Killercon; BookExpo America; World Fantasy Convention, RWA, Romantic Times.

TIPS "Research your field and contact professional writers' organizations to see who is looking for what. Finish your novel before querying agents. Read my book, *An Insider's Guide to Getting an Agent*, to get a sense of how agents operate. Read agent blogs-agentinthemiddle.blogspot.com and ravenousromance. blogspot.com."

ⓘ JAMES PETER ASSOCIATES, INC.

P.O. Box 358, New Canaan CT 06840. (203)972-1070. E-mail: gene_brissie@msn.com. Website: www.james peterassociates.com. **Contact:** Gene Brissie. Represents 75 individual and 6 corporate clients. 15% of clients are new/unpublished writers. Currently handles: nonfiction books 100%.

REPRESENTS nonfiction books. **Considers these nonfiction areas:** anthropology, archeology, architecture, art, biography, business, current affairs, dance, design, ethnic, film, gay/lesbian, government, health, history, language, literature, medicine, military, money, music, popular culture, psychology, self-help, theater, travel, war, women's issues, women's studies, memoirs (political, business).

⸻ "We are especially interested in general, trade and reference nonfiction." Does not want to receive children's/young adult books, poetry or fiction.

HOW TO CONTACT Submit proposal package, outline, SASE. Prefers to read materials exclusively. Responds in 1 month to queries. Obtains most new clients through recommendations from others, solicitations, contact with people who are doing interesting things.

TERMS Agent receives 15% commission on domestic sales. Agent receives 20% commission on foreign sales. Offers written contract.

🐚 PFD GROUP LTD.

Drury House, 34-43 Russell Street, London WC2B 5HA United Kingdom. (44)(207)344-1000. Fax: (44)(207)836-9539. E-mail: info@pfd.co.uk. Website: www.pfd.co.uk.

- "Peters Fraser and Dunlop offers its clients something unique in British agenting. Calling on our many areas of expertise, we work closely together to deliver an unparalleled full service, covering all aspects of publishing and media businesses. We have an active Television Division that represents broadcasters. We work with TV companies to come up with complementary programming as well selling film and television rights for our book clients. We have a Public Speaking Division for clients who wish to give lectures and speak at events. Our Foreign Rights Division is there to make sure that our authors' work is sold and published in foreign language markets. We have a Digital Division that represents our clients in the rapidly changing online world. Overall, this team ensures that all our clients' talents and opportunities are given the fullest possible professional attention."

MEMBER AGENTS Rowan Lawton (books), Caroline Michel (books), Michael Sissons and Fiona Petheram (books), Annabel Merullo (books), Claire Daniel (foreign rights), Robert Caskie (books and journalism).

ALISON J. PICARD, LITERARY AGENT

P.O. Box 2000, Cotuit MA 02635. Phone/Fax: (508)477-7192. E-mail: ajpicard@aol.com. **Contact:** Alison Picard. Represents 48 clients. 30% of clients are new/unpublished writers. Currently handles: nonfiction books 40%, novels 40%, juvenile books 20%.

- Prior to becoming an agent, Ms. Picard was an assistant at a literary agency in New York.

REPRESENTS nonfiction books, novels, juvenile. **Considers these nonfiction areas:** animals, autobiography, biography, business, child guidance, cooking, cultural interests, current affairs, diet/nutrition, economics, education, environment, ethnic, foods, gay/lesbian, government, health, history, how-to, humor, inspirational, juvenile nonfiction, law, medicine, memoirs, metaphysics, military, money, multicultural, New Age, parenting, popular culture, politics, psychology, religious, science, self-help, technology, travel, true crime, war, women's issues, women's studies, young adult. **Considers these fiction areas:** action, adventure, contemporary issues, crime, detective, erotica, ethnic, family saga, feminist, gay, glitz, historical, horror, humor, juvenile, lesbian, literary, mainstream, multicultural, mystery, New Age, picture books, police, psychic, romance, sports, supernatural, thriller, young adult.

- 🔑 "Many of my clients have come to me from big agencies, where they felt overlooked or ignored. I communicate freely with my clients and offer a lot of career advice, suggestions for revising manuscripts, etc. If I believe in a project, I will submit it to a dozen or more publishers, unlike some agents who give up after four or five rejections." No science fiction/fantasy, Western, poetry, plays or articles.

HOW TO CONTACT Query with SASE. Accepts simultaneous submissions. Responds in 2 weeks to queries. Responds in 4 months to mss. Obtains most new clients through recommendations from others, solicitations.

TERMS Agent receives 15% commission on domestic sales. Agent receives 20% commission on foreign sales. Offers written contract, binding for 1 year; 1-week notice must be given to terminate contract.

RECENT SALES *Zitface*, by Emily Ormand (Marshall Cavendish); *Totally Together*, by Stephanie O'Dea (Running Press); *The Ultimate Slow Cooker Cookbook*, by Stephanie O'Dea (Hyperion); Two Untitled Cookingbooks, by Erin Chase (St. Martin's Press); *A Journal of the Flood Year*, by David Ely (Portobello Books—United Kingdom, L'Ancora—Italy); *A Mighty Wall*, by John Foley (Llewellyn/Flux); *Jelly's Gold*, by David Housewright (St. Martin's Press).

TIPS "Please don't send material without sending a query first via mail or e-mail. I don't accept phone or fax queries. Always enclose an SASE with a query."

⚫ PINDER LANE & GARON-BROOKE ASSOCIATES, LTD.

159 W. 53rd St., Suite 14C, New York NY 10019. Website: www.pinderlane.com. Member of AAR. Signatory of WGA.

MEMBER AGENTS Robert Thixton, pinderl@rcn.com; Dick Duane, pinderl@rcn.com.

⌐ This agency specializes in mainstream fiction and nonfiction. Does not want to receive screenplays, TV series teleplays, or dramatic plays.
HOW TO CONTACT Query with SASE. *No unsolicited mss.* Obtains most new clients through referrals.
TERMS Agent receives 15% commission on domestic sales. Agent receives 30% commission on foreign sales. Offers written contract.

◎ PIPPIN PROPERTIES, INC.

155 E. 38th St., Suite 2H, New York NY 10016. (212)338-9310. Fax: (212)338-9579. E-mail: info@pippinproperties.com. Website: www.pippinproperties.com. **Contact:** Holly McGhee. Represents 52 clients. Currently handles: juvenile books 100%.

• Prior to becoming an agent, Ms. McGhee was an editor for 7 years and in book marketing for 4 years. Prior to becoming an agent, Ms. van Beek worked in children's book editorial for 4 years.

MEMBER AGENTS Holly McGhee, Elena Mechlin, Joan Slattery.
REPRESENTS Juvenile.
⌐ "We are strictly a children's literary agency devoted to the management of authors and artists in all media. We are small and discerning in choosing our clientele." Actively seeking middle grade and young adult novels.
HOW TO CONTACT Query via e-mail. Include a synopsis of the work(s), your background and/or publishing history, and anything else you think is relevant. Accepts simultaneous submissions. Responds in 3 weeks to queries if interested. Responds in 10 weeks to mss. Obtains most new clients through recommendations from others.
TERMS Agent receives 15% commission on domestic sales. Agent receives 25% commission on foreign sales. Offers written contract; 30-day notice must be given to terminate contract. Charges for color copying and UPS/FedEx.
TIPS "Please do not start calling after sending a submission."

◑ ALIČKA PISTEK LITERARY AGENCY, LLC

302A W. 12th St., #124, New York NY 10014. E-mail: alicka@apliterary.com. Website: www.apliterary.com. **Contact:** Alička Pistek. Represents 15 clients. 50% of clients are new/unpublished writers. Currently handles: nonfiction books 60%, novels 40%.

• Prior to opening her agency, Ms. Pistek worked at ICM and as an agent at Nicholas Ellison, Inc. Alička has an M.A. in German Translation and a B.A. in Linguistics from the University of California, San Diego. She has studied and worked in the UK, Germany and Prague, Czech Republic.

MEMBER AGENTS Alička Pistek.
REPRESENTS nonfiction books, novels. **Considers these nonfiction areas:** animals, anthropology, autobiography, biography, child guidance, current affairs, environment, government, health, history, how-to, language, law, literature, medicine, memoirs, military, money, parenting, politics, psychology, science, self-help, technology, travel, war, creative nonfiction. **Considers these fiction areas:** crime, detective, ethnic, family saga, historical, literary, mainstream, mystery, police, romance, suspense, thriller.
⌐ Does not want to receive fantasy, science fiction or Western's.
HOW TO CONTACT Agency only accepts queries via e-mail. Send e-query to info@apliterary.com. Include name, address, e-mail, and phone number, title, word count, genre of book, a brief synopsis, and relevant biographical information. Accepts simultaneous submissions. Responds in 2 months to queries. Will only respond if interested. Responds in 8 weeks to mss.
TERMS Agent receives 15% commission on domestic sales. Agent receives 20% commission on foreign sales. Offers written contract. This agency charges for photocopying more than 40 pages and international postage.
TIPS "Be sure you are familiar with the genre you are writing in and learn standard procedures for submitting your work. A good query will go a long way."

◑ PMA LITERARY AND FILM MANAGEMENT, INC.

45 W. 21st St., Suite 401, New York NY 10010. (212)929-1222. Fax: (212)206-0238. E-mail: queries@pmalitfilm.com. Website: www.pmalitfilm.com. **Contact:** Peter Miller. Address for packages is P.O. Box 1817, Old Chelsea Station, New York NY 10113. Represents more than 100 clients. 50% of clients are new/unpublished writers. Currently handles: nonfiction books 40%, novels 30%, juvenile books 5%, movie scripts 25%.

- In his time in the literary world, Mr. Miller has successfully managed more than 1,000 books and dozens of motion picture and television properties. He is the author of *Author! Screenwriter!*

MEMBER AGENTS Peter Miller (big nonfiction, business, true crime, religion); Adrienne Rosado (literary and commercial fiction, young adult).

REPRESENTS nonfiction books, novels, juvenile, movie, TV, TV movie. **Considers these nonfiction areas:** autobiography, biography, business, child guidance, cooking, cultural interests, current affairs, diet/nutrition, economics, ethnic, foods, humor, inspirational, investigative, memoirs, money, parenting, popular culture, religious, satire, self-help, sports, true crime. **Considers these fiction areas:** action, adventure, crime, detective, erotica, ethnic, experimental, gay, historical, humor, inspirational, juvenile, lesbian, literary, mainstream, mystery, police, psychic, religious, romance, satire, supernatural, suspense, thriller, women's, young adult. **Considers these script areas:** action/adventure, comedy, mainstream, romantic comedy, romantic drama, thriller.

☞ "PMA believes in long-term relationships with professional authors. We manage an author's overall career—hence the name—and have strong connections to Hollywood." Actively seeking new ideas beautifully executed. Does not want to receive poetry, stage plays, picture books and clichés.

HOW TO CONTACT Query with SASE. Submit publishing history, author bio. Send no attachments or mss of any kind unless requested. Any unsolicited material will be discarded. See full submission guidelines online. Accepts simultaneous submissions. Responds in 5-7 days for e-mail queries. Responds in 4-6 weeks to mss; 6 months for paper submissions. Obtains most new clients through recommendations from others, solicitations, conferences.

TERMS Agent receives 15% commission on domestic sales. Agent receives 25% commission on foreign sales. Offers written contract; 30-day notice must be given to terminate contract. This agency charges for approved expenses, such as photocopies and overnight delivery.

RECENT SALES *For the Sake of Liberty*, by M. William Phelps (Thomas Dunne Books); *The Haunting of Cambria*, by Richard Taylor (Tor); *Cover Girl Confidential*, by Beverly Bartlett (5 Spot);

Ten Prayers God Always Says Yes To!, by Anthony DeStefano (Doubleday); *Miss Fido Manners: The Complete Book of Dog Etiquette*, by Charlotte Reed (Adams Media); film rights to *Murder in the Heartland*, by M. William Phelps (Mathis Entertainment); film rights to *The Killer's Game*, by Jay Bonansinga (Andrew Lazar/Mad Chance, Inc.).

WRITERS CONFERENCES A full list of Mr. Miller's speaking engagements is available online.

TIPS "Don't approach agents before your work is ready and always approach them as professionally as possible. Don't give up."

🌑 PONTAS AGENCY

Sèneca, 31, principal 08006 Barcelona Spain. This agency has other offices in Germany. Website: www.pontas-agency.com.

MEMBER AGENTS Anna Soler-Pont; Martina Torrades; Carina Brandt; Marc de Gouvenain (represents authors from Scandinavia and the Pacific all over the world, both for publishing and for film rights).

REPRESENTS nonfiction books, novels, movies.

☞ Does not want original film screenplays.

HOW TO CONTACT For book submissions, send by air mail: *curriculum vitae*, with contact details. Details of previously published works. Short synopsis of the work. A printed and bound copy.

⊘ THE POYNOR GROUP

13454 Yorktown Dr., Bowie MD 20715. (301)805-6788. E-mail: jpoynor@aol.com. **Contact:** Jay Poynor, president. Represents 30 clients.

REPRESENTS **Considers these nonfiction areas:** autobiography, biography, business, cooking, cultural interests, diet/nutrition, economics, ethnic, foods, health, inspirational, medicine, multicultural, religious. **Considers these fiction areas:** juvenile, mystery, romance, suspense.

HOW TO CONTACT Mail: query with SASE; e-mail: query only.

⬤ HELEN F. PRATT INC.

1165 Fifth Ave., New York NY 10029. (212)722-5081. Fax: (212)722-8569. E-mail: hfpratt@verizon.net. **Contact:** Helen F. Pratt. Member of AAR.

MEMBER AGENTS Helen Pratt (illustrated books, fashion/decorative design nonfiction); Seamus Mullarky (does not accept unsolicited queries).

REPRESENTS nonfiction books, illustrated books. **Considers these nonfiction areas:** biography, cookbooks, gardening, memoirs, psychology, and especially gardening. **Considers these fiction areas:**, children's and young adult.

HOW TO CONTACT Query with SASE. Include illustrations if possible.

LINN PRENTIS LITERARY

155 East 116th St., #2F, New York NY 10029. Fax: (212)875-5565. E-mail: ahayden@linnprentis.com; linn@linnprentis.com. Website: www.linnprentis.com. **Contact:** Amy Hayden, acquisitions director; Linn Prentis, agent; Jordana Frankel, assistant. Represents 18-20 clients. 25% of clients are new/unpublished writers. Currently handles: nonfiction books 5%, novels 65%, story collections 7%, novella 10%, juvenile books 10%, scholarly books 3%.

- Prior to becoming an agent, Ms. Prentis was a nonfiction writer and editor, primarily in magazines. She also worked in book promotion in New York. Ms. Prentis then worked for and later ran the Virginia Kidd Agency. She is known particularly for her assistance with manuscript development.

REPRESENTS nonfiction books, novels, short story collections, novellas (from authors whose novels I already represent), juvenile (for older juveniles), scholarly, anthology. **Considers these nonfiction areas:** juvenile, animals, art, biography, current affairs, education, ethnic, government, how-to, humor, language, memoirs, music, photography, popular culture, sociology, women's. **Considers these fiction areas:** adventure, ethnic, fantasy, feminist, gay, glitz, historical, horror, humor, juvenile, lesbian, literary, mainstream, mystery, thriller.

"Because of the Virginia Kidd connection and the clients I brought with me at the start, I have a special interest in sci-fi and fantasy, but, really, fiction is what interests me. As for my nonfiction projects, they are books I just couldn't resist." Actively seeking hard science fiction, family saga, mystery, memoir, mainstream, literary, women's. Does not want to "receive books for little kids."

HOW TO CONTACT Query with SASE. Submit synopsis. No phone or fax queries. No snail mail. E-mail queries to ahayden@linnprentis.com. Include first ten pages and synopsis as either attachment or as text in the e-mail. Accepts simultaneous submissions. Obtains most new clients through recommendations from others, solicitations.

TERMS Agent receives 15% commission on domestic sales. Agent receives 20% commission on foreign sales. Offers written contract; 60-day notice must be given to terminate contract.

RECENT SALES Sold 15 titles in the last year. *The Sons of Heaven*, *The Empress of Mars*, and *The House of the Stag*, by Kage Baker (Tor); the last has also been sold to Dabel Brothers to be published as a comic book/graphic novel; *Indigo Springs* and a sequel, by A.M. Dellamonica (Tor); Wayne Arthurson's debut mystery plus a second series book; *Bone Crossed* and *Cry Wolf* for *New York Times* #1 bestselling author Patricia Briggs (Ace/Penguin). "The latter is the start of a new series."

TIPS "Consider query letters and synopses as writing assignments. Spell names correctly."

AARON M. PRIEST LITERARY AGENCY

708 3rd Ave., 23rd Floor, New York NY 10017-4201. (212)818-0344. Fax: (212)573-9417. Website: www.aaronpriest.com. Estab. 1974. Member of AAR. Currently handles: nonfiction books 25%, novels 75%.

MEMBER AGENTS Aaron Priest, querypriest@aaronpriest.com (thrillers, commercial fiction, biographies); Lisa Erbach Vance, queryvance@aaronpriest.com (general fiction, international fiction, thrillers, upmarket women's fiction, historical fiction, narrative nonfiction, memoir); Lucy Childs Baker, querychilds@aaronpriest.com (literary and commercial fiction, memoir, edgy women's fiction); Nicole Kenealy, querykenealy@aaronpriest.com (young adult fiction, narrative nonfiction, how-to, political, and pop-culture, literary and commercial fiction, specifically dealing with social and cultural issues).

Does not want to receive poetry, screenplays or sci-fi.

HOW TO CONTACT Query one of the agents using the appropriate e-mail listed on the website. "Please do not submit to more than 1 agent at this agency. We urge you to check our website and consider each agent's emphasis before submitting. Your query letter should be about one page long and describe your work as well as your background. You may also paste the first chapter of your work in the body of the e-mail. Do not send attachments." Accepts simultaneous submissions. Responds in 3 weeks, only if interested.

TERMS Agent receives 15% commission on domestic sales. This agency charges for photocopying and postage expenses.

RECENT SALES *Divine Justice*, by David Baldacci; *The White Mary*, by Kira Salak; *Long Lost*, by Harlan Coben; *An Accidental Light*, by Elizabeth Diamond; *Trust No One*, by Gregg Hurwitz; *Power Down*, by Ben Coes.

PROSPECT AGENCY, LLC

Attn: Submissions, 285 Fifth Ave., PMB 445, Brooklyn NY 11215. (718)788-3217. E-mail: esk@prospectagency.com. Website: www.prospectagency.com. **Contact:** Becca Stumpf, Emily Sylvan Kim. Represents 15 clients. 50% of clients are new/unpublished writers. Currently handles: novels 66%, juvenile books 33%.

• Prior to starting her agency, Ms. Kim briefly attended law school and worked for another literary agency.

MEMBER AGENTS Emily Sylvan Kim; Becca Stumpf (adult and young adult literary, mainstream fiction; nonfiction interests include narrative nonfiction, journalistic perspectives, fashion, film studies, travel, art, and informed analysis of cultural phenomena. She has a special interest in aging in America and environmental issues); Rachel Orr (fiction and nonfiction, particularly picture books, beginning readers, chapter books, middle grade, young adult novels); Teresa Kietlinski (artists who both write and illustrate).

REPRESENTS nonfiction books, novels, juvenile. **Considers these nonfiction areas:** art, biography, history, juvenile nonfiction, law, memoirs, popular culture, politics, science, travel, prescriptive guides. **Considers these fiction areas:** action, adventure, detective, erotica, ethnic, frontier, juvenile, literary, mainstream, mystery, picture books, romance, suspense, thriller, Westerns, young adult.

➤ "We are currently looking for the next generation of writers to shape the literary landscape. Our clients receive professional and knowledgeable representation. We are committed to offering skilled editorial advice and advocating our clients in the marketplace." Actively seeking romance, literary fiction, and young adult submissions. Does not want to receive poetry, short stories, textbooks, or most nonfiction.

HOW TO CONTACT Upload outline and 3 sample chapters to the website. Accepts simultaneous submissions. Responds in 3 weeks to queries. Responds in 1 month to mss. Obtains most new clients through recommendations from others, conferences, unsolicited mss.

TERMS Agent receives 15% commission on domestic sales. Agent receives 20% commission on foreign sales. Offers written contract.

RECENT SALES *BADD,* by Tim Tharp (Knopf); *Six,* by Elizabeth Batten-Carew (St. Martin's); *Rocky Road,* by Rose Kent (Knopf); *Mating Game*, by Janice Maynard (NAL); *Golden Delicious*, by Aaron Hawkins (Houghton Mifflin Harcourt); *Damaged*, by Pamela Callow (Mira); *Seduced by Shadows*, by Jessica Slade (NAL); *Identity of Ultraviolet*, by Jake Bell (Scholastic); *Quackenstein*, by Sudipta Bardhan-Quallen (Abrams); *Betraying Season*, by Marissa Doyle (Holt); *Sex on the Beach*, by Susan Lyons (Berkley).

WRITERS CONFERENCES "Please see our website for a complete list of attended conferences."

SUSAN ANN PROTTER, LITERARY AGENT

320 Central Park West, Suite 12E, New York NY 10025. **Contact:** Susan Protter. Member of AAR. Other memberships include Authors Guild.

• Prior to opening her agency, Ms. Protter was associate director of subsidiary rights at Harper & Row Publishers.

HOW TO CONTACT *"We are currently not accepting new unsolicited submissions."*

P.S. LITERARY AGENCY

20033-520 Kerr St., Oakville ON L6K 3C7 Canada. E-mail: query@psliterary.com. Website: www.psliterary.com. **Contact:** Curtis Russell, principal agent. Estab. 2005. Currently handles: nonfiction books 50%, novels 50%.

REPRESENTS nonfiction, novels, juvenile books. **Considers these nonfiction areas:** autobiography, biography, business, child guidance, cooking, current affairs, diet/nutrition, economics, environment, foods, government, health, history, how-to, humor, law, memoirs, military, money, parenting, popular culture, politics, science, self-help, sports, technology, true crime, war, women's issues, women's studies. **Considers these fiction areas:** action, adventure, detective, erotica, ethnic, family saga, historical, horror, humor, juvenile, literary, mainstream, mystery, picture books, romance, sports, thriller, women's, young adult.

☞ "What makes our agency distinct: We take on a small number of clients per year in order to provide focused, hands-on representation. We pride ourselves in providing industry-leading client service." Actively seeking both fiction and nonfiction. Seeking both new and established writers. Does not want to receive poetry or screenplays.

HOW TO CONTACT Accepts queries by e-mail/mail, but prefers e-mail. Submit query, synopsis, and bio. Accepts simultaneous submissions. Responds in 4-6 weeks to queries/proposals; mss 4-8 weeks. Obtains most new clients through solicitations.

TERMS Agent receives 15% commission on domestic sales. Agent receives 25% commission on foreign sales. We offer a written contract, with 30-days notice terminate. Fees for postage/messenger services only if project is sold.

TIPS "Please review our website for the most up-to-date submission guidelines. We do not charge reading fees. We do not offer a critique service."

✚ ◑ PUBLICATION RIOT GROUP

E-mail: submissions@priotgroup.com. Website: www.priotgroup.com. **Contact:** Donna Bagdasarian.

• Prior to being an agent, Ms. Bagdasarian worked as an acquisitions editor. Previously, she worked for the William Morris and Maria Carvainis agencies.

REPRESENTS nonfiction books, novels. **Considers these nonfiction areas:** memoirs, popular culture, politics, science, sociology. **Considers these fiction areas:** ethnic, historical, literary, mainstream, thriller, women's.

☞ "The company is a literary management company, representing their authors in all processes of the entertainment trajectory: from book development, to book sales, to subsidiary sales in the foreign market, television and film." Does not want science fiction and fantasy.

HOW TO CONTACT Query via e-mail with a short sample.

⊘ JOANNA PULCINI LITERARY MANAGEMENT

E-mail: info@jplm.com. Website: www.jplm.com. **Contact:** Joanna Pulcini.

☞ "JPLM is not accepting submissions at this time; however, I do encourage those seeking representation to read the 'Advice to Writers' essay on our website for some guidance on finding an agent."

HOW TO CONTACT Do not query this agency until they open their client list.

RECENT SALES *TV*, by Brian Brown; *The Movies That Changed Us*, by Nick Clooney; *Strange, But True*, by John Searles; *The Intelligencer*, by Leslie Silbert; *In Her Shoes* and *The Guy Not Taken*, by Jennifer Weiner.

● QUEEN LITERARY AGENCY

420 W. End Ave., Suite 8A, New York NY 10024. (212)974-8333. Fax: (212)974-8347. E-mail: lqueen@queenliterary.com. Website: www.queenliterary.com. **Contact:** Lisa Queen.

• Prior to her current position, Ms. Queen was a former publishing executive and most recently head of IMG Worldwide's literary division.

REPRESENTS nonfiction books, novels.

☞ Ms. Queen's specialties: "While our agency represents a wide range of nonfiction titles, we have a particular interest in business books, food writing, science and popular psychology, as well as books by well-known chefs, radio and television personalities, and sports figures."

HOW TO CONTACT Query with SASE.

RECENT SALES *The Female Brain*, by Louann Brizendine; *Does the Noise in My Head Bother You?* by Steven Tyler; *What I Cannot Change*, by LeAnn Rimes and Darrell Brown.

◑ QUICKSILVER BOOKS: LITERARY AGENTS

508 Central Park Ave., #5101, Scarsdale NY 10583. Phone/Fax: (914)722-4664. E-mail: quicksilverbooks@hotmail.com. Website: www.quicksilverbooks.com. **Contact:** Bob Silverstein. Represents 50 clients. 50% of clients are new/unpublished writers. Currently handles: nonfiction books 75%, novels 25%.

• Prior to opening his agency, Mr. Silverstein served as senior editor at Bantam Books and managing editor at Dell Books/Delacorte Press.

REPRESENTS nonfiction books, novels. **Considers these nonfiction areas:** anthropology, archeology, autobiography, biography, business, child guidance, cooking, cultural interests, current affairs, diet/nutrition, economics, environment, ethnic, foods, health, history, how-to, inspirational, language, medicine, memoirs, New Age, parenting, popular culture, psychology, religious, science, self-help, sociology, sports, true crime, women's issues, women's studies. **Considers these fiction areas:** action, adventure, glitz, mystery, suspense, thriller.

⚤━➤ This agency specializes in literary and commercial mainstream fiction and nonfiction, especially psychology, New Age, holistic healing, consciousness, ecology, environment, spirituality, reference, self-help, cookbooks and narrative nonfiction. Does not want to receive science fiction, pornography, poetry or single-spaced mss.

HOW TO CONTACT Query with SASE. Authors are expected to supply SASE for return of ms and for query letter responses. Accepts simultaneous submissions. Responds in 2 weeks to queries. Responds in 1 month to mss. Obtains most new clients through recommendations, listings in sourcebooks, solicitations, workshop participation.

TERMS Agent receives 15% commission on domestic sales. Agent receives 20% commission on foreign sales. Offers written contract.

RECENT SALES *Simply Mexican*, by Lourdes Castro (Ten Speed Press); *Indian Vegan Cooking*, by Madhu Gadia (Perigee/Penguin); *Selling Luxury*, by Robin Lent & Genevieve Tour (Wiley); *Get the Job You Want, Even When No One's Hiring*, by Ford R. Myers (Wiley); *Matrix Meditations*, by Victor & Kooch Daniels (Inner Traditions Bear & Co.); *Macrobiotics for Dummies* (Wiley); *The Power of Receiving* (Tarcher); *Eat, Drink, Think in Spanish* (Ten Speed Press); *Nice Girls Don't Win at Life* (Broadway).

WRITERS CONFERENCES National Writers Union.

TIPS "Write what you know. Write from the heart. Publishers print, authors sell."

❶ THE SUSAN RABINER LITERARY AGENCY, INC.

315 W. 39th St., Suite 1501, New York NY 10018. (212)279-0316. Fax: (212)279-0932. E-mail: susan@rabiner.net. Website: www.rabinerlit.com. **Contact:** Susan Rabiner.

• Prior to becoming an agent, Ms. Rabiner was editorial director of Basic Books. She is also

the co-author of *Thinking Like Your Editor: How to Write Great Serious Nonfiction and Get it Published* (W.W. Norton).

MEMBER AGENTS Susan Rabiner; Sydelle Kramer; Helena Schwarz; Holly Bemiss. See the website for individual agent e-mails.

REPRESENTS nonfiction books, novels, textbooks. **Considers these nonfiction areas:** autobiography, biography, business, economics, education, government, health, history, inspirational, law, medicine, philosophy, politics, psychology, religious, science, sociology, sports, technology.

⚤━➤ "Representing narrative nonfiction and big-idea books—work that illuminates the past and the present. I look for well-researched, topical books written by fully credentialed academics, journalists, and recognized public intellectuals with the power to stimulate public debate on a broad range of issues including the state of our economy, political discourse, history, science, and the arts."

HOW TO CONTACT Query by e-mail only, with cover letter and proposal for nonfiction. Accepts simultaneous submissions. Responds in 2 weeks if your project fits the profile of the agency. Obtains most new clients through recommendations from others.

TERMS Agent receives 15% commission on domestic sales. Agent receives 20% commission on foreign sales. Offers written contract; 1-month notice must be given to terminate contract.

❶ LYNNE RABINOFF AGENCY

72-11 Austin St., No. 201, Forest Hills NY 11375. (718)459-6894. E-mail: Lynne@lynnerabinoff.com. **Contact:** Lynne Rabinoff. Represents 50 clients. 50% of clients are new/unpublished writers. Currently handles: nonfiction books 99%, novels 1%.

• Prior to becoming an agent, Ms. Rabinoff was in publishing and dealt with foreign rights.

REPRESENTS nonfiction books. **Considers these nonfiction areas:** anthropology, archeology, autobiography, biography, business, cultural interests, current affairs, economics, ethnic, government, history, inspirational, law, memoirs, military, popular culture, politics, psychology, religious, science, technology, women's issues, women's studies.

⚤━➤ "This agency specializes in history, political issues, current affairs and religion."

HOW TO CONTACT Query with SASE or e-mail. Submit proposal package, synopsis, 1 sample chapter, author bio. Responds in 3 weeks to queries. Responds in 1 month to mss. Obtains most new clients through recommendations from others.

TERMS Agent receives 15% commission on domestic sales. Agent receives 20% commission on foreign sales. Offers written contract; 60-day notice must be given to terminate contract. This agency charges for postage.

RECENT SALES *The Confrontation*, by Walid Phares (Palgrave); *Flying Solo*, by Robert Vaughn (Thomas Dunne); *Thugs*, by Micah Halpern (Thomas Nelson); *Size Sexy*, by Stella Ellis (Adams Media); *Cruel and Usual*, by Nonie Darwish (Thomas Nelson); *Now They Call Me Infidel*, by Nonie Darwish (Sentinel/Penguin); *34 Days*, by Avid Issacharoff (Palgrave).

RAINES & RAINES

103 Kenyon Rd., Medusa NY 12120. (518)239-8311. Fax: (518)239-6029. **Contact:** Theron Raines (member of AAR); Joan Raines; Keith Korman. Member of AAR. Represents 100 clients.

REPRESENTS nonfiction books, novels. **Considers these nonfiction areas:** action/adventure, autobiography/biography, finance/investing, history, military/war, narrative, pychology, all subjects. **Considers these fiction areas:** action, adventure, crime, detective, fantasy, frontier, historical, mystery, picture books, police, science fiction, suspense, thriller, Westerns, whimsical.

HOW TO CONTACT Query with SASE. Responds in 2 weeks to queries.

TERMS Agent receives 15% commission on domestic sales. Agent receives 20% commission on foreign sales. Charges for photocopying.

RED SOFA LITERARY

2163 Grand Ave., #2, St. Paul MN 55105. (651)224-6670. E-mail: dawn@redsofaliterary.com. Website: www.redsofaliterary.com. **Contact:** Dawn Frederick, agent and owner. Represents 10 clients. 60% of clients are new/unpublished writers. Currently handles: nonfiction books 97%, novels 2%, story collections 1%.

- Prior to her current position, Ms. Frederick spent 5 years at Sebastian Literary Agency. In addition, Ms. Frederick worked more than 10 years in indie and chain book stores, and at an independent children's book publish-

er. Ms. Frederick has a master's degree in library and information sciences from an ALA-accredited institution.

REPRESENTS Nonfiction books and young-adult fiction. **Considers these nonfiction areas:** animals, anthropology, archeology, cooking, crafts, cultural interests, current affairs, diet/nutrition, ethnic, foods, gay/lesbian, government, health, history, hobbies, humor, investigative, law, medicine, popular culture, politics, satire, sociology, true crime, women's issues, women's studies, extreme sports.

HOW TO CONTACT Query by e-mail or mail with SASE. No attachments, please. Submit full proposal plus 3 sample chapters and any other pertinent writing samples. Accepts simultaneous submissions. Responds in 3 weeks to queries. Responds in 6 weeks to mss. Obtains most new clients through recommendations from others, solicitations.

TERMS Agent receives 15% commission on domestic sales. Agent receives 20% commission on foreign sales. Offers written contract. May charge a one-time $100 fee for partial reimbursement of postage and phone expenses incurred if the advance is below $15,000.

WRITERS CONFERENCES SDSU Writers' Conference.

TIPS "Truly research the agents you query. Avoid e-mailing and/or snail mailing every literary agent your book idea. Due to the large volume of queries received, the process of reading queries for unrepresented categories (by the agency) becomes tedious. Investigate online directories, printed guides like *Writer's Market*, individual agent websites, and more, before assuming every literary agent in this industry would represent your book idea. Each agent has a vision of what he/she wants to represent and will communicate this information accordingly; we're simply waiting for those specific book ideas to come in our direction."

THE REDWOOD AGENCY

474 Wellesley Ave., Mill Valley CA 94941. (415)381-2269, ext. 2. E-mail: info@redwoodagency.com. E-mail: query@redwoodagency.com. Website: www.redwoodagency.com. **Contact:** Catherine Fowler, founder. Adheres to AAR canon of ethics. Currently handles: nonfiction books 100%.

- Prior to becoming an agent, Ms. Fowler was an editor, subsidiary rights director and associate publisher for Doubleday, Simon & Schuster and Random House for her 20 years in NY publishing. Content exec for web startups Excite and WebMD.

REPRESENTS nonfiction books, novels. **Considers these nonfiction areas:** business, cooking, diet/nutrition, environment, gardening, health, humor, medicine, memoirs, parenting, popular culture, psychology, satire, self-help, women's issues, women's studies, narrative, parenting, aging, reference, lifestyle, cultural technology. **Considers these fiction areas:** literary, mainstream, suspense, women's, quirky.

✂➼ "Along with our love of books and publishing, we have the desire and commitment to work with fun, interesting and creative people, to do so with respect and professionalism, but also with a sense of humor." Actively seeking high-quality, nonfiction works created for the general consumer market, as well as projects with the potential to become book series. Does not want to receive fiction. Do not send packages that require signature for delivery.

HOW TO CONTACT Query via e-mail only. While we redesign website, submit "quick query" to: query@redwoodagency.com. See all guidelines online. Obtains most new clients through recommendations from others, solicitations.

TERMS Offers written contract. Charges for copying and delivery charges, if any, as specified in author/agency agreement.

RED WRITING HOOD INK

2075 Attala Rd. 1990, Kosciusko MS 39090. (662)582-1191. Fax: (662)796-3095. E-mail: redwritinghoodink@gmail.com. Website: www.redwritinghoodink.net. **Contact:** Sheri Ables. Adheres to AAR canon. Currently handles: nonfiction books 100%.

• Prior to her current position, Ms. Ables was an agent of the Williams Agency. In addition, she worked for an agency in Oregon from 1996-1997. Collectively, the staff of RWHI has more than 25 years of experience in the publishing industry.

MEMBER AGENTS Sheri Ables, agent; Terri Dunlap, literary assistant (terri@redwritinghoodink.net).

REPRESENTS nonfiction books.

✂➼ Biography, children's, crime and thrillers, entertainment, general fiction, health, history, inspirational, mystery/suspense, romantic fiction, general nonfiction, self-help.

HOW TO CONTACT Send cover letter and 2-page synopsis by e-mail or mail. If mailing, include SASE.

TERMS Agent receives 15% commission on domestic sales. Agent receives 20% commission on foreign sales.

TIPS Writers: View submission guidelines prior to making contact.

◑ HELEN REES LITERARY AGENCY

14 Beacon St., Suite 710, Boston MA 02108. (617)227-9014. Fax: (617)227-8762. E-mail: reesagency@reesagency.com. Website: http://reesagency.com. **Contact:** Joan Mazmanian, Ann Collette, Helen Rees, Lorin Rees. Estab. 1983. Member of AAR. Other memberships include PEN. Represents more than 100 clients. 50% of clients are new/unpublished writers. Currently handles: nonfiction books 60%, novels 40%.

MEMBER AGENTS Ann Collette (literary, mystery, thrillers, suspense, vampire, and women's fiction; in nonfiction, she prefers true crime, narrative nonfiction, military and war, work to do with race and class, and work set in or about Southeast Asia. Ann can be reached at: Agent10702@aol.com), Lorin Rees (literary fiction, memoirs, business books, self-help, science, history, psychology, and narrative nonfiction. lorin@reesagency.com).

REPRESENTS nonfiction books, novels. **Considers these nonfiction areas:** autobiography, biography, business, current affairs, economics, government, health, history, law, medicine, money, politics, women's issues, women's studies. **Considers these fiction areas:** historical, literary, mainstream, mystery, suspense, thriller.

HOW TO CONTACT Query with SASE, outline, 2 sample chapters. No unsolicited e-mail submissions. No multiple submissions. Responds in 3-4 weeks to queries. Obtains most new clients through recommendations from others, conferences, submissions.

TERMS Agent receives 15% commission on domestic sales. Agent receives 20% commission on foreign sales.

RECENT SALES Sold more than 35 titles in the last year. *Get your Ship Together*, by Capt. D. Michael Abrashoff; *Overpromise and Overdeliver*, by Rick Berrara; *Opacity* by Joel Kurtzman; *America the Broke*, by Gerald Swanson; *Murder at the B-School*, by Jeffrey Cruikshank; *Bone Factory*, by Steven Sidor; *Father Said*, by Hal Sirowitz; *Winning*, by Jack Welch; *The Case for Israel*, by Alan Dershowitz; *As the Future Catches You*, by Juan Enriquez; *Blood Makes the Grass*

Grow Green, by Johnny Rico; *DVD Movie Guide*, by Mick Martin and Marsha Porter; *Words that Work*, by Frank Luntz; *Stirring It Up*, by Gary Hirshberg; *Hot Spots*, by Martin Fletcher; *Andy Grove: The Life and Times of an American*, by Richard Tedlow; *Girls Most Likely To*, by Poonam Sharma.

REGAL LITERARY AGENCY

236 W. 26th St., #801, New York NY 10001. (212)684-7900. Fax: (212)684-7906. E-mail: info@regal-literary.com. Website: www.regal-literary.com. **Contact:** Barbara Marshall. London Office: 36 Gloucester Ave., Primrose Hill, London NW1 7BB, United Kingdom, uk@regal-literary.com. Estab. 2002. Member of AAR. Represents 70 clients. 20% of clients are new/unpublished writers.

MEMBER AGENTS Michelle Andelman joined in 2009. Markus Hoffmann joined Regal Literary in 2006. He had been a literary scout and foreign rights agent on both sides of the Atlantic, most recently as Foreign Rights Manager at Aitken Alexander Associates in London and then Director of International Scouting at Maria Campbell Associates in New York. His main interests are international and literary fiction, crime, (pop) cultural studies, current affairs, economics, history, music, popular science, and travel literature. He also looks after foreign rights for the agency and the London and Frankfurt Book Fairs every year. He's the trumpeter of Half on Signature, the finest R & B band on the international publishing circuit. Lauren Pearson started her career at the Russell & Volkening Literary Agency, and after stints at Tina Brown's *Talk* magazine and the Chicago-based *Modern Luxury* magazine group, she joined Regal Literary in 2004. In 2007, she moved across the pond to set up our London office. In addition to handling UK rights for the agency, she is looking to represent European-based writers of literary and commercial fiction, memoir, narrative nonfiction, and young adult and children's books. If it makes sense for your primary agent to be based in London, she's your gal. She likes anything pop culture or crime-related, and is an avid late-night watcher of *Law & Order* reruns and the British detective drama *Dalziel and Pascoe*. She is a graduate of Duke University and the Radcliffe Publishing Course. With more than a decade of experience in the book publishing industry, Michael Psaltis is a partner in The Culinary Cooperative, as well as the head of his own agency, Psaltis Literary. Michael began his book publishing career working with an independent book marketing company, then with a book publicist and then at a small press before becoming an agent at a boutique literary agency. For nine years he worked with the Book Industry Study Group (BISG), a non-profit organization that studies and reports on all aspects of the book industry. Joseph Regal got his first job in publishing at the Russell & Volkening Literary Agency in 1991. There he worked with Pulitzer Prize-winning bestselling authors Anne Tyler, Eudora Welty, Annie Dillard, Howell Raines, and Peter Taylor, as well as Tony Award-winner Ntozake Shange, Nobel Prize-winner Nadine Gordimer, and TV anchorman and novelist Jim Lehrer. After leaving music for publishing, he founded Regal Literary Inc. in 2002. He graduated from Columbia College magna cum laude. His primary interests are literary fiction, international thrillers, history, science, photography, music, culture, and whimsy. After graduating from Middlebury College, Michael Strong was a sailing instructor at the Hurricane Island Outward Bound School, a carpenter in Berkeley, California, an English teacher at a school for dyslexic students, and a graduate student in English at UNC-Chapel Hill, where he read for Carolina Quarterly. He was a PhD candidate at the Program in Comparative Literature and Literary Theory at the University of Pennsylvania, where he taught classes on technology and ethics, wrote a dissertation on *Finnegans Wake*, and was Assistant Director of the Penn National Commission. After 7 years in digital marketing at Sotheby's, he now handles marketing and publicity at Regal Literary. He yearns for fine literary fiction and ambitious thrillers, and for nonfiction about art, politics, science, business, sports, and he loves boats and the oceans.

Actively seeking literary fiction and narrative nonfiction. Does not want romance, science fiction, horror, screenplays.

HOW TO CONTACT "Query with SASE. No phone calls or e-mail queries. Submissions should consist of a 1-page query letter detailing the book in question, as well as the qualifications of the author. For fiction, submissions may also include the first 10 pages of the novel or one short story from a collection. We do not consider romance, science fiction, poetry, or screenplays." Accepts simultaneous submissions.

Responds in 2-3 weeks to queries. Responds in 4-12 weeks to mss.

TERMS Agent receives 15% commission on domestic sales. Agent receives 20% commission on foreign sales. "We charge no reading fees."

RECENT SALES Audrey Niffenegger's *The Time Traveler's Wife* (Mariner) and *Her Fearful Symmetry* (Scribner), Gregory David Roberts' *Shantaram* (St. Martin's), Josh Bazell's *Beat the Reaper* (Little, Brown), John Twelve Hawks' *The Fourth Realm Trilogy* (Doubleday), James Reston, Jr.'s *The Conviction of Richard Nixon* (Three Rivers) and *Defenders of the Faith* (Penguin), Michael Psilakis' *How to Roast a Lamb: New Greek Classic Cooking* (Little, Brown), Colman Andrews' *Country Cooking of Ireland* (Chronicle) and *Reinventing Food: Ferran Adria and How He Changed the Way We Eat* (Phaidon).

TIPS "We are deeply committed to every aspect of our clients' careers and are engaged in everything from the editorial work of developing a great book proposal or line editing a fiction manuscript to negotiating state-of-the-art book deals and working to promote and publicize the book when it's published. We are at the forefront of the effort to increase authors' rights in publishing contracts in a rapidly changing commercial environment. We deal directly with co-agents and publishers in every foreign territory and also work directly and with co-agents for feature film and television rights, with extraordinary success in both arenas. Many of our clients' works have sold in dozens of translation markets, and a high proportion of our books have been sold in Hollywood. We have strong relationships with speaking agents, who can assist in arranging author tours and other corporate and college speaking opportunities when appropriate. We also have a staff publicist and marketer to help promote our clients and their work."

⊘ JODY REIN BOOKS, INC.

7741 S. Ash Ct., Centennial CO 80122. (303)694-9386. Website: www.jodyreinbooks.com and www.bookproposalpro.com. **Contact:** Winnefred Dollar. Member of AAR. Resigned to design software for writers. Other memberships include Authors' Guild. Currently handles: nonfiction books 100%.

- Prior to opening her agency, Ms. Rein worked for 13 years as an acquisitions editor for Contemporary Books and as executive editor for Bantam/Doubleday/Dell and Morrow/Avon.

REPRESENTS nonfiction books, novels. **Considers these nonfiction areas:** business, child guidance, cultural interests, current affairs, dance, economics, environment, ethnic, film, government, history, humor, law, music, parenting, popular culture, politics, psychology, satire, science, sociology, technology, theater, women's issues, women's studies. **Considers these fiction areas:** literary, mainstream.

⊶ This agency is no longer actively seeking new clients.

TERMS Agent receives 15% commission on domestic sales. Agent receives 25% commission on foreign sales. Agent receives 20% commission on film sales. Offers written contract. Charges clients for express mail, overseas expenses, photocopying mss.

RECENT SALES *How to Remodel a Man*, by Bruce Cameron (St. Martin's Press); *8 Simple Rules for Dating My Teenage Daughter*, by Bruce Cameron (ABC/Disney); *Unbound* and *Skeletons on the Zahara*, by Dean King (Little, Brown); *Halfway to Heaven* and *The Big Year*, by Mark Obmascik (The Free Press); *The Rhino With Glue-On Shoes*, by Dr. Lucy Spelman (Random House); *See You in a Hundred Years*, by Logan Ward (Bantam).

TIPS Jody Rein's new software, book proposal pro, can be found at bookproposalpro.com. "Do your homework before submitting. Make sure you have a marketable topic and the credentials to write about it. Agents and editors seek well-written books on fresh and original nonfiction topics that have broad appeal, as well as novels written by authors who have spent years developing their craft. Authors must be well established in their fields and have strong media experience."

● THE AMY RENNERT AGENCY

98 Main St., #302, Tiburon CA 94920. E-mail: queries@amyrennert.com. **Contact:** Amy Rennert.

REPRESENTS nonfiction books, novels. **Considers these nonfiction areas:** autobiography, biography, health, history, medicine, memoirs, sports, lifestyle, narrative nonfiction. **Considers these fiction areas:** literary, mystery.

⊶ "The Amy Rennert Agency specializes in books that matter. We provide career management for established and first-time authors, and our breadth of experience in many genres enables us to meet the needs of a diverse clientele."

HOW TO CONTACT We now prefer to receive submissions by e-mail. For nonfiction, send cover letter and attach a Word file with proposal/first chapter. For fiction—and sometimes memoir—send cover letter and attach a Word file with 10-20 pages.

TIPS Due to the high volume of submissions, it is not possible to respond to each and every one. Please understand that we are only able to respond to queries that we feel may be a good fit with our agency.

JODIE RHODES LITERARY AGENCY

8840 Villa La Jolla Dr., Suite 315, La Jolla CA 92037-1957. Website: jodierhodesliterary.com. **Contact:** Jodie Rhodes, president. Member of AAR. Represents 74 clients. 60% of clients are new/unpublished writers. Currently handles: nonfiction books 45%, novels 35%, juvenile books 20%.

- Prior to opening her agency, Ms. Rhodes was a university-level creative writing teacher, workshop director, published novelist, and vice president/media director at the N.W. Ayer Advertising Agency.

MEMBER AGENTS Jodie Rhodes; Clark McCutcheon (fiction); Bob McCarter (nonfiction).

REPRESENTS nonfiction books, novels. **Considers these nonfiction areas:** autobiography, biography, child guidance, cultural interests, ethnic, government, health, history, law, medicine, memoirs, military, parenting, politics, science, technology, war, women's issues, women's studies. **Considers these fiction areas:** ethnic, family saga, historical, literary, mainstream, mystery, suspense, thriller, women's, young adult.

- "Actively seeking witty, sophisticated women's books about career ambitions and relationships; edgy/trendy young adult and teen books; narrative nonfiction on groundbreaking scientific discoveries, politics, economics, military; and important current affairs by prominent scientists and academic professors." Does not want to receive erotica, horror, fantasy, romance, science fiction, religious/inspirational, or children's books (does accept young adult/teen).

HOW TO CONTACT Query with brief synopsis, first 30-50 pages, SASE. Do not call. Do not send complete ms unless requested. This agency does not return unrequested material weighing a pound or more that requires special postage. Include e-mail address with query. Accepts simultaneous submissions. Responds in 3 weeks to queries. Obtains most new clients through recommendations from others, agent sourcebooks.

TERMS Agent receives 15% commission on domestic sales. Agent receives 20% commission on foreign sales. Offers written contract; 1-month notice must be given to terminate contract. Charges clients for fax, photocopying, phone calls, postage. Charges are itemized and approved by writers upfront.

RECENT SALES Sold 42 titles in the last year. *The Ring*, by Kavita Daswani (HarperCollins); *Train to Trieste*, by Domnica Radulescu (Knopf); *A Year With Cats and Dogs*, by Margaret Hawkins (Permanent Press); *Silence and Silhouettes*, by Ryan Smithson (HarperCollins); *Internal Affairs*, by Constance Dial (Permanent Press); *How Math Rules the World*, by James Stein (HarperCollins); *Diagnosis of Love*, by Maggie Martin (Bantam); *Lies, Damn Lies, and Science*, by Sherry Seethaler (Prentice Hall); *Freaked*, by Jeanne Dutton (HarperCollins); *The Five Second Rule*, by Anne Maczulak (Perseus Books); *The Intelligence Wars*, by Stephen O'Hern (Prometheus); *Seducing the Spirits*, by Louise Young (The Permanent Press), and more.

TIPS "Think your book out before you write it. Do your research, know your subject matter intimately, and write vivid specifics, not bland generalities. Care deeply about your book. Don't imitate other writers. Find your own voice. We never take on a book we don't believe in, and we go the extra mile for our writers. We welcome talented, new writers."

JONNE RICCI LITERARY AGENCY

P.O. Box 13410, Palm Desert CA 92255. Website: jonnericciliteraryagency.net/. **Contact:** Jonne Ricci. Other memberships include Better Business Bureau of Southland (California). Follows AAR guidelines. Currently handles: novels, juvenile books.

- "We represent authors who have special writing skills and want to see their books published. We encourage first-time writers to contact us. Our agency is committed to finding new talent, and we don't charge fees for reading or evaluating material. We urge you to learn more about our agency. Explore our Webscape and see if your work fits with us. Our agency represents writers of literary fiction. We are most interested in crime, mystery, romance, Westerns, thrillers and adventure. We also specialize in Christian themes. If you feel your work fits with us, please send (in hard copy only, no submissions via e-mail) a query with synopsis (3 pages or fewer) and the first few chapters (30 pages or fewer), all of which should be double spaced. SASE."

🌐 THE LISA RICHARDS AGENCY

108 Upper Leeson St., Dublin 4 Republic of Ireland ,Ireland. (03)(531)637-5000. Fax: (03)531/667-1256. E-mail: info@lisarichards.ie. Website: www.lisa richards.ie. **Contact:** Chairman: Alan Cook; Directors: Lisa Cook (managing) Miranda Pheifer, Fergus Cronin, Patrick Sutton. Actors' Agents: Lisa Cook, Richard Cook, Jonathan Shankey, Rose Parkinson. Comedy Agents: Jennifer Wilson, Christine Dwyer. Literary Agent: Faith O'Grady. Voice Overs: Lorraine Cummins. Corporate Bookings: Evan Kenny. Estab. 1989.

MEMBER AGENTS Faith O'Grady (literary).

REPRESENTS movie, TV, broadcast. **Considers these nonfiction areas:** biography, current affairs, history, memoirs, popular culture, travel, politics. **Considers these script areas:** comedy, general scipts.

HOW TO CONTACT Submit proposal package, synopsis, 2-3 sample chapters, query letter with SAE.

RECENT SALES Clients include Denise Deegan, Arlene Hunt, Roisin Ingle, Declan Lynch, Jennifer McCann, Sarah O'Brien, Kevin Rafter.

◑ ANGELA RINALDI LITERARY AGENCY

P.O. Box 7877, Beverly Hills CA 90212-7877. (310)842-7665. Fax: (310)837-8143. E-mail: amr@rinaldiliterary.com. Website: www.rinaldiliterary.com. **Contact:** Angela Rinaldi. Member of AAR. Represents 50 clients. Currently handles: nonfiction books 50%, novels 50%.

- Prior to opening her agency, Ms. Rinaldi was an editor at NAL/Signet, Pocket Books and Bantam, and the manager of book development for *The Los Angeles Times*.

REPRESENTS nonfiction books, novels, TV and motion picture rights (for clients only). **Considers these nonfiction areas:** biography, business, health books that address specific issues, career, personal finance, self help, true crime, women's issues/studies, current issues, psychology, popular reference, prescriptive and proactive self help, and books by journalists, academics, doctors and therapists, based on their research, motivational. **Considers these fiction areas:** commercial/literary fiction, upmarket contemporary women's fiction, suspense, literary historical thrillers like Elizabeth Kostova's *The Historian*, gothic suspense like Diane Setterfield's *The Thirteenth Tale* and Matthew Pearl's *The Dante Club*, women's book club fiction—novels where the story lends itself to discussion like Kim Edwards' *The Memory Keeper's Daughter*.

☛ Actively seeking commercial and literary fiction. Does not want to receive humor, techno thrillers, KGB/CIA espionage, drug thrillers, Da Vinci-code thrillers, category romances, science fiction, fantasy, horror, Westerns, film scripts, poetry, category romances, magazine articles, religion, occult, supernatural.

HOW TO CONTACT For fiction, send first 3 chapters, brief synopsis, SASE or brief e-mail inquiry with the first 10 pages pasted into the e-mail—no attachments unless asked for. For nonfiction, query with detailed letter or outline/proposal, SASE or e-mail—no attachments unless asked for. Do not send certified or metered mail. Responds in 6 weeks to queries that are posted; e-mail queries 2-3 weeks.

TERMS Agent receives 15% commission on domestic sales. Agent receives 25% commission on foreign sales. Offers written contract.

● ANN RITTENBERG LITERARY AGENCY, INC.

15 Maiden Lane, Suite 206, New York NY 10038. Website: www.rittlit.com. **Contact:** Ann Rittenberg, president; Penn Whaling, associate. Member of AAR. Currently handles: fiction 75%, nonfiction 25%.

REPRESENTS Considers these nonfiction areas: memoirs, women's issues, women's studies. **Considers these fiction areas:** literary, thriller, upmarket fiction.

☛ This agent specializes in literary fiction and literary nonfiction. Does not want to receive screenplays, straight genre fiction, poetry, self-help.

HOW TO CONTACT Query with SASE. Submit outline, 3 sample chapters, SASE. Query via postal mail *only*. Accepts simultaneous submissions. Responds in 6 weeks to queries. Responds in 2 months to mss. Obtains most new clients through referrals from established writers and editors.

TERMS Agent receives 15% commission on domestic sales. Agent receives 20% commission on foreign

sales. Offers written contract. This agency charges clients for photocopying only.

RECENT SALES *The Given Day*, by Dennis Lehane; *My Cat Hates You*, by Jim Edgar; *Never Wave Goodbye*, by Doug Magee; *House and Home*, by Kathleen McCleary; *Nowhere to Run*, by C.J. Box; and *Daughter of Kura*, by Debra Austin.

RIVERSIDE LITERARY AGENCY

41 Simon Keets Rd., Leyden MA 01337. (413)772-0067. Fax: (413)772-0969. E-mail: rivlit@sover.net. Website: www.riversideliteraryagency.com. **Contact:** Susan Lee Cohen.

✇➥ Represents adult fiction and nonfiction.

HOW TO CONTACT Query with SASE. Accepts simultaneous submissions. Responds in 2 weeks to queries. Obtains most new clients through referrals.

TERMS Agent receives 15% commission on domestic sales. Offers written contract. Charges clients for foreign postage, photocopying large mss, express mail deliveries, etc.

ⓞ LESLIE RIVERS, INTERNATIONAL (LRI)

P.O. Box 940772, Houston TX 77094-7772. (281)493–5822. Fax: (281)493–5835. E-mail: LRivers@Leslie Rivers.com. Website: www.leslierivers.com. **Contact:** Judith Bruni. Adheres to AAR's canon of ethics. Represents 20 clients. 80% of clients are new/unpublished writers.

- Prior to becoming agents, members were in marketing, sales, project management, customer satisfaction, writers, and publishing assistants.

MEMBER AGENTS Judith Bruni, literary agent and founder; Mark Bruni, consulting editor.

REPRESENTS novels. **Considers these nonfiction areas:** , "Open to all genres, as long as the author is established with a platform." **Considers these fiction areas:** All fiction genres, but no children's.

✇➥ "LRI collaborates with creative professionals and offers a customized, boutique service, based on the client's individual requirements. LRI maintains flexible hours to accommodate specific client needs. Its primary focus since 2005 is a high-end, no-fee based literary agency for authors. LRI provides high quality service, feedback, and recommendations at no charge, which include readings, proofreading, editing—including content editing, analysis, feedback, and recommendations. Send only your

finest work." Actively seeking fiction/novels only—all subgenres. Does not want to receive children's books or poetry or nonfiction.

HOW TO CONTACT Query via e-mail with Microsoft Word attachments. Submit synopsis, author bio, 3 chapters or 50 pages, whichever is longer. Prefers an exclusive read, but will consider simultaneous queries. Responds in 1-2 months to queries. Responds in 4-6 months to mss. Obtains most new clients through recommendations from others or solicitations.

TERMS Agent receives 15% commission on domestic sales. Agent receives 25% commission on foreign sales. Offers written contract; 90-day notice must be given to terminate contract. This agency charges for postage, printing, copying, etc. If no sale is made, no charges are enforced.

RECENT SALES *Secrets of the Sands*, by Leona Wisoker (Mercury Retrograde Press). Other clients include Brinn Colenda, Carol Gambino, Don Armijo and Fred Stawitz: co-authors of *Homeboy's Soul: Pride, Terror & Street Justice in America*; Fletcher F. Cockrell, author of *Dismissed With Prejudice*, Kathy J. Keller, author of *The Butterfly Clinic*, Leona Wisoker, author of *Secrets of the Sands, Book 1 of The Children of the Desert*, Michael Eldrige, Patricia Forehand, RC (Ruth) White, author of *Devil's Trace*, also *The Ascension at Antioch*, Rhiannon Lynn, Skott Darlow.

ⓞ RLR ASSOCIATES, LTD.

Literary Department, 7 W. 51st St., New York NY 10019. (212)541-8641. Fax: (212)262-7084. E-mail: sgould@rlrassociates.net. Website: www.rlrassociates. net. **Contact:** Scott Gould. Member of AAR. Represents 50 clients. 25% of clients are new/unpublished writers. Currently handles: nonfiction books 70%, novels 25%, story collections 5%.

REPRESENTS nonfiction books, novels, short story collections, scholarly. **Considers these nonfiction areas:** animals, anthropology, archeology, art, autobiography, biography, business, child guidance, cooking, cultural interests, current affairs, decorating, diet/nutrition, economics, education, environment, ethnic, foods, gay/lesbian, government, health, history, humor, inspirational, interior design, language, law, memoirs, money, multicultural, music, parenting, photography, popular culture, politics, psychology, religious, science, self-help, sociology, sports, technology, translation, travel, true crime, women's issues, women's studies. **Considers these fiction areas:** action, adventure, cartoon, comic books, crime, detective, ethnic, experimental, family saga, feminist, gay, historical, horror, humor, lesbian, literary, mainstream, multicultural, mystery, police, satire, sports, suspense.

8—☞ "We provide a lot of editorial assistance to our clients and have connections." Actively seeking fiction, current affairs, history, art, popular culture, health and business. Does not want to receive screenplays.

HOW TO CONTACT Query by either e-mail or mail. Accepts simultaneous submissions. Responds in 4-8 weeks to queries. Obtains most new clients through recommendations from others.

TERMS Agent receives 15% commission on domestic sales. Agent receives 20% commission on foreign sales. Offers written contract.

RECENT SALES Clients include Shelby Foote, The Grief Recovery Institute, Don Wade, Don Zimmer, The Knot.com, David Plowden, PGA of America, Danny Peary, George Kalinsky, Peter Hyman, Daniel Parker, Lee Miller, Elise Miller, Nina Planck, Karyn Bosnak, Christopher Pike, Gerald Carbone, Jason Lethcoe, Andy Crouch.

TIPS "Please check out our website for more details on our agency."

⬤ B.J. ROBBINS LITERARY AGENCY

5130 Bellaire Ave., North Hollywood CA 91607-2908. E-mail: Robbinsliterary@gmail.com or amy.bjrobbins literary@gmail.com. **Contact:** (Ms.) B.J. Robbins or Amy Maldonado. Member of AAR. Represents 40 clients. 50% of clients are new/unpublished writers. Currently handles: nonfiction books 50%, novels 50%.

REPRESENTS nonfiction books, novels. **Considers these nonfiction areas:** autobiography, biography, cultural interests, current affairs, dance, ethnic, film, health, humor, investigative, medicine, memoirs, music, popular culture, psychology, self-help, sociology, sports, theater, travel, true crime, women's issues, women's studies. **Considers these fiction areas:** crime, detective, ethnic, literary, mainstream, mystery, police, sports, suspense, thriller.

HOW TO CONTACT Query with SASE. Submit outline/proposal, 3 sample chapters, SASE. Accepts e-mail queries (no attachments). Accepts simultaneous submissions. Responds in 2-6 weeks to queries.

Responds in 6-8 weeks to mss. Obtains most new clients through conferences, referrals.

TERMS Agent receives 15% commission on domestic sales. Agent receives 20% commission on foreign sales. Offers written contract; 3-month notice must be given to terminate contract. This agency charges clients for postage and photocopying (only after sale of ms).

RECENT SALES Sold 15 titles in the last year. *The Sweetness of Tears*, by Nafisa Haji (William Morrow); *Paper Dollhouse: A Memoir*, by Dr. Lisa M. Masterson; *The Sinatra Club*, by Sal Polisi and Steve Dougherty (Gallery Books); *Getting Stoned With Savages*, by J. Maarten Troost (Broadway); *Hot Water*, by Kathryn Jordan (Berkley); *Between the Bridge and the River*, by Craig Ferguson (Chronicle); *I'm Proud of You* by Tim Madigan (Gotham); *Man of the House*, by Chris Erskine (Rodale); *Bird of Another heaven*, by James D. Houston (Knopf); *Tomorrow They Will Kiss* by Eduardo Santiago (Little, Brown); *A Terrible Glory*, by James Donovan (Little, Brown); *The Writing on My Forehead*, by Nafisa Haji (Morrow); *Seen the Glory*, by John Hough Jr. (Simon & Schuster); *Lost on Planet China*, by J. Maarten Troost (Broadway).

WRITERS CONFERENCES Squaw Valley Writers Workshop; San Diego State University Writers' Conference.

THE ROBBINS OFFICE, INC.

405 Park Ave., 9th Floor, New York NY 10022. (212)223-0720. Fax: (212)223-2535. Website: www.robbinsoffice. com. **Contact:** Kathy P. Robbins, owner.

MEMBER AGENTS Kathy P. Robbins; David Halpern.

REPRESENTS nonfiction books, novels. **Considers these nonfiction areas:** history, politics, journalism, regional interest, memoirs.

8—☞ This agency specializes in selling serious nonfiction, as well as commercial and literary fiction.

HOW TO CONTACT Accepts submissions by referral only.

TERMS Agent receives 15% commission on domestic sales. Agent receives 15% commission on foreign sales. Agent receives 15% commission on film sales. Bills back specific expenses incurred in doing business for a client.

➕⬤ RODEEN LITERARY MANAGEMENT

3501 N. Southport #497, Chicago IL 60657. E-mail: info@rodeenliterary.com. E-mail: submissions@

rodeenliterary.com. Website: www.rodeenliterary.
com. **Contact:** Paul Rodeen. Estab. 2009.

- Paul Rodeen established Rodeen Literary
Management in 2009 after 7 years of experi-
ence with the literary agency Sterling Lord
Literistic, Inc.

REPRESENTS nonfiction books, novels, juvenile
books, illustrations, graphic novels. **Considers
these fiction areas:** picture books, young adult,
middle grade fiction.

⚭━ Actively seeking "writers and illustrators of
all genres of children's literature including
picture books, early readers, middle-grade
fiction and nonfiction, graphic novels, and
comic books, as well as young adult fiction
and nonfiction." This is primarily an agency
devoted to children's books.

HOW TO CONTACT Unsolicited submissions are
accepted by e-mail only to submissions@rodeen
literary.com. Cover letters with contact information
should be included and a maximum of 50 sample
pages. Accepts simultaneous submissions. Response
time varies.

📞📀 ROGERS, COLERIDGE & WHITE

20 Powis Mews, London England W11 1JN, United Kingdom. (44)(207)221-3717. Fax: (44)(207)229-
9084. E-mail: info@rcwlitagency.co.uk. Website:
www.rcwlitagency.co.uk. **Contact:** David Miller,
agent. Estab. 1987.

- Prior to opening the agency, Ms. Rogers was an
agent with Peter Janson-Smith; Ms. Coleridge
worked at Sidgwick & Jackson, Chatto & Win-
dus, and Anthony Sheil Associates; Ms. White
was an editor and rights director for Simon &
Schuster; Mr. Straus worked at Hodder and
Stoughton, Hamish Hamilton, and Macmillan; Mr. Miller worked as Ms. Rogers' assistant and was treasurer of the AAA; Ms. Waldie
worked with Carole Smith.

MEMBER AGENTS Deborah Rogers; Gill Coleridge;
Pat White (illustrated and children's books); Peter
Straus; David Miller; Zoe Waldie (fiction, biogra-
phy, current affairs, narrative history); Laurence
Laluyaux (foreign rights); Stephen Edwards (foreign
rights); Peter Robinson; Sam Copeland; Catherine
Pellegrino; Hannah Westland; Jenny Hewson.

REPRESENTS nonfiction books, novels, juvenile.
Considers these nonfiction areas: biography, cooking, current affairs, diet/nutrition, foods, humor,
satire, sports, narrative history. **Considers these fiction areas:** , Considers most fiction categories.

⚭━ "Young adult and children's fiction should
be submitted via e-mail to clairewilson@rc-
wlitagency.com. We do not accept any other
e-mail submissions unless by prior arrangement with individual agents." Does not want
to receive plays, screenplays, technical books
or educational books.

HOW TO CONTACT "Submit synopsis, proposal,
sample chapters, bio, SAE by mail. Submissions
should include a cover letter with brief bio and the
background to the book. In the case of fiction, they
should consist of the first 3 chapters or approximately
the first 50 pages of the work to a natural break and
a brief synopsis. Nonfiction submissions should take
the form of a proposal, up to 20 pages in length explaining what the work is about and why you are best
placed to write it. Material should be printed out in
12-point font, in double-spacing and on one side only
of A4 paper. We cannot acknowledge receipt of material, nor can we accept responsibility for anything
you send us, so please retain a copy of material submitted. Material will be returned only if sent with
an adequately stamped and sized SASE; if return
postage is not provided the material will be recycled.
We do not accept e-mail submissions unless by prior
arrangement with individual agents. We will try to
respond within 6-8 weeks of receipt of your material,
but please appreciate that this isn't always possible as
we must give priority to the authors we already represent." Responds in 6-8 weeks to queries. Obtains most
new clients through recommendations from others,
solicitations, conferences.

TERMS Agent receives 15% commission on domestic sales. Agent receives 20% commission on foreign
sales. Offers written contract.

📀 LINDA ROGHAAR LITERARY AGENCY, LLC

133 High Point Dr., Amherst MA 01002. (413)256-1921.
E-mail: contact@lindaroghaar.com. Website: www.
lindaroghaar.com. **Contact:** Linda L. Roghaar. Represents 50 clients. 10% of clients are new/unpublished
writers. Currently handles: nonfiction books 100%.

- Prior to opening her agency, Ms. Roghaar worked in retail bookselling for 5 years and as a publishers' sales rep for 15 years.

REPRESENTS nonfiction books. **Considers these nonfiction areas:** animals, anthropology, archeology, autobiography, biography, education, environment, history, inspirational, popular culture, self-help, women's issues, women's studies.

HOW TO CONTACT Query with SASE. Accepts simultaneous submissions. Responds in 3 months to queries. Responds in 4 months to mss.

TERMS Agent receives 15% commission on domestic sales. Agent receives negotiable commission on foreign sales. Offers written contract.

RECENT SALES *Handmade Home,* by Amanda Soule (Shambhala); *Vintage Knits,* by Debbie Brisson (aka Stitchy McYarnpants) and Carolyn Sheridan (Wiley); *TYV Crafting for Kids,* by Jennifer Casa (Wiley); *The White Hand Society,* by Peter Conners (City Lights); *The Writing Warrior,* by Laraine Herring (Shambhala); *All Wound Up,* by Stephanie Pearl-McPhee (Andrews McMeel).

◑ RITA ROSENKRANZ LITERARY AGENCY

440 West End Ave., #15D, New York NY 10024-5358. (212)873-6333. Website: www.ritarosenkranzliterary agency.com. **Contact:** Rita Rosenkranz. Member of AAR. Represents 35 clients. 30% of clients are new/unpublished writers. Currently handles: nonfiction books 99%, novels 1%.

- Prior to opening her agency, Ms. Rosenkranz worked as an editor at major New York publishing houses.

REPRESENTS nonfiction books. **Considers these nonfiction areas:** animals, anthropology, art, autobiography, biography, business, child guidance, computers, cooking, crafts, cultural interests, current affairs, dance, decorating, economics, ethnic, film, gay, government, health, history, hobbies, how-to, humor, inspirational, interior design, language, law, lesbian, literature, medicine, military, money, music, nature, parenting, personal improvement, photography, popular culture, politics, psychology, religious, satire, science, self-help, sports, technology, theater, war, women's issues, women's studies.

⚷— "This agency focuses on adult nonfiction, stresses strong editorial development and refinement before submitting to publishers, and brainstorms ideas with authors." Actively seeks au-

thors who are well paired with their subject, either for professional or personal reasons.

HOW TO CONTACT Send query letter only (no proposal) via regular mail or e-mail. Submit proposal package with SASE only on request. No fax queries. Accepts simultaneous submissions. Responds in 2 weeks to queries. Obtains most new clients through directory listings, solicitations, conferences, word of mouth.

TERMS Agent receives 15% commission on domestic sales. Agent receives 20% commission on foreign sales. Offers written contract, binding for 3 years; 3-month written notice must be given to terminate contract. Charges clients for photocopying. Makes referrals to editing services.

RECENT SALES Sold 35 titles in the last year. *29 GIFTS: How a Month of Giving Can Change Your Life* by Cami Walker (DaCapo Press), *Writers Gone Wild: The Feuds, Frolics and Follies of Literature's Great Adventurers, Drunkards, Lovers, Iconoclasts, and Misanthropes,* by Bill Peschel (Perigee), *Study Your Brains Out!* by Anne Crossman (Ten Speed Press).

TIPS "Identify the current competition for your project to make sure the project is valid. A strong cover letter is very important."

● ANDY ROSS LITERARY AGENCY

767 Santa Ray Ave., Oakland CA 94610. (510)238-8965. E-mail: andyrossagency@hotmail.com. Website: www.andyrossagency.com. **Contact:** Andy Ross. Represents 30 clients. 20% of clients are new/unpublished writers. Currently handles: nonfiction books 100%.

REPRESENTS nonfiction books, scholarly. **Considers these nonfiction areas:** anthropology, autobiography, biography, child guidance, cultural interests, current affairs, education, environment, ethnic, government, history, language, law, literature, military, parenting, popular culture, politics, psychology, science, sociology, technology, war.

⚷— "This agency specializes in general nonfiction, politics and current events, history, biography, journalism, and contemporary culture." Actively seeking narrative nonfiction. Does not want to receive personal memoir, fiction, poetry, juvenile books.

HOW TO CONTACT Query via e-mail only. Accepts simultaneous submissions. Responds in 1 week to queries.

TERMS Agent receives 15% commission on domestic sales. Agent receives 20% commission on foreign sales through a sub-agent. Offers written contract.

● ROSS YOON AGENCY

1666 Connecticut Ave. N.W., Suite 500, Washington DC 20009. (202)328-3282. Fax: (202)328-9162. E-mail: submissions@rossyoon.com. Website: http://rossyoon.com. **Contact:** Jennifer Manguera. Member of AAR. Represents 200 clients. 75% of clients are new/unpublished writers. Currently handles: nonfiction books 95%.

MEMBER AGENTS Gail Ross (represents important commercial nonfiction in a variety of areas and counts top doctors, CEO's, prize-winning journalists, and historians among her clients. She and her team work closely with first-time authors; gail@rossyoon.com), Howard Yoon (nonfiction topics ranging from current events and politics to culture to religion and history, to smart business; he is also looking for commercial fiction by published authors; howard@rossyoon.com).

REPRESENTS nonfiction books. **Considers these nonfiction areas:** anthropology, archeology, autobiography, biography, business, cultural interests, economics, education, environment, ethnic, gay/lesbian, government, health, inspirational, investigative, law, medicine, money, politics, psychology, religious, science, self-help, sociology, sports, technology, true crime. **Considers these fiction areas:** occasional commercial fiction.

⊶ "This agency specializes in adult trade nonfiction."

HOW TO CONTACT "Send proposals by e-mail with a cover letter, résumé, brief synopsis of your work, and several sample chapters. We also accept query letters. No longer accepting submissions by mail." Accepts simultaneous submissions. Responds in 4-6 weeks to queries. Obtains most new clients through recommendations from others.

TERMS Agent receives 15% commission on domestic sales. Agent receives 25% commission on foreign sales. Charges for office expenses.

THE ROTHMAN BRECHER AGENCY

9250 Wilshire Blvd., Penthouse, Beverly Hills CA 90212. (310)247-9898. E-mail: reception@rothmanbrecher.com. **Contact:** Andrea Kavoosi. Signatory of WGA.

REPRESENTS TV, movie scripts, feature film.

HOW TO CONTACT Referrals only.

● JANE ROTROSEN AGENCY LLC

318 E. 51st St., New York NY 10022. (212)593-4330. Fax: (212)935-6985. Website: www.janerotrosen.com. Estab. 1974. Member of AAR. Other memberships include Authors Guild. Represents more than 100 clients. Currently handles: nonfiction books 30%, novels 70%.

MEMBER AGENTS Jane R. Berkey; Andrea Cirillo; Annelise Robey; Meg Ruley; Christina Hogrebe; Peggy Gordijn, director of rights.

REPRESENTS nonfiction books, novels. **Considers these nonfiction areas:** autobiography, biography, business, child guidance, cooking, current affairs, diet/nutrition, economics, environment, foods, health, how-to, humor, investigative, medicine, money, parenting, popular culture, psychology, satire, self-help, sports, true crime, women's issues, women's studies. **Considers these fiction areas:** crime, family saga, historical, mystery, police, romance, suspense, thriller, women's.

HOW TO CONTACT Query with SASE to the attention of "Submissions." Find appropriate agent contact/e-mail on website. Responds in 2 weeks to writers who have been referred by a client or colleague. Responds in 2 months to mss. Obtains most new clients through recommendations from others.

TERMS Agent receives 15% commission on domestic sales. Agent receives 20% commission on foreign sales. Offers written contract, binding for 3 years; 2-month notice must be given to terminate contract. Charges clients for photocopying, express mail, overseas postage, book purchase.

● THE DAMARIS ROWLAND AGENCY

91 Country Route 61, Chatham NY 12037. **Contact:** Damaris Rowland. Member of AAR.

REPRESENTS nonfiction books, novels.

⊶ This agency specializes in women's fiction, literary fiction and nonfiction, and pop fiction.

HOW TO CONTACT Query with synopsis, SASE. Obtains most new clients through recommendations from others, solicitations, conferences.

TERMS Agent receives 15% commission on domestic sales. Agent receives 20% commission on foreign sales. Offers written contract.

◑ ◎ THE RUDY AGENCY

825 Wildlife Lane, Estes Park CO 80517. (970)577-8500. Fax: (970)577-8600. E-mail: mak@rudyagency.com. Website: www.rudyagency.com. **Contact:** Maryann Karinch. Adheres to AAR canon of ethics. Represents 15 clients. 50% of clients are new/unpublished writers. Currently handles: nonfiction books 100%.

- Prior to becoming an agent, Ms. Karinch was, and continues to be, an author of nonfiction books—covering the subjects of health/medicine and human behavior. Prior to that, she was in public relations and marketing: areas of expertise she also applies in her practice as an agent.

MEMBER AGENTS Maryann Karinch (nonfiction: health/medicine, culture/values, history, biography, memoir, science/technology, military/intelligence).

REPRESENTS nonfiction books, textbooks with consumer appeal. **Considers these nonfiction areas:** anthropology, archeology, autobiography, biography, business, child guidance, computers, cultural interests, current affairs, economics, education, ethnic, gay/lesbian, government, health, history, how-to, language, law, literature, medicine, memoirs, military, money, music, parenting, popular culture, politics, psychology, science, sociology, sports, technology, true crime, war, women's issues, women's studies.

- ⚷ ➶ "We support authors from the proposal stage through promotion of the published work. We work in partnership with publishers to promote the published work and coach authors in their role in the marketing and public relations campaigns for the book." Actively seeking projects with social value, projects that open minds to new ideas and interesting lives, and projects that entertain through good storytelling. Does not want to receive poetry, children's/juvenile books, screenplays/plays, art/photo books, novels/novellas, religion books, and joke books or books that fit in to the impulse buy/gift book category.

HOW TO CONTACT "Query us. If we like the query, we will invite a complete proposal. No phone queries." Accepts simultaneous submissions. Responds in 8 weeks to mss. Obtains most new clients through recommendations from others, solicitations.

TERMS Agent receives 15% commission on domestic sales. Offers written contract, binding for 1 year.

RECENT SALES Sold 11 titles in the last year. *Live From Jordan: Letters Home From My Journal Through the Middle East*, by Benjamin Orbach (Amacom); *Finding Center: Strategies to Build Strong Girls & Women*, by Maureen Mack (New Horizon Press); *Crossing Fifth Avenue to Bergdorf Goodman: An Insider's Account on the Rise of Luxury Retailing*, by Ira Neimark (SPI Books); *Hamas vs. Fatah: The Struggle for Palestine*, by Jonathan Schanzer (Palgrave Macmillan); *The New Rules of Etiquette and Entertaining*, by Curtrise Garner (Adams Media); *Comes the Darkness, Comes the Light*, by Vanessa Vega (Amacom); *Murder in Mayberry*, by Mary and Jack Branson (New Horizon Press); *Not My Turn to Die*, by Savo Heleta.

WRITERS CONFERENCES BookExpo of America; industry events.

TIPS "Present yourself professionally. I tell people all the time: Subscribe to *Writer's Digest* (I do), because you will get good advice about how to approach an agent."

◑ RUSSELL & VOLKENING

50 W. 29th St., Suite 7E, New York NY 10001. (212)684-6050. Fax: (212)889-3026. Website: www.randvinc.com. **Contact:** Joy Azmitia (chick-lit, multicultural fiction, romance, humor, and nonfiction in the areas of travel, pop culture, and philosophy: joy@randvinc.com). Member of AAR. Represents 140 clients. 20% of clients are new/unpublished writers. Currently handles: nonfiction books 45%, novels 50%, story collections 3%, novella 2%.

REPRESENTS nonfiction books, novels, short-story collections. **Considers these nonfiction areas:** anthropology, architecture, art, autobiography, biography, business, cooking, cultural interests, current affairs, design, education, environment, ethnic, film, gay/lesbian, government, health, history, language, law, military, money, music, photography, popular culture, politics, psychology, science, sociology, sports, technology, true crime, war, women's issues, women's studies, creative nonfiction. **Considers these fiction areas:** action, adventure, crime, detective, ethnic, literary, mainstream, mystery, picture books, police, sports, suspense, thriller.

- ⚷ ➶ This agency specializes in literary fiction and narrative nonfiction. Actively seeking novels.

HOW TO CONTACT Query only with SASE to appropriate person. Responds in 4 weeks to queries.

TERMS Agent receives 15% commission on domestic sales. Agent receives 20% commission on foreign sales. Charges clients for standard office expenses relating to the submission of materials.

TIPS "If the query is cogent, well written, well presented, and is the type of book we'd represent, we'll ask to see the manuscript. From there, it depends purely on the quality of the work."

● REGINA RYAN PUBLISHING ENTERPRISES, INC.

251 Central Park W., 7D, New York NY 10024. (212)787-5589. E-mail: queries@reginaryanbooks.com. Website: www.reginaryanbooks.com. **Contact:** Regina Ryan. Currently handles: nonfiction books 100%.

- Prior to becoming an agent, Ms. Ryan was an editor at Alfred A. Knopf, editor-in-chief of Macmillan Adult Trade, and a book producer.

MEMBER AGENTS Regina Ryan; Sharona Moskowitz (for fiction queries).

REPRESENTS nonfiction books. **Considers these nonfiction areas:** animals, architecture, gardening, government, history, law, memoirs, parenting, politics, psychology, travel, women's issues, women's studies, narrative nonfiction; natural history (especially birds and birding); popular science, adventure, lifestyle, business, sustainability, mind-body-spirit, relationships.

HOW TO CONTACT Query by e-mail or mail with SASE. No telephone queries. Does not accept queries for juvenile or fiction. Accepts simultaneous submissions. Tries to respond in 1 month to queries. Obtains most new clients through recommendations from others.

TERMS Agent receives 15% commission on domestic sales. Agent receives 15% commission on foreign sales. Offers written contract. Charges clients for all out-of-pocket expenses (e.g., long distance calls, messengers, freight, copying) if it's more than just a nominal amount.

RECENT SALES *Backyard Bird Feeding*, by Randi Minetor (Globe Pequot Press); *In Search of Sacco and Vanzetti*, by Susan Tejada (Univ. Press of New England); *Trouble Shooting the Vegetable Garden*, by David Deardorff and Kathryn Wadsworth (Timber Press); *When Johnny Comes Marching Home: What Vets Need, What They Don't Need and What All of Us Can Do to Help*, by Paula Caplan (MIT Press); *Everything Changes: The Insider's Guide to Cancer in Your 20's and 30's*, by Kairol Rosenthal (Wiley); *Angel of Death Row: My Life as a Death Penalty Defense Lawyer*, by Andrea Lyon (Kaplan Publishing).

TIPS "An analysis of why your proposed book is different and better than the competition is essential; a sample chapter is helpful."

● THE SAGALYN AGENCY

4922 Fairmont Ave., Suite 200, Bethesda MD 20814. (301)718-6440. Fax: (301)718-6444. E-mail: query@sagalyn.com. Website: www.sagalyn.com. Estab. 1980. Member of AAR. Currently handles: nonfiction books 85%, novels 5%, scholarly books 10%.

MEMBER AGENTS Raphael Sagalyn; Bridget Wagner, Shannon O'Neill.

REPRESENTS nonfiction books. **Considers these nonfiction areas:** autobiography, biography, business, economics, history, inspirational, memoirs, popular culture, science, technology, journalism.

➤ Does not want to receive stage plays, screenplays, poetry, science fiction, fantasy, romance, children's books or young adult books.

HOW TO CONTACT Please send e-mail queries only (no attachments). Include 1 of these words in the subject line: query, submission, inquiry.

TIPS "We receive 1,000-1,200 queries a year, which in turn lead to 2 or 3 new clients. Query via e-mail only. See our website for sales information and recent projects."

● SALKIND LITERARY AGENCY

Part of Studio B, 734 Indiana St., Lawrence KS 66044. (785)371-0101. E-mail: neil@studiob.com. Website: www.salkindagency.com. **Contact:** Neil Salkind. Represents 200 clients. 25% of clients are new/unpublished writers. Currently handles: nonfiction books 60%, scholarly books 20%, textbooks 20%.

- Prior to becoming an agent, Mr. Salkind authored numerous trade and textbooks.

MEMBER AGENTS Greg Aunapu, Lynn Haller, Malka Margolies, Neil J. Salkind.

➤ Mr. Aunapu represents both fiction and nonfiction, including true crime, technology, biography, history, narrative nonfiction, memoir (by people who have accomplished something great in their fields), finance, current affairs, politics, pop culture, psychology, relationships, science and travel. Fiction includes suspense/thrillers, mystery, detective, adventure, humor, science fiction and modern urban fantasy. Submission guidelines can be found at www.gregaunapu.com. Nonfiction queries should be in book-proposal format; fiction queries should include a complete book synopsis, the first 25 pages of the manuscript, and an author biography. He can be reached at greg@studiob.com. Ms. Haller represents nonfiction authors, with a special interest in business, technology, and how-to. Queries should include a book proposal, a bio and writing samples. She can be reached at lynn@studiob.com. Ms. Lawler represents fiction and nonfiction authors. Her nonfiction interests include narrative nonfiction, self-help and some how-to. She is interested in genre fiction, including mystery and science fiction/fantasy. She does NOT represent children's or young adult. Please query with a book proposal (for nonfiction) and the first chapter of the manuscript (for fiction). She can be reached at jennifer@studiob.com. Ms. Margolies represents predominantly nonfiction. Her interests include history, current events, cultural issues, religion/spirituality, nutrition and health, women's issues, parenting, and the environment. She is not interested in science fiction, fantasy, how-to or children's books. She can be reached at malka@studiob.com. Mr. Salkind represents these nonfiction areas: business, cooking, crafts, health, how-to, photography and visual arts, science, and self-help. He also represents textbooks and scholarly books. Does not want "to receive book proposals based on ideas where potential authors have not yet researched what has been published."

HOW TO CONTACT Query electronically. Obtains most new clients through recommendations from others.

TERMS Agent receives 15% commission on domestic sales. Agent receives 15% commission on foreign sales.

🌐 SALOMONSSON AGENCY

Svartensgatan 4, 116 20 Stockholm, Sweden. E-mail: info@salomonssonagency.com. Website: www.salomonssonagency.com. **Contact:** Niclas Salomonsson. Estab. 2000. Currently handles: novels 100%.

MEMBER AGENTS Niclas Salomonsson, Szilvia Monar, Leyla Belle Drake.

REPRESENTS novels.

🔑— "Salomonsson Agency is one of the leading literary agencies in Scandinavia. We focus on fiction from the Nordic countries."

HOW TO CONTACT This agency focuses on Scandinavian authors.

RECENT SALES 9-book deal with Random House Canada regarding Liza Marklund; 2-book deal with HarperCollins US regarding Sissel-Jo Gazan; 8-book deal with Doubleday UK regarding Liza Marklund.

🅓 VICTORIA SANDERS & ASSOCIATES

241 Avenue of the Americas, Suite 11 H, New York NY 10014. (212)633-8811. Fax: (212)633-0525. E-mail: queriesvsa@hotmail.com. Website: www.victoriasanders.com. **Contact:** Victoria Sanders, Diane Dickensheid. Estab. 1992. Member of AAR. Signatory of WGA. Represents 135 clients. 25% of clients are new/unpublished writers. Currently handles: nonfiction books 30%, novels 70%.

MEMBER AGENTS Tanya McKinnon, Victoria Sanders, Chris Kepner (include the first three chapters in the body of the e-mail. At the moment, he is especially on the lookout for quality nonfiction), Bernadette Baker-Baughman.

REPRESENTS nonfiction books, novels. **Considers these nonfiction areas:** autobiography, biography, cultural interests, current affairs, dance, ethnic, film, gay/lesbian, government, history, humor, language, law, literature, music, popular culture, politics, psychology, satire, theater, translation, women's issues, women's studies. **Considers these fiction areas:** action, adventure, contemporary issues, ethnic, family saga, feminist, gay, lesbian, literary, thriller.

HOW TO CONTACT Query by e-mail only.

TERMS Agent receives 15% commission on domestic sales. Agent receives 20% commission on foreign sales. Offers written contract. Charges for photocopying, messenger, express mail. If in excess of $100, client approval is required.

RECENT SALES Sold 20+ titles in the last year.

TIPS "Limit query to letter (no calls) and give it your best shot. A good query is going to get a good response."

⚫ SANDUM & ASSOCIATES

144 E. 84th St., New York NY 10028-2035. (212)737-2011. **Contact:** Howard E. Sandum.

☛ This agency specializes in general nonfiction and occasionally literary fiction.

HOW TO CONTACT Query with synopsis, bio, SASE. Do not send full ms unless requested.

TERMS Agent receives 15% commission on domestic sales. Charges clients for photocopying, air express, long-distance telephone/fax.

🌐 LENNART SANE AGENCY

Hollandareplan 9, S-374 34, Karlshamn, Sweden. 0046 45412356. Fax: 0046 45414920. E-mail: info@lennart saneagency.com. Website: www.lennartsaneagency. com. **Contact:** Lennart Sane. Represents 20+ clients.

MEMBER AGENTS Lennart Sane, agent; Philip Sane, agent; Lina Hammarling, agent.

REPRESENTS nonfiction books, novels, juvenile.

☛ Lennart Sane Agency AB "represents the literary rights of authors, agents, and publishers, in the markets of fiction, nonfiction, and film." This European agency deals in a lot of translation rights, and North American authors are best *not* to query this agency without a strong referral.

HOW TO CONTACT Query with SASE. "We do not accept unsolicited submissions. We accept new material by referral only."

⬤ SCHIAVONE LITERARY AGENCY, INC.

236 Trails End, West Palm Beach FL 33413-2135. (561)966-9294. Fax: (561)966-9294. E-mail: profschia@aol.com. Website: www.publishersmarket place.com/members/profschia; blog site: www. schiavoneliteraryagencyinc.blogspot.com. **Contact:** Dr. James Schiavone, CEO, corporate offices in Florida; Jennifer DuVall, president, New York office. New York office: 3671 Hudson Manor Terrace, No. 11H, Bronx NY 10463-1139, (718)548-5332; Fax: (718)548-5332; E-mail: jendu77@aol.com. Other memberships include National Education Association. Represents 60+ clients. 2% of clients are new/unpublished writers. Currently handles: nonfiction books 50%, novels 49%, textbooks 1%.

- Prior to opening his agency, Dr. Schiavone was a full professor of developmental skills at the City University of New York and author of 5 trade books and 3 textbooks. Jennifer DuVall has many years of combined experience in office management and agenting.

REPRESENTS nonfiction books, novels, juvenile, scholarly, textbooks. **Considers these nonfiction areas:** animals, anthropology, archeology, autobiography, biography, child guidance, cultural interests, current affairs, education, environment, ethnic, gay/lesbian, government, health, history, how-to, humor, investigative, juvenile nonfiction, language, law, literature, medicine, military, parenting, popular culture, politics, psychology, satire, science, sociology, spirituality, true crime. **Considers these fiction areas:** ethnic, family saga, historical, horror, humor, juvenile, literary, mainstream, science fiction, young adult.

☛ This agency specializes in celebrity biography and autobiography and memoirs. Does not want to receive poetry.

HOW TO CONTACT Query with SASE. Do not send unsolicited materials or parcels requiring a signature. Send no e-attachments. Accepts simultaneous submissions. Responds in 2 weeks to queries. Responds in 6 weeks to mss. Obtains most new clients through recommendations from others, solicitations, conferences.

TERMS Agent receives 15% commission on domestic sales. Agent receives 20% commission on foreign sales. Offers written contract. Charges clients for postage only.

WRITERS CONFERENCES Key West Literary Seminar; South Florida Writers' Conference; Tallahassee Writers' Conference, Million Dollar Writers' Conference; Alaska Writers Conference.

TIPS "We prefer to work with established authors published by major houses in New York. We will consider marketable proposals from new/previously unpublished writers."

WENDY SCHMALZ AGENCY

P.O. Box 831, Hudson NY 12534. (518)672-7697. E-mail: wendy@schmalzagency.com. Website: www. schmalzagency.com. **Contact:** Wendy Schmalz. Estab. 2002. Member of AAR. Represents 35 clients. 10% of clients are new/unpublished writers.

☛ Actively seeking young adult novels, middle grade novels. Obtains clients through recommendations from others. Not looking for picture books, science fiction or fantasy.

TERMS Agent receives 15% commission on domestic sales. Agent receives 20% on foreign sales. Agent receives 25% for Asian sales.

⊘ HAROLD SCHMIDT LITERARY AGENCY

415 W. 23rd St., #6F, New York NY 10011. **Contact:** Harold Schmidt, Acquisitions. Estab. 1984. Member of AAR. Represents 3 clients.

REPRESENTS nonfiction, fiction. **Considers these fiction areas:** contemporary issues, gay, literary, original quality fiction with unique narrative voices, high quality psychological suspense and thrillers, likes offbeat/quirky.

⌐⊶ Actively seeking novels.

HOW TO CONTACT Query by mail with SASE (or e-mail address); do not send material without being asked. No telephone or e-mail queries. We will respond if interested. Do not send material unless asked as it cannot be read or returned.

⊕⊘ SUSAN SCHULMAN LITERARY AGENCY

454 W. 44th St., New York NY 10036. (212)713-1633. Fax: (212)581-8830. E-mail: schulmanqueries@yahoo. com. **Contact:** Susan Schulman. Estab. 1980. Member of AAR. Signatory of WGA. Other memberships include Dramatists Guild. 10% of clients are new/unpublished writers. Currently handles: nonfiction books 50%, novels 25%, juvenile books 15%, stage plays 10%.

MEMBER AGENTS Linda Kiss, director of foreign rights; Katherine Stones, theater; Emily Uhry, submissions editor.

REPRESENTS Considers these nonfiction areas: anthropology, archeology, autobiography, biography, business, child guidance, cooking, cultural interests, current affairs, dance, diet/nutrition, economics, education, environment, ethnic, foods, gay/lesbian, government, health, history, how-to, inspirational, investigative, language, law, literature, medicine, memoirs, money, music, parenting, popular culture, politics, psychology, religious, self-help, sociology, sports, true crime, women's issues, women's studies. **Considers these fiction areas:** action, adventure, crime, detective, feminist, historical, humor, inspirational, juvenile, literary, mainstream, mystery, picture books, police, religious, suspense, women's, young adult.

⌐⊶ "We specialize in books for, by and about women and women's issues including nonfiction self-help books, fiction and theater projects. We also handle the film, television and allied rights for several agencies, as well as foreign rights for several publishing houses." Actively seeking new nonfiction. Considers plays. Does not want to receive poetry, television scripts or concepts for television.

HOW TO CONTACT Query with SASE. Submit outline, synopsis, author bio, 3 sample chapters, SASE. Accepts simultaneous submissions. Responds in 6 weeks to queries. Responds in 6 weeks to mss. Obtains most new clients through recommendations from others, solicitations, conferences.

TERMS Agent receives 15% commission on domestic sales. Agent receives 20% commission on foreign sales. Offers written contract; 30-day notice must be given to terminate contract.

RECENT SALES Sold 50 titles in the last year; hundred of subsidiary rights deals.

WRITERS CONFERENCES Geneva Writers' Conference (Switzerland); Columbus Writers' Conference; Skidmore Conference of the Independent Women's Writers Group.

TIPS "Keep writing!"

⊕ JONATHAN SCOTT, INC

Chicago IL (312)339-7300. E-mail: jon@jonathan scott.us; scott@jonathanscott.us. Website: www. jonathanscott.us. **Contact:** Jon Malysiak, Scott Adlington. Estab. 2005. Represents 40 clients. 75% of clients are new/unpublished writers. Currently handles: nonfiction books 90%, novels 10%.

MEMBER AGENTS Scott Adlington (narrative nonfiction, sports, health, wellness, fitness, environmental issues); Jon Malysiak (narrative nonfiction and fiction, current affairs, history, memoir, business).

REPRESENTS nonfiction books.

⌐⊶ "We are very hands-on with our authors in terms of working with them to develop their proposals and manuscripts. Since both of us come from publishing backgrounds—editorial and sales—we are able to give our authors a perspective of what goes on within the publishing house from initial consideration through the entire development, publication, marketing and sales processes." Categories of health/fitness, cooking, sports history, narrative nonfiction, memoir, parenting, general business, and travel essay and all other nonfiction categories. We also represents books to be sold into film, television and other subsidiary channels. To find out about literary representation, please contact Jon Malysiak, with a query e-mail describing your book idea and/or a proposal.

HOW TO CONTACT "We only accept electronic submissions. Query by e-mail describing your book idea and/or a proposal." Accepts simultaneous submissions. Responds in 1-2 weeks to queries. Responds in 4-6 weeks to mss. Obtains most new clients through recommendations from others, solicitations, contacting good authors for representation.

TERMS Agent receives 15% commission on domestic sales. Agent receives 20% commission on foreign sales. Offers written contract; 30-day notice must be given to terminate contract.

TIPS "Platform, platform, platform. We can't emphasize this enough. Without a strong national platform, it is nearly impossible to get the interest of a publisher. Also, be organized in your thoughts and your goals before contacting an agent. Think of the proposal as your business plan. What do you hope to achieve by publishing your book? How can your book change the world?"

● SCOVIL GALEN GHOSH LITERARY AGENCY, INC.

276 Fifth Ave., Suite 708, New York NY 10001. (212)679-8686. Fax: (212)679-6710. E-mail: info@sgglit.com. Website: www.sgglit.com. **Contact:** Russell Galen. Estab. 1992. Member of AAR. Represents 300 clients. Currently handles: nonfiction books 60%, novels 40%.

MEMBER AGENTS Jack Scovil, jackscovil@sgglit.com; Russell Galen, russellgalen@sgglit.com (novels that stretch the bounds of reality; strong, serious nonfiction books on almost any subject that teach something new; no books that are merely entertaining, such as diet or pop psych books; serious interests include science, history, journalism, biography, business, memoir, nature, politics, sports, contemporary culture, literary nonfiction, etc.); Anna Ghosh, annaghosh@sgglit.com (strong nonfiction proposals on all subjects, as well as adult commercial and literary fiction by both unpublished and published authors; serious interests include investigative journalism, literary nonfiction, history, biography, memoir, popular culture, science, adventure, art, food, religion, psychology, alternative health, social issues, women's fiction, historical novels and

literary fiction); Ann Behar, annbehar@sgglit.com (juvenile books for all ages).

REPRESENTS nonfiction books, novels.

HOW TO CONTACT E-mail queries strongly preferred. Accepts simultaneous submissions.

● SCRIBBLERS HOUSE, LLC LITERARY AGENCY

P.O. Box 1007, Cooper Station, New York NY 10276-1007. (212)714-7744. E-mail: query@scribblershouse.net. Website: www.scribblershouse.net. **Contact:** Stedman Mays, Garrett Gambino. 25% of clients are new/unpublished writers.

MEMBER AGENTS Stedman Mays, Garrett Gambino.

REPRESENTS nonfiction books, novels, occasionally. **Considers these nonfiction areas:** biography, business, diet/nutrition, economics, health, history, how-to, language, literature, medicine, memoirs, money, parenting, popular culture, politics, psychology, self-help, sex, spirituality, the brain; personal finance; writing books; relationships; gender issues;. **Considers these fiction areas:** crime, historical, literary, suspense, thriller, women's.

HOW TO CONTACT "Query via e-mail. Put 'nonfiction query' or 'fiction query' in the subject line followed by the title of your project (send to our submissions e-mail on our website). Do not send attachments or downloadable materials of any kind with query. We will request more materials if we are interested. Usually respond in 2 weeks to 2 months to e-mail queries if we are interested (if we are not interested, we will not respond due to the overwhelming amount of queries we receive). We are only accepting e-mail queries at the present time." Accepts simultaneous submissions.

TERMS Agent receives 15% commission on domestic sales. Charges clients for postage, shipping and copying.

TIPS "If you must send by snail mail, we will return material or respond to a U.S. Postal Service-accepted SASE. (No international coupons or outdated mail strips, please.) Presentation means a lot. A well-written query letter with a brief author bio and your credentials is important. For query letter models, go to the bookstore or online and look at the cover copy and flap copy on other books in your general area of interest. Emulate what's best. Have an idea of other notable books that will be perceived as being in the same vein as yours. Know what's fresh about your project and articulate it in as few words as possible. Consult our website for the most up-to-date information on submitting."

○ SCRIBE AGENCY, LLC

5508 Joylynne Dr., Madison WI 53716. E-mail: what theshizzle@scribeagency.com. E-mail: submissions@scribeagency.com. Website: www.scribeagency.com. **Contact:** Kristopher O'Higgins. Represents 11 clients. 18% of clients are new/unpublished writers. Currently handles: novels 98%, story collections 2%.

- "We have 17 years of experience in publishing and have worked on both agency and editorial sides in the past, with marketing expertise to boot. We love books as much or more than anyone you know. Check our website to see what we're about and to make sure you jive with the Scribe vibe."

MEMBER AGENTS Kristopher O'Higgins; Jesse Vogel.

REPRESENTS nonfiction books, novels, short-story collections, novellas, anthologies. **Considers these nonfiction areas:** cooking, diet/nutrition, ethnic, foods, gay/lesbian, humor, memoirs, popular culture, satire, women's issues, women's studies. **Considers these fiction areas:** detective, erotica, experimental, fantasy, feminist, gay, horror, humor, lesbian, literary, mainstream, mystery, psychic, science fiction, thriller.

➤ Actively seeking excellent writers with ideas and stories to tell.

HOW TO CONTACT E-queries only: submissions@scribeagency.com. See the website for submission info, as it may change. Responds in 3-4 weeks to queries. Responds in 5 months to mss.

TERMS Agent receives 15% commission on domestic sales. Agent receives 20% commission on foreign sales. Offers written contract. Charges for postage and photocopying.

RECENT SALES Sold 3 titles in the last year.

WRITERS CONFERENCES BookExpo America; The Writer's Institute; Spring Writer's Festival; WisCon; Wisconsin Book Festival; World Fantasy Convention.

SECRET AGENT MAN

P.O. Box 1078, Lake Forest CA 92609-1078. (949)698-6987. E-mail: scott@secretagentman.net. E-mail: query@secretagentman.net. Website: www.secretagentman.net. **Contact:** Scott Mortenson.

REPRESENTS novels. **Considers these fiction areas:** detective, mystery, religious, suspense, thriller, Westerns.

➤ Actively seeking selective mystery, thriller, suspense and detective fiction. Does not want to receive scripts or screenplays.

HOW TO CONTACT Query with SASE. Query via e-mail or snail mail; include sample chapter(s), synopsis and/or outline. Prefers to read the real thing rather than a description of it. Obtains most new clients through recommendations from others, solicitations.

LYNN SELIGMAN, LITERARY AGENT

400 Highland Ave., Upper Montclair NJ 07043. (973)783-3631. **Contact:** Lynn Seligman. Other memberships include Women's Media Group. Represents 32 clients. 15% of clients are new/unpublished writers. Currently handles: nonfiction books 60%, novels 40%.

- Prior to opening her agency, Ms. Seligman worked in the subsidiary rights department of Doubleday and Simon & Schuster, and served as an agent with Julian Bach Literary Agency (which became IMG Literary Agency). Foreign rights are represented by Books Crossing Borders, Inc.

REPRESENTS nonfiction books, novels. **Considers these nonfiction areas:** interior, anthropology, art, biography, business, child guidance, cooking, current affairs, education, ethnic, government, health, history, how-to, humor, language, money, music, nature, photography, popular culture, psychology, science, self-help, sociology, film, true crime, women's. **Considers these fiction areas:** detective, ethnic, fantasy, feminist, historical, horror, humor, literary, mainstream, mystery, romance, contemporary, gothic, historical, regency, science fiction.

➤ "This agency specializes in general nonfiction and fiction. I also do illustrated and photography books and have represented several photographers for books."

HOW TO CONTACT Query with SASE. Prefers to read materials exclusively. Accepts simultaneous submissions. Responds in 2 weeks to queries. Responds in 2 months to mss. Obtains most new clients through referrals from other writers and editors.

TERMS Agent receives 15% commission on domestic sales. Agent receives 25% commission on foreign sales. Charges clients for photocopying, unusual postage, express mail, telephone expenses (checks with author first).

RECENT SALES Sold 15 titles in the last year. Lords of Vice series, by Barbara Pierce; Untitled series, by Deborah Leblanc.

◑ SERENDIPITY LITERARY AGENCY, LLC

305 Gates Ave., Brooklyn NY 11216. (718)230-7689. Fax: (718)230-7829. E-mail: rbrooks@serendipity lit.com; info@serendipitylit.com. Website: www. serendipitylit.com. **Contact:** Regina Brooks. Represents 50 clients. 50% of clients are new/unpublished writers. Currently handles: nonfiction books 50%.

- Prior to becoming an agent, Ms. Brooks was an acquisitions editor for John Wiley & Sons, Inc. and McGraw-Hill Companies.

MEMBER AGENTS Regina Brooks, Dawn M. Hardy (dawn@serendipitylit.com), Karen Thomas (karen@serendipitylit.com), Folade Bell (folade@ serendipitylit.com).

REPRESENTS nonfiction books, novels, juvenile, scholarly, children's books. **Considers these nonfiction areas:** biography, business, Christian nonfiction, cooking, crafts, cultural interests, current affairs, design, economics, education, ethnic, foods, health, history, inspirational, juvenile nonfiction, medicine, memoirs, metaphysics, money, multicultural, New Age, popular culture, politics, psychology, religious, science, self-help, sports, technology, women's issues, women's studies, narrative; popular science, contemporary culture. **Considers these fiction areas:** action, adventure, confession, ethnic, historical, juvenile, literary, multicultural, mystery, picture books, romance, suspense, thriller, Christian fiction, spiritual, commercial fiction, young adult novels.

- ☞ African-American nonfiction, commercial fiction, young adult novels with an urban flair and juvenile books. No stage plays, screenplays or poetry.

HOW TO CONTACT Prefers to read materials exclusively. For nonfiction, submit proposal, outline, 1 sample chapter (electronically), SASE. Write the field on the back of the envelope. For adult fiction, please send a query letter that includes basic information that describes your project. Your query letter should include the title, premise and length of the manuscript. See our guidelines onine. Write the genre of your book on the back of your envelope. Based on your initial query letter and synopsis, our office may request sample chapters or your ms in its entirety. Responds in 4-6 weeks to queries. Responds in 2

months to mss. Obtains most new clients through conferences, referrals.

TERMS Agent receives 15% commission on domestic sales. Agent receives 20% commission on foreign sales. Offers written contract; 2-month notice must be given to terminate contract. Charges clients for office fees, which are taken from any advance.

RECENT SALES *A Wreath for Emmitt Till*, by Marilyn Nelson (Houghton Mifflin); *A Song for Present Existence*, by Marilyn Nelson and Tonya Hegamin (Scholastic); *Ruby and the Booker Boys*, by Derrick Barnes (Scholastic); *Brenda Buckley's Universe and Everything In It*, by Sundee Frazier (Delacorte Books for Young Readers); *Wait Until the Black Girl Sings*, by Bil Wright Simon and Schuster (Scholastic); *First Semester*, by Cecil R. Cross II (KimaniTru/ Harlequin).

TIPS "See *Writing Great Books for Young Adults*. Looking for high concept ideas with big hooks."

◐● SEVENTH AVENUE LITERARY AGENCY

2052-124th St., South Surrey BC Canada. (604)538-7252. Fax: (604)538-7252. E-mail: info@seventhavenuelit.com. Website: www.seventhavenuelit.com. **Contact:** Robert Mackwood, director. Currently handles: nonfiction books 100%.

REPRESENTS nonfiction books. **Considers these nonfiction areas:** autobiography, biography, business, computers, economics, health, history, medicine, science, sports, technology, travel, lifestyle.

- ☞ Seventh Avenue Literary Agency is both a literary agency and personal management agency. (The agency was originally called Contemporary Management.) Actively seeking nonfiction. Does not want to receive fiction, poetry, screenplays, children's books, young adult titles, or genre writing such as science fiction, fantasy, or erotica.

HOW TO CONTACT Query with SASE. Submit outline, synopsis, 1 sample chapter (nonfiction), publishing history, author bio, table of contents with proposal or query. Send 1-2 chapters and submission history if sending fiction. No e-mail attachments. Provide full contact information. For fiction queries only contact Gloria Goodman: hettyphil@ sympatico.ca. Obtains most new clients through recommendations from others, some solicitations. Does not add many new clients.

TIPS "If you want your material returned, please include an SASE with adequate postage; otherwise, material will be recycled. (U.S. stamps are not adequate; they do not work in Canada.)"

◐ THE SEYMOUR AGENCY

475 Miner St., Canton NY 13617. (315)386-1831. E-mail: marysue@twcny.rr.com; nicole@theseymour agency.com. Website: www.theseymouragency.com. **Contact:** Mary Sue Seymour, Nicole Resciniti. Member of AAR. Signatory of WGA. Other memberships include RWA, Authors Guild. Represents 50 clients. 5% of clients are new/unpublished writers. Currently handles: nonfiction books 50%, fiction 50%.

- Ms. Seymour is a retired New York State certified teacher.

MEMBER AGENTS Mary Sue Seymour (accepts queries in Christian, inspirational, romance and nonfiction, Nicole Resciniti (accepts queries in same categories as Ms. Seymour in addition to action/suspense/thriller, mystery, sci-fi, fantasy, and young adult/children's).

REPRESENTS nonfiction books, novels. **Considers these nonfiction areas:** business, health, how-to, self-help, Christian books, cookbooks, any well-written nonfiction that includes a proposal in standard format and 1 sample chapter. **Considers these fiction areas:** action, fantasy, mystery, religious, romance, science fiction, suspense, thriller, young adult.

HOW TO CONTACT Query with SASE, synopsis, first 50 pages for romance. Accepts e-mail queries. Accepts simultaneous submissions. Responds in 1 month to queries. Responds in 3 months to mss.

TERMS Agent receives 12-15% commission on domestic sales.

RECENT SALES Dinah Bucholz's *The Harry Potter Cookbook* to Adams Media.com; Vannetta Chapman's *A Simple Amish Christmas* to Abingdon Press; Shelley Shepard Gray's current book deal to Harper Collins; Shelley Galloway's multibook deal to Zondervan; Beth Wiseman's Christmas two novellas and multibook deal to Thomas Nelson; Mary Ellis's multibook deal to Harvest House, Barbara Cameron's novellas to Thomas Nelson and multibook deal to Abingdon Press.

DENISE SHANNON LITERARY AGENCY, INC.

20 W. 22nd St., Suite 1603, New York NY 10010. (212)414-2911. Fax: (212)414-2930. E-mail: info@deniseshannon agency.com. E-mail: submissions@deniseshannon agency.com. Website: www.deniseshannonagency.com. **Contact:** Denise Shannon, founder; Lea Beresford, agent. Estab. 2002. Member of AAR.

- Prior to opening her agency, Ms. Shannon worked for 16 years with Georges Borchardt and International Creative Management.

REPRESENTS nonfiction books, novels. **Considers these nonfiction areas:** biography, business, health, narrative nonfiction; politics; journalism; memoir; social history. **Considers these fiction areas:** literary.

⛏ "We are a boutique agency with a distinguished list of fiction and nonfiction authors."

HOW TO CONTACT Query by e-mail to submissions @deniseshannonagency.com, or by mail with SASE. Submit query with description of project, bio, SASE. See guidelines online.

TIPS "Please do not send queries regarding fiction projects until a complete manuscript is available for review. We request that you inform us if you are submitting material simultaneously to other agencies."

◐ THE ROBERT E. SHEPARD AGENCY

4804 Laurel Canyon Blvd., Box 592, Valley Village CA 91607-3717. (818)508-0056. E-mail: mail@shepard agency.com. Website: www.shepardagency.com. **Contact:** Robert Shepard. Other memberships include Authors Guild. Represents 70 clients. 15% of clients are new/unpublished writers. Currently handles: nonfiction books 90%, scholarly books 10%.

- Prior to opening his agency, Mr. Shepard was an editor and a sales and marketing manager in book publishing; he now writes, teaches courses for nonfiction authors and speaks at many writers' conferences.

REPRESENTS nonfiction books, scholarly, appropriate for trade publishers. **Considers these nonfiction areas:** business, cultural interests, current affairs, economics, gay/lesbian, government, health, history, law, parenting, popular culture, politics, psychology, sports, Judaica; narrative nonfiction; science for laypeople.

⛏ This agency specializes in nonfiction, particularly key issues facing society and culture. Actively seeking works by experts recognized in their fields whether or not they're well-known to the general public, and books that offer fresh perspectives or new information even when the subject is familiar. Does not want to receive autobiographies, art books, memoir, spirituality or fiction.

HOW TO CONTACT Query either by e-mail or by regular mail with SASE (if you want material to be returned). Accepts simultaneous submissions. Responds in 4-6 weeks to queries. Responds in 6 weeks to proposals. Do not sent ms unless specifically requested to do so. Obtains most new clients through recommendations from others, solicitations.

TERMS Agent receives 15% commission on domestic sales. Agent receives 20% commission on foreign sales. Offers written contract, binding for term of project or until canceled; 30-day notice must be given to terminate contract. Charges clients for phone/fax, photocopying, postage (if and when the project sells).

RECENT SALES Sold 10 titles in the last year. *A Few Seconds of Panic*, by Stefan Fatsis (Penguin); *Big Boy Rules*, by Steve Fainaru (Da Capo Press); *The Fois Gras Wars*, by Mark Caro (Simon & Schuster).

TIPS "We pay attention to detail. We believe in close working relationships between the author and agent, and in building better relationships between the author and editor. Please do your homework! There's no substitute for learning all you can about similar or directly competing books and presenting a well-reasoned competitive analysis in your proposal. Be sure to describe what's new and fresh about your work, why you are the best person to be writing on your subject, everything editors will need to know about your work, and how the book will serve the needs or interests of your intended readers. Don't work in a vacuum: Visit bookstores, talk to other writers about their experiences and let the information you gather inform the work that you do as an author."

◐ WENDY SHERMAN ASSOCIATES, INC.

27 W. 24th St., New York NY 10010. (212)279-9027. E-mail: wendy@wsherman.com. E-mail: submissions@wsherman.com. Website: www.wsherman.com. **Contact:** Wendy Sherman. Member of AAR. Represents 50 clients. 30% of clients are new/unpublished writers.

- Prior to opening the agency, Ms. Sherman served as vice president, executive director, associate publisher, subsidiary rights director, and sales and marketing director for major publishers.

MEMBER AGENTS Wendy Sherman (board member of AAR), Kim Perel.

REPRESENTS Considers these nonfiction areas: memoirs, psychology, narrative; practical. **Considers these fiction areas:** mainstream fiction that hits the sweet spot between literary and commercial.

☞ "We specialize in developing new writers, as well as working with more established writers. My experience as a publisher has proven to be a great asset to my clients."

HOW TO CONTACT Query via e-mail. Accepts simultaneous submissions. Responds in 1 month to queries. Obtains most new clients through recommendations from others.

TERMS Agent receives 15% commission on domestic sales. Agent receives 20% commission on foreign and film sales. Offers written contract.

RECENT SALES *Exposure*, by Therese Fowler, *It's All Relative*, by Wade Rouse. *In Stitches,* by Dr. Tony Youn, *Daughters of the Witching Hill*, by Mary Sharratt; *The Sweet By and By*, by Todd Johnson; *Supergirls Speak Out*, by Liz Funk; *Love in 90 Days* and *Sealing the Deal*, by Dr. Diana Kirschner; *A Long Time Ago* and *Essentially*, by Brigid Pasulka; *Changing Shoes*, by Tina Sloan.

TIPS "The bottom line is: Do your homework. Be as well prepared as possible. Read the books that will help you present yourself and your work with polish. You want your submission to stand out."

● ROSALIE SIEGEL, INTERNATIONAL LITERARY AGENCY, INC.

1 Abey Dr., Pennington NJ 08534. (609)737-1007. Fax: (609)737-3708. Website: http://rosaliesiegel.com. **Contact:** Rosalie Siegel. Member of AAR. Represents 35 clients. 10% of clients are new/unpublished writers. Currently handles: nonfiction books 45%, novels 45%, young adult books and short-story collections for current clients 10%.

HOW TO CONTACT Obtains most new clients through referrals from writers and friends.

TERMS Agent receives 15% commission on domestic sales. Agent receives 20% commission on foreign sales. Offers written contract; 2-month notice must be given to terminate contract. Charges clients for photocopying.

❶ SIGNATURE LITERARY AGENCY

4200 Wisconsin Ave., NW, #106-233, Washington, DC 20016. Address for agents Gary Heidt and Amy Tipton is 101 W. 23rd St., Suite 346, New York, NY 10011. Website: www. signaturelit.com.

MEMBER AGENTS Ellen Pepus; Gary Heidt; Amy Tipton. Each agent's e-mail is (firstname)@signaturelit.com.

HOW TO CONTACT E-queries only. Responds if interested. Responds to queries in one month; responds to submissions in 3 months.

RECENT SALES *Delicious and Suspicious*, by Riley Adams; *Fall for Anything*, by Courtney Summers; *How to Live Safely in a Science Fictional Universe*, by Charles Yu; *Hunted by the Others* (series), by Jess Haines.

❷❶ JEFFREY SIMMONS LITERARY AGENCY

15 Penn House, Mallory St., London NW8 8SX, England. (44)(207)224-8917. E-mail: jasimmons@unicom box.co.uk. **Contact:** Jeffrey Simmons. Represents 43 clients. 40% of clients are new/unpublished writers. Currently handles: nonfiction books 65%, novels 35%.

- Prior to becoming an agent, Mr. Simmons was a publisher. He is also an author.

REPRESENTS nonfiction books, novels. **Considers these nonfiction areas:** autobiography, biography, current affairs, film, government, history, language, memoirs, music, popular culture, sociology, sports, translation, true crime. **Considers these fiction areas:** action, adventure, confession, crime, detective, family saga, literary, mainstream, mystery, police, suspense, thriller.

- ⚷ "This agency seeks to handle good books and promising young writers. My long experience in publishing and as an author and ghostwriter means I can offer an excellent service all around, especially in terms of editorial experience where appropriate." Actively seeking quality fiction, biography, autobiography, showbiz, personality books, law, crime, politics, and world affairs. Does not want to receive science fiction, horror, fantasy, juvenile, academic books, or specialist subjects (e.g., cooking, gardening, religious).

HOW TO CONTACT Submit sample chapter, outline/proposal, SASE (IRCs if necessary). Prefers to read materials exclusively. Responds in 1 week to queries. Responds in 1 month to mss. Obtains most new clients through recommendations from others, solicitations.

TERMS Agent receives 10-15% commission on domestic sales. Agent receives 15% commission on foreign sales. Offers written contract, binding for lifetime of book in question or until it becomes out of print.

TIPS "When contacting us with an outline/proposal, include a brief biographical note (listing any previous publications, with publishers and dates). Preferably tell us if the book has already been offered elsewhere."

❶ BEVERLEY SLOPEN LITERARY AGENCY

131 Bloor St. W., Suite 711, Toronto ON M5S 1S3, Canada. (416)964-9598. Fax: (416)921-7726. E-mail: beverly@slopenagency.ca. Website: www.slopenagency.ca. **Contact:** Beverley Slopen. Represents 70 clients. 20% of clients are new/unpublished writers. Currently handles: nonfiction books 60%, novels 40%.

- Prior to opening her agency, Ms. Slopen worked in publishing and as a journalist.

REPRESENTS nonfiction books, novels, scholarly, textbooks, college. **Considers these nonfiction areas:** anthropology, archeology, autobiography, biography, business, current affairs, economics, investigative, psychology, sociology, true crime, women's issues, women's studies. **Considers these fiction areas:** literary, mystery, suspense.

- ⚷ "This agency has a strong bent toward Canadian writers." Actively seeking serious nonfiction that is accessible and appealing to the general reader. Does not want to receive fantasy, science fiction, or children's books.

HOW TO CONTACT Query with SAE and IRCs. Returns materials only with SASE (Canadian postage only). Accepts simultaneous submissions. Responds in 2 months to queries.

TERMS Agent receives 15% commission on domestic sales. Agent receives 10% commission on foreign sales. Offers written contract, binding for 2 years; 3-month notice must be given to terminate contract.

RECENT SALES *Solar Dance*, by Modris Eksteins (Knopf Canada); *God's Brain*, by Lionel Tiger & Michael McGuire (Prometheus Books); *What They Wanted*, by Donna Morrissey (Penguin Canada, Premium/DTV Germany); *The Age of Persuasion*, by Terry O'Reilly & Mike Tennant (Knopf Canada, Counterpoint US); *Prisoner of Tehran*, by Marina Nemat (Penguin Canada, Free Press US,

John Murray UK); *Race to the Polar Sea*, by Ken McGoogan (HarperCollins Canada, Counterpoint US); *Transgression*, by James Nichol (HarperCollins US, McArthur Canada, Goldmann Germany); *Vermeer's Hat*, by Timothy Brook (HarperCollins Canada, Bloomsbury US); *Distantly Related to Freud*, by Ann Charney (Cormorant).

TIPS "Please, no unsolicited manuscripts."

◉ SLW LITERARY AGENCY

4100 Ridgeland Ave., Northbrook IL 60062. (847)509-0999. Fax: (847)509-0996. E-mail: shariwenk@gmail.com. **Contact:** Shari Wenk. Currently handles: nonfiction books 100%.

REPRESENTS nonfiction books. **Considers these nonfiction areas:** sports.

⌐ "This agency specializes in representing books written by sports celebrities and sports writers."

HOW TO CONTACT Query via e-mail, but note the agency's specific specialty.

● ◐ ROBERT SMITH LITERARY AGENCY, LTD.

12 Bridge Wharf, 156 Caledonian Rd., London NI 9UU, England. (44)(207)278-2444. Fax: (44)(207)833-5680. E-mail: robertsmith.literaryagency@virgin.net. **Contact:** Robert Smith. Other memberships include AAA. Represents 40 clients. 10% of clients are new/unpublished writers. Currently handles: nonfiction books 80%, syndicated material 20%.

• Prior to becoming an agent, Mr. Smith was a book publisher.

REPRESENTS nonfiction books, syndicated material. **Considers these nonfiction areas:** autobiography, biography, cooking, diet/nutrition, film, foods, health, investigative, medicine, memoirs, music, popular culture, self-help, sports, theater, true crime, entertainment.

⌐ "This agency offers clients full management service in all media. Clients are not necessarily book authors. Our special expertise is in placing newspaper series internationally." Actively seeking autobiographies.

HOW TO CONTACT Submit outline/proposal, SASE (IRCs if necessary). Prefers to read materials exclusively. Responds in 2 weeks to queries. Obtains most new clients through recommendations from others, direct approaches to prospective authors.

TERMS Agent receives 15% commission on domestic sales. Agent receives 20% commission on foreign sales. Offers written contract, binding for 3 months; 3-month notice must be given to terminate contract. Charges clients for couriers, photocopying, overseas mailings of mss (subject to client authorization).

RECENT SALES *Lawro*, by Mark Lawrenson (Penguin); *Enter the Dragon*, by Theo Paphitis (Orion); *Strong Women*, by Roberta Kray (Little, Brown); *Home From War*, by Martyn and Michelle Compton (Mainstream); *Diary of a Japanese P.O.W* by John Baxter (Aurum Press); *A Different Kind of Courage* by Gretel Wachtel and Claudia Strachan (Mainstream); *Drawing Fire*, by Len Smith (HarperCollins); *Mummy Doesn't Love You*, by Alexander Sinclair (Ebury Press); *Forgotten*, by Les Cummings (Macmillan); *Suffer the Little Children*, by Frances Reilly (Orion).

VALERIE SMITH, LITERARY AGENT

1746 Route 44-55, Box 160, Modena NY 12548. **Contact:** Valerie Smith. Represents 17 clients. Currently handles: nonfiction books 2%, novels 75%, story collections 1%, juvenile books 20%, scholarly books 1%, textbooks 1%.

REPRESENTS nonfiction books, novels, juvenile, textbooks. **Considers these nonfiction areas:** agriculture horticulture, cooking, how to, self help. **Considers these fiction areas:** fantasy, historical, juvenile, literary, mainstream, mystery, science, young, women's/chick lit.

⌐ "This is a small, personalized agency with a strong long-term commitment to clients interested in building careers. I have strong ties to science fiction, fantasy and young adult projects. I look for serious, productive writers whose work I can be passionate about." Does not want to receive unsolicited mss.

HOW TO CONTACT Query with synopsis, bio, 3 sample chapters, SASE. Contact by snail mail only. Obtains most new clients through recommendations from others.

TERMS Agent receives 15% commission on domestic sales. Agent receives 20% commission on foreign sales. Offers written contract; 6-week notice must be given to terminate contract.

MICHAEL SNELL LITERARY AGENCY

P.O. Box 1206, Truro MA 02666-1206. (508)349-3718. E-mail: snellliteraryagency@yahoo.com. Website:

http://michaelsnellagency.com. **Contact:** Michael Snell. Represents 200 clients. 25% of clients are new/unpublished writers. Currently handles: nonfiction books 90%, novels 10%.

- Prior to opening his agency, Mr. Snell served as an editor at Wadsworth and Addison-Wesley for 13 years.

MEMBER AGENTS Michael Snell (business, leadership, pets, sports); Patricia Snell (business, business communications, parenting, relationships).

REPRESENTS nonfiction books. **Considers these nonfiction areas:** agriculture, horticulture, crafts, interior, newage, animals, pets, anthropology, art, business, child, computers, cooking, current affairs, education, ethnic, gardening, gay, government, health, history, how-to, humor, language, military, money, music, nature, photography, popular culture, psychology, recreation, religion, science, self help, sex, spirituality, sports, fitness, film, travel, true crime, women's, creative nonfiction.

👉 This agency specializes in how-to, self-help, and all types of business, business leadership, entrepreneurship, and books for small business owners from low-level how-to to professional and reference. Especially interested in business management, strategy, culture building, performance enhancement, marketing and sales, finance and investment, marketing and sales, finance and investment, career development, executive skills, leadership and organization development. Actively seeking strong book proposals in any area of business where a clear need exists for a new business book. Does not want to receive fiction, children's books, or complete mss (considers proposals only).

HOW TO CONTACT Query by mail with SASE, or e-mail. Prefers to read materials exclusively. Responds in 1 week to queries. Responds in 2 weeks to mss. Obtains most new clients through unsolicited mss, word of mouth, *Literary Market Place, Guide to Literary Agents.*

TERMS Agent receives 15% commission on domestic sales. Agent receives 15% commission on foreign sales.

RECENT SALES *Change the Culture/Change the Game,* by Roger Connors and Tom Smith (Portfolio); *How Did That Happen? Holding*

Other People Accountable for Results the Positive, Principled Way, by Roger Connors and Tom Smith (Portfolio/Penguin); *Recovering the Lost River: Rewilding Salmon, Recivilizing Humans, Removing Dams,* by Steve Hawley (Beacon Press); *Feeding Your Leadership Pipeline,* by Dan Tobin (Berrett-Kohler); *Next Generation Leadership,* by William J. Byron (Scranton Univ. Press); *Just Business,* by Martin Sanbu (Prentice-Hall); *Strategic Customer Service,* by John Goodman (Amacom Books); *The Emotionally Intelligent Team,* by Marcia Hughes (Jossey-Bass); *Iron Butterflies; Strong Women Leaders Changing the World,* by Birute Regine (Prometheus); *Sell Anything to Anyone Anytime,* by Dave Kahle (Career Press).

TIPS "Send a maximum 1-page query with SASE. Brochure on 'How to Write a Book Proposal' is available on request with SASE. We suggest prospective clients read Michael Snell's book, *From Book Idea to Bestseller* (Prima 1997), or or visit the company's website for detailed information on how to write a book proposal plus a model proposal.

🗝 SPECTRUM LITERARY AGENCY

320 Central Park W., Suite 1-D, New York NY 10025. Fax: (212)362-4562. Website: www.spectrumliterary agency.com. **Contact:** Eleanor Wood, president. Estab. 1976. SFWA. Represents 90 clients. Currently handles: nonfiction books 10%, novels 90%.

MEMBER AGENTS Eleanor Wood, Justin Bell.

REPRESENTS nonfiction books, novels. **Considers these fiction areas:** fantasy, historical, mainstream, mystery, romance, science fiction, suspense.

👉 Mr. Bell is actively seeking submissions in mysteries and a select amount of nonfiction

HOW TO CONTACT Query with SASE. Submit author bio, publishing credits. No unsolicited mss will be read. Queries and submissions by snail mail only. Ms. Wood and other agents have different addresses—see the website for full info. Responds in 1-3 months to queries. Obtains most new clients through recommendations from authors.

TERMS Agent receives 15% commission on domestic sales. Deducts for photocopying and book orders.

TIPS "Spectrum's policy is to read only book-length manuscripts that we have specifically asked to see. Unsolicited manuscripts are not accepted. The letter should describe your book briefly and include pub-

lishing credits and background information or qualifications relating to your work, if any."

SPENCERHILL ASSOCIATES

P.O. Box 374, Chatham NY 12037. (518)392-9293. Fax:
(518)392-9554. E-mail: submissions@spencerhillasso-
ciates.com. Website: www.spencerhillassociates.com.
Contact: Karen Solem or Jennifer Schober (please refer to their website for the latest information). Member of AAR. Represents 96 clients. 10% of clients are
new/unpublished writers.

- Prior to becoming an agent, Ms. Solem was
editor-in-chief at HarperCollins and an associate publisher.

MEMBER AGENTS Karen Solem; Jennifer Schober;
Nalini Akolekar.

REPRESENTS novels. **Considers these fiction areas:** crime, detective, historical, inspirational, literary, mainstream, police, religious, romance, thriller,
young adult.

- "We handle mostly commercial women's fiction, historical novels, romance (historical,
contemporary, paranormal, urban fantasy),
thrillers and mysteries. We also represent
Christian fiction only—no nonfiction." No
nonfiction, poetry, science fiction, children's
picture books or scripts.

HOW TO CONTACT Query submissions@spencer
hillassociates.com with synopsis and first three chapters attached as a .doc or .rtf file. "Please note: We no
longer accept queries via the mail." Responds in 6-8
weeks to queries "if we are interested in pursuing."

TERMS Agent receives 15% commission on domestic sales. Agent receives 20% commission on foreign
sales. Offers written contract; 3-month notice must
be given to terminate contract.

PHILIP G. SPITZER LITERARY AGENCY, INC.

50 Talmage Farm Lane, East Hampton NY 11937.
(631)329-3650. Fax: (631)329-3651. E-mail: Luc.
Hunt@spitzeragency.com. Website: www.spitzer
agency.com. **Contact:** Luc Hunt. Member of AAR.
Represents 60 clients. 10% of clients are new/unpub-
lished writers. Currently handles: nonfiction books
35%, novels 65%.

- Prior to opening his agency, Mr. Spitzer served
at New York University Press, McGraw-Hill and
the John Cushman Associates literary agency.

REPRESENTS nonfiction books, novels. **Considers
these nonfiction areas:** biography, history, investigative, sports, travel, true crime. **Considers these
fiction areas:** crime, detective, literary, mainstream,
mystery, police, sports, suspense, thriller.

- This agency specializes in mystery/suspense,
literary fiction, sports and general nonfiction
(no how-to).

HOW TO CONTACT Query with SASE. Responds
in 2 weeks to queries. Responds in 6 weeks to mss.
Obtains most new clients through recommendations from others.

TERMS Agent receives 15% commission on domestic sales. Agent receives 20% commission on foreign
sales. Charges clients for photocopying.

WRITERS CONFERENCES London Bookfair,
Frankfurt, BookExpo America.

P. STATHONIKOS AGENCY

146 Springbluff Heights S.W., Calgary Alberta T3H
5E6 ,Canada. (403)245-2087. Fax: (403)245-2087. E-
mail: pastath@telus.net; stathonp@cadvision.com.
Contact: Penny Stathonikos.

- Prior to becoming an agent, Ms. Stathonikos
was a bookstore owner and publisher's representative for 10 years.

REPRESENTS nonfiction books, novels, juvenile.

- Children's literature, some young adult. Does
not want to receive romance, fantasy, historical fiction, plays, movie scripts or poetry.

HOW TO CONTACT Query with SASE. Submit
outline. Responds in 1 month to queries. Responds
in 2 months to mss.

TERMS Agent receives 10% commission on domestic sales. Agent receives 15% commission on foreign
sales. Charges for postage, telephone, copying, etc.

TIPS "Do your homework—read any of the Writer's
Digest market books, join a writers' group and check
out the local bookstore or library for similar books.
Know who your competition is and why your book
is different."

NANCY STAUFFER ASSOCIATES

1540 Boston Post Rd., P.O. Box 1203, Darien CT 06820.
(203)202-2500. Fax: (203)655-3704. E-mail: Stauffer
Assoc@optonline.net. Website: publishersmarketplace.
com/members/nstauffer. **Contact:** Nancy Stauffer Ca-
hoon. Other memberships include Authors Guild. 5%

of clients are new/unpublished writers. Currently handles: nonfiction books 15%, novels 85%.

REPRESENTS Considers these nonfiction areas: cultural interests, current affairs, ethnic, creative nonfiction (narrative). **Considers these fiction areas:** contemporary, literary, regional.

HOW TO CONTACT Obtains most new clients through referrals from existing clients.

TERMS Agent receives 15% commission on domestic sales. Agent receives 20% commission on foreign sales. Agent receives 15% commission on film sales.

RECENT SALES *The Magic and Tragic Year of My Broken Thumb*, by Sherman Alexie; *Bone Fire*, by Mark Spragg; *Claiming Ground*, by Laura Bell; *The Best Camera is the One That's With You*, by Chase Jarvis.

STEELE-PERKINS LITERARY AGENCY

26 Island Ln., Canandaigua NY 14424. (585)396-9290. Fax: (585)396-3579. E-mail: pattiesp@aol.com. **Contact:** Pattie Steele-Perkins. Member of AAR. Other memberships include RWA. Currently handles: novels 100%.

REPRESENTS novels. **Considers these fiction areas:** romance, women's, category romance, romantic suspense, historical, contemporary, multi-cultural and inspirational.

HOW TO CONTACT Submit synopsis and one chapter via e-mail (no attachments) or snail mail. Snail mail submissions require SASE. Accepts simultaneous submissions. Responds in 6 weeks to queries. Obtains most new clients through recommendations from others, queries/solicitations.

TERMS Agent receives 15% commission on domestic sales. Offers written contract, binding for 1 year; 1-month notice must be given to terminate contract.

RECENT SALES Sold 130 titles last year. This agency prefers not to share specific sales information.

WRITERS CONFERENCES RWA National Conference; BookExpo America; CBA Convention; Romance Slam Jam, Romantic Times.

TIPS "Be patient. E-mail rather than call. Make sure what you are sending is the best it can be."

STERLING LORD LITERISTIC, INC.

65 Bleecker St., 12th Floor, New York NY 10012. (212)780-6050. Fax: (212)780-6095. E-mail: info@sll.com. Website: www.sll.com. Member of AAR. Signatory of WGA. Represents 600 clients. Currently handles: nonfiction books 50%, novels 50%.

MEMBER AGENTS Sterling Lord; Peter Matson; Philippa Brophy (represents journalists, nonfiction writers and novelists, and is most interested in current events, memoir, science, politics, biography, and women's issues); Chris Calhoun; Claudia Cross (a broad range of fiction and nonfiction, from literary fiction to commercial women's fiction and romance novels, to cookbooks, lifestyle titles, memoirs, serious nonfiction on religious and spiritual topics, and books for the CBA marketplace); Robert Guinsler (literary and commercial fiction, journalism, narrative nonfiction with an emphasis on pop culture, science and current events, memoirs and biographies); Laurie Liss (commercial and literary fiction and nonfiction whose perspectives are well developed and unique); Judy Heiblum (fiction and nonfiction writers, looking for distinctive voices that challenge the reader, emotionally or intellectually. She works with journalists, academics, memoirists, and essayists, and is particularly interested in books that explore the intersections of science, culture, history and philosophy. In addition, she is always looking for writers of literary fiction with fresh, uncompromising voices); Neeti Madan (memoir, journalism, history, pop culture, health, lifestyle, women's issues, multicultural books and virtually any intelligent writing on intriguing topics. Neeti is looking for smart, well-written commercial novels, as well as compelling and provocative literary works); George Nicholson (writers and illustrators for children); Jim Rutman; Ira Silverberg; Douglas Stewart (literary fiction, narrative nonfiction, and young adult fiction).

HOW TO CONTACT Query with SASE by snail mail. Include synopsis of the work, a brief proposal or the first three chapters of the manuscript, and brief bio or resume. Does not respond to unsolicited e-mail queries. Responds in 1 month to mss.

TERMS Agent receives 15% commission on domestic sales. Agent receives 20% commission on foreign sales. Offers written contract. Charges clients for photocopying.

STERNIG & BYRNE LITERARY AGENCY

2370 S. 107th St., Apt. #4, Milwaukee WI 53227-2036. (414)328-8034. Fax: (414)328-8034. E-mail: jackbyrne@hotmail.com. Website: www.sff.net/people/jackbyrne. **Contact:** Jack Byrne. Other memberships include SFWA, MWA. Represents 30 clients. 10% of clients are new/unpublished writers. Currently handles: nonfiction books 5%, novels 90%, juvenile books 5%.

REPRESENTS nonfiction books, novels, juvenile. **Considers these fiction areas:** fantasy, horror, mystery, science fiction, suspense.

> 🔑 "Our client list is comfortably full, and our current needs are therefore quite limited." Actively seeking science fiction/fantasy and mystery by established writers. Does not want to receive romance, poetry, textbooks or highly specialized nonfiction.

HOW TO CONTACT Query with SASE. Prefers e-mail queries (no attachments); hard copy queries also acceptable. Responds in 3 weeks to queries. Responds in 3 months to mss.

TERMS Agent receives 15% commission on domestic sales. Agent receives 20% commission on foreign sales. Offers written contract; 2-month notice must be given to terminate contract.

TIPS "Don't send first drafts, have a professional presentation (including cover letter) and know your field. Read what's been done—good and bad."

STIMOLA LITERARY STUDIO, INC.

308 Livingston Ct., Edgewater NJ 07020. Phone/Fax: (201)945-9353. E-mail: info@stimolaliterarystudio.com. Website: www.stimolaliterarystudio.com. **Contact:** Rosemary B. Stimola. Estab. 1997. Member of AAR. Represents 45 clients. 15% of clients are new/unpublished writers. Currently handles: 10% novels, 90% juvenile books.

MEMBER AGENTS Rosemary B. Stimola.

HOW TO CONTACT Query via e-mail (no unsolicited attachments). Obtains most new clients through referrals. Unsolicited submissions are still accepted. Accepts simultaneous submissions. Responds in 3 weeks to queries "we wish to pursue further." Responds in 2 months to requested mss.

TERMS Agent receives 15% commission on domestic sales. Agent receives 20% (if subagents are employed) commission on foreign sales.

RECENT SALES Sold 40 books for young readers in the last year. Among these, *A Touch Mortal*, by Leah Clifford (Greenwillow/Harper Collins); *Black Hole Sun*, by David Gill (Greenwillow/Harper Collins); *Dot*, by Patricia Intriago (FSG/Macmillan); *Inside Out and Back Again*, by Thanhha Lai (Harper Collins); *The Fox Inheritance*, by Mary Pearson

(Henry Holt/Macmillan); *Henry Aaron's Dream*, by Matt Tavares (Candlewick Press); *Throat*, by R.A. Nelson (Knopf/RH).

WRITERS CONFERENCES Will attend: ALA Midwinter, ALA Annual, BEA, Bologna Book Fair, NTCE, SCBWI-Illinois regional conference; SCBWI Annual Winter Conference in New York, SCBWI-New York Metro.

TIPS Agent is hands-on, no-nonsense. May request revisions. Does not edit but may offer suggestions for improvement. Well-respected by clients and editors. "A firm but reasonable deal negotiator."

◑ STRACHAN LITERARY AGENCY

P.O. Box 2091, Annapolis MD 21404. E-mail: query@strachanlit.com. Website: www.strachanlit.com. **Contact:** Laura Strachan.

> • Prior to becoming an agent, Ms. Strachan was (and still is) an attorney.

REPRESENTS nonfiction books, novels. **Considers these nonfiction areas:** narrative. **Considers these fiction areas:** literary and up-market commercial.

> 🔑 "This agency specializes in literary fiction and narrative nonfiction."

HOW TO CONTACT E-mail queries only with brief synopsis and bio; no attachments or samples unless requested.

RECENT SALES *The Interventionist* (Hazelden); *The Golden Bristled Boar* (UVA Press); *Poser* (Walker).

● ROBIN STRAUS AGENCY, INC.

229 E. 79th St., Suite 5A, New York NY 10075. (212)472-3282. Fax: (212)472-3833. E-mail: info@robinstrausagency.com. Website: www.robinstrausagency.com. **Contact:** Ms. Robin Straus. Estab. 1983. Member of AAR.

> • Prior to becoming an agent, Ms. Straus served as a subsidiary rights manager at Random House and Doubleday and worked in editorial at Little, Brown.

REPRESENTS Represents high quality adult fiction and nonfiction including literary and commercial fiction, narrative nonfiction, women's fiction, memoirs, history, biographies, books on psychology, popular culture and current affairs, science, parenting, and cookbooks.

> 🔑 Does *not* represent juvenile, young adult, science fiction/fantasy, horror, romance, Westerns, poetry or screenplays.

HOW TO CONTACT If you prefer to submit your queries electronically, please note that we do not download manuscripts. All materials must be included in the body of the e-mail. We do not respond to any submissions that do not include a SASE. No metered postage.

TERMS Agent receives 15% commission on domestic sales. Agent receives 20% commission on foreign sales. Offers written contract. Charges for photocopying, express mail services, messenger and foreign postage, galleys and books for submissions, etc. as incurred.

● PAM STRICKLER AUTHOR MANAGEMENT

134 Main St., New Paltz NY 12561. (845)255-0061. E-mail: pamstrickleragency@gmail.com. Website: www.pamstrickler.com. **Contact:** Pamela Dean Strickler. Member of AAR. Also an associate member of the Historical Novel Society and member of RWA.

- Prior to opening her agency, Ms. Strickler was senior editor at Ballantine Books.

REPRESENTS novels. **Considers these fiction areas:** historical, romance, women's.

✂ Does not want to receive nonfiction or children's books.

HOW TO CONTACT Please, no unsolicited manuscripts. Prefer e-mail queries, including a one-page letter with a brief description of your plot, plus the first 10 pages of your novel all pasted into the body of the e-mail. Sorry, unknown attachments will not be opened.

● REBECCA STRONG INTERNATIONAL LITERARY AGENCY

235 W. 108th St., #35, New York NY 10025. (212)865-1569. E-mail: info@rsila.com. Website: www.rsila.com. **Contact:** Rebecca Strong. Estab. 2004.

- Prior to opening her agency, Ms. Strong was an industry executive with experience editing and licensing in the U.S. and U.K. She has worked at Crown/Random House, Harmony/Random House, Bloomsbury and Harvill.

REPRESENTS nonfiction books, novels. **Considers these nonfiction areas:** biography, business, health, history, memoirs, science, travel.

✂ "We are a consciously small agency selectively representing authors all over the world."

Does not want to receive poetry, screenplays or any unsolicited mss.

HOW TO CONTACT E-mail submissions only; subject line should indicate "submission query"; include cover letter with proposal. For fiction, include 1-2 complete chapters only. Accepts simultaneous submissions. Responds in 6-8 weeks to queries. Obtains most new clients through recommendations from others, conferences.

TERMS Agent receives 15% commission on domestic sales. Agent receives 20% commission on foreign sales. Offers written contract, binding for 10 years; 30-day notice must be given to terminate contract.

TIPS "I represent writers with prior publishing experience only: journalists, magazine writers or writers of fiction who have been published in anthologies or literary magazines. There are exceptions to this guideline but not many."

● THE STROTHMAN AGENCY, LLC

197 Eighth St., Flagship Wharf - 611, Charlestown MA 02129. (617)742-2011. Fax: (617)742-2014. E-mail: strothmanagency@gmail.com. Website: www.strothmanagency.com. **Contact:** Wendy Strothman, Lauren MacLeod. Member of AAR. Other memberships include Authors' Guild. Represents 50 clients. Currently handles: nonfiction books 70%, novels 10%, scholarly books 20%.

- Prior to becoming an agent, Ms. Strothman was head of Beacon Press (1983-1995) and executive vice president of Houghton Mifflin's Trade & Reference Division (1996-2002).

MEMBER AGENTS Wendy Strothman; Lauren MacLeod.

REPRESENTS nonfiction books, novels, scholarly, young adult, middle grade. **Considers these nonfiction areas:** business, current affairs, environment, government, history, language, law, literature, politics, travel. **Considers these fiction areas:** literary, young adult, middle grade.

✂ "Because we are highly selective in the clients we represent, we increase the value publishers place on our properties. We specialize in narrative nonfiction, memoir, history, science and nature, arts and culture, literary travel, current affairs, and some business. We have a highly selective practice in literary fiction, young adult and middle grade fiction, and nonfiction. We are now opening our doors to more commercial fiction but *only* from authors who have a platform. If you have a platform, please mention it in your query letter. The Strothman Agency seeks out scholars, journalists, and other acknowledged and emerging experts in their fields. We are now actively looking for authors of well-written young adult fiction and nonfiction. Browse the Latest News to get an idea of the types of books that we represent. For more about what we're looking for, read Pitching an Agent: The Strothman Agency on the publishing website www.strothmanagency.com." Does not want to receive commercial fiction, romance, science fiction or self-help.

HOW TO CONTACT Accepts queries only via e-mail at strothmanagency@gmail.com. See submission guidelines online. Accepts simultaneous submissions. Responds in 4 weeks to queries. Responds in 6 weeks to mss. Obtains most new clients through recommendations from others.

TERMS Agent receives 15% commission on domestic sales. Agent receives 20% commission on foreign sales. Offers written contract; 30-day notice must be given to terminate contract.

THE STUART AGENCY

260 W. 52 St., #24C, New York NY 10019. (212)586-2711. Fax: (212)977-1488. E-mail: andrew@stuartagency.com. Website: http://stuartagency.com. **Contact:** Andrew Stuart. Estab. 2002.

- Prior to his current position, Mr. Stuart was an agent with Literary Group International for five years. Prior to becoming an agent, he was an editor at Random House and Simon & Schuster.

REPRESENTS nonfiction books, novels. **Considers these nonfiction areas:** biography, ethnic, government, history, memoirs, multicultural, psychology, science, sports, narrative nonfiction. **Considers these fiction areas:** ethnic, literary.

HOW TO CONTACT Query by e-mail or mail with SASE. Do not send any materials besides query/SASE unless requested.

SUBIAS

One Union Square W., # 913, New York NY 10003. (212)445-1091. Fax: (212)898-0375. E-mail: mark@marksubias.com. Website: http://marksubias.com.

Contact: Mark Subias. Represents 35 clients. Currently handles: stage plays 100%.

REPRESENTS stage plays.

➤ This agency is not currently representing movie scripts.

HOW TO CONTACT Query with SASE.

❶ EMMA SWEENEY AGENCY, LLC

245 E. 80th St., Suite 7E, New York NY 10075. E-mail: queries@emmasweeneyagency.com. Website: www.emmasweeneyagency.com. Member of AAR. Other memberships include Women's Media Group. Represents 80 clients. 5% of clients are new/unpublished writers. Currently handles: nonfiction books 50%, novels 50%.

- Prior to becoming an agent, Ms. Sweeney was director of subsidiary rights at Grove Press. Since 1990, she has been a literary agent.

MEMBER AGENTS Emma Sweeney, president; Eva Talmadge, rights manager and agent (represents literary fiction, young adult novels and narrative nonfiction; considers these nonfiction areas: popular science, pop culture and music history, biography, memoirs, cooking, and anything relating to animals; considers these fiction areas: literary of the highest writing quality possible, young adult).

REPRESENTS nonfiction books, novels.

➤ "We specialize in quality fiction and nonfiction. Our primary areas of interest include literary and women's fiction, mysteries and thrillers; science, history, biography, memoir, religious studies and the natural sciences." Does not want to receive romance, Westerns or screenplays.

HOW TO CONTACT Send query letter and first ten pages in body of e-mail (no attachments) to queries@emmasweeneyagency.com. No snail mail queries.

TERMS Agent receives 15% commission on domestic sales. Agent receives 10% commission on foreign sales.

WRITERS CONFERENCES Nebraska Writers' Conference; Words and Music Festival in New Orleans.

❶ THE SWETKY AGENCY

2150 Balboa Way, No. 29, St. George UT 84770. (435)313-8006. E-mail: fayeswetky@amsaw.org. Website: www.amsaw.org/swetkyagency/index.html. **Contact:** Faye M. Swetky. Other memberships include American Society of Authors and Writers. Represents 20+ clients. 90% of clients are new/unpublished writers. Currently handles: nonfiction books 45%, novels 45%, movie scripts 10%, TV scripts 20%.

• Prior to becoming an agent, Ms. Swetky was an editor and corporate manager. She has also raised and raced thoroughbred horses.

REPRESENTS nonfiction books, novels, short-story collections, juvenile, movie, TV, movie scripts, feature film, MOW, sitcom, documentary. **Considers these nonfiction areas:** all major genres. **Considers these fiction areas:** all major genres. **Considers these script areas:** action, biography, cartoon, comedy, contemporary, detective, erotica, ethnic, experimental, family, fantasy, feminist, gay, glitz, historical, horror, juvenile, mainstream, multicultural, multimedia, mystery, psychic, regional, religious, romantic comedy, romantic drama, science, sports, teen, thriller, Westerns.

⚷ "We handle only book-length fiction and nonfiction and feature-length movie and television scripts. Please visit our website before submitting. All agency-related information is there, including a sample contract, e-mail submission forms, policies, clients, etc." Actively seeking marketable full-length material. Do not send unprofessionally prepared mss and/or scripts.

HOW TO CONTACT See website for submission instructions. Accepts e-mail queries only. Accepts simultaneous submissions. Response time varies. Obtains most new clients through queries.

TERMS Agent receives 15% commission on domestic sales. Agent receives 20% commission on foreign sales. Agent receives 20% commission on film sales. Offers written contract, binding for 6 months; 30-day notice must be given to terminate contract.

RECENT SALES *DOC—The Life and Legend of the Man Behind Wyatt Earp*; *Growing Fruit and Vegetables in Pots*; *Doc Holliday*. Others in negotiation.

TIPS "Be professional. Have a professionally-prepared product."

STEPHANIE TADE LITERARY AGENCY

P.O. Box 235, Durham PA 18039. (610)346-8667. **Contact:** Stephanie Tade.

• Prior to becoming an agent, Ms. Tade was an executive editor at Rodale Press. She was also an agent with the Jane Rotrosen Agency.

MEMBER AGENTS Stephanie Tade, Dana Bacher.

REPRESENTS nonfiction books, novels. **Considers these nonfiction areas:** celebrity, health/fitness, history, medicine, relationships/dating, self-help, self-improvement, spirituality, women's issues. **Considers these fiction areas:** commercial, historical, romance, young adult.

⚷ novels

HOW TO CONTACT Query by mail with SASE. Does not accept e-mail queries.

❶ TALCOTT NOTCH LITERARY

2 Broad St., Second Floor, Suite 10, Milford CT 06460. (203)876-4959. Fax: (203)876-9517. E-mail: editorial @talcottnotch.net. Website: www.talcottnotch.net. **Contact:** Gina Panettieri, President. Represents 35 clients. 25% of clients are new/unpublished writers. Currently handles: nonfiction books 50%, novels 20%, story collections 5%, juvenile books 20%, scholarly books 10%.

• Prior to becoming an agent, Ms. Panettieri was a freelance writer and editor.

MEMBER AGENTS Gina Panettieri (nonfiction, mystery); Rachel Dowen (children's fiction, mystery).

REPRESENTS nonfiction books, novels, juvenile, scholarly, textbooks. **Considers these nonfiction areas:** animals, anthropology, art, biography, business, computers, cooking, current affairs, decorating, education, environment, ethnic, gay/lesbian, government, health, history, interior design, investigative, juvenile nonfiction, memoirs, metaphysics, military, money, music, New Age, popular culture, psychology, science, sociology, sports, technology, true crime, women's issues, women's studies. **Considers these fiction areas:** action, adventure, crime, detective, fantasy, juvenile, mystery, police, romance, suspense, thriller, young adult.

HOW TO CONTACT Query via e-mail (preferred) with first ten pages of the ms within the body of the e-mail, not as an attachment, or with SASE. Accepts simultaneous submissions. Responds in 1 week to queries. Responds in 4-6 weeks to mss.

TERMS Agent receives 15% commission on domestic sales. Agent receives 20% commission on foreign sales. Offers written contract, binding for 1 year.

RECENT SALES Sold 36 titles in the last year. *Delivered From Evil*, by Ron Franscell (Fairwinds) and *Sourtoe* (Globe Pequot Press); *Hellforged*, by Nancy Holzner (Berkley Ace Science Fiction); *Welcoming Kitchen*; *200 Allergen- and Gluten-*

Free Vegan Recipes, by Kim Lutz and Megan Hart (Sterling); *Dr. Seteh's Love Prescription*, by Dr. Seth Meyers (Adams Media); *The Book of Ancient Bastards*, by Brian Thornton (Adams Media); *Hope in Courage*, by Beth Fehlbaum (Westside Books) and more.

TIPS "Know your market and how to reach them. A strong platform is essential in your book proposal. Can you effectively use social media/Are you a strong networker: Are you familiar with the book bloggers in your genre? Are you involved with the interest-specific groups that can help you? What can you do to break through the 'noise' and help present your book to your readers? Check our website for more tips and information on this topic."

PATRICIA TEAL LITERARY AGENCY

2036 Vista Del Rosa, Fullerton CA 92831-1336. Phone/Fax: (714)738-8333. **Contact:** Patricia Teal. Member of AAR. Other memberships include RWA, Authors Guild. Represents 20 clients. Currently handles: nonfiction books 10%, fiction 90%.

REPRESENTS nonfiction books, novels. **Considers these nonfiction areas:** animals, autobiography, biography, child guidance, health, how-to, investigative, medicine, parenting, psychology, self-help, true crime, women's issues, women's studies. **Considers these fiction areas:** glitz, mainstream, mystery, romance, suspense.

⚭ This agency specializes in women's fiction, commercial how-to, and self-help nonfiction. Does not want to receive poetry, short stories, articles, science fiction, fantasy, or regency romance.

HOW TO CONTACT Published authors only may query with SASE. Accepts simultaneous submissions. Responds in 10 days to queries. Responds in 6 weeks to mss. Obtains most new clients through conferences, recommendations from authors, editors.

TERMS Agent receives 10-15% commission on domestic sales. Agent receives 20% commission on foreign sales. Offers written contract, binding for 1 year. Charges clients for ms copies.

RECENT SALES Sold 30 titles in the last year. *Texas Rose*, by Marie Ferrarella (Silhouette); *Watch Your Language*, by Sterling Johnson (St. Martin's Press); *The Black Sheep's Baby*, by Kathleen Creighton (Silhouette); *Man With a Message*, by Muriel Jensen

(Harlequin).

WRITERS CONFERENCES RWA Conferences; Asilomar; BookExpo America; Bouchercon; Maui Writers Conference.

TIPS "Include SASE with all correspondence. I am taking on published authors only."

TESSLER LITERARY AGENCY, LLC

27 W. 20th St., Suite 1003, New York NY 10011. (212)242-0466. Fax: (212)242-2366. E-mail: michelle@tessleragency.com. Website: www.tessleragency.com. **Contact:** Michelle Tessler. Member of AAR.

• Prior to forming her own agency, Ms. Tessler worked at Carlisle & Co. (now a part of Inkwell Management). She has also worked at the William Morris Agency and the Elaine Markson Literary Agency.

REPRESENTS nonfiction books, novels.

⚭ "The Tessler Agency is a full-service boutique agency that represents writers of literary fiction and high-quality nonfiction in the following categories: popular science, reportage, memoir, history, biography, psychology, business and travel."

HOW TO CONTACT Submit query through website only.

THE AGENCY GROUP, LLC

142 W. 57th St., 6th Floor, New York NY 10019. (212)581-3100. E-mail: sarahstephens@theagencygroup.com. Website: www.theagencygroup.com. **Contact:** Marc Gerald, agent. Represents 50 clients. 10% of clients are new/unpublished writers. Currently handles: nonfiction books 60%, novels 30%, multimedia 10%.

• Prior to becoming an agent, Mr. Gerald owned and ran an independent publishing and entertainment agency.

MEMBER AGENTS Marc Gerald; Sarah Stephens, Caroline Greeven.

REPRESENTS nonfiction books, novels. **Considers these nonfiction areas:** anthropology, archeology, architecture, art, autobiography, biography, business, child guidance, cooking, cultural interests, dance, decorating, design, economics, environment, ethnic, finance, foods, government, health, history, how-to, humor, interior design, investigative, law, medicine, memoirs, money, nature, nutrition, parenting, personal improvement, popular culture, politics, psychology, satire, self-help, sports, true crime. **Considers these fiction areas:** action, adventure, cartoon, comic books, commercial, confession, contemporary issues, crime, detective, erotica, ethnic, experimental, family saga, feminist, frontier, gay, glitz, hi-lo, historical, horror, humor, inspirational, juvenile, lesbian, literary, mainstream, metaphysical, military, multicultural, multimedia, mystery, New Age, occult, picture books, plays, poetry, poetry in translation, police, psychic, regional, religious, romance, satire, short-story collections, spiritual, sports, supernatural, suspense, thriller, translation, war, Westerns, women's, young adult.

�—⚓ "While we admire beautiful writing, we largely represent recording artists, celebrities, authors, and pop culture and style brands with established platforms. When we represent fiction, we work almost exclusively in genre and in areas of expertise. We tend to take a non-linear approach to content—many of our projects ultimately have a TV/film or digital component." This agency is only taking on new clients through referrals.

HOW TO CONTACT We are currently not accepting submissions except by referral. Accepts simultaneous submissions. Responds in 1 month to queries. Responds in 3 months to mss. Obtains most new clients through recommendations from others.

TERMS Agent receives 15% commission on domestic sales. Agent receives 20% commission on foreign sales. Offers written contract. Charges clients for office fees (only for mss that have been sold).

ⓘ THE AHEARN AGENCY, INC.

2021 Pine St., New Orleans LA 70118. E-mail: pahearn@aol.com. Website: www.ahearnagency.com. **Contact:** Pamela G. Ahearn. Other memberships include MWA, RWA, ITW. Represents 35 clients. 20% of clients are new/unpublished writers. Currently handles: novels 100%.

- Prior to opening her agency, Ms. Ahearn was an agent for 8 years and an editor with Bantam Books.

REPRESENTS **Considers these fiction areas:** action, adventure, contemporary issues, crime, detective, ethnic, family saga, feminist, glitz, historical, humor, literary, mainstream, mystery, police, psychic, regional, romance, supernatural, suspense, thriller.

�—⚓ Handles women's fiction and suspense fiction only. Does not want to receive category romance, science fiction or fantasy.

HOW TO CONTACT Query with SASE. Accepts simultaneous submissions. Responds in 8 weeks to queries. Responds in 10 weeks to mss. Obtains most new clients through recommendations from others, solicitations, conferences.

TERMS Agent receives 15% commission on domestic sales. Agent receives 20% commission on foreign sales. Offers written contract, binding for 1 year; renewable by mutual consent.

RECENT SALES *The Ronin's Mistress*, by Laura Joh Rowland; *How to Woo a Reluctant Lady*, Jeffies; *The Things That Keep Us Here*, by Carla Buckley.

WRITERS CONFERENCES Moonlight & Magnolias; RWA National Conference; Thriller Fest; Florida Romance Writers; Bouchercon; Malice Domestic.

TIPS "Be professional! Always send in exactly what an agent/editor asks for—no more, no less. Keep query letters brief and to the point, giving your writing credentials and a very brief summary of your book. If one agent rejects you, keep trying—there are a lot of us out there!"

ⓘ THE AUGUST AGENCY, LLC

E-mail: submissions@augustagency.com. Website: www.augustagency.com. **Contact:** Cricket Freemain, Jeffery McGraw. Estab. 2004. Represents 25-40 clients. 50% of clients are new/unpublished writers. Currently handles: nonfiction books 75%, novels 20%, other 5% other.

- Before opening The August Agency, Ms. Freeman was a freelance writer, magazine editor and independent literary agent. Mr. McGraw worked as an editor for HarperCollins and publicity manager for Abrams.

MEMBER AGENTS Jeffery McGraw (politics/current affairs, entertainment, business, psychology, self-help, narrative nonfiction, contemporary women's fiction, literary fiction); Cricket Freeman (mystery/crime fiction, chick lit, thrillers).

REPRESENTS nonfiction books, novels. **Considers these nonfiction areas:** interior design, biography, business, child guidance, cooking, current affairs, ethnic, gay, government, health, history, how to, humor, memoirs, military, money, music, pop culture, psychology, self help, sociology, sports, film, true crime, women's, inspirational. **Considers these fiction areas:** psychic, adventure, detective, ethnic, family, gay, historical, humor, literary, mainstream, mystery, thriller, smart chick lit (non-genre romance).

ℂ➞ "We actively pursue a diverse array of writers to represent with an emphasis in the following areas: popular culture, arts, entertainment, women's fiction (not genre romance), general fiction biographies and memoirs, creative narrative nonfiction, media/current events (seasoned journalists receive special favor here), political science, social sciences, history, economics, business, and technology." Does not want academic textbooks, children's books, cozy mysteries, horror, poetry, science fiction/fantasy, short story collections, Westerns, screenplays, genre romance or previously self-published works.

HOW TO CONTACT Submit book summary (1-2 paragraphs), chapter outline (nonfiction only), first 1,000 words or first chapter, total page/word count, brief paragraph on why you have chosen to write the book. Send via e-mail only (no attachments). Responds in 2-3 weeks to queries if we are interested. Responds in 3 months to mss. Obtains most new clients through recommendations from others, solicitations, conferences.

TERMS Agent receives 15% commission on domestic sales. Agent receives 20% commission on foreign sales. Offers written contract; 1-month notice must be given to terminate contract.

WRITERS CONFERENCES Surrey International Writers' Conference; Southern California Writers' Conference; Naples Writers' Conference, et al.

● THE AXELROD AGENCY

55 Main St., P.O. Box 357, Chatham NY 12037. (518)392-2100. E-mail: steve@axelrodagency.com. Website: www.axelrodagency.com. **Contact:** Steven Axelrod. Member of AAR. Represents 15-20 clients. 1% of clients are new/unpublished writers. Currently handles: novels 95%.

- Prior to becoming an agent, Mr. Axelrod was a book club editor.

REPRESENTS novels. **Considers these fiction areas:** mystery, romance, women's.

HOW TO CONTACT Query with SASE. Accepts simultaneous submissions. Responds in 3 weeks to queries. Responds in 6 weeks to mss. Obtains most new clients through recommendations from others.

TERMS Agent receives 15% commission on domestic sales. Agent receives 20% commission on foreign sales. No written contract.

WRITERS CONFERENCES RWA National Conference.

● THE BARBARA BOVA LITERARY AGENCY

3951 Gulf Shore Blvd., No. PH 1-B, Naples FL 34103. (239)649-7263. Fax: (239)649-7263. E-mail: michael burke@barbarabovaliteraryagency.com. Website: www.barbarabovaliteraryagency.com. **Contact:** Ken Bova, Michael Burke. Represents 30 clients. Currently handles: nonfiction books 20%, fiction 80%.

REPRESENTS nonfiction books, novels. **Considers these nonfiction areas:** biography, history, science, self help, true crime, women's, social sciences. **Considers these fiction areas:** adventure, crime, detective, mystery, police, science fiction, suspense, thriller, women's, young adult, teen lit.

ℂ➞ This agency specializes in fiction and nonfiction, hard and soft science. No scripts, poetry or children's books.

HOW TO CONTACT Query through website. No attachments. We accept short (3-5 pages) e-mail queries. All queries should have the word "query" in the subject line. Include all information as you would in a standard, snail mail query letter, such as pertinent credentials, publishing history and an overview of the book. Include a word count of your project. You may include a short synopsis. We're looking for quality fiction and nonfiction. Obtains most new clients through recommendations from others.

TERMS Agent receives 15% commission on domestic sales. Agent receives 20% commission on foreign sales. Charges clients for overseas postage, overseas calls, photocopying, shipping.

RECENT SALES Sold 24 titles in the last year. *The Green Trap* and *The Aftermath*, by Ben Bova; *Empire* and *A War of Gifts*, by Orson Scott Card; *Radioman*, by Carol E. Hipperson.

TIPS "We also handle foreign, movie, television, and audio rights."

✪●◎ THE BUKOWSKI AGENCY

14 Prince Arthur Ave., Suite 202, Toronto Ontario M5R 1A9, Canada. (416)928-6728. Fax: (416)963-9978. E-mail: assistant@thebukowskiagency.com;

info@thebukowskiagency.com. Website: www.the-bukowskiagency.com. **Contact:** Denise Bukowski. Represents 70 clients.

- Prior to becoming an agent, Ms. Bukowski was a book editor.

REPRESENTS nonfiction books, novels.

8—¶ "The Bukowski Agency specializes in international literary fiction and up-market nonfiction for adults. Bukowski looks for Canadian writers whose work can be marketed in many media and territories, and who have the potential to make a living from their work." Actively seeking nonfiction and fiction works from Canadian writers. Does not want submissions from American authors, nor genre fiction, poetry, children's literature, picture books, film scripts or television scripts.

HOW TO CONTACT Query with SASE. Submit proposal package, outline/proposal, synopsis, publishing history, author bio. Send submissions by snail mail only. See online guidelines for nonfiction and fiction specifics. No unsolicited fiction. The Bukowski Agency is currently accepting nonfiction submissions from prospective authors who are residents in Canada. We ask for exclusivity for 6 weeks after receipt to allow time for proper consideration. Please see our nonfiction submission guidelines for more details on submitting proposals for nonfiction. Submissions should be sent by mail, in hard copy only. Responds in 6 weeks to queries.

THE CHOATE AGENCY, LLC

1320 Bolton Rd., Pelham NY 10803. E-mail: mickey@thechoateagency.com. Website: www.thechoateagency.com. **Contact:** Mickey Choate. Estab. 2004. Member of AAR.

REPRESENTS nonfiction books, novels. **Considers these nonfiction areas:** history; memoirs by journalists, military or political figures, biography; cookery/food; journalism; military science; narrative; politics; general science; natural science, wine/spirits. **Considers these fiction areas:** historical, mystery, thriller, select literary fiction, strong commercial fiction.

8—¶ The agency does not handle genre fiction, chic-lit, cozies, romance, self-help, confessional memoirs, spirituality, pop psychology, religion, how-to, New Age titles, children's books, poetry, self-published works or screenplays.

HOW TO CONTACT Query with brief synopsis and bio. This agency prefers e-queries, but accepts snail mail queries with SASE.

❶❷ THE CHUDNEY AGENCY

72 North State Rd., Suite 501, Briarcliff Manor NY 10510. (914)488-5008. E-mail: steven@thechudneyagency.com. Website: www.thechudneyagency.com. **Contact:** Steven Chudney. Estab. 2001. Other memberships include SCBWI. 90% of clients are new/unpublished writers.

- Prior to becoming an agent, Mr. Chudney held various sales positions with major publishers.

REPRESENTS novels, juvenile. **Considers these nonfiction areas:** juvenile. **Considers these fiction areas:** historical, juvenile, literary, mystery, suspense, young adult.

8—¶ This agency specializes in children's and teens books, and wants to find authors who are illustrators as well. "At this time, the agency is only looking for author/illustrators (one individual), who can both write and illustrate wonderful picture books. The author/illustrator must really know and understand the prime audience's needs and wants of the child reader! Storylines should be engaging, fun, with a hint of a life lessons and cannot be longer than 800 words. With chapter books, middle grade and teen novels, I'm primarily looking for quality, contemporary literary fiction: novels that are exceedingly well-written, with wonderful settings and developed, unforgettable characters. I'm looking for historical fiction that will excite me, young readers, editors, and reviewers, and will introduce us to unique characters in settings and situations, countries, and eras we haven't encountered too often yet in children's and teen literature." Does not want to receive any fantasy or science fiction; board books or lift-the-flap books, fables, folklore, or traditional fairytales, poetry or mood pieces, stories for all ages (as these ultimately are too adult oriented), message-driven stories that are heavy-handed, didactic or pedantic.

HOW TO CONTACT No snail-mail submissions. Queries only. Submit proposal package, 4-6 sample chapters. For children's, submit full text and 3-5 illustrations. Accepts simultaneous submissions.

Responds in 2-3 weeks to queries. Responds in 3-4 weeks to mss.

TERMS Agent receives 15% commission on domestic sales. Agent receives 20% commission on foreign sales. Offers written contract, binding for 1 year; 30-day notice must be given to terminate contract.

TIPS "If an agent has a website, review it carefully to make sure your material is appropriate for that agent. Read lots of books within the genre you are writing; work hard on your writing; don't follow trends—most likely, you'll be too late."

◑ THE CREATIVE CULTURE, INC.

47 E. 19th St., Third Floor, New York NY 10003. (212)680-3510. Fax: (212)680-3509. Website: www. thecreativeculture.com/about. **Contact:** Debra Goldstein. Estab. 1998. Member of AAR.

• Prior to opening her agency, Ms. Goldstein and Ms. Gerwin were agents at the William Morris Agency; Ms. Naples was a senior editor at Simon & Schuster.

MEMBER AGENTS Debra Goldstein (self-help, creativity, fitness, inspiration, lifestyle); Mary Ann Naples (health/nutrition, lifestyle, narrative nonfiction, practical nonfiction, literary fiction, animals/vegetarianism); Laura Nolan (literary fiction, parenting, self-help, psychology, women's studies, current affairs, science); Karen Gerwin (pop culture, lifestyle, parenting, humor, memoir/narrative nonfiction, women's interests, and a very limited selection of fiction [no genre categories, i.e. thrillers, romance, sci-fi/fantasy, etc.]; Matthew Elblonk (literary fiction, humor, pop culture, music and young adult. Interests also include commercial fiction, narrative nonfiction, science, and he is always on the lookout for something slightly quirky or absurd).

REPRESENTS nonfiction books, novels.

⚬━ We are known for our emphasis on lifestyle books that enhance readers' overall well-being—be it through health, inspiration, entertainment, thought-provoking ideas, life management skills, beauty and fashion, or food. Does not want to receive children's books, poetry, screenplays or science fiction.

HOW TO CONTACT Query with bio, book description, 4-7 sample pages (fiction only), SASE. We only reply if interested. Please see the titles page to get a sense of the books we represent. Responds in 2 months to queries.

⊘◉ THE DENISE MARCIL LITERARY AGENCY, INC.

156 Fifth Ave., Suite 625, New York NY 10010. (212)337-3402. Fax: (212)727-2688. Website: www.denise marcilagency.com. **Contact:** Denise Marcil, Anne Marie O'Farrell. Member of AAR.

• Prior to opening her agency, Ms. Marcil served as an editorial assistant with Avon Books and as an assistant editor with Simon & Schuster.

MEMBER AGENTS Denise Marcil (women's commercial fiction, thrillers, suspense, popular reference, how-to, self-help, health, business, and parenting); Anne Marie O'Farrell.

⚬━ This agency is currently not taking on new authors. We are currently seeking self-help and popular reference books, including parenting, business, spirituality, and biographies. We are looking for authors with national platforms such as national seminars, columns, television and radio shows. We do not represent science fiction, children's books, or political nonfiction.

HOW TO CONTACT The best way to query is with a well-written and compelling one-page query letter and SASE. (Do not send a query by fax or e-mail.) Query letters for Denise Marcil should be sent to 156 Fifth Ave., Suite 823, New York NY 10010. Query letters for Anne Marie O'Farrell should be sent to 86 Dennis St., Manhasset NY 11030. We do not respond to unsolicited e-mail queries.

TERMS Agent receives 15% commission on domestic sales. Agent receives 20% commission on foreign sales. Offers written contract, binding for 2 years. Charges $100/year for postage, photocopying, long-distance calls, etc.

RECENT SALES For Denise Marcil: *A Chesapeake Shores Christmas*, by Sherryl Woods; *Prime Time Health*, by William Sears, M.D. and Martha Sears, R.N.; *The Autism Book*, by Robert W. Sears, M.D.; *The Yellow House and The Linen Queen* by Patricia Falvey; *The 10-Minute Total Body Breakthrough*, by Sean Foy. For Anne Marie O'Farrell: *Think Confident, Be Confident*, by Leslie Sokol Ph.d and Marci G. Fox, Ph.d; *Hell Yes*, by Elizabeth Baskin; *Breaking Into the Boys Club*, by Molly Shepard, Jane K. Stimmler, and Peter Dean.

❶ THE DOE COOVER AGENCY

P.O. Box 668, Winchester MA 01890. (781)721-6000. Fax: (781)721-6727. E-mail: info@doecooveragency. com. Website: http://doecooveragency.com. Represents more than 100 clients. Currently handles: non-fiction books 80%, novels 20%.

MEMBER AGENTS Doe Coover (general nonfiction, including business, cooking/food writing, health and science); Colleen Mohyde (literary and commercial fiction, general nonfiction), Member AAR; Amanda Lewis (young adult & children's books); Associate: Frances Kennedy.

REPRESENTS Considers these nonfiction areas: autobiography, biography, business, cooking, economics, foods, gardening, health, history, nutrition, science, technology, social issues, narrative nonfiction. **Considers these fiction areas:** commercial, literary.

👉 This agency specializes in general nonfiction, particularly biography, business, cooking and food writing, health, history, popular science, social issues, gardening, and humor. The agency does not accept romance, fantasy, science fiction, poetry or screenplays.

HOW TO CONTACT Query with SASE. E-mail queries are acceptable—please check website for submission guidelines. No unsolicited mss, please. Accepts simultaneous submissions. Responds in 4-6 weeks to queries. Obtains most new clients through recommendations from others, solicitations.

TERMS Agent receives 15% commission on domestic sales. Agent receives 10% of original advance commission on foreign sales. No reading fees.

RECENT SALES Sold 25-30 titles in the last year. *As Always, Julia, Letters of Julia Child and Avis De Voto Food, Friendship and the Making of a Masterpiece*, selected and edited by Joan Reardon (Houghton Mifflin Harcourt); *Confessions of a Tarot Card Reader*, by Jane Stern (The Globe Pequot Press); *The Farm*, by Ian Knauer (Houghton Mifflin Harcourt); *Bottling the Gods: Why Global Development Has Gone Unnecessarily Wrong for So Long*, by Edward Carr (Palgrave/St. Martin's); *The Sewing Book*, by Tanya Whelan (Potter Craft); *The Gourmet Cookie Book: The Single Best Cookie Recipe From 1941-2009*, by Gourmet Magazine (Houghton Mifflin Harcourt); *Shades of Grey*, by Clea Simon (Severn House UK); *Cloud County Revival: How Wind Energy is*

Breathing New Life Into America's Heartland, by Philip Warburg (Beacon Press). Movie/TV MOW script(s) optioned/sold: *Keeper of the House*, by Rebecca Godwin, *Mr. White's Confession* by Robert Clark. Other clients include: WGBH, New England Aquarium, Blue Balliett, David Allen, Jacques Pepin, Deborah Madison, Rick Bayless, Suzanne Berne, Adria Bernardi, Paula Poundstone.

❶ THE EBELING AGENCY

P.O. Box 790267, Pala HI 96779. (808)579-6414. Fax: (808)579-9294. E-mail: kristina@ebelingagency.com; ebothat@yahoo.com. Website: www.ebelingagency.com. **Contact:** Michael Ebeling or Kristina Holmes. Represents 6 clients. 50% of clients are new/unpublished writers. Currently handles: nonfiction books 100%.

• Prior to becoming an agent, Mr. Ebeling established a career in the publishing industry through long-term author management. He has expertise in sales, platforms, publicity and marketing. Ms. Holmes joined the agency in 2005 and considers many types of projects. She is interested in books that take a stand, bring an issue to light or help readers.

MEMBER AGENTS Michael Ebeling, ebothat@yahoo. com; Kristina Holmes, kristina@ebelingagency.com.

REPRESENTS nonfiction books. **Considers these nonfiction areas:** animals, anthropology, archeology, architecture, art, autobiography, biography, business, child guidance, cooking, cultural interests, current affairs, dance, diet/nutrition, design, economics, education, environment, ethnic, foods, gay/lesbian, government, health, history, how-to, humor, inspirational, law, medicine, memoirs, money, music, parenting, photography, popular culture, politics, psychology, religious, satire, science, self-help, spirituality, sports, technology, travel, women's issues, women's studies, food/fitness, computers.

👉 "We accept very few clients for representation. To be considered, an author needs a very strong platform and a unique book concept. We represent nonfiction authors, most predominantly in the areas of business and self-help. We are very committed to our authors and their messages, which is a main reason we have such a high placement rate. We are always looking at new ways to help our authors gain the exposure they need to not only get published, but develop a successful literary career." Actively seeking well-written nonfiction material with fresh perspectives written by writers with established platforms. Does not want to receive fiction, poetry or children's lit.

HOW TO CONTACT E-mail query and proposal to either Mr. Ebling or Ms. Holmes. E-queries only. Accepts simultaneous submissions. Responds in 4-6 weeks to queries. Obtains most new clients through recommendations from others, solicitations.

TERMS Agent receives 15% commission on domestic sales. Agent receives 20% commission on foreign sales. Offers written contract; 60-day notice must be given to terminate contract. There is a charge for normal out-of-pocket fees, not to exceed $200 without client approval.

WRITERS CONFERENCES BookExpo America; San Francisco Writers' Conference.

TIPS "Approach agents when you're already building your platform, you have a well-written book, you have a firm understanding of the publishing process, and you have come up with a complete competitive proposal. Know the name of the agent you are contacting. You're essentially selling a business plan to the publisher. Make sure you've made a convincing pitch throughout your proposal, as ultimately, publishers are taking a financial risk by investing in your project."

THE FIELDING AGENCY, LLC

269 S. Beverly Dr., No. 341, Beverly Hills CA 90212. (310)276-7517. E-mail: wlee@fieldingagency.com; query@fieldingagency.com. Website: www.fieldingagency.com. **Contact:** Whitney Lee. Currently handles: nonfiction books 25%, novels 35%, juvenile books 35%, other 5% other.

• Prior to her current position, Ms. Lee worked at other agencies in different capacities.

REPRESENTS nonfiction books, novels, short-story collections, juvenile. **Considers these nonfiction areas:** animals, anthropology, archeology, architecture, art, autobiography, biography, business, child guidance, cooking, crafts, cultural interests, current affairs, decorating, diet/nutrition, design, economics, education, environment, ethnic, foods, gay/lesbian, government, health, history, hobbies, how-to, humor, investigative, juvenile nonfiction, language, law, literature, medicine, memoirs, military, money, parenting, popular culture, politics, psychology, satire, science, self-help, sociology, sports, technology, translation, true crime, war, women's issues, women's

studies. **Considers these fiction areas:** action, adventure, cartoon, comic books, crime, detective, ethnic, family saga, fantasy, feminist, gay, glitz, historical, horror, humor, juvenile, lesbian, literary, mainstream, mystery, picture books, police, romance, satire, suspense, thriller, women's, young adult.

☛ "We specialize in representing books published abroad and have strong relationships with foreign co-agents and publishers. For books we represent in the U.S., we have to be head-over-heels passionate about it because we are involved every step of the way." Does not want to receive scripts for TV or film.

HOW TO CONTACT Query with SASE. Submit synopsis, author bio. Accepts queries by e-mail and snail mail. Accepts simultaneous submissions. Obtains most new clients through recommendations from others.

TERMS Agent receives 15% commission on domestic sales. Agent receives 20% commission on foreign sales. Offers written contract, binding for 9-12 months.

WRITERS CONFERENCES London Book Fair; Frankfurt Book Fair; Bologna Book Fair.

THE FOLEY LITERARY AGENCY

34 E. 38th St., New York NY 10016-2508. (212)686-6930. **Contact:** Joan Foley, Joseph Foley. Estab. 1956. Represents 10 clients. Currently handles: nonfiction books 75%, novels 25%.

REPRESENTS nonfiction books, novels. **Considers these nonfiction areas:** business services.

HOW TO CONTACT Query with letter, brief outline, SASE. Responds promptly to queries. Obtains most new clients through recommendations from others (rarely taking on new clients).

TERMS Agent receives 10% commission on domestic sales. Agent receives 15% commission on foreign sales.

THE FRIEDRICH AGENCY

19 W. 21st St., Suite 201, New York NY 10010. E-mail: mfriedrich@friedrichagency.com; pcirone@friedrichagency.com; lcarson@friedrichagency.com. Website: www.friedrichagency.com. **Contact:** Molly Friedrich. Member of AAR. Represents 50+ clients.

• Prior to her current position, Ms. Friedrich was an agent at the Aaron Priest Literary Agency.

MEMBER AGENTS Molly Friedrich, Founder and Agent (open to queries); Paul Cirone, Foreign

Rights Director and Agent (open to queries); Lucy Carson, assistant.

REPRESENTS full-length fiction and nonfiction.

HOW TO CONTACT Query with SASE by mail, or e-mail. See guidelines on website.

RECENT SALES *Vanished,* by Joseph Finder, *T is for Trespass,* by Sue Grafton, *Look Again,* by Lisa Scottoline, *Olive Kitteridge,* by Elizabeth Strout. Other clients include Frank McCourt, Jane Smiley, Esmeralda Santiago, Terry McMillan, Cathy Schine, and more.

☉ THE GARAMOND AGENCY, INC.

12 Horton St., Newburyport MA 01950. E-mail: query@garamondagency.com. Website: www. garamondagency.com. Other memberships include Author's Guild.

MEMBER AGENTS Lisa Adams; David Miller.

REPRESENTS nonfiction books. **Considers these nonfiction areas:** business, economics, government, history, law, politics, psychology, science, technology, social science, narrative nonfiction.

&—☛ "We work closely with our authors through each stage of the publishing process, first in developing their books and then in presenting themselves and their ideas effectively to publishers and to readers. We represent our clients throughout the world in all languages, media and territories through an extensive network of subagents." No proposals for children's or young adult books, fiction, poetry, or memoir.

HOW TO CONTACT Queries sent by e-mail may not make it through the spam filters on our server. Please e-mail a brief query letter only, we do not read unsolicited manuscripts submitted by e-mail under any circumstances. See website.

RECENT SALES *Fifty-Nine in '84,* by Edward Achorn (Harper Collins); *Counterclockwise,* by Ellen J. Langer (Ballantine); *Too Big To Know,* by David Weinberger (Basic Books); *The Complete Psalms,* by Pamela Greenberg (Bloomsbury). See website for other clients.

TIPS "Query us first if you have any questions about whether we are the right agency for your work."

● THE GERNERT COMPANY

136 E. 57th St., 18th Floor, New York NY 10022. (212)838-7777. Fax: (212)838-6020. E-mail: info@ thegernertco.com. Website: www.thegernertco.com. **Contact:** Sarah Burnes.

• Prior to her current position, Ms. Burnes was with Burnes & Clegg, Inc.

MEMBER AGENTS Sarah Burnes (commercial fiction, adventure and true story); Stephanie Cabot (literary fiction, commercial fiction, historical fiction); Chris Parris-Lamb; Seth Fishman; Logan Garrison; Will Roberts; Erika Storella; Anna Worrall. At this time, Courtney Gatewood and Rebecca Gardner are closed to queries.

REPRESENTS nonfiction books, novels.

HOW TO CONTACT Queries should be addressed to a specific agent via the e-mail subject line. Please send a query letter, either by mail or e-mail, describing the work you'd like to submit, along with some information about yourself and a sample chapter if appropriate. Please do not send e-mails to individual agents; use info@thegernertco.com and indicate which agent you're querying. See company website for more instructions. Obtains most new clients through recommendations from others, solicitations.

RECENT SALES *House of Joy,* by Sarah-Kate Lynch (Plume); *Mudbound,* by Hillary Jordan (Algonquin); *The Reluctant Diplomat: Peter Paul Rubens and His Secret Mission to Save Europe From Itself,* by Mark Lamster (Talese).

◑☉ THE GREENHOUSE LITERARY AGENCY

11308 Lapham Dr., Oakton VA 22124. E-mail: submissions@greenhouseliterary.com. Website: www. greenhouseliterary.com. **Contact:** Sarah Davies. Other memberships include SCBWI. Represents 20 clients. 100% of clients are new/unpublished writers. Currently handles: juvenile books 100%.

• Prior to becoming an agent, Ms. Davies was the publishing director of Macmillan Children's Books in London.

REPRESENTS juvenile. **Considers these fiction areas:** juvenile, young adult.

&—☛ "We exclusively represent authors writing fiction for children and teens. The agency has offices in both the U.S. and U.K., and Sarah Davies (who is British) personally represents authors to both markets. The agency's commission structure reflects this—taking 15% for sales to both U.S. and U.K., thus treating both as 'domestic' market.'" All genres of children's and young adult fiction—ages 5+. Does not want to receive nonfiction, poetry, picture books (text or illustration), work aimed at adults, short stories, educational or religious/inspirational work, preschool/novelty material, or screenplays.

HOW TO CONTACT E-queries only as per guidelines given on website. Query should contain one-paragraph synopsis, one-paragraph bio, up to 5 sample pages pasted into e-mail. Replies to all submissions mostly within 2 weeks, but leave 6 weeks before chasing for response. Responds in 6-8 weeks to requested full mss. Our current policy on picturebooks is that we do not solicit either texts or illustrators but *do* represent picturebooks by authors whom we have already taken on for their older, longer work. Responds in 6 week to queries. Obtains most new clients through recommendations from others, solicitations, conferences.

TERMS Agent receives 15% commission on domestic sales. Agent receives 25% commission on foreign sales. Offers written contract. This agency charges very occasionally for copies for submission to film agents or foreign publishers.

RECENT SALES *Princess for Hire*, by Lindsey Leavitt (Hyperion); *What Happened on Fox Street*, by Tricia Springstubb (Harpercollins); *The Replacement*, by Brenna Yovanoff (Razorbill); *Just Add Magic*, by Cindy Callaghan (Aladdin).

WRITERS CONFERENCES Bologna Children's Book Fair, SCBWI conferences, BookExpo America.

TIPS "Before submitting material, authors should read the Greenhouse's 'Top 10 Tips for Authors of Children's Fiction,' which can be found on our website."

THE GUMA AGENCY

P.O. Box 503, Kensington MD 20895. E-mail: matthew@gumaagency.com. **Contact:** Matthew Guma.

REPRESENTS **Considers these nonfiction areas:** autobiography/biography, business/economics, celebrity, child guidance/parenting, health/fitness, narrative, relationships/dating, religious/inspirational, science, spirituality.

HOW TO CONTACT Accepts e-mail queries only.

● THE HELEN BRANN AGENCY, INC.

94 Curtis Rd., Bridgewater CT 06752. Fax: (860)355-2572. Member of AAR.

HOW TO CONTACT Query with SASE.

◐ THE JEFF HERMAN AGENCY, LLC

P.O. Box 1522, Stockbridge MA 01262. (413)298-0077. Fax: (413)298-8188. E-mail: jeff@jeffherman.com. Website: www.jeffherman.com. **Contact:** Jeffrey H. Herman. Represents 100 clients. 10% of clients are new/unpublished writers. Currently handles: nonfiction books 85%, scholarly books 5%, textbooks 5%.

- Prior to opening his agency, Mr. Herman served as a public relations executive.

MEMBER AGENTS Deborah Levine, vice president (nonfiction book doctor); Jeff Herman.

REPRESENTS nonfiction books. **Considers these nonfiction areas:** business, economics, government, health, history, how-to, law, medicine, politics, psychology, self-help, spirituality, technology, popular reference.

This agency specializes in adult nonfiction.

HOW TO CONTACT Query with SASE. Accepts simultaneous submissions.

TERMS Agent receives 15% commission on domestic sales. Offers written contract. Charges clients for copying and postage.

RECENT SALES *Days of Our Lives* book series; *H&R Block* book series. Sold 35 titles in the last year.

◐ THE JENNIFER DECHIARA LITERARY AGENCY

31 East 32nd St., Suite 300, New York NY 10016. (212)481-8484. Fax: (212)481-9582. E-mail: jenndec@aol.com; stephenafraser@verizon.net. Website: www.jdlit.com. **Contact:** Jennifer DeChiara, Stephen Fraser. Represents 100 clients. 50% of clients are new/unpublished writers. Currently handles: nonfiction books 25%, novels 25%, juvenile books 50%.

- Prior to becoming an agent, Ms. DeChiara was a writing consultant, freelance editor at Simon & Schuster and Random House, and a ballerina and an actress.

MEMBER AGENTS Jennifer DeChiara, Stephen Fraser, Dorothy Spencer (adult fiction and nonfiction).

REPRESENTS nonfiction books, novels, juvenile. **Considers these nonfiction areas:** autobiography, biography, child guidance, cooking, crafts, criticism, cultural interests, current affairs, dance, decorating, education, environment, ethnic, film, finance, foods, gay, government, health, history, hobbies, how-to, humor, interior design, investigative, juvenile nonfiction, language, law, lesbian, literature, medicine, memoirs, military, money, music, nature, nutrition, parenting, personal improvement, photography, popular culture, politics, psychology, satire, science, self-help, sociology, sports, technology, theater, true crime, war, women's issues, women's studies, celebrity biography. **Considers these fiction areas:** confession, crime, detective, ethnic, family saga, fantasy, feminist, gay, historical, horror, humor, juvenile, lesbian, literary, mainstream, mystery, picture books, police, regional, satire, sports, suspense, thriller, young adult, chick lit; psychic/supernatural; glitz.

8—➤ "We represent both children's and adult books in a wide range of ages and genres. We are a full-service agency and fulfill the potential of every book in every possible medium—stage, film, television, etc. We help writers every step of the way, from creating book ideas to editing and promotion. We are passionate about helping writers further their careers, but are just as eager to discover new talent, regardless of age or lack of prior publishing experience. This agency is committed to managing a writer's entire career. For us, it's not just about selling books, but about making dreams come true. We are especially attracted to the downtrodden, the discouraged, and the downright disgusted." Actively seeking literary fiction, chick lit, young adult fiction, self-help, pop culture, and celebrity biographies. Does not want Westerns, poetry, or short stories.

HOW TO CONTACT Query with SASE. Accepts simultaneous submissions. Responds in 3-6 months to queries. Responds in 3-6 months to mss. Obtains most new clients through recommendations from others, conferences, query letters.

TERMS Agent receives 15% commission on domestic sales. Agent receives 20% commission on foreign sales. Offers written contract.

RECENT SALES Sold more than 100 titles in the past year. *The Chosen One*, by Carol Lynch Williams (St. Martin's Press); *The 30-Day Heartbreak Cure*, by Catherine Hickland (Simon & Schuster); *Naptime for Barney*, by Danny Sit (Sterling Publishing); *The Screwed-Up Life of Charlie the Second*, by Drew Ferguson (Kensington); *Heart of a Shepherd*, by Rosanne Parry (Random House); *Carolina Harmony*, by Marilyn Taylor McDowell (Random House); *Project Sweet Life*, by Brent Hartinger

(HarperCollins). Movie/TV MOW scripts optioned/sold: *The Elf on the Shelf*, by Carol Aebersold and Chanda Bell (Waddell & Scorsese); *Heart of a Shepherd*, by Rosanne Parry (Tashtego Films); *Geography Club*, by Brent Hartinger (The Levy Leder Company). Other clients include Sylvia Browne, Matthew Kirby, Sonia Levitin, Susan Anderson, Michael Apostolina.

◑ THE JOAN BRANDT AGENCY

788 Wesley Dr., Atlanta GA 30305-3933. (404)351-8877. **Contact:** Joan Brandt.

• Prior to her current position, Ms. Brandt was with Sterling Lord Literistic.

REPRESENTS nonfiction books, novels, short story collections. **Considers these nonfiction areas:** investigative, true crime. **Considers these fiction areas:** family saga, historical, literary, mystery, suspense, thriller, women's.

HOW TO CONTACT Query letter with SASE. Accepts simultaneous submissions.

TERMS Agent receives 15% commission on domestic sales. Agent receives 20% commission on foreign sales. No written contract.

◑ THE JOY HARRIS LITERARY AGENCY, INC.

381 Park Avenue S., Suite 428, New York NY 10016. (212)924-6269. Fax: (212)725-5275. E-mail: submissions@jhlitagent.com; contact@jhlitagent.com. Website: joyharrisliterary.com. **Contact:** Joy Harris. Member of AAR. Represents more than 100 clients. Currently handles: nonfiction books 50%, novels 50%.

REPRESENTS nonfiction books, novels, and young adult. **Considers these fiction areas:** ethnic, experimental, family saga, feminist, gay, glitz, hi-lo, historical, humor, lesbian, literary, mainstream, multicultural, multimedia, mystery, regional, satire, short-story collections, spiritual, suspense, translation, women's, young adult.

8—➤ We do not accept unsolicited manuscripts, and are not accepting poetry, screenplays, or self-help submissions at this time.

HOW TO CONTACT Visit our website for guidelines. Query with sample chapter, outline/proposal, SASE. Accepts simultaneous submissions. Responds in 2 months to queries. Obtains most new clients through recommendations from clients and editors.

TERMS Agent receives 15% commission on domestic sales. Agent receives 20% commission on foreign sales. Charges clients for some office expenses.

● THE LA LITERARY AGENCY

P.O. Box 46370, Los Angeles CA 90046. (323)654-5288. E-mail: ann@laliteraryagency.com; mail@laliteraryagency.com. Website: www.laliteraryagency.com. **Contact:** Ann Cashman.

- Prior to becoming an agent, Mr. Lasher worked in publishing in New York and Los Angeles.

MEMBER AGENTS Ann Cashman, Eric Lasher, Maureen Lasher.

REPRESENTS nonfiction books, novels. **Considers these nonfiction areas:** animals, anthropology, archeology, architecture, art, autobiography, biography, business, child guidance, cooking, cultural interests, current affairs, diet/nutrition, design, economics, environment, ethnic, foods, government, health, history, how-to, investigative, law, medicine, parenting, popular culture, politics, psychology, science, self-help, sociology, sports, technology, true crime, women's issues, women's studies, narrative nonfiction. **Considers these fiction areas:** action, adventure, crime, detective, family saga, feminist, historical, literary, mainstream, police, sports, thriller.

HOW TO CONTACT Prefers submissions by mail but welcomes e-mail submissions as well. Nonfiction: query letter and book proposal; fiction: query letter and first 50 (double-spaced) pages. Query with outline, 1 sample chapter.

RECENT SALES *Full Bloom: The Art and Life of Georgia O'Keeffe*, by Hunter Druhojowska-Philp (Norton); *And the Walls Came Tumbling Down*, by H. Caldwell (Scribner); *Italian Slow & Savory*, by Joyce Goldstein (Chronicle); *A Field Guide to Chocolate Chip Cookies*, by Dede Wilson (Harvard Common Press); *Teen Knitting Club* (Artisan); *The Framingham Heart Study*, by Dr. Daniel Levy (Knopf).

● THE LITERARY GROUP INTERNATIONAL

14 Penn Plaza, Suite 925, New York NY 10122. (646)442-5896. E-mail: js@theliterarygroup.com. Website: www.theliterarygroup.com. **Contact:** Frank Weimann. 1900 Ave. of the Stars, 25 Fl., Los Angeles CA 90067; (310)282-8961; Fax: (310) 282-8903. 65% of clients are new/unpublished writers. Currently handles: nonfiction books 50%, fiction 50%.

MEMBER AGENTS Frank Weimann.

REPRESENTS nonfiction books, novels, graphic novels. **Considers these nonfiction areas:** animals, anthropology, biography, business, child guidance, crafts, creative nonfiction, current affairs, education, ethnic, film, government, health, history, humor, juvenile nonfiction, language, memoirs, military, multicultural, music, nature, popular culture, politics, psychology, religious, science, self-help, sociology, sports, travel, true crime, women's issues, women's studies. **Considers these fiction areas:** adventure, contemporary issues, detective, ethnic, experimental, family saga, fantasy, feminist, historical, horror, humor, literary, multicultural, mystery, psychic, romance, sports, thriller, young adult, regional, graphic novels.

8—★ This agency specializes in nonfiction (memoir, military, history, biography, sports, how-to).

HOW TO CONTACT Query with SASE. Prefers to read materials exclusively. Only responds if interested. Obtains most new clients through referrals, writers conferences, query letters.

TERMS Agent receives 15% commission on domestic sales. Agent receives 20% commission on foreign sales. Offers written contract; 30-day notice must be given to terminate contract.

RECENT SALES *One From the Hart*, by Stefanie Powers with Richard Buskin (Pocket Books); *Sacred Trust, Deadly Betrayal,* by Keith Anderson (Berkley); *Gotti Confidential*, by Victoria Gotti (Pocket Books); *Anna Sui's* illustrated memoir (Chronicle Books); *Mani*a, by Craig Larsen (Kensington); *Everything Explained Through Flowcharts*, by Doogie Horner (HarperCollins); *Bitch*, by Lisa Taddeo (TOR); film rights for *Falling Out of Fashion*, by Karen Yampolsky to Hilary Swank and Molly Smith for 2S Films.

WRITERS CONFERENCES San Diego State University Writers' Conference; Maui Writers' Conference; Agents and Editors Conference; NAHJ Convention in Puerto Rico, others.

● THE MARSH AGENCY, LTD

50 Albemarle St., London England W1S 4BD United Kingdom. (44)(207)399-2800. Fax: (44)(207)399-2801. Website: www.marsh-agency.co.uk. Estab. 1994.

MEMBER AGENTS Jessica Woollard, Stephanie Ebdon, Charlotte Bruton, Hannah Ferguson.

REPRESENTS nonfiction books, novels.

8—★ "This agency was founded as an international rights specialist for literary agents and publishers in the United Kingdom, the U.S., Canada and New Zealand, for whom we sell foreign rights on a commission basis. We work directly with publishers in all the major territories and in the majority of the smaller ones; sometimes in conjunction with local representatives." Actively seeking crime novels.

HOW TO CONTACT Query with SASE or use online submission form. Incluce a brief cover letter with your contact details and any relevant information, including any previously published work and any experience which relates to the book's subject matter; a short synopsis. Fiction: outline the plot and main characters. Nonfiction: a summary of the work and chapter outlines. First three chapters (no more than 100 pages) double spaced with all pages numbered. Obtains most new clients through recommendations from others, solicitations.

RECENT SALES A full list of clients and sales is available online.

TIPS "Use this agency's online form to send a generic e-mail message."

◐⊘ THE MARY CUNNANE AGENCY

PO Box 336, Bermagui, NSW 2546, Australia. E-mail: christine@cunnaneagency.com. E-mail: mary@cunnaneagency.com. Website: www.cunnaneagency.com. Australian Literary Agents Association

MEMBER AGENTS Mary Cunnane: mary@cunnaneagency.com.

⚭─┮ "Full-service literary agency representing book authors to publishers in Australia and around the world. We handle adult fiction and nonfiction." This agency does not work with North American authors. We do not represent science fiction, fantasy, romance novels, new age/spiritual books or children's books.

HOW TO CONTACT We prefer an initial inquiry by phone, e-mail or letter telling us something about the project and prospective author. If e-mailing, then please address your inquiry to Mary Cunnane and copy Christine Poulton. Please do not send files in excess of 10 megabytes. If we are interested, we will ask you to send the entire ms along with a SASE sufficiently large to post the ms back to you. We strive to read and respond within 4-6 weeks of receipt of the ms. Our server and Hotmail accounts do not work well together, so please try to avoid such accounts.

◑ THE MCGILL AGENCY, INC.

10000 N. Central Expressway, Suite 400, Dallas TX 75231. (214)390-5970. E-mail: info.mcgillagency@gmail.com. **Contact:** Jack Bollinger. Estab. 2009. Represents 10 clients. 50% of clients are new/unpublished writers.

MEMBER AGENTS Jack Bollinger (eclectic tastes in nonfiction and fiction); Amy Cohn (nonfiction interests include women's issues, gay/lesbian, ethnic/cultural, memoirs, true crime; fiction interests include mystery, suspense and thriller).

REPRESENTS Considers these nonfiction areas: biography, business, child guidance, current affairs, education, ethnic, gay, health, history, how-to, memoirs, military, psychology, self-help, true crime, women's issues. **Considers these fiction areas:** historical, mainstream, mystery, romance, thriller.

HOW TO CONTACT Query via e-mail. Responds in 2 weeks to queries and 6 weeks to mss. Obtains new clients through conferences.

TERMS Agent receives 15% commission.

➕◑ THE MCVEIGH AGENCY

345 W. 21st St., New York NY 10011-3035. E-mail: queries@themcveighagency.com. Website: www.themcveighagency.com. **Contact:** Linda Epstein. Estab. 2009.

REPRESENTS Considers these nonfiction areas: biography, history, memoirs. **Considers these fiction areas:** commercial, crime, literary, mainstream, picture books, young adult, graphic novels, middle grade.

⚭─┮ Actively seeking genre mashups, a book that combines two common but disparate themes and combines them to comic or dramatic effect. As far as middle grade and young adult, this agency seeks everything but especially scary books, historical steampunk and books that would appeal to children of color.

HOW TO CONTACT E-query. In the subject line of your e-mail, please write "Query," then the type of manuscript (e.g. young adult, middle grade, picture book, adult, nonfiction) and then the title of your book. The body of your e-mail should consist of your query letter, followed by the first 20 pages of your ms (for fiction) or your full proposal (for nonfiction). Please do not add your ms as an attachment. If the agency is interested in reading more, they'll request that you e-mail the full ms.

TIPS "I am a very hands-on, old-school agent who likes to edit manuscripts as much as I like to negotiate deals. My favorite agents were always what I called "honest sharks," out to get the best deal for their client, always looking ahead, but always conducted business in such a way that everyone came away as happy as possible. In short, they had integrity and determination to represent their clients to the best of their abilities, and that's what I aspire to."

THE MITCHELL J. HAMILBURG AGENCY

149 S. Barrington Ave., #732, Los Angeles CA 90049. (310)471-4024. Fax: (310)471-9588. **Contact:** Michael Hamilburg. Estab. 1937. Signatory of WGA. Represents 70 clients. Currently handles: nonfiction books 70%, novels 30%.

REPRESENTS nonfiction books, novels. **Considers these nonfiction areas:** anthropology, biography, business, child, cooking, current affairs, education, government, health, history, memoirs, military, money, psychology, recreation, regional, self help, sex, sociology, spirituality, sports, travel, women's, creative nonfiction; romance; architecture; inspirational; true crime. **Considers these fiction areas:** glitz, New Age, adventure, experimental, feminist, humor, military, mystery, occult, regional, religious, romance, sports, thriller, crime; mainstream; psychic.

HOW TO CONTACT Query with outline, 2 sample chapters, SASE. Responds in 1 month to mss. Obtains most new clients through recommendations from others, conferences, personal search.

TERMS Agent receives 10-15% commission on domestic sales.

THE NED LEAVITT AGENCY

70 Wooster St., Suite 4F, New York NY 10012. (212)334-0999. Website: www.nedleavittagency.com. **Contact:** Ned Leavitt. Member of AAR. Represents 40+ clients.

MEMBER AGENTS Ned Leavitt, founder and agent; Britta Alexander, agent; Jill Beckman, editorial assistant.

REPRESENTS nonfiction books, novels.

⌇ "We are small in size but intensely dedicated to our authors and to supporting excellent and unique writing."

HOW TO CONTACT This agency now only takes queries/submissions through referred clients. Do *not* cold query.

TIPS "Look online for this agency's recently changed submission guidelines." For guidance in the writing process we strongly recommend the following books: *Writing Down the Bones,* by Nathalie Goldberg; *Bird by Bird,* Anne Lamott.

✚☺ THE RIGHTS FACTORY

P.O. Box 499, Station C, Toronto ON M6J 3P6, Canada. (416)966-5367. Website: www.therightsfactory.com.

MEMBER AGENTS Sam Hiyate, Alisha Sevigny, Ali McDonald.

⌇ "The Rights Factory is an agency that deals in intellectual property rights to entertainment products, including books, comics and graphic novels, film, television, and video games. We license rights in every territory by representing three types of clients."

HOW TO CONTACT There is a submission form on this agency's website.

RECENT SALES *Beauty, Pure & Simple*, by Kristen Ma; *Why Mr. Right Can't Find You*, by J.M. Kearns; *Tout Sweet: Hanging Up My High Heels for a New Life in France*, by Karen Wheeler; *The Orange Code*, by Arkadi Kuhlmann and Bruce Philp.

ⓘ THE ROSENBERG GROUP

23 Lincoln Ave., Marblehead MA 01945. (781)990-1341. Fax: (781)990-1344. Website: www.rosenberggroup.com. **Contact:** Barbara Collins Rosenberg. Estab. 1998. Member of AAR. Recognized agent of the RWA. Represents 25 clients. 15% of clients are new/unpublished writers. Currently handles: nonfiction books 30%, novels 30%, scholarly books 10%, college textbooks 30%.

• Prior to becoming an agent, Ms. Rosenberg was a senior editor for Harcourt.

REPRESENTS nonfiction books, novels, textbooks, college textbooks only. **Considers these nonfiction areas:** current affairs, foods, popular culture, psychology, sports, women's issues, women's studies, women's health, wine/beverages. **Considers these fiction areas:** romance, women's.

⌇ Ms. Rosenberg is well-versed in the romance market (both category and single title). She is a frequent speaker at romance conferences. Actively seeking romance category or single title in contemporary romantic suspense, and the historical subgenres. Does not want to receive inspirational, time travel, futuristic or paranormal.

HOW TO CONTACT Query with SASE. No e-mail or fax queries; will not respond. See guidelines on website. Responds in 2 weeks to queries. Responds in 4-6 weeks to mss. Obtains most new clients through recommendations from others, solicitations, conferences.

TERMS Agent receives 15% commission on domestic sales. Agent receives 15% commission on foreign sales. Offers written contract; 1-month notice must be given to terminate contract. Charges maximum of $350/year for postage and photocopying.

RECENT SALES Sold 27 titles in the last year.

WRITERS CONFERENCES RWA National Conference; BookExpo America.

🌑 THE SCIENCE FACTORY

Scheideweg 34C, 20253 Hamburg, Germany. 44 (0)207 193 7296. E-mail: info@sciencefactory.co.uk. Website: www.sciencefactory.co.uk. **Contact:** Peter Tallack. Estab. 2008.

- Prior to his current position, Mr. Tallack was a director of the U.K. agency Conville & Walsh, publishing director at Weidenfeld & Nicolson, and on the editorial staff of the science journal *Nature*.

REPRESENTS Considers these nonfiction areas: all areas of serious popular nonfiction, particularly science, history and current affairs. **Considers these fiction areas:** At present is not considering fiction.

8—π "This agency specializes in representing authors aiming to satisfy the public's intellectual hunger for serious ideas. Experience of dealing directly in all markets, media and languages across the world." Actively seeking popular science nonfiction, particularly from public intellectuals, academics and journalists.

TIPS The Science Factory is the trading name of The Science Factory Ltd. Registered Office: The Courtyard, Shoreham Rd., Upper Beeding, Steyning, West Sussex BN44 3TN, UK. Registered in England and Wales: Company No. 06498410. UK VAT Registration No. GB 938 1678 84. German VAT Registration No. DE 274 9743 26.

⬤ THE SPIELER AGENCY

27 W. 20th St., Suite 305, New York NY 10011. E-mail: thespieleragency@gmail.com. **Contact:** Katya Balter,

acquisitions. Represents 160 clients. 2% of clients are new/unpublished writers.

- Prior to opening his agency, Mr. Spieler was a magazine editor.

MEMBER AGENTS Joe Spieler, Eric Myers.

REPRESENTS nonfiction books, novels, children's books. **Considers these nonfiction areas:** autobiography, biography, business, child guidance, current affairs, economics, environment, film, gay/lesbian, government, history, law, memoirs, money, music, parenting, politics, sociology, spirituality, theater, travel, women's issues, women's studies. **Considers these fiction areas:** feminist, gay, lesbian, literary, mystery, children's books, middle grade and young adult novels.

HOW TO CONTACT Accepts electronic submissions, or send query letter and sample chapters. Returns materials only with SASE; otherwise materials are discarded when rejected. Accepts simultaneous submissions. Cannot guarantee a personal response to all queries. Obtains most new clients through recommendations, listing in *Guide to Literary Agents*.

TERMS Agent receives 15% commission on domestic sales. Charges clients for messenger bills, photocopying, postage.

WRITERS CONFERENCES London Book Fair.

TIPS "Check www.publishersmarketplace.com/members/spielerlit/."

⊕ THE STRINGER LITERARY AGENCY, LLC

E-mail: stringerlit@comcast.net. Website: www.stringerlit.com. **Contact:** Marlene Stringer.

REPRESENTS Considers these nonfiction areas: history, military, music, parenting, science, sports, middle grade. **Considers these fiction areas:** fantasy, historical, mystery, romance, science fiction, thriller, women's, young adult.

8—π This agency specializes in fiction. Does not want to receive picture books, plays, short stories or poetry.

HOW TO CONTACT Electronic submissions only. Accepts simultaneous submissions.

RECENT SALES *Out for Blood* and *Stolen*, by Alyxandra Harvey (Walker Books); *Change of Heart*, by Shari Maurer, (WestSide Books); *I Stole Johnny Depp's Alien Girlfriend*, by Gary Ghislain (Chronicle Books); *The Land of Hope & Glory Trilogy*, by Geoffrey Wilson to Hodder; *... And On The Piano, Nicky Hopkins!* by Julian Dawson (Plus One Press);

Poison Kissed, by Erica Hayes, St. Martin's; *Possum Summer*, by Jen K. Blom, Holiday House; *An Echo Through the Snow to Forge*.

TIPS "If your manuscript falls between categories, or you are not sure of the category, query and we'll let you know if we'd like to take a look. We strive to respond as quickly as possible. If you have not received a response in the time period indicated, please re-query."

✪ THE UNTER AGENCY

23 W. 73rd St., Suite 100, New York NY 10023. (212)401-4068. E-mail: Jennifer@theunteragency. com. Website: www.theunteragency.com. **Contact:** Jennifer Unter. Estab. 2008.

- Ms. Unter began her book publishing career in the editorial department at Henry Holt & Co. She later worked at the Karpfinger Agency while she attended law school. She then became an associate at the entertainment firm of Cowan, DeBaets, Abrahams & Sheppard LLP where she practiced primarily in the areas of publishing and copyright law.

REPRESENTS **Considers these nonfiction areas:** biography, environment, foods, health, memoirs, popular culture, politics, travel, true crime, nature subjects. **Considers these fiction areas:** commercial, mainstream, picture books, young adult.

⚷ This agency specializes in children's and nonfiction but does take quality fiction.

HOW TO CONTACT Send an e-query.

◑ THREE SEAS LITERARY AGENCY

P.O. Box 8571, Madison WI 53708. (608)834-9317. E-mail: queries@threeseaslit.com. Website: http://three-seasagency.com. **Contact:** Michelle Grajkowski, Cori Deyoe. Estab. 2000. Member of AAR. Other memberships include RWA. Represents 55 clients. 10% of clients are new/unpublished writers. Currently handles: nonfiction books 5%, novels 80%, juvenile books 15%.

- Since starting her agency, Ms. Grajkowski has sold more than 350 titles worldwide. Her authors have appeared on all the major lists including *The New York Times* and *USA Today*. Prior to joining the agency in 2006, Ms. Deyoe was a multi-published author. She represents a wide range of authors and has sold many projects at auction.

MEMBER AGENTS Michelle Grajkowski; Cori Deyoe.

REPRESENTS nonfiction, novels, juvenile.

⚷ 3 Seas focuses primarily on romance (including contemporary, romantic suspense, paranormal, fantasy, historical and category), women's fiction, mysteries, nonfiction, young adult and children's stories. "Currently, we are looking for fantastic authors with a voice of their own." 3 Seas does not represent poetry, screenplays or novellas.

HOW TO CONTACT E-mail queries only. For fiction titles, query with first chapter and synopsis embedded in the e-mail. For nonfiction, query with complete proposal and first chapter. For picture books, query with complete text. One sample illustration may be included. Accepts simultaneous submissions. Responds in 1 month to queries. Obtains most new clients through recommendations from others, conferences.

TERMS Agent receives 15% commission on domestic sales. Agent receives 20% commission on foreign sales. Offers written contract.

RECENT SALES Clients include *New York Times* bestselling authors: Katie MacAlister, Kerrelyn Sparks and C.L. Wilson. Other award-winning authors include: Alexis Morgan, Donna MacMeans, Anna DeStefano, Laura Marie Altom, Cathy McDavid, Trish Milburn, Winnie Griggs, Carla Capshaw, Lisa Mondello, Tricia Mills, Tracy Madison, Keri Mikulski, Lori McDonald, R. Barri Flowers, Jennifer Brown, Kristi Gold and Susan Gee Heino.

◎ ANN TOBIAS: A LITERARY AGENCY FOR CHILDREN'S BOOKS

520 E. 84th St., Apt. 4L, New York NY 10028. E-mail: AnnTobias84@hotmail.com. **Contact:** Ann Tobias. Estab. 1988. Represents 25 clients. 10% of clients are new/unpublished writers. Currently handles: juvenile books 100%.

- Prior to opening her agency, Ms. Tobias worked as a children's book editor at Harper, William Morrow and Scholastic.

REPRESENTS juvenile and young adult. **Considers these nonfiction areas:** juvenile nonfiction, young adult. **Considers these fiction areas:** picture books, poetry, poetry in translation, young adult, illustrated mss; mid-level novels.

⚷ This agency specializes in books for children.

HOW TO CONTACT For all age groups and genres: Send a one-page letter of inquiry accompanied by a one-page writing sample, double-spaced. No attachments will be opened. Responds in 2 months to mss. Obtains most new clients through recommendations from editors.

TERMS Agent receives 15% commission on domestic sales. Agent receives 20% commission on foreign sales. This agency charges clients for photocopying, overnight mail, foreign postage, foreign telephone.

WRITERS CONFERENCES 3LiteraryAgents.com. For questions, contact info@3literaryagents.com.

TIPS "Read at least 200 children's books in the age group and genre in which you hope to be published. Follow this by reading another 100 children's books in other age groups and genres so you will have a feel for the field as a whole."

☯● TRANSATLANTIC LITERARY AGENCY

2 Bloor St., Suite 3500, Toronto ON M4W 1A8, Canada. E-mail: info@tla1.com. Website: www.tla1.com. Represents 250 clients. 10% of clients are new/unpublished writers. Currently handles: nonfiction books 30%, novels 15%, juvenile books 50%, textbooks 5%.

MEMBER AGENTS Lynn Bennett, Lynn@tla1.com (juvenile and young adult fiction); Shaun Bradley, Shaun@tla1.com (literary fiction and narrative nonfiction); Marie Campbell, Marie@tla1.com (literary juvenile and young adult fiction); Andrea Cascardi, Andrea@tla1.com (literary juvenile and young adult fiction); Samantha Haywood, Sam@tla1.com (literary fiction, narrative nonfiction and graphic novels); Don Sedgwick, Don@tla1.com (literary fiction and narrative nonfiction).

REPRESENTS nonfiction books, novels, juvenile. **Considers these nonfiction areas:** autobiography, biography, business, current affairs, economics, environment. **Considers these fiction areas:** juvenile, literary, mainstream, mystery, suspense, young adult.

☛ "In both children's and adult literature, we market directly into the United States, the United Kingdom and Canada." Actively seeking literary children's and adult fiction, nonfiction. Does not want to receive picture books, poetry, screenplays or stage plays.

HOW TO CONTACT Submit e-query with synopsis, 2 sample chapters, bio. Always refer to the website as guidelines will change. Also refer to website for appropriate agent contact info to send e-query. Responds in 2 weeks to queries. Obtains most new clients through recommendations from others.

TERMS Agent receives 15% commission on domestic sales. Agent receives 20% commission on foreign sales. Offers written contract; 45-day notice must be given to terminate contract. This agency charges for photocopying and postage when it exceeds $100.

RECENT SALES Sold 250 titles in the last year.

● S©OTT TREIMEL NY

434 Lafayette St., New York NY 10003. (212)505-8353. E-mail: general@scotttreimelny.com. Website: ScottTreimelNY.blogspot.com; www.ScottTreimelNY.com. **Contact:** John M. Cusick. Member of AAR. Other memberships include Authors Guild, SCBWI. 10% of clients are new/unpublished writers. Currently handles: junvenile/teen books 100%.

- Prior to becoming an agent, Mr. Treimel was an assistant to Marilyn E. Marlow at Curtis Brown, a rights agent for Scholastic, a book packager and rights agent for United Feature Syndicate, a freelance editor, a rights consultant for HarperCollins Children's Books, and the founding director of Warner Bros. Worldwide Publishing.

REPRESENTS nonfiction books, novels, juvenile, children's, picture books, young adult.

☛ This agency specializes in tightly focused segments of the trade and institutional markets. Career clients.

HOW TO CONTACT Submissions accepted only via website.

TERMS Agent receives 15% commission on domestic sales. Agent receives 20% commission on foreign sales. Offers verbal or written contract. Charges clients for photocopying, express postage, messengers, and books needed to sell foreign, film and other rights.

RECENT SALES *The Hunchback Assignments*, by Arthur Slade (Random House, HarperCollins Canada; HarperCollins Australia); *Shotgun Serenade*, by Gail Giles (Little, Brown); *Laundry Day*, by Maurie Manning (Clarion); *The P.S. Brothers*, by Maribeth Boelts (Harcourt); *The First Five Fourths*, by Pat Hughes (Viking); *Old Robert and the Troubadour Cats*, by Barbara Joosse (Philomel); *Ends*, by David Ward (Abrams); *Dear Canada*, by Barbara Haworth-Attard (Scholastic); *Soccer Dreams*, by Maribeth Boelts (Candlewick); *Lucky*

Me, by Richard Scrimger (Tundra); *Play, Louie, Play*, by Muriel Harris Weinstein (Bloomsbury).

WRITERS CONFERENCES SCBWI NY, NJ, PA, Bologna; The New School; Southwest Writers' Conference; Pikes Peak Writers' Conference.

TIPS "We look for dedicated authors and illustrators able to sustain longtime careers in our increasingly competitive field. I want fresh, not derivative story concepts with overly-familiar characters. We look for gripping stories, characters, pacing, and themes. We remain mindful of an authentic (to the age) point-of-view, and look for original voices. We spend significant time hunting for the best new work, and do launch debut talent each year. It is best *not* to send manuscripts with lengthy submission histories already."

TRIADA U.S. LITERARY AGENCY, INC.

P.O. Box 561, Sewickley PA 15143. (412)401-3376. E-mail: uwe@triadaus.com. Website: www.triadaus. com. **Contact:** Dr. Uwe Stender. Member of AAR. Represents 65 clients. 20% of clients are new/unpublished writers.

REPRESENTS fiction, nonfiction. **Considers these nonfiction areas:** biography, business, cooking, diet/nutrition, economics, education, foods, health, how-to, memoirs, popular culture, science, sports, advice, relationships, lifestyle. **Considers these fiction areas:** action, adventure, crime, detective, ethnic, historical, horror, juvenile, literary, mainstream, mystery, occult, police, romance, women's, especially young adult, women's fiction, and mysteries.

"We are looking for great writing and story platforms. Our response time is fairly unique. We recognize that neither we nor the authors have time to waste, so we guarantee a 5-day response time. We usually respond within 24 hours. " Actively looking for both fiction and nonfiction in all areas.

HOW TO CONTACT E-mail queries preferred; otherwise query with SASE. Accepts simultaneous submissions. Responds in 1-5 weeks to queries. Responds in 2-6 weeks to mss. Obtains most new clients through recommendations from others, conferences.

TERMS Agent receives 15% commission on domestic sales. Agent receives 20% commission on foreign sales. Offers written contract; 30-day notice must be given to terminate contract.

RECENT SALES *The Man Whisperer*, by Samantha

Brett and Donna Sozio (Adams Media); *Whatever Happened to Pudding Pops*, by Gael Fashingbauer Cooper and Brian Bellmont (Penguin/Perigee); *86'd*, by Dan Fante (Harper Perennial); *Hating Olivia*, by Mark SaFranko (Harper Perennial); *Everything I'm Not Made Me Everything I Am*, by Jeff Johnson (Smiley Books).

TIPS "I comment on all requested manuscripts that I reject."

TRIDENT MEDIA GROUP

41 Madison Ave., 36th Floor, New York NY 10010. (212)262-4810. E-mail: ellen.assistant@tridentmedia group.com. Website: www.tridentmediagroup.com. **Contact:** Ellen Levine. Member of AAR.

MEMBER AGENTS Kimberly Whalen, whalen. assistant@tridentmediagroup (commercial fiction and nonfiction, women's fiction, suspense, paranormal, and pop culture); Eileen Cope, ecope@ tridentmediagroup.com (narrative nonfiction, history, biography, pop culture, health, literary fiction, short-story collections); Scott Miller, smiller@ tridentmediagroup.com (thrillers, crime, mystery, young adult, children's, narrative nonfiction, current events, military, memoir, literary fiction, graphic novels, pop culture); Alex Glass, aglass@ tridentmediagroup (thrillers, literary fiction, crime, middle grade, pop culture, young adult, humor, narrative nonfiction); Melissa Flashman, mflashman@ tridentmediagroup.com (narrative nonfiction, serious nonfiction, pop culture, lifstyle); Alyssa Henkin, ahenkin@tridentmediagroup.com (juvenile, children's, young adult); Stephanie Maclean (romance, women's fiction and young adult); Don Fehr (literary and commercial novelists, narrative nonfiction, memoirs, biography, travel, science/medical/health related titles); Alanna Ramirez (literary fiction, narrative nonfiction, memoir, pop culture, food and wine, lifestyle books); John Silbersack (commercial and literary fiction, science fiction and fantasy, narrative nonfiction, young adult, thrillers).

REPRESENTS nonfiction books, novels, short-story collections, juvenile. **Considers these nonfiction areas:** autobiography, biography, current affairs, government, humor, law, memoirs, military, multicultural, popular culture, politics, true crime, war, women's issues, women's studies, young adult. **Considers these fiction areas:** crime, detective, humor, juvenile, literary, military, multicultural, mystery, police, short story collections, suspense, thriller, women's, young adult.

🔑 Actively seeking new or established authors in a variety of fiction and nonfiction genres.

HOW TO CONTACT Query with SASE or via e-mail. Check website for more details.

TIPS "If you have any questions, please check FAQ page before e-mailing us."

✛ ◑ UPSTART CROW LITERARY

P.O. Box 25404, Brooklyn NY 11202. E-mail: info@ upstartcrowliterary.com. E-mail: chris.submission@ gmail.com. Website: www.upstartcrowliterary.com. **Contact:** Chris Richman. Estab. 2009.

MEMBER AGENTS Michael Stearns; Chris Richman (special interest in books for boys, books with unforgettable characters, and fantasy that doesn't take itself too seriously); Danielle Chiotti (books ranging from contemporary women's fiction to narrative nonfiction, from romance to relationship stories, humorous tales and young adult fiction); Ted Malawer (accepting queries only through conference submissions and client referrals).

REPRESENTS Considers these fiction areas: women's, young adult, middle grade.

HOW TO CONTACT This agency likes submissions sent via e-mails to Chris Richman or Danielle Chiotti.

VAN DIEST LITERARY AGENCY

P.O. Box 1482, Sisters OR 97759. Website: www.christian literaryagency.com.

MEMBER AGENTS David Van Diest, Sarah Van Diest.

🔑 Christian books. "We are actively looking to discover and bring to market a few authors with fresh perspectives on timely subjects."

HOW TO CONTACT "Before submitting a proposal or manuscript, we ask that you submit an online query found on the 'Contact Us' page. We will contact you if we would like to receive a full proposal."

◑ VENTURE LITERARY

2683 Via de la Valle, G-714, Del Mar CA 92014. (619)807-1887. Fax: (772)365-8321. E-mail: submissions@ ventureliterary.com. Website: www.ventureliterary. com. **Contact:** Frank R. Scatoni. Represents 50 clients. 40% of clients are new/unpublished writers. Currently handles: nonfiction books 80%, novels 20%.

• Prior to becoming an agent, Mr. Scatoni worked as an editor at Simon & Schuster.

MEMBER AGENTS Frank R. Scatoni (general nonfiction, biography, memoir, narrative nonfiction, sports, serious nonfiction, graphic novels, narratives).

REPRESENTS nonfiction books, novels, graphic novels, narratives. **Considers these nonfiction areas:** anthropology, biography, business, cultural interests, current affairs, dance, economics, environment, ethnic, government, history, investigative, law, memoirs, military, money, multicultural, music, popular culture, politics, psychology, science, sports, technology, true crime, women's issues, women's studies. **Considers these fiction areas:** action, adventure, crime, detective, literary, mainstream, mystery, police, sports, suspense, thriller, women's.

🔑 Specializes in nonfiction, sports, biography, gambling and nonfiction narratives. Actively seeking nonfiction, graphic novels and narratives. Does not want fantasy, sci-fi, romance, children's picture books, Westerns.

HOW TO CONTACT Considers e-mail queries only. No unsolicited mss and no snail mail whatsoever. See website for complete submission guidelines. Obtains most new clients through recommendations from others.

TERMS Agent receives 15% commission on domestic sales. Agent receives 20% commission on foreign sales. Offers written contract.

RECENT SALES *The 9/11 Report: A Graphic Adaptation*, by Sid Jacobson and Ernie Colon (FSG); *Having a Baby* by Cindy Margolis (Perigee/Penguin); *Phil Gordon's Little Blue Book*, by Phil Gordon (Simon & Schuster); *Atomic America*, by Todd Tucker (Free Press); *War as They Knew It*, by Michael Rosenberg (Grand Central); *Game Day*, by Craig James (Wiley); *The Blueprint*, by Christopher Price (Thomas Dunne Books).

◑ VERITAS LITERARY AGENCY

601 Van Ness Ave., Opera Plaza, Suite E, San Francisco CA 94102. (415)647-6964. Fax: (415)647-6965. E-mail: submissions@veritasliterary.com. Website: www.veritasliterary.com. **Contact:** Katherine Boyle. Member of AAR. Other memberships include Author's Guild.

REPRESENTS nonfiction books, novels. **Considers these nonfiction areas:** current affairs, memoirs, popular culture, politics, true crime, women's issues, young adult, narrative nonfiction, art and music biography, natural history, health and wellness, psychology, serious religion (no New Age), and popular science. **Considers these fiction areas:** commercial, fantasy, literary, mystery, science fiction, young adult. ☛ Does not want to receive romance, poetry or children's books.

HOW TO CONTACT This agency accepts short queries or proposals via e-mail only. "If you are sending a proposal or a manuscript after a positive response to a query, please write 'Requested Material' on the subject line and include the initial query letter."

Ⓞ BETH VESEL LITERARY AGENCY

80 Fifth Ave., Suite 1101, New York NY 10011. (212)924-4252. E-mail: mlindley@bvlit.com. **Contact:** Julia Masnik, assistant. Represents 65 clients. 10% of clients are new/unpublished writers. Currently handles: nonfiction books 75%, novels 10%, story collections 5%, scholarly books 10%.

- Prior to becoming an agent, Ms. Vesel was a poet and a journalist.

REPRESENTS nonfiction books, novels. **Considers these nonfiction areas:** autobiography, biography, business, cultural interests, economics, ethnic, health, how-to, investigative, medicine, memoirs, psychology, true crime, women's issues, women's studies, cultural criticism. **Considers these fiction areas:** crime, detective, literary, police, Francophone novels.

☛ "My specialties include serious nonfiction, psychology, cultural criticism, memoir, and women's issues." Actively seeking cultural criticism, literary psychological thrillers, and sophisticated memoirs. No uninspired psychology or run-of-the-mill first novels.

HOW TO CONTACT Query with SASE. Accepts simultaneous submissions. Responds in 2 weeks to queries. Responds in 1 month to mss. Obtains most new clients through referrals, reading good magazines, contacting professionals with ideas.

TERMS Agent receives 15% commission on domestic sales. Agent receives 20% commission on foreign sales. Offers written contract.

RECENT SALES Sold 10 titles in the last year. *Life With Pop,* by Janis Spring, Ph.D (Avery); *American Scandal,* by Laura Kipnis (Metropolitan); *Bird in Hand,* by Christina Baker Kline (William Morrow); *Reimagining the South,* by Tracy Thompson (Simon & Schuster); *Are Fathers Necessary,* by Raul Raeburn (Simon & Schuster); *Blind Date,* by Virginia Vitzhum

(Workman); *Bipolar Breakthrough,* by Ron Fieve (Rodale).

WRITERS CONFERENCES Squaw Valley Writers Workshop, Iowa Summer Writing Festival.

TIPS "Try to find out if you fit on a particular agent's list by looking at his/her books and comparing yours. You can almost always find who represents a book by looking at the acknowledgements."

⊘ RALPH M. VICINANZA LTD.

303 W. 18th St., New York NY 10011. (212)924-7090. Fax: (212)691-9644. Member of AAR.

MEMBER AGENTS Ralph M. Vicinanza; Chris Lotts; Christopher Schelling.

HOW TO CONTACT This agency takes on new clients by professional recommendation only.

TERMS Agent receives 15% commission on domestic sales. Agent receives 20% commission on foreign sales.

◑Ⓞ WADE & DOHERTY LITERARY AGENCY

33 Cormorant Lodge, Thomas Moore St., London E1W 1AU England. (44)(207)488-4171. Fax: (44)(207)488-4172. E-mail: bd@rwla.com. Website: www.rwla.com. **Contact:** Robin Wade. Estab. 2001.

- Prior to opening his agency, Mr. Wade was an author; Ms. Doherty worked as a production assistant, editor and editorial director.

MEMBER AGENTS Robin Wade, Broo Doherty.

REPRESENTS fiction and nonfiction, including children's books.

☛ "We are young and dynamic and actively seek new writers across the literary spectrum." Does not want to receive poetry, plays or short stories.

HOW TO CONTACT Submit synopsis (1-6 pages), bio, first 10,000 words via e-mail (Word or pdf documents only). If sending by post, include SASE or IRC. Responds in 1 week to queries. Responds in 1 month to mss.

TERMS Agent receives 10% commission on domestic sales. Agent receives 20% commission on foreign sales. Offers written contract; 1-month notice must be given to terminate contract.

TIPS "We seek manuscripts that are well written, with strong characters and an original narrative voice. Our absolute priority is giving the best possible service to the authors we choose to represent, as well as maintaining routine friendly contact with them as we help develop their careers."

◑ WALES LITERARY AGENCY, INC.

P.O. Box 9426, Seattle WA 98109-0426. (206)284-7114. E-mail: waleslit@waleslit.com. Website: www.waleslit. com. **Contact:** Elizabeth Wales, Neal Swain. Member of AAR. Other memberships include Book Publishers' Northwest, Pacific Northwest Booksellers Association, PEN. Represents 60 clients. 10% of clients are new/unpublished writers. Currently handles: nonfiction books 60%, novels 40%.

- Prior to becoming an agent, Ms. Wales worked at Oxford University Press and Viking Penguin.

MEMBER AGENTS Elizabeth Wales; Neal Swain.

⚷— This agency specializes in quality fiction and nonfiction. Does not handle screenplays, children's literature, genre fiction, or most category nonfiction.

HOW TO CONTACT Accepts queries sent with cover letter and SASE, and e-mail queries with no attachments. No phone or fax queries. Accepts simultaneous submissions. Responds in 2 weeks to queries, 2 months to mss.

TERMS Agent receives 15% commission on domestic sales. Agent receives 20% commission on foreign sales.

RECENT SALES *The Dirty Doll Diaries: A novel,* by Cinthia Ritchie (Grand Central/Hachette, 2011); *Heat: A Natural and Unnatural History,* by Bill Streever (Little, Brown, 2012); *Cheesemonger: A Life on the Wedge, by Gordon Edgar (Chelsea Green, 2010); Special Exits: My Parents: A Memoir* by Joyce Farmer (Fantagraphics, 2010); *Unterzakhn: A Graphic Novel,* by Leela Corman (Schocken/Pantheon, 2010).

WRITERS CONFERENCES Pacific Northwest Writers Conference, annually; and others.

TIPS "We are especially interested in work that espouses a progressive cultural or political view, projects a new voice, or simply shares an important, compelling story. We also encourage writers living in the Pacific Northwest, West Coast, Alaska, and Pacific Rim countries, and writers from historically underrepresented groups, such as gay and lesbian writers and writers of color, to submit work (but does not discourage writers outside these areas). Most importantly, whether in fiction or nonfiction, the agency is looking for talented storytellers."

◑ JOHN A. WARE LITERARY AGENCY

392 Central Park W., New York NY 10025-5801. (212)866-4733. Fax: (212)866-4734. **Contact:** John Ware. Represents 60 clients. 40%% of clients are new/unpublished writers. Currently handles: nonfiction books 75%, novels 25%.

- Prior to opening his agency, Mr. Ware served as a literary agent with James Brown Associates/Curtis Brown, Ltd., and as an editor for Doubleday.

REPRESENTS nonfiction books, novels. **Considers these nonfiction areas:** Americana, anthropology, biography, current affairs, history, investigative journalism, sports, language, music, nature, popular culture, psychology (academic credentials required), true crime, women's issues, social commentary, folklore. **Considers these fiction areas:** detective, mystery, thriller, accessible literary non-category fiction.

⚷— Does not want personal memoirs.

HOW TO CONTACT Query with SASE. Send a letter only. Accepts simultaneous submissions. Responds in 2 weeks to queries.

TERMS Agent receives 15% commission on domestic sales, 20% commission on foreign sales, film. Charges clients for courier and messenger service and photocopying.

RECENT SALES *Ironmen,* by Chris Ballard (Hyperion); *Knights of The Sea,* by David Hanna (New American Library); *Velva Jean Learns to Fly,* by Jennifer Niven (Plume); *Kosher USA,* by Roger Horowitz (Columbia); *The River's Own,* by Travis Hugh Culley (Random House).

TIPS "Writers must have appropriate credentials for authorship of proposal (nonfiction); no publishing track record required. I am open to good writing and interesting ideas by new or veteran writers."

◑ WATERSIDE PRODUCTIONS, INC.

2055 Oxford Ave., Cardiff CA 92007. (760)632-9190. Fax: (760)632-9295. E-mail: admin@waterside.com. Website: www.waterside.com. Estab. 1982.

MEMBER AGENTS Bill Gladstone; Margot Maley Hutchison; Carole Jelen McClendon; Lawrence Jackel; Neil Gudovitz; David Nelson; Kimberly Brabec.

REPRESENTS nonfiction books. **Considers these nonfiction areas:** architecture, art, autobiography, biography, business, child guidance, computers, cultural interests, design, economics, environment, ethnic, health, how-to, humor, medicine, money, parenting, popular culture, psychology, sociology, sports, technology, travel, cookbooks, natural health, real estate, lifestyles and more.

O– Specializes in computer books, how-to, business, and health titles.

HOW TO CONTACT "Please read each agent bio [on the website] to determine who you think would best represent your genre of work. When you have chosen your agent, please write his or her name in the subject line of your e-mail and send it to admin@waterside.com with your query letter in the body of the e-mail and your proposal or sample material as an attached word document." Obtains most new clients through referrals from established client and publisher list.

TIPS "For new writers, a quality proposal and a strong knowledge of the market you're writing for goes a long way toward helping us turn you into a published author. We like to see a strong author platform. Two foreign rights agents on staff—Neil Gudovitz and Kimberly Brabec—help us with overseas sales."

● WATKINS LOOMIS AGENCY, INC.

P.O. Box 20925, New York NY 10025. (212)532-0080. Fax: (646)383-2449. E-mail: assistant@watkinsloomis. com. Website: www.watkinsloomis.com. Estab. 1980. Represents 50+ clients.

MEMBER AGENTS Gloria Loomis, president, Julia Masnik, junior agent.

REPRESENTS nonfiction, novels, short-story collections. **Considers these nonfiction areas:** autobiography, biography, cultural interests, current affairs, environment, ethnic, history, popular culture, technology, investigative journalism. **Considers these fiction areas:** literary, short-story collections.

O– This agency specializes in literary fiction and nonfiction.

HOW TO CONTACT No unsolicited mss. This agency does not guarantee a response to queries.

TERMS Agent receives 15% commission on domestic sales. Agent receives 20% commission on foreign sales.

● WAXMAN LITERARY AGENCY, INC.

80 Fifth Ave., Suite 1101, New York NY 10011. (212)675-5556. Fax: (212)675-1381. E-mail: scottsubmit@waxmanagency.com. Website: www.waxmanagency. com. **Contact:** Scott Waxman. Represents 60 clients.

50% of clients are new/unpublished writers. Currently handles: nonfiction books 80%, novels 20%.

• Prior to opening his agency, Mr. Waxman was an editor at HarperCollins.

MEMBER AGENTS Scott Waxman (all categories of nonfiction, commercial fiction—specifically suspense/thriller), Byrd Leavell, Farley Chase, Holly Root.

REPRESENTS Considers these nonfiction areas: prescriptive, historical, sports, narrative, pop culture, humor, memoir, biography, celebrity. **Considers these fiction areas:** literary, contemporary, commercial, young adult.

O– "We're looking for new novelists with nonpublished works."

HOW TO CONTACT Please visit our website. Accepts simultaneous submissions.

TERMS Agent receives 15% commission on domestic sales. Agent receives 10% commission on foreign sales. Offers written contract; 2-month notice must be given to terminate contract.

◎ IRENE WEBB LITERARY

551 W. Cordova Rd., #238, Santa Fe NM 87505. (505)988-1817. E-mail: webblit@gmail.com. Website: www.irenewebb.com. **Contact:** Irene Webb.

REPRESENTS nonfiction books, novels. **Considers these nonfiction areas:** animals, environment, health, memoirs, popular culture, self-help, spirituality, sports, true stories. **Considers these fiction areas:** commercial, crime, horror, mystery, suspense, thriller, women's, young adult, middle grade, literary and commercial fiction.

O– "Irene Webb Literary is known as one of the top boutique agencies selling books to film and TV. We have close relationships with top film producers and talent in Hollywood." Does not want to receive unsolicited mss or screenplays.

HOW TO CONTACT Query via e-mail only. Obtains most new clients through recommendations from others, solicitations.

RECENT SALES *Secrets of a Soap Opera Diva*, by Victoria Rowell (Atria); *Now I Can See the Moon*, by Elaine Hall (Harper Studio); *Dead Write*, by Sheila Low (NAL); *East to the Dawn*, by Susan Butler (Fox Studio for the Amelia Earhart story starring Hilary Swank).

✚ ◑ WEED LITERARY

27 West 20th St., New York NY 10011. E-mail: info@weedliterary.com. Website: www.weedliterary.com. **Contact:** Elisabeth Weed. Estab. 2007.

- Prior to forming her own agency, Ms. Weed was an agent at Curtis Brown and Trident Media Group.

REPRESENTS nonfiction, fiction, novels. **Considers these fiction areas:** literary, women's.

☞ This agency specializes in upmarket women's fiction. Does not want to receive picture books, mysteries, thrillers, romance or military.

HOW TO CONTACT Send a query letter.

RECENT SALES *Life Without Summer*, by Lynne Griffin (St. Martin's Press); *Time of My Life*, by Allison Winn Scotch (Shaye Areheart Books); and *The Last Will of Moira Leahy*, by Therese Walsh (Shaye Areheart Books).

WRITERS CONFERENCES Muse and the Marketplace (Boston, annual).

● THE WENDY WEIL AGENCY, INC.

232 Madison Ave., Suite 1300, New York NY 10016. (212)685-0030. Fax: (212)685-0765. E-mail: wweil@wendyweil.com. Website: www.wendyweil.com. Estab. 1987. Member of AAR. Currently handles: nonfiction books 20%, novels 80%.

MEMBER AGENTS Wendy Weil (commercial fiction, women's fiction, family saga, historical fiction, short stories); Emily Forland; Emma Patterson.

REPRESENTS nonfiction books, novels.

☞ "The Wendy Weil Agency, Inc. represents fiction and nonfiction for the trade market. We work with literary and commercial fiction, mystery/thriller, memoir, narrative nonfiction, journalism, history, current affairs, books on health, science, popular culture, lifestyle, social activism, and art history. It is a full-service literary agency that handles around 100 authors, among them Pulitzer Prize winners, National Book Award winners, *New York Times* bestsellers." Does not want to receive screenplays or textbooks.

HOW TO CONTACT "Accepts queries by regular mail and e-mail, however, we cannot guarantee a response to electronic queries. Query letters should be no more than 2 pages, which should include a bit about yourself and an overview of your project. If you'd like, you're welcome to include a separate synopsis along with your query. For queries via regular mail, please be sure to include a SASE for our reply. Snail mail queries are preferred." Responds in 4-6 weeks. Obtains most new clients through recommendations from others, solicitations.

● CHERRY WEINER LITERARY AGENCY

28 Kipling Way, Manalapan NJ 07726-3711. (732)446-2096. Fax: (732)792-0506. E-mail: cherry8486@aol.com. **Contact:** Cherry Weiner. Represents 40 clients. 10% of clients are new/unpublished writers. Currently handles: nonfiction books 10-20%, novels 80-90%.

REPRESENTS nonfiction books, novels. **Considers these nonfiction areas:** self-help. **Considers these fiction areas:** action, adventure, contemporary issues, crime, detective, family saga, fantasy, frontier, historical, mainstream, mystery, police, psychic, romance, science fiction, supernatural, thriller, Western.

☞ *This agency is currently not accepting new clients except by referral or by personal contact at writers' conferences.* Specializes in fantasy, science fiction, Western, mysteries (both contemporary and historical), historical novels, Native-American works, mainstream and all genre romances.

HOW TO CONTACT Query with SASE. Prefers to read materials exclusively. Responds in 1 week to queries. Responds in 2 months to mss that I have asked for.

TERMS Agent receives 15% commission on domestic sales. Agent receives 15% commission on foreign sales. Offers written contract. Charges clients for extra copies of mss, first-class postage for author's copies of books, express mail for important documents/mss.

RECENT SALES Sold 70 titles in the last year. This agency prefers not to share information on specific sales.

TIPS "Meet agents and publishers at conferences. Establish a relationship, then get in touch with them and remind them of the meeting and conference."

● THE WEINGEL-FIDEL AGENCY

310 E. 46th St., 21E, New York NY 10017. (212)599-2959. **Contact:** Loretta Weingel-Fidel. Currently handles: nonfiction books 75%, novels 25%.

- Prior to opening her agency, Ms. Weingel-Fidel was a psychoeducational diagnostician.

REPRESENTS nonfiction books, novels. **Considers these nonfiction areas:** art, autobiography, biography, dance, memoirs, music, psychology, science, sociology, technology, women's issues, women's studies, investigative journalism. **Considers these fiction areas:** literary, mainstream.

ⓞ—ⲧ This agency specializes in commercial and literary fiction and nonfiction. Actively seeking investigative journalism. Does not want to receive genre fiction, self-help, science fiction or fantasy.

HOW TO CONTACT Accepts writers by referral only. No unsolicited mss.

TERMS Agent receives 15% commission on domestic sales. Agent receives 20% commission on foreign sales. Offers written contract, binding for 1 year with automatic renewal. Bills sent back to clients are all reasonable expenses, such as UPS, express mail, photocopying, etc.

TIPS "A very small, selective list enables me to work very closely with my clients to develop and nurture talent. I only take on projects and writers about which I am extremely enthusiastic."

ⓞ TED WEINSTEIN LITERARY MANAGEMENT

307 Seventh Ave., Suite 2407, Dept. GLA, New York NY 10001. E-mail: tw@twliterary.com. E-mail: submissions@twliterary.com. Website: www.twliterary.com. **Contact:** Ted Weinstein. Member of AAR. Represents 75 clients. 50% of clients are new/unpublished writers. Currently handles: nonfiction books 100%.

REPRESENTS Considers these nonfiction areas: biography, business, current affairs, economics, government, health, history, investigative, law, medicine, popular culture, politics, science, self-help, technology, travel, true crime, lifestyle, narrative journalism, popular science.

HOW TO CONTACT Please visit website for detailed guidelines before submitting. E-mail queries only. Responds in 3 weeks to queries.

TERMS Agent receives 15% commission on domestic sales. Agent receives 20% commission on foreign sales. Agent receives 20% commission on film sales. Offers written contract, binding for 1 year. Charges clients for photocopying and express shipping.

TIPS "Accepts e-mail queries *only*; paper submissions are discarded. See agency's website for full guidelines."

ⓞ LARRY WEISSMAN LITERARY, LLC

526 8th St., #2R, Brooklyn NY 11215. E-mail: lw submissions@gmail.com. **Contact:** Larry Weissman. Represents 35 clients. Currently handles: nonfiction books 80%, novels 10%, story collections 10%.

REPRESENTS nonfiction books, novels, short-story collections. **Considers these fiction areas:** literary.

ⓞ—ⲧ "Very interested in established journalists with bold voices. Interested in anything to do with food. Fiction has to feel 'vital' and short stories are accepted, but only if you can sell us on an idea for a novel, as well." Nonfiction, including food and lifestyle, politics, pop culture, narrative, cultural/social issues, journalism. No genre fiction, poetry or children's.

HOW TO CONTACT "Send e-queries only. If you don't hear back, your project was not right for our list."

TERMS Agent receives 15% commission on domestic sales. Agent receives 20% commission on foreign sales.

ⓞⓞ WESTWOOD CREATIVE ARTISTS, LTD.

94 Harbord St., Toronto ON M5S 1G6, Canada. (416)964-3302. Fax: (416)975-9209. E-mail: wca_office@wcaltd.com. Website: www.wcaltd.com. Represents 350+ clients.

MEMBER AGENTS Deborah Wood, book-to-film agent; Ahston Westwood, book-to-film agent; Linda McKnight, literary agent; Jackie Kaiser, literary agent; Hilary McMahon, literary agent; Bruce Westwood, literary agent; John Pearce, literary agent; Natasha Daneman, subsidiary rights director; Michael Levine, film and TV agent; Chris Casuccio, administrative assistant.

HOW TO CONTACT Query with SASE. Use a referral to break into this agency. Accepts simultaneous submissions.

RECENT SALES *A Biography of Richard Nixon*, by Conrad Black (Public Affairs); *The New Cold War: Revolutions; Rigged Elections and Pipeline Politics in the Former Soviet Union*, by Mark MacKinnon (Carroll & Graf).

ⓞ WHIMSY LITERARY AGENCY, LLC

New York/Los Angeles E-mail: whimsynyc@aol.com. Website: http://whimsyliteraryagency.com/. **Contact:** Jackie Meyer. Other memberships include Center for Independent Publishing Advisory Board. Represents 30 clients. 20% of clients are new/unpublished writers. Currently handles: nonfiction books 100%.

- Prior to becoming an agent, Ms. Meyer was with Warner Books for 19 years; Ms. Vezeris and Ms. Legette have 30 years experience at various book publishers.

MEMBER AGENTS Jackie Meyer; Olga Vezeris (fiction and nonfiction); Nansci LeGette, senior associate in LA.

REPRESENTS nonfiction books. **Considers these nonfiction areas:** agriculture, art, biography, business, child guidance, cooking, education, health, history, horticulture, how-to, humor, interior design, memoirs, money, New Age, popular culture, psychology, religious, self-help, true crime, women's issues, women's studies. **Considers these fiction areas:** mainstream, religious, thriller, women's.

⚷ "Whimsy looks for projects that are concept- and platform-driven. We seek books that educate, inspire and entertain." Actively seeking experts in their field with good platforms.

HOW TO CONTACT Send a query letter via e-mail. Send a synopsis, bio, platform, and proposal. No snail mail submissions. Responds "quickly, but only if interested" to queries. Does not accept unsolicited mss. Obtains most new clients through recommendations from others, solicitations.

TERMS Agent receives 15% commission on domestic sales. Agent receives 20% commission on foreign sales. Offers written contract. Charges for posting and photocopying.

AUDREY R. WOLF LITERARY AGENCY

2510 Virginia Ave. N.W., #702N, Washington DC 20037. **Contact:** Audrey Wolf. Member of AAR.
HOW TO CONTACT Query with SASE.

◯ WOLFSON LITERARY AGENCY

P.O. Box 266, New York NY 10276. E-mail: query@ wolfsonliterary.com. Website: www.wolfsonliterary. com. **Contact:** Michelle Wolfson. Adheres to AAR canon of ethics. Currently handles: nonfiction books 70%, novels 30%.

- Prior to forming her own agency, Ms. Wolfson spent two years with Artists & Artisans, Inc. and two years with Ralph Vicinanza, Ltd.

REPRESENTS nonfiction books, novels. **Considers these nonfiction areas:** business, child guidance, economics, health, how-to, humor, medicine, memoirs, parenting, popular culture, satire, self-help, women's issues, women's studies. **Considers these**

fiction areas: mainstream, mystery, romance, suspense, thriller, women's, young adult.

⚷ Actively seeking commercial fiction, mainstream, mysteries, thrillers, suspense, women's fiction, romance, young adult, practical nonfiction (particularly of interest to women), advice, medical, pop culture, humor, business.

HOW TO CONTACT E-queries only! Accepts simultaneous submissions. Responds only if interested. Positive response is generally given within 2-4 weeks. Responds in 3 months to mss. Obtains most new clients through recommendations from others, solicitations.

TERMS Agent receives 15% commission on domestic sales. Agent receives 25% commission on foreign sales. Offers written contract; 30-day notice must be given to terminate contract.

WRITERS CONFERENCES SDSU Writers' Conference; New Jersey Romance Writers of America Writers' Conference; American Independent Writers Conference in Washington DC.

TIPS "Be persistent."

⊘ WOLGEMUTH & ASSOCIATES, INC

8600 Crestgate Circle, Orlando FL 32819. (407)909-9445. Fax: (407)909-9446. E-mail: ewolgemuth@ wolgemuthandassociates.com. **Contact:** Erik Wolgemuth. Member of AAR. Represents 60 clients. 10% of clients are new/unpublished writers. Currently handles: nonfiction books 90%, novella 2%, juvenile books 5%, multimedia 3%.

- "We have been in the publishing business since 1976, having been a marketing executive at a number of houses, a publisher, an author, and a founder and owner of a publishing company."

MEMBER AGENTS Robert D. Wolgemuth; Andrew D. Wolgemuth; Erik S. Wolgemuth.

REPRESENTS Material used by Christian families.

⚷ "We are not considering any new material at this time."

TERMS Agent receives 15% commission on domestic sales. Offers written contract, binding for 2-3 years; 30-day notice must be given to terminate contract.

❶⊘ WORDSERVE LITERARY GROUP

10152 S. Knoll Circle, Highlands Ranch CO 80130. Website: www.wordserveliterary.com. **Contact:** Greg Johnson; Rachelle Gardner. Represents 100 clients.

20% of clients are new/unpublished writers. Currently handles: nonfiction books 50%, novels 35%, juvenile books 10%, multimedia 5%.

- Prior to becoming an agent in 1994, Mr. Johnson was a magazine editor and freelance writer of more than 20 books and 200 articles.

MEMBER AGENTS Greg Johnson; Rachelle Gardner.

REPRESENTS **Considers these nonfiction areas:** biography, child guidance, inspirational, memoirs, parenting, self-help. **Considers these fiction areas:** historical, inspirational, mainstream, spiritual, suspense, thriller, women's.

⚶ Materials with a faith-based angle, whether fiction or nonfiction, are of interest.

HOW TO CONTACT This agency's submission guidelines are constantly changing; with that in mind, they have asked that all writers check the website before submitting to make sure Wordserve's agents are open to queries at the current time. Accepts simultaneous submissions. Responds in 4 weeks to queries. Responds in 2 months to mss. Obtains most new clients through recommendations from others.

TERMS Agent receives 15% commission on domestic sales. Agent receives 10-15% commission on foreign sales. Offers written contract; up to 60-day notice must be given to terminate contract.

RECENT SALES Sold 1,500 titles in the last 15 years. Redemption series, by Karen Kingsbury (Tyndale); *Loving God Up Close*, by Calvin Miller (Warner Faith); *Christmas in My Heart* by Joe Wheeler (Tyndale). Other clients include Doug Fields, Wanda Dyson, Catherine Martin, David Murrow, Leslie Haskin, Gilbert Morris, Robert Wise, Jim Burns, Wayne Cordeiro, Denise George, Susie Shellenberger, Tim Smith, Athol Dickson, Patty Kirk, John Shore, Marcus Bretherton, Rick Johnson.

TIPS "We are looking for good proposals, great writing and authors willing to market their books, as appropriate. Also, we're only looking for projects with a faith element bent. See the website before submitting."

⬤ WRITERS HOUSE

21 W. 26th St., New York NY 10010. (212)685-2400. Fax: (212)685-1781. E-mail: mmejias@writershouse.com; smalk@writershouse.com. Website: www.writershouse.com. **Contact:** Michael Mejias. Estab. 1973. Member of AAR. Represents 440 clients. 50% of clients

are new/unpublished writers. Currently handles: nonfiction books 25%, novels 40%, juvenile books 35%.

REPRESENTS nonfiction books, novels, juvenile. **Considers these nonfiction areas:** animals, art, autobiography, biography, business, child guidance, cooking, decorating, diet/nutrition, economics, film, foods, health, history, humor, interior design, juvenile nonfiction, medicine, military, money, music, parenting, psychology, satire, science, self-help, technology, theater, true crime, women's issues, women's studies. **Considers these fiction areas:** adventure, cartoon, contemporary issues, crime, detective, erotica, ethnic, family saga, fantasy, feminist, frontier, gay, hi-lo, historical, horror, humor, juvenile, literary, mainstream, military, multicultural, mystery, New Age, occult, picture books, police, psychic, regional, romance, spiritual, sports, thriller, translation, war, Westerns, women's, young adult, cartoon.

⚶ This agency specializes in all types of popular fiction and nonfiction. Does not want to receive scholarly, professional, poetry, plays or screenplays.

HOW TO CONTACT Query with SASE. Please send us a query letter of no more than 2 pages, which includes your credentials, an explanation of what makes your book unique and special, and a synopsis. (If submitting to Steven Malk: Writers House, 7660 Fay Ave., #338H, La Jolla CA 92037) Responds in 6-8 weeks to queries. Obtains most new clients through recommendations from authors and editors.

TERMS Agent receives 15% commission on domestic sales. Agent receives 20% commission on foreign sales. Offers written contract, binding for 1 year. Agency charges fees for copying mss/proposals and overseas airmail of books.

TIPS "Do not send manuscripts. Write a compelling letter. If you do, we'll ask to see your work. Follow submission guidelines and please do not simultaneously submit your work to more than one Writer's House agent."

⬤ WRITERS' REPRESENTATIVES, LLC

116 W. 14th St., 11th Floor, New York NY 10011-7305. Fax: (212)620-0023. E-mail: transom@writersreps.com. Website: www.writersreps.com. Represents 130 clients. 10% of clients are new/unpublished writers. Currently handles: nonfiction books 90%, novels 10%.

• Prior to becoming an agent, Ms. Chu was a lawyer; Mr. Hartley worked at Simon & Schuster, Harper & Row and Cornell University Press.

MEMBER AGENTS Lynn Chu; Glen Hartley; Christine Hsu.

REPRESENTS nonfiction books, novels. **Considers these fiction areas:** literary.

8—¬ Serious nonfiction and quality fiction. No motion picture or television screenplays.

HOW TO CONTACT Query with SASE. Prefers to read materials exclusively. Considers simultaneous queries, but must be informed at time of submission.

TERMS Agent receives 15% commission on domestic sales. Agent receives 20% commission on foreign sales.

TIPS "Always include a SASE; it will ensure a response from the agent and the return of your submitted material."

⊘ THE WYLIE AGENCY

250 West 57th St., Suite 2114, New York NY 10107. (212)246-0069. Fax: (212)586-8953. E-mail: mail@wylieagency.com. Website: www.wylieagency.com. Ovreseas address: 17 Bedford Square, London WC1B 3JA, United Kingdom; mail@wylieagency.co.uk.

MEMBER AGENTS Andrew Wylie, Sarah Chalfant; Scott Moyers.

REPRESENTS nonfiction books, novels.

8—¬ High-profile and prolific authors. This agency is not currently accepting unsolicited submissions, so do not query unless you are asked.

HOW TO CONTACT This agency does not currently take unsolicited queries/proposals.

⊘ YATES & YATES

1100 Town & Country Rd., Suite 1300, Orange CA 92868. E-mail: e-mail@yates2.com. Website: www.yates2.com. Represents 60 clients.

REPRESENTS nonfiction books. **Considers these nonfiction areas:** autobiography, biography, business, current affairs, memoirs, politics, sports, religious.

RECENT SALES *No More Mondays*, by Dan Miller (Doubleday Currency).

● ZACHARY SHUSTER HARMSWORTH

1776 Broadway, Suite 1405, New York NY 10019. (212)765-6900. Fax: (212)765-6490. E-mail: kfleury@zshliterary.com. Website: www.zshliterary.com. **Contact:** Kathleen Fleury. Alternate address: 535 Boylston St., 11th Floor, Boston MA 02116. (617)262-2400. Fax: (617)262-2468. Represents 125 clients. 20% of clients are new/unpublished writers. Currently handles: nonfiction books 45%, novels 45%, story collections 5%, scholarly books 5%.

• "Our principals include two former publishing and entertainment lawyers, a journalist and an editor/agent. Lane Zachary was an editor at Random House before becoming an agent."

MEMBER AGENTS Esmond Harmsworth (commercial mysteries, literary fiction, history, science, adventure, business); Todd Shuster (narrative and prescriptive nonfiction, biography, memoirs); Lane Zachary (biography, memoirs, literary fiction); Jennifer Gates (literary fiction, nonfiction); Colleen Rafferty; Janet Silver; Mary Beth Chappell; Joanne Wyckoff. You can e-mail any agent on the website online form.

REPRESENTS nonfiction books, novels. **Considers these nonfiction areas:** animals, autobiography, biography, business, current affairs, economics, gay/lesbian, government, health, history, how-to, investigative, language, law, literature, memoirs, money, music, politics, psychology, science, self-help, sports, technology, true crime, women's issues, women's studies. **Considers these fiction areas:** detective, ethnic, feminist, gay, historical, lesbian, literary, mainstream, mystery, suspense, thriller.

8—¬ Check the website for updated info.

HOW TO CONTACT Cannot accept unsolicited submissions. Query with SASE. Obtains most new clients through recommendations from others.

TERMS Agent receives 15% commission on domestic sales. Agent receives 20% commission on foreign sales. Offers written contract, binding for 1 work only; 30-day notice must be given to terminate contract.

● KAREN GANTZ ZAHLER LITERARY MANAGEMENT AND ATTORNEY AT LAW

860 Fifth Ave., Suite 7J, New York NY 10065. (212)734-3619. E-mail: karen@karengantzlit.com. Website: www.karengantzlit.com. **Contact:** Karen Gantz Zahler. Currently handles: nonfiction books 95%, novels 5%, film/TV scripts.

• Prior to her current position, Ms. Gantz Zahler practiced law at two law firms, wrote two cookbooks, *Taste of New York* (Addison-Wesley) and *Superchefs* (John Wiley & Sons). She also participated in a Presidential Advisory Committee on Intellectual Property, U.S. Department of Commerce. She currently chairs Literary and Media Committee at Harmone Club NYC.

REPRESENTS nonfiction books, novels, very selective. "We are hired for two purposes: one as lawyers to negotiate publishing agreements, option agreements and other entertainment deals, and two as literary agents to help in all aspects of the publishing field. Ms. Gantz is both a literary agent and a literary property lawyer. Thus, her firm involves themselves in all stages of a book's development, including the collaboration agreement with the writer, advice regarding the book proposal, presentations to the publisher, negotiations including the legal work for the publishing agreement and other rights to be negotiated, and work with the publisher and public relations firm so that the book gets the best possible media coverage. We do extensive manuscript reviews for a few." Actively seeking nonfiction. "We assist with speaking engagements and publicity."

HOW TO CONTACT Accepting queries and summaries by e-mail only. Check the website for complete submission information. Responds in 4 weeks to queries. Obtains most new clients through recommendations from others, solicitations.

RECENT SALES *A Promise to Ourselves,* by Alec Baldwin (St. Martin's Press 2008); *Take the Lead, Lady! Kathleen Turner's Life Lessons,* by Kathleen Turner in collaboration with Gloria Feldt (Springboard Press 2007); *Tales of a Neo-Con,* by Benjamin Wattenberg (Tom Dunne 2008); *Beyond Control,* by Nancy Friday (Sourcebooks 2009); more sales can be found online.

TIPS "Our dream client is someone who is a professional writer and a great listener. What writers can do to increase the likelihood of our retainer is to write an excellent summary and provide a great marketing plan for their proposal in an excellent presentation. Any typos or grammatical mistakes do not resonate well. If we want to review your project, we will ask you to send a copy by snail mail with an envelope and return postage enclosed. We don't call people unless we have something to report."

❶ HELEN ZIMMERMANN LITERARY AGENCY

3 Emmy Lane, New Paltz NY 12561. (845)256-0977. Fax: (845)256-0979. E-mail: Helen@ZimmAgency.com. Website: www.zimmermannliterary.com. **Contact:** Helen Zimmermann. Estab. 2003. Represents 25 clients. 50% of clients are new/unpublished writers. Currently handles: nonfiction books 80%, fiction 20%.

- Prior to opening her agency, Ms. Zimmermann was the director of advertising and promotion at Random House and the events coordinator at an independent bookstore.

REPRESENTS nonfiction books, novels. **Considers these nonfiction areas:** animals, child guidance, diet/nutrition, how-to, humor, memoirs, popular culture, sports. **Considers these fiction areas:** family saga, historical, literary, mystery, suspense. "As an agent who has experience at both a publishing house and a bookstore, I have a keen insight for viable projects. This experience also helps me ensure every client gets published well, through the whole process." Actively seeking memoirs, pop culture, women's issues and accessible literary fiction. Does not want to receive horror, science fiction, poetry or romance.

HOW TO CONTACT Accepts e-mail queries only. E-mail should include a short description of project and bio, whether it be fiction or nonfiction. Accepts simultaneous submissions. Responds in 2 weeks to queries. Responds in 1 month to mss. Obtains most new clients through recommendations from others, solicitations.

TERMS Agent receives 15% commission on domestic sales. Offers written contract; 30-day notice must be given to terminate contract. Charges for photocopying and postage (reimbursed if project is sold).

RECENT SALES *She Bets Her Life: Women and Gambling,* by Mary Sojourner (Seal Press); *Seeds: One Man's Quest to Preserve the Trees of America's Most Famous People,* by Rick Horan (HarperCollins); *Saddled,* by Susan Richards (Houghton Mifflin Harcourt); *Final Target,* by Steven Gore (HarperPerennial); *Liberated Body, Captive Mind: A WWII POW Memoir,* by Normal Bussel (Pegasus Books).

WRITERS CONFERENCES BEA/Writer's Digest Books Writers' Conference, Portland, ME Writers Conference, Berkshire Writers and Readers Conference.

○ RENÈE ZUCKERBROT LITERARY AGENCY

115 West 29th St., 3rd Floor, New York NY 10001. (212)967-0072. Fax: (212)967-0073. E-mail: renee@rzagency.com. E-mail: submissions@rzagency.com. Website: rzagency.com. **Contact:** Renèe Zuckerbrot. Member of AAR. Represents 30 clients. Currently handles: nonfiction 30%, fiction 70%.

- Prior to becoming an agent, Ms. Zuckerbrot worked as an editor at Doubleday as well as in the editorial department at Putnam.

REPRESENTS nonfiction books, novels, short-story collections.

☞ Literary fiction, short-story collections, mysteries, thrillers, women's fiction, slipstream/speculative, narrative nonfiction (focusing on science, history and pop culture). No business books, self-help, spirituality or romance. No screenplays.

HOW TO CONTACT Query by mail, e-mail at: submissions@rzagency.com. Include a description of your manuscript or proposal. Include your publishing history, if applicable. Include a brief personal bio. Include a SASE or an e-mail address. Accepts simultaneous submissions. Responds in 4 weeks.

TERMS Agent receives 15% commission on domestic sales. Agent receives 25% commission on foreign sales.

RECENT SALES *Pretty Monster,* by Kelly Link (Penguin); *Manhattan Primeval,* by Eric Sanderson (Abrams); *Everything Asian,* by Sung Woo (Dunne/St. Martin's); *The Dart League King,* by Keith Lee Morris (Tin House); *Pleasure Bound: Victorian Sex Rebels and the New Eroticism* by Deborah Lutz (W.W. Norton)]; *Clinton St. Baking Company Cookbook: Breakfast, Brunch and Beyond From New York's Favorite Neighborhood Restaurant,* by DeDe Lahman & Neil Kleinberg (Little Brown).

RENÈE ZUCKERBROT LITERARY AGENCY

115 West 29th St., 3rd Floor, New York NY 10001. (212)967-0072. Fax: (212)967-0073. E-mail: renee@rzagency.com. E-mail: submissions@rzagency.com. Website: rzagency.com. **Contact:** Renèe Zuckerbrot. Represents 30 clients. Currently handles: novels, other 30& nonfiction and 70% fiction.

- Prior to becoming an agent, Ms. Zuckerbrot worked as an editor at Doubleday as well as in the editorial department at Putnam.

REPRESENTS nonfiction books, novels, short story collections.

☞ Literary and commercial adult and young adult fiction, short story collections, mysteries, thrillers, women's fiction, slipstream/speculative, narrative nonfiction (focusing on science, history and pop culture). "Looking for writers with a unique voice." No business books, self-help, spirituality or romance. No screenplays.

HOW TO CONTACT Query by e-mail: submissions@rzagency.com. Include a synopsis, publication history and a brief personal bio. Include a brief personal bio. You may include a sample chapter. Query by snail mail: Please include an SASE or an e-mail address. Responds in approximately 4 weeks.

TERMS Agent receives 15% commission on domestic sales. Agent receives 25% commission on foreign sales (10% to RZA; 15% to foreign rights co-agent).

CONFERENCES

Attending a writers' conference that includes agents gives you the opportunity to learn more about what agents do and to show an agent your work. Ideally, a conference should include a panel or two with a number of agents to give writers a sense of the variety of personalities and tastes of different agents.

Not all agents are alike: Some are more personable, and sometimes you simply click better with one agent versus another. When only one agent attends a conference, there is a tendency for every writer at that conference to think, "Ah, this is the agent I've been looking for!" When the number of agents attending is larger, you have a wider group from which to choose, and you may have less competition for the agent's time.

Besides including panels of agents discussing what representation means and how to go about securing it, many of these gatherings also include time—either scheduled or impromptu—to meet briefly with an agent to discuss your work.

If they're impressed with what they see and hear about your work, they will invite you to submit a query, a proposal, a few sample chapters, or possibly your entire manuscript. Some conferences even arrange for agents to review manuscripts in advance and schedule one-on-one sessions during which you can receive specific feedback or advice regarding your work. Such meetings often cost a small fee, but the input you receive is usually worth the price.

Ask writers who attend conferences and they'll tell you that, at the very least, you'll walk away with new knowledge about the industry. At the very best, you'll receive an invitation to send an agent your material!

Many writers try to make it to at least one conference a year, but cost and location can count as much as subject matter when determining which one to attend. There are

At the beginning of some listings, you will find one or more of the following symbols:

➕ conference new to this edition

♻ Canadian conference

🌀 International conference

Find a pull-out bookmark with a key to symbols on the inside cover of this book.

conferences in almost every state and province that can provide answers to your questions about writing and the publishing industry. Conferences also connect you with a community of other writers. Such connections help you learn about the pros and cons of different agents, and they can also give you a renewed sense of purpose and direction in your own writing.

SUBHEADS

In this section, each listing is divided into subheads to make locating specific information easier. In the first section, you'll find contact information for conference contacts. You'll also learn conference dates, specific focus, and the average number of attendees. Finally, names of agents who will be speaking or have spoken in the past are listed along with details about their availability during the conference. Calling or e-mailing a conference director to verify the names of agents in attendance is always a good idea.

COSTS: Looking at the price of events, plus room and board, may help writers on a tight budget narrow their choices.

ACCOMMODATIONS: Here, conferences list overnight accommodations and travel information. Often conferences held in hotels will reserve rooms at a discount rate and may provide a shuttle bus to and from the local airport.

ADDITIONAL INFORMATION: This section includes information on conference-sponsored contests, individual meetings, the availability of brochures, and more.

ABROAD WRITERS CONFERENCES

17363 Sutter Creek Rd., Sutter Creek CA 95685. (209)296-4050. E-mail: abroadwriters@yahoo.com. Website: www.abroad-crwf.com/index.html. "Abroad Writers' Conferences are devoted to introducing our participants to world views here in the United States and abroad. Throughout the world we invite several authors to come join us to give readings and to participate on a panel. Our discussion groups touch upon a wide range of topics from important issues of our times to publishing abroad and in the United States. Our objective is to broaden our cultural and scientific perspectives of the world through discourse and writing."

COSTS Prices start at $2,750. Discounts and upgrades may apply. Particpants must apply to program no later than 3 months before departure. To secure a place you must send in a deposit of $700. Balance must be paid in full twelve weeks before departure. See website for pricing details.

ADDITIONAL INFORMATION Agents participate in conference. Application is online at website.

ALGONKIAN FIVE-DAY NOVEL CAMP

2020 Pennsylvania Ave. NW, Suite 443, Washington DC 20006. E-mail: algonkian@webdelsol.com. Website: fwwriters.algonkianconferences.com. Conference duration: 5 days. Average attendance: 12 students maximum per workshop. "During 45+ hours of actual workshop time, students will engage in those rigorous narrative and complication/plot exercises necessary to produce a publishable manuscript. Genres we work with include general commercial fiction, literary fiction, serious and light women's fiction, mystery/cozy/thriller, SF/F, young adult, and memoir/narrative nonfiction. The three areas of workshop emphasis will be premise, platform, and execution.

COSTS $865.

ACCOMMODATIONS Offers overnight accommodations. Price includes tuition, private cottage room for five nights, breakfast and lunch. Transportation to and from the conference and dinner are not included.

ADDITIONAL INFORMATION For brochure, visit website. "The Algonkian Park is located 30 miles from Washington, D.C. A good map and directions can be found here. It is 12 miles from Dulles International Airport (the perfect place to fly into—cab fares from Dulles to Algonkian are about $25). The

cottages are fully furnished with TV, phones, linens, dishes, central air and heat. All cottages feature fireplaces, decks with grills, equipped kitchens, cathedral ceilings, and expansive riverside views of the Potomac. Participants each have their own room in the cottage. The address of the Algonkian Park Management headquarters is 47001 Fairway Drive, Sterling, Virginia, and their phone number is 703-450-4655. If you have any questions about the cottages or facilities, ask for Lawan, the manager."

AMERICAN CHRISTIAN WRITERS CONFERENCES

P.O. Box 110390, Nashville TN 37222-0390. (800)219-7483. Fax: (615)834-7736. E-mail: acwriters@aol.com. Website: www.acwriters.com. **Contact:** Reg Forder, director. Estab. 1981. Conference duration: 2 days. Average attendance: 60. Annual conferences promoting all forms of Christian writing (fiction, nonfiction, scriptwriting). Conferences are held throughout the year in 36 U.S. cities. ACW hosts dozens of annual one-, two-, and three-day writers conferences across America taught by editors and professional freelance writers. These conferences provide excellent instruction, networking opportunities, and valuable one-on-one time with editors. For schedule, click on city name for an online brochure.

COSTS $150 for one day, $250 for two days, plus meals and accommodations.

ACCOMMODATIONS Special rates are available at the host hotel (usually a major chain like Holiday Inn).

ADDITIONAL INFORMATION Send a SASE for conference brochures/guidelines.

AMERICAN INDEPENDENT WRITERS (AIW) AMERICAN WRITERS CONFERENCE

1001 Connecticut Ave. NW, Ste. 701, Washington DC 20036. (202) 775-5150. Fax: (202) 775-5810. E-mail: info@amerindywriters.org. E-mail: donald@amerindywriters.org. Website: www.amerindywriters.org. **Contact:** Donald O. Graul Jr., Executive Director. Estab. 1975. Annual conference held in June. Conference duration: Saturday. Average attendance: 350. "Gives participants a chance to hear from and talk with dozens of experts on book and magazine publishing as well as meet one-on-one with literary agents." Site: George Washington University Conference Center. Past keynote speakers included Erica Jong, Diana Rehm, Kitty Kelley, Lawrence Block, John Barth, Stephen Hunter, Francine Prose.

AMERICAN INDEPENDENT WRITERS (AIW) SPRING WRITERS CONFERENCE

1001 Connecticut Ave. NW, Suite 701, Washington DC 20036. (202)775-5150. Fax: (202)775-5810. E-mail: info@amerindywriters.org; donald@amerindywriters.org. Website: www.amerindywriters.org. **Contact:** Donald O. Graul, Jr. Estab. 1975. Annual conference held in June. Average attendance: 350. Focuses on fiction, nonfiction, screenwriting, poetry, children's writing, and technical writing. Gives participants the chance to hear from and talk with dozens of experts on book and magazine publishing, as well as on the craft, tools, and business of writing. Speakers have included Erica Jong, John Barth, Kitty Kelley, Vanessa Leggett, Diana McLellan, Brian Lamb, and Stephen Hunter. New York and local agents attend the conference.

ADDITIONAL INFORMATION See the website or send a SASE in mid-February for brochures/guidelines and fees information.

ART WORKSHOPS IN GUATEMALA

4758 Lyndale Ave. S, Minneapolis MN 55419-5304. (612)825-0747. E-mail: info@artguat.org. Website: www.artguat.org. **Contact:** Liza Fourre, director. Estab. 1995.

COSTS See website; includes tuition, lodging, breakfast, ground transportation.

ACCOMMODATIONS All transportation and accommodations included in price of conference.

ADDITIONAL INFORMATION Conference information available now. For brochure/guidelines visit website, e-mail, fax or call. Accepts inquiries by e-mail, phone.

ASJA WRITERS CONFERENCE

American Society of Journalists and Authors, 1501 Broadway, Suite 403, New York NY 10036. (212)997-0947. Fax: (212)937-2315. E-mail: asjaoffice@asja.org; director@asja.org. Website: www.asja.org/wc. **Contact:** Alexandra Owens, exec. director. Estab. 1971. Annual conference held in April. Conference duration: 3 days. Average attendance: 600. Covers nonfiction. Held at the Roosevelt in New York. Speakers have included Arianna Huffington, Kitty Kelley, Barbara Ehrenreich, Stefan Fatsis.

COSTS $200+, depending on when you sign up (includes lunch). Check website for updates.

ACCOMMODATIONS The hotel holding our conference always blocks out discounted rooms for attendees.

ADDITIONAL INFORMATION Brochures available in February. Registration form is on the website. Inquire by e-mail or fax. Sign up for conference updates on website.

ASPEN SUMMER WORDS LITERARY FESTIVAL & WRITING RETREAT

Aspen Writers' Foundation, 110 E. Hallam St., #116, Aspen CO 81611. (970)925-3122. Fax: (970)925-5700. E-mail: info@aspenwriters.org. Website: www.aspenwriters.org. Estab. 1976. Annual conference held the fourth week of June. Conference duration: 5 days. Average attendance: 150 at writing retreat; 300+ at literary festival. Retreat for fiction, creative nonfiction, poetry, magazine writing, food writing, and literature. Festival includes author readings, craft talks, panel discussions with publishing industry insiders, professional consultations with editors and agents, and social gatherings. Retreat faculty members in 2007: Andrea Barzi, Katherine Fausset, Anjali Singh, Lisa Grubka, Amber Qureshi, Joshua Kendall, Keith Flynn, Robert Bausch, Amy Bloom, Percival Everett, Danzy Senna, Bharti Kirchner, Gary Ferguson, Dorianne Laux. Festival presenters include (in 2007): Ngugi Wa Thiong'o, Wole Soyinka, Chimamanda Ngozi Adichie, Alaa Al Aswany, Henry Louis Gates, Jr., Leila Aboulela, and many more!

COSTS Check website each year for updates.

ACCOMMODATIONS Discount lodging at the conference site will be available. Future rates to be announced. Free shuttle around town.

ADDITIONAL INFORMATION Workshops admission deadline is April 15. Manuscripts for juried workshops must be submitted by April 15 for review and selection. 10-page limit for workshop application manuscript. A limited number of partial-tuition scholarships are available. Deadline for agent/editor meeting registration is May 27th. Brochures available for SASE, by e-mail and phone request, and on website.

ASSOCIATED WRITING PROGRAMS ANNUAL CONFERENCE

Mail Stop 1E3, George Mason University, Fairfax VA 22030-4444. (703)993-4301. Fax: (703)993-4302. E-mail: conference@awpwriter.org. Website: www.awpwriter.org. Estab. 1992. Annual conference held between February and April. Average attendance: More than 8,000. The conference focuses on fiction, poetry, and creative writing and features 350 presentations—including readings, lectures, panel discussions and forums—plus hundreds of book signings, receptions, dances, and informal gatherings.

ACCOMMODATIONS Upcoming conferences include Washington D.C. (February 2011) and Chicago (February- March 2012).

AUSTIN FILM FESTIVAL & CONFERENCE

1801 Salina St., Suite 210, Austin TX 78702. (512)478-4795; (800)310-FEST. Fax: (512)478-6205. Website: www.austinfilmfestival.com. **Contact:** Maya Perez, conference director. Estab. 1994. Annual conference held in October (Oct. 20-23, 201—Early discount registration available through May 31, 2011; Oct. 18-25, 2012). Conference duration: 4 days. Average attendance: 2,200. This festival is the first organization of its kind to focus on writers' unique creative contribution to the film and television industries. The conference takes place during the first four days of the festival. The event presents more than 75 panels, round tables and workshops that address various aspects of screenwriting and filmmaking. The Austin Film Festival is held in downtown Austin at the Driskill and Stephen F. Austin hotels. The AFF boasts a number of events and services for emerging and professional writers and filmmakers. Past participants include Robert Altman, Wes Anderson, James L. Brooks, Joel & Ethan Coen, Russell Crowe, Barry Levinson, Darren Star, Robert Duvall, Buck Henry, Dennis Hopper, Lawrence Kasdan, John Landis, Garry Shandling, Bryan Singer, Oliver Stone, Sandra Bullock, Harold Ramis, Danny Boyle, Judd Apatow, Horton Foote, and Owen Wilson.

COSTS Approximately $300 for early bird entries (includes entrance to all panels, workshops, and round-tables during the 4-day conference, as well as all films during the 8-night film exhibitions and the opening and closing night parties). Go online for other offers.

ACCOMMODATIONS Discounted rates on hotel accommodations are available to attendees if the reservations are made through the Austin Film Festival office.

ADDITIONAL INFORMATION The Austin Film Festival furthers the art and craft of filmmaking by inspiring and championing the work of screenwriters, filmmakers, and all artists who use the language of film to tell a story. The Austin Film Festival is considered one of the most accessible festivals, and Austin is the premier town for networking because when industry people are here, they are relaxed and friendly. The Austin Film Festival holds annual screenplay/teleplay and film competitions, as well as a Young Filmmakers Program. Check online for competition details and festival information. Inquire via e-mail or fax.

AUSTRALIAN POETRY FESTIVAL

Poets Union and the Australian Poetry Centre, P.O. Box 755, Potts Point NSW 1335 Australia. (61)(2)9357 6602. Fax: (61)(2)9818-5377. E-mail: info@poetsunion.com; martinlangford@bigpond.com. Website: www.poetsunion.com. Estab. 1998. "The Australian Poetry Festival is a joint festival to be hosted by the Poets Union and the Australian Poetry Centre on September 3, 4 and 5, 2010, in Sydney, and in other locations." This is biennial. Check website for 2012 information later in the year.

AWP ANNUAL CONFERENCE AND BOOKFAIR

MS 1E3, George Mason Univ., Fairfax VA 22030. (703)993-4317. E-mail: conference@awpwriter.org. Website: www.awpwriter.org/conference. www.facebook.com/awpwriter **Contact:** Anne Le, conference coordinator. Estab. 1967.

COSTS Early registration fees: $40 student; $140 AWP member; $160 non-member.

ACCOMMODATIONS Provide airline discounts and rental-car discounts. Special rate at Hilton Chicago & Palmer House Hilton Hotels.

ADDITIONAL INFORMATION 2012 AWP Annual Conference & Bookfair, Chicago, IL. February 29-March 3, 2012. MS 1E3, George Mason University, Fairfax VA 22030. Annual. Conference duration: 4 days. AWP holds its Annual Conference in a different region of North America in order to celebrate the outstanding authors, teachers, writing programs, literary centers, and small press publishers of that region. The annual conference typically features 350 presentations: readings, lectures, panel discussions and forums—plus hundreds of book signings, receptions, dances, and informal gatherings. The conference attracts more than 8,000 attendees and more than 500 publishers. All genres are represented. "We will offer 175 panels on everything from writing to teaching to critical analysis." Previously, Art Spiegelman was the keynote speaker. Others readers were Charles Baxter, Isaiah Sheffer, Z.Z. Packer, Nareem Murr, Marilynne Robinson; 2008: John Irving, Joyce Carol Oates, among others.

BACKSPACE AGENT-AUTHOR SEMINAR

P.O. Box 454, Washington MI 48094-0454. (732)267-6449. Fax: (586)532-9652. E-mail: chrisg@bksp.org. Website: www.bksp.org. Estab. 2006. 2010 conference is over and was a success. Main conference duration: 1 day. Average attendance: 100. Annual seminar held in November. Panels and workshops designed to educate and assist authors in search of a literary agent to represent their work. Only agents will be in program. Past speakers have included Scott Hoffman, Dan Lazar, Scott Miller, Michael Bourret, Katherine Fausset, Jennifer DeChiara, Sharlene Martin and Paul Cirone.

COSTS All 3 days (May 26–28; includes Agent-Author Seminar, Conference Program, Book Signing & Cocktail Reception, Donald Maass workshop) $700. **Backspace Members Receive a $120 discount on a 3-day registration! First 2 days** (May 26-27; includes Agent-Author Seminar, Conference Program, Book Signing & Cocktail Reception) $550. **Day, 1 only** (May 26; Agent-Author Seminar, small-group workshops and agent panels) $325. **Day 2 only** (May 27; Conference Program, Book Signing & Cocktail Reception) $250. **Day 3 only** (May 28; Donald Maass workshop) $150. Tickets for the Friday evening cocktail reception may be purchased for $85; each one reception ticket is included with the 3-day, 2-day and Friday only (May 27) registrations. **EXTRA EVENING WORKSHOP!** Jeff Kleinman from Folio Literary Management, assisted by Andrea Walker, Vice President and Editorial Director of Reagan Arthur Books, an imprint of Little, Brown, will hold his always-popular Buy This Book! role-playing workshop from 7–9 p.m. on Thursday, May 26. **Cost for the 2-hour workshop is $45** .

ADDITIONAL INFORMATION The Backspace Agent-Author Seminar offers plenty of face time with attending agents. This casual, no-pressure seminar is a terrific opportunity to network, ask questions, talk about your work informally and listen from the people who make their lives selling books.

⊕ BACKSPACE WRITERS CONFERENCE & AGENT AUTHOR SEMINAR

P.O. Box 454, Washington MI 48094. (732)267-6449. E-mail: karendionne@bksp.org. Website: www.backspacewritersconference.com. **Contact:** Christopher Graham or Karen Dionne, co-founders.

COSTS $200-700; offers member, group, and student discounts along with additional workshops that are priced separately.

ACCOMMODATIONS "We offer a special conference rate at the Radisson Martinique for conference attendees. Average price of $199-279/night, must be booked 30 days in advance." The Radisson Martinique in Manhattan NY is located in Mid-town Manhattan, just a few blocks from Madison Square Garden/NY Penn Station.

ADDITIONAL INFORMATION 2011 dates: May 31-June 2. Dates for the November 2011 Agent-Author Seminar: Nov. 3rd and 4th. Conference duration: 3 days. Average attendance: 150-200. "We focus on all genres, from nonfiction to literary fiction and everything in between, covering all popular genres from mysteries, and thrillers to young adult and romance. Formal pitch sessions are a staple at most writers' conferences. However, in planning our Backspace events, we discovered that agents hate conducting pitch sessions almost as much as authors dread doing them. In fact, many of the agents we've talked to are happy to sit on a panel or conduct a workshop, but decline to participate in formal pitch sessions. The goal of the Backspace Agent-Author Seminars is to help authors connect with agents—lots of agents—thereby giving authors the opportunity to ask questions specific to their interests and concerns. We facilitate this through small group workshops of usually no more than 10 writers and 2 agents. Workshops concentrate on query letters and opening pages. That's why we've built so much free time into the program. The full 15 minutes between panels also allows plenty of opportunity for seminar registrants to talk to agents. Many of the agents will also be available during the noon hour. Remember, agents attend conferences because they want to help authors. They're looking for new talent, and welcome the chance to hear about your work. Instead of a tense, angst-filled pitch session where it's difficult for all but the most confident authors to put their best foot forward, an interesting, relaxed, enjoyable conversation leaves a much more positive impression. And even if authors don't get the chance to mention their project, the pleasant conversation gives the author a point of reference when sending a formal query letter to the agent's office after the seminar is over." 2011 agents in attendance: Jeff Kleinman, Donald Maass, Sharlene Martin, Lois Winston, Jennifer De Chiara, Rebecca Strauss, Kristin Nelson, Kathleen Ortiz, Scott Hoffman, Rachel Vogel, Meredith Barnes,

Roseanne Wells, Suzie Townsend, Tamar Rydzinski, April Eberhardt, Diana Fox. Editors: Rachel Griffiths (Scholastic), Brenda Copeland (St. Martin's). See website for more information. Brochures available in January. Accepts inquiries by e-mail and phone. Agents and editors attend conference."

BALTIMORE WRITERS' CONFERENCE

PRWR Program, Linthicum Hall 218K, Towson University, 8000 York Rd., Towson MD 21252. (410)704-5196. E-mail: prwr@towson.edu. Website: www.towson.edu/writersconference. Estab. 1994. "Annual conference held in November at Towson University. Conference duration: 1 day. Average attendance: 150-200. Covers all areas of writing and getting published. Held at Towson University. Session topics include fiction, nonfiction, poetry, magazine and journals, agents and publishers. Sign up the day of the conference for quick critiques to improve your stories, essays, and poems."

COSTS $75-95 (includes all-day conference, lunch and reception). Student special rate of $35 before mid-October, $50 thereafter.

ACCOMMODATIONS Hotels are close by, if required.

ADDITIONAL INFORMATION Writers may register through the BWA website. Send inquiries via e-mail.

BIG SUR WRITING WORKSHOPS

Henry Miller Library, Highway One, Big Sur CA 93920. Phone/Fax: (831)667-2574. E-mail: magnus@henrymiller.org. Website: www.henrymiller.org/CWW. Annual workshops are held the first weekend of December and the first weekend of March every year for children's/young adult writing and in March for adult fiction and nonfiction.

ACCOMMODATIONS See location online at website. It has changed.

○ BLOODY WORDS

64 Shaver Ave., Toronto ON M9B 3T5 Canada. E-mail: registration@bloodywords2011.com; carosoles@rogers.com; cheryl@freedmanandsister.com; amummenhoff@rogers.com; info@bloodywords.com. Website: www.bloodywords.com. **Contact:** Caro Soles. Estab. 1999. Annual conference usually held in June. 2011 dates: June 3-5. Conference duration: 3 days.

COSTS $175. Includes banquet.

ACCOMMODATIONS A special rate will be available at The Hotel Grand Pacific *downtown Victoria*

on the inner harbour.

ADDITIONAL INFORMATION Registration is available online. Send inquiries via e-mail. Guest of Honour ~ Michael Slade; International Guest of Honour ~ Tess Gerritsen; Local Guest of Honour ~ William Deverell. Suggested Topics: Crime Writers of Canada Pre-Conference Workshop, VIB W Social-Business Networking: How to Schmooze like a Pro; What Makes For Good Writing? Cozy Chicks & Hard-Boiled Dicks; Inside a Murderer's Mind; Cold Cases: Researching Historical Mysteries; Points of View: Speaking from the Margins; Where Life Meets Art; Short and Twisted; Michael Slade's Shock Theatre; Michael Slades Ghost Walk.

○ BLOODY WORDS MYSTERY CONFERENCE

12 Roundwood Court, Toronto ON M1W 1Z2 Canada. Phone/fax: (416)497-5293. E-mail: soles@sff.net. Website: www.bloodywords.com. Estab. 1999.

COSTS $175 Canadian (includes the banquet and all panels, readings, dealers' room and workshop).

ACCOMMODATIONS Offers block of rooms in hotel; list of optional lodging available. Check website for details.

ADDITIONAL INFORMATION Sponsors short mystery story contest—5,000 word limit; judges are experienced editors of anthologies; fee is $5 (entrants must be registered). Conference information is available now. For brochure visit website. Accepts inquiries by e-mail and phone. Agents and editors participate in conference. "This is a conference for both readers and writers of mysteries, the only one of its kind in Canada. We also run 'The Mystery Cafe,' a chance to get to know a dozen or so authors, hear them read and ask questions (half hour each)."

● BLUE RIDGE "AUTUMN IN THE MOUNTAINS" NOVEL RETREAT

(800)588-7222. E-mail: ylehman@bellsouth.net. Website: www.lifeway.com/novelretreat. **Contact:** Yvonne Lehman, director. Estab. 2007. Annual retreat held in October at Ridgecrest/LifeWay Conference Center near Asheville NC. Retreat duration: Sunday through lunch on Thursday. Average attendance: 55. All areas of novel writing is included. For beginning and advanced novelists. Site: LifeWay/Ridgecrest Conference Center, 20 miles east of Asheville, NC. Faculty: Dr. Dennis Hensley, Dr. Angela Hunt, Ray Blackston, Jeff Gerke, Deborah Raney, Ann Tatlock, Yvonne

Lehman. No editors or agents. Mornings: large group class. Afternoons: writing time and workshops. Evening: discussion and faculty panel.

COSTS Retreat Tuition: $315; Room: $69-89; Meals: $124.

ACCOMMODATIONS Mountain Laurel Hotel on campus.

BLUE RIDGE "SUMMER IN THE MOUNTAINS" NOVEL RETREAT

(800)588-7222. E-mail: ylehman@bellsouth.net. Website: www.gideonfilmfestival.com. **Contact:** Yvonne Lehman, Director. Held along with the Gideon Media Arts Conference August 6-11, 2011. For beginning and advanced novelists. Faculty: Andrea Boeshaar, Lynette Eason, Eva Marie Everson, Jeff Gerke, Rene Gutteridge, Dr. Dennis Hensley, Yvonne Lehman, Deborah Raney, Rebeca Seitz, Ann Tatlock.

COSTS Tuition $315, Room $69-89, Meals $159.

BLUE RIDGE MOUNTAIN CHRISTIAN WRITERS CONFERENCE

E-mail: ylehman@bellsouth.net. Website: www.lifeway.com/christianwriters. Annual conference held in May (May 9-13, 2011). Conference duration: Sunday through lunch on Thursday. Average attendance: 400. A training and networking event for both seasoned and aspiring writers that allows attendees to interact with editors, agents, professional writers, and readers. Workshops and continuing classes in a variety of creative categories are also offered.

COSTS $375 (includes sessions and a banquet). See website for next year's costs.

ACCOMMODATIONS $54-84, depending on room size, at the LifeWay Ridgecrest Conference Center near Asheville, North Carolina.

ADDITIONAL INFORMATION The event also features a contest for unpublished writers and ms critiques prior to the conference.

✪ BOOMING GROUND ONLINE WRITERS STUDIO

Buch E-462, 1866 Main Mall, UBC, Vancouver BC V6T 1Z1 Canada. Fax: (604)648-8848. E-mail: contact@boomingground.com. Website: www.boomingground.com. **Contact:** Jordan Hall, director.

BREAD LOAF WRITERS' CONFERENCE

Middlebury College, Middlebury VT 05753. (802)443-5286. Fax: (802)443-2087. E-mail: ncargill@middle bury.edu. Website: www.middlebury.edu/blwc. Estab. 1926. Annual conference held in late August. Conference duration: 11 days. Offers workshops for fiction, nonfiction, and poetry. Agents, editors, publicists, and grant specialists will be in attendance.

COSTS $2,345 (includes tuition, housing).

ACCOMMODATIONS Bread Loaf Campus in Ripton, Vermont.

ADDITIONAL INFORMATION 2011 Conference Dates: August 10-20. Location: mountain campus of Middlebury College. Average attendance: 230.

CALIFORNIA CRIME WRITERS CONFERENCE

cosponsored by Sisters in Crime/Los Angeles and the Southern California Chapter of Mystery Writers of America. No public address available. E-mail: sistersincrimela@gmail.com. Website: www.ccwconference.org. Estab. 1995. Annual. Conference held June 11-12, 2011; following years TBO. Average attendance: 200. Two-day conference on mystery and crime writing. Offers craft, forensic and career-building sessions, two keynote speakers, author and agent panels and book signings. Breakfast and lunch both days included.

ADDITIONAL INFORMATION Conference information is available on the website.

CLARION WEST WRITERS WORKSHOP

P.O. Box 31264, Seattle WA 98103-1264. (206)322-9083. E-mail: info@clarionwest.org. Website: www.clarionwest.org. Contact us through our webform. **Contact:** Leslie Howle, Workshop Director. Clarion West is an intensive 6-week workshop for writers preparing for professional careers in science fiction and fantasy, held annually in Seattle, Wash. Usually goes from mid-June through end of July. Conference duration: 6 weeks. Average attendance: 18. Held near the University of Washington. Deadline for applications is March 1. Instructors are well-known writers and editors in the field.

COSTS $3200 (for tuition, housing, most meals). Limited scholarships are available based on financial need.

ACCOMMODATIONS Workshop tuition, dormitory housing and most meals: $3,200. Students stay onsite in workshop housing at one of the University of Washington's sorority houses. "Students write their own stories every week while preparing critiques of all the other students' work for classroom sessions. This gives participants a more focused, professional approach to their writing. The core of the workshop remains speculative fiction, and short stories (not novels) are the focus." Conference information available in Fall. For brochure/guidelines send SASE, visit website, e-mail or call. Accepts inquiries by e-mail, phone, SASE. Limited scholarships are available, based on financial need. Students must submit 20-30 pages of ms with 4-page biography and $40 fee ($30 if received prior to Feb. 10) for applications sent by mail or e-mail to qualify for admission.

ADDITIONAL INFORMATION This is a critique-based workshop. Students are encouraged to write a story every week; the critique of student material produced at the workshop forms the principal activity of the workshop. Students and instructors critique mss as a group. Conference guidelines are available for a SASE. Visit the website for updates and complete details.

⊕ COD WRITERS' CONFERENCE

P.O. Box 408, Osterville MA 02655. E-mail: writers@capecodwriterscenter.org. Website: www.capecodwriterscenter.org. **Contact:** Nancy Rubin Stuart, Artistic Director. Duration: Third week in August, 5 days. Offers workshops in fiction, commercial fiction, nonfiction, poetry, screen writing, digital communications, getting published, manuscript evaluation, mentoring sessions with faculty. Held at the Craigville Conference Center in a Cape Cod village overlooking Nantucket Sound.

COSTS Vary, average for one 5-day class and registration: $200.

CRESTED BUTTE WRITERS CONFERENCE

P.O. Box 1361, Crested Butte CO 81224. Website: www.crestedbuttewriters.org/conf.php. **Contact:** Barbara Crawford or Theresa Rizzo, co-coordinators. Estab. 2006.

COSTS $330 Nonmembers, $300 members, $297 Early Bird, The Sandy Writing Contest Finalist $280, and groups of 5 or more $280.

ACCOMMODATIONS The conference is held at the scenic Elevation Hotel, located at the Crested Butte Mountain Resort at the base of the ski mountain (Mt. Crested Butte, CO). The quaint historic town lies nestled in a stunning mountain valley 3 short miles from the resort area of Mt. Crested Butte. A free bus runs frequently between the two towns. The closest airport is 10 miles away, in Gunnison CO. Our website lists 3 lodging options besides rooms at the Event Facility. All condos, motels and hotel options offer special conference rates. No special travel arrangements are made through the conference; however, information for car rental from Gunnison airport or the Alpine Express shuttle is listed on the conference FAQ page.

ADDITIONAL INFORMATION Our conference workshops address a wide variety of writing craft and business. Our most popular workshop is Our First Pages Readings—with a twist. Agents and editors read opening pages volunteered by attendees-with a few best selling authors' openings mixed in. Think the A/E can identify the bestsellers? Not so much. Each year one of our attendees has been mistaken for a best seller and obviously garnered requests from some on the panel. Agents attending: Stephen Barr—Writers House; Marisa Corvisiero—L. Perkins Agency; and Helen Breitwieser—Cornerstone Literary. The agents will be speaking. and available for meetings with attendees through our Pitch and Pages system. Editors attending: Holly Blanck—St. Martin's Press and Mike Braff-Del Rey/Spectra. Award-winning Authors: Robin D. Owens, Sophie Littlefield, Juliet Blackwell and Kaki Warner. Writers may request additional information by e-mail.

DINGLE WRITING COURSES

Ballintlea, Ventry Co Kerry Ireland. Phone/Fax: (353)(66)915-9815. E-mail: info@dinglewritingcourses.ie. Website: www.dinglewritingcourses.ie. Estab. 1996. Workshops held in September and October. Average attendance: 14. Creative writing weekends for fiction, poetry, memoir, novel, starting to write, etc. Our courses take place over a weekend in a purpose-built residential centre at Inch on the Dingle peninsula. They are designed to meet the needs of everyone with an interest in writing. All our tutors are well-known writers, with experience tutoring at all levels. See courses and tutors online at website.

COSTS 420–445 euros. Some bursaries are available from county arts officers.

ACCOMMODATIONS Provides overnight accommodations.

ADDITIONAL INFORMATION Some workshops require material to be submitted in advance. Accepts inquiries by e-mail, phone, and fax.

EAST TEXAS CHRISTIAN WRITERS CONFERENCE

The School of Humanities, Dr. Jerry L. Summers, Dean, Scarborough Hall, East Texas Baptist Univ., 1209 N. Grove, Marshall TX 75670. (903)923-2269. E-mail: jhopkins@etbu.edu; contest@etbu.edu. Website: www.etbu.edu/News/CWC. Estab. 2002. Annual conference held 2nd weekend of April. Average attendance: 125. Conference offers: contact, conversation, and exchange of ideas with other aspiring writers; outstanding presentations and workshop experiences with established authors, agents, editors, and publishers; potential publishing and writing opportunities; networking with other writers with related interests; promotion of both craft and faith; and one-on-one consultations with agents, editors, and publishers. Speakers have included Vickie Phelps, Terry Burns, Robert Darden, Bill Keith, Miriam Hees, Lenora Worth, Donn Taylor, and Mary Lou Redding. Offers an advanced track and teen track beginner, intermediate, and advanced level contest. Partial scholarships available for students only.

COSTS Visit website.

ACCOMMODATIONS Visit website for a list of local hotels offering a discounted rate.

FESTIVAL OF FAITH AND WRITING

Department of English, Calvin College, 1795 Knollcrest Circle SE, Grand Rapids MI 49546. (616)526-6770. E-mail: ffw@calvin.edu. Website: www.calvin.edu/festival. **Contact:** English Dept. Estab. 1990. Biennial festival held in April. Conference duration: 3 days. The festival brings together writers, editors, publishers, musicians, artists, and readers to discuss and celebrate insightful writing that explores issues of faith. Focuses on fiction, nonfiction, memoir, poetry, drama, children's, young adult, academic, film, and songwriting. Past speakers have included Joyce Carol Oates, Salman Rushdie, Patricia Hampl, Thomas Lynch, Leif Enger, Marilynne Robinson and Michael Chabon. Agents and editors attend the festival.

COSTS Consult festival website.

ACCOMMODATIONS Shuttles are available to and from local hotels. Shuttles are also available for overflow parking lots. A list of hotels with special rates for conference attendees is available on the festival website. High school and college students can arrange on-campus lodging by e-mail.

ADDITIONAL INFORMATION Online registration opens in October. Accepts inquiries by e-mail and phone.

FISHTRAP, INC.

400 Grant Street, P.O. Box 38, Enterprise OR 97828-0038. E-mail: director@fishtrap.org. Website: www.fishtrap.org. **Contact:** Barbara Dills, Interim Director. In 21 years, Fishtrap has hosted over 200 published poets, novelists, journalists, song writers, and nonfiction writers as teachers and presenters. Although workshops are kept small, thousands of writers, teachers, students and booklovers from around the west have participated in Fishtrap events on a first come first served basis. Writer workshops geared toward beginner, intermediate, advanced and professional levels. Open to students, scholarships available. A series of writing workshops and a writers' gathering is held each July. During the school year Fishtrap brings writers into local schools and offers workshops for teachers and writers of children's and young adult books. Other programs include writing and K-12 teaching residencies, writers' retreats, and lectures. College credit available for many workshops. See website for full program descriptions and to get on the e-mail and mail lists.

FLATHEAD RIVER WRITERS CONFERENCE

P.O. Box 7711, Kalispell MT 59904-7711. E-mail: answers@authorsoftheflathead.org. Website: www.authorsoftheflathead.org. **Contact:** Director. Estab. 1990.

ACCOMMODATIONS Rooms are available at a discounted rate.

ADDITIONAL INFORMATION Come prepared to learn from renowned speakers and enjoy this spectacular area near Glacier National Park. Confirmed presenters for Oct. 1–2, 2011: Agents Deborah Herman of The Jeff Herman Agency, Katharine Sands of the Sarah Jane Freymann Literary Agency, children's book Author Kathi Appelt, best-selling memoir Author Laura Munson. "Watch our website for additional speakers and other details. Register early as seating is limited."

THE GLEN WORKSHOP

Image, 3307 Third Avenue W., Seattle WA 98119. (206)281-2988. Fax: (206)281-2335. E-mail: glenworkshop@imagejournal.org; jmullins@imagejournal.org. Website: www.imagejournal.org/glen. Estab. 1991. Annual workshop held in August. Conference duration: 1 week. Workshop focuses on fiction, poetry, spiritual writing, playwriting, screenwriting, songwriting, and mixed media. Writing classes combine general instruction and discussion with the workshop experience, in which each individual's works are read and discussed critically. Held at St. John's College in Santa Fe, N.M. Faculty has included Scott Cairns, Jeanine Hathaway, Bret Lott, Paula Huston, Arlene Hutton, David Denny, Barry Moser, Barry Krammes, Ginger Geyer, and Pierce Pettis. The Glen Workshop combines an intensive learning experience with a lively festival of the arts. It takes place in the stark, dramatic beauty of the Sangre de Cristo mountains and within easy reach of the rich cultural, artistic, and spiritual traditions of northern New Mexico. Lodging and meals are included with registration at affordable rates. A low-cost "commuter" rate is also available for those who wish to camp, stay with friends, or otherwise find their own food and lodging.

COSTS See costs online. A limited number of partial scholarships are available.

ACCOMMODATIONS Offers dorm rooms, dorm suites, and apartments.

ADDITIONAL INFORMATION Like *Image*, the Glen is grounded in a Christian perspective, but its tone is informal and hospitable to all spiritual wayfarers. Depending on the teacher, participants may need to submit workshop material prior to arrival (usually 10-25 pages).

GOTHAM WRITERS' WORKSHOP

WritingClasses.com, 555 Eighth Ave., Suite 1402, New York NY 10018. (212)974-8377. Fax: (212)307-6325. E-mail: dana@write.org. Website: www.writingclasses. com. Estab. 1993. Online classes are held throughout the year. There are four terms of NYC classes, beginning in January, April, June/July, and September/October. Offers craft-oriented creative writing courses in general creative writing, fiction writing, screenwriting, nonfiction writing, article writing, stand-up comedy writing, humor writing, memoir writing, novel writing, children's book writing, playwriting, poetry, songwriting, mystery writing, science fiction writing, romance writing, television writing, article writing, travel writing, business writing and classes on freelancing, selling your screenplay, how to blog, nonfiction book proposal, and getting published. Also, the Workshop offers a teen program, private instruction, mentoring program, and classes on selling your work.

Classes are held at various schools in New York City as well as online at www.writingclasses.com. Agents and editors participate in some workshops.

COSTS $395/10-week workshops; $125 for the four-week online selling seminars and 1-day intensive courses; $295 for 6-week creative writing and business writing classes.

ADDITIONAL INFORMATION "Participants do not need to submit workshop material prior to their first class." Sponsors a contest for a free 10-week online creative writing course (value=$420) offered each term. Students should fill out a form online at www. writingclasses.com to participate in the contest. The winner is randomly selected. For brochure send e-mail, visit website, call or fax. Accepts inquiries by e-mail, phone, fax. Agents and editors participate in some workshops.

GREATER LEHIGH VALLEY WRITERS GROUP 'THE WRITE STUFF' WRITERS CONFERENCE

3650 Nazareth Pike, PMB #136, Bethlehem PA 18020-1115. E-mail: writestuffchair@glvwg.org. Website: www.glvwg.org/. **Contact:** Donna Brennan. Estab. 1993.

COSTS Members, $100 (includes Friday evening session and all Saturday workshops, 2 meals, and a chance to pitch to an editor or agent); non-members, $120. Late registration, $135. Pre-conference workshops require an additional fee.

ADDITIONAL INFORMATION "The Writer's Flash contest is judged by conference participants. Write 100 words or less in fiction, creative nonfiction, or poetry. Brochures available in January by SASE, or by phone, e-mail, or on website. Accepts inquiries by SASE, e-mail or phone. Agents and editors attend conference. Greater Lehigh Valley Writer's Group hosts a friendly conference has remained one of the most friendly conferences and gives you the most for your money. Breakout rooms offer craft topics, business of publishing, editor and agent panels. Book fair with book signing by published authors and presenters."

GREEN LAKE CHRISTIAN WRITERS CONFERENCE

W2511 State Road 23, Green Lake Conference Center, Green Lake WI 54941-9599. (920)294-3323. E-mail: program@glcc.org. Website: www.glcc.org. Estab. 1948. Conference duration: 1 week. Attendees may be well-published or beginners, may write for secular and/or Christian markets. Leaders are experienced writing teachers. Attendees can spend 11.5 contact hours in the workshop of their choice: fiction, nonfiction, poetry, inspirational/devotional. Seminars include specific skills: marketing, humor, songwriting, writing for children, self-publishing, writing for churches, interviewing, memoir writing, the magazine market. Evening: panels of experts will answer questions. Social and leisure activities included. GLCC is in south central WI, has 1,000 acres, 2.5 miles of shoreline on Wisconsin's deepest lake, and offers a resort setting.

ACCOMMODATIONS Hotels, lodges and all meeting rooms are a/c. Affordable rates, excellent meals.

ADDITIONAL INFORMATION Brochure and scholarship info from website or contact Jan White (920-294-7327). To register, call 920-294-3323.

GREEN MOUNTAIN WRITERS CONFERENCE

47 Hazel St., Rutland VT 05701. (802)236-6133. E-mail: ydaley@sbcglobal.net. Website: www.vermont-writers.com. Estab. 1999. "Annual conference held in the summer. Covers fiction, creative nonfiction, poetry, journalism, nature writing, essay, memoir, personal narrative, and biography. Held at an old dance pavillion on on a remote pond in Tinmouth, Vermont. Speakers have included Stephen Sandy, Grace Paley, Ruth Stone, Howard Frank Mosher, Chris Bohjalian, Joan Connor, Yvonne Daley, David Huddle, David Budbill, Jeffrey Lent, Verandah Porche, Tom Smith, and Chuck Clarino."

COSTS $500 before July 1; $525 after July 1. Partial scholarships are available.

ACCOMMODATIONS "We have made arrangements with a major hotel in nearby Rutland and 3 area bed and breakfast inns for special accommodations and rates for conference participants. You must make your own reservations."

ADDITIONAL INFORMATION Participants' mss can be read and commented on at a cost. Sponsors contests. Conference publishes a literary magazine featuring work of participants. Brochures available in January on website or for SASE, e-mail. Accepts inquiries by SASE, e-mail, phone. "We offer the opportunity to learn from some of the nation's best writers at a small, supportive conference in a lakeside setting that allows one-to-one feedback. Participants often continue to correspond and share work after confer-

ences." Further information available on website, by e-mail or by phone.

⊕ HAIKU NORTH AMERICA CONFERENCE

1275 Fourth St. PMB #365, Santa Rosa CA 95404. E-mail: welchm@aol.com. Website: www.haiku northamerica.com. **Contact:** Michael Dylan Welch. Five days, held every two years at varying locations throughout North America. Dates: August 3-7, 2011 (Eleventh) biennial conference. 2013 dates to be determined. Site: Seattle Center, Seattle, Wash.

ACCOMMODATIONS Typically around $200, including a banquet and some additional meals. Accommodations at discounted hotels nearby are an additional cost. Information available on website as details are finalized closer to the conference date.

ADDITIONAL INFORMATION Past conferences have been held in San Francisco (twice), Toronto, Portland (Oregon), Chicago, Boston, New York City, Port Townsend (Washington), Winston-Salem (North Carolina), and Ottawa (Ontario). In the words of Jim Kacian, founder of the Haiku Foundation, "Haiku North America ... is intellectually diverse, socially expansive, emotionally gratifying, and provides more than any other single experience the sense that haiku is a literary force to be reckoned with and capable of work that matters in the rest of the world."

HEART TALK

Women's Center for Ministry, Western Seminary, 5511 SE Hawthorne Blvd., Portland OR 97215-3367. (800)517-1800, ext. 1931. Fax: (503)517-1889. E-mail: wcm@westernseminary.edu. Website: www.western seminary.edu/women. Estab. 1998. Biannual conference held in March. Conference alternates between writing one year and speaking the next. Provides inspirational training for beginning and advanced writers/speakers. Workshops may include writing fiction, nonfiction, children's books, publishing, trends, dialogue, book proposals, websites, blogs, etc. Editors/publicists available for one-on-one consultations. Past speakers have included Robin Jones Gunn, Deborah Hedstrom-Page, Patricia Rushford, Sally Stuart, and many more.

COSTS 2008: $65. See website for more information.

ACCOMMODATIONS Western Seminary has a chapel and classrooms to accommodate various size groups. The campus has a peaceful, park-like setting with beautiful lawns, trees, and flowers, plus an inviting fountain and pond. Please check website for further details as they become available.

ADDITIONAL INFORMATION Conference information is available online, by e-mail, phone, or fax.

HIGHLIGHTS FOUNDATION FOUNDERS WORKSHOPS

814 Court St., Honesdale PA 18437. (570)253-1172. Fax: (570)253-0179. E-mail: contact@highlights foundation.org. Website: www.highlightsfoundation. org/pages/current/FWsched_preview.html. **Contact:** Kent L. Brown, Jr. Estab. 2000. Conference duration: 3-7 days. Average attendance: limited to 10-14. Genre specific workshops and retreats on children's writing: fiction, nonfiction, poetry, promotions. "Our goal is to improve, over time, the quality of literature for children by educating future generations of children's authors." Highlights Founders' home in Boyds Mills, PA.

COSTS Previous costs ranged from $795-1195, including meals, lodging, materials, and much more. "Our scholarship-aid program serves those who may not be able to bear the costs of our programs. In the past, more than 100 individuals received scholarships or other financial aid."

ACCOMMODATIONS Coordinates pickup at local airport. Offers overnight accommodations. Participants stay in guest cabins on the wooded grounds surrounding Highlights Founders' home adjacent to the house/conference center.

ADDITIONAL INFORMATION Some workshops require pre-workshop assignment. Brochure available for SASE, by e-mail, on website, by phone, by fax. Accepts inquiries by phone, fax, e-mail, SASE. Editors attend conference. "Applications will be reviewed and accepted on a first-come, first-served basis, applicants must demonstrate specific experience in writing area of workshop they are applying for—writing samples are required for many of the workshops."

HIGHLIGHTS FOUNDATION WRITERS WORKSHOP AT CHAUTAUQUA

814 Court St., Honesdale PA 18431. (570)253-1192. Fax: (570)253-0179. E-mail: contact@highlights foundation.org. Website: www.highlightsfoundation. org. Estab. 1985. 814 Court St., Honesdale, PA 18431. (570)253-1192. E-mail: contact@highlightsfoundation.org. Website: www.highlightsfoundation.org. Annual conference held July 16-23, 2011. Average attendance: 100. Workshops are geared toward those who write for children at the beginner, intermediate, and advanced levels. Offers seminars, small group workshops, and one-on-one sessions with authors, editors, illustrators, critics, and publishers. Workshop site is the picturesque community of Chautauqua, New York. Speakers have included Bruce Coville, Candace Fleming, Linda Sue Park, Jane Yolen, Patricia Gauch, Jerry Spinelli, Eileen Spinelli, Joy Cowley and Pam Munoz Ryan.

COSTS Previous cost was $2,400 (includes all meals, conference supplies, gate pass to Chautauqua Institution).

ACCOMMODATIONS We coordinate ground transportation to and from airports, trains, and bus stations in the Erie, PA and Jamestown/Buffalo, NY area. We also coordinate accommodations for conference attendees.

ADDITIONAL INFORMATION "We offer the opportunity for attendees to submit a manuscript for review at the conference. Workshop brochures/guidelines are available upon request."

HOFSTRA UNIVERSITY SUMMER WRITING WORKSHOPS

University College for Continuing Education, 250 Hofstra University, Hempstead NY 11549-2500. (516)463-7600. Fax: (516)463-4833. E-mail: ce@hofstra.edu. Website: ce.hofstra.edu/summerwriters. Estab. 1972. 37th Annual Summer Writers Program. July 5-15, 2011. Hofstra University's two-week Summer Writers Program, a cooperative endeavor of the Creative Writing Program, the English Department, and Hofstra University Continuing Education (Hofstra CE), offers 8 classes which may be taken on a noncredit or credit basis, for both graduate and undergraduate students. Led by master writers, the Summer Writing Program operates on the principle that true writing talent can be developed, nurtured and encouraged by writer-in-residence mentors. Through instruction, discussion, criticism and free exchange among the program members, writers begin to find their voice and their style. The program provides group and individual sessions for each writer. The Summer Writing Program includes a banquet, guest speakers, and exposure to authors such as Oscar Hijuelos, Robert Olen Butler (both Pulitzer Prize winners), Maurice Sendak, Cynthia Ozick, Nora Sayre, and Denise Levertov. Often agents, editors, and publishers make presentations during the conference, and authors and students read from published work and works in progress. These presentations and the conference banquet offer additional opportunities to meet informally with participants, master writers and guest speakers. Average attendance: 65. Conference offers workshops in short fiction, nonfiction, poetry, and occasionally other genres such as screenplay writing or writing for children. Site is the university campus on Long Island, 25 miles from New York City.

COSTS Check website for current fees. Credit is available for undergraduate and graduate students. Choose one of 9 writing genres and spend two intensive weeks studying and writing in that genre.

ACCOMMODATIONS Free bus operates between Hempstead Train Station and campus for those commuting from New York City on the Long Island Rail Road. Dormitory rooms are available.

ADDITIONAL INFORMATION Students entering grades 9–12 can now be part of the Summer Writers Program with a special section for high school students. Through exercises and readings, students will learn how to use their creative impulses to improve their fiction, poetry and plays and learn how to create cleaner and clearer essays. During this intensive 2-week course, students will experiment with memoir, poetry, oral history, dramatic form and the short story, and study how to use character, plot, point of view and language.

HOW TO BE PUBLISHED WORKSHOPS

P.O. Box 100031, Birmingham AL 35210-3006. E-mail: mike@writing2sell.com. Website: www.writing2sell.com. **Contact:** Michael Garrett. Estab. 1986. Workshops are offered continuously year-round at various locations. Conference duration: 1 session. Average attendance: 10-15. Workshops to move writers of category fiction closer to publication. Workshops held at college campuses and universities. Themes include Marketing, Idea Development and manuscript critique. Special critique is offered, but advance submission is not required. Workshop information available on website. Accepts inquiries by e-mail.

COSTS $49-79.

ADDITIONAL INFORMATION "Special critique is offered, but advance submission is not required." Workshop information available on website. Accepts inquiries by e-mail.

INTERNATIONAL WOMEN'S WRITING GUILD "REMEMBER THE MAGIC" ANNUAL SUMMER CONFERENCE

P.O. Box 810, Gracie Station, New York NY 10028-0082. (212)737-7536. E-mail: dirhahn@aol.com. Website: www.iwwg.com. **Contact:** Hannelore Hahn, Exec. Director. Estab. 1978.

COSTS $1,399 for 7 days. Five day, weekend and commuter rates are also available. Includes meals and lodging.

ACCOMMODATIONS Modern, air-conditioned and non-air-conditioned dormitories—single and/or double occupancy. Meals served cafeteria-style with choice of dishes. Variety of fresh fruits, vegetables and salads have been found plentiful, even by vegetarians. Conference information is available now. E-mail, call visit website or fax. "The conference is for women only."

IOWA SUMMER WRITING FESTIVAL

C215 Seashore Hall, University of Iowa, Iowa City IA 52242. (319)335-4160. Fax: (319)335-4743. E-mail: iswfestival@uiowa.edu. Website: www.uiowa.edu/~iswfest. Estab. 1987. Annual festival held in June and July. Conference duration: Workshops are 1 week or a weekend. Average attendance: Limited to 12 people/class, with over 1,500 participants throughout the summer. "We offer courses across the genres: novel, short story, poetry, essay, memoir, humor, travel, playwriting, screenwriting, writing for children, and women's writing. Held at the University of Iowa campus." Speakers have included Marvin Bell, Lan Samantha Chang, John Dalton, Hope Edelman, Katie Ford, Patricia Foster, Bret Anthony Johnston, Barbara Robinette Moss, among others.

COSTS $560 for full week; $280 for weekend workshop. Housing and meals are separate. See registration info online.

ACCOMMODATIONS Accommodations available at area hotels. Information on overnight accommodations available by phone or on website.

ADDITIONAL INFORMATION Brochures are available in February. Inquire via e-mail or on website.

IWWG EARLY SPRING IN CALIFORNIA CONFERENCE

International Women's Writing Guild, P.O. Box 810, Gracie Station, New York NY 10028-0082. (212)737-7536. Fax: (212)737-9469. E-mail: iwwg@iwwg.org.

Website: www.iwwg.org. **Contact:** Hannelore Hahn, Exec. Director. Estab. 1976. Annual conference held in March. Average attendance: 50. Conference promotes creative writing, personal growth, and voice. Site is a Redwood Forest mountain retreat in Santa Cruz, California.

COSTS $350/members; $380/nonmembers for weekend program with room and board; $125 for weekend program without room and board.

ACCOMMODATIONS All participants stay at the conference site or may commute.

ADDITIONAL INFORMATION Brochures/guidelines are available online or for a SASE. Inquire via e-mail or fax.

IWWG MEET THE AGENTS/MEET THE AUTHORS PLUS ONE DAY WRITING WORKSHOP

c/o International Women's Writing Guild, P.O. Box 810, Gracie Station, New York NY 10028-0082. (212)737-7536. Fax: (212)737-9469. E-mail: dirhahn@ aol.com. Website: www.iwwg.org. Estab. 1980. Workshops are held April 16-17 and October 15-16. Average attendance: 200. Workshops promote creative writing and professional success. A 1-day writing workshop *Memoir & Metaphor: Illuminating Your Life Through Writing*, is offered on Saturday. Sunday morning includes a discussion with up to 10 recently published IWWG authors and a book fair during lunch. On Sunday afternoon, up to 10 literary agents introduce themselves, and then members of the audience speak to the agents they wish to meet. Many as-yet-unpublished works have found publication in this manner. Speakers have included Regina Ryan, Rita Rosenkranz, and Diana Finch.

COSTS $190/members for the weekend/ $220/nonmembers for the weekend (includes lunch); $125 members/$135 nonmembers for Saturday (includes lunch); $125 members/$135 nonmembers for all day Sunday (includes lunch); $85 members/$95 nonmembers for Sunday afternoon.

JACKSON HOLE WRITERS CONFERENCE

PO Box 1974, Jackson WY 83001. (307)413-3332. E-mail: nicole@jacksonholewritersconference.com. Website: www.jacksonholewritersconference.com. Estab. 1991. Annual conference held in June. For 2010: June 24-27. Conference duration: 4 days. Average attendance: 110. Covers fiction, creative nonfiction, and young adult and offers ms critiques from authors, agents, and editors. Agents in attendance will take pitches from writers. Paid manuscript critique programs are available.

COSTS $355-385, includes all workshops, speaking events, cocktail party, BBQ, and goodie bag with dining coupons. $75 spouse/guest registration; $50 ms evaluation; $75 extended ms evaluation. "You must register for conference to be eligible for manuscript evaluation."

ADDITIONAL INFORMATION Held at the Center for the Arts in Jackson, Wyoming and online.

JENNY MCKEAN MOORE COMMUNITY WORKSHOPS

English Department, George Washingtion University, 801 22nd St. NW, Rome Hall, Suite 760, Washington DC 20052. (202) 994-6180. Fax: (202) 994-7915. E-mail: tvmallon@gwu.edu. Website: www.gwu.edu/~english/creative_jennymckeanmoore.html. **Contact:** Thomas Mallon, Director of Creative Writing. Estab. 1976. Workshop held each semester at the university. Average attendance: 15. Concentration varies depending on professor—usually fiction or poetry. The Creative Writing department brings an established poet or novelist to campus each year to teach a writing workshop for GW students and a free community workshop for adults in the larger Washington community.

COSTS : N/A.

ADDITIONAL INFORMATION Admission is competitive and by ms.

KENYON REVIEW WRITERS WORKSHOP

The Kenyon Review, Kenyon College, Gambier OH 43022. (740)427-5207. Fax: (740)427-5417. E-mail: reacha@kenyon.edu. Website: www.kenyonreview.org. Estab. 1990. Annual 8-day workshop held in June. Participants apply in poetry, fiction, or creative nonfiction, and then participate in intensive daily workshops which focus on the generation and revision of significant new work. Held on the campus of Kenyon College in the rural village of Gambier, Ohio. Workshop leaders have included David Baker, Ron Carlson, Rebecca McClanahan, Rosanna Warren and Nancy Zafris.

COSTS $1,995 (includes tuition, housing, meals).

ACCOMMODATIONS Participants stay in Kenyon College student housing.

KENYON REVIEW WRITERS WORKSHOP

Kenyon College, Gambier OH 43022. Website: www.
kenyonreview.org. Estab. 1990.

COSTS $1,995 includes tuition, room and board.

ACCOMMODATIONS The workshop operates a
shuttle to and from Gambier and the airport in Columbus, Ohio. Offers overnight accommodations.
Participants are housed in Kenyon College student
housing. The cost is covered in the tuition.

ADDITIONAL INFORMATION Application includes
a writing sample. Admission decisions are made on a
rolling basis. Workshop information is available online at www.kenyonreview.org/workshops in November. For brochure send e-mail, visit website, call, fax.
Accepts inquiries by SASE, e-mail, phone, fax.

KILLER NASHVILLE

P.O. Box 680686, Franklin TN 37068-0686. (615)599-
4032. E-mail: contact@killernashville.com. Website:
www.killernashville.com. Jaden Terrell, Exec. Dir.
Contact: Clay Stafford. Estab. 2006. Annual. Next
events: Aug. 24–26, 2012. Conference duration: 3 days.
Average attendance: 200+. Conference designed for
writers and fans of mysteries and thrillers, including fiction and nonfiction authors, playwrights, and
screenwriters. There are many opportunities for authors to sign books. 2011 guest of honor is Donald
Bain. 2012 guest of honor To Be Announced. Agents,
editors and industry professionals have included Jill
Marr (Sandra Dijkstra Agency), Carey Nelson Burch
(William Morris Agency), Lucienne Diver (The
Knight Literary Agency), Miriam Kress (Irene Goodman Literary Agency), Deni Dietz (Five Star/Cengage)
and Maryglenn McCombs (Oceanview Publishing).
Event includes book signings and panels. Past panel-
ists included authors Michael Connelly, Carol Higgins
Clark, Bill Bass, Gregg Hurwitz, Hallie Ephron, Chris
Grabenstein, Rhonda Pollero, P.J.Parrish, Reed Far-
rel Coleman, Kathryn Wall, Mary Saums, Don Bruns,
Bill Moody, Richard Helms, Alexandra Sokoloff, and
Steven Womack.

COSTS Signings events are free; current prices for
events available on website.

ADDITIONAL INFORMATION "Additional information about registration is provided at www.Kill-
erNashville.com."

LEAGUE OF UTAH WRITERS' ANNUAL ROUNDUP

P.O. Box 18430, Kearns UT 84118. E-mail: ediddy.
luw@gmail.com; writerscache435@gmail.com. Website: www.luwriters.org/index.html. **Contact:** Edwin
Smith, president; Tim Keller, president elect. Website:
www.luwriters.org/index.html Annual conference,
Writer workshops geared toward beginner, intermediate or advanced writers.

COSTS Early bird registration (Deadline August 26)
is $120 for members; or $150 after August 26. Cost
for non-members is $180. Price includes 3 meals, all
workshops, general sessions, a syllabus, handouts and
conference packet.

ACCOMMODATIONS Roundup will be held at The
Riverwoods Conference Center with lodging available at the Marriott Springhill Suites, (adjacent to
the Conference Center) phone 435-750-5180 in Logan, Utah, September 16–17, 2011.

ADDITIONAL INFORMATION Check website www.
luwriters.org for updates, and specifics.

THE MACDOWELL COLONY

100 High St., Peterborough NH 03458. (603)924-3886.
Fax: (603)924-9142. E-mail: admissions@macdowell
colony.org. Website: www.macdowellcolony.org. Estab. 1907. Open to writers, playwrights, composers,
visual artists, film/video artists, interdisciplinary artists and architects. Applicants send information and
work samples for review by a panel of experts in each
discipline. Application form submitted online at www.
macdowellcolony.org/apply.html. Work samples and
completed application forms must still be mailed. See
application guidelines for details.

COSTS Travel reimbursement and stipends are available for participants of the residency, based on need.
There are no residency fees.

MAGNA CUM MURDER

Magna Cum Murder Crime Writing Festival, The E.B.
and Bertha C. Ball Center, Ball State University, Mun-
cie IN 47306. (765)285-8975. Fax: (765)747-9566. E-
mail: magnacummurder@yahoo.com; kennisonk@
aol.com. Website: www.magnacummurder.com. Estab. 1994. Annual conference held in October. Average attendance: 300. Festival for readers and writers of
crime writing. Held in the Horizon Convention Center. Usually 30-40 mystery writers are in attendance
and there are presentations from agents, editors and

professional writers. The website has the full list of attending speakers.

COSTS Check website for updates.

MARK TWAIN CREATIVE WRITERS WORKSHOPS

5101 Rockhill Rd., Kansas City MO 64110-2499. (816)235-1168. Fax: (816)235-2611. E-mail: BeasleyM@umkc.edu. **Contact:** Betsy Beasley, admin. associate. Estab. 1990.

COSTS Fees for regular and noncredit courses.

ACCOMMODATIONS Offers list of area hotels or lodging options.

ADDITIONAL INFORMATION Submit for workshop 6 poems/one short story prior to arrival. Conference information is available in March by SASE, e-mail or on website. Editors participate in conference.

MONTROSE CHRISTIAN WRITERS' CONFERENCE

218 Locust St., Montrose PA 18801. (570)278-1001 or (800)598-5030. Fax: (570)278-3061. E-mail: info@montrosebible.org. Website: www.montrosebible.org. Estab. 1990. "Annual conference held in July. Offers workshops, editorial appointments, and professional critiques. We try to meet a cross-section of writing needs, for beginners and advanced, covering fiction, poetry, and writing for children. It is small enough to allow personal interaction between attendees and faculty. Speakers have included William Petersen, Mona Hodgson, Jim Fletcher, and Terri Gibbs."

COSTS Previous registration (tuition) was $155.

ACCOMMODATIONS Will meet planes in Binghamton, NY, and Scranton, PA. On-site accomodations: room and board $285–330/conference; $60–70/day including food (previous rates). RV court available.

ADDITIONAL INFORMATION "Writers can send work ahead of time and have it critiqued for a small fee." The attendees are usually church related. The writing has a Christian emphasis. Conference information available in April. For brochure send SASE, visit website, e-mail, call or fax. Accepts inquiries by SASE, e-mail, fax, phone.

MOUNT HERMON CHRISTIAN WRITERS CONFERENCE

37 Conference Drive, Mount Hermon CA 95041. E-mail: info@mounthermon.org. Website: www.mounthermon.org/writers. Estab. 1970. Annual profes-

sional conference (always held over the Palm Sunday weekend, Friday noon through Tuesday noon). Average attendance: 450. Sponsored by and held at the 440-acre Mount Hermon Christian Conference Center near San Jose, California in the heart of the coastal redwoods, we are a broad-ranging conference for all areas of Christian writing, including fiction, nonfiction, fantasy, children's, teen, young adult, poetry, magazines, inspirational and devotional writing. This is a working, how-to conference, with Major Morning tracks in all genres (including a track especially for teen writers), and as many as 20 optional workshops each afternoon. Faculty-to-student ratio is about 1 to 6. The bulk of our more than 70 faculty members are editors and publisher representatives from major Christian publishing houses nationwide. Speakers have included T. Davis Bunn, Debbie Macomber, Jerry Jenkins, Bill Butterworth, Dick Foth and others.

COSTS Registration fees include tuition, all major morning sessions, keynote sessions, and refreshment breaks. Room and board varies depending on choice of housing options. See website for current costs.

ACCOMMODATIONS Registrants stay in hotel-style accommodations. Meals are buffet style, with faculty joining registrants. See website Nov. 1 for cost updates.

ADDITIONAL INFORMATION "The residential nature of our conference makes this a unique setting for one-on-one interaction with faculty/staff. There is also a decided inspirational flavor to the conference, and general sessions with well-known speakers are a highlight. Registrants may submit 2 works for critique in advance of the conference, then have personal interviews with critiquers during the conference. All conference information is online by December 1 of each year. Send inquiries via e-mail. Tapes of past conferences are also available online."

NANCY SONDEL'S PACIFIC COAST CHILDREN'S WRITERS WORKSHOP

P.O. Box 244, Aptos CA 95001. Website: www.childrenswritersworkshop.com. Estab. 2003. "Our seminar serves semi-advanced through professional-level adult writers. A concurrent, intergenerational workshop is open to students age 14 and up, who give adults target-reader feedback. Intensive focus on craft as a marketing tool. Team-taught master classes (open clinics for manuscript critiques) explore such topics as "Envision and Edit Your Whole Novel" and "Story Architecture and Arcs." Continuous close contact with faculty, who have included literary agent Andrea Brown and Dial Books senior editor Kate Harrison. **Next seminars:** October 7-9, 2011 and October 5-7, 2012. Registration limited to 12 adults and 6 teens. "For the most critique options, submit sample chapters and synopsis with e-application by mid May; open until filled. **Content:** Character-driven novels with protagonists ages 11 and older. Collegial format; 90 percent hands-on, with dialogues between seasoned faculty and savvy, congenial peers. Our faculty critiques early as well as optional later chapters, plus synopses. Our pre-workshop anthology of peer manuscripts maximizes learning and networking. Several enrollees have landed contracts as a direct result of our seminar. **Details:** "Visit our website and e-mail us via the contact form."

COSTS Approx $450 (teens) to $600; includes lodging, most meals, and up to two in-person faculty critiques of partials. Optional: whole-novel critiques, plus two consults with editor or agent, for additional $400-$600. Limited work scholarships.

ACCOMMODATIONS Our venue, Pajaro Dunes Conference Center and Resort, offers free use of business center with DSL Internet access in enrollees' beachfront townhomes.

NATCHEZ LITERARY AND CINEMA CELEBRATION

P.O. Box 1307, Natchez MS 39121-1307. (601)446-1208. Fax: (601)446-1214. E-mail: carolyn.smith@colin.edu. Website: www.colin.edu/nlcc. Estab. 1990. Annual conference held in February. Conference duration: 5 days. Conference focuses on all literature, including film scripts. Each year's conference deals with some general aspect of Southern history. Speakers have included Eudora Welty, Margaret Walker Alexander, William Styron, Willie Morris, Ellen Douglas, Ernest Gaines, Elizabeth Spencer, Nikki Giovanni, Myrlie Evers-Williams, and Maya Angelou.

NATIONAL WRITERS ASSOCIATION FOUNDATION CONFERENCE

P.O. Box 4187, Parker CO 80134. (303)841-0246. Fax: (303)841-2607. E-mail: natlwritersassn@hotmail.com. Website: www.nationalwriters.com. **Contact:** Sandy Whelchel. Estab. 1926. Annual conference held the second week of June in Denver. Conference duration:

1 day. Average attendance: 100. Focuses on general writing and marketing.

COSTS Approximately $100.

ADDITIONAL INFORMATION Awards for previous contests will be presented at the conference. Brochures/guidelines are online, or send a SASE.

THE NEW LETTERS WEEKEND WRITERS CONFERENCE

University of Missouri-Kansas City, 5101 Rockhill Rd., Kansas City MO 64110-2499. (816)235-1168. Fax: (816)235-2611. E-mail: newletters@umkc.edu. Website: http://cas.umkc.edu/ce/. **Contact:** Betsey Beasley. Estab. 1970s (as The Longboat Key Writers Conference). Annual conference held in late June. Conference duration: 3 days. Average attendance: 75. The conference brings together talented writers in many genres for seminars, readings, workshops, and individual conferences. The emphasis is on craft and the creative process in poetry, fiction, screenwriting, playwriting, and journalism, but the program also deals with matters of psychology, publications, and marketing. The conference is appropriate for both advanced and beginning writers. The conference meets at the university's beautiful Diastole Conference Center. Two- and 3-credit hour options are available by special permission from director Robert Stewart.

COSTS Participants may choose to attend as a noncredit student or they may attend for 1 hour of college credit from the University of Missouri-Kansas City. Conference registration includes Friday evening reception and keynote speaker, Saturday and Sunday continental breakfast and lunch.

ACCOMMODATIONS Registrants are responsible for their own transportation, but information on area accommodations is available.

ADDITIONAL INFORMATION Those registering for college credit are required to submit a ms in advance. Ms reading and critique are included in the credit fee. Those attending the conference for noncredit also have the option of having their ms critiqued for an additional fee. Brochures are available for a SASE after March. Accepts inquiries by e-mail and fax.

NEW YORK COMIC BOOK MARKETPLACE

(formerly known as Big Apple Con), 401 Seventh Ave. 33rd St., New York NY 10001-2062. (347)581-6166. E-mail: mikecarbo@gmail.com. Website: www.nycbm. com. **Contact:** Michael Carbonaro. "Annual comic book show. Located directly across from Madison Square Garden and Penn Station."

NIMROD ANNUAL WRITERS' WORKSHOP
800 S. Tucker Dr., Tulsa OK 74104. (918)631-3080. E-mail: nimrod@utulsa.edu. Website: www.utulsa.edu/nimrod. **Contact:** Eilis O'Neal, managing editor. Estab. 1978. Annual conference held in October. Conference duration: 1 day. Offers one-on-one editing sessions, readings, panel discussions, and master classes in fiction, poetry, nonfiction, memoir, and fantasy writing. Speakers have included Myla Goldberg, B.H. Fairchild, Colum McCann, Molly Peacock, Peter S. Beagle, Robert Olen Butler, and Marvin Bell. Full conference details are online in August.

COSTS Approximately $50. Lunch provided. Scholarships available for students.

ADDITIONAL INFORMATION *Nimrod International Journal* sponsors *Nimrod* Literary Awards: The Katherine Anne Porter Prize for fiction and The Pablo Neruda Prize for poetry. Poetry and fiction prizes: $2,000 each and publication (1st prize); $1,000 each and publication (2nd prize). Deadline: must be postmarked no later than April 30.

NORTH CASCADES INSTITUTE 2011 WRITING RETREATS
North Cascades Institute, 810 Highway 20, Secro-Wooley WA 98284-9394. (360)856-5700 ext. 209. Fax: (360)859-1934. E-mail: nci@ncascades.org. Website: www.ncascades.org. **Contact:** Deb Martin, registrar. Estab. 1999. Writing in the North Cascades: *The Art of the Essay* with Lyanda Lynn Haupt October 7-9 (Fri-Sun) North Cascades Environmental Learning Center. Cost ranges from $275-515 depending on accommodations. Join award-winning writer Lyanda Lynn Haupt in this inspiring class for writers of all experience levels. The essay is a wondrous form, and can contain anything a writer brings to it—obscure connections, questions without answers, observations, information, inspiration. It is the perfect form for exploring and deepening the human connection with the natural world. Essays offer freedom of expression, but in order to be good, an essay must also have clarity of vision, a consistent voice, a well-woven structure and a solid sense of craft. Work on all of these through writing exercises, readings and one-on- one coaching with Lyanda to invigorate your writing practice as you complete an essay over this autumn weekend in the North Cascades. Writing in the North Cascades:

The Art of the Quest Narrative with Nick O'Connell. August 22-24 (Mon-Wed). North Cascades Environmental Learning Center. Cost ranges from $275-515 depending on accommodations A quest narrative is one of the oldest and steadfast ways of telling a story. Join Seattle-based author and writing instructor Nick O'Connell to learn about and practice writing the quest narrative, an adaptable form that can be used to craft personal essays, travelogue, memoir, fiction and nature writing. Together, we'll learn how we can employ the quest narrative form to write about seeking to reconcile with your family, searching for the perfect glass of Pinot Noir wine or attempting to scale Mt. Rainier. Scholarships, teacher hours and academic credits are available.

COSTS Writing in the North Cascades: *The Art of the Essay* with Lyanda Lynn Haupt. October 7-9 (Fri-Sun) North Cascades Environmental Learning Center. Cost ranges from $275-515 depending on accommodations. Writing in the North Cascades: *The Art of the Quest Narrative* with Nick O'Connell. August 22-24 (Mon-Wed). North Cascades Environmental Learning Center. Cost ranges from $275-515 depending on accommodations.

NORWESCON
P.O. Box 68547, Seattle WA 98168-9986. (425)243-4692. Fax: (520)244-0142. E-mail: info@norwescon.org. Website: www.norwescon.org. Estab. 1978. Annual conference held on Easter weekend. Average attendance: 2,800. General multitrack convention focusing on science fiction and fantasy literature with wide coverage of other media. Tracks cover science, socio-cultural, literary, publishing, editing, writing, art, and other media of a science fiction/fantasy orientation. Agents will be speaking and available for meetings with attendees.

ACCOMMODATIONS Conference is held at the Doubletree Hotel Seattle Airport.

ADDITIONAL INFORMATION Brochures are available online or for a SASE. Send inquiries via e-mail.

ODYSSEY FANTASY WRITING WORKSHOP
P.O. Box 75, Mont Vernon NH 03057. E-mail: jcavelos@sff.net. Website: www.odysseyworkshop.org. Saint Anselm College 100 Saint Anselm Drive, Manchester, N.H., 03102. Estab. 1996. Annual workshop held in June (through July). Conference duration: 6 weeks. Average attendance: 16. A workshop

for fantasy, science fiction, and horror writers that combines an intensive learning and writing experience with in-depth feedback on students' mss. Held on the campus of Saint Anselm College in Manchester, New Hampshire. Speakers have included George R.R. Martin, Elizabeth Hand, Jane Yolen, Harlan Ellison, Melissa Scott and Dan Simmons. **COSTS** In 2010: $1,900 tuition, $775 housing (double room), $1,550 (single room); $35 application fee, $400-600 food (approximate), $450 processing fee to receive college credit.

ADDITIONAL INFORMATION Students must apply and include a writing sample. Application deadline April 10. Students' works are critiqued throughout the 6 weeks. Workshop information available in October. For brochure/guidelines send SASE, e-mail, visit website, call or fax. Accepts inquiries by SASE, e-mail, fax, phone.

PACIFIC NORTHWEST WRITER ASSN. SUMMER WRITER'S CONFERENCE

PMB 2717, 1420 NW Gilman Blvd., Ste. 2, Issaquah WA 98027. E-mail: staff@pnwa.org. Website: www. pnwa.org. Writer conference geared toward beginner, intermediate, advanced and professional levels. Meet agents and editors. Learn craft from renowned authors. Uncover new marketing secrets. PNWA's 56th Annual Conference will be held August 4-7, 2011, at the Hyatt Regency, Bellevue, WA 98004.

PIMA WRITERS' WORKSHOP

Pima College, 2202 W. Anklam Rd., Tucson AZ 85709-0170. (520)206-6084. Fax: (520)206-6020. E-mail: mfiles@pima.edu. Website: www.pima.edu. **Contact:** Meg Files, director. Estab. 1988. Annual conference held in May. Conference duration: 3 days. 2011 dates: May 27-29. Average attendance: 300. Features a dozen authors, editors, and agents talking about writing and publishing fiction, nonfiction, poetry, and stories for children. Speakers have included Larry McMurtry, Barbara Kingsolver, Jerome Stern, Connie Willis, Jack Heffron, Jeff Herman, and Robert Morgan. Agents will be speaking and available for meetings with attendees. **COSTS** $100 (can include ms critique). Participants may attend for college credit, in which case there are fees for Arizona residents and for out-of-state residents. Meals and accommodations are not included. **ACCOMMODATIONS** Information on local accommodations is made available. Special workshop rates

are available at a specified hotel close to the workshop site (about $70/night).

ADDITIONAL INFORMATION Sessions are held in the Center for the Arts on Pima Community College's West campus. The workshop atmosphere is casual, friendly, and supportive, and guest authors are very accessible. Readings and panel discussions are offered, as well as talks and manuscript sessions. Participants may have up to 20 pages critiqued by the author of their choice. Mss must be submitted 3 weeks before the workshop. Conference brochure/guidelines available for SASE. Accepts inquiries by e-mail.

POETRY WEEKEND INTENSIVES

40 Post Ave., Hawthorne NJ 07506. (973)423-2921. Fax: (973)523-6085. E-mail: mariagillan@verizon. net. Website: www.pccc.edu/poetry. **Contact:** Maria Mazziotti Gillan, executive director. Estab. 1997. **ACCOMMODATIONS** $375, including meals. Offers a $25 early bird discount. Housing in on-site facilities included in the $375 price. Location: generally at Glastonbury Abbey, in Hingham, MA; also several other convents and monasteries.

ADDITIONAL INFORMATION Usually held 2 times/year in June and December. Average attendance: 26. Additional Information: Individual poetry critiques available. Poets should bring poems to weekend. Registration form available for SASE or by fax or e-mail. Maria Mazziotti Gillan is the director of the Creative Writing Program of Binghamton University, exec. director of the Poetry Center at Passaic County Community College, and edits *Paterson Literary Review*. Laura Boss is the editor of *Lips* magazine. Fifteen professional development credits are available for each weekend.

THE PUBLISHING GAME

Peanut Butter & Jelly Press, P.O. Box 590239, Newton MA 02459. E-mail: alyza@publishinggame.com. Website: www.publishinggame.com. **Contact:** Alyza Harris, manager. Estab. 1998. Conference held monthly, in different locales across North America: Boston, New York City, Washington DC, Boca Raton, San Francisco, Los Angeles, Seattle, Chicago. Conference duration: 9 a.m. to 4 p.m. Maximum attendance: 18 writers. "A one-day workshop on finding a literary agent, self-publishing your book, creating a publishing house and promoting your book to bestsellerdom!" Site: "Elegant hotels across the country. Boston locations alternate between the Four Seasons

Hotel in downtown Boston and The Inn at Harvard in historic Harvard Square, Cambridge." Fiction panels in 2005 included Propel Your Novel from Idea to Finished Manuscript; How to Self-Publish Your Novel; Craft the Perfect Book Package; How to Promote Your Novel; Selling Your Novel to Bookstores and Libraries. Workshop led by Fern Reiss, author and publisher of The Publishing Game series.

COSTS $195.

ACCOMMODATIONS "All locations are well-known hotels easily accessible by public transportation." Offers discounted conference rates for participants who choose to arrive early. Offers list of area lodging.

ADDITIONAL INFORMATION Brochures available for SASE. Accepts inquiries by SASE, e-mail, phone, fax, but e-mail preferred. Agents and editors attend conference. "If you're considering finding a literary agent, self-publishing your book or just want to sell more copies of your book, this conference will teach you everything you need to know to successfully publish and promote your work."

ROBERT QUACKENBUSH'S CHILDREN'S BOOK WRITING AND ILLUSTRATING WORKSHOP

460 E. 79th St., New York NY 10075. Phone/fax: (212)861-2761. E-mail: rqstudios@aol.com. Website: www.rquackenbush.com. Annual workshop held during the second week in July. Conference duration: 4 days. Average attendance: Enrollment limited to 10. Workshops promote writing and illustrating books for children and are geared toward beginners and professionals. Generally focuses on picture books, easy-to-read books, and early chapter books. Held at the Manhattan studio of Robert Quackenbush, author and illustrator of more than 200 books for children. All classes led by Robert Quackenbush.

COSTS $750 tuition covers all the costs of the workshop but does not include housing and meals. A $100 nonrefundable deposit is required with the $650 balance due three weeks prior to attendance.

ACCOMMODATIONS A list of recommended hotels and restaurants is sent upon receipt of deposit to applicants living out of the area of New York City.

ADDITIONAL INFORMATION Class is for beginners and professionals. Critiques during workshop. Private consultations also available at an hourly rate. "Programs suited to your needs; individualized schedules can be designed. Write or phone to discuss your

goals and you will receive a prompt reply." Conference information available 1 year prior to conference. For brochure, send SASE, e-mail, visit website, call or fax. Accepts inquiries by fax, e-mail, phone, SASE.

ROCKY MOUNTAIN FICTION WRITERS COLORADO GOLD

Rocky Mountain Fiction Writers, P.O. Box 545, Englewood CO 80151. E-mail: conference@rmfw.org. Website: www.rmfw.org. Estab. 1983. Annual conference held in September. Conference duration: 3 days. Average attendance: 300+. Themes include general novel-length fiction, genre fiction, contemporary romance, mystery, science fiction/fantasy, mainstream, and history. New in 2012: Friday morning master classes. Speakers have included Joseph Finder, Brenda Novak, Connie Willis, James O. Born, Eldon Thompson. Approximately 13 editors/agents attend annually.

COSTS Costs available online.

ACCOMMODATIONS Special rates will be available at conference hotel.

ADDITIONAL INFORMATION Editor-conducted workshops are limited to 8 participants for critique, with auditing available. Pitch appointments available at no charge.

○ SAGE HILL WRITING EXPERIENCE

Box 1731, Saskatoon SK S7K 2Z4 Canada. Phone/Fax: (306)652-7395. E-mail: sage.hill@sasktel.net. Website: www.sagehillwriting.ca. Annual workshops held in late July/August and May. Conference duration: 10-14 days. Average attendance: 40/summer program; 8/spring program. Sage Hill Writing Experience offers a special working and learning opportunity to writers at different stages of development. Top-quality instruction, low instructor-student ratio, and the beautiful Sage Hill setting offer conditions ideal for the pursuit of excellence in the arts of fiction, poetry and playwriting. The Sage Hill location features individual accommodations, in-room writing areas, lounges, meeting rooms, healthy meals, walking woods, and vistas in several directions. Classes being held (may vary from year to year) include: Introduction to Writing Fiction & Poetry, Fiction Workshop, Writing Young Adult Fiction Workshop, Poetry Workshop, Poetry Colloquium, Fiction Colloquium, Novel Colloquium, Playwriting Lab, Fall Poetry Colloquium, and Spring Poetry Colloquium. Speakers have included Nicole Brossard, Steven Galloway, Robert Currie, Jeanette Lynes, Karen Solie and Colleen Murphy.

COSTS Summer program: $1,095 (includes instruction, accommodation, meals). Fall Poetry Colloquium: $1,375. Scholarships and bursaries are available.

ACCOMMODATIONS Located at Lumsden, 45 kilometers outside Regina.

ADDITIONAL INFORMATION For Introduction to Creative Writing, send a 5-page sample of your writing or a statement of your interest in creative writing and a list of courses taken. For workshop and colloquium programs, send a résumé of your writing career and a 12-page sample of your work, plus 5 pages of published work. Guidelines are available for SASE. Inquire via e-mail or fax.

SAN DIEGO STATE UNIVERSITY WRITERS' CONFERENCE

SDSU College of Extended Studies, 5250 Campanile Dr., San Diego State University, San Diego CA 92182-1920. (619)594-2517. Fax: (619)594-8566. E-mail: sdsuwritersconference@mail.sdsu.edu. Website: www.ces.sdsu.edu/writers. Estab. 1984. SDSU College of Extended Studies, 5250 Campanile Drive, San Diego CA 92182-1920. (619) 594-2517. Fax: (619) 594-8566. E-mail: sdsuwritersconference@mail.sdsu.edu. Website: www.ces.sdsu.edu/writers. Annual conference held in January/February. Conference duration: 2 days. Average attendance: 375. Covers fiction, nonfiction, scriptwriting and e-books. Held at the Doubletree Hotel in Mission Valley. Each year the conference offers a variety of workshops for the beginner and advanced writers. This conference allows the individual writer to choose which workshop best suits his/her needs. In addition to the workshops, editor reading appointments and agent/editor consultation appointments are provided so attendees may meet with editors and agents one-on-one to discuss specific questions. A reception is offered Saturday immediately following the workshops, offering attendees the opportunity to socialize with the faculty in a relaxed atmosphere. Last year, approximately 60 faculty members attended.

COSTS Approximately $365-485 (2011-12 costs will be published with a fall update of the website).

ACCOMMODATIONS Doubletree Hotel (800)222-TREE. Attendees must make their own travel arrangements.

SAN FRANCISCO WRITERS CONFERENCE

1029 Jones St., San Francisco CA 94109. (415)673-0939. Fax: (415)673-0367. E-mail: Barbara@sfwrit

ers.org. **Contact:** Barbara Santos, marketing director. Estab. 2003. 1029 Jones St, San Francisco CA 94109. (415) 673-0939 or (866) 862-739. Fax: (415) 673-0367. E-mail: sfwriters@aol.com. Website: www.sfwriters.org. 3 days. "Annual conference held Presidents' Day weekend in February. Average attendance: 400+. Top authors, respected literary agents, and major publishing houses are at the event so attendees can make face-to-face contact with all the right people. Writers of nonfiction, fiction, poetry, and specialty writing (children's books, cookbooks, travel, etc.) will all benefit from the event. There are important sessions on marketing, self-publishing, technology, and trends in the publishing industry. Plus, there's an optional 4-hour session called Speed Dating for Agents where attendees can meet with 20+ agents. Speakers have included Jennifer Crusie, Richard Paul Evans, Jamie Raab, Mary Roach, Jane Smiley, Debbie Macomber, Firoozeh Dumas, Zilpha Keatley Snyder, Steve Berry, Jacquelyn Mitchard. More than 20 agents and editors participate each year, many of whom will be available for meetings with attendees."

COSTS $600+ with price breaks for early registration (includes all sessions/workshops/keynotes, Speed Dating with Editors, opening gala at the Top of the Mark, 2 continental breakfasts, 2 lunches). Optional Speed Dating for Agents is $50.

ACCOMMODATIONS The Intercontinental Mark Hopkins Hotel is a historic landmark at the top of Nob Hill in San Francisco. Elegant rooms and first-class service are offered to attendees at the rate of $159/night. The hotel is located so that everyone arriving at the Oakland or San Francisco airport can take BART to either the Embarcadero or Powell Street exits, then walk or take a cable car or taxi directly to the hotel.

ADDITIONAL INFORMATION "Present yourself in a professional manner and the contact you will make will be invaluable to your writing career. Brochures and registration are online."

✚ SAN FRANCISCO WRITING FOR CHANGE CONFERENCE

1029 Jones St., San Francisco CA 94109. (415)673-0939. E-mail: Barbara@sfwriters.org. Website: SFWritingforChange.org. **Contact:** Barbara Santos, marketing director. Estab. 2004. Annual conference held in Fall 2011 and hotel TBD. Average attendance: 200.

COSTS Costs: $495; early discounts available. Includes over 30 workshops, two keynotes with luncheons, Sunday breakfast, social events, editor and agent consultations.

ACCOMMODATIONS Check website for special attendance rates on rooms and parking. Public transportation and taxis are readily available. Classes and keynote meals will be on three levels of the hotel (elevator).

ADDITIONAL INFORMATION "The limited number of attendees (150) and excellent presenter-to-attendee ratio make this a highly effective and productive conference. The presenters are major names in the publishing business, but take personal interest in the projects discovered at this event each year." Guidelines available on website, e-mail, and fax.

☺ SASKATCHEWAN FESTIVAL OF WORDS

217 Main St. N., Moose Jaw SK S6J 0W1 Canada. (306)691-0557. Fax: (306)693-2994. E-mail: festivaloperations@sasktel.net. Website: www.festivalofwords. com. Estab. 1997. Annual festival held in July. 2011 Dates: July 14-17. Festival duration: 4 days. Average attendance: 4,000.

☺ SCBWI—CANADA EAST

Canada. Website: www.scbwicanada.org/east. **Contact:** Lizann Flatt, Regional Advisor. Writer and illustrator events geared toward all levels. Usually offers one event in spring and another in the fall. Check website Events pages for updated information.

SCBWI--MIDATLANTIC;
ANNUAL FALL CONFERENCE

P.O. Box 3215, Reston VA 20195-1215. E-mail: scbwimidatlantic@gmail.com. Www.SCBWI-MidAtlantic.org. **Contact:** Sydney Dunlap and Erin Teagan, conference co-chairs. Ellen Braaf, regional advisor. Conference takes place Saturday, October 22, 2011 in Arlington, VA from 8 to 5. Keynote speaker TBA. For updates and details visit website. Registration limited to 200. Conference fills quickly.

COSTS $115 for SCBWI members; $145 for nonmembers. Includes continental breakfast. Lunch is on your own. (The food court at the Ballston Common Mall is two blocks away.)

⊕ SCBWI—NEW JERSEY;
ANNUAL SUMMER CONFERENCE

SCBWI-New Jersey: Society of Children's Book Writers & Illustrators, New Jersey NJ Website: www. newjerseyscbwi.com. **Contact:** Kathy Termean, re-

gional advisor. This weekend conference is held in the beginning of June in Princeton, NJ. Multiple one-on-one critiques; "How-to" workshops for every level, first page sessions, agent pitches and interaction with the faculty of editors, agents, art director and authors are some of the highlights of the weekend. On Friday attendees can sign up for writing intensives or register for illustrators' day with the art directors. Published authors attending the conference can sign up to participate in the bookfair to sell and autograph their books. Illustrators have the opportunity to display their artwork. Attendees have the option to participate in group critiques after dinner on saturday evening and attend a mix and mingle with the faculty on Friday night. Meals are included with the cost of admission. Conference is known for its high ratio of faculty to attendees and interaction opportunities.

SCBWI—NEW JERSEY;
FIRST PAGE SESSIONS

New Jersey NJ E-mail: njscbwi@newjerseyscbwi. com; kathy@newjerseyscbwi.com; laurie@newjerseyscbwi.com. Website: www.newjerseyscbwi.com. Held 4 times a year in Princeton, NJ. Two editors/agents give their first impression of a first page and let participants know if they would read more. These sessions are held late afternoon during the week and are limited to 30 people. Attendees can choose to have dinner with the editors after the session. Please visit www.newjerseyscbwi.com for more information.

SCBWI SOUTHERN BREEZE
SPRINGMINGLE CONFERENCE

P.O. Box 26282, Birmingham AL 35260. E-mail: jskittinger@gmail.com. Website: www.southern-breeze. net. **Contact:** Jo Kittinger, co-regional advisor. Estab. 1992.

COSTS About $200; SCBWI non-members pay about $30 more. Some meals are included.

ACCOMMODATIONS Individuals make their own reservations. Ask for the Southern Breeze group rate in the conference site's hotel.

ADDITIONAL INFORMATION Manuscript and portfolio critiques available for an additional fee. Mss must be sent ahead of time. Visit website for details. Accepts inquiries by SASE, e-mail.

SCBWI–VENTURA/SANTA BARBARA; FALL CONFERENCE

Simi Valley CA 93094-1389. E-mail: alexisinca@aol. com. **Contact:** Alexis O'Neill, Regional Advisor. Estab. 1971. "The Society of Children's Book Writers and Illustrators is the largest professional writing organization in the world, with more than 13,000 members located around the globe. SCBWI is dedicated to assisting individuals working in the fields of children's books, multimedia, magazines, film, and television. Whether a beginner, a famous author or illustrator, an educator, a bookstore owner, an editor, or an enthusiast, SCBWI has much to offer everyone, including two annual international conferences, regional events, work-in-progress grants, a bi-monthly newsletter, informational publications, marketing data, and a supportive community with a shared passion."

SCBWI WINTER CONFERENCE ON WRITING AND ILLUSTRATING FOR CHILDREN

8271 Beverly Blvd., Los Angeles CA 90048. (323)782-1010. Fax: (323)782-1892. E-mail: scbwi@scbwi.org. Website: www.scbwi.org. **Contact:** Stephen Mooser. Estab. 2000. (formerly SCBWI Midyear Conference), Society of Children's book Writers and Illustrators. Annual. Conference held in February. Average attendance: 1,000. Conference is to promote writing and illustrating for children: picture books; fiction; non-fiction; middle grade and young adult; network with professionals; financial planning for writers; marketing your book; art exhibition; etc. Site: Manhattan.

COSTS See website for current cost and conference information.

ADDITIONAL INFORMATION SCBWI also holds an annual summer conference in August in Los Angeles. See the listing in the West section or visit website for details.

☼ THE SCHOOL FOR WRITERS SUMMER WORKSHOP

The Humber School for Writers, Humber Institute of Technology & Advanced Learning, 3199 Lake Shore Blvd. W., Toronto ON M8V 1K8 Canada. (416)675-6622. E-mail: antanas.sileika@humber.ca; hilary. higgins@humber.ca. Website: www.creativeandper-formingarts.humber.ca/content/writers.html. Annual workshop held second week in July. Conference duration: 1 week. Average attendance: 100. New writ-

ers from around the world gather to study with faculty members to work on their novel, short stories, poetry, or creative nonfiction. Agents and editors participate in conference. Include a work-in-progress with your registration. Faculty has included Martin Amis, David Mitchell, Rachel Kuschner, Peter Carey, Roddy Doyle, Tim O'Brien, Andrea Levy, Barry Unsworth, Edward Albee, Ha Jin, Julia Glass, Mavis Gallant, Bruce Jay Friedman, Isabel Huggan, Alistair MacLeod, Lisa Moore, Kim Moritsugu, Francine Prose, Paul Quarrington, Olive Senior, and D.M. Thomas, Annabel Lyon, Mary Gaitskill, M. G. Vassanji.

COSTS $949/Canadian residents before June 11; $1,469/non-Canadian residents before June 11; $999/Canadian residents after June 11; $1,519/non-Canadian residents after June 11 (includes panels, classes, lunch). Some limited scholarships are available.

ACCOMMODATIONS Approximately $75/night. See http://conference.humber.ca for a pair of modest college dorm rooms. Nearby hotels are also available.

ADDITIONAL INFORMATION Accepts inquiries by e-mail, phone, and fax.

SEACOAST WRITERS ASSOCIATION SPRING AND FALL CONFERENCES

59 River Rd., Stratham NH 03885-2358. (603)742-1030. E-mail: patparnell@comcast.net. Website: www.seacoastwritersassociation.org. **Contact:** Pat Parnell, conf. coordinator. Seacoast Writers Association is a non-profit, member-supported organization dedicated to providing area writers with resources that enable them to hone their writing skills. We also work to supply members with practical information that may assist them in publishing their work, such as workshops in preparing manuscripts, submitting work, writing query letters, finding agents, researching markets, self-publishing and so forth. SWA members receive discounted admission to SWA events. SWA organizes 2 one-day writers' conferences each year. We also sponsor an annual writers' contest and publish *Currents,* an anthology of prize winning poetry, short fiction and personal essays. SWA also publishes the *Seacoast Writer,* a quarterly newsletter for members. Conferences held in May and October. Conference duration: 1 day. Average attendance: 60. Our conferences offer workshops covering various aspects of fiction, nonfiction and poetry. Site: McConnell Center, 61 Locust St., Dover NH.

COSTS Approx. $50.

ADDITIONAL INFORMATION "We sometimes include critiques. It is up to the workshop presenter." Spring meeting includes a contest. Categories are fiction, nonfiction (essays) and poetry. Judges vary from year to year. Conference and contest information available for SASE November 1, April 1, and September 1. Accepts inquiries by SASE, e-mail and phone. For further information, check the website www.seacoastwritersassociation.org, or visit us on Facebook: Seacoastwritersassociation.

SEWANEE WRITERS' CONFERENCE

735 University Ave., 123 Gailor Hall, Stamlor Center, Sewanee TN 37383-1000. (931) 598-1654. E-mail: kewilson@sewanee.edu. Website: www.sewanee writers.org. **Contact:** Kevin Wilson. Estab. 1990. 735 University Ave., Sewanee TN 37383-1000. (931) 598-1654. E-mail: swc@sewanee.edu. Website: www.sewaneewriters.org. Annual conference held in the second half of July. Conference duration: 12 days. Average attendance: 144. "We offer genre-based workshops in fiction, poetry, and playwriting. The conference uses the facilities of Sewanee: The University of the South. The university is a collection of ivy-covered Gothic-style buildings located on the Cumberland Plateau in mid-Tennessee. Editors, publishers, and agents structure their own presentations, but there is always opportunity for questions from the audience." Previous faculty included fiction writers Richard Bausch, Tony Earley, Diane Johnson, Randall Kenan, Jill McCorkle, Alice McDermott, Erin McGraw, and Steve Yarbrough; poets Daniel Anderson, Claudia Emerson, Debora Greger, Andrew Hudgins, William Logan, Alan Shapiro, Dave Smith, and Greg Willimson; and playwrights Lee Blessing and Dan O'Brien. Visiting agents include Gail Hochman and Georges Borchardt. A score of writing professionals will visit.

COSTS $1,700 (includes tuition, board, single room, sports and fitness center access).

ACCOMMODATIONS Participants are housed in single rooms in university dormitories. Bathrooms are shared by small groups. Motel or B&B housing is available, but not abundantly so.

ADDITIONAL INFORMATION "Complimentary chartered bus service is available from the Nashville Airport to Sewanee and back on the first and last days of the conference. We offer each partici-pant (excepting auditors) the opportunity for a private manuscript conference with a member of the faculty. These manuscripts are due 1 month before the conference begins. Brochures/guidelines are free. The conference provides a limited number of fellowships and scholarships; these are awarded on a competitive basis."

SHEVACON 19

PO Box 7622, Roanoke VA 24019. (540)248-4152. E-mail: Shevacon@shevacon.org. Website: www.shevacon.org. **Contact:** Lynn Bither, chairperson. Estab. 1993. Annual conference held in March. Conference focuses on writing, art, and gaming in the science fiction, fantasy, and horror genres.

COSTS See website for rates.

ACCOMMODATIONS There is special rate at the Sheraton Roanoke Hotel & Conference Center, Virginia. "Shuttles from the airport are available; we do not have airline discounts." Offers overnight accomodations; "individuals must make their own reservations." For brochure send SASE or visit website. Accepts inquiries by mail, e-mail or phone.

ADDITIONAL INFORMATION New dates: March 4-6, 2011. "SheVaCon is celebrating its 19th year as the largest Multi-Media Science Fiction & Fantasy convention in Southwestern Virginia. We offer many fun events and great programming focusing on sci-fi, fantasy, and horror. Workshops, panel discussions, art show & artist alley, dealer's room, costumed fandom groups, auctions, computer and console gaming, RPG/LARP gaming, Video and Anime screenings.. and so much more! There is more parking and we can open sooner on Friday the 4th. Confirmed guests are listed on the website and we are updating regularly."

SILKEN SANDS CONFERENCE

Gulf Coast Chapter RWA, P.O. Box 1815, Ocean Springs MS 39566. (228)875-3864. E-mail: jillian chantal@gmail.com. Website: www.gccrwa.com. **Contact:** Jillian Chantal. Estab. 1995. Annual conference. Held March 16-18, 2012 in Pensacola Beach, FL. Average attendance: 100. Focuses on romance, fiction including paranormal, inspirational, romantic suspense, category.

COSTS To be announced.

ADDITIONAL INFORMATION Brochures available for SASE, e-mail, phone or on website. Accepts inquiries by e-mail. Agents and editors participate in conference. The conference is noted for its relaxed, enjoyable atmosphere where participants can immerse themselves in the total writing experience from the moment they arrive.

SITKA CENTER FOR ART AND ECOLOGY

P.O. Box 65, Otis OR 97368. E-mail: info@sitkacenter.org. Website: www.sitkacenter.org. **Contact:** Jalene Case, program manager. Estab. 1970.
COSTS "Workshops are generally $60-500; they do not include meals or lodging."
ACCOMMODATIONS Does not offer overnight accommodations. Provides a list of area hotels or lodging options.
ADDITIONAL INFORMATION Brochure available in February of each year by SASE, phone, e-mail, fax or visit website. Accepts inquiries by SASE, e-mail, phone, fax.

SOCIETY OF CHILDREN'S BOOK WRITERS & ILLUSTRATORS ANNUAL SUMMER CONFERENCE ON WRITING AND ILLUSTRATING FOR CHILDREN

8271 Beverly Blvd., Los Angeles CA 90048-4515. (323)782-1010. Fax: (323)782-1892. E-mail: scbwi@scbwi.org. Website: www.scbwi.org. Estab. 1972. Annual conference held in early August. Conference duration: 4 days. Average attendance: 1,000. Held at the Century Plaza Hotel in Los Angeles. Speakers have included Andrea Brown, Steven Malk, Scott Treimel, Ashley Bryan, Bruce Coville, Karen Hesse, Harry Mazer, Lucia Monfried, and Russell Freedman. Agents will be speaking and sometimes participate in ms critiques.
COSTS Approximately $400 (does not include hotel room).
ACCOMMODATIONS Information on overnight accommodations is made available.
ADDITIONAL INFORMATION Ms and illustration critiques are available. Brochure/guidelines are available in June online or for SASE.

SOUTH COAST WRITERS CONFERENCE

Southwestern Oregon Community College, P.O. Box 590, 29392 Ellensburg Avenue, Gold Beach OR 97444. (541)247-2741. Fax: (541)247-6247. E-mail: scwc@socc.edu. Website: www.socc.edu/scwriters. Estab. 1996. Annual conference held Presidents Day weekend in February. Conference duration: 2 days. Covers fiction, historical, poetry, children's, nature, and marketing. John Daniel is the next scheduled keynote speaker and presenters include John Daniel, Linda Barnes, Jayel Gibson, Kim Griswell, Diane Hammond, Leigh Anne Jasheway, Marianne Monson, Rebecca Olson, Dennis Powers, Keith Scales, Erica Wheeler, Jaimal Yogis.
ADDITIONAL INFORMATION See website for cost and additional details.

⊕ SOUTHERN EXPRESSIONS AUTHOR CONFERENCE

P.O. Box 10294, Gulfport MS 39505-0294. (228)239-3575. E-mail: writerpllevin@gmail.com. Website: www.gcwriters.org/. **Contact:** Philip L. Levin. Estab. 2010. Annual conference held October 14, 15, 16. 3 days. Average attendance: 120. Held at the refurbished Mary C. O'Keefe Cultural Center for the Arts in Ocean Springs, MS, Southern Expressions includes 18 speakers, including 4 literary agents, special demonstrations, keynotes by famous published authors, a Friday night cocktail party with silent auction, a Sunday morning brunch and author signing. The conference is sponsored by the IP Casino, Resort and Spa.
COSTS $200 with $25 GCWA discount for members.
ACCOMMODATIONS Room block reserved at the IP Casino, Resort and Spa. Shuttle provided between the IP and the conference. In addition, the city of Ocean Springs is providing transportation from designated parking spots to the art fair which is two blocks from the conference.
ADDITIONAL INFORMATION Brochures are available online or for SAE. Inquire via e-mail.

SOUTHERN LIGHTS CONFERENCE

First Coast Romance Writers, P.O. Box 32456, Jacksonville FL 32237. E-mail: conference@firstcoastromancewriters.com. Website: www.firstcoastromancewriters.com. Estab. 1995. Annual conference held on March 12, 2011. Conference duration: 1 day. Offers workshops, author panels, industry expert sessions, editor/agent appointments, and a keynote address. Speakers include CL Wilson, Vic Digenti, Tessa Woodward (Avon Publishing) and Emmanuelle Morgan (literary agent).

SOUTHWEST WRITERS CONFERENCE MINI-CONFERENCE SERIES

3721 Morris St. NE, Suite A, Albuquerque NM 87111. (505)265-9485. E-mail: swwriters@juno.com. Website: www.southwestwriters.com. **Contact:** Conference Chair. Estab. 1983. Annual mini-conferences held throughout the year. Average attendance: 50.

Speakers include writers, editors, agents, publicists, and producers. All areas of writing, including screenwriting and poetry, are represented.

COSTS Fee includes conference sessions and lunch.

ACCOMMODATIONS Usually have official airline and hotel discount rates.

ADDITIONAL INFORMATION Sponsors a contest judged by authors, editors from major publishers, and agents from New York, Los Angeles, etc. There are 14 categories. Deadline: May 1; late deadline May 16. Entry fee ranges from $10-60. There are bi-monthly contests with various themes: $10 entry fee. See website for details. Brochures/guidelines are available online or for a SASE. Inquire via e-mail or phone. A one-on-one appointment may be set up at the conference with the editor or agent of your choice on a first-registered, first-served basis.

SPLIT ROCK ARTS PROGRAM

360 Coffey Hall, 1420 Eckles Ave., St. Paul MN 55108-6084. Website: www.cce.umn.edu/Split-Rock-Arts-Program. Summer workshops and seasonal retreats, including autobiography, poetry, fiction, creative nonfiction, memoir, writing for children; book arts, comic illustration, calligraphy, picture books illustration, graphic novel, and a variety of special topics and forms, are taught by renowned writers and illustrators. Held on the Twin Cities campus and at the University's Cloquet Forestry Center in northern Minnesota. Writing instructors for 2010-11 includes: Jessica Abel, Brenda Cardenas, Nancy Carlson, Jack El-Hai, Heid Erdrich, John Hildebrand, Jim Moore, Gregory Orfalea, Shannon Olson, Sun Yung Shin, Joyce Sutphen, Richard Terrill, Catherine Watson, and more. Three-day seasonal retreats are offered in February, April, and October; weeklong and three-day summer workshops and retreats are offered in June and July. Registration limited to 17 per workshop/retreat. Graduate/undergraduate credit, scholarships and on-campus accommodations available.

COSTS: Workshop: $370-555. Registration is ongoing.

SQUAW VALLEY COMMUNITY OF WRITERS

P.O. Box 1416, Nevada City CA 95959-1416. (530)470-8440. E-mail: info@squawvalleywriters.org. Website: www.squawvalleywriters.org. **Contact:** Brett Hall Jones, executive director. Estab. 1969.

COSTS Tuition is $800, which includes 6 dinners.

ACCOMMODATIONS The Community of Writers rents houses and condominiums in the Valley for participants to live in during the week of the conference. Single room (one participant): $725/week. Double room (twin beds, room shared by conference participant of the same sex): $350/week. Multiple room (bunk beds, room shared with 2 or more participants of the same sex): $210/week. All rooms subject to availability; early requests are recommended. Can arrange airport shuttle pick-ups for a fee.

ADDITIONAL INFORMATION Admissions are based on submitted ms (unpublished fiction, one or two stories or novel chapters); requires $35 reading fee. Submit ms to Brett Hall Jones, Squaw Valley Community of Writers, P.O. Box 1416, Nevada City, CA 95959. Brochure/guidelines available March by phone, e-mail or visit website. Accepts inquiries by SASE, e-mail, phone. Agents and editors attend/participate in conferences.

STELLARCON

Box F4, Brown Annex, Elliott University Center, UNCG, Greensboro NC 27412. (336)294-8041. E-mail: info@stellarcon.org. Website: www.stellarcon.org. Estab. 1976. Annual conference held in March. Average attendance: 500. Conference focuses on general science fiction, fantasy, horror with an emphasis on literature, and comics. Held at the Radisson Hotel in High Point, N.C.

STONY BROOK SOUTHAMPTON SCREENWRITING CONFERENCE

Stony Brook Southampton, 239 Montauk Highway, Southampton NY 11968. (631)632-5007. E-mail: southamptonwriters@notes.cc.sunysb.edu. Website: www.sunysb.edu/writers/screenwriting/. **Contact:** Conference Coordinator. "The Southampton Screenwriting Conference welcomes new and advanced screenwriters, as well as all writers interested in using the language of film to tell a story. The five-day residential conference will inform, inspire, challenge, and further participants understanding of the art of the screenplay and the individual writing process. Our unique program of workshops, seminars, panel presentations, and screenings will encourage and motivate attendees under the professional guidance of accomplished screenwriters, educators, and script analysts."

COSTS Residential $1495, Non-Residential $1300.

ADDITIONAL INFORMATION Space is limited.

TAOS SUMMER WRITERS' CONFERENCE

Department of English Language and Literature, MSC 03 2170, University of New Mexico, Albuquerque NM 87131-0001. (505)277-5572. Fax: (505)277-2950. E-mail: taosconf@unm.edu. Website: www.unm.edu/~taosconf. Estab. 1999. Annual conference held in July. Conference duration: 7 days. Offers workshops in novel writing, short story writing, screenwriting, poetry, creative nonfiction, travel writing, historical fiction, memoir, and revision. Participants may also schedule a consultation with a visiting agent/editor.

COSTS $325/weekend; $625/week; discounted tuition rate of $275/weekend workshop with weeklong workshop or master class registration.

ACCOMMODATIONS $69-109/night at the Sagebrush Inn; $89/night at Comfort Suites.

TEXAS CHRISTIAN WRITERS' CONFERENCE

7401 Katy Freeway, Houston TX 77092. (713)686-7209. E-mail: dannywoodall@yahoo.com. Martha Rogers **Contact:** Danny Woodall. Estab. 1990. Open conference for all interested writers. "Focus on all genres." Sponsors a contest for short fiction; categories include articles, devotionals, poetry, short story, book proposals, drama. Fees: $8-15. Conference information available with SASE or e-mail to Danny Woodall. Agents participate in conference. Senior discounts available.

COSTS $65 for members of IWA, $80 nonmembers, discounts for seniors (60+) and couples, meal at noon, continental breakfast and breaks.

ACCOMMODATIONS Offers list of area hotels or lodging options.

ADDITIONAL INFORMATION Open conference for all interested writers. Sponsors a contest for short fiction; categories include articles, devotionals, poetry, short story, book proposals, drama. Fees: $8-15. Conference information available with SASE or e-mail to Danny Woodall, danny.woodall@yahoo.com. Agents participate in conference. (For contest information, contact patav@aol.com.)

THRILLERFEST

PO Box 311, Eureka CA 95502. E-mail: infocentral@thrillerwriters.org. Website: www.thrillerfest.com. **Contact:** Shirley Kennett. Grand Hyatt New York. 109 E. 42nd St. New York, NY 10017. Estab. 2006. 2010 conference: July 7-10 in Manhattan. Conference duration: 4 days. Average attendance: 700. Conference "dedicated to writing the thriller and promoting the enjoyment of reading thrillers." Speakers have included David Morrell, Sandra Brown, Eric Van Lustbader, David Baldacci, Brad Meltzer, Steve Martini, R.L. Stine, Katherine Neville, Robin Cook, Andrew Gross, Kathy Reichs, Brad Thor, Clive Cussler, James Patterson, Donald Maass, and Al Zuckerman. Two days of the conference is CraftFest, where the focus is on writing craft, and two days is ThrillerFest, which showcase the author-fan relationship. Also featured are AgentFest, a unique event where authors can pitch their work face-to-face to forty top literary agents; and the international Thriller Awards and Banquet.

COSTS Price will vary from $200 to $1,000 dollars depending on which events are selected. Various package deals are available offering savings, and Early Bird pricing is offered beginning August of each year.

ACCOMMODATIONS Grand Hyatt in New York City.

TMCC WRITERS' CONFERENCE

5270 Neil Road, Reno NV 89502. (775)829-9010. Fax: (775)829-9032. E-mail: wdce@tmcc.edu. Website: wdce.tmcc.edu. Estab. 1991. Annual conference held in April. Average attendance: 125. Focuses on fiction, poetry, and memoir, plus an assortment of other forms of writing, such as screenwriting, thrillers, mysteries, and nonfiction. There is always an array of speakers and presenters with impressive literary credentials, including agents and editors. Speakers have included Dorothy Allison, Karen Joy Fowler, James D. Houston, James N. Frey, Gary Short, Jane Hirschfield, Dorrianne Laux, Kim Addonizio, Amy Rennert, and Laurie Fox.

COSTS $99 for a full-day seminar; $15 for 15 minute one-on-one appointment with an agent or editor.

ACCOMMODATIONS The Nugget offers a special rate and shuttle service to the Reno/Tahoe International Airport, which is less than 20 minutes away.

ADDITIONAL INFORMATION "The conference is open to all writers, regardless of their level of experience. Brochures are available online and mailed in the fall. Send inquiries via e-mail."

TONY HILLERMAN WRITERS CONFERENCE

1063 Willow Way, Santa Fe NM 87505. (505)471-1565. E-mail: wordharvest@wordharvest.com. Website: www.wordharvest.com. Estab. 2001. Annual conference held in November. Conference duration: 3 days.

Average attendance: 100. Workshops on writing good dialogue, building your platform, writing series that sell, and adding humor to your writing are geared toward mystery writers. Held at the Inn & Spa at Loretto in Sante Fe, N.M. Speakers have included Tony Hillerman, Michael McGarrity, J.A. Jance, Margaret Coel, Sean Murphy, Virginia Swift, James D. Doss, Gail Larsen, Luther Wilson, Bill O'Hanlon, Steve Havill, Sandi Ault, Judith Van Gieson, Pari Noskin Taichert and Craig Johnson. 2008 guests include: James Rollins, Michael McGarrity, Craig Johnson, Pari Noskin Taichert and Sandi Ault. The conference has both a short story writing contest and a novel writing contest.

Costs $250 up, depending on if attendees want an entire weekend pass or just one day. Full cost information available online.

ACCOMMODATIONS Approximately $110/night at the Inn & Spa at Loretto.

UCLA EXTENSION WRITERS' PROGRAM

10995 Le Conte Ave., #440, Los Angeles CA 90024. (310)825-9415 or (800)388-UCLA. Fax: (310)206-7382. E-mail: writers@uclaextension.edu. Website: www.uclaextension.org/writers. Estab. 1891. "As America's largest and most comprehensive continuing education creative writing and screenwriting program, the UCLA Extension Writers' Program welcomes and trains writers at all levels of development whose aspirations range from personal enrichment to professional publication and production. Taught by an instructor corps of 250 professional writers, the Writers' Program curriculum features 530 annual open-enrollment courses onsite and online in novel writing, short fiction, personal essay, memoir, poetry, playwriting, writing for the youth market, publishing, feature film writing, and television writing, and is designed to accommodate your individual writing needs, ambitions, and lifestyle. Special programs and services include certificate programs in creative writing, feature film writing, and television writing; a four-day Writers Studio which attracts a national and international audience; nine-month master classes in novel writing and feature film writing; an online screenwriting mentorship program; one-on-one script and manuscript consultation services; literary and screenplay competitions; advisors who help you determine how best to achieve your personal writing goals; and free annual public events such as Writers Faire and Publication Party which allow you to extend your writing education and network with the literary and entertainment communities."

COSTS Depends on length of the course.

ACCOMMODATIONS Students make their own arrangements. Out-of-town students are encouraged to take online courses.

ADDITIONAL INFORMATION Some advanced-level classes have ms submittal requirements; see the UCLA Extension catalog or see website.

⊕ UNIVERSITY OF NORTH FLORIDA WRITERS CONFERENCE

12000 Alumni Dr., Jacksonville FL 32224-2678. (904)620-4200. E-mail: sharon.y.cobb@unf.edu. Website: www.unfwritersconference.com. **Contact:** Sharon Y. Cobb, conference director. Estab. 2009.

COSTS See website for current registration fees. Full conference attendees receive: workshops, critiques by faculty and fellow students, lunches, Friday wine/cheese reception, and book signings.

ACCOMMODATIONS Nearby accommodations are listed on website. There is free parking provided at the University Center.

ADDITIONAL INFORMATION Annual conference held in August. Next conference held August 5–7, 2011 (also August 3–5, 2012). Conference duration: 3 days. Average attendance: 200. Short workshops on craft, genre, marketing and getting published. Writers may submit pitches to agents, editors, and film producers through the conference's Writers Pitch Book. Brochures and guidelines available for SASE and on website, or by e-mail.

VERMONT COLLEGE OF FINE ARTS POSTGRADUATE WRITERS' CONFERENCE

36 College St., Montpelier VT 05651. (802)828-8835. E-mail: pgconference@vermontcollege.edu. Website: www.vermontcollege.edu/post-graduate-writers-conference. Estab. 1996. 16th annual conference for writers with MFAs or equivalent preparation on the historic campus of Vermont College of Fine Arts. August 9-15, 2011. Features intensive small-group workshops taught by an award-winning faculty, plus readings, craft talks, writing exercise sessions and individual consultations. Conference size: 70 participants. Workshops in creative nonfiction, novel, short story, poetry, poetry manuscript and writing for young people.

COSTS Costs: $850 or $975 (poetry ms)/tuition,

$330/private room, $180/shared room, $175/meals. Limited scholarships are available.

ACCOMMODATIONS Single or double rooms are available in the VCFA campus dormitories.

VIRGINIA FESTIVAL OF THE BOOK

Virginia Festival of the Book Foundation for the Humanities, 145 Ednam Dr., Charlottesville VA 22903-4629. (434)982-2983. Fax: (434)296-4714. E-mail: vabook@virginia.edu; spcoleman@virginia.edu. Website: www.vabook.org. Susan Coleman, Director, VA Center for the Book **Contact:** Nancy Coble Damon, Program Director. Estab. 1995. Annual Virginia Festival of the Book, March 16–20, 2011. Average attendance: 22,000. Festival held to celebrate books and promote reading and literacy.

COSTS See website for 2011 rates. Most events are free and open to the public. Two luncheons, a breakfast, and a reception require tickets.

ACCOMMODATIONS Overnight accommodations available.

ADDITIONAL INFORMATION "The festival is a five-day event featuring authors, illustrators, and publishing professionals. Authors must apply to the festival to be included on a panel. Preferred method of application is by use of online form. Information is available on the website and inquiries can be made via e-mail, fax, or phone."

WESLEYAN WRITERS CONFERENCE

Wesleyan University, 294 High St., Room 207, Middletown CT 06459. (860)685-3604. Fax: (860)685-2441. E-mail: agreene@wesleyan.edu. Website: www.wesleyan.edu/writers. Estab. 1956. Annual conference held the third week of June. Average attendance: 100. Focuses on the novel, fiction techniques, short stories, poetry, screenwriting, nonfiction, literary journalism, memoir, mixed media work and publishing. The conference is held on the campus of Wesleyan University, in the hills overlooking the Connecticut River. Features a faculty of award-winning writers, seminars and readings of new fiction, poetry, nonfiction and mixed media forms—as well as guest lectures on a range of topics including publishing. Both new and experienced writers are welcome. Participants may attend seminars in all genres. Speakers have included Esmond Harmsworth (Zachary Schuster Agency), Daniel Mandel (Sanford J. Greenburger Associates), Dorian Karchmar, Amy Williams (ICM and Collins McCormick), Mary Sue Rucci (Simon & Schuster),

Denise Roy (Simon & Schuster), John Kulka (Harvard University Press), Julie Barer (Barer Literary) and many others. Agents will be speaking and available for meetings with attendees. Participants are often successful in finding agents and publishers for their mss. Wesleyan participants are also frequently featured in the anthology *Best New American Voices*.

ACCOMMODATIONS Meals are provided on campus. Lodging is available on campus or in town.

ADDITIONAL INFORMATION Ms critiques are available, but not required. Scholarships and teaching fellowships are available, including the Joan Jakobson Awards for fiction writers and poets; and the Jon Davidoff Scholarships for nonfiction writers and journalists. Inquire via e-mail, fax, or phone.

WESTERN RESERVE WRITERS & FREELANCE CONFERENCE

7700 Clocktower Dr., Kirtland OH 44094. (440) 525-7812. E-mail: deencr@aol.com. Website: www.deannaadams.com. **Contact:** Deanna Adams, director/conference coordinator. Estab. 1983. Biannual. Last conference held September 25, 2010. Conference duration: One day. Average attendance: 120. "The Western Reserve Writers Conferences are designed for all writers, aspiring and professional, and offer presentations in all genres—nonfiction, fiction, poetry, essays, creative nonfiction and the business of writing, including Web writing and successful freelance writing." Site: Located in the main building of Lakeland Community College, the conference is easy to find and just off the I-90 freeway. The fall 2010 conference featured top notch presenters from newspapers and magazines, along with published authors and freelance writers. Presentations included how to draft a standout book proposal and novel synopsis, creating credible characters, contracts/copyrights, public speaking, tips on storytelling for both fiction and nonfiction writers, and when and how to get an agent. Included throughout the day are one-on-one editing consults, Q&A panel, and book sale/author signings.

COSTS Fall all-day conference, includes lunch: $95. Spring half-day conference, no lunch: $69.

ADDITIONAL INFORMATION Additional information brochures for the conferences are available by January (for spring conference) and July (for fall). Also accepts inquiries by e-mail and phone, or see website. Editors and agents often attend the conferences.

WILDACRES WRITERS WORKSHOP

233 S. Elm St., Greensboro NC 27401. (336)370-9188. E-mail: judihill@aol.com. Website: www.wildacres writers.com. Estab. 1985. Annual residential work shop held in July. Conference duration: 1 week. Average attendance: 100. Workshop focuses on novel, short story, flash fiction, poetry, and nonfiction. 10 on faculty include Ron Rash, Carrie Brown, Dr. Janice Fuller, Phillip Gerard, Luke Whisnant, Dr. Joe Clark, John Gregory Brown, Dr. Phebe Davidson, Lee Zacharias, and Vicki Lane.

COSTS See website for pricing.

ADDITIONAL INFORMATION Include a 1-page writing sample with your registration. See the website for information.

WILLAMETTE WRITERS CONFERENCE

2108 Buck St., Portland OR 97068. (503)305-6729. Fax: (503)452-0372. E-mail: wilwrite@willamette writers.com. Website: www.willamettewriters.com. Estab. 1968. Annual conference held in August. Average attendance: 600. "Williamette Writers is open to all writers, and we plan our conference accordingly. We offer workshops on all aspects of fiction, nonfiction, marketing, the creative process, etc. Also, we invite top-notch inspirational speakers for keynote addresses. We always include at least 1 agent or editor panel and offer a variety of topics of interest to screenwriters and fiction and nonfiction writers." Speakers have included Laura Rennert, Kim Cameron, Paul Levine, Angela Rinaldi, Robert Tabian, Joshua Bilmes and Elise Capron. Agents will be speaking and available for meetings with attendees.

COSTS Pricing schedule available online.

ACCOMMODATIONS If necessary, arrangements can be made on an individual basis. Special rates may be available.

ADDITIONAL INFORMATION Brochure/guidelines are available for a catalog-sized SASE.

◐ WINCHESTER WRITERS' CONFERENCE, FESTIVAL AND BOOKFAIR, AND WEEKLONG WRITING WORKSHOPS

University of Winchester, Winchester Hampshire WA S022 4NR United Kingdom. 44 (0) 1962 827238. E-mail: Barbara.Large@winchester.ac.uk. Website: www.writersconference.co.uk. **Contact:** Barbara Large.

WISCONSIN BOOK FESTIVAL

222 S. Bedford St., Suite F, Madison WI 53703. (608)262-0706. Fax: (608)263-7970. E-mail: alison@wisconsinbookfestival.org. Website: www.wisconsinbookfestival.org. Estab. 2002. Annual festival held in October. Conference duration: 5 days. The festival features readings, lectures, book discussions, writing workshops, live interviews, children's events, and more. Speakers have included Michael Cunningham, Grace Paley, TC Boyle, Marjane Satrapi, Phillip Gourevitch, Myla Goldberg, Audrey Niffenegger, Harvey Pekar, Billy Collins, Tim O'Brien and Isabel Allende.

COSTS All festival events are free.

WISCONSIN REGIONAL WRITERS' ASSOCIATION CONFERENCES

No public address available, E-mail: vpresident@wrwa.net. Website: www.wrwa.net. Estab. 1948. Annual conferences are held in May and September. Conference duration: 1-2 days. Provides presentations for all genres, including fiction, nonfiction, scriptwriting, and poetry. Presenters include authors, agents, editors, and publishers. Speakers have included Jack Byrne, Michelle Grajkowski, Benjamin Leroy, Richard Lederer, and Philip Martin.

COSTS $40-75.

ACCOMMODATIONS Provides a list of area hotels or lodging options. "We negotiate special rates at each facility. A block of rooms is set aside for a specific time period."

ADDITIONAL INFORMATION Award winners receive a certificate and a cash prize. First place winners of the Jade Ring contest receive a jade ring. Must be a member to enter contests. For brochure, call, e-mail or visit website in March/July.

WOMEN WRITING THE WEST

8547 E. Araphoe Rd., Box J-541, Greenwodd Village CO 80112-1436. E-mail: WWW1@lohseworks.com; info@WomenWritingtheWest.org. Website: www.womenwritingthewest.org. Annual conference held in September. Covers research, writing techniques, multiple genres, marketing/promotion, and more. Agents and editors will be speaking and available for one-on-one meetings with attendees. Conference location changes each year.

ACCOMMODATIONS See website for location and accommodation details.

WORDS & MUSIC

624 Pirate's Alley, New Orleans LA 70116. (504)586-1609. Fax: (504)522-9725. E-mail: info@wordsandmusic.org. Website: www.wordsandmusic.org. Estab. 1997. Annual conference held the first week in November. Conference duration: 5 days. Average attendance: 300. Presenters include authors, agents, editors and publishers. Past speakers included agents Deborah Grosvenor, Judith Weber, Stuart Bernstein, Nat Sobel, Jeff Kleinman, Emma Sweeney, Liza Dawson and Michael Murphy; editors Lauren Marino, Webster Younce, Ann Patty, Will Murphy, Jofie Ferrari-Adler, Elizabeth Stein; critics Marie Arana, Jonathan Yardley, and Michael Dirda; fiction writers Oscar Hijuelos, Robert Olen Butler, Shirley Ann Grau, Mayra Montero, Ana Castillo, H.G. Carrillo. Agents and editors critique manuscripts in advance; meet with them one-on-one during the conference.

COSTS See website for a costs and additional information on accommodations.

ACCOMMODATIONS Hotel Monteleone in New Orleans.

WRANGLING WITH WRITING

Society of Southwestern Authors, (520)546-9382. Fax: (520)751-7877. E-mail: Mike_Rom@hotmail.com. Website: www.ssa-az.org/conference.htm. **Contact:** Mike Rom. Estab. 1972. Held in late September; visit website for specific dates. Conference duration: 2 days. Average attendance: 300. Conference offers 36 workshops covering all genres of writing, plus pre-scheduled one-on-one interviews with 30 agents, editors, and publishers representing major book houses and magazines. Speakers have included Ray Bradbury, Clive Cussler, Elmore Leonard, Ben Bova, Sam Swope, Richard Paul Evans, Bruce Holland Rogers, and Billy Collins.

COSTS See website for costs. Five meals included.

ADDITIONAL INFORMATION Brochures/guidelines are available as of July 15 by e-mail address above. Two banquets will include editor and agent panels for all attendees, and Saturday evening winning plays from contestants will be presented.

♻ WRITE! CANADA

The Word Guild, P.O. Box 1243, Trenton ON K8V 5R9 Canada. E-mail: info@thewordguild.com; writecanada@rogers.com. Website: www.writecanada.org. Conference duration: 3 days. Annual conference for writers who are Christian of all types and at all stages. Offers solid instruction, stimulating interaction, exciting challenges, and worshipful community.

WRITE ON THE SOUND WRITERS' CONFERENCE

Edmonds Arts Commission, 700 Main St., Edmonds WA 98020. (425)771-0228. Fax: (425)771-0253. E-mail: wots@ci.edmonds.wa.us. Website: www.ci.edmonds.wa.us/ArtsCommission/wots.stm. Estab. 1985. Annual conference held in October. Conference duration: 2.5 days. Average attendance: 200. Features over 30 presenters, a literary contest, ms critiques, a reception and book signing, onsite bookstore, and a variety of evening activities. Held at the Frances Anderson Center in Edmonds, just north of Seattle on the Puget Sound. Speakers have included Elizabeth George, Dan Hurley, Marcia Woodard, Holly Hughes, Greg Bear, Timothy Egan, Joe McHugh, Frances Wood, Garth Stein and Max Grover.

COSTS See website for more information.

ADDITIONAL INFORMATION Brochures are available in July. Accepts inquiries via phone, e-mail, and fax.

WRITERS@WORK CONFERENCE

P.O. Box 540370, North Salt Lake UT 84054-0370. (801)292-9285. E-mail: lisa@writersatwork.org. Website: www.writersatwork.org. Estab. 1985. Annual conference held in June. Conference duration: 5 days. Average attendance: 250. Morning workshops (3 hours/day) focus on novel, advanced fiction, generative fiction, nonfiction, poetry, and young adult fiction. Afternoon sessions will include craft lectures, discussions, and directed interviews with authors, agents, and editors. In addition to the traditional, one-on-one manuscript consultations, there will be many opportunities to mingle informally with agents/editors. Held at the Alta Lodge in Alta Lodge, Utah in 2011. Speakers have included Steve Almond, Bret Lott, Shannon Hale, Emily Forland (Wendy Weil Agency), Julie Culver (Folio Literary Management, Chuck Adams (Algonquin Press), and Mark A. Taylor (Juniper Press).

COSTS See website for pricing informaiton.

ACCOMMODATIONS Onsite housing available. Additional lodging and meal information is on the website.

WRITERS' CONFERENCE AT OCEAN PARK

14 Temple Ave., P.O. Box 7296, Ocean Park ME 04063-2823. (401)598-1424. E-mail: jbrosnan@jwu.edu. Website: www.oceanpark.org/programs/education/writers/writers.html#. Other addresses: P.O. Box 7146, Ocean Park, ME 04063-7146; P.O. Box 172, Assonet, MA 02702 (mailing address for conference). Estab. 1941. Annual conference held in mid-August. Conference duration: 4 days. Average attendance: 50. "We try to present a balanced and eclectic conference. In addition to time and attention given to poetry, we also have children's literature, mystery writing, travel, fiction, nonfiction, journalism, and other issues of interest to writers. Our speakers are editors, writers, and other professionals. Our concentration is, by intention, a general view of writing to publish with supportive encouragement. We are located in Ocean Park, a small seashore village 14 miles south of Portland. Ours is a summer assembly center with many buildings from the Victorian age. The conference meets in Porter Hall, one of the assembly buildings which is listed in the National Register of Historic Places. Speakers have included Michael C. White (novelist/short story writer), Betsy Shool (poet), Suzanne Strempek Shea (novelist), John Perrault (poet), Josh Williamson (newspaper editor), Dawn Potter (poet), Bruce Pratt (fiction writer), Amy McDonald (children's author), Anne Wescott Dodd (nonfiction writer), Kate Chadbourne (singer/songwriter), Wesley McNair (poet/Maine faculty member), and others. We usually have about 8 guest presenters each year." Publishers, writers and editors will be speaking, leading workshops, and will be available for meetings with attendees.

COSTS $200. The fee does not include housing or meals, which must be arranged separately by conferees.

ACCOMMODATIONS "An accommodations list is available. We are in a summer resort area where motels, guest houses, and restaurants abound."

ADDITIONAL INFORMATION We have 6 contests for various genres. An announcement is available in the spring. The prizes (all modest) are awarded at the end of the conference and only to those who are registered. Send SASE in June for the conference program.

WRITERS' INSTITUTE

21 North Park St., Room 7331, Madison WI 53715. (608)265-3972. Fax: (608)265-2475. E-mail: lscheer@dcs.wisc.edu. Website: www.uwwritersinstitute.org. **Contact:** Laurie Scheer. Estab. 1989. Conference speakers are judges. For brochure send e-mail, visit website, call, fax. Accepts inquiries by SASE, e-mail, phone, fax. Agents and editors participate in conference.

COSTS $245 includes materials, breaks.

ACCOMMODATIONS Provides a list of area hotels or lodging options.

ADDITIONAL INFORMATION Sponsors contest. Submit 1-page writing sample and $10 entry fee. Conference speakers are judges. For brochure send e-mail, visit website, call, fax. Accepts inquiries by SASE, e-mail, phone, fax. Agents and editors participate in conference.

2012 WRITERS' LEAGUE OF TEXAS AGENTS CONFERENCE

Writers' League of Texas, 611 S. Congress Ave., Suite 130, Austin TX 78704. (512)499-8914. Fax: (512)499-0441. E-mail: wlt@writersleague.org. Website: www.writersleague.org. Estab. 1982. Annual conference held in the summer. Conference duration: 3 days. Average attendance: 300. "The Writers' League of Texas Agents Conference is the place to meet agents and editors to learn the latest trends in publishing. This event provides writers with the opportunity to meet top literary agents and editors from New York and the West Coast. Topics include: finding and working with agents and publishers, writing and marketing fiction and nonfiction, dialogue, characterization, voice, research, basic and advanced fiction writing, the business of writing, and workshops for genres." Speakers have included Malaika Adero, Stacey Barney, Sha-Shana Crichton, Jessica Faust, Dena Fischer, Mickey Freiberg, Jill Grosjean, Anne Hawkins, Jim Hornfischer, Jennifer Joel, David Hale Smith and Elisabeth Weed.

COSTS $309 member/$439 nonmember.

ACCOMMODATIONS 2011 event are at the Hyatt Regency Austin, 208 Barton Springs Road, Austin, TX 78704. Check back often for new information.

ADDITIONAL INFORMATION Contests and awards programs are offered separately. Brochures are available upon request.

WRITERS' LEAGUE OF TEXAS WORKSHOPS AND SUMMER WRITING RETREAT

611 S. Congress Ave., Suite 130, Austin TX 78704. (512)499-8914. Fax: (512)499-0441. E-mail: wlt@writersleague.org. Website: www.writersleague.org. **Contact:** Sara Kocek, program coordinator.

COSTS $49-359 (Writers' League members receive

discounts).

ADDITIONAL INFORMATION "Classes and workshops provide practical advice and guidance on the craft of writing for writers at all stages of their career." Retreat: Annual Summer Writing Academy in Alpine, TX, is a weeklong writing intensive with five tracks. Special presentations: "The Secrets of the Agents" series of workshops with visiting literary agents. Classes and Workshops: Topics: E-publishing; creative nonfiction; screenwriting; novel writing; short fiction; journaling; manuscript revision; memoir writing; poetry; essays; freelance writing; publicity; author/book websites; and blogging. Instructors include Carol Dawson, Karleen Koen, Kirsten Cappy, Eric Butterman, Cyndi Hughes, Scott Wiggerman, Debra Monroe, Jennifer Ziegler, W.K. Stratton. Workshops are held in Austin unless otherwise indicated; some courses are available online. Course descriptions are available at www.writersleague.org.

WRITERS RETREAT WORKSHOP

P.O. Box 4236, Louisville KY 40204. E-mail: wrw04@netscape.net. Website: www.writersretreatworkshop.com. Estab. 1987. Annual workshop held in summer (2011 dates: June 17–26). Conference duration: 10 days. Focuses on fiction and narrative nonfiction books in progress (all genres). This is an intensive learning experience for small groups of serious-minded writers. Founded by the late Gary Provost (one of the country's leading writing instructors) and his wife Gail (an award-winning author). The goal is for students to leave with a solid understanding of the marketplace, as well as the craft of writing a novel. Held at Saint Josephs Retreat Center in Owensboro, Ky. in 2011. Speakers have included Becky Motew, Donald Maass, Jennifer Crusie, Michael Palmer, Nancy Pickard, Elizabeth Lyon, Lauren Mosko (Writer's Digest Books), Adam Marsh (Reece Halsey North), and Peter H. McGuigan (Sanford J. Greenburger Literary Agency).

COSTS $1,850-1,945 (includes meals, housing, consultations, materials). Scholarships are available.

WRITERS WEEKEND AT THE BEACH

P.O. Box 877, Ocean Park WA 98640. (360)262-0160. E-mail: bhansen6@juno.com. Estab. 1992. Annual conference held in March. Conference duration: 2 days. Average attendance: 35-40. A retreat for writers with an emphasis on poetry, fiction, and nonfiction. Held at the Ocean Park Methodist Retreat Center & Camp.

Speakers have included Wayne Holmes, Miralee Ferrell, Jim Whiting, Birdie Etchison, Colette Tennant, Gail Dunham, Linda Clare and Marion Duckworth.

COSTS $195-205 (includes lodging, meals, full workshop); $145/everything but lodging; $95/Saturday only (includes lunch); $25/Sunday critique session (includes brunch); $10/Saturday evening only.

ACCOMMODATIONS Offers on-site overnight lodging.

THE WRITERS WORKSHOP

PO Box 329, Langley WA 98260. E-mail: bob@bobmayer.org. Website: www.bobmayer.org. **Contact:** Bob Mayer. Estab. 2002.

COSTS Varies depending on venue.

ADDITIONAL INFORMATION Limited to eight participants and focused on their novel and marketability.

WRITERS WORKSHOP IN SCIENCE FICTION

English Department/University of Kansas, Wesoce Hall, 1445 Jayhawk Blvd., Room 3001, Lawrence KS 66045-7590. (785)864-3380. Fax: (785)864-1159. E-mail: jgunn@ku.edu. Website: www.ku.edu/~sfcenter. Estab. 1985. Annual workshop held in late June/early July (2011: June 26-July 8). Average attendance: 10. Conference for writing and marketing science fiction. Classes meet in university housing on the University of Kansas campus. Workshop sessions operate informally in a lounge. Speakers have included Frederik Pohl, Kij Johnson, James Gunn, and Chris McKitterick.

COSTS See website for tuition rates, dormitory housing costs, and deadlines.

ACCOMMODATIONS Housing information is available. Several airport shuttle services offer reasonable transportation from the Kansas City International Airport to Lawrence.

ADDITIONAL INFORMATION Admission to the workshop is by submission of an acceptable story. Two additional stories should be submitted by the middle of June. These 3 stories are distributed to other participants for critquing and are the basis for the first week of the workshop. One story is rewritten for the second week. Send SASE for brochure/guidelines. This workshop is intended for writers who have just started to sell their work or need that extra bit of understanding or skill to become a published writer.

WRITE-TO-PUBLISH CONFERENCE

WordPro Communication Services, 9118 W. Elmwood Dr., Suite 1G, Niles IL 60714-5820. (847)296-3964. Fax: (847)296-0754. E-mail: lin@writetopublish.com. Website: www.writetopublish.com. **Contact:** Lin Johnson, director. Estab. 1971. Annual. Conference held June 8–11, 2011 and June 6–9, 2012. Average attendance: 250. Conference on "writing all types of manuscripts for the Christian market." Site: Wheaton College, Wheaton, IL (Chicago).

COSTS approximately $480.

ACCOMMODATIONS In campus residence halls or discounted hotel rates. Cost approximately $270-350.

ADDITIONAL INFORMATION Optional ms evaluation available. College credit available. Conference information available in January. For details, visit website, or e-mail brochure@writetopublish.com. Accepts inquiries by e-mail, fax, phone.

WRITING FOR THE SOUL

Jerry B. Jenkins Christian Writers Guild, 5525 N. Union Blvd., Suite 200, Colorado Springs CO 80918. (866)495-5177. Fax: (719)495-5181. E-mail: leilani@christianwritersguild.com. Website: www.christianwritersguild.com. **Contact:** Leilani Squires, admissions manager. Annual conference held in February. Workshops and continuing classes cover fiction, nonfiction and magazine writing, children's books, and teen writing. Appointments with more than 30 agents, publishers, and editors are also available. The keynote speakers are nationally known, leading authors. The conference is hosted by Jerry B. Jenkins.

COSTS $649/Guild members; $799/nonmembers.

ACCOMMODATIONS $159/night at the Grand Hyatt in Denver.

⊕ WRITING WORKSHOP AT CASTLE HILL

1 Depot Rd., P.O. Box 756, Truro MA 02666-0756. E-mail: cherie@castlehill.org. Website: www.castlehill.org. Poetry, fiction, memoir workshops geared toward intermediate and advanced levels. **Open to students.** Workshops by Keith Althaus: Poetry; Anne Bernays: Elements of Fiction; Elizabeth Bradfield: Poetry in Plein Air & Broadsides and Beyond: Poetry as Public Art; Melanie Braverman: In Pursuit of Exactitude: Poetry; Josephine Del Deo: Preoccupation in Poetry; Martin Espada: Barbaric Yamp: A Poetry Workshop; Judy Huge: Finding the Me in Memoir; Justin Kaplan: Autobiography. See website under Summer 2011 Writers for dates and more information.

THE HELENE WURLITZER FOUNDATION

P.O. Box 1891, Taos NM 87571. (505)758-2413. Fax: (575)758-2559. E-mail: hwf@taosnet.com. Website: www.wurlitzerfoundation.org. **Contact:** Michael A. Knight, executive director. Estab. 1953. The foundation offers residencies to artists in the creative fields—visual, literary and music composition. There are three 13-week sessions from mid-January through November annually. Application deadline: January 18 for following year. For application, request by e-mail or visit website to download.

ACCOMMODATIONS "Provides individual housing in fully furnished studio/houses (casitas), rent and utility free. Artists are responsible for transportation to and from Taos, their meals, and the materials for their work. Bicycles are provided upon request."

GENERAL INDEX

LITERARY AGENTS SPECIALTIES INDEX

Seligman, Literary Agent, Lynn 260
Serendipity Literary Agency, LLC 261
Smith, Literary Agent, Valerie 265
Spectrum Literary Agency 266
Spencerhill Associates 267
Strickler Author Management, Pam 270
Tade Literary Agency, Stephanie 272
The Agency Group, LLC 273
The Ahearn Agency, Inc. 274
The August Agency, LLC 274
The Choate Agency, LLC 276
The Chudney Agency 276
The Fielding Agency, LLC 279
The Joan Brandt Agency 282
The Joy Harris Literary Agency, Inc. 282
The LA Literary Agency 283
The Literary Group International 283
The McGill Agency, Inc. 284
The Natasha Kern Literary Agency 201
The Stringer Literary Agency, LLC 286
Triada U.S. Literary Agency, Inc. 289
Weiner Literary Agency, Cherry 294
Wordserve Literary Group 296
Writers House 297
Zachary Shuster Harmsworth 298
Zimmermann Literary Agency, Helen 299

HORROR
Amsterdam Agency, Marcia 138
Bent Agency, The 143
Brown, Ltd., Curtis 151
Cameron & Associates, Kimberley 154
Croce Agency, The 160
D4EO Literary Agency 161
DeChiara Literary Agency, The Jennifer 281
Goumen & Smirnova Literary Agency 186
Harwood Limited, Antony 192
Jabberwocky Literary Agency 198
Linn Prentis Literary 239
Maass Literary Agency, Donald 218
Mainhardt Agency, Ricia 219
Marshall Agency, The Evan 283
McCarthy Creative Services 224
Perkins Agency, L. 234
Picard, Literary Agent, Alison J. 236
P.S Literary Agency 240
RLR Associates, Ltd. 249
Schiavone Literary Agency, Inc. 257
Scribe Agency, LLC 260
Seligman, Literary Agent, Lynn 260
Sternig & Byrne Literary Agency 268
The Agency Group, LLC 273
The Fielding Agency, LLC 279
The Literary Group International 283
Triada U.S. Literary Agency, Inc. 289
Webb Literary, Irene 293
Writers House 297

HUMOR
Alive Communications, Inc. 136
Artists and Artisans Inc. 140
Bradford Literary Agency 147
Brown, Ltd., Curtis 151
Chamein Canton Agency 155
D4EO Literary Agency 161
Daniel Literary Group 162
DeChiara Literary Agency, The Jennifer 281
Dupree/Miller and Associates Inc. Literary 168
Golomb Literary Agency, The Susan 185
Greenburger Associates, Inc., Sanford J. 188
Green Literary Agency, LLC, Kathryn 189
Harwood Limited, Antony 192
Henshaw Group, Richard 193
International Transactions, Inc. 198
Jabberwocky Literary Agency 198
JET Literary Associates 199
Langlie, Literary Agent, Laura 207
Larsen/Elizabeth Pomada, Literary Agents, Michael 208
Levine Literary Agency, Paul S. 211
Linn Prentis Literary 239
Lippincott Massie McQuilkin 213
Lyons Literary, LLC 217
Mainhardt Agency, Ricia 219
Marshall Agency, The Evan 283
McBride Literary Agency, Margret 223
McCarthy Creative Services 224
Mendel Media Group, LLC 225

Mura Literary, Dee 228
Picard, Literary Agent, Alison J. 236
PMA Literary and Film Management, Inc. 237
P.S Literary Agency 240
RLR Associates, Ltd. 249
Schiavone Literary Agency, Inc. 257
Schulman Literary Agency, Susan 258
Scribe Agency, LLC 260
Seligman, Literary Agent, Lynn 260
The Agency Group, LLC 273
The Ahearn Agency, Inc. 274
The August Agency, LLC 274
The Fielding Agency, LLC 279
The Joy Harris Literary Agency, Inc. 282
The Literary Group International 283
The Mitchell J. Hamilburg Agency 285
Trident Media Group 289
Writers House 297

Inspirational
Alive Communications, Inc. 136
Browne & Miller Literary Associates 151
Crichton & Associates 160
Daniel Literary Group 162
Dupree/Miller and Associates Inc. Literary 168
Hartline Literary Agency 191
Hawkins & Associates, Inc., John 192
Hidden Value Group 194
Hurst Literary Management, Andrea 196
Larsen/Elizabeth Pomada, Literary Agents, Michael 208
Levine Literary Agency, Paul S. 211
Lindstrom Literary Management, LLC 212
Living Word Literary Agency 215
MacGregor Literary Inc. 219
Marshall Agency, The Evan 283
Mendel Media Group, LLC 225
Northern Lights Literary Services, LLC 231
PMA Literary and Film Management, Inc. 237
Schulman Literary Agency, Susan 258
Spencerhill Associates 267
The Agency Group, LLC 273
The Natasha Kern Literary Agency 201
Wordserve Literary Group 296

JUVENILE
Brown Literary Agency, Inc., Andrea 150
Browne, Ltd., Pema 152
Brown, Ltd., Curtis 151
Brown Associates, Inc., Marie 151
Chamein Canton Agency 155
D4EO Literary Agency 161
DeChiara Literary Agency, The Jennifer 281
Dijkstra Literary Agency, Sandra 165
Dunham Literary, Inc. 168
Dwyer & O'Grady, Inc. 169
Grayson Literary Agency, Ashley 188
Green Literary Agency, LLC, Kathryn 189
Grinberg Literary Agency, Jill 190
Hurst Literary Management, Andrea 196
Janklow & Nesbit Associates 199
KT Literary, LLC 205
Langlie, Literary Agent, Laura 207
Linn Prentis Literary 239
Maccoby Literary Agency, Gina 218
Mainhardt Agency, Ricia 219
McCarthy Agency, LLC, The 223
Mendel Media Group, LLC 225
Mura Literary, Dee 228
Muse Literary Management 229
Pavilion Literary Management 234
Picard, Literary Agent, Alison J. 236
PMA Literary and Film Management, Inc. 237
Poynor Group, The 238
Prospect Agency, LLC 240
P.S Literary Agency 240
Schiavone Literary Agency, Inc. 257
Schulman Literary Agency, Susan 258
Serendipity Literary Agency, LLC 261
Smith, Literary Agent, Valerie 265
Talcott Notch Literary 272
The Agency Group, LLC 273
The Chudney Agency 276
The Fielding Agency, LLC 279
The Greenhouse Literary Agency 280

Transatlantic Literary Agency 288
Triada U.S. Literary Agency, Inc. 289
Trident Media Group 289
Writers House 297

LESBIAN
Anderson Literary Management, LLC 139
DeChiara Literary Agency, The Jennifer 281
Dystel & Goderich Literary Management 169
Fairbank Literary Representation 175
Greenburger Associates, Inc., Sanford J. 188
Harwood Limited, Antony 192
Hawkins & Associates, Inc., John 192
International Transactions, Inc. 198
Jabberwocky Literary Agency 198
JET Literary Associates 199
Larsen/Elizabeth Pomada, Literary Agents, Michael 208
Levine Literary Agency, Paul S. 211
Linn Prentis Literary 239
Lippincott Massie McQuilkin 213
Lyons Literary, LLC 217
Mainhardt Agency, Ricia 219
Mendel Media Group, LLC 225
Mura Literary, Dee 228
Picard, Literary Agent, Alison J. 236
PMA Literary and Film Management, Inc. 237
RLR Associates, Ltd. 249
Sanders & Associates, Victoria 256
Scribe Agency, LLC 260
The Agency Group, LLC 273
The Fielding Agency, LLC 279
The Joy Harris Literary Agency, Inc. 282
The Spieler Agency 286
Zachary Shuster Harmsworth 298

LITERARY
Aitken Alexander Associates 136
Alive Communications, Inc. 136
Altshuler Literary Agency, Miriam 137
Amster Literary Enterprises, Betsy 138
Anderson Literary Management, LLC 139
Artists and Artisans Inc. 140
Avenue A Literary 141
Barer Literary, LLC 142
Barrett Books, Inc., Loretta 142
Belli Literary Agency (LBLA), Lorella 143
Bleecker Street Associates, Inc. 144
Bond Literary Agency 145
Brandt & Hochman Literary Agents, Inc. 147
Braun Associates, Inc., Barbara 148
Brick House Literary Agents 148
Browne, Ltd., Pema 152
Browne & Miller Literary Associates 151
Brown Literary Agency, Inc., Andrea 150
Brown, Ltd., Curtis 151
Brown Associates, Inc., Marie 151
Castiglia Literary Agency 155
Congdon Associates Inc., Don 158
Cornerstone Literary, Inc. 159
Crichton & Associates 160
Croce Agency, The 160
D4EO Literary Agency 161
Daniel Literary Group 162
Davis Wager Literary Agency 163
DeChiara Literary Agency, The Jennifer 281
DeFiore & Co. 163
Delbourgo Associates, Inc., Joelle 164
Dijkstra Literary Agency, Sandra 165
Donovan Literary, Jim 166
Dreisbach Literary Management 167
Dunham Literary, Inc. 168
Dupree/Miller and Associates Inc. Literary 168
Dystel & Goderich Literary Management 169
Eady Associates, Toby 170
Ellison Agency, The Nicholas 173
Eth Literary Representation, Felicia 174
Fairbank Literary Representation 175
Finch Literary Agency, Diana 176
FinePrint Literary Management 176
Fletcher & Company 178
Folio Literary Management, LLC 178
Foundry Literary + Media 179
Fox Literary 179
Franklin Associates, Ltd., Lynn C. 180
Frederick Hill Bonnie Nadell, Inc. 182
Freymann Literary Agency, Sarah Jane 182

WRITER'S DIGEST

Is Your Manuscript Ready?

Trust 2nd Draft Critique Service to prepare your writing to catch the eye of agents and editors. You can expect:

- Expert evaluation from a hand-selected, professional critiquer
- Know-how on reaching your target audience
- Red flags for consistency, mechanics, and grammar
- Tips on revising your work to increase your odds of publication

Visit WritersDigestShop.com/2nd-draft for more information.

THE PERFECT COMPANION TO *WRITER'S MARKET*

The Writer's Market Guide to Getting Published

Learn exactly what it takes to get your work into the marketplace, get it published, and get paid for it!

Available from WritersDigestShop.com and your favorite book retailers.

To get started, join our mailing list: WritersDigest.com/enews

FOLLOW US ON:

 Find more great tips, networking and advice by following @writersdigest

 And become a fan of our Facebook page facebook.com/writersdigest